THE MAKING OF PAUL

The Making of Paul

Constructions of the Apostle in Early Christianity

Richard I. Pervo

FORTRESS PRESS
MINNEAPOLIS

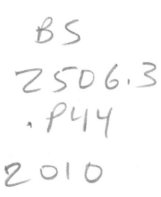

THE MAKING OF PAUL
Constructions of the Apostle in Early Christianity

Unless otherwise noted, Scripture quotations are taken from the *New Revised Standard Bible*, copyright © 1989 by the Division of Christian Education of the National Council of Churches of Christ in the USA. Used by permission. All rights reserved.

Cover images: Detail of the vault mosaics, Scala / Art Resource, NY; Majolica plate, Réunion des Musées Nationaux / Art Resource, NY; *Master of Soriguerola*, Scala / Art Resource, NY
Cover design: Paul Boehnke
Book design: Michelle L. N. Cook

Library of Congress Cataloging-in-Publication Data
Pervo, Richard I.
  The making of Paul : constructions of the Apostle in early Christianity / Richard I. Pervo.
    p. cm.
  Includes bibliographical references (p.   ) and indexes.
  ISBN 978-0-8006-9659-7 (alk. paper)
  1. Paul, the Apostle, Saint. I. Title.
  BS2506.3.P44 2010
  225.9'2—dc22
                          2009040664

The paper used in this publication meets the minimum requirements of American National Standard for Information Sciences — Permanence of Paper for Printed Library Materials, ANSI Z329.48-1984.

Manufactured in the U.S.A.

Contents

Preface

THIS BOOK MIGHT be called a commentary upon one of the most abused passages in the Pauline correspondence—1 Cor. 9:19-22,[1] which reads:

> *19* For though I am free with respect to all,
> I have made myself a slave to all,
> so that I might win more of them.
> *20* To the Jews I became as a Jew,
> in order to win Jews.
> *21* To those under the law I became as one under the law
> (though I myself am not under the law)
> so that I might win those under the law.
> To those outside the law I became as one outside the law
> (though I am not free from God's law but am under Christ's law)
> so that I might win those outside the law.
> *22* To the weak I became weak,
> so that I might win the weak.
> I have become all things to all people,
> that I might by all means save some.

This carefully fashioned rhetorical piece (the climax of Paul's argument that the essence of freedom resides in the possibility of renouncing one's due) refers to the poles, or boundaries, of his missionary strategy. The apostle could not "become a Jew" because he *was* a Jew.[2] Concessions to Torah would have been restricted to circumstances in which there was no substantial body of gentile believers; for the weak he was prepared to adapt his own behavior, as a limited strategy.[3] In the course of time, Paul would become something like all things to all people: a gentile to the gentiles, a sinner for the sinners, a Gnostic for the Gnostics, a radical for the radicals, a conservative for the conservatives... The objective of this book is to describe how this protean apostle came to take his shapes.

SOMETIME DURING THE opening years of the fourth decade of the Common Era, one Paul, a Greek-speaking Diaspora Jew who belonged to the Pharisaic party, underwent an important change. Hitherto an opponent of the people who followed Jesus of Nazareth, he joined that very group and became a missionary to the gentile world. As an element of that missionary activity Paul would, from time to time, compose letters, a number of which have survived. This heritage makes him unique, for he is the only Christian of the first two generations whose direct first-person testimony survives, the sole example prior to Ignatius, a bishop of Antioch executed at Rome in the first third of the second century.

Views and opinions, prejudices and conclusions, attitudes and convictions about the early Christian missionary Paul are as numerous as needles in a pine forest, but there is probably one matter about which the majority of Paul's subsequent admirers, despisers, and ignorers would happily agree: the historical Paul was not "all things to all people." Persons of that ilk exist, the most famous of which enjoy the sort of immortality fiction alone can bestow: Polonius. To move closer to Paul's own time: the community that produced the Dead Sea Scrolls had a properly scriptural phrase for this type, "seekers after smooth things."[4] Seekers after smooth things we shall always have with us, reconcilers at times, sycophants at others, oily manipulators or astute pourers of oil upon troubled waters. Of all the accusations made against Paul, the least probable is that he sought to say only what others wished to hear—which is not to say that this accusation was not circulated (cf. Gal. 5:11).

No one approaches Paul in influence upon the theology and history of Christianity. Those who prefer quantitative approaches might note that, of the twenty-seven writings comprising the New Testament, thirteen are letters attributed to Paul, while a fourteenth, Hebrews, owes its place to association with him. Pauline influence of one sort or another can be attributed to at least three of the other letters (1 and 2 Peter, James), while his practice of writing letters influenced the prevalence of this form (Jude, possibly 2 and 3 John, and very probably Revelation). Paul is the principal character in Acts, the largest work in the New Testament Canon, while his thought influenced the Gospels of Matthew (negatively) and Luke (positively). Only Mark and John stand quite outside of the Pauline orbit—and a case for indirect influence upon Mark can be advanced. No person is named more often than Paul in the surviving Christian literature of the second century.[5] The ultimate result of this influence is that:

Paul is one of the leading *heroes* of the Christian life, faith, and story. He is also a *villain* worthy of comparison with Judas. Finally, he is the archetypical *victim*, worthy of comparison with Jesus. Many of those who celebrate Paul as their hero also rejoice in his victimization, an understanding that has played a major role in Pauline scholarship of the last century and a half. The villain role, for its part, retains much vitality. Many persons have a substantial investment in Paul as either villain or victim. One whose research focus is ancient popular narrative can confirm that victims and villains tend to yield good propaganda or melodrama. As scholarly categories they are somewhat wanting. The following caricature is one that few would accept in so unvarnished a form, but it has elements that continue to exert a pull upon popular scholarship and understanding. It was still current when I began my graduate studies in 1971.

At some point, probably around the turn of the first century CE, the letters of Paul were gathered into a collection and circulated among believers. Why this happened is, to plunder Eph. 5:32, a great mystery.[6] In due course Marcion, who alone of second-century Christians really understood Paul (although he, in fact, misunderstood him), acquired the franchise to the Pauline legacy.[7] In orthodox circles the apostle went under a cloud, from which he was ultimately extricated through substantial revision of both the corpus of writings and his theology, not to mention the appearance of the book of Acts. To all intents and purposes Abraham was left without a legitimate heir, for the Paulinism of Irenaeus and his successors was no more than the debased offspring of a concubine.

Thirteen centuries later, at the time of the Reformation,[8] the real Paul was excavated from the accumulated debris of the patristic and medieval eras. Thereafter one task, at least for Protestant historians of interpretation, became the exposure of the extent to which earlier interpreters had not understood Paul. Since the Enlightenment, it has transpired that even the canonical Paul is something of a hybrid creature. Johann S. Semler (1725–1791) and Ferdinand C. Baur (1792–1860), among others, demonstrated that it is not possible to make a sharp distinction between Scripture and Tradition.[9] Scripture is itself the product of tradition and contains Pauline letters that Paul did not write. The real Paul is to be discovered in the contingent, historical circumstances of his seven undisputed—but not integral—letters,[10] with greater or lesser supplements from Acts. Paul, like his Lord, was not betrayed by external enemies but from within the circle of his own students who sold out his theology while concocting letters in his name, as well as other texts relating to him.

NOW THERE IS more than a little truth, if little nuance, in this caricature, but it is not without flaws. The dual impact of Christian ecumenism and postmodernism has challenged the claim to be able to make a timeless and definitive interpretation of Paul. Even among the mainstream of traditional, Western, interpreters there is no reigning consensus about the center of Paul's own theology, and this tradition can no longer claim either objectivity or exclusive authority. The thrust of the following pages is toward defining profiles of Paul and Paulinism in terms of the needs, questions, and values of the persons, groups, or movements represented in various texts. Specifically, I wish to describe how Paul becomes a, even *the*, pillar and founder of catholic Christianity, by which I mean the emerging "great church" of the period from 150–250 CE, and later. In order to accomplish this great task Paul (not unlike Jesus) had to die.

The canonical Acts reports in ch. 9 what is called the Conversion of Paul. This account includes the traditional signs attending the overpowering and conversion of one who resists the divine will, and presents the event as an epiphany, as a manifestation of heavenly light. The form of this presentation is quite appropriate, for the result of that change was an explosion. The world has not been the same since; that explosion still affects us, with echoes yet resounding, in settings both familiar and strange. The question of who Paul was and is has received a variety of answers, more than one of which is reflected in the New Testament. One often hears that history is written by the winners. This is an important half-truth, or more than a half-truth, but it is not the full truth.[11] It is more apposite to say that historians enjoy one great blessing, the advantage of hindsight, and one tormenting curse, the disadvantage of hindsight. Knowing the effects, researchers are prone to rummage through the data in pursuit of their causes. Much is overlooked in that process. One feature of this book is to attend to some of what has been overlooked without neglecting the broad picture.

The New Testament as we have it reflects to a remarkable extent the influence of Pauline Christianity in both favorable and hostile ways. The forms of Christianity that eventually triumphed were Greek-speaking and gentile in orientation. Only relatively less advanced traces of "Jewish Christianity" and "Judeo-Christianity," that is, movements more closely linked to traditional Jewish observance, emerge within the New Testament canon, which consists entirely of documents written in Greek.[12] This is not to say that the picture of Paul arising from the New Testament texts alone is one that Paul would have painted—far from it.

The portraits of Paul that emerge in early (and subsequent) Christianity do not arise from any concern to preserve history for the benefit of subsequent investigators; they seek to address the problems of those churches in their own times. In those endeavors, they found the letters of Paul and images of him to be both valuable and vexing. But both images and epistles endured, surprisingly. Why should letters written by a missionary to churches that he could not visit in person just then have survived? The answer is far from obvious.

It is easier to understand the impact of Paul's mission. Many of the communities of believers in Asia Minor, Macedonia, and Greece traced their origins to him. Paul was, however, a controversial figure, both during and after his lifetime, and the blessing of Pauline origins could be regarded as mixed. The canonical figure of Paul is shaped, and largely still determined, by the book of Acts. This, the second of two anonymous volumes written by an author traditionally known as Luke, stands in the current New Testament as a bridge between the Gospels and the Epistles.[13] At its conclusion Paul has arrived in Rome, where, although in theory a prisoner, he will carry out an unhindered mission. The next document is none other than Paul's letter to the Romans. Placed as it is, Acts serves as a hermeneutical key to Paul, as the pattern by which Paul is to be interpreted. As such, it bears comparison with the letters.

The above summary points out one aspect of Paul's biography that the author of Acts did not choose to mention: his execution by the Roman government. For many, this fate was an embarrassment. A cursory reading of Acts reveals that Paul, following his miraculous conversion, promptly repaired to Jerusalem and conferred with the apostles there; that he carried out a mission always in touch with the leaders of the Jerusalem church; that his labors began, whenever possible, within the local synagogues, and that the gentile mission proper followed only upon rejections by the majority of the Jewish people (rejections repeated at every key point in the story); that Paul was a powerful preacher and worker of miracles; and that his theology was the quite congruent with that of Peter and James.

One would not gather, from reading Acts, that Paul ever engaged in a lengthy conflict with other followers of Jesus, and that relations between him and Jerusalem were often strained. Nor would one imagine, from this account, that Paul ever wrote a letter. This is not precisely the picture that emerges from reading Paul, who reports conflict with Peter, difficulties in relationships with Jerusalem, accusations of inability to preach effectively or to work adequate miracles, and so on. Nor do these letters permit any doubt that Paul had a particular theological understanding often at odds with the views of others.[14] Dissonance between Acts and the letters is but one of many complicated issues requiring exploration.[15]

SINCE THIS IS not intended to be a comprehensive monograph, it is selective in approach. The governing method is to concentrate upon a number of entire works rather than piecemeal examination of a broad range of texts. Organization of a study like this is another challenge. Shall one follow a strictly chronological line or divide the material into categories? The chronological approach permits something approximating a continuous narrative. Categorical structures allow the comparison of apples with apples. Selection of categories is problematic and may require extensive justification. Geography is another component deserving attention. How, for example, were people utilizing Pauline letters and stories in Rome in 100, 150, and 175 CE? No solution is ideal. The path chosen here is mixed. After an introduction comes a chapter showing how Paul became, and remained, a book. The next three chapters use genre—letters and narratives—as their basis, at which point the method shifts to a thematic analysis. Compromise applies also to the chronological range. The thematic survey closes c. 180, with the synthesis of Irenaeus of Lyons. This is an intelligent stopping point. With regard to genres, however, these limits have been surpassed, since it is easier—albeit potentially more deceptive—for readers to connect letters attributed to Paul and material about him to earlier writings of similar type. These genres come to their own conclusions, at different times. All choices involve compromises and the absence of perfect symmetry. My hope is that the structure will be useful for readers.

The story of this book is nearly as complicated as its subject. Its genesis was a series of lectures on the urban background of nascent Christianity delivered in the mid-1980s at the Church of the Ascension, Chicago. In 1991, at the suggestion of Helmut Koester, a contract to produce a manuscript on "Paul in History and Tradition" was executed. Basic research was facilitated by a graduate seminar on the subject at Notre Dame in 1992, followed by an upper level undergraduate course at Northwestern University in 1997, along with a regularly offered course on selected Pauline Epistles at Seabury-Western Theological Seminary in Evanston. Intermittent work continued until 2000, but much of my energy had been diverted to the preparation of a number of essays on ancient fiction in the context of early Judaism and early Christianity, and by the obligation to execute a commentary on Acts. Research and writing on Acts occupied me entirely from Winter 2002 until Spring 2007. Only in May of that year did I return to this project, a draft of which was completed in May 2008. An advantage of this delay is that ideas, like a good wine, have been given time to mature.

This is the only book I have written that has taken shape in the course of teaching over many years in various settings and courses. It is therefore dedicated, with gratitude, to my students at various institutions, from 1971 to 2001. Specific thanks are due to Philip Sellew, Julian V. Hills, François Bovon, Abraham Malherbe, Mark Reasoner, Clare Rothschild, and Matthew Skinner.

INTRODUCTION

In CARTHAGE ON a (presumably) hot 17 July in the year 180 CE, the proconsul (Roman governor) of Africa, P. Vigellius Saturninus, took up the case of twelve professed Christians (nine men and three women) from the town of Scillium.[1] Through their spokesperson, Speratus, the accused rejected both the emperor and the "empire of this world" (*Acts of the Scillitan Martyrs* §6). The patient governor urged them to swear by the genius of the emperor and to offer prayers for his welfare. The prisoners refused. In due course (§12) the governor asked Speratus about the contents of his case (*capsa*). "Books and letters of a just man named Paul" (*libri et epistulae Pauli viri iusti*), he replied. These books would have been seized with the prisoners. The group refused a postponement of thirty days, were duly sentenced, and promptly executed by the sword.

This account raises a number of questions, such as: What were the contents of that *capsa*, properly a container for scrolls?[2] The most likely answer is books and letters written by Paul. Slightly less arguable is "(some) books as well as letters of Paul."[3] What books written by Paul might this case have held? The *Acts of Paul*? One hypothesis is that the books included a copy of the Third Gospel. That would suggest that these Christians could have been followers of Marcion, who regarded an edition of Luke as a Pauline gospel and accepted this, together with an edition of Paul's letters, as the authoritative Christian scripture, a "New Testament."[4]

One might also ask from what letters of Paul these believers learned to reject the emperor's authority. Romans 13:1-7 does not promote this posture, while 1 Tim. 1:1-2 enjoins prayer for the emperor. The Scillitan martyrs evidently advocated a rather radical Paulinism, more akin to that of the aforementioned *Acts of Paul*[5] than to the eventual corpus of thirteen letters. This two-page Latin account of a trial reveals strongly divergent appropriations of the legacy of the self-described "apostle to the gentiles" (Gal. 1:16) in the early church. Among these divergent appropriations is the most famous portrait of Paul, known from the book of Acts, in which Paul, who is not an apostle, gives constant priority to evangelizing Jews.[6] There have always been many Pauls.

The thesis of the present book is that the only real Paul is the dead Paul. This contests the standard—and far from erroneous—view that, unlike Jesus, whose words survive only in writings by others (e.g. the various Gospels), Paul's actual thoughts are directly accessible in a number of letters, in addition to which are letters not written by Paul but attributed to him, and other texts, such as the canonical book of Acts and the *Acts of Paul*.[7]

A quantity of Paul's *ipsissima verba* (actual words) certainly survive in his letters, but they do so as the result of a process that included the selection of certain letters, the probable rejection of others, at least some editing—everyone must concede that the external addresses, like those now placed on envelopes and at the head of a communication, have been lost—and the arrangement of these into a collection (an important activity, for what comes first helps determine the meaning of what follows and the occupant of the final position leaves an enduring impression), as well as the combination of multiple letters into one, the composition of what are called pseudo-Pauline letters (letters that Paul did not write), and various narratives about Paul.[8] Paul's epistles were not discovered, like thousands of ancient letters, through the labors of modern archaeologists,[9] nor were they preserved for the benefit of future historians or theologians. They were edited and copied to meet the needs of early Christians. This is an obvious but very important point: the Pauline letters that have come down to us represent Paul as some early believers wished him to be received and understood.

▇Table 1: Paul vs. Jesus?

(Note: The underlined words show contrasts between the two passages.)

Jesus Tradition (Luke 12:49-53)[10]
Jesus said, "Whoever comes to me and <u>does not hate father and mother, wife and chil-</u>
<u>dren</u>, brothers and sisters, yes, and even life itself, cannot be my disciple." (Luke 14:26)
Jesus said, "I came to bring fire to the earth, and how I wish it were already kindled! I have
a baptism with which to be baptized, and what stress I am under until it is completed! Do
you think that I have come to bring peace to the earth? No, I tell you, but rather division!
<u>From now on five in one household will be divided, three against two and two against</u>
<u>three; they will be divided: father against son and son against father, mother against</u>
<u>daughter and daughter against mother, mother-in-law against her daughter-in-law and</u>
<u>daughter-in-law against mother-in-law.</u>"

Pauline Tradition (Col. 3:18-21)[11]
<u>Wives, be subject to your husbands</u>, as is fitting in the Lord. Husbands, love your wives
and never treat them harshly. <u>Children, obey your parents in everything</u>, for this is your
acceptable duty in the Lord. Fathers, do not provoke your children, or they may lose
heart.

Why does the Christian church revere the Gospels and confess Jesus
Christ as its Lord and Savior, but prefer the more conventional ethics of the
Pauline tradition to the robust teachings of Jesus? Outside of a general dis-
taste for parent-bashing and wife-beating, the underlying question is the
mystery of how an utterly rural Galilean prophet became an object of worship in the cities of the Roman Empire. This is, from what the apostle would
call "the human perspective," the problem of why Christianity became an
international gentile religion. When the credit for this accomplishment is
awarded, one villain and one hero tower above all rivals. The hero is, of
course, Paul. The name of the villain, as all realize, is...Paul, beside whom,
in the eyes of more than a few, Judas begins to acquire a bit of luster.

How did this come about? How is it that a Greek-speaking Diaspora
Pharisee could launch an operation that would command the allegiance
of one third of the world's people by the end of the second millennium?
How could these small and isolated bands of believers become within a
few decades the normative form of the Jesus-movement and grow into
the established religion of the Western world?

Intellectual Backgrounding (and Foregrounding)

At one time Protestant scholarship, in particular, saw the task of analyzing pre- (and post-) Augustinian[12] exegesis of Paul as demonstrating how "they" misunderstood him.[13] Today, that task involves showing how these interpreters *understood* Paul.[14] Three of the most important reasons for this shift are: (1) the impact of ecumenism, which has brought scholars of varying traditions into conversation with one another; (2) the evolution of historical criticism, which summons researchers to treat their sources with respect; and (3) various impulses of postmodernism, including admiration for a plurality of views and suspicion about "pure objectivity." In fewer words: it is no longer possible to assume that there is a "correct" interpretation of Paul against which all others may be measured. If the "Paulinism" of Irenaeus of Lyon (c. 180) and that of Clement of Alexandria (c. 200) was affected by the issues and methods of their times, so also were the interpretations of Paul by Martin Luther and Karl Barth, in the sixteenth and twentieth centuries, respectively. The capacity to inspire different interpretations in response to the needs of various generations is now viewed as a sign of Paul's success.

By that criterion, few persons have been more successful. Paul has played a major role in nearly all of the movements for renewal and reform, as well as conflicts within Christianity. One example is the development of "proto-orthodox" or "early Catholic" Christianity. Rebelling against this early synthesis, Marcion of Sinope, who was active from the second quarter of the second century, sought to purge Christian thought and practice of all that did not conform to his understanding of Paul. The church he created constituted a formidable rival to the emerging "great Church." It lasted for centuries. The other formidable rival of emerging Christianity was Gnosticism, not a single church, but a variety of movements that shared a number of typical features, classically a strong dualism between matter and spirit, between the true god and the material universe. Both "Gnostic" and "orthodox" Christians appealed to Paul in defense of their views. Mani (216–277), the founder of a Gnostic world religion, took Paul as his model.[15] The medieval Christian heresies of the Paulicians and Bogomils in the east and the Cathari in the west made considerable use of Paul in expanding their views. The Cathari constituted a serious threat to catholic Christianity in the twelfth and thirteenth centuries.[16]

A survey of highlights of the impact of Romans alone yields an impressive narrative. In response to a child's *"tolle, lege"* ("pick up and read"), Augustine picked up and read Rom. 13:13: "let us live honorably as in the day, not in reveling and drunkenness, not in debauchery and licentiousness, not in quarreling and jealousy" (*Confessions* 8.12). From Romans 5 Augustine (who was engaged in a theological debate[17]) developed a view of original sin, a notion destined to have vast consequences for Western history. The brilliant twelfth-century theologian Peter Abelard drew substantially upon the arguments of Romans. A course of lectures on Romans and other Pauline epistles by John Colet (1466[?]–1519) marked a new approach to biblical interpretation, the impact of Humanism, which encouraged the exploration of critical issues and attention to historical context. Romans formed the subject of Martin Luther's first lectures on the New Testament at the new university of Wittenberg (1515–16).

One notable outcome of that Augustinian monk's attempt to understand Romans was the Protestant Reformation. Romans also played a major role in the development of the magnificent theological edifice designed by John Calvin. It is not an egregious exaggeration to say that Western Christianity split over the interpretation of Romans—not only Protestants from papalists, but also Calvinists from Lutherans. In 1738, an Anglican priest found his heart "strangely warmed" as he heard a reading of Luther's Preface to Romans. His name was John Wesley. In 1918, as the Great War that demolished "Christendom" drew towards an end, there appeared the first major writing of a young theologian. Karl Barth's commentary on Romans marked the demise of the old Liberal theology and the beginning of Neo-Orthodoxy. The Pauline legacy is, by any criterion, rich.

Another factor that has shaped recent assessment of this legacy is a shift in the nature of religious authority. Classical Protestant Orthodoxy, that is, seventeenth-century Lutheranism and Calvinism, identified Scripture—the books of the Hebrew Bible and the New Testament—as the sole basis of doctrinal and other authority. The Roman Catholic Church (as well as the eastern Orthodox and, to a lesser degree, Anglicans) also assigned a place to tradition, but Scripture was the chief official source for all Christians. Fundamental to the various parties' view of the Bible was the principle that the quality of "apostolicity" implied that apostles or their associates composed all of the New Testament texts.

The eighteenth century saw the rise of a critical skepticism that emphasized reason. This generated widespread challenges to traditional authority.[18] Questions were raised about the authorship of the Pastoral

Epistles (1 and 2 Timothy, Titus), for example.[19] This constituted a serious breach in the fortress of critical orthodoxy. If Paul (or Peter, and so on) did not compose some of the epistles transmitted under his name, the canon was no longer a secure basis for doctrine and discussion.[20] This view set the terms of the debate for about a century and a half. To state that Paul did not write 2 Timothy or Ephesians was to deny those texts authority.[21] Supporters of the tradition understood themselves as obliged to defend the Pauline authorship of the disputed epistles, while some liberals rejoiced in repudiating texts of whose teachings they disapproved.

This debate has largely abated during the last generation, not because defenders of the Pauline authorship of disputed epistles no longer exist, but because it is widely agreed that to call a certain text "inauthentic" does not mean that it is bad, or unworthy of inclusion in the New Testament. The present consensus is that Paul wrote seven epistles: Romans, 1 and 2 Corinthians, Galatians, Philippians, 1 Thessalonians, and Philemon. These are "undisputed." This book regards the others (Ephesians, Colossians, 2 Thessalonians, 1 and 2 Timothy, and Titus) as post-Pauline compositions. The object is not to strip away this unseemly husk to reveal the "real Paul," but to utilize the Deutero-Pauline letters as components of the developing Pauline legacy.

Behind this change stand not only convincing scholarly arguments but also changed understandings. As indicated above, at one time scholars opposed to certain views could help denounce them by arguing that the views in question were not from the pens of Peter, Paul, James, and others. Inauthentic texts were not apostolic and thus not authoritative. In short, if not by Paul or whomever, "kick it out." This is no longer true. Arguments that a particular text was not written by its traditional or alleged author are attempts to provide a historical context and framework rather than to invalidate the material or to discharge it from the Bible.

The understanding of the functioning of pseudonymity has also changed. On the one hand, prior to modern printing and copyrights, the attribution of a text to a certain person had more to do with the authority invoked than with authorship. The production of pseudepigraphical compositions was an accepted and honored practice by students or admirers. The leading motive for such compositions was to provide fresh formulations of the master's thought for a new situation, to make it "relevant" and "contemporary."[22] Finally, the general prejudice against the works of followers, "epigonids" or the like, is not warranted. Is Deutero-Isaiah an inferior work? Certainly not to Christians.

Excursus: Research on the Pauline Legacy

A full history of Paulinism would be a difficult project, probably beyond the scope of any single scholar.[23] Present-day scholarship focuses upon the reception of Paul. Two seminal works appeared in German in 1979, followed by an American dissertation in 1981. The value of these three contributions will be recognized by all who consult the subsequent footnotes.

Andreas Lindemann's *Paulus im ältesten Christentum* (Paul in Primitive Christianity) is noteworthy for its comprehensiveness and critical insight. If the book before you is selective, Lindemann approaches the encyclopedic. I am not attempting to replace him. A merit of Ernst Dassmann's engagingly titled *Der Stachel im Fleisch* (The Thorn in the Flesh)[24] is that he pursues his study through Irenaeus (180 CE), whereas Lindemann, whose research has concentrated upon Christian writings of the period up to c. 100 CE, closes with Marcion and the earliest apologists. On the other hand, Lindemann recognizes the value of the editing of the corpus for understanding the issues. Dassmann, a historian of early Christianity, is rather more moderate in his critical approach. The nearly simultaneous publication of these two studies indicates the congruity of method and view among Protestant and Roman Catholic scholars in Germany. The year 1981 saw the appearance of a Yale dissertation by David Rensberger, titled "As the Apostle Teaches: The Development of the use of Paul's Letters in Second-Century Christianity." This contribution was never published, primarily because of the recent appearance of Lindemann and Dassmann. In retrospect, this is regrettable, for Rensberger has a number of useful insights.

Subsequent decades have seen a profusion of work on individual studies and groups, such as the Pastoral Epistles and Colossians/Ephesians. Both particular and general studies have often appeared in collections of essays, most of which contain valuable contributions.[25] Contemporary attention to reception has not neglected the subsequent task of construction, since one cannot properly describe the subsequent Use and application of Paul without attending to the resulting portrait of the apostle. Finally, study of the reception of Paul cannot neglect divergent reception, that is, the continuing presence of intra-Pauline conflicts, which mark the process from beginning to end.

In the End, Paul...

In Romans 15, Paul spoke of his plans to take to Jerusalem a collection raised by his gentile communities to Jerusalem. For Paul, the collection was a tool for forging church unity, an attempt to find a platform for unity that was not based upon perfect agreement in belief and practice. Just as his letters were instruments for the organization of individual churches, so the collection served to remind all believers of their fundamental unity in Christ and of their origins, with which the collection forged a concrete link. Romans 15:30-31 indicates that Paul had fears about the results, fears attributed to the designs of unbelievers. This is most probably the last time Paul's voice is heard from his surviving writings. For the results of that collection the only witness is the ambiguous hints of Acts 20–21.[26] In any case, the apostle was arrested in Jerusalem, sent eventually to Rome, and there executed. His last mission was on behalf of Church unity. This theme of unity assumed a growing role among his followers in the period after his death.

Among the crucial decades of nascent Christianity, that of 60s may be no less important than the 30s. Under Nero the East was recovering in the 60s from the rapacity of earlier Roman exploitation. The emperor himself would make a concert tour of Greece, crowning his triumphs with a proclamation of liberation. On the microscopically minute end of the scale, the fire ignited by Jesus had given birth to a number of vibrant if dimly visible movements. Three leaders of the movements were most prominent. One was James, a notably pious brother of Jesus who lived in Jerusalem. Although willing to include gentiles, James was most concerned for those who remained loyal to Israelite tradition and observed Torah. He was far from the most conservative early believer, but he lined up on the right, as it were. Paul, for his part, was not the most radical, but he represented the claim that gentiles could receive the promises of God without conforming to Torah. Lodge him on the left. Between these two stood a figure and symbol of moderation, Simon, nicknamed "the rock."[27] Peter, as we call him, pursued compromises that would strive to avoid offending the observant while incorporating gentiles. During the 60s, Paul was executed in Rome, according to tradition; Peter likewise, according to a somewhat mistier tradition; and James in Jerusalem, according to Josephus.[28] In 66, Judea and neighboring regions erupted in revolt, the results of which devastated the country and destroyed the Temple, which, together with that "land," had long been the glue that bound the people together. A minor—at that time—result of the revolt was the disruption of the Christian community in Jerusalem.[29] Out of this cauldron of discontinuity there would emerge in subsequent generations two new "religions": (an increasingly gentile) Christianity and formative Rabbinic Judaism.[30] For all the survivors, the crisis was acute. So long as the temple had constituted the basis for Jewish unity, room remained for a diversity of sects. The Pharisaic party, which had a program that did not require a temple, provided the dominant contribution to a new synthesis. Representatives of various "Jesus-movements" offered, for their part, rival syntheses. The ultimately decisive "orthodox" Christian synthesis emerged during the final quarter of the second century in the work of Irenaeus of Lyons.[31] Earlier attempts at syntheses permeate the New Testament texts, the vast majority of which were written in the period *after* the deaths of Paul and the other apostles, in the 60s and later.

With the departure of the founders, a crisis of authority broke out. How were these nascent communities to be managed? One possibility was reliance upon direct revelation, the work of the Spirit in the life and worship of the community.[32] Others appealed to the authority of Jesus manifested in his teachings, now being collected and beginning to achieve written form.[33] Those who belonged to the Pauline circle worshiped the exalted Christ and made relatively limited use of stories, traditions, and sayings of or about the "earthly" Jesus prior to his passion.[34] Leaders and others may have wished to support their authority by appeal to Paul, but he was gone. The communities founded by Paul (and his network) faced problems both numerous and large.[35] His followers, including, no doubt, some of his co-workers, had to struggle to maintain that heritage. One effort to preserve this inheritance emerges in Deutero-Paulinism, which is an element of what scholars call emergent early catholicism. This concept refers, in large part, to the gradual emergence of communities organized under episcopal leadership, with clear and comprehensive regulations and a theology based upon a synthesis of various trends, characteristics of which include suspicion of some of the more adventurous speculative approaches and a firm inclination to reject moral experimentation. Others took different paths. That was a long-term result. In the short term, matters were more fluid.

From the available data it is reasonable to postulate the emergence of one or more Pauline "schools," in more or less the sense of ancient philosophy:[36] a nucleus of pupils engaged in the study and application of the master's words. Ancient schools derived from authorities. If one task of those involved in such a school was to preserve and transmit the writings of a master, an equally important responsibility was to interpret and update these teachings. Since the (written or oral) words of the master were the basis of authority in schools, the tendency to issue works under his name was quite customary. This practice, which we call pseudonymity, strikes present-day readers as quite improper. These values should not be imposed upon antiquity. It is not accidental that no Christian work from the period c. 60–c. 125 appears under the name of its actual author. All are either anonymous or pseudonymous. Authorship, for many ancient texts, refers more to authority and intellectual orientation than to composition. The use of such names as Plato, Enoch, or Paul as authorities relates to their authority or to the system invoked.

One mark of school activity is that Paul became an object of reading, whether at worship, in small groups, or in private. Public reading is mandated in 1 Thess. 5:27.[37] Reading as a reflective activity is apparent in Eph. 3:3-4 ("how the mystery was made known to me by revelation, as I have written briefly. When you read this you can perceive my insight into the mystery of Christ"). These verses indicate that Paul is now a written text for study, discussion, and reflection.[38]

The production of various Deutero-Pauline epistles, as these texts are called, witnesses to the *success and form* of Paul's technique of writing letters. Just as the transformation of Jesus' parables and the production of new parables testify to the power of that form,[39] so these later epistles show that Paul's authority endured and that his methods were deemed worthy of emulation. Individuals will have different positions about the authorship of this or that epistle, but all should understand and agree that their existence manifests flattery in its least adulterated form. One object of such "school" activity was to foster a sense of universalism, *to make the local work of Paul in various places catholic.* The social, rather than the historical, moral, or ideological, implications of pseudonymity are linked to the pursuit of broadened horizons. These "schools" sought to stabilize communities and relate them to the larger whole. Community growth, inter-connections with other churches, and interaction with the non-Christian world are all aspects of this phenomenon. Another is the subtle transformation of the understanding of Paul as an example and source of assistance for believers. These activities reflect variable stances toward the authority of Israelite scriptures.[40] Ephesus is the most likely seat for the earliest of such activities, which may have begun in Paul's lifetime.[41]

The attempts to maintain Pauline communities after his martyrdom, to build connections with other parts of the Jesus movement/nascent Christian Church, resulted in a number of activities:[42]

The development, as noted, of so-called early Catholicism, linked relatively conservative bodies in various locations to one another through communication and the sharing of various resources, including money.

The production of Deutero-Pauline letters was a major feature of this process.[43]

The formation of a collection of Pauline epistles to be shared among the faithful and used as an authority included editorial efforts to transform the apostle's communications addressed to particular communities into general communications to all believers.

The composition of narrative and other texts about Paul, from which varied texts it is possible to discern underlying narratives. Letters contain or, more often, presume a story. One of the challenges of reading other people's mail is the reconstruction of those underlying narratives. As in the case of Jesus "the teacher," legends and stories about Paul developed. These legends, which often competed with one another, *preceded* the use of his letters in a wider sense—collected and shared—although, in the course of time, the letters could be included within them.[44]

The "canonical," in several senses, form of this narrative constitutes what could be called, with some hesitation based upon both propriety and taste, a "paulology."[45] After his death, Paul was widely celebrated as a missionary, pastor, and martyr. Some of the motifs related to this postmortem portrait of Paul are common to such otherwise different works as Colossians, Ephesians, Acts, the Pastoral Epistles, 1 Clement, and the *Acts of Paul*. In outline form, with intentionally "creedal" wording, these are:

> Paul, the missionary/apostle to the gentiles,
> evangelized the entire world and is now a figure within salvation
>   history.
> Having once been an (essentially polytheist) unbeliever and persecutor,
>   Paul subsequently converted by the power of Christ. Paul
>   is a Redeemed Persecutor, the prototypical arch-sinner
>   who became beneficiary of grace.
> Paul suffered and died, a martyr whose commitment to the gospel was
>   sealed by his salutary passion and death.
>   Paul remains as a hero,
>   a bearer of salvation,

a teacher of the church.

As a teacher Paul is a promulgator of virtuous conduct,

an opponent of false teaching and will brook no deviation,

and a champion of unity and ecclesiastical consolidation.[46]

The portraits of Paul arising in early (and subsequent) Christianity did not, to reiterate, derive from a concern to preserve history for the benefit of subsequent investigators, but from the problems of those churches in their own times. These challenges helped to motivate the collection of Paul's highly esteemed letters.

Each of the elements in the foregoing narrative outline has some basis in Paul's life and writings, but they emerge in new forms and with new meanings after the crises following his death, the Jewish revolt, the proliferation of Jesus movements and followers, and various pressures upon believers in the Christ. This construct, this paulology, is not by necessity linked to Paul as a writer of letters—witness Acts. Others, however, continued the tradition of letter writing, seeking to enhance these images by means of texts purportedly written by Paul, as well as letters inspired by Pauline practice. The bare bones of this outline require a bit of flesh.

The Apostle

In the Deutero-Pauline letters and the *Acts of Paul* Paul is, in most instances, the only apostle.[47] Paul becomes *the* apostle without peer, even to those who have not heard him. "His apostleship transcends the particularities of time and place and encompasses the world."[48] He alone writes, speaks, and acts.[49]

The absent, suffering Paul became a substitute for the visiting Paul. This is to say that the martyr death of Paul both ruptured his relation to the communities he served and gave impetus to collect his letters as the apostolic deposit and bequest to his followers.[50] In some ways the dead Paul was more acceptable than a living apostle. One could more readily take exception to the letters of a living Paul; his death colored and changed the reception of his words. Just as the post-mortem Jesus became a universal savior, so the dead Paul greatly expanded the influence of his living predecessor.

Evangelist of the Entire World

As the apostle *par excellence*, Paul's apostolic field is not a single province, but "all creation."[51] Paul is not just the "minister" of the gospel but of the church (Col. 1:24-25). The strength of Paul's authority is apparent in the effort to ascribe universality to his jurisdiction. Paul is the one apostle to all members of the one church, present and future. From the perspective of the object of unity, the Paul of the canonical Acts presents less of a contrast to the figure of the Deutero-Pauline letters than is sometimes asserted. Although not an apostle in Acts—the title is restricted to followers of the earthly Jesus—he is, like them, a witness,[52] and, more importantly, gentile missionary *extraordinaire*. Peter, rather than Paul, had, with divine prodding, initiated the gentile mission, but Paul was its effective agent. For Acts, as for Ephesians, the success of the gentile mission raises the question of unity among Jewish and gentile believers. Once again, it is possible to point to the continuation of themes addressed already by Paul in Romans. Acts also affirms that Paul's arrest came as a result of his quest for unity. If the Paul of Acts is not in a literal sense the sole missionary to "the ends of the earth" (Acts 1:8), he is the essential instrument of that program. (In later texts *kēryx* ["herald"], with its sacral and universal connotations, emerges as a preferred description of Paul's role.[53]) Ephesians trumpets a Paul who is more universal mystagogue than world-wide evangelist (Eph. 3:9). The concept of universality admits considerable variation.

To create a universal audience for Paul's message, the apostle's followers were obliged to let Paul's principle of not issuing orders to communities that he had not founded languish. Already in Colossians, "Paul" begins to address those who had not heard him (1:4). Ephesians does speak of "apostles" (somewhat awkwardly as figures of the apparent past),[54] but there is no doubt that Paul is the only significant representative of this group. The Pastoral Epistles (1 and 2 Timothy, Titus) likewise do not make the explicit claim that Paul is the only apostle, but he alone exercises and deputizes authority in the church.

Later acts and letters integrate the two approaches of the Deutero-Pauline letters and the canonical acts. *Third Corinthians*,[55] the Coptic *Apocalypse of Paul*, and the *Epistula Apostolorum*[56] link Paul, his teaching, and the subsequent gentile mission with the Twelve. The *Acts of Paul* does not provide details about other apostles, but leaves no doubt that Paul proclaims the words and deeds of Christ (that is, the contents of the written Gospels) in harmony with others.[57] The purpose of displaying Paul as more or less the only apostle and as the evangelist of the whole (gentile) world is not simply to glorify Paul, nor is it to denigrate other apostles. Behind this image lies the goal of forging unity among a number of scattered and diverse communities. It is typical of the process of heroization that Paul needs no more than a few weeks to plant a successful mission and move on. The author of Acts is obliged to provide a rationale for lengthy stays, as in the vision of 18:9-11.[58]

Several strategies served this pursuit of unity and universality. The geographical symbolism of Acts (1:8; 13:47)[59] and *1 Clement* (5:7, above) is apparent. Colossians and Ephesians are notable for their use of *pas* ("all, every").[60] Every nation, person, race, and place is embraced. The cosmic christology and ecclesiology developed in those texts also serves to give the one church a single, worldwide horizon. Ephesians takes the process a step further by omitting personal greetings or local details: only the bearer, Tychichus, is named (6:21). This lack of detail and engagement with the readers, who are not even addressed with the characteristic "sisters and brothers," is often laid against the text. Presuming that the writer could have concocted any details desired, or, like the author of Colossians, borrowed them,[61] it is more likely that the author eschewed such devices in order to enhance the general applicability of the message.[62]

Redeemed Sinner

New believers can identify with the "redeemed persecutor" who had been converted from a sinful life. Although this view is at some variance with Paul's own self-understanding,[63] it constituted an important model for those who had turned away from the evils of the world. Among the most edifying, if least historically defensible, elements of the post-Pauline construct is the portrayal of "the pre-Christian Paul" as a vicious sinner, the veritable enemy of the people of God, and, more or less, as a gentile. First Timothy 1:12-17 is perhaps the most thoroughgoing example of this tendency:

> I am grateful to Christ Jesus our Lord, who has strengthened me, because he judged me faithful and appointed me to his service, even though I was formerly a *blasphemer*, a persecutor, and a *man of violence*. But I received mercy because I had acted ignorantly in unbelief, and the grace of our Lord overflowed for me with the faith and love that are in Christ Jesus. The saying is sure and worthy of full acceptance, that Christ Jesus came into the world to save *sinners—of whom I am the foremost*. But for that very reason I received mercy, so that in me, as the foremost, Jesus Christ might display the utmost patience, making me an example to those who would come to believe in him for eternal life. To the King of the ages, immortal, invisible, the only God, be honor and glory forever and ever. Amen. (Emphasis added.)

Of the several terms, only "persecutor" belongs to Paul's self-description.[64] The epithets "blasphemer" and "violent person" in v. 13[65] do not correspond to Paul's view of his career, nor does he describe himself as the "foremost of sinners" (vv. 15-16). "Ignorance" (v. 13) brings to mind Acts 3:17; 17:30, and Eph. 4:18, where the term serves to explain, if not to excuse, *gentile* behavior.[66] The pre-conversion Paul of 1 Timothy is as ignorant as the idolatrous Athenians. The contrast between "pagan" and "Christian" Paul is central to the moral teaching of the Pastorals and their emphasis upon "law and order." Paul is the prototypical sinner[67] and therefore the model convert.

First Timothy is not the sole witness to this tendency. The quite assuredly pre-Lucan legend of "The Conversion of Paul" (Acts 9) includes this remarkable phrase: "Who are you, Lord?" (v. 5). Such a question belongs to a polytheistic milieu, in which one needs to know just which particular god's ire has been aroused and the reason for the epiphany. It is therefore quite at home in "conversion stories,"[68] but scarcely appropriate in the present context. Saul, as he is called in Acts, is quite aware of whom he is persecuting, and he had not learned at the feet of Gamaliel or elsewhere that there were many true lords. The persecutor presented here is a typical enemy of the people of God, and to all intents and purposes a polytheist sinner.[69]

Acts depicts the persecuting Paul as a bloodthirsty beast, the personification of *mania* ("raging insanity").[70] Only the most vicious and twisted of officials would seize *and bind* women no less than men. In Acts 26:10, Paul advises Agrippa that he had consistently voted for the death penalty against followers of Jesus. The confrontation with the risen one transformed Paul from darkness to light, error to truth, madness[71] to moderation, "*le miracle des miracles*."[72]

The Paul of Eph. 3:8 is pleased to characterize himself as "the most insignificant of saints."[73] This interesting modification of 1 Cor. 15:9 ("least among the *apostles*") follows the same path. Paul has a past so sinful that he could scarcely dare raise his head but for the grace of God.[74] Ephesians 2:3—"All of us once lived among them in the passions of our flesh, following the desires of flesh and senses, and we were by nature children of wrath, like everyone else"[75]—indicates that this understanding of the pre-Christian Paul had taken hold by the close of the first century.[76]

The parenetic and catechetical utility of this contrast between wretched sinner and mild-mannered apostle is patent. Paul illuminates both virtue and vice, with conversion providing the means and point of radical change, the pivot for the shift of eons now construed in terms of individual conversions. No longer the immediate agent of gentile conversions, Paul becomes the very model of the modern majority, a gentile convert, a figure with whom such converts can identify and to whom they may look for both inspiration and guidance.[77]

Suffering and Saving

Paul's life as a Christian missionary was, so to speak, no bed of roses. Rather than regard his misfortunes as inexplicable, due to bad luck or the like, the historical Paul regarded his suffering as authentication of his apostolic credentials,[78] verification that he was an imitator of Christ. Post-Pauline products did not neglect this feature of his existence. They intensified it.

Paul's proper place was in jail. To the undisputed "imprisonment epistles," Philippians and Philemon, were added Colossians, Ephesians, 2 Timothy, *3 Corinthians*, and *Laodiceans*. Acts reports a number of apprehensions and incarcerations, culminating with the arrest in Jerusalem of ch. 21.[79] For the residue of Acts, Paul remains, at least technically, a prisoner. In *1 Clem.* 5:7, the number of his imprisonments has reached the altogether satisfactory total of seven.[80] The *Acts of Paul* reports imprisonments in Iconium,[81] Ephesus,[82] Philippi,[83] and Rome.[84]

In all of these contexts the theme of imprisonment gave scope for the development of rhetorical pathos with its capacity for moving the reader. Second Timothy 4 is the most extravagant example of this potential. No doubt such stories provided inspiration to Christians faced with actual arrest and imprisonment. In the epistolary tradition, imprisonment also functions as an element of post-mortem *parousia* ("presence"). Superficially, the apostle cannot visit in person because he is in prison. The continuing vitality of epistolary *parousia* is affirmed by an imitator, Polycarp:

> Not that I should be taking on myself to write to you in this way about the life of holiness, my brothers and sisters, if you yourselves had not invited me to do so. For I am as far as anyone else of my sort from having the wisdom of our blessed and glorious Paul. During his residence with you he gave the people of those days clear and sound instruction in the word of truth, while he was there in person among them; and even after his departure he still sent letters that, if you study them attentively, will enable you to make progress in the faith which was delivered to you. (*Smyrn.* 3.1-3)[85]

At a symbolic level, imprisonment gives scope for the use of bonds and prison as images for death.[86] It is possible that this symbolism provided a kind of cloak for authors (and readers?) of pseudonymous texts. Presence through absence is used in Acts at the point of Paul's greatest success: the mission to Ephesus. Paul is rarely "off-stage" from Acts 15 through 28, but he is not described as personally active in 19:13-20, 23-40. Explanations of this odd phenomenon tend to focus upon the apologetic desire to remove Paul as far as possible from the riot. This has merit, but it is also valid, and perhaps more cogent, to look to the Ephesian church of Luke's era, where Paul was present by reputation and by legend, in message and in memory. The absent Paul continues to care for the flock.[87]

Later tradition and literature glorify and magnify Paul's suffering, which becomes a leading means through which the gospel is spread (Col. 1:24-28).[88] Rather than inhibit his work, suffering provides the central impetus to growth.[89] In the canonical and apocryphal Acts persecution is a leading motive of the plot.[90] Persecution, intended to suppress the mission, backfires because it does no more than drive the apostle on to new sites. If the various Acts give full range to the possibility for edifying narrative, the Pastorals provide occasion for making the moral implications and example clear. Second Timothy 3:10-11, for instance, says:

> Now you have observed my teaching, my conduct, my aim in life, my faith, my patience, my love, my steadfastness, my persecutions and suffering the things that happened to me in Antioch,[91] Iconium, and Lystra. What persecutions I endured! Yet the Lord rescued me from all of them.

Utilizing persecution as the mainspring of mission in the narrative works may appear to be a relatively harmless literary device. By reading these accounts together with the epistles, one perceives the underlying *theologoumenon*: because Paul's suffering enables the gospel to spread, it has soteriological significance.[92] In the undisputed correspondence, Paul had already played with the correspondence between absent savior and absent apostle, with the themes of *parousia* and *apousia* (presence and absence).[93] Following his death, the absent, suffering Paul became a substitute for the visiting Paul. Like Jesus, who had also suffered, he remained "present in spirit." Colossians 2:5—"For though I am absent in body, yet I am with you in spirit, and I rejoice to see your morale and the firmness of your faith in Christ"—doubtless takes its impetus from expressions such as that found in 1 Cor. 5:3,[94] but there has been a major shift. Paul, like the Christ of Matthew (Matt. 28:18-20, and so on), is always with his followers, observing—rather like Santa Claus in the cautionary song—the actions of those around him.

Although Colossians is apparently the earliest of the Deutero-Paulines and closest to Paul in thought and style, this text assimilates Paul to Christ in some remarkable ways. Not only is the apostle present in spirit, but his sufferings also have a vicarious effect. Accommodations of Paul's "passion" to that of his master raise few questions so long as they are regarded as imitating Christ. Some texts may, however, go beyond such "mere" parallelism.

Best known are the "Jesus–Paul parallels" of Luke and Acts,[95] where the narrator's intentions become patent in the reciprocity of "influences." At points, Luke may have adjusted the Gospel account to correspond with that of Acts.[96] In any case, the similarities are numerous enough to demand attention. The author intended to show a close correspondence between the ministry and passion of the two leading heroes (and others). Why, then, does Luke not narrate the death of Paul, an event of which he was surely aware?[97] There are strong arguments for interpreting Acts 27–28 as a symbolic narration of Paul's death and resurrection.[98] Such readings are open to challenge. In this instance, the Lucan parallels and the internal imagery of Luke and Acts provide both impetus and control. Those who prefer a "concrete" reading of the surface text must deal not only with the problem of the length of the account, exciting as it is, but also with Paul's essentially free status following his delivery from the deep. Has the narrator forgotten (for a while) that Paul is supposed to be a prisoner?[99]

If the living and abiding Paul with whom Acts leaves the reader has experienced a kind of crossing over from death to life, the narrators of Colossians and Ephesians speak from heaven, as it were, to believers urged to share with him the heavenly throne of God.[100] Second Thessalonians also grounds salvation with Paul and his colleagues.[101] The narrative approach of the *Acts of Paul* is quite explicit.[102]

Paul the Teacher

The general tendency of the post-Pauline period was to promote Paul as a "teacher of righteousness" (e.g., *1 Clem.* 5:7). The "righteousness" (*dikaiosynē*) in view was not justification by faith but proper conduct.[103] This view of the apostle as first and foremost an instructor in good behavior dominated proto-orthodox writing until the late second century.

The value of Paul's words for hammering false teachers was also prominent in the first three decades of the second century (note Acts, Pastoral Epistles, Polycarp), but then fell into desuetude. Here the impact of Marcion and various "Gnostics" is apparent. Until Irenaeus (c. 180), the major exponents of Pauline theology belonged to the heretical side of the eventual division. The proto-orthodox stressed his moral message. The nature of that message was crystallized in the "Household Codes" that first appeared in Colossians and remained prominent in texts directly or indirectly associated with Paul (Ephesians, 1 Peter, *1 Clement*, the Pastoral Epistles, Ignatius, Polycarp).[104]

The Codes show Paul as also a general manager of families and communities who is able to issue firm, universally applicable instructions. They presume, in conjunction with the ancient world in general, a society that is both stable and congruent with the universal (as they saw it) empire. The Deutero-Pauline tendency to shift from temporal (eschatological) to spatial categories and images is another means through which universalism is implemented.[105]

CONCLUSION

There are a number of ways in which the formation and proliferation of traditions about Jesus and Paul are similar. In both cases, followers set out to preserve his heritage by producing texts from oral and written traditions. The process included the amalgamation of different genres, the editing of multiple texts into one, experiments with different sorts of editions, and the production of "apocrypha."[106]

Universalism was another interest. In this matter Paul had a head start, as it were, through his explicitly gentile and ecumenical mission, but followers took pains to make his occasional letters to specific communities applicable to believers everywhere. Matthew, John, and Luke (as well as the composer of Mark 16:9-20[107]) sought to establish the worldwide, inclusive character of the Jesus movement. Universalism is not simply a missionary ideal. It serves also to make the particular Galilean and Judean teachings of Jesus and the occasional instructions of Paul to particular communities general.[108]

Paul came to have an advantage that Jesus lacked: a sinful past that in itself exemplified the benefits of conversion. He was a figure with whom gentile converts could find identification as well as inspiration. Both Jesus and Paul gathered disciples or followers to whom they delivered their message and over whom they exercised spiritual and pastoral care.[109] For both Jesus and Paul, heroic suffering came to play a decisive role. The gospels that achieved normative status among mainstream believers were those based upon the "creedal" shape introduced by Mark, namely, the suffering, dying, and rising Son of God. What validated Jesus' message and saved his followers was not the specific content of his ethical teaching, nor his great deeds, but the offering of his own life on the cross. In the course of time Paul's suffering not only acquires romantic hues; it also comes to have redemptive significance. The bringer of salvation is also a savior. It need not be said that a rather full repertory of saving deeds, exorcisms, healings, and resurrections, accompanied that emphasis.

This is not to suggest that Paul becomes a competitor with his Lord for membership in the Holy Trinity. The goal of this survey is to state that the development of writings about and of Jesus and Paul followed some similar lines because they were responses to similar problems and elements of projects seeking to maintain and nurture the heritage of faith.

This introduction has presented a summary of the big picture, the major limbs of the tree, at a high level of generalization. Hereafter the subject will be twigs and leaves, as well as various small branches. (See the diagram of the Pauline "family tree," Appendix.) This is to say that this introduction really is an introduction, a map of the sites to be visited and a structure to be held in mind while examining the various texts.

The following table attempts to highlight the extent to which problems about authorship and whether the canonical text is a single letter pervade the corpus.

Table 2: Letters Attributed to Paul in the Early Church

(Note: The letter marks should be viewed loosely as an academic metaphor. An "A" does not represent excellence, however. A high "grade" of authenticity indicates a high degree of scholarly consensus that the text was written by Paul; a high "grade" of integrity indicates that the extant "letter" corresponds to the original scope of a single document.)

Text	Authenticity	Integrity
Romans	A	B+[118]
1 Corinthians	A	B+[119]
2 Corinthians	A	C-[120]
Galatians	A	A
Ephesians[110]	C-	A
Philippians	A	B-[121]
Colossians	C	B[122]
1 Thessalonians	A	A-[123]
2 Thessalonians	C	A(-)[124]
1 Timothy	D	A[125]
2 Timothy	D	A
Titus	D	A
Philemon	A	A
Hebrews[111]	D-	A-
3 Corinthians[112]	F	A
Laodiceans[113]	F[117]	A[125]
Paul and Seneca[114]	F	A
Alexandrians[115]	F	—
Others[116]	F	—

Only in the cases of Galatians and (the tiny) Philemon is there a high degree of agreement that the texts were, in fact, written by Paul and preserved intact. Both the order, placement, and contents of the Pauline corpus varied considerably in ancient manuscripts and lists.

1. Paul Becomes a Book

The Introduction claimed that various apostolic letters played an important role in the post-Pauline Christian world. The object of the present chapter is to show how Paul became a book. The analogy with Jesus is again useful. Just as Jesus became a story contained within a book (the Gospel[s]), so Paul survived in the form of a book—collected letters. This may seem too obvious to note, but it is a fact of considerable importance that is readily ignored or denied. Although some letters may have continued to enjoy an independent existence, since the first quarter of the first century, Paul has been known through collected epistles. In both gospels and letter-collections, what has survived or been invented or modified is the result of choices related to perceived current needs.

There were stories about Jesus, but much of the tradition contained what Jesus *said*. Those who disseminated these teachings were not concerned with the preservation of gossip or trivia. We do not learn whether, for example, Jesus was bald or what his preferences in food and beverages were.[1] The teachings of Jesus were applied to issues in the lives and communities of his followers. Now, those who promulgated these teachings were unencumbered by actual writings of Jesus, who never published. Paul had not been so wise. Already in his lifetime he was known—and sometimes criticized—for being more potent in writing than in person.[2] Paul had developed the letter as a pastoral and administrative instrument for the management of his communities. Now absent, like Jesus, Paul could continue to address the faithful through letters. The editing of letters, the production of new letters, and the formation of collections proceeded simultaneously. These activities should be studied in conjunction with one another to gain insight into the process by which Paul's authority was consolidated and extended. The object of this activity was not, to reiterate, preservation of historical data or the maintenance of sacred words. It was urgent, immediate, and practical. Before investigating the process, it will be useful to reflect briefly upon the nature of letters and about collections of letters.

What is a Letter?

Letters are social documents.[3] Unlike epic poems or novels, which may indeed have social functions and reflect social realities or desires, letters are elements of social relations and, if genuine letters, are not to be read as tracts. The consistent form of the Greek personal letter shows that a letter is a substitute for a meeting. A letter is one half of a dialogue or a substitute for an actual dialogue, in which the writer speaks to a person or persons as though they were present. A letter is speech in the medium of writing; this in apparent in its form, which corresponds to a visit or an interview. Reduced to its absolute essentials, that form is: greeting, conversation, farewell. Letters are addressed to individuals or groups from whom the sender is separated by physical or social distance. One will misunderstand letters if one focuses only upon the ideas within them.

Letters involve different types of social relationships: hierarchical, between superiors and subordinates and vice-versa, between equals, and within a family network. Some letters have an official character, including royal decrees and communications of a governor to an emperor, such as Pliny's famous letters to Trajan.[4] Other letters are literary, including epistles in verse. Such classifications should not be viewed as absolute. The letters of Paul were real, but they were neither private (even Philemon addresses a community) nor devoid of literary and formal features. They were intended as a form of apostolic "visit" (*parousia*) to be read aloud to communities (1 Thess. 5:27, cited below).

One must also take with utmost seriousness the function of letters. They are irrevocably dialectical in character. The letter is an appropriate genre for a movement that understands itself to be in the process of formation, on the way. In the time of Paul, this was true in the historical sense, but even today it remains an essential aspect of Christian self-understanding. If a believer were to try to read the mind of the Holy Spirit, so to speak—a risky proposition—one might well say that precisely these factors have led to the canonization of Paul's letters: their understanding of theology as dialectic and as always in process. The ephemeral and ad hoc character of these epistles says something about the totality of the theological enterprise. The difficulty of accepting this leads some to wish to treat Paul's letters as if they had been dropped from the sky on tablets of stone. That is a serious error. These letters are exploratory probes. All of these unremarkable facts about the nature, character, and function of letters generated difficulties for subsequent readers.

If the teachings of Jesus later had to address a broader range of situations than their original circumstances, the same requirement applied to Paul's letters. In a sentence, the problem is: "What does what Paul may have said to his converts at Corinth at some particular time and in some particular setting have to do with *me*?" Reading other people's mail can be difficult, as centuries of attempts to interpret Paul demonstrate. The first task of those who wished to keep alive the voice of Paul was to share his words in such a way that they would address those of other and later situations. Paul's letters were *particular*.[5] His followers had to make them *general*. The story of the process by which the particularity of Pauline correspondence became catholic is not exciting, but it both reflected *and* created pictures of Paul.

Collected Letters

Collections of correspondence issued today are quite like those prepared in antiquity. These may be prepared or initiated by the author, but more commonly stem from the work of later editors. At present one may see "complete" collections prepared for historical research, but, now as then, selection was normal. Editors typically exclude whatever is deemed trivial or unimportant,[6] possibly also items deemed unflattering or offensive. Modern collections are usually chronological, although they may be grouped under thematic heads in order of composition. Chronological considerations could also play a part in ancient collections.[7] The activity of different editors can result in multiple editions over the course of time. Concerns about forgery are not an important factor in modern collections.

That was not the case in antiquity, where concerns about forgery loomed large, and for good reason. Of the thirteen letters that have come down under the name of Plato, seven, at most, are considered genuine. The philosophic tradition found letters an effective medium of communication. Most of these, such as the letters of various Cynics, are undisputed forgeries. A number of the collections of intellectual letters have, or are approaching, the form of epistolary novels.[8] These collections have value in assessing the Pastoral Epistles and the correspondence between Paul and Seneca.[9] In most cases, these collections were planned and executed as such. Other collections, like the *Moral Epistles* of Seneca, used the letter form to evoke intimacy but were not dispatched as actual letters.[10] These collections remain important to the interpreter of Paul, especially the use of letters in the philosophical tradition, as these focused, particularly in the Hellenistic and Roman eras, upon moral advice. An important phenomenological parallel is the letters of Epicurus, which were written to communities of his followers.[11]

The Latin letters of Cicero and the Younger Pliny are examples of actual letters individually dispatched to their recipients. David Trobisch, who focused upon collections generated by their authors, investigated about two hundred ancient collections and constructed the following general model of development. First, authors prepare letters for formal publication. These editions are subsequently expanded, and further editions emerge. In due course, comprehensive editions pulled together all known and available predecessors.[12] As his focus indicates, Trobisch wished to make a case for regarding Paul as the driving factor behind the collection of his letters. This remains possible. Trobisch argued that the original collection generated by Paul included Romans, the Corinthian correspondence, and Galatians.[13] This effectively makes Paul the editor of canonical 1 and 2 Corinthians, a conclusion that the reconstruction of the latter renders unlikely.[14] One might also ask whether the apostle wished people to learn about the extent to which his authority was challenged and whether he wished to invite believers to compare and contrast Romans and Galatians, for example. This collection would have provided potential opponents with formidable ammunition. One must also note that this hypothetical collection evidently had not reached Rome by the end of the first century.[15]

It is legitimate to ask whether those first responsible for collecting Pauline correspondence were aware of the tradition of literary letters. This is a possibility, but it requires evidence before it can be posited as the basis of a theory.[16] Nonetheless, Trobisch has done a service by raising the question of Pauline impetus, in addition to his broad research. If Paul did not publish a small collection of his correspondence, he may well have begun the practice of using them for further reflection. Romans, for example, includes reworked material from Galatians and 1 Corinthians. Paul also almost certainly attended to the making of copies of his letters.

My Introduction posited Ephesus as one likely site for a "Pauline school" (or "schools"). Ephesus is also the most likely site for the production of the corpus.[17] Producers of this collection had several tasks, including selection, arrangement, editorial modification, consolidation, and the composition of new items. Letters of Paul kept appearing until the fourth century. No Bible of today contains the epistle to the Laodiceans, but many medieval Bibles did. Armenian Christians of another era could long profit from a third letter to the Corinthians. The earliest lists[18] of Paul's letters do not contain 1 and 2 Timothy and Titus, but the oldest extant text of Paul's letters does include Hebrews, which is anonymous and not by Paul.

Arrangement is also crucial. The first and last items in a literary catalogue or collection are important. What comes first and what appears last helps establish meaning. One edition, utilized by Marcion, an ardent Paulinist of the second century, put the red-hot letter to the Galatians first. A different impression arises from opening with Romans, wherein Paul was at his diplomatic best. The oldest preserved text, P46,[19] begins with Romans, followed by Hebrews. That edition stemmed from Alexandria, whose scholars wanted Hebrews to be Pauline and prominent because it justified their "allegorical" method of interpretation.[20]

The Collection of Paul's Letters

Church history indicates that the initial impetus was toward enrichment, expansion of the body of Pauline letters through the addition of other letters until the late second century (and beyond). In contemporary terms, this would be called the promotion of diversity and pluralism. The ultimate harvest yielded fourteen Pauline letters (including the anonymous Hebrews)[21] and seven others (the revealingly named "catholic" or "general" epistles).[22] The building of a collection indicates that Paul's letters were viewed as authoritative, but it does not mean that these works were regarded as part of a "canon" of inspired sacred scripture. The term "canon" is best restricted to the fourth and later centuries, when church councils and leaders could promulgate rules and attempt to make generally binding decisions. Inspiration was a broad concept in the early church, not restricted to the original apostles and those of the first Christian generation.[23] The most widely received canonical collection includes:

Letters of Paul, arranged by those addressed to:
communities (10),[24]
individuals (4).
Other letters (the catholic epistles: James, 1-2 Peter, 1-3 John, Jude).
All of these letters were edited, to a lesser or greater degree. This activity included:

1. *Selection* of the letters to be included.
2. *Arrangement* in order by one or more of these criteria:
    a. doctrine—for example, placing first that letter deemed most important for revealing Paul's thought;
    b. length—from longest to shortest, a criterion that is still visible in the current arrangement;
    c. type, community, followed by individual—as still enshrined in contemporary Bibles;
    d. Presumed chronological order of composition.
3. *Generalization* through such means as omitting the address (e.g., "at Rome"), or universalizing it (1 Cor. 1:2).
4. The *combination* of multiple letters into one, for various reasons.
5. *Interpolations* and *deletions*, reflecting diverse tendencies.
6. Composition of *inscriptions, prefaces, and subscripts*, providing data about the contents, time of composition, and provenance.
7. *Liturgical* changes for lectionary purposes, as well as the addition of blessings, doxologies, and final "amens."
8. *Removal* of personal names.
9. The *composition* of Pseudonymous letters.[25]

The foregoing summary is not a tidy set of universally recognized facts. Competing views and theories exist. The next task will be to develop the arguments implied in the foregoing sketch. This entails immersion in a welter of details, varied hypotheses, and efforts to see whether and which trees constitute a grove. Behind the following exposition lie myriad hours of patient scholarly research conducted over many generations—indeed, over nearly two millennia. One point of departure is comparison of lists deduced from writers or manuscripts:

Table 3: The Order of Pauline Letters in Various Early Sources

Marcion[26]	P46[28]	Muratori[30]	Claromontanus[31]	Gelasianum[33]
Galatians	Romans	1 Corinthians	Romans	Romans
1 Corinthians	Hebrews	2 Corinthians	1 Corinthains	1 Corinthians
2 Corinthians	1 Corinthians	Ephesians	2 Corinthians	2 Corinthians
Romans	2 Corinthians	Philippians	Galatians	Ephesians
1 Thessalonians	Ephesians	Colossians	Ephesians	1 Thessalonians
2 Thessalonians	Galatians	Galatians	1 Timothy	2 Thessalonians
Laodiceans[27]	Philippians	1 Thessalonians	Titus	Galatians
Colossians	Colossians	2 Thessalonians	Colossians	Philippians
Philippians	1 Thessalonians	Romans	Philemon[32]	Colossians
Philemon	2 Thessalonians	Titus		1 Timothy
	Philemon[29]	1 Timothy		2 Timothy
		2 Timothy		Titus
		Philemon		Philemon
		Rejected:		
		Laodiceans		
		Alexandrians		
		Others		

Ambrosiaster[34]	Victorinus of Petau[36]	Augustine[37]	Syriac[38]
Romans	Romans	Romans	Galatians
1 Corinthians	1 Corinthians	1 Corinthians	1 Corinthians
2 Corinthians	2 Corinthians	2 Corinthians	2 Corinthians
Galatians	Ephesians	Galatians	Romans
Ephesians	1 Thessalonians	Ephesians	Hebrews
Philippians[35]	2 Thessalonians	Philippians	Colossians
1 Thessalonians	Galatians	1 Thessalonians	Ephesians
2 Thessalonians	Philippians	2 Thessalonians	Philippians
Titus	Colossians	Colossians	1 Thessalonians
Colossians	1 Timothy	1 Timothy	2 Thessalonians
1 Timothy	2 Timothy	2 Timothy	2 Timothy[39]
2 Timothy	Titus	Titus	Titus
Philemon	Philemon	Philemon	Philemon
Hebrews			

These lists are useful for evaluating the growth and development of the corpus.[40] They illuminate the processes of *selection* and *arrangement*. The two earliest known collections, for example, do not contain the Pastoral Epistles. This supports the judgment that they are Deutero-Pauline. The fluctuating position and occasional absence of Hebrews reflects ambivalence about this anonymous letter, which was accepted early in the East but with reluctance in the West.[41] Hebrews was found, or listed, in three general places: within the letters to communities (usually either after Romans, as in P46, or after 2 Corinthians), after the church letters, or after the Pauline letters (as found in modern English Bibles).[42] The early Eastern theologians Clement of Alexandria and Origen sought a *rationale* for including of Hebrews among Paul's epistles. They did not have to argue for its inclusion.[43]

The two dominant criteria are arrangement by length, from longest to shortest, a system found in other ancient collections of texts, and the separation of community letters from those addressed to persons. The fluctuating position of Colossians in the Latin tradition lends some support that this letter was once combined with Philemon, the contents of which formed its conclusion.[44] It is highly tempting to attribute the initial place of Galatians in Marcion's list to theological motivation: this is Paul's most cogent statement of his view of salvation apart from the Torah and of his independence from other apostles. The same order in Syriac lists suggests caution—although these lists may have derived from Marcion's edition.[45]

Selection implies that not all of Paul's correspondence was preserved. The most interesting of items known to be lost would be the letter of Paul to Corinth, mentioned in 1 Cor. 5:9. No collection had room for letters *to* Paul (cf. 1 Cor. 7:1), a loss lamented by scholars, if not others. The apostle doubtless wrote a number of administrative letters in relation to the funds he raised for Jerusalem and about other matters, as well as shorter personal communications.[46] Letters treating the collection survive in 2 Corinthians 8 and 9. Philippians 4:10-20 was evidently a short note of thanks.[47] Philemon is an extant personal note (although even this addresses a house-church [v. 2]). John Knox recognized that the primary question raised by Philemon was the fact of its survival.[48] The chief reason for the disappearance of administrative material was its particularity (not to mention possible banality). The traces that exist indicate that such correspondence may have been relatively substantial.[49]

The Circulation of Paul's Letters

The circulation of letters constitutes an appropriate point of departure, since this was the basis of Paul's literary influence and also touches upon the question of the apostle's own role in the collection and distribution of his letters. Paul intended that his letters be read aloud to the entire community. He did not speak to one section of the community (e.g., women or "the strong") out of the hearing of others. First Thessalonians 5:27 probably represents the typical situation: "I adjure you by the Lord that this letter be read to all the believers."[50] Could all of the believers at

Thessalonica assemble in one place? This is possible, but such was not the case for Galatians, where the letter is addressed "to the churches of Galatia" (1:2).[51] By one means or another, the letter would have to be read to each community. Was Paul able to send multiple copies by the hand of one or more couriers? If a single courier read the letter in each place, some (especially those who agreed with Paul) may have had a copy made for local use. Wherever there was more than one house-church, the publication would have required separate readings. This was certainly the case in Rome (Rom. 16:5, 10, 11, 14, 15). In any particular place the leadership could have blocked public reading of a letter. Traveling messengers would also require support; refusal of this assistance would disrupt their mission.[52]

Colossians 4:16, which reads "And when this letter has been read among you, have it read also in the church of the Laodiceans; and see that you read also the letter from Laodicea," presents an explicitly different situation. The author encourages the sharing of correspondence to particular churches with other communities. Believers are directed to read one another's mail.[53] Although there is a clear motive for this direction—Colossae was essentially deserted when the letter was written—the movement toward a wider audience is clear.[54] It is noteworthy that the impetus toward sharing letters appears at the same time as Deutero-Pauline correspondence. The phenomena are complementary. With this trend went a desire to make letters more general in application. Extant examples of this process are discussed in what follows.

The Address of Ephesians
Ephesians 1:1 reads:

> Paul, an apostle of Christ Jesus by the will of God, to the saints who are <u>in Ephesus</u> and are faithful in Christ Jesus: (NRSV)

> *Variant:* Paul, an apostle of Christ Jesus by the will of God, to the saints who are also faithful in Christ Jesus: (RSV)

Marcion knew canonical Ephesians as "the letter to the Laodiceans."[55] The RSV reading has the best textual support,[56] but the NRSV editors determined that *something* must have stood in this place originally. "Ephesians" is most likely original, but "Laodiceans" indicates that the blank form is very old.

The Address of Romans:

Romans 1:7 reads:

> To all God's beloved <u>in Rome</u>, who are called to be saints:
> Grace to you and peace from God our Father and the Lord Jesus
> Christ.

> *Variant reading*: To all God's beloved, who are called to be saints: Grace
> to you and peace from God our Father and the Lord Jesus Christ.[57]

> *Another Variant*: To all who are in the love of God.[58]

Romans 1:15 reads:

> hence my eagerness to proclaim the gospel to you also who are <u>in
> Rome</u>.

> *Variant reading*: hence my eagerness to proclaim the gospel to you
> also.[59]

The effect of the omission of an addressee in Romans, where the omission is clearly secondary, and Ephesians, where it may be primary, is to make the letters applicable to all believers everywhere. These letters are no longer particular.[60] In the case of Romans difficulties remained, as in chs. 15–16, which contain a good deal of particular information.[61]

The history of the text of Romans illustrates the desire to portray Paul as a catholic, in the sense of both universal and orthodox, missionary and theologian. One well-attested edition contained Romans 1–14, without specification of the recipients. As Harry Gamble, following Nils Dahl,[62] has shown, the object of this edition was to provide the Pauline message in a form addressed to all Christians everywhere. One need not work through the manuscripts to see the issue. An edition of Romans that ended with ch. 14 eliminated all of the personal data that restricted the letter in time and place.

In addition to the fourteen-chapter edition of Romans known to and accepted by Marcion, Irenaeus, and Tertullian, there is also some evidence for an edition comprising chs. 1–15.[63] The discovery of P46, with a doxology at the end of Romans 15, was hailed as support for the theory that Romans 16 represents a separate letter originally sent to Ephesus.

This theory has fallen into disfavor among the Romans specialists,[64] and Peter Lampe would even question the existence of a fifteen-chapter edition.[65] His argument against Rom. 15:33 as the original ending is not without force, but this is not the same as proving that no such edition ever existed in antiquity, and Lampe does not deal with Harry Gamble's patristic evidence. Kurt Aland questioned the setting for an edition of fifteen chapters, while Gamble is content to see it as another general edition.[66] Reasons for the excision of Romans 16 appear clear enough, since it is little more than a recommendation with a long list of greetings, that is, data not useful for later readers.[67]

Chapter 15 is, from this perspective, more perplexing. In the case of vv. 1-13, it is easier to envision *theological* reasons for excision than considerations of extraneous content.[68] The balance of the chapter (Rom. 15:14-33) relates Paul's personal plans. In this case, the reason for omission could be particularity, but such details occur elsewhere and serve to lend verisimilitude to the Pastorals, for example.[69] One reason for omitting this statement of plans was the knowledge that they had not been fulfilled. The collection, which may have been rejected by the Jerusalem church, was too touchy a subject for Luke to address directly.[70] As a project for the promotion of Christian unity it was a failure, and orthodox leaders of the second century had little motivation to speak of unsuccessful fund-raising ventures or fruitless gestures toward unity.[71] Another reason is that Paul had been executed before he had the opportunity to visit Spain.[72] Desire to avoid depicting an apostle formulating plans that remained unfulfilled would also contribute to the motivation for deleting Romans 15.

In due course, the opposite motive—that apostolic plans were divinely authorized and would occur, willy-nilly—came into play. Reinforcing this tendency was an interest in making the journeys of apostles as comprehensive as possible, both to promote universalism and to provide various locales with apostolic foundations.[73] During the second and later centuries, Paul's visit to Spain became an accomplished fact.[74] In the developing context of this legendary belief that Paul did reach Spain, one may posit a setting for a fifteen-chapter edition of Romans. An editor with access to the full text (which never vanished) and "knowledge" of the mission to Spain would have had the motivation to include within a collection Romans 1–15, omitting the personal greetings as extraneous and inconsistent with such traditions as found in the *Acts of Peter*. This editor may have been responsible for the doxology, which has many affinities with ch. 15.[75] In this edition, Romans may have stood last in the collection.[76] In summary: some early editions of Romans presented an abbreviated letter addressed in timeless fashion to all believers. This set the tone for the interpretation of Romans for some eighteen centuries.

Two further examples of the tendency to make letters more generally applicable follow:

The Address (and Content) of Galatians
Galatians 1:1-2:

> Paul an apostle—sent neither by human commission nor from human authorities, but through Jesus Christ and God the Father, who raised him from the dead—and all the members of God's family who are with me, To the churches of Galatia:

The term Galatia is not precise at all. Up to this day New Testament scholars cannot settle the question of the precise address. Galatia is either a geographical region or the Roman province. In both cases it covers a huge area. None of Paul's other letters has a comparable address.[77]

Galatians is quite atypical. Not only are the addressees vague, but the text also lacks any personal information about Paul's travel plans, offers no greetings, makes no reference to the activities of fellow workers, and includes no personal names. Information about the Collection is also lacking, although 1 Cor. 16:1 indicates that Paul had given direction to "the churches of Galatia."[78] Since the relative date of Galatians is uncertain—it may postdate 1 Corinthians—this could refer to a lost letter. Another possibility is that this material was removed, along with personal data. The original address may have specified the particular communities. These names could have been deleted, perhaps because subsequent traditions focused upon the Province of Galatia (Acts, Pastorals, *Acts of Paul*) rather than upon the presumably original addressees in the territory, probably in the cities of Ancyra, Pessinus, Tavium, and Gordium. These foundations may have fallen out of the Pauline orbit (cf. 1 Pet 1:1). Acts has no details about Paul's missionary labor there (cf. Acts 16:6; 18:23). Galatians has the marks of an edited text oriented to believers everywhere. This hypothetical editing has, unlike the other examples, left no traces in the manuscript tradition.

The Address of 1 Corinthians

First Corinthians 1:1-2 reads:

> Paul, called to be an apostle of Christ Jesus by the will of God, and our
> brother Sosthenes,
>> To the church of God that is in Corinth, to those who are sanctified
> in Christ Jesus, called to be saints, *together with all those who in every*
> *place call on the name of our Lord Jesus Christ, both their Lord and ours.*
>
> *Variant*: To the church of God, to those who are sanctified in Christ
> Jesus, that is in Corinth...[79]

The variant indicates that the verse order has been disturbed. The
cause of this is due to varied placement or non-placement of the words
"which is in Corinth."[80] The italicized clause universalizes the letter. Note
in this connection 1 Cor. 16:19: "The churches of Asia send greetings.
Aquila and Prisca, together with the church in their house, greet you
warmly in the Lord." Some witnesses omit all[81] or the first part of v. 19.[82]
The reason for that omission is apparent: it conflicts with the general
address of 1:2. That generalization appears to be a secondary addition to
1 Corinthians, perhaps introduced for the widespread circulation of this
particular epistle, or for a collection that began with the Corinthian correspondence.[83] These examples illustrate efforts to answer the question:
Why does what Paul said to believers at Rome or Corinth have any relevance to me? In the case of Romans and 1 Corinthians, less possibly that
of Ephesians, and possibly Galatians, these alterations may attest to the
circulation of these documents as individual letters. A competing understanding was expressed in a collection of seven letters to seven churches.

This hypothetical collection is inferred from various data. The most
important of these data are the Muratorian List, the relative length, and the
prologues to the epistles found in a number of Old Latin manuscripts.[84]

Lines 39-63 of the Muratorian fragment read as follows:[85]

> The epistles, however, *40* of Paul themselves make clear to those who
> wish to know it which there are (i.e. from Paul), from what place and for
> what cause they were written. First of all to the Corinthians (to whom)
> he forbids the heresy of schism, then to the Galatians (to whom he for-
> bids circumcision), and then to the Romans, (to whom) he explains that
> Christ *45* is the rule of the scriptures and moreover their principle, he

has written at considerable length. We must deal with these severally, since the blessed apostle Paul himself, following the rule of his predecessor John,[86] writes by name only to seven churches in the following order: *50* to the Corinthians the first (epistle), to the Ephesians the second, to the Philippians the third, to the Colossians the fourth, to the Galatians the fifth, to the Thessalonians the sixth, to the Romans the seventh. Although he wrote to the Corinthians and to the *55* Thessalonians once more for their reproof, it is yet clearly recognizable that over the whole earth one church is spread. For John also in the Revelation writes indeed to seven churches, yet speaks to all. But to Philemon one, *60* and to Titus one, and to Timothy two, (written) out of goodwill and love, are yet held sacred to the glory of the catholic church for the ordering of ecclesiastical discipline.[87]

The text is evidently a pastiche. Lines 41-45 look as if they were derived from the prologues (see below). Line 46 takes up the model of seven letters to seven churches, invoking the "rule" of John, a point repeated in lines 57-59. In lines 54-55, the text recognizes the existence of 2 Corinthians and 2 Thessalonians. The "individual letters" appear as an afterthought in lines 59-63. It is possible that an earlier text was "corrected" by adding data that reflected a thirteen-letter collection. At the core, however, the list identifies seven letters, beginning with Corinth and ending with Rome. That order would jibe with the universal address of 1 Cor. 1:1b and the doxology of Rom. 16:25-27.[88]

As lines 56-59 assert, seven is a symbol of completeness and thus of universality.[89] This number was achieved by combining into single letters the correspondence with Corinth and Thessalonica. John Knox argued that the openings of 2 Corinthians and 2 Thessalonians are essentially secondary, based upon those of the respective "first" epistles.[90] The priority of Corinthians reflects the principle of length. The familiar thirteen-letter edition is also determined, in general, by length. In the seven-letter edition, however, the Corinthian correspondence was the longest, followed, according to that criterion, by Romans, Ephesians, Thessalonians, Galatians, Philippians, and Colossians (in which epistle Philemon may have been embedded). The placement of Romans at the end in Muratori shows the tug of another criterion: presumed chronological order. In short, the principle of length explains the place of Corinthians.[91]

Excursus: The Number Seven

Seven is the most important symbolic number in the Bible.[92] It signifies totality and is thus the symbol of completeness and perfection.[93] The ground for this is the week, which represents the structure of creation. Outside of the Jewish realm, the seven planets contributed to this understanding.[94] Groups of seven are common in John and Revelation. Philo, as might be expected, developed this symbolism.[95]

Seven became a standard number for letter collections. Pride of place belongs to the seven letters in Revelation 2–3, in which the number is a synecdoche, that is, a symbol of universality, as noted in the Muratorian List.[96] The eventual canon of the New Testament includes seven catholic letters. The (probably) original collection of Ignatius' letters totals seven, as does that of Dionysius of Corinth (c. 170).[97] The fourteen letters of the most widely accepted Pauline canon could be advertised as twice seven and thus as participating in the symbolism. From these data two conclusions can be drawn. The more important is that "seven" equals "all." The second is that the tendency of collections to fall into groups of seven is more likely to reflect art than actuality.

The so-called Marcionite Prologues to the Letters of Paul[98] offer brief prefaces of a fixed form for Galatians, Corinthians, Romans, Thessalonians, Ephesians, Colossians, Philippians, Philemon. Corinthians will serve as an example:

> The Corinthians are Achaeans. They similarly [to the Galatians] heard the true message from the Apostle, but were led astray in various ways by false apostles, some toward the wordy eloquence of philosophy, others induced toward the sect of the Jewish law. The Apostle summons them back to the true evangelical wisdom. He wrote to them from Ephesus, Timothy serving as his agent. (author's trans.)

This preface envisions a single letter to Corinth, which may have followed that to the Galatians.[99] The contents, however, relate to both of the canonical epistles. "Philosophy" is applicable to 1 Corinthians 1–4, while "Judaizing" summarizes the conflict addressed in 2 Corinthians. The Thessalonian correspondence likewise receives a single (complementary) preface.[100] These prologues therefore reflect an edition of (probably) seven letters to seven communities. This lost edition shows that it was acceptable to combine pieces of Pauline correspondence into a single letter. That practice may have preceded the construction of the seven-letter edition.

Partition Theories

Partition theories have once more become acceptable. Proposals that one or more of the Pauline letters is the result of combinations of parts of originally independent pieces have long met resistance on the grounds that priority should be given to the extant text and that every effort should be advanced to support its integrity. This view of "integrity" as the default position sounds reasonable, but it lacks cogency, for it does not recognize the principle that Paul's letters have come down in a book that had no interest in preserving the original texts of each piece of correspondence, but rather in presenting the message of the apostle to all believers everywhere. The evidence for the seven-letter edition presumes combination of all correspondence to one site in a single letter. Other examples of this practice are available.[101] The principle that gives priority to the assumption of integrity is not valid. Combinations should occasion no surprise. Each proposal should be examined on its merits rather than relegated to the status of a "mere" hypothesis. To reiterate: preparation of Paul's correspondence for a book makes amalgamation of letters highly probable.

Partition hypotheses have been advanced for Romans,[102] 1 Corinthians,[103] 2 Corinthians, Philippians, and 1 Thessalonians,[104] while Colossians has been construed as an amalgam based upon an authentic letter of Paul,[105] and a venerable theory views sections of the Pastorals as authentic personal notes of Paul.[106] Two of these possibilities will be surveyed here. The purpose of this exploration is not to impugn the canonical text but to illustrate the freedom with which early Christians could handle Pauline correspondence in their attempts to make the apostle useful and relevant for later times, as well as the theological perspectives that informed them.

Corinthians

Second Corinthians is the most illuminating example of the editing of Pauline material. This letter did not circulate outside of a collection. It was evidently edited between c. 100 and 120. *First Clement* knows 1 Corinthians, probably through an individual copy,[107] but does not show awareness of 2 Corinthians, a text that would have been most useful for its purpose of recalling the Corinthian believers to obey their lawful leaders. Acts shows knowledge of 2 Corinthians, but it is possible that the author had access to but a component of the canonical letter.[108]

A substantial majority of scholars believes that canonical 2 Corinthians is a composite text.[109] The simplest theory envisions chs. 1–9 and 10–13 as parts of two different letters.[110] The transition between 9:15 and ch. 10 is unparalleled outside of that between Philippians 2 and 3, which is likewise probably due to the merger of different pieces of correspondence. The following partition hypothesis is intended as a prelude to the principal object: examination of the form and function of canonical 2 Corinthians as a Deutero-Pauline text.

First Corinthians 16:5 envisions a visit by Paul to gather the collection, preceded by a visit from Timothy. Second Corinthians 1:15 has the same visit in view, but 2 Cor. 2:1 reveals that it was canceled because of a "painful visit," about which nothing certain is known. Problems increase when 2 Cor. 8:16-18, which speaks of a visit by Titus and an unnamed "brother," is compared to 2 Cor. 12:14, which speaks of a third visit. Paul's plans had gone awry due to difficulties with Corinth. Because Paul tends to associate discussion of the collection with travel plans, the collection is a good point of departure. Although both 2 Corinthians 8 and 9 treat the collection, they do not relate to one another. The two chapters differ in tone, form, purpose, and style, even in destination. They certainly differ in strategy. Second Corinthians 8 is written to Corinth and recommends Titus and another believer.[111] In ch. 8, Macedonia is held up as a model of generosity, yet ch. 9 speaks of the generosity of Achaea in an appeal to *Macedonia*. Fundraisers have often used such tactics, but rarely in a manner that allows each party to hear what was said to the other. These are parts of once-distinct pieces of correspondence: ch. 8 was a letter of recommendation for Titus, and ch. 9 was the particular application of what we should label a "stewardship sermon."

Chapters 1–7 and 10–13 address a problem brought about by the incursion of rival missionaries. These pieces do not constitute a logical sequence, for ch. 1 opens with a celebration of a conflict resolved, whereas in chs. 10–13 the argument is both bitter and current. The tone of the letter moves from joy to sorrow, with an interlude presenting two different views on the collection. Bad as this is, deconstruction is not over.

Chapters 1–7 do not constitute a unity. The report breaks off at 2:13 and resumes at 7:5. There is no parallel for such a lengthy excursus in the Pauline letters. Second Corinthians 2:14 is from the thanksgiving portion of a letter, the opening of which has been deleted. Thanksgivings normally follow the opening (e.g., Rom. 1:8-17; 1 Cor. 1:4-9). Second Corinthians 2:14—7:4 is therefore a large fragment of a letter embedded into another fragment: 1:1—2:13; 7:5-16.

Second Corinthians 6:14—7:1 presents another difficulty. This is an abruptly inserted bit of advice (parenesis). Once more there is no clear reason for changing the subject.[112] A plea for openness appears in 6:13, and in 6:14—7:1 there is a demand for narrowness. The content essentially equates Christ and Beliar as two cosmic powers.[113] The theology is dualistic, with cosmic overtones. Critics have found many correspondences with the literature from Qumran. Its perspective is highly sectarian and, unlike Paul, rules out mixed marriages and association with polytheists. This passage is an interpolation.[114] It contradicts Pauline theology and was not written by the apostle.

When arranged in reasonable chronological order these fragments appear as follows:

▓ Table 4: The Order of Letter Fragments in 2 Corinthians

Chronological Order		*Order as the Fragments Now Appear*	
A[115]	a forensic defense (2:14—7:4)	1:1—2:13	Letter C (first part)
B	an apology of the Socratic sort (10:1—13:10)[116]	2:14—6:13	Letter A (first part)
C	a friendly letter of advice (1:1—2:13; 7:5-16)[117]	6:14—7:1	Letter F (insertion)
D	an administrative letter of recommendation (ch. 8)	7:2-4	Letter A (second part)
E	an advisory letter on stewardship (ch. 9)	7:5-16	Letter C (second part)
F	a piece of non-Pauline apocalyptic advice (6:14—7:1)	8	Letter D
		9	Letter E
		10:1—13:10	Letter B

The canonical text was produced c. 90–100 CE, perhaps in relation to post-Pauline conflicts at Ephesus.[118] Ephesus is the most likely place of origin, for two additional reasons. The first is that Paul's correspondence with Corinth was written at Ephesus, at which place copies would logically be kept. The second is that the text has affinities with Ephesians, which was probably composed at Ephesus. Both letters are nearly devoid of personal names, a sign of the post-Pauline lack of interest in particularity.[119] The opening of 2 Corinthians is due, to an indeterminable extent, to the editor. The address in 1:1-2 appears to be modeled upon that of 1 Corinthians: "Paul, an apostle of Christ Jesus by the will of God, and Timothy our brother, To the church of God that is in Corinth, including all the saints throughout Achaia." The addition of "all Achaea" reflects the contents of the edited text (2 Cor. 8–9) and may reflect the evident expansion found in the second half of 1 Cor. 2:2.[120]

In contrast to the conventional form of the Pauline letter, 2 Corinthians opens (1:3-7) with a *berakah* or *eulogia* ("Blessed are you, Lord our God"), a blessing, rather than the standard thanksgiving ("We/I give you thanks...").[121] The only other examples in the New Testament of an opening blessing instead of a thanksgiving are Eph. 1:3-14 and 1 Pet 1:3-12. This relationship is not merely formal. Both the parallels and the function pertain to a Deutero-Pauline situation. Pauline thanksgivings are specific, related to the particular occasions of the letters. Blessings, on the other hand, tend to have a general character, and are more suitable for works with a wider application.[122] Use of this generalized language in 2 Corinthians and the other texts is a sign of the post-Pauline effort to make apostolic teaching applicable to a variety of situations. In this instance, the blessing is a reflection upon the relation of "affliction" to "consolation." One might think that it was written to a community experiencing harassment or even persecution.

The interpretation of Paul's sufferings in vv. 4-6 closely resembles that of Col. 1:24, which views apostolic afflictions as a vicarious activity that continues the passion of Christ into the present, with redemptive significance. In these verses of Colossians there emerges an image of the apostle characteristic of the second and later generations.[123] The figure of the suffering apostle is an object for the development of rhetorical pathos and attendant manipulation, without a sense of "the irony of affliction"[124] that characterized Paul's own reflections.[125]

The fulsome, pleonastic language of 2 Cor. 1:3-7, with its repetitious quality, alliteration, other sonorous effects, and genitive constructions, is equally reminiscent of the style of Ephesians. Ten uses of *parakaleō* and *paraklēsis* ("console," "consolation") may be too much of a good thing.[126] In particular, the phrase "father of mercies" in v. 3 has but one parallel, namely, "father" with a qualitative genitive plural (Eph. 1:17). The openings of canonical 2 Corinthians and Ephesians thus exhibit similarities in both form and style. They need not be the work of the same person, but they arguably derive from the same workshop, as it were. Ephesians may be the earliest witness to some of the correspondence utilized in the composition of 2 Corinthians.[127] These intertextual relations offer hints about the formation of the Pauline corpus and the workings of a "Pauline school," with particular reference to the composition of 2 Corinthians.

The editor used Letter C (1:1—2:13; 7:5-16) as the basis. The presumption was that good relations between apostle and community were the normal and normative state of affairs. Into this text Letter A (2:14—7:4) was inserted. The image utilized in 2:14-16 is that of a triumphal procession. Religious processions then began, as they may now, with incense, an offering consumed by fire. Paul, in accordance with his view of the apostolic role (e.g. 1 Cor. 4:9; cf. Rom. 8:31-36), viewed himself as the enemy victim, who would be executed at the climax of the procession.[128] The editor transformed (perhaps by misunderstanding) this image. By introducing it after Paul's description of his arrival in Macedonia (2:13, resumed at 7:5[129]) he presented the apostle's career as a triumphal procession across the Mediterranean world. This is an idealized view characteristic of later generations.[130] When an editor set out to produce a fresh letter from fragments of Pauline correspondence, s/he operated with these two principles: that Paul's relations with his converts were friendly and that his career was triumphal. That the contents of Letter B (2 Cor. 10–13) did not support these principles was not relevant. Paul is being squeezed into the mold of a later generation.

The insertion of 6:14—7:1 may evidence a need to "correct," at least to supplement, Paul. The dualistic quality of this passage evokes Colossians and Ephesians. Like parts of Ephesians, it bears a strong resemblance to the Qumran texts.[131] By means that can only be guessed, Qumran-like material, probably in Greek, was available to Christians in Ephesus by the end of the first century. This passage is, at best, half-digested and was evidently inserted in support of the strong separation of believers from the world.[132] Its moralistic apocalypticism is also somewhat evocative of

Revelation (which is usually located in Ephesus). The editor of canonical 2 Corinthians was evidently less theologically sophisticated than the author of Ephesians. Moral advice (parenesis) was a common feature of Pauline letters (cf. Rom. 12:1—15:13; Gal. 5:13—6:10; 1 Thess. 4:1-12; 5:1-22). The editor apparently thought that parenesis was a good thing and supplied some, selecting a piece that would quash any suggestion of openness toward the general society.

The placement of Letter B is equally conventional. Warnings about false prophets (whose appearance could be depicted as signs of the end) often came at the close of texts.[133] Chapters 10—13, with their attack upon false apostles, were suitable in this position.[134] Prior to this polemic, the editor enclosed two pieces dealing with the perennial problem of fundraising and the proper use of resources.[135] The canonical text of 2 Corinthians serves, like other Deutero-Pauline letters (note, in particular 2 Timothy), as a general testament from the apostle, exhorting the faithful to harmony, obedience, generosity, and steadfast resistance to false teachers. By the close of the first century, the view that heretics did not appear until after the departure of the apostles had begun to exercise its appeal.[136] Second Corinthians 10—13 allows readers to understand the apostle as warning them about false teachers who would appear in later, that is, their own, times. This assemblage was valuable for a good eighteen centuries— and remains so. Only when critics seeking to reconstruct the career of the apostle and those exercising literary-critical skills approached the text did the composite character of 2 Corinthians become apparent. Canonical 2 Corinthians is now a testament to the lack of interest on the part of those who conserved Paul's words in preserving what he wrote in proper order. The occasion for them was not "the opponents of Paul in 2 Corinthians," but what the apostle said of enduring value to believers everywhere. Canonical Philippians will now come before the eye of the astute and merciless critic.

Philippians

As in the case of 2 Corinthians, there are questions about whether Philippians is a single document.[137] More scholars defend the unity of Philippians than uphold the integrity of 2 Corinthians, and it is possible to read Philippians sequentially, if not smoothly. The simplest division is to view 1:1—3:1 as one letter and 3:2—4:23 as another. This deals with the nearly impossible transition between 3:1 and 3:2, but does not resolve other difficulties. Some of these are sequential. Philippians 2:25-30 reports that

Epaphroditus had been ill but has now returned to Philippi. This does not mesh with 4:18, which reveals that Epaphroditus brought money to Paul. This indicates that the thank-you passage in 4:10-20 is out of place. As one learned from one's mother, this matter should have received prompt attention. Again, 4:10 implies the renewal of a relationship, another indicator that things are out of place. Whereas 1:12-18 views prospects for release as good, and 2:19-24 look forward to travel, 4:10-20 reflect a different situation. The circumstances envisioned in the last chapter of Philippians are different from those in chs. 1–2. Other considerations relate to form and style.

The letter has too many conclusions. Chapter 4 moves toward a close in vv. 4-7, 9, 20, and 21-23. Verse 9 looks like a final blessing, but vv. 19-20 are a closing. This contributes to the stylistic problem. Joy is a good thing, but excessive exhortation to exhibit this quality produces a cloying effect. Weariness is a more likely result than happiness. If Paul wrote 4:4-23 in this order, he was not in his best form.[138] Formally, chs. 1–2 and parts of ch. 4 seem to be a friendly letter that makes frequent use of the conventions of friendship (such as sharing and equality). Philippians 4:10-20 can stand alone. Because of the issues of sequence, it is desirable to regard this unit as originally a short note of thanksgiving, acknowledging the Philippians' gift.

The transition between 3:1 and 3:2 is, as noted, all but impossible, presenting an abrupt change of form and content. Philippians 3:1b/2-21 (4:1?) represent a testament, or farewell speech[139] in a form suitable to religious debates. This example contains a biographical section, ethical admonition, and a closing blessing/curse. The harsh polemic of this passage is not consistent with 1:15-18, in which Paul looks upon his rivals in an almost nonchalant manner.

When the difficulties of sequence, form, and style are taken into account, it is preferable to view canonical Philippians as a compilation. Letter A (4:10-20[140]) is a thank you note that shows no knowledge about conflict within the community (which had sent a note with Epaphroditus, who became ill and did not return promptly). Letter B (1:1—3:1[a] plus elements of ch. 4[141]) is a friendly pastoral letter, with plans for a visit in the not too distant future. Paul reveals that his incarceration was held against him. His efforts to secure release may have caused controversy. Letter C (3:1b[2]—3:21/4:1[142]) arose in unclear circumstances. Paul may or may not have been imprisoned. This may have preceded or followed a visit.[143] Even a reasonable conjecture about the date and provenance (place of origin) of canonical Philippians is difficult to advance. Ephesus is a good possibility, since the individual pieces of correspondence were presumably available there. Philippi could be another. The Philippians and Thessalonians—Paul's Macedonian converts in general—enjoyed good relations with their founder. One result of this was a lack of lengthy correspondence. Unlike the Corinthians, the Philippians did not cause Paul any (known) major difficulties. The text may have been assembled at Philippi, to provide that community with at least a modest letter from the apostle. This would require an exchange of correspondence with Ephesus, at least. On the whole, Ephesus is a more likely location for preparation of the edition.[144]

Canonical Philippians is the work of a less sophisticated implied editor than the implied redactor who produced of 2 Corinthians. "Implied" holds open the possibility that the same person produced both—few persons produce work of uniform quality. Once more the basis is a positive, friendly letter. In this case the editor did not wish to end with polemical material. Denunciation of false teachers is sandwiched between units that praise the Philippian believers. Joy is the framing element. As in 1 Cor. 16:1-4, discussion of money comes toward the end. Rather than ask for funds, however, the apostle thanks his converts for their generosity. The best came last. Because of ch. 4, readers will not readily suspect that the opponents denounced in ch. 3 gained any adherents at Philippi. Philippians 4:10-20 receives end-stress. To a later generation, this unit would look like an appeal for "support of the clergy." Whereas his rivals are engaged in pursuing their own interests (Phil. 1:15-17), Paul does not require support, useful as it is. This is an implicit admonition against greed, especially greedy leaders, a theme common in Deutero-Pauline and related literature.[145]

Read as a Deutero-Pauline composition, canonical Philippians envisions the situation after Paul's death. Although a prisoner, Paul is present in his words, continuing to care for his flock. This understanding was facilitated by the use of "prison" as a metaphor for "death."[146] The Deutero-Pauline letters prefer the image of Paul as a prisoner.[147] This utility is confirmed by the use made of Philippians by the author of Colossians.[148] Second Corinthians and Philippians, despite the differences in content and editorial technique, reflect a similar pattern. The apostle enjoys happy relations with the communities he founded. While absent, he continues to offer them warnings against (future) false teachers and sound advice on life together and the use of resources. The historical Paul, who struggled to cope with personal and missionary ups and downs, has been flattened out. The specifics of history have given way to a picture of stable and lasting value. These conflated texts are not due to haphazard assembly of fragments. They have much in common with the pseudonymous epistles to be discussed in the subsequent chapter.

Interpolations and Glosses

For ancient texts in general, the presence of some interpolations (additions inserted into the text) are rather the norm than rare and isolated exceptions.[149] Copyists saw themselves as free, even obliged, to alter texts, including not only changes of words and phrases, but also the insertion of additions. Some of these began as "glosses," marginal notes such as are still entered by hand into printed books, and were later introduced into the text by subsequent copyists.[150] The vast majority of interpolations within the Pauline corpus do not appear in printed editions, as they are not supported by the canons of New Testament textual criticism.[151] Most scholars take a conservative approach to this question, but a few argue for extensive expansions of Paul's original text. A few examples will receive detailed treatment, serving as illustrations of the general tendencies of emerging orthodoxy.

First Corinthians 14:31-39 reads:

For you can all prophesy one by one, so that all may learn and all be encouraged. And the spirits of prophets are subject to the prophets, for God is a God not of disorder but of peace. [*As in all the churches of the saints, women should be silent in the churches. For they are not permitted to speak, but should be subordinate, as the law also says. If there is anything they desire to know, let them ask their husbands at home. For it is shameful for a woman to speak in church. Or did the word of God originate with you? Or are you the only ones it has reached?*] Anyone who claims to be a prophet, or to have spiritual powers, must acknowledge that what I am writing to you is a command of the Lord. Anyone who does not recognize this is not to be recognized. So, my friends, be eager to prophesy, and do not forbid speaking in tongues.

The bracketed and italicized words in vv. 33b-36 are almost certainly an interpolation.[152] The source of v. 34 is 1 Timothy:

Table 5: The Source of 1 Corinthians 14:34

1 Cor. 14:34[153]	1 Tim. 2:11-13
A. The women should keep silent in the churches.	A. Let a woman learn in silence
C. For they are not permitted to speak,[154]	B. with full submission[156]
B. but should be subordinate,[155]	C. I permit[157] no woman to teach
	D. or to have authority over a man,
	E. She is to keep silent.
F. As even the law says.	F. For Adam was formed first, then Eve.

Arguments against the originality of this passage are numerous:

- The textual tradition shows fluctuation.[158] Although all known manuscripts contain this material, its varied location indicates that it was not present in some early witnesses.

- It disrupts the context, which treats prophecy. Verse 37 follows v. 33a without difficulty; v. 33b does not follow v. 33a.

- The passage conflicts with 1 Cor. 11:2-16, which presumes that women exercise a prophetic ministry.

- The language has its closest parallels in Deutero-Pauline literature. (See Table 4.)

- The text views "the Law" (Torah) as fully authoritative. When Paul appeals to the Torah, he cites a particular text. This view of Law is essentially the concept of the Pastorals (1 Tim. 1:8-11).

- Paul normally speaks about the conduct of both women and men (e.g., 1 Cor. 7; 11:2-16).

- The paragraph presumes the household model of the church and assumes that women are married. This is the position of the Pastor (as the author of 1 and 2 Timothy and Titus is conveniently known), but not of Paul (1 Cor. 7), who favors celibacy.

These verses, which contradict not only such general statements as Gal. 3:26-28, but important passages in this very letter, are a second-century interpolation that addresses conflicts about the ministry of women.[159] The interpolator used two key words as the basis for introducing the passage: "be silent" (*sigaō*) in v. 30, and "be subject to" (*hypotassomai*) in v. 32. The context is important, for 1 Corinthians 14 is the only discussion within the corpus of guidelines for prophecy.[160] The function of this addition in the Pauline Corpus is clear: it harmonizes 1 Corinthians with the Pastoral Epistles. Attempts to set Paul against Paul are vitiated.[161] The interpolation is also a witness to the elimination of women from leadership positions within Christian communities.[162]

The next example takes up an equally uncomfortable subject: anti-Judaism. First Thessalonians 2:13/14-16 reads:

> We also constantly give thanks to God for this, that when you received the word of God that you heard from us, you accepted it not as a human word but as what it really is, God's word, which is also at work in you believers. For you, brothers and sisters, became imitators of the churches of God in Christ Jesus that are in Judea, for you suffered the same things from your own compatriots as they did from the Jews, who killed both the Lord Jesus and the prophets, and drove us out; they displease God and oppose everyone by hindering us from speaking to the Gentiles so that they may be saved. Thus they have constantly been filling up the measure of their sins; but God's wrath has overtaken them at last.

First Thessalonians 2:13/14-16 is most probably an interpolation from the early second century.[163] On virtually every ground—language, ideas, structure, dating—this passage is inconsistent with the views of Paul expressed elsewhere. The differences are:

- The form resumes, in 2:13, the thanksgiving section (1 Thess. 1:2-10) without need.[164]
- The passage is marked by non-Pauline use of Pauline terms and concepts, as well as some rare or non-Pauline language. Paul did not ask people to be imitators of churches (v. 14), but of *him*, as he imitated Christ (1 Cor. 11:1; 1 Thess. 1:6). The object of imitation, literally, "the churches of God that are in Judea in Jesus Christ," is odd and not Pauline.[165]
- The view of the Jewish people here is not that of Paul. In contrast to Rom. 9:11, this passage presents five accusations in staccato fashion: "the Jews" (a) have caused believers in both Judea and Macedonia to suffer, (b) have killed the prophets and Jesus, (c) have driven Paul (and co-workers?) out of communities, (d) do not please God, and (e) are misanthropes.

- In consequence, the destruction of Jerusalem in 70 CE is to be viewed as the wrath of God, an enduring divine punishment.[166]
- The author of 2 Thessalonians, who imitates 1 Thessalonians closely and is fond of apocalyptic vengeance, does not reflect this passage.[167]
- Polemic is out of place here; the material does not cohere with the context.

The point of view expressed belongs to the end of the first century or later, when Christians engaged in bitter controversy with those who remained loyal to traditional Judaism. Matthew 21:33-46 and Luke 11:47-52/Matt. 23:29-32 exemplify the tendency to vilify "the Jews" as murderers of prophets. The viewpoint is particularly congenial with that of Acts. It is quite possible that this passage was written by someone who had read Acts 17:1-5 (Luke's story of the founding of the mission at Thessalonica, in which Jews stir up a mob leading to Paul's departure). Like the author of Acts, the interpolator exploits ancient anti-Semitism, one characteristic of which was the charge that the Jews were hostile to gentiles (*odium generis humani*).[168] This passage, which can only be squeezed into Paul's views by tortuous rationalizations, brings 1 Thessalonians and the entire corpus into line with the Gospels (especially Matthew, Luke, and John) and Acts.

The conclusion to Romans offers insights into the construction of the corpus. If Romans 16 is a part of the original letter, then vv. 17-20a are probably secondary.[169] The reasons for this hypothesis are clear. The material disrupts a long list of greetings to and from, a list that began in 16:3 with greetings to persons and resumes with greetings from persons in v. 21. It is difficult to imagine that Paul would have written this long letter on a variety of important subjects, tossing in a warning against false teachers in a few vague and stereotyped phrases only at the close. Warnings against false prophets are common in the final portions of Jewish and Christian texts.[170] These verses serve the purpose of showing that Paul attacked false teachers in every letter. This admonition, which unlike the detailed dialectic of the undisputed letters provides no specifics beyond conventional polemic, does not supply weapons with which to combat heretics, though it does portray Paul as their staunch opponent. The crucial factor here is thus the image rather than the content. As is characteristic of post-Pauline developments,[171] one can speak of dissent as an offense, appeal to a fixed teaching (*didachē*), characterize opponents as those who seduce innocent people[172] with smooth speech, and command that opponents be avoided rather than refuted. The Paul of Rom. 16:17-20a speaks with an authority otherwise restricted by the historical Paul to communities that he had founded. That reservation was of no help to those seeking to make his message universal. The interpolator was insensitive to a Pauline principle that had become dysfunctional.

The last ten verses of canonical Romans thus reveal the kind of Paul many in the second century required.[173] The blessing/grace at the end of v. 20 floats about, in longer and shorter forms. Many D-text witnesses[174] omit it here, but place it after v. 23. Others locate it after v. 27.[175] The NRSV reads as follows:

> 23 Gaius, who is host to me and to the whole church, greets you. Erastus, the city treasurer, and our brother Quartus, greet you. [omit v. 24] 25 Now to God who is able to strengthen you according to my gospel and the proclamation of Jesus Christ, according to the revelation of the mystery that was kept secret for long ages 26 but is now disclosed, and through the prophetic writings is made known to all the Gentiles, according to the command of the eternal God, to bring about the obedience of faith—27 to the only wise God, through Jesus Christ, to whom be the glory forever! Amen.

The textual tradition is quite complex.[176] The doxology clearly intended to mark the close of Romans. It may have appeared at the end of ch. 14 in an edition that closed the corpus with the fourteen-chapter edition of Romans.[177] It also appears after ch. 15,[178] as well as at the close of ch. 16. Some witnesses omit it altogether, while others include it more than once. The textual evidence includes six locations for this doxology.[179] This fulsome, if almost untranslatable, conclusion uses the ripe liturgical language of the second century[180] to provide a fitting conclusion that conforms Pauline teaching to the message of Jesus and the theology of a later era. Paul did not compose it.[181]

Other passages in Romans have come into question. Rudolph Bultmann's shrewd eye identified a number of possible glosses in the text: 2:1, which may have come from the Sermon on the Mount (cf. Matt. 7:1-5) and is moralistic; 2:16, in which "gospel" has a formal sense, being in effect the "new law" and a criterion for judgment;[182] 6:17b, "to the form of teaching to which you were entrusted" (cf. 1 Tim. 1:16; 2 Tim. 2:13;

50 ❉ The Making of Paul

2 Thess. 3:9), which takes a moralizing approach to Paul as a model of Christian behaviour; as well as 7:25b, 8:1, 10:17, and 13:5.[183] These arguable glosses treat "Gospel" as a formal category, stress judgment, and portray Paul as a general model of Christian virtue. If Paul is not quite a preacher of salvation by good works, some of the rough edges to justification by faith have been trimmed.

Longer interpolations in Romans have also been proposed. William O. Walker lists the following examples: 1:18—2:29; 1:19—2:1; 1:32; 3:12-18; 3:24-26; 4:14; 4:17; 4:18-29; 5:1; 5:6-7; 5:12-21; 5:17; 6:13, 19; 8:9-11; 9:5; 10:9; 10:17; 11:6; 12:11; 13:1-7; 14:6; 15:4; ch. 16; 16:5.[184] These judgments are disputable, but they cannot be dismissed out of hand. Refutations must be as thoughtful and detailed as the proposals they would reject. As Paul's most important letter, Romans was that most subject to modification. Close behind came 1 Corinthians, a letter that was immensely popular in early Christianity because of its pastoral utility.

In addition to the omission of the addressee and evident expansion in 1 Cor. 1:2b (above), 1 Corinthians is noteworthy for its references to universal teaching: 4:17; 7:17; 11:16; cf. 14:33 (part of the interpolation discussed above). Paul presented the same teaching everywhere. This claim both refutes the contention that Paul was opportunistically inconsistent, saying what pleased his audience, and/or that he engaged in secret teaching.[185] Some of these may have been "universalizing" additions.[186] First Corinthians 4:6b is evidently a gloss. The NRSV rendition, "so that you may learn through us the meaning of the saying, 'Nothing beyond what is written,'" masks very obscure Greek. The phrase "not beyond that which is written" evidently began as a gloss, subsequently inserted into the text with an expansion.[187]

A number of passages in 1 Corinthians have attracted suspicion:[188] Corinthians 2:6-16; 7:29-31; 10:1-22; 11:3-16;[189] 11:23-26; 12:31b—14:1a; 15:3-11; 15:21-22; 15:29-34;[190] 15:31c; 15:44b-48; 15:56.[191] The majority of scholars are reluctant to accept these proposals, but the individual and collective forces of the arguments deserve consideration, for these problems address genuine difficulties in the material. Two extremes are questionable. One is to propose partition or interpolation[192] as a prompt solution to anomalies. Scholars must confront a large number of Gordian knots. Alexander the Great's solution is not always a viable option. The other is to go to almost any length to defend the integrity of a letter or the originality of a particular passage. New Testament scholarship offers more examples of the latter than of the former.

Liturgical changes include both alterations for reading aloud and pious additions that also serve as a kind of punctuation mark.[193] In reading Paul's letters to an assembled community, it was customary to begin with "sisters and brothers." Since Paul often used this word (*adelphoi*, a marker of "fictive kinship"), some of these lectionary additions can become textual variants—that is, possible original readings. The practice witnesses to the understanding that Paul always addresses all believers.[194] On Rom. 16:25-27, the fullest example of a post-Pauline doxology, see above.[195] The final "amen" to Galatians is considered part of the original text, but every epistle received this conclusion in the course of textual history.[196]

Deletions

This study has already considered material deemed irrelevant and/or particular, such as lists of greetings and other personal details.[197] Deletions could also be theological. Marcion removed many positive references to the God or faith of Israel, believing that these passages were interpolations. His approach was theological rather than historical-critical, and proto-orthodox theologians had to develop critical methods in order to attempt refutation of his claims. That he was able to produce his edition of Paul and claim its originality is a testimony to the frequency of interpolations in the era of manuscripts.[198] First Corinthians 7:21 is one interesting possibility. The verse is a notorious difficulty because the verb "make use of" has no object. The two possibilities are "freedom" and "slavery." Paul may have written "freedom," deleted by an editor interested in preserving the status quo.[199] The opposite—deletion of "slavery" in the interests of manumission—is possible, but the tendency observed in the process indicates that subsequent alterations tend to represent a conservative point of view.

Editions properly include a number of what are now called "user friendly" devices, including prefaces, inscriptions, "chapter divisions," and subscripts. These offered data about such subjects as contents, time of composition, and provenance. An example of one type of preface, the so-called Marcionite Prologues, has been considered.[200] Those who open a copy of the 1611 av or "King James" version of the Bible to Romans will observe a title: "The Epistle of Paul to the Romans." Its descendant, the nrsv, differs only in using the word "letter." Is this title an original part of the text? Few would think so. It is the product of editorial activity, a welcome convenience for the reader. The earliest ancestors of these editors used but two words: "To [the] Romans." The absence of an author's name indicates that Romans was viewed as part of a *book*, the collected letters of Paul, of which this work constituted a chapter, as it were.[201] By the Middle Ages these titles had become a bit more ornate, such as "The Letter of the Holy and Wholly Blessed Apostle Paul..."[202] At the close of Romans the reader of the AV will find these words, "Written to the Romans from Corinth, *and sent* by Phebe servant of the church at Cenchrea" (marked by distinct type and a mark such as ¶ in more recent editions). This material is absent from the RSV/NRSV. Few would judge this "subscript" to be part of the original text, but it derives from ancient manuscripts.[203] Chapter divisions (sometimes superior to the medieval divisions still in use) may go back to the third century.[204] They are attested from the fourth century and found in most subsequent manuscripts.

One objective of the present study has been to show how the composition of pseudo-Pauline letters was a part of the project aimed at making Paul a teacher and authority for all believers. In different ways, the production of Colossians, Ephesians, 2 Thessalonians, the formation of a corpus of Paul's letters, Acts, the Pastorals Epistles, *3 Corinthians*, the *Acts of Paul,* and other works serve similar purposes, even if, as is quite arguable in the case of the Pastorals and the *Acts of Paul,*[205] they take opposing stands.

Efforts to facilitate understanding of these letters as addressed to all believers are one dimension of another achievement of the post-mortem Paul: universalism. During his career, Paul sought to make believers in one community aware of others. One objective of the collection he raised for Jerusalem was to help Christians elsewhere appreciate that there were other believers. Similarly, Paul saw no geographic barriers to the scope of his mission.

This ideal gave rise to a grand vision in the minds of some of Paul's followers, who imbued this notion with vivid theology and implemented it with much hard work. The task of making Paul's local work universal was a component of the creation of a universal church. He became the "herald" who "taught righteousness to the whole world, having traveled to the limits of the west," as an early Christian letter has it (*1 Clem.* 5:7).[206] For Luke, "the ends of the earth" is a central symbol and Paul the principal instrument of its expression (Acts 1:8; 13:47).

The theological and ecclesiological horizons of this task unfold in two later letters, Colossians and Ephesians, which emphasize language of space rather than of time. This is to say that the structure of Christian existence comes less from a sense of the nearness of the end than from a picture of the universe in which earth is joined to heaven and in which the journey of faith is not so much progress through time as movement upwards. Christ, the savior of the universe, rules the church from heaven. Ephesians 1:22-23 reads: "*God* has put all things under *Christ's* feet and has made him the head over all things for the church, which is his body, the fullness of him who fills all in all."

The practical application of this belief generated abundant contact, interaction, and communication between and among these congregations. When the difficulties and expense of travel are taken into account, the frequency and extent to which these small and poor churches made contact with one another is surprising. There are no real analogies from any other ancient religious movements, with the possible and partial exception of Judaism.[207] This practice, another development of the Pauline heritage, happily embraced also by those who did not agree with Paul, contributed, as cause and effect, to some of the distinguishing features of the Christian religion and gave no small impetus to its eventual success within the Roman Empire and beyond. Because these groups communicated with one another, they laid the grounds for a supra-local organization matched by no other cult. Because they communicated with one another, Christian groups in various places discovered differences in matters of practice and belief that they deemed it necessary to resolve.

Because doctrinal developments became the subject of rapid and widespread discussion, Christianity developed one of its most peculiar characteristics: the production of careful and detailed binding statements of belief. There is a line, however unsteady and occasionally dotted, between Paul's letters to Corinth in the 50s and the first ecumenical council of Christian bishops that met at Nicea in 325—and all subsequent councils, synods, conventions, and assemblies. This line is a bit less apparent than the linkage between Paul's letters and the pastoral letters of bishops today, but it can be traced.

Through this process, in which Paul became the evangelist of the entire world, whose message was broadcast to all, the successors of Paul helped the young congregations gain *stability*, a crucial element to their ongoing vitality and growth. Multiple sources of authority could be confusing. The Pauline traditions, like those associated with Peter, James, and others, sought to avoid such confusion. The eventual solution, promulgated already in the book of Acts, maintains that all of the leaders, Peter, Paul, and James, and so on, taught the same thing and enjoyed a nearly perfect harmony.

Scholars can deconstruct and explode this hypothesis with the tip of a learned finger, to be sure, but its *function* is important. The object was the pursuit of *unity*, an ever-present and always elusive goal from the earliest times. The concept of unity is an inheritance from Israel: the one people of the one God. All early Christians agreed that unity did not mean complete uniformity; problems arose in the identification of those matters in which agreement, let alone uniformity, was paramount. In this discussion Paul has always been a, if not *the*, pivotal figure, the paradoxical apostle who died in an attempt to achieve some kind of unity, yet who was subsequently fashioned into the apostle of disunity.

THE FORMATION OF THE PAULINE CORPUS

Various theories have sought to account for the origin of the collection.[208] The "snowball" approach, which goes back to the great nineteenth-century scholars Theodor Zahn and Adolf von Harnack, envisions a gradual accumulation of letters, as communities shared their texts with one another. A basis for this could have been local collections, such as Macedonia (Philippians, 1 and 2 Thessalonians), Achaea (Corinthian correspondence), and Asia Minor (Philemon, Colossians, Ephesians). In due course these small collections were merged. This is logical, but little evidence can be introduced in its support. Philemon evidently owes its preservation to Colossians,[209] but the author of the latter already had access to Philippians,[210] and a corpus consisting almost entirely of Colossians and Ephesians would draw attention to the latter's use of the former. Three was an appealing number. A sub-group is formed by 1, 2, and 3 John; the same is true, to an extent, of 1 and 2 Peter and Jude.[211] One group of three, published as such, was the Pastoral Epistles.[212] The "snowball" hypothesis seeks to account for the different arrangements in various lists and manuscripts by appeal to probability, but this evidence already reflects the existence of relatively full editions rather than their predecessors. This hypothesis appreciates the phenomenon of growth: the corpus tended to expand over time. It also recognizes the value of Paul's letters after his death and the perceived drive toward collecting them, but does not take into account the evident neglect of others, notably 2 Corinthians.

Neglect was the basis of Edgar J. Goodspeed's theory.[213] He presumed that the appearance of Acts led to interest in Paul, and, in due course, in his letters, which were collected by a diligent admirer and published with Ephesians, composed by the collector, as a preface.[214] Goodspeed made some useful advances. He proposed that the publication of the corpus was a single, rather than a gradual, event and assigned the collector a role in the editorial process. He intimated, but did not sketch out, the existence of a "Pauline school."[215] His theory has not gained wide acceptance. Paul was not forgotten after his death, Acts leads no one to suspect that Paul wrote letters that could be uncovered by research, and Ephesians contains more (revisionist) theology than Goodspeed contemplated. If the "snowball" hypothesis is too gradual, Goodspeed did not take into account antecedent impulses and activities.

Walter Schmithals also assigned the editor a major role in the preparation of the corpus, which he envisioned as containing seven community letters assembled from sixteen fragments.[216] Like Goodspeed, he proposes one principal editor working in one place—Corinth in this case. The concept of a major editor has merit, as does the linkage of editing to the formation of the corpus. The data suggest more than one editorial hand at work, even if a principal editor be recognized,[217] and Schmithals' complicated partition argument has won little support. The theory of an initial large edition prepared in a single place is more probable than theories of haphazard growth. Moreover, it is difficult to envision how the seven-letter collection could have given rise to a corpus composed of discrete epistles. Ephesus is, as Goodspeed argued, a more probable location for the activity.

David Trobisch, like Schmithals, relates the question of content to that of origins. Trobisch, as already indicated, is almost alone in arguing that Paul was directly responsible for generating the collection. Trobisch envisioned two ancient editions. One consisted of Romans, Hebrews, 1 Corinthians, and Ephesians. The other included Romans, 1 and 2 Corinthians, Galatians, Ephesians, Philippians, Colossians, 1 and 2 Thessalonians, 1 and 2 Timothy, Titus, and Philemon. The former edition was edited to remove references to specific communities and other particulars. The eventual *corpus Paulinum* derives from a blending of these two editions. Each of these proposals has merit, but none has carried the day.

Some letters may have circulated individually. This is certain in the case of 1 Corinthians, known to *1 Clement*,[218] and highly probable for Romans (presumably in the short edition of chs. 1–14), and possible for others. Kurt Aland thinks, on the basis of textual data, that individual letters circulated as late as c. 200.[219] Smaller collections may have existed. It is likely that these, with the exception of the Pastoral Epistles, derived from larger editions. Economic and labor factors should be given their due. Copying the entire collection was an expensive and time-consuming task. Individuals may have copied/had copied a single letter, or several letters, from the larger corpus and have taken or had sent this material elsewhere.[220]

The earliest data are intertextual, most of which can be located in Asia Minor. Colossians utilized Philemon and Philippians; Ephesians utilized Colossians and other letters. Second Thessalonians borrowed heavily from 1 Thessalonians.[221] Luke and Acts show the existence of a substantial collection in the second (possibly the third) decade of the second century.[222] Nothing can be conjectured about the structure and shape of the collection used by Luke, for it does not even acknowledge the letters, let alone cite any by name. The existence of this collection, which shows no traces of 2 Thessalonians (a letter Luke may have known but not found useful[223]), or, not surprisingly, of the Pastoral Epistles, does not obviate the possibility that other collections existed. The Pastoral Epistles are familiar with a collection of letters. By the third decade of the second century a collection was known to Marcion in Pontus, Ignatius in Antioch, and Polycarp in Smyrna. The near certainty of a collection or collections in the first third of the second century does not answer all of the questions pursued by those who have attempted to trace the origins of the corpus.

Several apparent presuppositions require attention. One has been a tendency to identify the circulation of letters with the existence of a collection. Another is a proclivity to confuse a collection with a *corpus*, that is, a somewhat official collection that intimates completeness. Most regrettable of all has been an implicit tendency to confuse the existence of a collection with canonization, the conclusion that the collection represents authoritative "scripture." It is difficult to imagine that any early Christian writings did not intend to possess some authority, but that authority had to be earned, as it were. The Gospel according to Mark intended to have authority, and evidently acquired it, but others, including the authors of Matthew, Luke, and, possibly, John, sought to supersede Mark. Had the letters of Paul been viewed as sacred texts from the outset, they would not have been so extensively edited. As authoritative texts they were both valuable and mutable.

Edited they were, and editions were numerous. When all of the factors discussed above are taken into account, editions of Pauline letters number in the hundreds, and the production of them has not ceased.[224] Each of the lists set out in Table 3 represents an edition. Simplification is both desirable and possible. By the late second century, two different editions can be positively identified, and the existence of a third can be inferred with high probability.

One is the basis of that outlined above,[225] an edition of separate letters arranged by length, first those to communities (Romans, Corinthians [2], Ephesians, Galatians, Philippians, Colossians, and Thessalonians [2]), followed by those to individuals, also arranged by length (Timothy [2], Titus, and Philemon). The latter category was a subsequent addition, as P46 indicates, although the Pastoral Epistles were known to Irenaeus (c. 175).[226] This edition presented what would become the dominant shape.[227] The edition utilized by Marcion included Galatians, (1 and 2) Corinthians, Romans (in the fourteen-chapter form), (1 and 2) Thessalonians, Laodiceans (= Ephesians), Colossians, Philippians, and Philemon.[228] This edition may have sought to arrange the correspondence in chronological order.[229] Although Marcion performed substantial editorial work of his own, he did not create its basic order and shape.[230] The position of the Corinthian correspondence before Romans in Marcion's edition suggests that the two canonical letters may have been combined, at least in an antecedent edition, and thus have been the largest letter. This, in turn, indicates a possible link between the edition of Marcion and the "seven letters to seven churches" edition described above.[231] A gap of about forty to not much more than fifty years separates the last known individual letter of Paul (Romans) and the preparation of a relatively full edition. Three factors indicate that Paul's epistles remained available, in some degree, after his death.

The first is an impetus toward circulation, already encouraged in the first Deutero-Pauline letter, Colossians.[232] Followers of the deceased apostle encouraged the use of his letters, as well as the production of imitations. The earliest catholic epistles, Hebrews, James, 1 Peter, and, possibly, Jude,[233] testify to the power of the letter form, which could also be used to criticize Paul's views (James). *1 Clement* is a more or less explicit adaptation of the Pauline literary type, although quite different in size and form. On the borderline stand the letters embedded in Revelation 2–3. These show Pauline influence—although somewhat anti-Pauline in content[234]—and may reflect a corpus of Pauline letters.[235] After the emergence of a corpus the production of letters, with or without acknowledgment of Paul, becomes a flood: the Pastorals, Polycarp, 2 and 3 John, (Jude,) Ignatius, and 2 Peter.

Second Thessalonians also presumes that readers will know Paul as a writer of letters: "I, Paul, write this greeting with my own hand. This is the mark *in every letter of mine*; it is the way I write" (2 Thess. 3:17).[236] That same letter also recognizes the possibility of forgeries, showing that this issue arose very early in the process: "not to be quickly shaken in mind or alarmed, either by spirit or by word *or by letter, as though from us,* to the effect that the day of the Lord is already here" (1 Thess. 2:2). Irony is present, for the putative Pauline epistle in mind may be 1 Thessalonians.

Ephesus was the most important center of Paul's mission and evidently the site from which he labored for the longest period of his short career as an independent missionary. There much of his correspondence was written. Ephesus is the most probable location of at least one "Pauline school," attested in the production of Colossians and Ephesians. There most of the early post-Pauline trajectories come to light, including Colossians/Ephesians, Luke/Acts, and the Pastorals. All of these show familiarity with Pauline correspondence. Ephesus was also the source of considerable diversity and disagreement.[237] Apollos was another independent missionary associated with both Paul and Ephesus. In due course, the Johannine tradition claimed Ephesus as its home. The city may have been the locale from which 2 and 3 John originated. Late in the second century, the *Acts of John* was able to exploit this relationship.[238] By this means the otherwise unknown John who wrote Revelation came to be identified with the Apostle John, identified with the Beloved Disciple of the Fourth Gospel,[239] and thus the author of five books representing three genres. As stated above, the letters embedded in Revelation 1–3 probably reflect Pauline practice. This gives rise to an intriguing question: Did the concept of seven letters to seven churches as a symbol of universality take its inspiration from Revelation or was the opposite the case? The former may be more likely, on chronological grounds.[240] If there is a relationship between the seven heavenly letters in Revelation and the Pauline corpus, the earliest edition may have been the seven-letter edition, which could have been utilized by Marcion.[241]

Less speculative are some key themes of the corpus. Universality is an important dimension of Ephesian Paulinism, reflected in Colossians, Ephesians, and Acts. Another characteristic is the portrait of Paul as the apostle of unity among believers in Jesus. First Corinthians, and, in particular, Romans, provided the basis for this theme, developed in Ephesians, Acts, and Ignatius.[242] In light of probable conflict among the diverse Christian groups in Ephesus from the 50s onward, this emphasis is quite intelligible. In time, this principle would harden into admonitions to obey the leadership and avoid conversation with rivals (Rom. 16:17-20, the Pastoral Epistles, Ignatius). Reliance upon strong leaders would become one of the hallmarks of early catholic Christianity.

These data support the view that the first relatively complete edition of Pauline letters was made in Ephesus c. 100: (1) Most of the material was available in Ephesus. (2) Concinnity of viewpoints among Ephesians, 2 Corinthians, and Acts. Qumran-like influence can be seen in Ephesians and the interpolation in 2 Cor. 6:14—7:1.[243] Canonical 2 Corinthians agrees with Acts in presenting Paul's missionary career as a triumphal movement through the Mediterranean world. Colossians, Ephesians, and Acts portray Paul as a universal missionary and advocate of unity among Christians. (3) Intertextuality: Colossians, almost certainly written at Ephesus, constituted the major source of Ephesians, while Luke and Acts, most probably composed at Ephesus, are the first witnesses of an extensive body of Pauline correspondence. (4) The use of letters by the prophet John (Rev. 1–3). (5) Ephesus included a number of diverse groups of believers who were sometimes in conflict. The promotion of Paul as the unifying apostle is unlikely in Pauline foundations, such as Corinth, and even less likely at Antioch, where Peter was the symbol of unity, while Alexandria betrays no early (prior to c. 150) Pauline influence.[244]

"Paulinism" at Ephesus was not unified: Ephesians utilizes Colossians, but blunts some of its trends, while Acts rejects any theology that has the aroma of cosmic speculation. The "Paul" of 2 Thessalonians favors the apocalyptic vengeance promoted by the book of Revelation. The world of the Pastorals is static, hierarchical, and disinclined to theological debate. The Pauline "schools," to continue the modern analogy, were more like rival faculties of theology located within the same metropolis, inimical to each other, but reading one another's literary output. Here also hardening is perceptible: if Paul and his colleagues formed an informal "wisdom seminar" in which various issues were discussed and the kind of dialectical model visible in his letters predominated—within limits, as his letters also indicate[245]—in time the model became that of master communicating material to pupil. This is highly apparent in the Pastoral Epistles, where real-life colleagues, Timothy and Titus, are treated as neophytes requiring advice on diet no less than data about doctrine (1 Tim. 5:23).

The arguments for Ephesus as the site of the first collection of Pauline letters are not decisive, but this hypothesis provides the best explication of the extant data and resolves more problems than it creates. The simplest solution is to presume that one person undertook the task of preparing an edition, with assistance from others, and that this editor was generally responsible for producing composite texts. For the author of the Third Gospel and Acts, Paul was already something like a "book," that is, a body of material. That author absorbed and transformed some key themes of Pauline theology, but he also included evidently intentional allusions to actual written words of Paul. Since Luke was quite capable of revising his sources, notably Mark, it is arguable that he wanted his readers to grasp these allusions, certainly not as citations from Romans or Galatians, the existence of which he does not acknowledge, but as the words of Paul. In his own way Luke puts forth the view that what Paul said to one church, he said to all. The "decree" of Acts 15:23-29 is in the form of a letter dealing with the conflict in Antioch and is thus addressed to Antioch and environs, but, as 16:4 indicates, it applies to all gentile believers.[246] Acts implicitly endorses the notion that apostolic letters apply to all believers everywhere. Luke may have derived this from the edition of the corpus he used.

The claim that Paul spoke to all, made emphatically by Tertullian and repeated by others as a self-understood fact,[247] represents the victory of the collected letters of Paul: no longer words addressed to individual communities in particular circumstances, but a message to all believers everywhere for all time. Different editions appeared, and the collection continued to grow, with or without official approval. Yet, from the early second century onward, Paul was encountered as a book, from which individual letters might be cited, but with awareness of, and often in the context of, the collection.

2. The Pseudepigraphic Pauline Letters

This chapter will examine a number of letters attributed to Paul that were written between the late first and the mid-fourth century, most of them in the period between c. 100 and c. 225. Only one of these texts, which is also the latest, the *Correspondence between Seneca and Paul*, has never found a place within a biblical manuscript or canon list. The six earliest: Ephesians, Colossians, 2 Thessalonians, 1 and 2 Timothy, and Titus are part of the universal Christian canon.[1] The most important fact communicated by the existence of pseudo-Pauline letters is that the apostle continued to have authority. They would not otherwise exist. This does not mean that Paul's authority was always and everywhere celebrated, but it does show that his words had a continuous influence in circles that eventually became dominant. Investigation of these letters will also demonstrate that a single form of Deutero-Pauline thought, with appropriate developments within that framework, cannot be traced. It is necessary to speak of "Deuteropaulinisms." The Deutero-Pauline letters first appeared within circles of Paul's personal followers and continued among those who wished to preserve—which always means to change—his heritage. One means for tracking the progress of the early Pauline heritage is the developmental model proposed by Margaret Y. MacDonald:[2]

(1) *Community Formation*, c. 35–55. This stage represents the missionary and pastoral work of the historical Paul, including the composition of the undisputed letters. Organization varies, and boundaries are broad.

(2) *Community Stabilization*, c. 60–100. Major extant products of this stage are Colossians and Ephesians (cf. 1 Peter; *1 Clement*). Boundaries become more fixed and ethics more conventional. Outsiders ought to find

the life of the church attractive. "Christianity" is becoming a "religion"[3] distinct from Judaism. Individual communities are linked in a broader network, that is, "churches" are part of "the church." Correspondingly, ecclesiology is assuming greater importance.

(3) *Community Protection*, c. 100–130. Second Thessalonians and the Pastoral Epistles (cf. Acts, Ignatius, and Polycarp) belong to this era. Rival teachings and aberrant behavior are major concerns. Christianity and Judaism are going their separate ways. To be "in the world" means acceptance of many of its institutions, mores, and manners. Government by properly qualified and selected leaders is a matter of considerable concern. Community protection continues to be a leading concern of the early apologists and opponents of "heresies," such as Justin and Irenaeus.

Like all social-scientific models, this scheme involves a high level of generalization. Elements of each of these stages are present throughout the present and subsequent eras. The model identifies the most prominent quality of each period. The chronology is also general and approximate. The task of Paul's followers was to make their founder a suitable agent and authority for stabilizing and protecting the communities he founded. That enterprise, rather than a comprehensive interpretation of the several pieces, is the focus of the present chapter. Colossians and Ephesians can be described as school products, for they represent efforts by devoted admirers of the apostle who have carefully studied at least some of his epistles and develop Pauline ideas for different circumstances.

Amalgamations, including 2 Corinthians, probably Philippians, and possibly others, are also Deutero-Pauline letters, for their editors shared some of the same views as those who composed pseudonymous epistles. These documents are early Patristic texts that verge upon the era of the Apostolic Fathers. Their editors did not neglect issues of their own times in their attempts to construct longer items of correspondence.

COLOSSIANS

The period from 1965–75 witnessed a major shift on the question of the authorship of Colossians.[4] Since the time of F. C. Baur, who accepted only four epistles as genuine, relatively few voices against the authenticity of Colossians appeared. During the decade mentioned, however, a number of convincing arguments against Pauline authorship emerged. The commentary of Eduard Lohse,[5] together with the stylistic arguments of W. Bujard,[6] swung the pendulum, so that Raymond Brown could estimate that in 1980 c. 60 per cent of scholars did not attribute this letter to Paul, Brown among them.[7] Vocabulary is a fluid entity, but one can point to some important words that are not used, including "sin," "justification," "believe," "freedom, "promise," "boast," "law," and "salvation." The absence of "my brothers and sisters," a term used by Paul even in Romans (e.g., 1:13) is striking.[8] This affectionate expression of "fictive kinship" is also missing in Ephesians and the Pastorals. Its absence portrays a distance between the author and the recipients. Also important are a number of words found in the undisputed epistles used by the author of Colossians with different meanings.

Style is more decisive than vocabulary. Whereas the undisputed letters are conversational, Colossians (followed by Ephesians) tends toward hymnic and liturgical language.[9] The lack of rhetorical directness is equally noteworthy. Rather than argue with opposing views, the author admonishes the readers to reject them. This is characteristic of the Deutero-Pauline environment. Colossians prefers long sentences (e.g., 1:3-8, 9-20) linked in an associative manner (without the customary Pauline connective devices[10]) that are loaded with participial phrases and relative clauses. Although Paul makes use of traditions and traditional materials, the volume of traditional material is considerably larger in Colossians than in the undisputed letters.[11] Reliance upon tradition is another indication of distance from Paul and of a desire to provide communities with a stable foundation.[12] Because of its style and utilization of tradition, Colossians is more "Jewish" in some ways than are the undisputed epistles; yet, remarkably, the letter contains not one citation of or reference to Israelite scripture. The earliest Deutero-Pauline letter exhibits no interest in preserving the Jewish scriptural heritage of the Jesus movement.[13]

Most decisive are theological differences, including matters of Christology, ecclesiology, eschatology, anthropology, ethics, and sacramental theology.[14] The theology of Colossians is, nevertheless, "Paulinist" in that it is a development of Pauline thought. It is also a coherent and consistent theology. Against any claims that these changes of style and thought are the result of Paul's ongoing development of his ideas are the hypothetical circumstances: if situated in the life of Paul, Colossians is best viewed in close proximity to Philemon and prior to Romans. The greeting list in Col. 4:10-14 represents Paul's Asian entourage.[15] Proximity to Romans is difficult, since Col. 2:12-13 conflicts with Rom. 6:5-6. Colossians is evidently later than Philemon, as 4:9 describes Onesimus as a coworker of Paul from Colossae, yet Philemon is later than Philippians, for Philemon 22 expects

Paul's imminent release. Appeals to changes in Pauline thought[16] require that Colossians be dated as late as possible, presumably being composed in Rome. That hypothesis, in turn, builds implicitly or explicitly upon the situation presumed by 2 Timothy.

Formally, Colossians is somewhat atypical in that it is a pastoral letter with an apparently polemical component.[17] Yet, unlike Ephesians, it has the qualities of a genuine epistle of the Pauline type, addressed to a specific situation. Was this letter actually dispatched to Colossae, in the Lykos Valley? Or was another destination (Ephesus?) in view? In this case, one can find a ready rationale for explaining how a pseudonymous text could be accepted, for Colossae had, in fact, been destroyed by an earthquake in 60–61.[18] Colossae had no more than a shadowy existence when the letter was written. This would explain how a letter from Paul had escaped wider attention. Colossians 4:16 may indicate the actual destination: Laodicea.[19] Ephesus is another possibility.

Colossians could have been written by an immediate follower of Paul, one whose acquaintance was not merely literary or through hearsay, probably in Ephesus. The range of dates would be somewhere from c. 60 (death of Paul) to c. 90+ (use of Colossians by Ephesians). Despite the relative proximity to Paul, the apostle stands at a rather formal distance from the community. No visit is contemplated. His absence is a fixed datum (2:4-5). This is a characteristic of much Deutero-Pauline literature.[20]

The historical Paul had to battle for the right to be accepted as a true apostle with a valid mission (Galatians, 2 Corinthians, Philippians 3). In the post-Pauline letters this situation no longer applies. Paul is not only *the* apostle; he is, to all intents and purposes, the *only* apostle.[21] The writers of the Deutero-Pauline letters were not explicit constructors of apostolic syntheses. They did not strive to equate Paul with Peter or James. The lack of interest in or appeal to other authorities reveals how narrow their orientation was. By contrast, Acts, which utilizes post-Pauline letters and belongs to the Deutero-Pauline world, accepts that Paul was not an apostle and demonstrates that the views of Peter, James, and Paul were more or less identical.

The most prominent shift is that mission and management have become increasingly universal, rather than local. This is apparent in the portrayal of Paul as a privileged universal herald of the worldwide message (Col. 1:8, 23, 26-28). Paul is "the *solus apostolus* who proclaims the *solus Christus*."[22] No other evangelists need apply. This magnification of Paul—the historical apostle would be astonished to learn of his standing—intends to defend the legitimacy of the Pauline, gentile mission. Despite the theoretically limited audience at Colossae (extended to Laodicea, 4:16), Paul's message and admonition are directed to everyone. The principle subsequently enunciated, that what Paul says to one community he says to all, is already operative in Colossians.[23] Hand in hand with the universality of Paul's mission walk a cosmic christology and a cosmic ecclesiology.

Paul viewed Christians as members of a body that has suffered, died, and risen, although believers in the present age must look forward to the resurrection. Through baptism Christians belong to this body of Christ.[24] Colossians and Ephesians present a corporate understanding of the church as a body the *head* of which is Christ who is now in heaven (Col. 1:18; Eph. 1:22-23). The body Christ heads embraces the universe. In a metaphor that would become enduring, Christ as king rules over a hierarchical pyramid, like the Roman emperor.[25] As a heavenly entity, the church resists classification as an institution or possession with the characteristics of a corporation.[26] The church is still an eschatological creation, but is depicted as a heavenly entity on earth that participates in celestial realities. This shift toward spatial metaphors/categories would have important consequences for the development of those movements labeled "Gnostic."

For Paul, ecclesiology was related to the justification of believers, who, as justified sinners, comprise the church and await ultimate deliverance. In Colossians and Ephesians, ecclesiology is linked to soteriology: Believers are delivered from evil via forgiveness of sins rather than through justification (1:13-14; 2:13; 3:13) and thus comprise the church. Grace, rather than faith, is the basis of salvation.[27] Since salvation resides in the heavenly body of Christ, christology takes on an ecclesiological dimension.[28] The object of these shifts was to promote confidence among believers and to show their empowerment for meeting the challenges of existence in the faith. A logically concomitant shift took place in the sphere of anthropology.

Colossians (and Ephesians) proffer a "less pessimistic" and more conventional view of what is vulgarly called "human nature."[29] Empowerment is not attributed to the Spirit,[30] but to baptism, specifically baptismal resurrection. Whereas Paul said that believers had been buried with Christ in baptism and *would* rise (Rom. 6:3-9), Colossians, followed less hesitantly by Ephesians (2:6), locates resurrection in baptism (Col. 2:12).[31] The ethical consequences of this state are patent: "So if you have been raised with Christ, seek the things that are above, where Christ is, seated at the right hand of God" (Col. 3:1). This preserves, on a new basis, the Pauline ethical paradigm of indicative and imperative, in which the fact of salvation ("you have been redeemed") makes possible the ethical demand ("so act like it"). This formula is quite unlike demands to shape up or face the consequences. Colossians 3:5-20 works out the contrast by building upon the imagery of clothing. Candidates for baptism remove their clothing for the rite and dress in festal garments after it has been performed. Metaphorically understood, the baptized cast off vices then robe themselves in virtues. Whereas Paul was wont to speak of identity with Christ through humiliation, Colossians portrays believers as exalted with Christ into the heavens.[32]

Ethical guidance of individuals by the Spirit is not advocated, nor will the author leave any room for the sort of ethical experimentation that made early Christian life in Corinth such a challenge for Paul (1 Corinthians). After the breathtaking description of sacramental empowerment comes a bath of cold water. Without further ado, the author propounds a version of the "Household Code," a new phenomenon in the Pauline world, as the apostle did not provide such fixed prescriptions for stable community life.[33] This pattern arose in discussions of social organization. The household was presumed to be both a microcosm and a cell of the larger society. If the entire society, the *polis*, were to be healthy, each cell must be sound.[34] Aristotle framed the discussion by identifying the reciprocal rights and obligations of three essential pairs: husbands/wives, parents/children, and owners/slaves.[35]

This model of relationships presumes, in accordance with ancient society in general and in distinction from much of the modern Western world, that society is stable and will remain so. It does not, for example, contemplate the possibility that slavery might cease to exist. Greco-Roman society in general strongly adhered to "ethical relativism."[36] Certain behaviors were appropriate to each sex and to the various social strata. What people were to do and not do depended upon their social position. The key to social harmony is the maintenance of proper relationships and boundaries. Household Codes encapsulate the essence of Greco-Roman family values.[37] In Colossians, the code bursts upon the Deutero-Pauline world, in which it will eventually commingle with descriptions of church order.[38] What has sparked this change?

Without doubt, more conservative social behavior is being recommended. This is not as strong a push to the ethical right as it may seem to modern readers.[39] In the ancient world, adherence to these principles was like announcing, "We brush our teeth regularly, pay for the merchandise we acquire, and do our part as good citizens." Concern about the views of outsiders has assumed a larger role. Paul was not indifferent to this issue (e.g., 1 Cor. 14:22-23; 1 Thess. 4:12). In Colossians, it has become a priority. For more than a hundred years, outsiders often viewed Christians as moral degenerates. Slanders about their orgies and unspeakable practices endured for centuries.[40] The author of Colossians was not pressing for change, urging obedience upon recalcitrant slaves, and authority for henpecked husbands, but for shared values.[41]

Shortly after propounding the code, the author speaks of behavior *vis-à-vis* outsiders (4:5). This suggests that attention is being directed toward the missionary implications of Christian behavior. Such a stance is characteristic of what Bryan Wilson designated a "conversionist sect," a group that desires both to remain pure and distinct but also to attract new members.[42] Both of these desires emerge in the "Household Codes," which reflect pressure for "respectability."[43] The author has not sold out to social conventions. Church and household polities are not identified.[44] The baptismal declaration of Col. 3:11, in contrast to Gal. 3:28, omits "male and female," but it does maintain the removal of religious distinction between slave and free.[45]

Clearly the most loaded section in Colossians is that dealing with the relations between slaves and masters. Servants are urged to follow the pace set by their owners when it comes to theology. The latter would probably be less inclined than some to presume that baptism should lead to prompt emancipation. This may be a bid to strengthen the leadership of patrons of house-churches.[46] The mixed state of affairs is apparent. Nympha (4:15) is the host and patron of a house-church, but women appear to be losing power in the communities.[47] Desire to conform to increasingly conservative Greco-Roman norms may have helped to motivate the introduction of the Code. The movement's attraction for women and slaves may also have created tensions in house-churches.[48] Colossians provides no support for ascetic tendencies within the Pauline tradition, most notably in the realm of marriage.[49] The false teaching attacked in 2:8-23 includes ascetic features.[50] Since asceticism practiced by religious groups could become a basis for public suspicion, avoidance of such displays could have both defensive and missionary dimensions.[51]

Several features of the post-Pauline world first appear in Colossians. Pathos colors the portrait of Paul the weary, hard-working, and suffering evangelist. Note 1:24-29 and the closing appeal to be mindful of his chains

(4:18; cf. 4:3). Pathos serves to aggrandize Paul's authority through, as contemporary English would have it, "laying a guilt trip" on the readers.[52] His struggle demonstrates his dedication and therefore his authority. Suffering is glorified. Related to this are what may be called novelistic details. These are particularly apparent when the greeting list in 4:10-14 is compared with its source in Philemon 23-24. Aristarchus has become a fellow prisoner; Mark is now the "cousin" of Barnabas, who may visit. These data point to a reconciliation between Paul and Barnabas.[53] Although concerned only with one apostle, Colossians already shows a tendency to idealize the "primitive" church: leaders do not have enduring quarrels. Luke receives that status he has enjoyed ever since: "the beloved physician."[54] The efforts devoted to bolstering these co-workers represent the voice of the absent apostle exhorting later believers to respect their leaders.

Paul's suffering is more than a prod to obedience. It is related to his absence. Rather than speak of plans for a visit, Paul stresses his suffering. That suffering is not just imitation of his master: it has soteriological significance. Paul suffers "for" the Colossians. It is a means of grace, for through it the message of salvation spreads. His suffering has an ecclesiological dimension. This epistle adumbrates a "paulology," as it were. Paul is becoming a redeemer figure. He is now part of the message.[55]

Colossians, in summary, exploits the literary convention of "absent in person, present in spirit" (Col. 2:5).[56] Paul's absence is now permanent; he is held in the "bonds of death," but he remains present through his letters. His presence is not restricted to the audience of this letter, for his scope is now general. Even for those who have not heard him, Paul is the apostle (Col. 1:7). The universality of Paul's reach is complemented by a universal ecclesiology with cosmic dimensions. He remains a missionary to gentiles. The community is of gentile origin (1:21; 2:13), and, despite the use of materials and methods from the Jewish wisdom movement,[57] ties to Israelite religion are essentially absent.[58] The role and function of apostles as bearers of tradition and the basis for authority continues, as for the historical Paul, with the sense that tradition is becoming more fixed and with particular emphasis upon ethical matters.[59] Church officers are not yet a subject for discussion or direction. Believers will adhere to general social conventions, avoiding what is extreme. This letter stands across the divide from the historical Paul, but the chasm is not vast. Nonetheless, this, the earliest Deutero-Pauline letter, already shows features that will characterize subsequent writings: a focus upon universalism, in which Paul addresses all creation, integration of christology with ecclesiology and the increased importance of the latter, as well as emphasis upon conventional behavior.[60] Communication of the Pauline legacy shows the attraction of the testamentary form, which played a large role in both the composition of Deutero-Pauline epistles and the editing of genuine fragments.[61]

EPHESIANS

The shift from Colossians to Ephesians brings both the familiar and much that is different.[62] The author of Ephesians either greatly admired Colossians, exhibiting flattery in its most sincere form, or wished to replace it. Just as modern scholars conclude that Matthew and Luke wished to replace Mark (a book that they wanted to vanish), it is arguable that the author of Ephesians wanted his text to replace Colossians.[63] Both follow a similar format, within the tradition of the Pauline epistle.[64] Each moves from top to bottom, as it were, beginning in the heavenly realm and moving into the nitty-gritty of domestic life.[65] Ephesians does not reject the cosmic ecclesiology of Colossians but blunts it by introducing a strong salvation-historical thrust. Things in heaven are as they ought to be; the problems are on earth.

An intertextual relationship between the two documents is indisputable. Examination shows that Ephesians has routinely commented upon and developed Colossians, one-third of which it has taken up. The contrary argument, that Colossians is an abbreviation of Ephesians, is not tenable, for many of the changes would be inexplicable.[66] For those who accept the Deutero-Pauline character of Colossians, arguments about the authenticity of Ephesians, which has been questioned since at least the late eighteenth century, are otiose.[67] A date of c. 90–100 is appropriate, for several reasons. Affinities in viewpoint with Luke and Acts (c. 115), which extend beyond Acts' borrowings from Ephesians,[68] are noteworthy. Equally striking are a number of words that occur in the New Testament only in Ephesians but also appear in the Apostolic Fathers.[69]

The shift toward universal application is nearly complete. Colossians attends to both local churches (4:15-17) and to the church at large. Ephesians considers the church only from its catholic perspective.[70] Although Ephesians has the framework of a letter, it does not engage a particular set of readers or take up particular local issues. Critics are tempted to call the work a treatise or sermon in letter form,[71] but such designations can obscure the author's pursuit of a pastoral purpose in conformity with the Pauline tradition.[72] The existence of a debate about the genre of Ephesians testifies to its generality. No co-authors are mentioned,[73] and greetings to individuals or groups are absent.[74] Only the bearer, Tychicus, is named (6:21), in bland imitation of Col. 4:7. To these data must be added the problem of the address.[75] The implied author is, to all intents and purposes, a stranger who introduces himself by summarizing his message.[76] The writer's model for this tactic was Romans, from which he has taken some of his major themes. The distance between "Paul" and his audience has widened. The foundation of the community, indeed the Christian community, belongs to the relatively distant past (Eph. 2:20). As in Acts, Paul's proclamation to the gentiles is a fact of salvation history rather than current experience. Since Ephesus was the most important of Paul's missionary bases, it is inconceivable that the historical Paul wrote this letter to that community.[77]

The Paul of Ephesians is a writer rather than a missionary who turns out letters while engaged in missions elsewhere. Ephesians 3:3-4 states: "and how the mystery was made known to me by revelation, as I wrote above in a few words, a reading of which will enable you to perceive my understanding of the mystery of Christ." Contrast this to 2 Cor. 1:12.[78] Paul is now a written text for study by the faithful.[79] Whereas Colossians relied upon two epistles, Ephesians works with a literary heritage, freely exploiting most of the correspondence.[80] To this extent it resembles a selective compendium of Pauline theology.[81] With its emphasis upon unity, Ephesians continues the project of Romans in different circumstances.[82] Both Romans and Ephesians look back upon the letters as givens. To this extent Goodspeed grasped the meaning of Ephesians.[83]

Although the author of Colossians utilized material from the Jewish tradition, the work envisions no audience other than gentiles[84] and attacks practices that might be associated with Judaism (although he does not label them as such). Ephesians, on the other hand, shows both the use of Jewish modes of thought and explicitly takes up the question of Jewish–gentile unity. It is characteristic of later New Testament writings to be "more Jewish" than earlier texts.[85] One possible reason for this was a hypothetical influx of Jews into the Christian movement after the First Jewish Revolt (66–73/4), an event which precipitated widespread hostility to Jews and increased their liabilities.[86] Another was a desire to preserve the Israelite heritage, both as a claim of legitimacy and against those Christians who would abandon it altogether. Like Luke/Acts, Ephesians focuses upon beginnings and the role of the church in the fulfillment of God's plan (1:4-10; 2:20).[87]

Ephesians also uses dualistic language and thought that shows some remarkable affinities with the world of Qumran.[88] One explanation for his influence is the possible presence of converts who had affinities with the Qumran community or movement. Similar influence is patent in 2 Cor. 6:14—7:1, where the thought is much less Christianized.[89] Among these similarities is the contrast between darkness and light, including the anthropological division of humanity into "children of darkness" and "children of light" (Eph. 5:8), emphasis upon the community as a temple (Eph. 2:21; but cf. 1 Cor. 3:16-17), description of God's plan as a "secret"/"mystery" (Eph. 1:9; 3:3, 4, 9; 6:19), a view of the cosmos as populated by angelic and demonic powers, military imagery (6:10-17), and a loaded style that piles up synonyms and uses many genitival expressions as adjectives.[90] The author of Ephesians wanted his words to sound "Jewish," not, however, by imitating the LXX, as did Luke, but by writing sonorous prose of a quasi-liturgical style.[91]

Although the audience is presumed to be gentile (note "you gentiles" at 2:11 and 3:1), the author is concerned about unity between Jews and gentiles.[92] Paul was likewise engaged with this issue, but not in abstract terms. Unity among believers, including those of gentile and Jewish background or orientation, was vital to him. His struggle was for acceptance of a mission that did not require gentiles to conform to Torah. In Ephesians the problem is different. Gentile Christians must be admonished not to look down on those of Jewish background or orientation (2:11-22). Acts also expresses interest in this issue. It is possible to read Acts 21:18-25 as a plea for acceptance of the Jewish minority, but Acts in general shows little appreciation for toleration.[93] The Paul of Acts also works for unity among Jewish and gentile believers, but is routinely thwarted by jealous and hostile Israelites. From the perspective of Acts, the quest for unity has failed and the blame for this is clear.

Intense concern for unity at every level, from the heaven above to the household below, permeates Ephesians.[94] As is often the case, calls for unity involve demands for compromise from those lacking formal power. This is, in fact, the ground of the Household Code in Eph. 5:21—6:9, unity based upon proper subordination with the concomitant demand for proper exercise of authority and responsibility. Paul's apostolic mission in Ephesians is the creation and maintenance of unity. In the light of the diverse movements visible in Ephesus at the close of the first century, this is intelligible—but it has resulted in the creation of a very different apostle. Paul the apostle of unity grounded in hierarchy will be a major figure from c. 100 onward.[95]

Ephesians is more interested in "political" unity on earth than in speculation about cosmic unity. The author, however, uses the cosmological scheme of Colossians as the indicative ground for the imperative for unity. The argument is, in effect, "don't worry about unity among heavenly entities, for God has taken care of that problem. Focus instead upon earthly unity." The cosmic reconciliation effected by Christ has implications for earth, as both model and source of power.

Ephesians' presentation of the Household Code exemplifies these trends.[96] The author has attempted to draw the code more firmly into a Jewish–Christian framework. The link between this set of regulations and the Decalogue is clear.[97] The entire passage is placed under the rubric of mutual subjection motivated by reverence for Christ (5:21).[98] To modern eyes, at least, this subverts the entire code. In fact it functions like the kind of general statement against, for example, discrimination that precedes the specific instance of discrimination (etc.) proposed. A New Testament example of this rhetorical device appears in Acts 10:34, where Peter first states that God does not discriminate and then gives an example of the sorts of persons in favor of whom God does discriminate.

Slavery dominated the code in Colossians; in Ephesians the most important subject is marriage, a theme which occupies twelve of the twenty-two verses. Here efforts to give the code a Christian basis are prominent.[99] The model is Christ/husband–church/wife. The essence of this comparison is not reciprocity.[100] Christ loves the church, which returns not love but reverence (note 5:33). Ephesians 5:31 places the provisions about marriage within the context of Gen. 2:24. In the background is a view of marriage as the restoration of the original unity of the human race. "One flesh" is understood as a sacramental union. This is indebted to Hellenistic Jewish speculation stimulated by Plato.[101] The first person was a bisexual being; sexual union was a means for restoration of the original one from two.[102] The author thus promotes, in distinction from Paul, a positive view of marriage[103] that complements his general exhortation to unity[104] and at the same time advocates Christian support of the social order. A christological feature is that the traditional metaphor of God as the spouse of Israel has been assigned to Christ and given an ontological basis.[105] The use of bridal imagery is another indicator that Ephesians stands near to the world of the Apostolic Fathers.[106] The amount of space devoted to marital union indicates that the position of wives was a male "problem"[107] One target may have been Christian wives of non-Christian men, who are told not to rock the boat.[108] In the language popularized by

Ernst Troeltsch, the ruling concept of community life is patriarchalism qualified by love.[109]

Of the three pairs of Gal. 3:26-28, Jew/Greek, free/slave, male/female, equality is a present reality for the first. Slaves are free only from an eschatological perspective. The author effectively endorses the program: "be good slaves and you'll go to heaven" (Eph. 6:8). Masters are, however, also to take eschatology into account (6:9). They, too, have a master. All are slaves of Christ. The eschatological view of equality is not very far from that of the historical Paul, but he would not view marriage as the sole option for women. Other differences are that dialectical argumentation and discussion have given way to concrete prescription, and the emancipation of slaves is not a topic for discussion. Ephesians 5:21-24 indicates that the household is, in some sense, a mirror or microcosm of the order of the cosmos: the church reflects the cosmos and the household the church.[110] The link between social structures and metaphysics is all but inseparable. This is not to imply that the church has sold out to the world. Ephesians is less positive about the world than much of the Deutero-Pauline tradition. Christians should separate themselves from its evil influences.[111] The author simultaneously urges conformity to general social norms and avoidance of assimilation into Greco-Roman society.

The integration of christology with ecclesiology is more thorough than in Colossians.[112] Eschatological emphasis lies upon the present. Colossians located resurrection in baptism but said that new life is "hidden in God" (3:3). Ephesians locates the baptized as seated with Christ in heaven (2:6). The object of this assertion is parenetic: those so enthroned are empowered for the new life. Other shifts are apparent. In place of grace as the means of justification—a juridical term not readily appealing to gentiles—is grace as the instrument of deliverance.[113] Salvation has replaced justification as the object and result of conversion. The miraculous dimension of justification has faded. Humans apparently possess by nature the capacity to grasp salvation.

The center of this activity is Paul, who, although he can still describe himself as a "minister" of the message (Eph 2:7, from Col. 1:29), is becoming a redeemer in his own right. To him was delivered the "mystery."[114] Comparison of 3:1-13 with its major source, the historical report in Galatians 1-2, is illuminating. This is a meditation on Paul's place in salvation history rather than an essay in apologetic biography. The apostle brings sinners from darkness to light (3:9).[115]

The "very leastest of saints" (Eph. 3:8)[116] characterizes the apostle as one with a past so sinful that he could scarcely dare raise his head but for the grace of God.[117] Ephesians 2:3—"All of us once lived among them in the passions of our flesh, following the desires of flesh and senses, and we were by nature children of wrath, like everyone else"—shows that this fictive Paul identifies himself with gentiles. This is another trend that will become predominant.[118] The author both idealizes Paul—there is no mention of his role as a persecutor—and denigrates him to the ranks of gentile sinners. Paul is a redeemed sinner with whom all may identify and also a sort of redeemed redeemer who liberates through his message.

The closing paraenesis is also remarkable.[119] Paul is, in the end, a prisoner, but not a typical detainee. He continues to speak freely, with boldness. This bondage is only apparent, for Christ has broken the bonds and defeated the powers of evil (cf. also Eph 4:9-10). The imagery speaks not of chains but of weapons (6:11-17). Believers require an ideal Paul, one who is a prisoner only in appearance. So, too, the powers of evil are unable to vanquish the faithful. Robert A. Wild calls this portrait "a mythologized Paul."[120] It is mirrored in the close of Acts, where Paul the prisoner also acts with boldness and freedom.[121]

Beyond the ethereal standing of the apostle, Ephesians, unlike some later texts, does not utilize church office as a means for guaranteeing "orthodox" tradition. Ephesians 4:11 revises 1 Cor. 12:28. Rather than speak of gifts of various types headed by "apostles, prophets, and teachers," the author identifies these gifts as "apostles, prophets, evangelists, pastors and teachers." These may be offices. Apostles and prophets belong to the past. The role of "evangelists" is uncertain. "Pastors and teachers" are evidently one group. Pastors are community leaders (cf. Acts 20:28), with whom the *magisterium* (authority to promulgate correct teaching) resides. This lack of attention to offices is appropriate for a text that concerns itself with the universal church rather than its local instantiations.[122] Ephesians also exhibits limited concern for false doctrine. Like the Pastorals, Ephesians speaks of "heresy" only in general terms. The faithful need but be admonished to avoid other doctrines. Refutation and debate are not on the agenda (Eph. 4:14; 5:6).

The Paul of Ephesians is without doubt the great apostle, imprisoned as he is. He is the designated communicator of the mystery of Christ to the gentiles and, by implication, the guarantor of apostolic tradition. No longer the missionary writing to those he has recently converted, Paul is now the guardian of a mystery. (Compare and contrast the exhortation to "guard the deposit" in 1 Tim. 6:20; 2 Tim. 1:14.[123]) Believers can identify with this former sinner who is a model of behavior. Although in theory a "confessor,"[124] he is, in fact, a martyr who has died for the faith. The apostle has become an archetype. The church for which he has given his life and of which he remains the teacher is the *una sancta*, the body of the faithful dispersed throughout the earth. The ecclesiology of Ephesians marches step for step with its apostle. The author looks beyond the picture of an apocalyptic sect to a universal church, which has acquired attributes from its head (Christ). Just as Christ has become "head" of the body of the church, so now he is the cornerstone, in contrast to 1 Cor. 3:10-17. The one Christ unites the one church.[125] Baptism incorporates believers into heaven and thus empowers them to thwart the forces of wickedness.

Ephesians and Colossians thus promote a legend of Paul that also appears in Acts, the Pastorals, and elsewhere: the apostle and missionary to the gentiles who evangelized the entire world, suffered and died, a redeemed vessel of redemption. Surrounded with a nimbus of martyrdom that embraces the world, Paul remains as a teacher of the whole church throughout all ages. Stability is a social goal, anchored in the desire to demonstrate that Christians are not threats to the social order and to maintain communities with appropriate boundaries.

2 THESSALONIANS

This brief letter of forty-seven verses is unlike Colossians and Ephesians in a number of important ways. Second Thessalonians addresses a specific situation, more specific than that of Colossians. A single theme, the nature and time of the end, pervades the entire letter. Marriage and family life (e.g., the Household Code) do not enter the discussion. Developed ecclesiology, dualistic thought, and emphases upon the worldwide scope of the gentile mission are lacking. There is no discussion of "Judaizing" practices or of the relationship of Jews to gentiles.[126] Pauline intertextuality is essentially limited to a single work: 1 Thessalonians.[127] Among the disputed epistles, there remains more scholarly support for the authenticity of 2 Thessalonians than for any of the others.

Although the authenticity of this letter has been questioned since the late eighteenth century, only in recent decades has the tide turned against Pauline composition.[128] The quantity of resemblances between 1 and 2 Thessalonians has no parallels in any two undisputed letters.[129] As always, solutions must account for both similarities and differences. They have identical senders (Paul, Silvanus, and Timothy), as well as nearly identical openings and closings.[130] The two follow a very similar outline.[131] One shared feature is noteworthy: both have two thanksgiving passages (1 Thess. 2:13; 2 Thess. 2:13-14), a practice not otherwise attested in undisputed letters. If, as argued above, 1 Thess. 2:13-16 is an interpolation, 2 Thessalonians is demonstrably Deutero-Pauline and not earlier than c. 100. Even for those who regard 1 Thess. 2:13 (with or without vv. 14-16) as original, the repetition testifies against authenticity, as this would be an egregious case of Paul imitating himself.

Linguistic issues also arise. The author uses many Pauline terms in ways different from the apostle. A number of typical Pauline idioms, including particles[132] and prepositions, which tend to be consistent indicators of individual style, are absent.[133] Stylistic peculiarities can be readily identified.[134] The most notable of these is the use of parallelism.[135] Synonymous and antithetic parallelism are characteristic of Hebrew poetry; they are not conducive to dialectic. Second Thessalonians is not, unlike 1 Thessalonians, part of a conversation. The use of long and involved sentences is evocative of Colossians and Ephesians. Paul's followers utilized a more complicated style than had their master.

Tone provides another indication of pseudonymity. The author does not seek to persuade his hearers. He is authoritative rather than argumentative, asserting the correct view and rejecting those of others without seeking to refute them. Second Thessalonians adopts a very impersonal style, with qualities of prophetic or official speech. The result resembles a didactic and authoritarian essay.

Theological differences are decisive. The author makes no reference to the death and resurrection of Christ. The christology is "high" in that the author attributes to the heavenly Lord qualities like those of God. Paul exhorted believers to an eschatological existence, equipped against evil for the present and prepared for the future. The author of 2 Thessalonians makes use of an eschatological timetable that stipulates a number of generally unpleasant events that will precede the *dénouement* of the cosmic drama (cf. Mark 13). These signs indicate that the end is not yet. People should continue their lives.

Efforts to press the thought of 2 Thessalonians into conformity with that of 1 Thessalonians require too great a sacrifice of Pauline integrity.[136] The most probable attempt to locate this letter within Paul's career dates it shortly after 1 Thessalonians, the earliest extant church letter. Yet 2 Thessalonians is quite aware of Paul as a letter writer (2:2; 3:17). No other letter so stresses this image.[137] Second Thessalonians 3:17 refers to "every letter," a difficult phrase if this was the second church letter Paul ever wrote.[138] In any case, it is rather early in the day for pseudonymous compositions to play so large a role. In conclusion, arguments against authenticity are more weighty than attempts to include it among the undisputed correspondence.

Most of the warmth of 2 Thessalonians is reserved for the (figurative) fires of Hell. This historical Paul said nothing about the fate of unbelievers. The author of this cold and impersonal communication has more to say about that matter than about the future joys of the elect, which are, at best, implicit.[139] A moralizing quality appears in the one specific element of Christian life that receives attention.[140] Here emerges the so-called "Protestant work ethic." The notion of work as a virtue is not Pauline, but it does surface in the Deutero-Pauline period.[141] In 2 Thessalonians, the apostle's practice of supporting himself is not a means of serving Christ but an admonition to goad the unproductive.[142] Concentration upon the horrors to be afforded the wicked, its "be good or else" method of exhortation, its authoritarian character, and its moralism suggest that 2 Thessalonians has been one of the most influential of Pauline epistles, an epitome of many issues that have led large numbers of people to find Christianity repulsive. It can be read as a manual of the "hell-fire and damnation" gospel that once characterized much American evangelical preaching.[143]

Agreement that this letter is post-Pauline leaves many questions unanswered. It is much too unlike Colossians or Ephesians to be associated with their immediate milieu. Date and situation remain unclear. Was this piece actually directed to Thessalonica or to another location? In favor of that destination is the scrupulous imitation of 1 Thessalonians, yet that is not decisive, for it is arguable that the author wished to modify implications of 1 Thessalonians' eschatology.

What scholars have referred to as "the Delay of the Parousia" (that is, the failure of the world to end within the generation after the crucifixion) brought forth a number of prospective solutions. Among these were explanations of the delay, such as: the need to evangelize the entire earth, a program visible in Luke and Acts; the translation of apocalyptic language into new categories, as seen in Colossians and Ephesians; and the revitalization of apocalyptic thought. Helmut Koester intelligently associates 2 Thessalonians with a revival of apocalyptic expectation and mentality.[144] The general result was to establish "eschatology" as a division of theology, i.e., doctrines about "the end," whenever that might occur, with a concomitant attention to the fate of the individual. Emerging proto-orthodoxy took up Luke's view of the church as a phenomenon in world history, together with the emphasis upon ecclesiology seen in Colossians–Ephesians, and attention to order, as in *1 Clement*, the Pastorals, Polycarp, and Ignatius. The shift from temporal to spatial categories yielded fruitful results in the movements called "Gnostic." For its part, apocalyptic revival has been a repeated phenomenon within history.

Elements of apocalyptic revival belong to the background of Mark (c. 80–85), and its effects persist and reverberate to the middle of the second century (2 Peter, the *Shepherd of Hermas*). Thereafter it is transformed in various ways (*Acts of Paul*, Montanism). Jude and, in particular, Revelation provide close contacts. The Anti-Christ of Rev. 20:1-3 has qualities like the counterpart in 2 Thess. 2:8-12. Both will enjoy a "parousia" (2:8-9).[145] This suggests that 2 Thessalonians stems from Asia Minor, possibly Ephesus. The earliest date would be c. 90. The command to observe "traditions" (2:15) evokes the atmosphere of the Pastorals.[146] Knowledge of the existence of a number of Pauline letters, the contents of which can evidently be consulted, pushes the likely date closer to c. 100.[147] Indeed, the existence of Pauline letters constitutes something of a problem. The possibility of forged letters (2 Thess. 2:2) motivates the writer to provide an authenticating signature (3:17). Identifying signatures (*sphragis* in Greek) are found in Gal. 6:11, Philemon 19, and 1 Cor. 16:21. Such defensiveness provokes suspicion. This letter stems from a milieu that was aware of Pauline letters and, possibly, debates about them. The phrase "in every letter" (3:17) intimates a collection,[148] but 2 Thessalonians presents itself as *the* letter to Thessalonica,[149] rather than as a sequel to 1 Thessalonians.

The Story of 2 Thessalonians

The understanding of 2 Thessalonians may be enhanced by viewing it as a narrative relating to events of the past, present, and future. Supernatural characters include God, the Lord Jesus Christ, his angels, Satan, and the great enemy of God, the "lawless one," and a mysterious restraining figure. Nothing is said about the past of God, the Lord, or the evil one. Human characters are Paul,[150] whose authority is not challenged, believers of various types, and unbelievers.

Paul, a figure of the relatively distant past, visited Thessalonica and evidently founded the community.[151] While there he taught and, later, wrote (2:15). Through his message believers became the chosen people of God (1:11). Among the things he taught was the sequence of events leading up to the end (2:5). Paul supported himself and demanded that those who would not work not be supported by the community (3:8, 10).[152] The purpose of his labor was to provide an example (3:9).

The community has been experiencing various forms of harassment (1:4-5).[153] Although they have remained steadfast, they have been agitated by claims that the "day of the Lord" has arrived (2:2). This view is probably not a form of "realized eschatology" so much as an assertion that the end is near. This message, which can be refuted (below), comes through three agencies: "Spirit," "word," and "a letter allegedly written" by Paul (2:2).[154] "Spirit" probably refers to oracles delivered by prophets, perhaps in a state of ecstasy. These are evidently local prophets, as the narrator introduces no claims about external trouble-makers. "Word" could refer to sermons delivered by members of the community or, slightly less probable, sayings attributed to Jesus. Paul is known as a writer of letters.

For the present, Paul advises the faithful that the purpose of their discomfort is to prove their worthiness for election (1:4-5). Their obligation is to abide by what he said and wrote (2:15)[155] and to avoid those who say otherwise (3:14). Those who do not adhere to the tradition are to be shunned. These persons are identified with the "disorderly" (3:6).[156] One may reasonably infer that these disorderly creatures are the agitators and/or their adherents.[157] Some of them have evidently ceased to work in expectation of the imminent end of the age, devoting their time to ruminations and reflections about its arrival. For now Paul offers comfort, oriented toward the future.

The principal source of consolation is the certainty that God will punish their enemies (1:5-10). The Lord Jesus will come as an agent of vengeance, assisted by punishing angels. This event is not yet at hand, for it will be preceded by rebellion, the appearance of the Anti-Christ, who will deify himself. An agent of restraint now prevents revelation of the Anti-Christ. When that restraint is removed, the Lord Jesus will almost literally "blow away" the evil one. He has taken on the characteristics of the "divine warrior" of the Hebrew Bible. Satan's activities prove the existence of the Anti-Christ. God has deluded the unbelievers in order to achieve their condemnation (2:11-12). The elect are to be confident that God will rescue them (3:2-5). Meanwhile...life goes on. The faithful will continue to live correctly, unperturbed by rumors of impending catastrophe. Peace is achievable.[158]

Although God is in charge, the Lord is his active agent, and Christ's activity is almost entirely oriented to the future destruction of the wicked.

Justice is paramount, while mercy is in short supply. Paul, although at one time present in person, is chiefly a writer of letters, the authenticity of which is a major concern (2:2; 3:17). His authority is absolute and command is his leading means of instruction. About community organization, worship, and life nothing is said beyond the inference that there is a common fund and the probability that prophetic communication takes place in assemblies. The agitators remain nameless. The refractory are to be shunned as a means of provoking repentance, not treated as outside the pale (3:15-16).

This is not a very edifying story, when so presented, and its implied narrator is the least creative of the various pseudo-Pauls. The author of 2 Thessalonians shows that no single image of Paul was promoted in the two generations following his death. Equally important are the characteristics shared by the picture of Paul in 2 Thessalonians with other Deutero-Pauline texts. He works by himself. Rather than serving as a medium of the tradition that he had received (see 1 Cor. 11:23-26; 15:3-8), Paul is the *source* of tradition. In so far as his gospel is the means of God's call, Paul has some of the qualities of a redeemer, a herald who brings salvation. He is the only authority figure who matters, and he uses his authority authoritatively, through pronouncement rather than conversation, command in place of dialogue. As in other Deutero-Pauline compositions, opponents are to be avoided rather than refuted. This letter also reflects the translation of faith and eschatology into formal categories, that is, doctrines. Faith is more nearly *fides quae*, what one believes (the creed), than power, while eschatology is finding a secure place as the doctrine of the last things. Luke and Acts follow a similar path. In 2 Thessalonians, hope is no longer a component of faith, but refers to confidence about the outcome of the last judgment. This opens the door to an individualistic eschatology. The historical Paul urged his converts to imitate him (1 Cor. 11:1). In the Deutero-Pauline world, this imitation is routinely concretized in imitation of one or more particular virtues. Finally, 2 Thessalonians shares with other post-Pauline letters an impersonal tone marked by the absence of references to specific individuals. Here, as elsewhere, Paul is a revered figure from the past who has valuable things to say to the faithful of later times. In rhetorical terms, 2 Thessalonians is engaged in the construction of a Pauline *ethos*, characterization rather than image-making.[159] Together with Colossians and Ephesians it represents a continuation of the Pauline practice of managing conflict *in absentia*. The author is a follower of the historical Paul in so far as s/he utilizes convictions about the future as pointers to how one should behave at the present time.

One may ask why this fairly mediocre piece, with its mechanical imitation of 1 Thessalonians, was received into the Pauline corpus.[160] Why would those who accepted Colossians and Ephesians also incorporate 2 Thessalonians, which may have opposed one or both of those letters?[161] Mediocrity and concern with the events of the end were not scarce commodities at the opening of the second century. The factors shared with other post-Pauline writings probably contributed to its acceptance. Its major utility may have been its value in opposing, on Paul's authority, those who urged believers to grab a white sheet and head for the mountaintop, as well as those advocating eschatological fulfillment in the present.

The Pastoral Epistles: 1 and 2 Timothy, Titus

Critical consensus against the authenticity of the Pastoral Epistles[162] is quite strong and has long prevailed.[163] The Pastorals seem to have had no circulation as separate letters. The indications are that they were written as a letter corpus and that from the beginning they circulated as a small collection. "The suggestion for the writing of a letter collection in the name of Paul would most probably come through acquaintance with an existing Pauline letter collection."[164] This evident fact, together with its distinctive vocabulary and style,[165] awareness of a written gospel,[166] possible awareness of Acts, non-Pauline theology,[167] apparent knowledge of Marcion and incipient Gnosis,[168] as well as similarity to Polycarp and other Apostolic Fathers[169] suggest a date of c. 120–25. Internal evidence supports the view that the Pastorals were written in Ephesus, a major battleground in the struggle over the Pauline heritage.[170] That these were the final additions to the corpus of Pauline letters that eventually found a place in the Christian canon is clear from the attestation.[171]

The Pastoral Epistles present a third stage of the history of the Pauline heritage and fate. In the case of Paul's own letters one sees, as noted, community-building as primary, the formation of a distinct sect. In Colossians and Ephesians the emphasis upon community stabilization is stronger. Second Thessalonians shares this perspective. In the Pastoral Epistles, the object is the maintenance and protection of communities regarded as stable. Stability and continuity are achievements and have become norms. The object of the texts is to protect communities from corruption, to guard the deposit. Paul is, as the traditional title suggests, rather more of a pastor than a missionary.

This collection confronts readers with the fragility of the Pauline inheritance and the problems its transmission to subsequent generations raised. Appropriate judgment requires evaluating a variety of solutions to these problems and reflection upon the merits and weaknesses of each. The historical Paul had not attempted to present an immutable gospel carved upon stone tablets. His writings were, to reiterate, occasional, models for dealing theologically with particular pastoral problems rather than catch-all solutions. These letters were often obscure, especially to those who were not part of the generating discussions that provoked the various pieces of correspondence. The epistles were provocative and stimulating documents with a proclivity to increase speculation through their incentive to reflection. The communities Paul had organized were vulnerable, for a number of reasons, many intentional. This vulnerability had already made them susceptible to disruptive forces within Paul's lifetime. If his converts at Corinth had problems while he was in Ephesus, how many more would erupt in the time after his departure and death? Colossians, Ephesians, and 2 Thessalonians exhibit responses to some of these issues. The Pastoral Epistles seek to tie up the package with secure twine. In them the shift from particular to general is complete and enduring.

Since the three letters cohere in many ways, particularly in viewpoint and themes, and contain a good deal of overlap, one may ask why the author issued three letters, instead of one. Granting the distinct character of 2 Timothy, two would also have been reasonable: one the equivalent of 1 Timothy and Titus, the other tantamount to 2 Timothy. Three is, however, a satisfactory and symbolic number, implying a true collection. One may invoke the narrative "rule of three"[172] and the artistic triptych.[173] Three is "just right." The repetitions serve both to reinforce various points and also to underscore the thesis that Paul delivered a similar message in all of his letters.

Because these three letters constitute a group (the Pastoral Epistles), they are appropriately studied as a unit. Since there are three letters (1 and 2 Timothy, Titus) differences among them should also be pursued. The preferable sequence is Titus, 1 Timothy, 2 Timothy.[174] This order appears in some ancient lists[175] and is supported by epistolary features. Titus has the most elaborate opening formula, while 2 Timothy has the fullest conclusion. First Timothy, for its part, is succinct in both opening and closing.[176] These data intimate that the original order has been displaced by the principle of placing under a single heading letters to a place (e.g., 1 and 2 Corinthians) or a person (1 and 2 Timothy).

Formally, each composition belongs to the general category of the parenetic letter, advice transmitted from a senior to his juniors, private letters addressed to individuals in both their private and public capacities. This was appropriate for the Greco-Roman world, in which members of the ruling class belonged to large social networks.[177] An even closer comparison can be found in collections of letters attributed to Socrates and other philosophers.[178] Because they tell a story, the Pastoral Epistles may be compared to ancient collections of fictitious letters that resemble epistolary novels.[179] Another basis for comparison, particularly in the case of 2 Timothy, is the fictitious testament, such as the *Testaments of the Twelve Patriarchs*. These also have novelistic qualities.

The Story of the Pastorals

Titus and Timothy certainly represent similar, but different, characters. Both are quite young,[180] and cannot be held to possess much in the way of experience, competence, or even intelligence, since they require instruction of the most rudimentary sort, such as "memory, maxims, and morals" that do not in any way differ from the moral advice given to catechumens and recent converts.[181] In background they differ. Titus is a convert from a sinful life[182] (a quality he shares with Paul), whereas Timothy comes from generations of devout believers[183] (a quality he shares with Paul). The two thus exemplify the potential for Christian leaders of quite distinct origins. Men from Christian families and those of polytheist origins are both potentially qualified for leadership.

Their roles have much in common. Both are charged with the tasks of oversight and instruction. They are very much Paul's agents, with major responsibilities but minimal authority.[184] Each comes into view from the point at which Paul last saw him.[185] Although Titus is, in effect, the "Metropolitan of Crete" and Timothy presides at Ephesus, each is nonetheless to hasten to Paul's side when required. Church leaders, apparently, are not to exercise creativity and personal judgment, but to turn always to Paul for guidance.

Their situations are not the same. Titus, himself a convert, appears to have responsibility for a relatively "new mission field";[186] Timothy is to govern an established metropolitan church. Opponents of the true faith are viewed as outsiders in Titus, insiders in the established community of 1 Timothy.[187] For his part, Timothy appears to be rather intimidated by these opponents and must be propped up with reminders of the endowments conveyed by his heritage and through the imposition of hands. Titus does not seem to require such detailed support. Readers of the two letters learn how leaders with different backgrounds and varying gifts are to deal with general situations.

Nothing in Titus and 1 Timothy locates them within a "late period" of Paul's missionary career. The apostle is engaged in his great missionary journey around the Aegean.[188] Except during the winter, Paul is constantly on the move, faithful to his missionary commission.[189] This, in turn, requires the use of deputies, to whom he writes letters on church management. Here, needless to say, one finds a very different picture from that in the undisputed letters. This author does not address his congregations in direct conversation aimed at persuasion, but speaks to their leaders. The apostle works through the chain of *command*.

The congregations require some attention, because the wolves are out there, and in force. These "opponents," as scholarship labels them, permeate the Pastoral Epistles, yet, for all of the references to false teachers, it is difficult to provide these deviants with a clear theological profile.[190] The reader is evidently expected to take note of a great deal of conflict and a number of general types of theological speculation with which it may be associated, but does not need to discover the ideological bases for the actual details, which are not particularly important. The fact of conflict casts its shadow over the Pastoral Epistles, which do not lack suggestions for dealing with it.

Order is the principal instrument for correction,[191] together with a strong disinclination to engage in debate. Enemies come from within and from without. The Pastor, as the author is conveniently denominated, wishes them handled with practice rather than with theory. He is not an executive who shows much interest in or patience with intellectual approaches, but is rather a proponent of the tried and true, good, old-fashioned methods. The church should follow the model of the well-managed Greco-Roman household, envisioned as a healthy organism which functions soundly when each member is performing its proper task in its proper place.[192] The wolves, alas, carry germs.

One surprising feature about the opponents is that, if their views are not clear, many of their names are.[193] This is not traditional. The historical Paul, for example, did not name his opponents.[194] Nor would Ignatius.[195] This quality gives the Pastoral Epistles a vividness, a sense of intimacy, and a realism that have more in common with narrative fiction than with other early Christian polemic.[196] It suggests that the work has some literary goals. Similar observations may be made about the abundance of personal references in the Pastoral Epistles, which surpass those of the church letters in detail and frequency.[197] Only in the Pastoral Epistles, for example, do readers learn of Paul's efforts to secure his cloak and obtain writing material (or writings).[198]

Second Timothy introduces a surprising change of circumstances. Paul is, for reasons the narrator does not clarify, in custody at Rome, where he has been through a hearing of his case (in whole or part), and does not have much hope for release. Nonetheless, his character shines through. He can reflect upon a long history of persecution and its place in his vocation, which Timothy is to share. This use of pathos in 2 Timothy is another clearly literary quality of the Pastoral Epistles. Paul is, to be sure, lonely and harried in his journeys, but, as the end approaches, the narrator pulls out all of the stops.[199] One cannot doubt that the reader is to be left in tears when the abandoned and shivering apostle has finished the enumeration of his woes.[200] At the narrative level, comparison with Acts 20:17-38 is both obvious and illuminating.[201]

The Pastoral Epistles communicate a good deal of information about Paul's life and character. Although Paul can refer at one point to the faith of his ancestors,[202] he is effectively a gentile, as it were, who has been converted from a sinful life.[203] The function of this fictional portrayal is obviously to provide a basis with which gentile converts and their children (the actual implied readers) may identify with the apostle. Since that conversion, his life has been marked by conscientious fidelity to his commission to serve as missionary and pastor. Readers see him acting in these capacities and follow him to the brink of his death.[204]

This understanding is quite congenial with the oft-stated thesis that the Pastoral Epistles seek to promulgate a portrait of Paul.[205] When read in the light of early Christian controversies, this portrait is usually characterized as "apologetic." Although this approach may have merit,[206] the foregoing reading suggests that priority belongs to the character of Paul as a *model*, in season and out, for the Christian life.[207] The reader is to follow Titus and Timothy in following Paul, not as an itinerant apostle, although possibly as a church leader, and certainly as a believer who leads a chaste, sober, just, and godly life with a clear conscience and sound doctrine. Readers are to be imitators of Titus and Timothy, even as the latter were to imitate Paul.[208] They belong to a third Christian generation,[209] and will give birth to a fourth, and so on. Although Paul is the formal author and *subject* of these documents, he is, in fact, their actual *object*.

The purpose of these texts is to create an image of Paul that will serve to direct and shape communities along particular lines. Because the object of this material is protection and maintenance, the Pastor has no need to speak about theological development.

This portrait is, to a far greater extent than in the epistles thus far surveyed, biographical, viewing the apostle from his pre-conversion wickedness to the point of his impending death. This is the same ground covered in Acts.[210] The contrast between "pagan" and "Christian" Paul is central to the moral teaching of the Pastorals and their emphasis upon "law and order." The apostle has been transformed into that romantic figure of edifying religious biography: the miscreant who has been led to abandon his wicked ways and give his life to the service of virtue.[211] No one could better serve as a model convert for those once enmeshed in worldly error and deceit. On this point the text is explicit: 1 Tim. 1:16 uses a term for "example" (*hypotypōsis*). The Pastor knew better, for he—no advocates for "she" command any following—had access to the letters of Paul. This portrait does not derive from an attempt at historical reconstruction but from the desire supply a model and inspiration for gentile converts of the Pastor's era. This picture of the former reprobate who changed his skin is not limited to this epistle. Acts has introduced a kindred Paul, while Ephesians had taken steps in the same direction.[212]

The middle portion of Paul's career is like that portrayed in Acts 13–19.[213] Paul is, as noted, busily engaged in his independent missionary work. Mission in the sense of forming new communities is not, however, the subject of 1 Timothy and Titus. The current task is to nurture churches that already exist. The apostle does not advise his assistants about how to convert polytheists (or Jews). He instructs them about how to manage established bodies.[214] Paul is, in more than one sense, the universal patriarch of the Christian church. Second Timothy 4:6-8 depicts Paul at the very moment of death. The end has arrived, as he indicates in a series of vivid and justly memorable images, derived from the ancient arena.[215] The picture of Paul at the respective closings of Ephesians, Acts, and 2 Timothy is remarkably similar.[216]

> 6 As for me, I am already being poured out as a *libation*, and the time of my departure has come.
>> 7 I have fought the good *fight* (*agōna*),
>> I have finished the *race*,
>> I have kept the faith (= my oath).

8 From now on there is reserved for me the *crown* of righteousness,

which the Lord, the righteous *judge*, will give me on that day,

and not only to me but also to all who have longed for his

appearing (*epiphaneian*).[217]

The athletic contest is a common metaphor for martyrdom.[218] The parallel with Acts is Paul's "testament" in 20:17-38 (note also 20:34). Both Acts and 2 Timothy view Paul's martyrdom as an event of the past. Acts and 2 Timothy portray, as does *1 Clement* 5, Paul as a triumphant hero of the faith. After this moving narration...life continues. Paul snaps out a series of crisp comments and instructions in vv. 9-15, then turns to reflections about his "first defense" (which the audience might interpret as a preliminary hearing), suggests that he may be acquitted (vv. 16-18),[219] and closes with conventional greetings in an atmosphere of "business as usual." These verses do not evoke the situation of a man on the brink of death.

Part of the reason for this surprising anti-climax is the literary background. The last words of a person about to shuffle off the mortal coil could be extensive and comprehensive.[220] The Pastoral Epistles reverse the conventional order. Rather than begin with the narrator at the point of death, all of the useful advice is "front-loaded."[221] The author's evident intent is to show that Paul continued to work to the very last moment: issuing orders and publishing warnings, conveying greetings. He remained in command; and he did not quit.[222]

Through a multitude of circumstantial details and their portrayal of Paul's career, beginning in Titus 1 and closing at 2 Timothy 4, the Pastoral Epistles create a plausible narrative world, concocting Pauline situations which appear utterly probable until one attempts to fit them into the evidence elsewhere available. This technique of verisimilitude is shared with the authors of fiction. So compelling are these vignettes and incidents that some have proposed the existence of authentic Pauline fragments woven into the present text.[223] Even if this were true, as it very probably is not,[224] the technique would still belong to the realm of verisimilitude. Much of the power of the work comes from this fictitious atmosphere, which, as indicated, resembles that of Acts.[225] In neither case is entertainment the primary object.

The picture of Paul constructed by the Pastor is not just background to support the message; it is a far from unimportant component of that message. Paul and his successors, of whom Timothy and Titus are models, are *leaders*, who function as patriarchal heads of their households, the local churches. Ephesians keeps the universal church before the reader's eye, with no attention to local communities. The Pastoral Epistles are nearly the exact opposite. Not for the Pastor is the cosmic Body of Christ. The Christian community in view is regional and local. Its model is secular: the household.[226] The common topic of household management is suitable for both home and church. Leaders must prove themselves as heads of families.[227] This leads to an intermingling of the Household Code with what will later emerge as the "Church Order."[228]

The Pastor was not pilfering items from an existing set of regulations. He was more of a creator of the genre than a borrower from it.[229] "Secular" is appropriate because the Pastoral Epistles are world embracing, not only because of their endorsement of general social values, but also because of the absence of world-rejecting language. It is symptomatic of this perspective that outsiders *must* think well of the church (1 Tim. 3:7). The chain of authority is God, Christ, Paul, Timothy/Titus, bishop(s), presbyters, deacons, men, women, children, and slaves. The "godliness" in mind is that which ranks a place above "cleanliness."[230] The goal is to be and to do what is "sound." Avoidance of excess lies at the heart of popular Greco-Roman ethics, exemplified by the Delphic maxim *mēden agan*, "nothing in excess." The health imagery of which the Pastor is so fond[231] epitomizes his concern for sound common sense. Common sense changes in places and eras, but the impetus toward rational behavior derives from Paul.[232] The historical apostle believed that it was preferable to conform in "non-essentials." Problems arise when these are deemed essential.[233] For the Pastor, this distinction was too subtle, a judgment for which he has had to pay a price since the nineteenth century. Followers of Christ are to be "good citizens."[234]

The door of emancipation has been slammed shut. In contrast to Colossians and Ephesians (Col. 4:1//Eph. 6:9), slaves are viewed solely from the perspective of their owners (1 Tim. 6:1-2; Titus 2:9-10). Children are objects (1 Tim. 3:4, 12; Titus 2:4).[235] Women receive substantial attention, more or less all of it disappointing to egalitarians. The full subordination of women is urged for reasons that go beyond any desire to avoid social criticism. In the face of such strong and pervasive regimentation, it is difficult to evade the conclusion that the Pastor does not simply wish to exclude women from leadership but that some women were attempting to exert or were exerting types of leadership that they may well have, not without reason, believed to have been traditional in Pauline communities.[236] Furthermore, some women may have been proponents of teachings rejected by the Pastor. This hypothesis is not the product of whistling in the dark, for a document that emerged about two generations later than the Pastoral Epistles, itself based upon earlier legends, portrays just such a woman: the virgin Thecla (or Thekla) of the *Acts of Paul*.[237] Thecla, who rejects marriage and becomes a missionary, is the kind of "silly woman" (2 Tim. 3:6) about whom the Pastor wishes to warn us.

Behind this misogyny stand popular prejudices about women and religion, such as the presumption that women were hysterical creatures, especially susceptible to bizarre religious impulses, and that they, through their lack of education and experience, as well as their constitutions, were vulnerable to unscrupulous missionaries in pursuit of their virtue or their money, if not both.[238] In addition, such missionaries could be purveyors of socially dangerous doctrines (2 Tim. 3:6).[239] Marriage was a central issue. Many women could have justifiably understood Paul (cf. 1 Cor. 7) as inviting them to claim their freedom. This freedom authorized emancipation from marital bonds, including rejection of marriage altogether. Against such views the Pastor advocates not just the desirability of marriage but its very necessity, with the fundamental duties of obedience to one's husband and avoidance of attention-getting behavior, notably through their silent and decorous behavior during worship.[240] The Pastor comes perilously close to saying that women are saved by child-bearing (1 Tim. 2:9-15).[241] The entire female sex must bear the burden of Eve's failure to resist enticement. Major efforts are required to control their labile nature, including substantial exercise in self-control.[242] Self-control was a general virtue. For women it often came down to modesty and chastity.[243]

Moreover, there is the question of the widows, who were organized as a group, that is, as a formally enrolled order within the church.[244] "Widow" is best understood as an unmarried woman, since the body evidently included those who had never married, divorcées, and actual widows.[245] Some of these women were rather independent and well to do; others were quite poor, belonging to the category of "widows and orphans." Among the never married were dedicated virgins, who could appeal to the authority of Paul (1 Cor. 7). From the earliest times (Acts 6:1-7), male church leaders found widows vexatious.[246] These women may have lacked much formal education, but they knew what sorts of wheels were likely to receive lubrication. Widows engaged in various types of ministry. Some, like Tabitha (Acts 9:36-41), were financially independent.[247] Others relied upon the Christian community for support. One purpose of the Pastor was financial: to reduce the monetary burden. He recommends that the order be limited to those for whom the church has social responsibility: women without means of support (e.g. from children or other relatives) who were beyond the age of marriage and childbearing.[248] Younger "widows" are to take on the role rejected by Thecla and become housewives. Limitation, better, suppression of widows is a goal of the Pastor.[249]

Economic issues were not the author's sole concern in the matter of widows. He devotes more space to that order than to the office of bishop. Constant prayer is recommended (1 Tim. 5:5).[250] This was an intelligible exchange: the feeble could pray while the vigorous worked, but it excludes teaching. The only instruction permitted to elderly women involves moral advice to young women (Titus 2:3-5). Other stereotypes emerge: the drunken old woman (Titus 2:3) and the "merry widow," common objects of calumny and gossip (1 Tim. 5:5-6).[251] The Pastor's rather overdetermined strictures about women challenge those who wish to find in Christian scripture norms for an abiding social order.

The theology of the Pastoral Epistles reflects Pauline roots channeled in fresh directions.[252] The Jewish past has become remote. Salvation history and linkage between Israel and the Church receive no attention. The most important figures in salvation history are Jesus and Paul. If scripture is honored (2 Tim. 3:16), its use is rather limited. A theology of the Holy Spirit is largely absent.[253] Christ's suffering and death play no theological role. God appears to be a highly remote, transcendent figure. The epiphany of Christ makes the gift of God immanent and available. This imagery derives from the cult of the Roman rulers.[254] Christ would deliver everyone from the perils of the future judgment. His arrival has made all things pure. This is the indicative that makes ethical living possible. Grace is educative, as set forth in the stirring words of Titus 2:9-15.[255] The ethics recommended by the Pastor are hierarchical, conventional, conservative, and rational. Threat of final judgment plays a leading role in motivating conduct.[256]

The historical Paul's ethical exhortations were soundly grounded upon his apocalyptically oriented soteriology, but their content is often prudent moral sense. He did not always set out ethical recommendations that were patently grounded in his theology, as subsequent arguments between progressives pursuing implications of his theology and conservatives appealing to his specific recommendations reveal. Diverse groups and individuals received aspects of Paul's rich inheritance and erected upon them more consistent systems of their own. Some replaced his distinctive theology with traditions derived from Diaspora Judaism and a biblical-bourgeois morality.[257] Of the various trends, both the apocalypticizing and the gnosticizing types retained features of Paul's thought, which led them to embrace a "sectarian" morality that (1) devalued the church as a body of the political sort, and (2) could quickly give Christianity a bad reputation. The Pastor may have realized that these "sectarian" solutions dealt with the problem of "the world" by cutting a knot left raveled by their common master, Paul. In such hands Christianity would soon become little more than a batch of syncretistic and fissiparous sects. The Pastoral Epistles, following Paul, reject ideas of escapism by apocalyptic or dualizing otherworldliness and try to carve out a sphere of Christian existence within the world. They seek to make possible a kind of social life that will be Christian without scandalizing the pagans, but yet will not sell out to them. This is the perspective of a "Conversionist Sect."[258] The Pastoral Epistles aim at the existence of an enduring body that will "whip the world into shape."

Their values are typically bourgeois, as were those of Paul, and thus utterly unremarkable. Good Christian citizens will be productive members of society. They will not raise questions by their conduct. Radical practices in the realms of sexual behavior, life-style, and gender roles, as noted, are shelved. The church is to be organized, inevitably for that era and in those conditions, along models of hierarchy, specifically patriarchy, and subordination. Freedom is no longer a value. Paul could regard washing dishes as the exercise of a valuable charisma. The Pastoral Epistles raise domestic life to the level of a sacred and redemptive vocation. Something has changed, but this is not totally alien; it is perverse—as were Marcion and others. These particular phenomena are noteworthy and outstanding, but they are secondary. Other social models can replace them, and a church somewhat comfortably ensconced within the world can dare to be a bit more experimental—and has. Where the Pastoral Epistles are truly harbingers of proto-orthodox "early Catholicism" emerges in their view of the church: a body now regulated by structure and conformed to "nature," as perceived, and in their program of transforming nature by grace.

Whatever one thinks about the ethical specifics of the Pastoral Epistles, their ground is theological and, as in Paul, ethical empowerment comes from grace. These texts are relevant to contemporary "mainstream" Christians, who must likewise reflect about the relation of Christ and culture without the expectation of an imminent end.[259] The portrait of Paul as a redeemed sinner is also a defense of the goodness of law.[260] No reader of these letters can find evidence that the apostle held an antinomian position. Whereas Acts depicts continuity with Israel in the story of salvation history, for the Pastor this continuity belongs to morality and piety.[261]

Church order is, by any standard of calculation, of great importance to the Pastor. Like Acts, 1 Peter, and *1 Clement*, the Pastoral Epistles reflect a fluid state between systems of governance by presbyters and the emerging bishop, deacon, and presbyter model[262] that will become normative.[263] Although the term "bishop" tellingly appears only in the singular, either "bishop" or "presbyter" is acceptable terminology for the community leader. Nothing is said about the liturgical functions of these officers.[264] Teaching is their most important role.[265] The ministry is acquiring the status of what we would call a "profession." This is one reason for the disappointingly minimal qualifications for these offices: they conform to those of other professions.[266] The church has become an institution. Stability is to be achieved not by appeal to a cosmic church or to the grace of baptism, but through structure. Many have found this change unpleasant. One thing that can be said in its favor is that, as an institution in its society, the church could survive.

Certain historical manifestations of Christianity (and other religions) may disappoint their readers—or worse. Historians cannot allow such disappointments to terminate reflection and research. Movements are to be assessed within their historical environment, and historians must attempt to evaluate them in terms of their objectives, to try to assess their fidelity to the roots and the success of the projects in which they were engaged. The first question to answer is not whether the various themes propounded in the Pastoral Epistles seem liberal or conservative, abhorrent or congenial, but whether they have some consistency and theological integrity within their historical and social contexts. The Pastoral Epistles do not claim to provide a normative social blueprint for all Christians of all times, but the New Testament is, in general, remarkably free of such blueprints.[267]

The Pastoral Epistles represent Paul as a strong, authoritative leader encouraging the selection of strong, authoritative leaders to succeed him. Those leaders the faithful are to obey. The Pastoral Epistles pursue this objective through a double pseudonymity, for both author and recipients are fictitious constructions. The truly implied readers[268] are thus permitted to look over the shoulders of "Timothy" and "Titus." Both present and potential leaders, as well as general members, were to find value in this short group of letters. Reading the Pastoral Epistles from a historical perspective is quite satisfying. They *exude* distance and rely upon authority that has the patina, indeed the halo, of antiquity. In these texts Paul is a hero of salvation history, not an apostle battling for recognition. If Moses was the Lawgiver, Paul serves as the herald announcing deliverance.[269] The heroization of Paul actually surpasses that of Acts.[270] "There is thus a continuing process of assimilation of the master by the disciple both in the Father's service and in death."[271] Paul is becoming an icon, fixed in time and space.

Every reading of the Pastoral Epistles has to account for this sense of distance, and there is little doubt that the most difficult readings are those that place the recipients within the life of Paul. Historical distance actualizes the text. Readers quite readily take up the Pastoral Epistles in terms of what Paul is saying to me/us *now* rather than what he said to Titus and Timothy *then*.

The six Deutero-Pauline letters considered thus far have been received into the universal Christian canon. They include one small collection (the Pastoral Epistles), two related pieces (Colossians and Ephesians), and one that is unique: 2 Thessalonians. With the possible exception of the last, all are associated with conflicts in Asia Minor, specifically Ephesus, over the course of a generation, from c. 80 to c. 125. All are intensely intra-Pauline. The late apostle to the gentiles was a recognized authority figure, but the meaning of his message, that is, his letters, is in considerable dispute. The most daring is Colossians, which, with its cosmic speculation and lack of interest in the Israelite heritage, reveals an incipient form of the "left-wing Paulinism" that will inspire Marcion. Ephesians blunts this approach by reframing the cosmic model in salvation-historical terms. Both Ephesians and Colossians show the transformation of Pauline ecclesiology in a universal direction. Their Paul envisions a universal church anchored in the heavens. For Ephesians, which had a substantial influence upon Acts, unity is a major concern, with particular application to Jewish-gentile unity. That unity was more theological than social, but it reflects an apparent influx of Jews toward the close of the first century. Second Thessalonians attacks both the "realized" eschatology discernible in Colossians/Ephesians and its basis in 1 Thessalonians.

Colossians/Ephesians and 2 Thessalonians also exhibit the promotion of conventional morality, most notably through the use of the Household Code and the promulgation of a work ethic. The Pastoral Epistles take this model a step further; the household is now the model for the church. The theology of the Pastoral Epistles is a more diluted Paulinism, with expressions of loyalty to Pauline concepts that are nonetheless based upon a different christological model. The end-time has become a formal category of theology rather the driving force of Christian existence. One may show ways in which each of these pseudonymous letters has preserved Paul's own thought and betrayed the same, but those issues are not the only matters requiring attention. All are best viewed as attempts to preserve Paul's heritage by proposing how he would have addressed subsequent situations. By that criterion they were successful, for they served both to support the authority of the founding missionary and to integrate his thought with other understandings of early Christianity.

The following section takes up correspondence that found limited or no place in Christian Bibles. *Third Corinthians*, *Laodiceans*, and the correspondence of Paul and Seneca represent a considerable advance in date. These texts show ongoing use of the pseudonymous letter in various circumstances.

3 Corinthians

The complex known as "3 Corinthians"[272] is traditionally divided into four components: I. Narrative Setting; II. The Letter from the Corinthians; III. Narrative; IV. Paul's Letter to Corinth. Although only IV is *3 Corinthians* proper, the title is applied to the entire complex.

> I. The Corinthians were gravely concerned about Paul because he was going to leave the world before the proper time. Simon and Cleobius had come to Corinth with this message: "There is no resurrection of the flesh but [only] of the spirit, and the human body is not a divine creation, and, with regard to the world, God neither created it nor knows it, nor has Jesus Christ been crucified—he was mere appearance[273], he was neither born of Mary nor was he of Davidic descent." In sum, they taught many things in Corinth, deceiving themselves and many others. When therefore the Corinthians heard...they sent [a letter to Paul] in Macedonia [by the hand of the deacons] Threptus and Eutychus.[274] The letter read:
>
> The Corinthians to the Apostle Paul[275]
>
> II. *1* Stephanas[276] and his fellow-presbyters Daphnus, Eubulus, Theophilus, and Zeno to Paul, who is in Christ: greetings.[277]
> *2* Two individuals have come to Corinth, Simon and Cleobius; they overthrew the faith of some[278] with corrupt words.

3 These[279] you will examine, *4* for we never heard such things either from you or from the others.[280] *5* But we maintain what we have received from you and from them. *6* As the Lord has shown us mercy, we should hear this from you again while you are still in the flesh. *7* Either come to us or write to us, *8* for we believe, as it was revealed to Theonoe,[281] that the Lord has delivered you from the hand of the lawless one. *9* They say and teach as follows: *10* The prophets are not to be utilized; *11* God is not almighty; *12* there is no resurrection of flesh; *13* God did not fashion the human race; *14* The Lord neither came in the flesh nor was he born of Mary; *15* the world is not of God but of angels. *16* Therefore, brother, please hasten here, so that the Corinthian church may continue without stumbling and the foolishness of these men may be exposed. Farewell in the Lord.

III. [282] *1* The deacons, Threptus and Eutychus, took the letter to Philippi. *2* When Paul received it, although he was in prison because of Stratonike, the wife of Apollophanes, he became quite upset, *3* and exclaimed "It would have been better had I died and were with the Lord than to remain in the flesh and to hear words that heap sorrow upon sorrow. *4* How dreadful it is to be in prison while Satan's wiles flourish!" *5* And in considerable affliction Paul wrote this reply to the letter.

Paul's Epistle to the Corinthians
[Concerning the Flesh][283]

IV. *1* Paul, the prisoner of Jesus Christ, to the believers at Corinth: greetings. *2* Since I am experiencing numerous misfortunes, I am not surprised that the teachings of the evil one are experiencing rapid success. *3* The Lord Christ will quickly come, since he is rejected by those who falsify his teaching. *4* For I delivered to you first of all what I received from the apostles before me who were always with Jesus Christ, *5* that our Lord Christ Jesus was of Davidic descent, born of Mary, into whom the Father sent the spirit from heaven[284] *6* that he might come into this world and liberate all flesh by his own flesh, and that he might raise us in the flesh from the dead as he has shown us by example. *7* Humanity was created by his Father *8* and was thus sought by God when lost, so that it might become alive by adoption. *9* For the almighty God of the universe, maker of heaven and earth, sent the prophets first to the Jews to deliver them from their sins, *10* as he desired to save the house of Israel; therefore he distributed some of the spirit of Christ and apportioned it to the prophets who proclaimed the true worship of God over a long period. *11* Yet the [evil] prince wished to be god himself and laid his hands on them and bound all human flesh to lust.[285] *12* But the almighty God, who is just, did not wish to nullify his own creation *13* and sent Spirit through fire into Mary the Galilean,[286] *15* that the evil one might be conquered by the same flesh by which he ruled and be convinced that he is not God. *16* For by his own body Jesus Christ saved all flesh, *17* so that he might exhibit a temple of righteousness in his own body *18* by which[287] we are liberated. *19* Those who impede the providence of God by denying that heaven and earth and all that is in them are works of the father are children of wrath, not of righteousness. *20* They possess the accursed faith of the serpent. *21.* Avoid them and keep your distance from their teaching.[288] *24* For those who tell you that there is no resurrection of the flesh there will be no resurrection—*25* Those who do not believe the one who thus [*in the* flesh] rose.[289] *26* For they do not know, Corinthians, about the sowing of wheat or other seeds that one casts naked upon the ground and dies, then rises by God's will, in a body and clothed. *27* God not only raises the sown body but also bestows upon it abundant blessings. *28* If we cannot develop a parable from seeds, *29* you know of Jonah, the son of Amathios who, when he refused to preach to the Ninevites, was swallowed up by a sea-monster. *30* After three days and three nights God heard the prayer of Jonah from the depths of Hades. No part of him was corrupted, not even a hair or an eyelid. *31* How much more, you of limited faith, will he raise those who have believed in Christ Jesus, as he himself was raised up? *32* When some Israelites threw a corpse on the bones of the prophet Elisha, the person's body was raised. So also will you, upon whom the body, bones, and Spirit of Christ have been thrown,[290] will be raised on that day with a whole body.[291] *34* If, however, you receive any different teaching, do not trouble me, *35* for I have shackles on my hands so that I may gain Christ and marks on my body so that I may attain to the resurrection of the dead. *36* Whoever abides by the rule which we have received through the blessed prophets and the holy gospel, shall receive a reward,[292] *37* but whoever transgresses these, and those who did so earlier will receive fire, *38* since they are godless persons, a generation of vipers.[293] *39* Rebuff them by the power of Christ. *40* Peace be with you.[294]

This material is transmitted in Greek (incomplete),[295] Latin, Coptic, Syriac, and Armenian. *Third Corinthians* was included, after 1 and 2 Corinthians, in many Armenian Bibles as late as the nineteenth century. Ephraem Syrus commented upon the epistle, which he regarded as genuine.[296] It is found in five Latin manuscripts., often with *Laodiceans*, at the close of the Pauline correspondence or of the New Testament, once with the specific stipulation that it is not authentic.[297]

The letter to Paul is, as characterized in Latin ms. L, a petition, that is, an example of deliberative rhetoric.[298] Verse 2 begins with a narrative summary, followed by a request for Paul to examine the opponents' claims, assurance that the community has remained steadfast, a renewal of the petition in vv. 6b-8, adding a rationale: Paul remains alive. Verse 7 is the thesis. Verses 9-15 narrate the opposing doctrine, in propositional (creedal) form, followed in v. 16 by a concluding repetition of the request. The narrative is essentially a summary of the creed.

Paul's response also follows a deliberative pattern.[299] After an introduction affirming the source of Pauline teaching (vv. 2-3), vv. 4-8 are narration, concluding with the thesis: the creator God seeks to restore the human race. Most of the letter is devoted to proof. Verses 9-21 conclude with the admonition to avoid the rival teachers. Verses 24-32 culminate with a subsidiary thesis: God will rescue humanity by raising the body. Verses 34-39 constitute an epilogue, in pathetic style, complementing the opening pathos of v. 2. Verses 36-37 contain a promise/threat ("judgment saying"). Verses 19-24 and 37-39 are parallel. The first set of proofs is "inartistic," essentially the creed in salvation-historical form. The second set involves an analogy from nature (vv. 26-29), followed by two historical examples in vv. 29-33.[300] In effect, this is a compressed statement of how to refute those who deny fleshly resurrection: first via the creed (i.e., this is what Christians have always believed) and then through arguments from creation and scripture. Framing the body are two personal evocations of *pathos* (IV.2, 34). These observations about structure show that neither letter, in particular Paul's response, is a careless pastiche of quotations from the correspondence, but organized prose persuasion.[301] The points raised in II.9-15 are taken up and refuted.[302]

The epistolary features resemble those in the letters in the Apostlic Fathers. Like the letters of Ignatius (e.g., *Romans*, Polycarp), the greeting is the standard *chairein* (lit., "rejoice"). The closing of II also follows the Greek convention of "farewell": *errōso/errōsthe*.[303] The opening of II is very similar to that of Polycarp's *Philippians*. Paul's letter (III), however, takes its opening from Colossians.

As embedded in the *Acts of Paul*, *3 Corinthians* is associated with a stay of Paul in Philippi (chs. 8/10). In the available fragments, this follows a sojourn in Ephesus, toward the close of which his departure for Macedonia is mentioned.[304] From the subsequent material (II.2 and *APl* 9/11-12), it appears that Paul had been condemned to labor in the mines. In ch. 11 (Rordorf),[305] he raises one Frontina, who has evidently been hurled (presumably from a rock or cliff) to her death because of her association with Paul.[306] At the close of that episode Paul goes from Philippi to Corinth. As the text stands, the narrator utilizes retardation, shifting, evidently at a moment of great anxiety in Philippi, to Corinth, where the believers are distraught by false teachers. Not until the letters have been reported does the narrative return to Paul's experiences at Philippi. The narrative interstices develop their own interest. Section I opens with anxiety about Paul's imminent death,[307] then reports the arrival of Simon and Cleobius. The danger is that the death of Paul will open the door to false teachers.[308] The Corinthians' letter (II.8) reports that this fear was relieved. Paul's response to the news about the visitors (III.3-5) echoes the opening of I. This is to say that *3 Corinthians* serves as an effective piece of retardation within the *Acts of Paul*. This does not establish its original place in that work.

That question has apparently been resolved: *3 Corinthians* was originally independent of the *Acts of Paul* and subsequently incorporated into it.[309] The principal arguments are literary. When Paul arrives in Corinth, the disturbance created by false teaching receives no mention. As far as this subsequent episode is concerned, the problem did not occur. Stephanas/us and the other leaders noted in II are not mentioned. Cleobius, a rival teacher in *3 Corinthians*, shares the name of an inspired believer at Corinth.[310] Finally, Paul's letter (IV.34) implied that no visit to Corinth was in the offing.[311] The character of Paul is notably different in *3 Corinthians*.

In the residue of the *Acts of Paul* he is a super apostle whose status often approaches, even rivals, that of Christ, working miracles and preaching powerful sermons.[312] *Third Corinthians* apparently subordinates him to the other apostles, who had instructed him in the faith (IV.4).[313] The source of that verse is Gal. 1:17, the meaning of which *3 Corinthians* has flipped upside down. Paul's claim that he did not visit the earlier apostles after his call is used here to acknowledge his inferiority.[314] The Corinthians address Paul as "brother" (II.1), rather than as "teacher" or "apostle."

Some overlap between *3 Corinthians* and the *Acts of Paul* nonetheless exists. A good example is the role of the pre-existent Christ in the inspiration of the prophets (IV.10). The theme also appears in *APl* 10/13.[315] This "Spirit Christology" serves admirably to unite the eras of salvation history.[316] One could argue that the editor introduced this theme into *3 Corinthians* to facilitate its integration into the *Acts of Paul. Third Corinthians* IV.11 follows IV.9 quite smoothly. If this hypothesis is accepted, it would imply that the editor was more interested in theological integration than in narrative continuity.[317] This particular theological theme is common enough in the second century and environs,[318] allowing the hypothesis that this agreement is too unremarkable to serve as a basis for regarding the correspondence as an integral part of the Acts.[319] An example of overlap created by the editor derives from III.2. Paul was in prison because of Stratonike the wife of Apollophanes when he received the Corinthians' letter. Readers will assume that Stratonike was converted to the celibate life by Paul, that her husband Apollophanes took exception to her behavior, and, finally, that he was highly placed and had the authority to have Paul jailed. For such readers Paul suffered because of his proclamation of celibacy and resurrection, the terms used to summarize his gospel in 3.5 (Thecla). The text of *3 Corinthians* itself does not demand abstinence. This continuity is a creation of the editor, who presumably accepted the necessity of avoiding sexual activity (and procreation).[320]

The letters contained in *3 Corinthians* were therefore composed separately and inserted into the text by a later editor who may or may not have been responsible for composition of the narrative portions I and III, since these generate a number of inconsistencies.[321] For some time, the letters circulated both as a component of the *Acts of Paul* and separately or within collections of the correspondence.[322] *Third Corinthians* was probably inserted into the *Acts of Paul* in the first half of the third century. One motive for this addition could have been a desire to give the *Acts* a more catholic flavor, since questions had been raised about its orthodoxy, most notably by Tertullian.[323] Tertullian's objections had more to do with practice than with belief, and it was difficult to claim that the book was highly deviant in doctrine. With the inclusion of *3 Corinthians*, however, the *Acts of Paul* could be viewed as a positive weapon in the arsenal of orthodoxy, a refutation of various heresies.[324] The original letters were probably written between 175 and 200.[325] They exhibit knowledge of various early Christian texts and appear, unlike the residue of the *Acts of Paul*, to envision communities governed by the three-fold ministry of bishop, presbyters, and deacons.[326] Theologically, they reflect a climate rather similar to that of Irenaeus, as they relate creation to redemption, emphasize the Incarnation, and place strong emphasis upon the physical human body ("flesh").[327] In line with other later Pauline writings, they omit reflection on such subjects as the cross, law, sin, and justification.[328]

The correspondence, its narrative setting, and its placement with the *Acts of Paul* reveal skill in novelistic technique. Like the Pastoral Epistles, but unlike 2 Thessalonians and Ephesians, the text presents an abundance of proper names. These create verisimilitude. The author drew these names from a variety of traditions, with the possible contribution of imagination.[329] At the head stands Stephanas, a firm link with 1 Corinthians (1:16; 16:15, 17). Theophilus could be the dedicatee of Luke and Acts (Luke 1:3; Acts 1:1). Eutychus is another link to Acts (20:7-12).[330] By bringing the Paul of the epistles and the Paul of Acts together this author complements, with a few deft strokes, one of Irenaeus' major projects. The framework is quite logical—until one attempts to coordinate it with other sources—and the setting: prison in Philippi, a debate about resurrection, is highly appropriate. Like the majority of Deutero-Pauline letters, *3 Corinthians* is a "prison epistle," with all of the pathos thereunto appertaining.[331]

The author was not devoid of wit. In 1 Cor. 5:9 Paul had referred to a letter that he had written; 1 Cor. 7:1 takes up a communication from Corinth. *Third Corinthians* fills these gaps. Corinth was an ideal site for questions about resurrection, notably because of Paul's lengthy argument in 1 Corinthians 15, a chapter that did not escape the attention of *3 Corinthians'* composer. *Third Corinthians* IV.3 draws upon 1 Cor. 15:3 (cf. 11:23), with an important modification: Paul transmitted the gospel he had received from the apostles who had associated with the earthly Jesus.[332] The purpose of this change is not to denigrate Paul but to argue, in the approved anti-heretical fashion, that Christians had held the views here defended from the very beginning, implying that they derived from the historical

Jesus. This assertion silently rebuffs claims of secret revelations by the risen Christ to various apostles, including Paul, and contentions that these views had been transmitted to followers of the original apostles.

The second part of Paul's *probatio* (IV.24-32) corresponds to statements in 1 Cor. 15:4, 24-25 to 1 Cor. 15:12; 26 to 15:36-38; 31 to 15:20.[333] In place of Paul's lengthy analogy from planting, the author offers a shorter analogy from nature (IV.26-27). Parallels to 1 Cor. 15:50-57 are lacking, and for good reason. First Corinthians 15:50—"What I am saying, brothers and sisters, is this: flesh and blood cannot inherit the kingdom of God, nor does the perishable inherit the imperishable"—constituted, if the metaphor is pardonable, a substantial thorn in the flesh to those who argued that Paul taught a fleshly resurrection.[334] Donald Penny aptly summarizes the difference: in 1 Corinthians 15, Paul opposes those who reject the resurrection of the dead; *3 Corinthians* uses the same data against those who reject the resurrection of the flesh. Penny also notes the implication: Paul pressed for discontinuity, while *3 Corinthians*, supports continuity between present and future existence.[335] "Heretical" writers of the second century constructed sustained and able arguments in support of resurrection as a "spiritual" phenomenon.[336]

The seed "parable" in IV.26-27 depends upon 1 Cor. 15:37-38, but, as is appropriate in a work devoted to ascribing creation to God, it makes a natural analogy to resurrection. Such arguments are frequent in early Christian "natural theology."[337] In *3 Corinthians* it is important that seeds "die"[338] prior to their "resurrection" and that they rise "clothed," that is, enfleshed. "Seed" was also an important concept in various "Gnostic" systems.[339] The author wished to suppress speculation about seeds by keeping to the tried-and-true track of homely wisdom. The examples provided are popular. The story of Jonah was one of the most common themes of early Christian art,[340] and the Elijah-Elisha cycle permeated the sources of the Gospels, receiving further development in Luke and Acts.[341]

Also congenial to the Corinthian situation is the arrival of "outside agitators"—Simon and Cleobius.[342] This reflects the circumstances of 2 Corinthians.[343] No place was more familiar with Pauline correspondence than that Roman colony (cf. also 2 Cor. 10:10) and data about letters from Macedonia to Corinth and vice versa (see 2 Cor. 7:5-9; 8:1; 9:2). The pseudonymous Pauline letter closing (IV.34-38) borrows from Gal. 6:16-17, an appropriate choice, as Galatians involved indirect conflict with rival teachers. Other clear borrowings are from Philippians, notably 3:11 in IV.35, another appropriate choice, as Paul was in Philippi at that time.

The Pastoral Epistles make important contributions to the mentality of the letters. Like the Pastor, the author of *3 Corinthians* urges that rivals be avoided.[344] Equally like the Pastor, this Paul sets out clear, simple creedal statements that are matters for adherence, not topics for discussion.[345] Second Timothy 2:18 is cited in II.2. Romans 1:2-3 and Luke 1 lie behind the creedal formulation of IV.5, but the author probably received this from earlier creedal statements rather than directly from those texts. Other allusions can be noted.[346] The author had access to a collection of Pauline epistles like that of Irenaeus, that is, one that included the Pastoral Epistles.

Also like the Pastoral Epistles, *3 Corinthians* appears to attack heresies in general rather than focus upon a specific variety of false teaching.[347] The consistency of the polemic here is, however, clearer. The text opposes any teaching that views creation as the work of inferior beings and consequently views matter as negative. Marcion and various "Gnostics" are in view. References to creation by angels,[348] the "Serpent" (IV.20; cf. 38), and "seeds" (IV.26) evoke the teachings of Saturnilus, Naasenes or Ophites, and Valentinians, respectively, while much of the heretical profile, including both hostility toward creation and rejection of Israelite scripture, fits Marcion. The author may have garnered these details from experience in a competitive religious environment, but it is also quite possible that he made use of heresiological material. One candidate would have been Irenaeus' treatise *Against the Heresies*, usually dated c. 180. This possibility gains force from the similarity between the theology of *3 Corinthians* and that of Irenaeus, noted above. Paul's letter takes up the birth of Jesus from two perspectives: its relation to creation (IV.5-11) and, more specifically, to redemption (IV. 12-18).[349] Use of Irenaeus would also fit the likely date of c. 175–200. Familiarity with the work of Irenaeus is thus a possibility.[350]

In conclusion, this text is an attempt to say what the Pastor would have said had he lived in the second half of the second century.[351] In style (authoritative prescriptions, refusal of dialogue with rival expressions of the faith) and form (letter), this material resembles the work of the Pastor, who was a principal model. In its use of novelistic detail and fictional composition, *3 Corinthians* also evokes the Pastoral Epistles, although the author did not regard those letters as fictions. In other ways *3 Corinthians* is unlike the work of the Pastor. Paul is no longer the only apostle; he is subordinate to Peter & Co., and his views have entered into a broader synthesis. The letters of Paul are part of a broader collection of authoritative texts, including the Gospels and Acts. Paul has taken his place as one representative of "apostolic orthodoxy."[352]

LAODICEANS

To the Laodiceans[353]

1 Paul, an apostle not of mortal authorization and not through a mortal agent, but through Jesus Christ, to the believers at Laodicea:[354] *2* Grace to you and peace from God the Father and the Lord Jesus Christ.[355]

3 I thank Christ in every prayer of mine, that you may continue and persevere in good works,[356] looking for that which is promised[357] in the day of judgment.[358] *4* Do not be troubled by the vain speeches of anyone who perverts the truth, that they may draw you aside from the truth of the Gospel[359] that I have preached.[360] *5* And now may God grant that my converts may attain to a perfect knowledge of the truth of the Gospel,[361]...be beneficent, and continue to do good works[362] which accompany salvation.[363]

6 And now my bonds, which I suffer in Christ, are manifest;[364] I rejoice and am glad in them.[365] *7* For I know that this shall eventuate in my everlasting salvation,[366] which will come about through your prayer and the assistance of the Holy Spirit. *8* Whether I live or die,[367] for me to live shall be a life to Christ, and to die will be joy.[368]

9 And our Lord [Christ] will grant us his mercy, that you may have the same love, and be like-minded.[369] *10* Wherefore, my beloved, as you have heard from me while I was present,[370] so remain steadfast and work in awe of God. So you will have eternal life.[371] *11* For it is God who is working in you;[372] Do what you do[373] without sliding back.[374] *13* For the rest, most beloved, rejoice in Christ[375] and beware of those seeking corrupting money.[376] *14* Let all your requests be manifest to God,[377] and remain steadfast[378] in the mind[379] of Christ.[380]

15 Do those things that are genuine, valid, and admirable.[381] Keep in mind what you have heard and received, and peace will be with you.

17 Salute all the believers with the holy kiss.[382] *18* All the believers send greetings.[383] *19* The grace of the Lord Jesus Christ be with your spirit.[384]

20 See that this letter is read to the Colossians[385] and that to the Colossians to you.

For Brook Foss Westcott (1825–1901), "The history of the Epistle to the Laodicenes [sic]...forms one of the most interesting episodes in the literary history of the Bible."[386] This was about the kindest thing anyone has said about this little letter in the last five hundred years—and the good bishop was not speaking of its contents.[387] *Laodiceans* was quite probably composed in Greek, but survives only in Latin and translations from it.[388] This epistle drew a flurry of criticism in the fourth century, but that activity was due to concentration upon fixing a scriptural canon and producing commentaries upon approved texts rather than to the sudden epiphany of this apocryphon. *Laodiceans'* clear but simple Trinitarian theological outlook, with roles for each person thereof, intimate a date of c. 200–c. 250. The assumption of a Western origin would suggest a date rather early in this period, when Greek was in wide use in the West.[389] That assumption cannot be supported by reference to the Muratorian List, for that document is not certainly Western or second century, and evidence for associating the letter in question with the *Laodiceans* mentioned there is, as will be shown, wanting.

Western origin is not improbable, but the question cannot be resolved on the basis of extant data. What is certain is that *Laodiceans* met strong and continuing disapproval in the East, resulting in its formal condemnation at Nicea II (787).[390] A different story emerged in the West, where the letter held a place in many bibles for a millennium, including translations into a number of European languages,[391] until it succumbed to the pressure of humanist criticism, which brought knowledge of Greek and use of critical method.[392] By the year 1600, *Laodiceans* had generally been ejected from Christian scripture.[393]

One could nonetheless make a case supporting the "authenticity" of *Laodiceans*, for most of it derives from Paul. Few apocrypha, however, have received proportionally more disdain than this short epistle. The most authoritative collection of Christian Apocrypha calls it "a worthless patching together of Pauline passages and phrases, mainly from the Epistle to the Philippians."[394] The view of *Laodiceans* as a pastiche, cento, or catena is general,[395] but it is inaccurate. The work has the formal features of a letter and is not a hodge-podge or a patchwork. *Laodiceans* closely follows Philippians, not only in phrases, but also in order. If this letter is worthless patchwork, the same judgment cannot easily be withheld from that canonical letter—indeed it is more applicable to it.

One apparent motive for the composition of *Laodiceans* was to fill in a gap caused by the reference to a letter associated with Laodicea in Col. 4:16. Verse 20, which evokes that passage, is decisive. Since Colossians is Deutero-Pauline, it is likely that Col. 4:16 promoted the sharing of Pauline correspondence among various communities in general. Colossians 4:16 speaks of a letter "from (*ek*) Laodicea," allowing the possibility that it referred to a letter written *to* Paul.[396] Lightfoot's arguments that a Pauline letter is in view are decisive.

Tradition—especially legendary tradition—hates vacuums with a passion that puts nature to shame, but the task of filling in gaps is not inherently shameful, for historians also practice it. Two examples from the Pauline tradition are the letter mentioned in 1 Cor. 5:9 and the "tearful letter" (2 Cor. 2:4). For more than a century, some scholars have located the former in the fragment 2 Cor. 6:14—7:1, while the latter is quite frequently identified with the fragment 2 Corinthians 10–13.[397] The author of *Laodiceans* filled the perceived gap by composition rather than by speculation, but the greatest crime, if one is to believe the critics, was not forgery but lack of imagination. Rather than represent the apostle as engaged in an anachronistic attack upon the evils of procreation[398] or the fantasies of the Valentinians, he reproduced, in a modest and conservative fashion, Paul's own words.

The more important question is why the author decided to produce a shortened edition of Philippians. As Philip Sellew has argued, *Laodiceans* looks like it has been based upon one of the documents used in the hypothetical composite that constitutes canonical Philippians: letter B (1:1—3:1[a] with elements of ch. 4).[399] This would require access to unedited correspondence, and would be compatible with a relatively early date. If, however, the source is the canonical letter found within a collection of epistles, as the apparent allusions suggest, it reveals an intelligent abbreviator, one who selected those portions of Philippians suitable for a friendly, parenetic letter. The indisputable merit of Sellew's hypothesis is his demonstration that an ancient editor with no interest in developing a partition hypothesis was able, through literary means, to isolate what historical critics regard as the core of Philippians. Moreover, that same editor wished to portray Paul primarily as a proponent of the gospel of joy and love. For this he has been portrayed at worst as worthless, better as "harmless,"[400] at best as a proponent of Marcion.[401]

The text has a clear structure:

I.	vv. 1-2	Epistolary greeting.
II.	vv. 3-5	Thanksgiving, closing with a prayer.
III.	vv. 6-8	Paul's situation. He is an example of joy in apparent misfortune.
IV.	vv. 9-16	Exhortations for the recipients, closing with an *inclusio* ("peace," v. 2).
V.	vv. (17) 18-20	Epistolary conclusion.

The cohesiveness of this structure is apparent in sections III–IV, the body. These are parallel, composed of similar subjects: salvation, good works, joy, prayer. Section III relates these to Paul, IV to the believers. Paul is an example of the Christian life, the object of which is salvation.

As in many of the pseudo-Pauline letters (Colossians, Ephesians, 2 Timothy, the Pastoral Epistles, *3 Corinthians*), the focus is upon the absent, imprisoned, suffering apostle. Although absent in person, he remains present through his words. Other Deutero-Pauline features include a brief, vague denunciation of rival teachers without any refutation of their views (v. 4), support for leaders who will succeed him (cf. the Pastorals), strong emphasis upon eschatology, with a tendency toward individualized eschatology and the final judgment (vv. 3, 5, 7, 10),[402] concern about greed (v. 13), exhortation to be faithful to tradition (v. 16), as well as strong moralism focused upon the doing of good works (vv. 3, 5, 10).

Despite the substantial amount of typical post-Pauline sentiment in this short letter, the author was a vigorous Paulinist whose thought was anchored in the "core" of the undisputed letters. This is most apparent in the opening, which is the most significant deviation from Philippians. Galatians 1:1, its model, sounds the purest note of the undiluted Pauline trumpet, a firm declaration of Paul's independent, heavenly message. Its thesis was often set aside in emerging orthodoxy, which either preferred to identify Paul's message with that of other apostles, as in Acts, or to claim that he was instructed by the followers of Jesus, as in *3 Corinthians* (IV.4). *Laodiceans* nonetheless immediately fends off (v. 3) two ideas associated with the radical Paul: that he was an antinomian, and that he taught a fully present eschatology (which was often associated with the concept of a present, "spiritual" resurrection). Verse 4 sounds a sharply Pauline note by referring to his own message, rather than to the apostolic teaching in general.

These virile Pauline assertions, as well as the propensity to change "God" to "Christ" (e.g., vv. 3, 13) led Adolph von Harnack,[403] followed by Gilles Quispel,[404] to view *Laodiceans* as a Marcionite product. A benefit of this hypothesis is that it takes note of the text's unabashed Paulinism. This proposal has received limited support. The evidence is thin and ambiguous, the hints of heresy are Deutero-Pauline in quality and lack Marcionite particulars.[405] Preference for "Christ" may be attributed to the influence of developing Trinitarian theology.

The Muratorian List (lines 63-68) speaks of "a letter to the Laodiceans and another to the Alexandrians that were forged in the name of Paul in support of Marcion's heresy, and many others that the catholic church cannot accept."[406] No evidence exists that Marcion's collection of Pauline letters contained a letter to the Alexandrians, and the initial title creates difficulties, for that collection already included a "Laodiceans," canonical Ephesians.[407] Tertullian does not accuse Marcion of introducing a pseudepigraphical epistle, a charge that he would have been most willing to deliver, but, instead, with altering the name of Ephesians.[408] Subsequent patristic writers (e.g. Epiphanius, *Panarion* 42.9) were unable to shed additional light on the matter.[409] In the West, which long exhibited reservations about Hebrews, *Laodiceans* could serve to provide the Pauline corpus with the mystically desirable fourteen (2 × 7) letters.[410] Ancient and modern attempts to drive *Laodiceans* into the Marcionite fold have been unsuccessful.

In sum, *Laodiceans* is neither jejune nor disorganized. The author selected elements of what is arguably Paul's most beautiful epistle to present a brief guide to the apostle's message. This letter could readily be memorized to serve as a companion in the Christian life. Probably issued in the first half of the third century, *Laodiceans* testifies to the existence of a mildly sanitized Paul, who remained nonetheless a living and vigorous herald of the gospel. It is an example of pseudepigraphical restraint. Had the author written not only from love of Paul but also with a particular and readily dateable agenda, his work would receive more scholarly attention. Its importance lies in the lack of such an agenda, for this is a portrait of Paul that wishes to be ordinary and is therefore evidence of normal—as opposed to elite—Christian activity.

Alexandrians

In addition to an allegedly Marcionite letter to the Laodiceans, the Muratorian List (lines 63-65) mentions a letter to the Alexandrians.[411] Theodor Zahn proposed that a fragment of this text survived in the eighth-century

Sacramentary and Lectionary of Bobbio.[412] The heading reads: "The Epistle of the apostle Paul to the Colossians."[413] What follows is not Colossians, nor does it bear any Pauline marks. The content is an exhortation to keep the commandments and to practice daily repentance.[414] The most likely explanation of the origin of this piece is that it is a fragment of a homily, portions of which were read in the Daily Office of the Benedictine Order.[415] Its firm reliance upon the commandments of the Hebrew Bible place it at a great remove from Marcion. *Alexandrians*, if it ever existed, has been lost.

The Correspondence between Paul and Seneca

This collection of fourteen letters (hereafter identified by Arabic numerals) is an interesting relic of the Christian mission to educated Romans in the fourth century.[416] Unlike the letters considered previously, *Paul and Seneca* never appeared within a biblical manuscript or as part of a discussion about canonicity.[417] The implication is that Western Christians acknowledged for a good millennium letters composed by Paul that did not merit biblical status and were presumably not inspired. Few would wish to claim inspiration of any sort for *Paul and Seneca*. A modern editor of some worthy's correspondence would pass over items of this sort, for they are brief paragraphs of generally bland material.[418]

The atmosphere of *Paul and Seneca* is that of the final chapter (the Martyrdom) of the *Acts of Paul*. The apostle is, to all intents, a free person. His movements appear to be unrestricted. Letters 1, 3, 5, 7, 9, 11–13 are attributed to Seneca, while Paul is assigned responsibility for 2, 4, 6, 8, 10, and 14. They are friendly letters, with expressions of gratitude (2), praise (1, 2, 7, 12, 14), advice (6, 14), and, as they develop, mild criticism (8, 13). Praise and blame lubricated the Greco-Roman social network. The author shows that Paul was accepted into the friendly circle of those who stood at the very apex of Roman imperial society.[419] Intimations of a nascent network appear in 6, where Paul greets Lucilius (the dedicatee of Seneca's letters), and 7, in which Seneca includes Theophilus (the dedicatee of Luke and Acts), in his salutation. Theophilus could also be viewed as a person of high standing.[420] One point that can be made in favor of the person(s) responsible for this corpus is, like *Laodiceans*, the exercise of restraint. Few would be surprised if this apocryphon had narrated Seneca's fervid embrace of the faith. *Paul and Seneca* is quite modest about such claims. This is an important clue to its function.

Restraint also characterized the earliest testimony to *Paul and Seneca*. Its date can be established by reference to Lactantius (*Div. Instit.* 6.24.13-14), who did not know of this work in 325, and Jerome (*Vir. ill.* 12), who discussed it c. 392.[421] Jerome was less than unequivocal in endorsing its authenticity, and scholars[422] have sometimes suspected that he had a different dossier. This hypothesis is a tribute to Jerome's intelligence, but they are very probably wrong.[423] Stylistic analysis places *Paul and Seneca* in the fourth century.[424] In truth, both Jerome and Augustine (Letter 153.14, whose remarks may be dependent upon Jerome—that is, he may not have known the letters directly) very much wanted them to be authentic. *Paul and Seneca* enjoyed considerable popularity during the Middle Ages, resulting in dozens of manuscripts, most of poor quality. Renaissance erudition extinguished respectable claims to their authenticity.[425]

Known Christian admiration for Seneca began with the claim of the uncompromising Tertullian that the Stoic philosopher was "frequently ours," that is, often Christian in sentiment.[426] His moral exhortations were viewed as highly congruent with those of writers like Paul. This was not coincidental, for Paul's letters show the influence of popular moral philosophy.[427] *Paul and Seneca* does not need to demonstrate that the apostle might have admired the philosopher; its ostensible purpose is to demonstrate admiration of Paul by Seneca. That the means for doing so was a batch of utterly trite little missives characterized as "pluperfect platitude"[428] may seem astonishing, but it was in fact quite astute. Cliché is a vital form of communication, for it establishes what speakers or writers and their audiences have in common. Cliché builds and nourishes relationships. It may also be a medium and mirror of intimacy.

Suppose that someone found in a family attic a series of postcards from T. S. Eliot to her grandparents, including a card from the Louvre with the words: "Having a fine time; wish you were here," and another from Rome remarking that the weather was hot but the food splendid, etc. These bits of pasteboard would not embellish the reputation of the author of the "Four Quartets." Their diction and sentiments would cause admirers to cringe. What they would show is that Eliot enjoyed a relationship with one's grandparents, wished to communicate with them, and that the relationship was sufficiently close that the famous author could communicate without care. "Having a fine time; wish you were here" expresses affection. Letters (including postcards) reflect bonds.

By producing this series of notes between Paul and Seneca the author has, *mutatis mutandis*, produced something like those hypothetical postcards from T. S. Eliot. The writer was a bit cleverer than is normally allowed. Abraham Malherbe has shown that s/he was thoroughly conversant with both literary clichés—not, after all, a great accomplishment—but also familiar with epistolary theory, and, evidently, with published correspondence.[429] *Paul and Seneca* possesses some of the features of a school exercise,[430] possibly suggesting that the author had not attained the highest level of education, but that writer did know how to exploit what s/he had learned.[431] The brevity and mediocrity of *Paul and Seneca* represents a strategic choice that was much more effective than an exchange of treatises. The problem for more recent critics has not been that *Paul and Seneca* is shallow, but that it was rather too subtle.

The question of integrity must be engaged before any discussion of structure. Letters 10-14 are dated. The dates are, in modern equivalents: (10) 27 June 58, (11) 28 March 64, (12) 23 March 59, (13) 6 July 58, (14) 1 August 58. Chronological order would yield this sequence: 10, 13, 14, 12, and 11. Letter 12 answers the issue raised in 10. Letter 11 is clearly out of place. Furthermore, it differs in style and content, offering historical examples in erroneous order,[432] a tag from Virgil,[433] the datum that both Christians and Jews were executed as arsonists under Nero, and (questionable) statistics about the fire at Rome.[434] Whereas the Nero of 7 could listen to Paul's letters with interest, the emperor of 11 has taken his traditional place in the tyrants' hall of fame.[435] Letter 11 therefore stems from a different hand. This person, who was probably also responsible for adding the dates,[436] wished to supply an intimation of the proper finale to Paul's life. Letter 11 is not a part of the "original" *Paul and Seneca*.[437] The enigma is how this item did not find a place at the close of the correspondence.[438]

The order of the closing letters is also uncertain. The sequence implied by the appended dates is clearly a secondary arrangement, related to the interpolated letter 11. In the present arrangement, 13 and 14 interrupt the back and forth sequence. It is arguable that an earlier edition concluded in this order: 10, 12, 14, and 13. Letter 13 was relocated before 14 when 11 was appended as a close to the collection. When that interpolated letter was inserted between 10 and 12, 13 and 14 remained in their order because a subsequent editor did not wish the collection to close with criticism of Paul. In the order 14-13 the collection closes with an *inclusio* of sorts with the first two letters: Paul expresses his admiration of Seneca's great learning while Seneca speaks of the power of the apostle's ideas. Letters 10, 12, 14, and 13 is thus the preferred order.

Thirteen/fourteen letters is scarcely the result of accident. Since much of the Latin-speaking west long expressed reluctance about Hebrews,[439] the number thirteen represented the total of Pauline letters received in at least some circles at Rome in the middle of the fourth century. The eventual addition of a fourteenth thus served, *inter alia*, to bring the total into conformity with what had eventually become the norm. The author evidently intended that the quantity of letters in this collection mirror that of Paul, another apt and possibly subtle touch.[440]

Paul and Seneca contains a discernible plot formed around the growing attraction of the characters to one another, enhanced by an abandoned sub-plot. Letter 1 plunges readers *medias in res*. Seneca writes about a discussion held the previous day in the gardens of Sallust about "secrets and other matters" (*de apocryphis et aliis rebus*).[441] Gardens were suitable locations for philosophical reflection among peers.[442] Readers will wish to know just what these "secrets" were. Paul, as Seneca states, was familiar with the conversation. In the initial sentence, the narrator both arouses interest and makes it clear to readers that this is mail addressed to someone else. One topic is not left to conjecture: the group read some of Paul's letters and admired his moral sentiments. That judgment forms the basis for subsequent developments.

Paul replies (2), apologizing for a delay due to the unavailability of a suitable messenger. He is pleased to receive the compliments of a great man, but makes it clear that he writes as a friend rather than as a mere flatterer.[443] In 3 the plot thickens. Seneca has produced some scrolls with the contents in proper rhetorical order.[444] These he will read to the Emperor (presumably in his capacity as tutor). He hopes that Paul will be present on that occasion. For readers these "scrolls" present more mystery. Is Seneca speaking of his own writings? Has he produced an intellectually suitable edition of Pauline thought? His closing is more intimate (*carissime*, "dearly beloved"). Paul's reply (4) expresses a desire for a personal meeting. In 5, Seneca laments Paul's absence. One may gather that personal meetings have occurred.

The philosopher wonders if Paul's absence is not due to Poppaea.[445] In conjunction with 6 and 8, the narrator is intimating a triangle: Nero/Poppaea/Seneca, the last two of whom have opposing views about Paul. Readers are not discouraged from suspecting that Poppaea's machinations will bring down both Paul and Seneca, but, once more, this is no more than an inference.[446] Letter 6, addressed also to Lucilius, is enigmatic, implying that Paul will not write openly about the empress. He nonetheless urges charity toward all. Only those who receive respect will consider personal moral reformation. In a few phrases the narrator reveals both Paul's generosity of spirit and his pastoral sagacity.

Letter 7 (in which Theophilus is a co-addressee) reports that Seneca has read Galatians and 1 and 2 Corinthians to the emperor.[447] Nero was moved, but wondered how someone of such limited education could emit such views. Seneca replied that God speaks out of the mouths of babes and added an historical example to prove his point.[448] At this, the middle point of the correspondence, the crucial issue emerges: how can educated people admire such poorly written letters? Seneca's answer conforms to patristic apologetics: power comes from weakness. God does not require fancy language; moreover, the message was initially addressed to those of lower status.[449]

The apostle ignores this issue in 8, underlining his fear that Seneca may attract the enmity of Poppaea.[450] Moreover, Nero is not an apt target for moral improvement. Paul is waving Seneca away from any attempts to bring the royal couple around—not for his own sake, of course, but for Seneca's. In 9 Seneca proposes a new beginning. The subject of M. and Mme. Nero has come to an end. Their differing views on this matter will not end the friendship. The narrator knows when to quit, a point not taken by the author of the evidently interpolated 11, who comes down hard on the emperor. The subject of imperial favor or disapproval will linger in the reader's mind for the residue of *Paul and Seneca*, but those who want to know how the story ended will have to read the final chapter of the *Acts of Paul*, a story with which all Roman Christians (and doubtless many non-Christians) were familiar.[451] Seneca's new start includes the kind provision of a book on excessive wordiness (*De copia verborum*).[452] The principal subject has come to the fore.

Without expressing thanks for the book (although he closes by calling Seneca his "most reverend teacher," *devotissime magister*), Paul devotes 10 to his practice of placing Seneca's name first.[453] This does nothing to abate the readers' anxiety. The two seem to be fiddling while Rome is in danger of conflagration. For his part, Seneca reassures Paul in 12 that he need not worry about the order of names, implying that they are equals, fellow Roman citizens. At this point, the letter-for-letter exchange is ruptured. This is probably intentional. The author is too intelligent to add a Pauline reply on the subject of whose name should enjoy precedence.

In letter 14, Paul continues to ignore Seneca's advice. The author might have allowed Paul to promise to attend to his Latin and let readers conclude that his execution brought the project to a premature close. Instead of this simple solution, Paul urges the more or less persuaded Seneca to use his eloquence in the service of the Church. The philosopher will be able to persuade temporal kings toward the path of righteousness. No answer to this appeal is offered. The narrator is speaking to a contemporary audience in an era when kings were Christian and presumably amenable to instruction. Hints of philosophical language reveal some familiarity with the Neo-Platonic tradition.[454] In his final words, Paul has become a (fourth-century) philosopher exhorting Seneca to teach Christian morality.[455] Seneca has become *noster* ("ours") and "we" have become philosophical theologians. The apostle and the philosopher *did* correspond, although the process took more than three centuries.

Letter 13 makes Seneca's theme, introduced in 7, explicit: Paul's letters lack clarity[456] and style. The philosopher entreats Paul to improve his Latinity. For the narrator, this question of style was not an issue of the long ago, nor was it limited to Paul. In the course of the fourth century, many members of the local Roman élite were attracted, for various reasons, to the church, but resistance was strong. One of the ostensible grounds for reluctance to accept the faith was the crudeness of Christian scripture, in particular the New Testament, which was read in the often barbarous Old Latin version. The Seneca of this correspondence recognized this issue, but it did not prevent him from admiring Paul and his writings. That, *enfin*, is the message of *Paul and Seneca*: do not despise Christianity because its primary texts lacked literary elegance.[457] If it was good enough for Seneca... Although the theoretical audience was the "cultured despisers of Christianity," its actual readership, as with most apologetic literature, consisted mainly of believers, whose sense of inferiority it addressed.

Paul and Seneca does exhibit a logical structure and plot development. It is appropriately compared with ancient epistolary novels, the majority of which dealt with the philosophical tradition.[458] "Epistolary novella" might be more appropriate, given the size of the work, but this series of short letters tells a coherent story, introduces a dramatic sub-plot to engage the reader, sprinkles the narrative with novelistic details, and carefully attends to epistolary conventions. As previously observed, the use of two correspondents permitted the author to introduce two voices, allowing for two direct points of view, as well as those of others (Nero, Poppea) communicated second hand.[459] As might be expected, much remains unsaid and readers sense that they are reading correspondence between two persons who knew more than they wrote and who did not need to explain details familiar to them. The author effectively depicts the development of a relationship initiated before the first letter. Paul and Seneca are *friends* who can speak candidly to one another. Convention and cliché are important elements of this portrayal and should not be attributed to a lack of intelligence or imagination. They effectively reinforce the theme of friendship. *Paul and Seneca* also allows the inference that both Paul and Seneca were victims of Jewish machinations supported by the empress. Under a tyrant like Nero and with fellow victims like Seneca, the execution of Paul was no embarrassment.

The image of Paul promoted in *Paul and Seneca* is, on the one hand, that of a thinker powerful enough to gain the friendship of a great philosopher, stylistic infelicities notwithstanding, and, on the other, that of a very modest, non-authoritarian apostle more concerned with the fate of others than of himself and rather shrewd in his judgments about character. This Paul speaks quite softly and has no need of the stick. He understood how to address people like Seneca and how to approach the most unlikely cases (Poppaea)—in short, this Paul is "all things to all people."[460]

For the author, Paul's letters were essentially a book[461] containing letters directed "to a city or provincial capital" (1.8). *Paul and Seneca* 7.2 speaks of those to "the Galatians, the Corinthians, and the Achaeans." Only one of these (Corinthians) could involve a "city or provincial capital." "Achaeans" evidently refers to 2 Corinthians (cf. 2 Cor. 1:1). One wonders if this was a designation in use at that time or an invention of the author. Since "letters to the Galatians and Corinthians" would have been acceptable, the term may refer to a title that sought to enhance the universality of Paul's correspondence.[462] It is certainly intelligent, given not only the address but also chs. 8 and 9 of canonical 2 Corinthians.[463] For the putative Seneca, Paul's correspondence represented a collection, like those of other writers (including Seneca), the central content of which was admirable exhortation to the moral life (Letter 1.9). The text of the corpus is the *Vetus Latina*, presumed to be the original.[464]

Conclusion

The Deutero-Pauline letters express a wide range of views, but some general trends are apparent. Only *Paul and Seneca* seeks to defend Paul, and that essentially because of his style. Otherwise the authority of Paul is presumed. Without that authority grounds for a pseudonymous writing would be absent. Nonetheless, the general trend is to make Paul more conservative in matters of ethics. Over the course of time one can detect a shift from Paul as essentially the only apostle to Paul as one of the apostles, all of whom stick to the same story, so to speak.[465] These letters testify (with blanks to be filled in by texts discussed in the following chapters) to the continuing interest in and value of Paul during the period from c. 60 to the close of the second century (and beyond). Another general tendency is toward a more complex style. Paul utilized elements of early Christian worship (e.g., Phil. 2:6-11). His followers practically wrote in liturgical language (e.g., Ephesians; cf. the Pastoral Epistles).

Intertextuality varies. Colossians uses two letters (Philippians and Philemon) as its major source. Ephesians follows Colossians closely enough to be labeled a new edition, but also exploits Romans and other letters. Second Thessalonians has a single model: 1 Thessalonians, while *Laodiceans* uses Philippians primarily. All the Deutero-Paulines look back upon the authentic letters, and all make use of one or more of them. These later epistles testify both to the success of Paul's chosen form and to the requirements to keep him up to date.[466]

Like some of the amalgamated letters, the Deutero-Paulines use various techniques to make their application general. Despite particular addressees, these texts are intended for all believers of every era. Specificity and particularity have given way to generality. False teachings may be addressed, but their individual character is difficult to isolate. In the case of the Pastoral Epistles and *3 Corinthians,* it appears that the authors have attempted to cover a range of deviant views rather than a particular "heresy."[467] The dominant principle is that false teachers are to be avoided rather than refuted. Conversation is not recommended. This is indirect testimony to either the acumen of the opponents or to the inability of these Paulinists, or to both. After Colossians and Ephesians, there is a decided decline in theological originality and emphasis. The pool of traditions drawn from expands, with limited use of traditions taken directly from Paul, although developments from Pauline roots are generally apparent. Each letter or group reveals different ideas about how best to preserve the Pauline legacy and thus conflicts over that legacy.

In general, links to the parent religion attenuate. Ephesians retains a strong interest in salvation history, but even there the focus is upon gentile believers. In this environment Paul tends to become a gentile, both through neglect of his Jewish background and emphasis upon his preconversion status as a wicked, essentially "pagan" sinner. The picture of

Paul's "conversion" is a Deutero-Pauline effort to transform him into a model gentile convert.

Various techniques establish plausibility. In addition to the conventional letter form and the presence of some Pauline phrases, the practice of using letters as substitutes or preparations for a visit is modified: Paul is normally in prison. Effectively, permanent absence has replaced future presence. This coincides with the theme of coming martyrdom. Pathos is always available, most explicitly in 2 Timothy. With this goes a tendency to view each letter as a testament of the (now martyred) Paul. Novelistic devices are most prominent in the Pastoral Epistles and *Paul and Seneca*, but each establishes some kind of fictional epistolary setting. This is worked out most thoroughly in *3 Corinthians*, probably because of its incorporation into the *Acts of Paul*.

A full and valid appreciation of these compositions would require a full description of the evolution of Christian history in various localities, for none of these epistles emerged within a vacuum. They are paragraphs within a lengthy history of conflict and development. Any appreciation of the Deutero-Paulines requires attention to both their environments and to the similarities and differences between and among them. Environmental factors are often difficult to identify beyond inferences from the texts themselves. This survey has attempted to emphasize positive features for each item and refrain from continual denunciations of the various authors as Judases betraying Paul for their own, probably shallow, objectives. All of these authors viewed themselves as faithful followers of the Apostle applying his thought and techniques to different situations.

3. Paul and the Epistolary Tradition in Early Christianity

This chapter explores a number of lines of inquiry. The most general is pursuit of the hypothesis that the success of Paul's practice is responsible for much of the epistolary tradition in early Christian literature. The thesis is perhaps too broad, but letters were not the only possible mode of communication. Outside of the Gospels, Acts, and Revelation, every book in the New Testament is classified as a letter, even where, as is partly applicable to Hebrews and fully applicable to 1 John, the documents are not letters. Also telling is the number of texts called letters, including *Barnabas*, *2 Clement*, and *Diognetus*, that are not such. Revelation, although not an epistle, begins with seven church letters (chs. 2–3) that exhibit awareness of the Pauline form.[1] The widespread use of letters as instruments of church policy in early Christianity took its impetus from the Pauline practice and is one indicator of knowledge about Paul during the period from c. 60–c. 100.[2]

Another category includes such writers as Ignatius and Polycarp, whose admiration for and imitation of Paul is explicit. Others use epistles to engage Paul critically or to modify his views. James, 2 Peter, and the so-called *Epistle of the Apostles* are examples of this technique, which is a negative testimony to the value of Paul's method: "If ya can't beat 'em, jine 'em."[3] The first item to be considered is Hebrews, a formally anonymous text that found a place in the Pauline corpus.

HEBREWS

Although Hebrews was not always accepted in the *Corpus Paulinum* in antiquity, it remained within the Pauline orbit, broadly construed.[4] The East in general supported its Pauline character.[5] Lingering doubts eventually vanished, so that for a millennium Hebrews had a secure place in the Pauline corpus, until its authorship was challenged in the period of the Renaissance and Reformation. Some continued to support the medieval tradition into the twentieth century, but critical scholarship has abandoned ascription of this letter to Paul.[6]

Although it does not include the Pastoral Epistles, the first extant edition of the Pauline corpus (P46, c. 200–225) places Hebrews second after Romans. P46 indicates that Hebrews was viewed as a letter written by Paul.[7] This ms. is of Egyptian provenance, and the first known discussion of authorship comes from the Egyptian authors Clement of Alexandria and Origen, for both of whom the tradition of Pauline authorship was a problem they dealt with by attributing the ideas to Paul and the style to another.[8]

Their comments have passed through the filter of Eusebius. In 6.14 of his *Ecclesiastical History*, the historian notes that Clement had commented upon "all of the canonical (ἐνδιάθηκος, lit. "covenanted") scripture."[9] Eusebius (6.14.2) cites Clement's view that Paul wrote the work in "Hebrew," while Luke rendered it into Greek.[10] Omission of the author's name (2-3) was due to the prejudice of the Hebrews against Paul. Eusebius adds another comment, evidently attributed to Clement's teacher Pantaenus,[11] that Paul omitted his name owing to modesty, since he was an apostle to the gentiles (4). These observations indicate that Clement knew Hebrews with its present opening—that is, without an epistolary prescript and with the title "To the Hebrews."[12]

Origen's views are reported in *H.E.* 6.25.11-14. After finding the style of Hebrews superior to that of Paul, Origen commends its ideas as "not inferior" to the apostle's. Subsequently, Eusebius cites Origen as suggesting that Hebrews was the work of someone who had taken notes of Paul's teaching. Any local community that accepts Hebrews as Pauline is commendable, according to Origen, since tradition supports Pauline authorship. To this he appends his famous observation that (only) God knows who wrote it. Thereafter he notes, without endorsement of either, the opinions that Clement of Rome or Luke were the authors. Origen thus thinks little of Clement of Alexandria's assertion that Luke wrote

Hebrews. These comments are summarized in detail to show that the claim that authorship has more to do with authority than with composition is not a modern dodge around the problem of pseudonymity.[13] Origen embraced it.[14]

Hebrews was known to *1 Clement*, which used it.[15] This helps to establish the date (before 100) and indicates that Hebrews was not generally attributed to Paul or to any other early Christian worthy, since *1 Clement* knows and cites 1 Corinthians as a letter of Paul.[16] In the course of the second century, Hebrews passed from unclear status among some at Rome to inclusion among Paul's letters in Alexandria. The course of this progress is not clear, but it is arguable that the "Pauline" Hebrews, which was used by "Gnostic" theologians at Rome,[17] was brought from there to Alexandria, where it was received in due course by Pantaenus and Clement, who made use of Valentinian and other works. The importance of Pauline attribution for these exegetes was that it bestowed apostolic authority upon the practice of learned, philosophical exegesis best known from the writings of Philo.[18] Paul is shown as a serious exegete of the LXX. Clement and Origen could claim that they were following a path that the apostle had laid out.

While Hebrews is formally a sermon,[19] it has a typical epistolary conclusion (13:20-25) that cannot be characterized as a later addition and is filled with Pauline reminiscences.[20] The extant text begins, however, in rhetorical fashion without any epistolary features.[21] The principal options are that the author closed his work in epistolary fashion to make personal contact with the audience or that an original epistolary beginning has not survived. The former possibility is anomalous. Although the hypothesis that the original epistolary prescript has been suppressed is not popular,[22] it is not without merit. With the crescent impetus to attribute Hebrews to Paul, an epistolary opening could not have survived. If the work ever had a prescript, it had been eliminated by the time Hebrews reached Alexandria, as Clement's authority Pantaenus could attribute it to the apostle. The epistolary format and the reference to Timothy as released from custody (13:23) suggest that the author was attempting to insinuate himself into the Pauline circle.[23] This hypothesis has been developed by Clare Rothschild to the point where it is now the strongest claim: Hebrews is a Deutero-Pauline letter that seeks, particularly through its epistolary closing, to gain a place among Pauline writings.

Hebrews has very little in common with Pauline theology, style, and exegesis of the LXX. The last is primary for Hebrews; its style approaches, and sometimes attains, the periodic,[24] and its theological orientation has quite different bases and interests from that of Paul. The same can be said, in differing degrees, for other disputed compositions. With Hebrews Paul had a foothold on the ladder leading to "philosophy," and theologians of the Greek East were quite happy to assist in his further ascent. The incorporation of Hebrews within the Pauline corpus aided the incorporation of Paul into the realm of higher education.[25]

JAMES

James complements Hebrews in that it has an epistolary prescript (not of the Pauline type) but no conclusion. Like Hebrews, James exhibits rather good Greek and is better understood as a sermon in the guise of a letter than as a true epistle.[26] This is another example of the value of an epistolary framework for sharing one's message with a (literally or figuratively) distant audience. By addressing the letter to "the twelve tribes in the Diaspora," the author is making a claim to universal authority, rather like that found in early editions of the Pauline corpus.[27] The authority in this case is Paul's rival, James. In eastern Syria James would become, with the support of Peter, the representative of anti-Pauline "Jewish Christianity."[28] This letter probably stems from western Syria, possibly Antioch.[29] Like Matthew, with which it has other common interests, James is harshly critical of the antinomian understanding of Paul's thought.[30] That circumstance arose when the original Pauline dialectic of faith rather than Torah as the basis for incorporation within the people of God had become a dead issue. This James, unlike the historical brother of Jesus, displays no interest in *kashrut* or other elements of observance. James' stress upon practical wisdom[31] implicitly opposes the wing of Paulinism (Colossians–Ephesians) that indulged in cosmic speculation related to the identification of Christ with heavenly Wisdom.[32] If this opposition is intended, James may have emerged after publication of the Pauline corpus, thus c. 100 or slightly later.[33]

James had some difficulties obtaining canonical status. It was not cited as an authoritative writing before the mid-third century, at the earliest. Jerome was still unenthusiastic at the end of the fourth century. James did not find a place in the Syriac Bible until the fifth century. Such sixteenth-century humanists as Cardinal Cajetan and Erasmus questioned attribution of the letter to the historical James, and Martin Luther's vigorous objections are well known.[34]

Luther was not without justification, as it were, for James took direct aim at Paul's doctrine of justification by faith.[35] An intertextual relationship is undisputable. Discussions of the contrast between "works" and "faith" were not common in early Judaism and early Christianity. Paul and "James" both engage in this rare debate; both use the same example (Abraham) and cite the same passage (Gen. 15:6) with the same deviation from the LXX; both use the verb "justify" in its theological sense of God's action toward humanity, rather than the common moral sense of acting properly.[36] Evidence for James' engagement with Pauline texts is clear from the following table:

▮ Table 6: Paul and James

Paul	James
Rom. 4:1-3: Τί οὖν ἐροῦμεν εὑρηκέναι Ἀβραὰμ τὸν προπάτορα ἡμῶν κατὰ σάρκα; 2 εἰ γὰρ Ἀβραὰμ ἐξ ἔργων ἐδικαιώθη, ἔχει καύχημα, ἀλλ οὐ πρὸς θεόν. τί γὰρ ἡ γραφὴ λέγει ἐπίστευσεν δὲ Ἀβραὰμ τῷ θεῷ καὶ ἐλογίσθη αὐτῷ εἰς δικαιοσύνην.	Jas 2:21-23: Ἀβραὰμ ὁ πατὴρ ἡμῶν οὐκ ἐξ ἔργων ἐδικαιώθη ἀνενέγκας Ἰσαὰκ τὸν υἱὸν αὐτοῦ ἐπὶ τὸ θυσιαστήριον; 22 βλέπεις ὅτι ἡ πίστις συνήργει τοῖς ἔργοις αὐτοῦ καὶ ἐκ τῶν ἔργων ἡ πίστις ἐτελειώθη, καὶ ἐπληρώθη ἡ γραφὴ ἡ λέγουσα· ἐπίστευσεν δὲ Ἀβραὰμ τῷ θεῷ, καὶ ἐλογίσθη αὐτῷ εἰς δικαιοσύνην. . .
(Gen 15:6, LXX: καὶ ἐπίστευσεν Ἀβραμ τῷ θεῷ, καὶ ἐλογίσθη αὐτῷ εἰς δικαιοσύνην)	
What then are we to say was gained by Abraham, our ancestor according to the flesh? 2 For if Abraham was justified by works, he has something to boast about, but not before God. 3 For what does the scripture say? "Abraham believed God, and it was reckoned to him as righteousness."	21 Was not our ancestor Abraham justified by works when he offered his son Isaac on the altar? 22 You see that faith was active along with his works, and faith was brought to completion by the works. 23 Thus the scripture was fulfilled that says, "Abraham believed God, and it was reckoned to him as righteousness." . . .

Paul	James
Gal. 2:16: εἰδότες δὲ ὅτι <u>οὐ</u> <u>δικαιοῦται ἄνθρωπος ἐξ ἔργων</u> <u>νόμου ἐὰν μὴ διὰ πίστεως</u> Ἰησοῦ Χριστοῦ, καὶ ἡμεῖς εἰς Χριστὸν Ἰησοῦν ἐπιστεύσαμεν, ἵνα δικαιωθῶμεν ἐκ πίστεως Χριστοῦ καὶ οὐκ ἐξ ἔργων νόμου, ὅτι ἐξ ἔργων νόμου οὐ δικαιωθήσεται πᾶσα σάρξ.	Jas 2:24: ὁρᾶτε ὅτι <u>ἐξ ἔργων</u> <u>δικαιοῦται ἄνθρωπος</u> καὶ οὐκ ἐκ πίστεως μόνον.
Yet we know that <u>a person is justi-</u> <u>fied not by the works of the law but</u> <u>through faith in Jesus Christ.</u> And we have come to believe in Christ Jesus, so that we might be justified by faith in Christ, and not by doing the works of the law, because no one will be justified by the works of the law.	You see that <u>a person is justified by</u> <u>works</u> and not by faith alone.

James may have been attacking a radical, antinomian form of Paulinism, but that cannot be demonstrated from the text, which does not reveal a caricature or other "misunderstanding" of Pauline theology, but opposes what Paul actually wrote. This does not exclude interpretations that Paul would have disowned; it does exclude suggestions that James did not disagree with Paul. James does not mention Paul's name. Two explanations for this omission are possible. One is the standard practice of leaving one's opponents anonymous.[38] Another is that the authority of Paul was too widely accepted for direct confrontation. The tradition of later "Jewish-Christianity," in which Paul is not directly named, supports the former understanding. For emerging anti-Paulinism, Paul was "that man."[39]

James' own view of the Torah is not unlike the perspective of Luke and Acts, *1 Clement*, some other apostolic fathers, and the subsequent apologists. The Torah is a useful source for moral guidance. James' anthropology is rather optimistic, like that of Matthew and unlike that of Paul. Trials and tests are opportunities to demonstrate righteousness (1:2-27). This epistle leaves no room for claims that "the Devil made me do it." People are responsible for their actions. The presumed ecclesiology, "synagogues" managed by presbyters, is decidedly non-Pauline. James 5:13-20 is a nascent church order, with emphasis upon pastoral care and mutual help. The letter of James promotes an urban, Greek-speaking Christianity that is decidedly non-Pauline in theology, structure, and ethical outlook. All in all, it is preferably viewed as criticism of the developments found in the current Deutero-Pauline tradition (specifically Ephesians and Colossians), a criticism that would apply even more vigorously to the (presumably later) Pastoral Epistles. Whether intended, as proposed by Margaret Mitchell, or otherwise, James serves to move Paul toward the center.[40]

1 PETER

The diversity of views about 1 Peter's relation to Paulinism can be illustrated by two authoritative introductions. Raymond Brown says, "We can think of 1 Peter as a largely independent work..."[41] Helmut Koester, for his part, asserts: "Everything is either Pauline or attributable to general Christian tradition."[42] One need not be an attorney to discover that these statements contain loopholes.[43] Different agenda are in view. Those who incline to agree with Brown wish to establish the right of 1 Peter to serious consideration as an important contribution to nascent Christianity.[44] Koester's view that this letter belongs to the realm of Deutero-Paulinism appears somewhat old-fashioned. First Peter *is* indebted to a broad range of tradition, some of which is shared with the genuine and pseudonymous Pauline texts.[45] Both views are overstated and both have merit.

What would have happened had this text been transmitted under the name of Paul?[46] The early church would have raised no particular objections (presuming that this letter had found its way into relatively early collections of the corpus), and it would have escaped the incipient critical eye of Renaissance and Reformation scholars. Not until the nineteenth century would challenges have been issued, and the question would not have been settled before the middle of the twentieth, with some continuing to support authenticity to this day. The question is not fair, since tradition carries considerable weight in these matters, but, had 1 John or Jude been attributed to Paul, objections would have arisen much earlier.

First Peter's relation to the Pauline tradition is important precisely because of, rather than in spite of, its relative independence. If later tradition sought to equalize Peter and Paul, sometimes to Paul's benefit,[47] this letter borrows from Paul to pay Peter. First Peter imitates specific Pauline and Deutero-Pauline formulae, links itself to the Pauline circle, and may well display specific knowledge of particular letters, as well as Pauline tradition received indirectly. The first two items seem beyond dispute, lending support to the third.[48]

The greeting opens with "Peter, an apostle of Jesus Christ," a formula found in 1 and 2 Corinthians, Ephesians, Colossians, and the Pastoral Epistles,[49] and concludes with the standard "grace to you and peace."[50] In place of a Thanksgiving period, 1 Peter, like Ephesians and canonical 2 Corinthians, has a *eulogia*/blessing. This formal choice is evocative of the Deutero-Pauline environment.[51] The final greeting, an exhortation to offer one another a kiss (5:14), is also a Pauline trait.[52] First Peter has the framework of a Pauline letter. These verbal features suggest a direct acquaintance with Romans at least, and possibly Ephesians.[53] First Peter 2:18—3:7 contains an example of the Household Code rather like that found in Colossians and Ephesians. Much of the evidence for Pauline influence suggests indirect contact.[54] Coupled with the direct influence of the epistolary structure, the data suggest that the author was familiar with a collection of Pauline epistles from which he drew concepts without resorting to direct quotation. This intimates a date of c. 100 or later.

The two proper names, Sylvanus and Mark, also have Pauline and, in the case of Mark, Deutero-Pauline, associations. In 5:12, Sylvanus may have the apparent function of participation in authorship that could be inferred from 1 Thess. 5:1, although the view that Sylvanus delivered the letter is equally possible.[55] Mark is evidently with Peter in Rome (5:12), as could be construed from Philemon 24 (cf. Col. 4:10).[56] The author utilized these links to Paul to enhance the authority of his letter and, in all probability, its Roman provenance.[57] The circumstances are quite different from those in the region of Antioch, where Peter was the primary authority. Luke also sought to enhance the status of Paul by associating him with Peter. Lindemann proposes that the mission in northern Asia Minor (the region addressed by 1 Peter) stemmed from Syria.[58] This is an intelligent hypothesis for which little concrete evidence exists. In various intended and unintended ways, 1 Peter takes a step toward the linkage of Peter and Paul as pillars of the early Roman community. *First Clement* vigorously asserts this point of view.

1 Clement

This review now takes up texts with undisputed links to Paul, since they explicitly invoke Paul's name as an authority. The earliest of these is *1 Clement*, which was written in the last decade of the first century.[59] The traditional title is a misnomer, for *1 Clement* is a letter written by one Christian community (Rome) to another (Corinth).[60] That the document had a single major author is likely, and that person may have been named Clement, but the title obscures what is a new departure in extant early Christian literature. In effect, *1 Clement* fulfills a Pauline dream: a community has become able to act on its own and to do so in relation to another group of believers. In the Pauline tradition, although not necessarily exclusively so, the text assumes that Christians at both Rome and Corinth constitute a single organization. This is debatable for Rome and may not have been the case at Corinth, but the assumption represents the importance of the concept of unity. Like Paul, *1 Clement* does not wish house-based communities to consider themselves independent, but as part of the same local community. This is the root of the conception that each city (and its environs) constituted a "diocese" that would eventually include parishes in addition to its cathedral.

The object of *1 Clement* is to persuade its Corinthian coreligionists to restore duly selected leaders (presbyters) who have been deposed for reason or reasons not clearly stated. Although this piece may strike many modern readers as unduly verbose (it is about 1.5 times the size of Romans), often turgid, and sometimes monotonous, it enjoyed both popularity and authority in the early church, as indicated by references to its use in worship, translation into several languages, and inclusion within biblical manuscripts and canon lists.[61] During the first half of the twentieth century, *1 Clement* was a touchstone of the controversy swirling around the concept of "Early Catholicism." In the eyes of some, not least the eyes of many German Protestants of that era, *1 Clement* represented a betrayal of the original Christian gospel, for it was held to present the church as an institution, set law over Spirit, and—worst of all—seemed to be an impertinent assertion of Roman authority. These qualities were all the more intolerable because the document was not composed in hapless ignorance of Paul's thought but gave the appearance of appealing to him for support.

Matters have changed. *First Clement* is now viewed as a less than full-blown instrument of proto-orthodoxy/Early Catholicism.[62] Its perspective is similar to that of Luke and Acts, which collaborate with, but do not fully endorse, the early catholic viewpoint.[63] *First Clement* does not, for example, advocate government by a single bishop, accompanied or assisted by presbyters and deacons. The Spirit has not been quenched.[64] The most striking feature of *1 Clement* is its substantial dependence upon the piety and thought of Diaspora Judaism.[65] Paul was indubitably Jewish, but his letters brim with a sense of apocalyptic newness that is absent from *1 Clement*. Scholars nurtured in Pauline thought have difficulty discovering the central Christian core of this letter. James raises similar questions. Both texts are, however, Christian, even if they do not always enunciate a vigorous and consistent soteriology.[66]

Paul had often cited Jewish scripture and made use of popular philosophical morality.[67] These items are the pillars upon which *1 Clement* erects its platform. The philosophical basis of this platform is different from that of Paul, for *1 Clement* grounds its views upon God's revelation in nature. Luke followed a similar path.[68] Both probably saw themselves as continuing the thought propounded in Rom. 1:18-32.[69] This letter can be viewed as a development of Romans written by someone with different presuppositions from Paul who had absorbed the content of the apostle's communication to the Roman community.[70]

First Clement has a sense of the indicative/imperative relationship,[71] as in 30:1, which says, in effect, "Act holy because you have been made holy." *First Clement* 31:2 claims that Abraham was "blessed" because "he did righteousness and truth through faith." This awkwardly literal rendition indicates that "righteousness" is something done, rather than a state. It is, in effect, a virtue comparable with truthfulness.[72] Like James, *1 Clement* combines Genesis 22 with Gen. 15:6.[73] The same passage from Genesis is cited in 10:6, with the conclusion, in the next verse, that Abraham received a son "because of his faith and hospitality."[74] For *1 Clement* faith is, in Lutheran terms, a "work." The author reveres Paul as a missionary hero of the faith and esteems his letters, but the core of Paul's theology does not appeal to him. Paul's authority, which is certainly under no cloud, does appeal, not least because of its value in chastising those Corinthians to whom Paul had once threatened to take a figurative rod (1 Cor. 4:21).

Measured by some Deutero-Pauline, let alone Pauline, standards, *1 Clement*'s social thought is staunchly conservative. Like Paul, *1 Clement* likens the "body politic" to the human body, but understands it in the traditional sense as an argument for subordination rather than equality in diversity.[75] *First Clement's* use of the Household Codes (1:3 and 21:6-8) address, unlike the examples in Colossians, Ephesians, and 1 Peter,[76] the male head of the household (*paterfamilias*) only. Women have duties rather than privileges and responsibilities. This orientation is comparable to the Pastoral Epistles. The letter's vigorous assertion of community harmony (*homonoia*)[77] does not refer to consensus reached through discussion but of obedience to properly authorized leaders. The essence of harmony is subordination to hierarchy. Greek and Roman authorities would have applauded.

This is the first known interpretation of Pauline theology, outside of the pseudonymous epistles, developed in any detail on the basis of (some of) Paul's letters. The apostle in view here stresses a rational and practical morality that emphasizes modesty, humility, and various other virtues, with particular emphasis upon unity in pursuit of the common good. All of these elements can be called legitimate expositions of elements present in Paul,[78] and they are typical of the subsequent generations of Christian missions.[79] The clearest shift is from focus upon redemption to the centrality of creation. This is quite apparent in *1 Clement's* argument for resurrection as a logical, natural phenomenon (chs. 24–26),[80] rather than an eschatological miracle of new creation.[81]

Others—Marcion and various "Gnostics"—would concentrate upon redemption, together with explicit denigration of creation. Both those who turned toward the "first article"[82] and those whose point of departure was the second could appeal to Paul for authorization. Colossians, followed by Ephesians, reflects fascination with the created order and relations between the heavenly and the earthly, but in ways quite different from *1 Clement*, for whom nature provides a model of order. The emphases upon the goodness of creation, accompanied by veneration for the Israelite tradition with its view of God as maker of all, and proper order, constituted the pillars upon which emergent orthodox Christianity would build its church. Irenaeus' praise for *1 Clement* and Luke/Acts is no surprise.

At the opening of ch. 47, the text makes the earliest extant explicit reference to a Pauline letter: "Take up the epistle of blessed Paul the apostle." For the first known time Paul's words are being applied to a fresh situation. Qualifications are in order, for Paul was the ideal person to cite in seeking to reprove Corinth, not least in a communication to them. *First Clement* can assume that 1 Corinthians had been preserved at Corinth and could be readily consulted. This is important, for it expects that, however occasional Paul's letters had been, they were not simply discarded after the passage of some time. Secondly, *1 Clement* 47 shows that a copy of this letter had also been shared with believers at Rome, probably carried there by one of his admirers. Thirdly, this shows that *1 Clement* was not aware of 2 Corinthians, as this, too, would have been of great value in the current situation.[83] *First Clement* therefore antedates the circulation of the published corpus.[84] First Corinthians would nevertheless do quite well for the present necessity. By 47:3, *1 Clement* notes that, even in that ideal age, the Corinthians were engaged in factionalism. This was not a peripheral issue, for unity and concord are central themes of 1 Corinthians.[85] This theme the author of *1 Clement* took from 1 Corinthians, with limited appropriation of its theological underpinnings, but a firm grasp of its purpose. The pastoral value of 1 Corinthians explains its considerable popularity in early Christianity.

The authority is a hero, already "blessed Paul," who is an apostle.[86] The ground for this veneration received early and ample preparation. After a brief description of the "golden age" at Corinth, the text identifies "jealousy and envy" as the cause of their decline (3:1-2).[87] Chapter 4 presents seven artistically arranged biblical examples of the effects of these two vices. The author then moves, in accordance with rhetorical practice, to more recent examples—Peter, Paul, and a "great multitude" of subsequent martyrs—closing with the general effects of jealousy upon family and civic life. The middle chapter of this unit (ch. 5) is a relatively elegant and stylistically complex treatment of Peter and Paul, who appear together for the first time as dual heroes.[88] The narrator does not claim that both died at Rome, or at the same time. Perhaps these data can be assumed, but their absence deserves attention.

1 Clement 5

This is an encomiastic comparison of the labours of Peter and Paul.

> (*Transition*) 5:1 But to stop giving ancient examples, let us come to those who became athletic contenders ($\dot{\alpha}\theta\lambda\eta\tau\dot{\alpha}\varsigma$) in quite recent times. We should consider the noble examples of our own generation.[89]
> (*Theme*) 5:2-3 Because of *jealousy and envy* the greatest and most upright pillars[90] were persecuted, and they struggled in the contest ($\ddot{\eta}\theta\lambda\eta\sigma\alpha\nu$[91]) even to death. We should set[92] before our eyes the good[93] apostles.

Table 7: Peter and Paul in 1 Clement

Peter

4 Πέτρον, ὃς <u>διὰ ζῆλον</u> ἄδικον
οὐχ ἕνα οὐδὲ δύο, ἀλλὰ
πλείονας ὑπήνεγκεν πόνους
There is Peter, who <u>because of</u>
unjust <u>jealousy</u> bore up under
hardships not just once or twice,
but many times;

Paul

5 <u>Διὰ ζῆλον</u> καὶ ἔριν Παῦλος
ὑπομονῆς βραβεῖον ὑπέδειξεν·

<u>Because of jealousy</u> and strife Paul
pointed the way to the prize for
endurance.

6 <u>ἑπτάκις δεσμὰ φορέσας,</u>
Seven times he bore chains;
φυγαδευθείς,
he was sent into exile
λιθασθείς,
and stoned;
κήρυξ γενόμενος ἔν τε τῇ ἀνατολῇ
καὶ ἐν τῇ δύσει,
he served as a herald in both the East and
the West;
τὸ γενναῖον τῆς πίστεως αὐτοῦ
κλέος ἔλαβεν,
and he received the noble reputation for
his faith.

7 δικαιοσύνην διδάξας ὅλον τὸν
κόσμον,
He taught righteousness to the whole
world,
καὶ ἐπὶ τὸ τέρμα τῆς δύσεως ἐλθὼν
and came to the limits of the West,

καὶ οὕτω μαρτυρήσας·[90]
and having thus borne his witness

καὶ μαρτυρήσας ἐπὶ τῶν ἡγουμένων,
bearing his witness before the rulers.

ἐπορεύθη εἰς τὸν ὀφειλόμενον
τόπον[91] τῆς δόξης.
<u>he went to the place</u> of glory that he
deserved.

οὕτως ἀπηλλάγη τοῦ κόσμου καὶ εἰς
τὸν ἅγιον τόπον ἐπορεύθη,
And so he was set free from this world
and transported up to the holy place,
ὑπομονῆς γενόμενος μέγιστος
ὑπογραμμός.
Having become the greatest example of
endurance.

This passage is an example of *syncrisis*, rhetorical comparison. Many of Plutarch's biographies ("Parallel Lives") are implicit or explicit comparisons.[96] If pressed to make a choice, one would conclude that, although they both number among the "greatest" apostles, Paul is more important than Peter, as he is "the greatest example of endurance." One cannot doubt that Paul receives more attention. The two sections utilize a parallel outline, with a number of identical words (underlined in the above table). Obvious rhetorical devices, such as anaphora (διά, "because of"), alliteration and rhyme (φορέσας, φυγαδευθείς, λιθασθείς, "wearing," "exiled," "stoned") enliven the composition. Rhetorical vigor derives from the series of succinct participial phrases, eight in the description of Paul. The chapter is framed with an inclusion: "example" and, for the Pauline section (vv. 5-7), "endurance."

In the background is the type of popular teaching called the "diatribe." Popular philosophers adopted the use of sports metaphors to portray life as a "struggle" and those who engaged it seriously as "athletes."[97] They also allegorized the labors of Heracles (Hercules in Latin) as deeds of virtue and his career as a mission of enlightenment.[98] In the course of time, such varied figures as Dionysus, Heracles, and Alexander the Great came to be viewed as the subjects of worldwide missions.[99] Just as Jews had claimed Moses as a hero of this sort, Christians now follow with similar comparisons and claims for their founders, the "pillars" of the structure of faith.

The martyrdoms of the apostles are attributed to "jealousy and envy" (v. 2), the sources of which are not specified. Perhaps the idea that machinations of some Jews led to their deaths was already current.[100] In any case the claim is typical: "Our opponents are not motivated by our ideas; they are jealous of our success."[101] Although Peter had to suffer "many hardships," not a single instance is mentioned. This may have been due to a lack of information;[102] another possibility is that he provides a foil for Paul, about whom information is relatively abundant. These few sentences show that, prior to the publication of the corpus, before Acts was written, before the Pastoral Epistles, more than a half century before the *Acts of Paul*, there was already the outline of a fully developed Paul legend, the focus of which was his universal mission, the importance of which is underlined by repetition. Universality was a vital component of the Deutero-Pauline program, emphasized already in the earliest extant pseudo-Pauline letter, Colossians, and a key feature in the formation of the corpus.[103] The number "seven," a symbol of universality,[104] plays a role here. Chapter 4 has seven references to "jealousy," followed by another seven in chs. 5–6. The claim that Paul had to undergo chains seven times (v. 6) probably has symbolic value. In effect, Paul went everywhere and wherever he went he was arrested.[105]

The expression "limits of the West," which, from the viewpoint of Rome, probably refers to the Atlantic,[106] raises the question of whether legend had already granted Paul a mission to Spain. Unless there had been a thorough disruption in Roman Christianity, this seems unlikely. Roman believers knew that Paul had not been released. The notion that Paul had been released after one trial in Rome and later re-arrested and executed is a relatively late attempt to account for the Pastoral Epistles.[107] A more likely sequence is that *1 Clement* helped to inspire the legend of a Pauline mission to Spain.[108] Another possibility is that this letter is utilizing a tradition developed in the East, where Rome could be viewed as the far West.[109] One item may have been added to the catalogue to conform to tradition: exile (v. 6). This is the primary meaning of φυγαδευθείς ("exiled"). Although Acts reports a number of occasions when Paul left or had to leave a city,[110] none of these is technically an exile, in which one is forced to leave a native city or to reside in a certain place. Exile was, however, a more or less required entry in the résumé of the qualified philosopher.[111] This participle has also motivated speculation that Paul was exiled to Spain.[112]

"Herald" is another term applied to philosophical missionaries[113] that is obviously suitable for Christians as well.[114] Heralds are messengers. The title underlines the evidently unique role of Paul as an itinerant missionary for whom geography alone set limits. Exaggerated as 5:6-7 are, they witness to the impact and reputation of "St. Paul the Traveler." The content of this herald's message can be summed up in two words: "teaching righteousness." The apostle is primarily a teacher, a role that became more important in the post-Pauline era.[115] What he taught was "righteousness"—not "justification by faith," but proper behavior.[116] Implicit and explicit (ch. 47) examples of that teaching permeate *1 Clement*. Paul was, first and foremost, a teacher of social ethics.

This epistle from one community not founded by Paul to a Pauline foundation represents both direct and evidently indirect applications of Pauline theology with a heroic portrait of the apostle that serves to underscore appeal to his message. In this first Roman evocation of his name, Paul is in no way subordinate to Peter. This was convenient for the argument advanced in ch. 47, but Peter also figured, in some capacity, as an authority at Corinth (1 Cor. 1:12; 3:22).[117] The view that Paul taught the entire world, a concept that is in conflict with, for example, the legend that the twelve apostles at Jerusalem divided the world into separate territories, each receiving one of these spheres by lot, would be a part of the program for the general relevance of Paul's letters. He went everywhere; therefore his writings are of use to all.

Ignatius of Antioch

Ignatius irrupts into church history through letters written over a brief period to six churches (Ephesus, Magnesia, Tralles, Rome, Philadelphia, and Smyrna) and one leader (Polycarp, Bishop of Smyrna), as Ignatius was being taken to Rome for execution.[118] Why he was condemned is not entirely clear. Ignatius was the leader, bishop, of the (or a) Christian community at Antioch.[119] He is the first real individual to emerge in early Christian literature since Paul. The bishop's vivid personality makes a striking—if not always completely positive—impression upon every reader. Although his letters now reside in temperate pages within enduring books, they were not composed, like Paul's, in varied degrees of harried leisure over some years, but in unsavory circumstances while traveling under guard.[120] From the historical perspective, Ignatius' letters are a lightning bolt momentarily silhouetting some surprising features of church history. In general, "psychologizing" interpretation of ancient texts, which often amounts to the attribution of a feeling to, for example, Paul and then explaining his words by reference to anger, anxiety, and so on, is not advisable, as such emotions can rarely be tested. In the case of Ignatius, a dead man walking, the procedure is less objectionable, for his emotions are often patent.[121]

Ignatius is the first Christian writer from Syrian Antioch to mention, let alone revere, Paul.[122] The conventional date for his journey to Rome is c. 105–115, but this is questionable.[123] The 1985 commentaries of Schoedel and Bauer/Paulsen do not discuss the date.[124] The traditional Trajanic date is based upon Eusebius, whose data are both vague and dubious.[125] His *Chronicle* indicates 107–108, but without evidence. The subsequent *Ecclesiastical History* was more general: under Trajan (98–117).[126] The chronicle of John Malalas, which also dates the event c. 108, is too unreliable to provide firm support.[127]

Two of Eusebius' major interests were locating early Christian leaders as early as possible (sometimes earlier than possible) and in demonstrating the succession of bishops in various sees from the time of the apostles. Eusebius (*H.E.* 3.22) states that the famous Ignatius was the second bishop at Antioch, succeeding Evodius, c. 100. Fourteen chapters later (3.36), Eusebius says that Ignatius was the second bishop "after Peter." Few today would credit the claim that Peter had been Bishop of Antioch.

Trajan's reign provides the framework for Eusebius' discussion of Ignatius. In chs. 34 and 35 of *H.E.* 3, he speaks of the death of Clement, Bishop of Rome, c. 100–101, and the accession of Justus to the episcopal throne at Jerusalem. Polycarp emerges in ch. 36 as the appointee (by "eye-witnesses and ministers of the Lord" [cf. Luke 1:2]) to the bishopric of Smyrna. Notable contemporaries included Papias and Ignatius. A firmer datum appeared in 3.33.3, where the historian cited the correspondence of Pliny with Trajan discussing the treatment of Christians (Pliny, *Epistles* 10.96-97, c. 110). Eusebius evidently viewed Trajan as an emperor under whom persecutions occurred and thus placed Ignatius' death within his reign.[128] This hypothesis does not constitute chronological evidence.[129] One of the contemporaries identified by Eusebius, Papias, is plausibly dated c. 130.[130] That date also fits Polycarp's *Philippians*.[131] Those who date Acts c. 115 and the Pastoral Epistles c. 120 will find 115 too early for Ignatius, and there is no weighty evidence for that traditional date. Schoedel allows a wide range of between 105 and 135.[132] The latter part of this is much more suitable for Ignatius' view of church organization, even if some of those he identifies as bishops were not in full possession of all the authority that he grants them. Ignatius may have been arguing for government by bishops, presbyters, and deacons more than building upon an established constitution, but his letters indicate that this was not simply a fantasy.[133] Ignatius falls squarely into the era of community protection rather than on the boundary between stabilization and protection.[134] A date of c. 130–140 is the preferable date for Ignatius.[135]

A number of matters troubled the bishop in the course of his compulsory travels.[136] One was the fate of believers at Antioch, now bereft of their leader. In Asia Minor he saw indications of conflicts about the faith. Finally, he feared what might happen at Rome, fears based less upon his own courage than because of anxiety that Roman believers might seek to purchase a stay of execution or even his release (*Rom.* 4; 7). On his path to Rome, Ignatius made contact with churches or delegates who had come to be with him. These encounters illuminate the support of Christian communities for one another. His *via dolorosa* was the subject of a major campaign involving considerable planning and expense.[137] Such mutual concern is unprecedented among Greco-Roman religions, with the qualified exception of Judaism.[138]

The collection of Ignatius' epistles grew in late antiquity to include thirteen letters, as well as numerous interpolations in the original seven. Comparison with the history of the Pauline corpus is inevitable. In addition, an abbreviated collection, extant only in Syriac, appeared. Patient scholarly investigation has established a consensus—not unanimity—that the "Middle Recension" of seven letters (those printed in editions and translations) is original.[139] A major impetus for the collection is known. In *Phil.* 13:2, Polycarp states that he is sending to Philippi, per their request, copies of letters that Ignatius had sent to him, along with others in his possession.

The form of these letters blends Pauline influence with Greco-Roman (and Hellenistic Jewish) conventions.[140] They have some of the features of the testament: instructions, bequests, and requests delivered by a person on his way to death. A number of known writings and traditions influenced Ignatius. The pursuit of intertextuality must take into account that Ignatius was not sitting in his episcopal study, as it were, with copies of texts close to hand. His allusions derive from memory.[141] Prominent and explicit is the influence of Paul. Matthew is also detectable, as would be expected from Antioch. Other synoptic allusions remain possible.[142] Influence from Johannine tradition is also apparent, although it is not possible to identify the use of an edition of the Fourth Gospel.[143] Other traditions, including some "mystic" trends that would later be associated with Gnosis, have been posited and argued.[144] John P. Meier views Ignatius as the builder of a synthesis based upon the major—Pauline, Synoptic, and Johannine—traditions.[145] This synthetic approach, which can be argued, in various ways, for others, including Matthew and Luke, may not have been intentional. If Ignatius' theological tool chest contained more items than Matthew's had, this is also relevant to the argument about date.

Ignatius had almost certainly made use of a collection of Pauline letters.[146] He did not have direct access to these texts while a prisoner on the road. This is the best explanation for his thorough immersion in Pauline thought, on the one hand, and the relative lack of direct quotations on the other. First Corinthians alone is certain (*Eph.* 16:1; 18:1; *Rom.* 5:1; 9:2; *Phld.* 3:3). Ignatius may have got that letter practically by heart. He knew that Paul wrote a number of letters.[147] The other most likely possibilities are Romans and Ephesians. These three were the most popular Pauline epistles in the first half of the second century. Peter is the only other apostle mentioned by name.[148]

Ignatius is famous for his support of the desire that the Christian community in each city be led by one bishop (monepiscopacy), assisted by a group of presbyters and some deacons. The house-church is no longer a primary unit. Ignatius' ideal is a single assembly meeting under the presidency of the bishop. This ideal could not always be met; the compromise is that no eucharistic assemblies be held without episcopal authorization (*Smyrn.* 8:1). The bishop–deacon model probably emerged in Pauline circles, around 100, although the traces of this are limited.[149] Governance by presbyters evidently derived from the synagogue. The latter is the structure preferred by Luke, for example, who, like *1 Clement* and the Pastoral Epistles, is willing to view the titles of bishop and presbyter as somewhat equivalent. Ignatius' imagery shows that his polity is a blend of these two systems.[150] Ignatius does not, unlike *1 Clement*, discuss succession (or the manner of episcopal election), and exhibits a number of charismatic qualities.[151]

For Ignatius, the office of the bishop was important as both the instrument and the symbol of community unity and as a means for combating rival teachings. In the language of today, he presents the bishop as the sacrament of unity of the local community. Through management of the various elements of the community—home-based groups, circles, conventicles—the bishop could seek to prevent the emergence of various trends, whether developed internally or through outside influence, that could produce distinctive doctrinal and social systems.

Ignatius' focus upon corporate unity derives from Paul. Unlike Paul, he reflects upon disunity as a cosmic phenomenon. Like Paul, he understands that (the restoration of) unity comes from above, not as the result of human effort. Unity is a gift. He has imbibed the legend that unity prevailed in apostolic times (*Eph.* 11:2—12:2), and his thought reflects the widely attested view that concord[152] requires subordination. For Ignatius, as for Paul, ethics involves the strengthening of community life rather than individual achievement.[153] The relation between indicative and imperative is alive in his thought: grace is power.[154] In the Deutero-Pauline tradition (cf. Luke/Acts, the Pastoral Epistles) Ignatius believes that the church must do business with the world and avoid offending unbelievers (*Trall.* 8:2).

Rudolph Bultmann, who had difficulty discovering "what it really is that makes I Clem. a Christian document," praises Ignatius as a theologian who "...confronted a genuine appropriation of the Christian kerygma, which had received its first theological explication at the hands of Paul."[155] An example of Ignatius' transformation of Pauline thought is the categories of "flesh" and "spirit."[156] For Paul, these are spheres of existence, fundamental orientations to life, rather than the opposition of material and immaterial. For Ignatius, they are still spheres, but each is a distinct substance, as it were. For the Bishop of Antioch, salvation involved overcoming the fundamental dualism of flesh and spirit. Through grace the "fleshly" is to be transformed. Ignatius' sacramental emphasis is wholly compatible with his understanding of these two entities. Despite his concern about flesh and spirit, Ignatius has almost nothing to say about creation. Redemption alone is significant. Contrast with *1 Clement* is noteworthy, as are affinities with the movements of Marcion and various "Gnostics." Ignatius shows that a Pauline theologian could essentially ignore Israelite scripture and be indifferent to the role of God as creator without joining the ranks of the "heretics." Matters had not yet crystallized. Opposition between flesh and spirit also illustrates Ignatius' love of polarity and antithesis, paradox and parallel. Opposition to Docetism—the view that Jesus was only apparently human[157]—was an important influence upon the development of Ignatius' ideas.[158] Like Paul, Ignatius sought to refute opposing doctrines rather than simply denounce them, although he followed the post-Pauline model that advised avoidance of rival teachers.[159] Also derived from Paul is his understanding of martyrdom as the imitation of Christ, unrestrained as his expressions may sometimes be. Paul's martyrdom was a source of encouragement to Ignatius. He was following the path of the great apostle.[160] Ignatius knew, identified with, and imitated Paul as an itinerant, a writer of letters, and a leader who suffered for his faith.

That path is depicted, in a manner familiar from *1 Clement*, canonical 2 Corinthians, and Acts, as a triumphal procession.[161] Like Heracles, Ignatius has traversed the world while fighting wild beasts (*Rom.* 5:1). He says in *Rom.* 2:2: "...God has deemed the bishop of Syria worthy to be found at the setting of the sun, after sending him from where it rises."[162] Passage from east to west is movement from life to death.[163] Despite the exuberant adaptation of his life to myth and his use of a regal style,[164] Ignatius retains Paul's paradoxical understanding of his place in the procession, as the victim to be offered (2 Cor. 2:14-17). The first part of *Rom.* 2:2 reads: "But grant me nothing more than to be poured out as a libation to God while there is still an altar at hand, that by becoming a chorus in love, you may sing forth to the Father in Jesus Christ,"[165] evoking Phil. 2:17 (cf. 2 Tim. 4:6).[166]

In the Greco-Roman world the arrival of a ruler or general was treated as an epiphany. The Roman triumph is the best-known type of these processions.[167] Ignatius utilizes the theme because his journey is a revelation of the power of Christ. Sacred processions were among the most important events on the religious calendars of Greco-Roman cities.[168] Ignatius' nickname (or baptismal name), "God-bearer," fits the picture of one who bears an image of the god in a procession. He exploits this theme in *Eph.* 9:2.[169] *Romans* 9:3 is redolent with the aroma of triumphal processions.[170] The world-conquering missions of gods and heroes have been accessorized with the features of a sacred parade. The impetus for this imagery was, as the texts cited above indicate, the mission of Paul.[171] Ignatius was an imitator of both the Paul of history and the Paul of legend.

Ignatius viewed himself as a bishop who imitated, rather than formally succeeded, the apostles, in particular Paul, whose practice of writing letters to various communities, in both their and his (cf. Romans) interests. Like *1 Clement*, he viewed Paul as both model and authority, but Ignatius developed a consistent theology with a christological center and basis, inspired by and rooted in Paul, although not exclusively so. He was the first creative Pauline theologian to find an eventual home in proto-orthodox circles. His only rival as an early original and creative Pauline theologian was Marcion of Sinope.

Polycarp of Smyrna

Polycarp (c. ?70–c. 155/6) has a small but comprehensive dossier.[172] He was the recipient of a letter from Ignatius, the author of correspondence to Philippi, and the subject of a narrative martyrdom. Polycarp's chief value for the ancient church was his value for stretching the length of the apostolic era into the final quarter of the second century. This enhanced his utility as an opponent of heretics. Irenaeus claims (*A.H.* 3.3.4, and in a letter to Florinus, cited by Eusebius, *H.E.* 5.20.5-6) that, while a boy, he saw Polycarp, who had been appointed by apostles to the bishopric of Smyrna[173] and that he spoke of his conversation with John and other companions of Jesus. This is very romantic, but it should be noted that, in Polycarp's correspondence, Paul appears as the only apostle worth naming (*Phil.* 9:1), and the letter makes no claims to have been an auditor of John or other eyewitnesses of the ministry of Jesus.[174] It is likely that Irenaeus has commingled traditions about John the traditional author of the Fourth Gospel and a figure known as "John the Elder." For Irenaeus, endorsed by Eusebius (who sought to stretch him even more thinly[175]), Polycarp was a link between apostolic and recent times. Stated otherwise, if historians of Christian origins could be granted one interview with a personage of the period 100–150, Polycarp would be the choice of many, for he could supply answers to numerous burning questions.[176]

The *Martyrdom of Polycarp* is an inspiring document that had a considerable influence upon the development of the genre of martyr acts, but it is literature from which facts must be extracted with caution.[177] Polycarp's *Philippians* has been less influential. A prime witness to this is the state of the text, which survives complete only in a not fully reliable Latin translation. The entire Greek ms. tradition derives from an archetype in which the last three words of *Phil.* 9:2 are omitted, followed by *Barnabas*, beginning at 5:7. At some point leaves must have been lost, and copyists were unable to recognize and, perhaps, to remedy the fault. All of ch. 9 and most of ch. 13 are available in Greek from Eusebius. Integrity issues also exist. The theory of P. N. Harrison[178] that chs. 13 and 14 derive from an earlier letter continues to have many adherents, although it has not gone unchallenged.[179] Compilation is intrinsically likely, but the argument has lost much of its cogency with the shift in the date of Ignatius. It is no longer necessary to date the final chapters c. 115, or earlier.[180] The more probable solution is to assign chs. 13 and 14 to the period of Ignatius' martyrdom and to date chs. 1–12 to c. 135. As Helmut Koester has demonstrated, the citations in chs. 1–12 reflect the existence of written gospels.[181]

Polycarp has no specific references to the LXX, although allusions are present. In *Phil.* 6:3, he refers to prophets who foretold the coming of Christ. This view is similar to those of Ignatius and of Luke.[182] In 12:2, he deprecates his knowledge of the scriptures, but does have a quote to offer. That appears to come from Eph. 4:26, but Ps. 4:5 may have been in mind. A *prima facie* argument could be advanced that Polycarp views Paul as "sacred scripture," but this passage is extant in Latin alone, limiting its force.[183] Ignatius and Polycarp moved in circles that were willing to assert that Jewish scripture supported the Christian position without engaging in detailed study of it.[184] The Pastoral Epistles are comparable in this regard.

Polycarp exhibits familiarity with a number of early Christian texts, including Matthew, Luke, Acts (probably), Romans, 1 and 2 Corinthians, Galatians, Ephesians, Philippians, 1 Thessalonians, the Pastoral Epistles (on which see also below), and *1 Clement*. Polycarp had access to a collection (perhaps collections, below) of the Pauline corpus.[185] In no case are these texts cited by name or as authoritative writings. The closest example of an exception appears in 11:2 (Latin), where, after stating, "the saints will judge the world" (1 Cor. 6:2), he says: "that is what Paul teaches."[186] Paul is the chief ecclesiastical authority for Polycarp. That authority seems unquestioned, either in Smyrna or in Philippi. Polycarp has no need to defend the apostle to the gentiles from criticism, nor is he engaged in an effort to revive interest in a vanished figure of the past.

The Bishop of Smyrna's Paul was not the red-hot author of Galatians, nor the missionary who sought to build a bridge between believers of Jewish and gentile backgrounds (cf. Romans, Ephesians). His Paul wears the garb of the Pastor. The congruence between Polycarp's *Philippians* and the Pastoral Epistles is strong enough to have prompted Hans von Campenhausen to argue that Polycarp was the author of the Pastoral Epistles.[187] A leading deficit of this argument is the absence of the "epiphany christology" of the Pastoral Epistles in Polycarp. The choices are that: (1) Polycarp utilized a different theology when composing the Pastoral Epistles; (2) both compositions derive from a kindred environment; (3) Polycarp employed an intertextual model (in effect, Polycarp dined richly from the morality of the Pastoral Epistles but left its theology languishing on the plate). The third option seems most likely. This does not conflict with the second, whereas the dissidence of the first option is difficult to explain. Polycarp may have known the Pastoral Epistles as an independent collection. At the very least, Polycarp and the Pastoral Epistles derive from a very similar world.

One reason for Polycarp's presentation of Paul may have been competing interpretations. Ignatius warned the Smyrneans about the dangers of Docetism (*Smyrn.* 2-3; cf. *Trall.* 10). In *Phil.* 7:1, Polycarp does the same, in words apparently drawn from 1 John (4:2-3 and 3:8).[188] Against denial of the incarnation he adduces "the witness of the cross,"[189] then goes on to speak of "distorting the words of the Lord" by denial of resurrection and judgment.[190] Chapters 8 and 9 develop this theme in regard to behavior. This indicates the coherence of the letter. It also indicates that the thrust is upon the positive features of Polycarp's exposition: the moral consequences of his view of saving events. These are far more important to him than the specifics of the views opposed. The essence of "heresy" is what corrodes community life and ethical standards. The views he opposes are too general to pin upon a known system, as the good bishop did not wish to describe a particular system and may not have been able to do so had he the mind.[191] This does not mean that Marcion, in some form or another, may not have been known to him.[192] Tradition associates

Polycarp with Marcion. According to Irenaeus (*A.H.* 3.3.4; Eusebius, *H.E.* 4.14.7), Polycarp identified the missionary from Sinope as "first-born of Satan," the epithet applied to false teachers in *Phil.* 7:1. The apophthegm is not historical in form; its function is to represent Polycarp as an opponent of Marcion, whom he may have encountered[193] and with whose teachings he probably had some familiarity.[194]

Polycarp preserves elements of Pauline theology, even if these are not fully integrated into a system.[195] While affirming (probably on the basis of Eph. 2:5, 8-9) that believers are saved by grace rather than works, and that salvation is the result of God's will (*Phil.* 1:3), and following this indicative with an imperative, he tends toward a moralism based upon the final judgment. This is quite apparent in 8:1-2, where Christ is the "down payment of our righteousness," a phrase that can be viewed positively as empowerment, followed by the imperative to imitate Christ, coupled with the view that Christ's passion was exemplary.[196] Neither the Holy Spirit nor the sacraments receive attention. The "weapons of righteousness" yield the fruit of well-managed households and communities (*Phil.* 4).[197] The contrast with Ignatius is acutely obvious. Realized eschatology, perhaps coupled with moral indifference, was a patent issue for Polycarp (*Phil.* 7), and this may well have been associated with enthusiastic emphasis upon spiritual gifts. The traditions behind the *Acts of Paul* (which arose in Asia Minor c. 175) exalt spiritual gifts and reject the model of the Household Codes.

The bishop doubtless viewed himself as a faithful follower of Paul. His theme, proposed by the Philippians according to 3:1, was righteousness in the sense of proper behavior. For Polycarp, righteousness involved the specifics of right behavior rather than the power of grace. Irenaeus, the Greek original of whose *magnum opus* was also lost, mentions (*A.H.* 3.3.4) a letter of Polycarp to the Philippians that he characterizes as "very powerful" or "exceptionally suitable" (ἱκανωτάτη). More recent reviews have tended to be less enthusiastic. Maxwell Staniforth calls him "the type of humble, pious pastor whom John Bunyan would have delighted to draw."[198] *Philippians* deserves a sympathetic reading.[199] It is a pastoral exercise in boundary maintenance.[200] Such exercises do not prize novelty.

For Polycarp, Paul was first and foremost a teacher of said righteousness. This view is consonant with that of *1 Clem.* 5:5 and is entirely characteristic of contemporary proto-orthodoxy. His correspondence exemplifies the nature of much Deutero-Pauline theology of his era, which is less "genuine Paul" seasoned with "disputed Paul" than the Paul of the Deutero-Pauline tradition to which the earlier letters are conformed. This

Paul is a true hero, the only apostle deserving mention—he is "glorious" and "blessed" (*Phil.* 2:2; 11:3[201])—whose presence guaranteed orthodoxy and orthopraxy. Polycarp deemed himself unworthy to untie the laces of Paul's sandals. He was no great thinker, but he was a leader and is probably representative of many lesser lights who did their part to preserve and build the early catholic church. To those facts the *Martyrdom* is an impressive witness.

2 Peter

Second Peter[202] is the latest writing admitted to the canon of the New Testament, into which it experienced considerable difficulty gaining admission.[203] On internal grounds, including the quality of its Greek and its sophisticated intellectual outlook, one could argue for a date of composition c. 150, but c. 130 seems more likely, since 2 Peter is evidently utilized in the *Apocalypse of Peter*, which is probably to be dated to c. 135.[204] Asia Minor is a likely place of composition. The author of 2 Peter produced a new edition of the Epistle of Jude, which is its major source.[205] Second Peter, with its competent Greek style and blatant pseudonymity, breathes the atmosphere of the Christian apocrypha.[206] Like 2 Timothy and other Deutero-Pauline compositions, 2 Peter has some of the features of a testament. Peter is fully confident of his authority and can adopt an imperial style.[207] This is a truly catholic epistle, addressed to all Christians (1:1-2).

To his side in a debate about the delay of the end, which is more a matter of dogma than of hope,[208] Peter summons his "beloved brother Paul" (3:15).[209] Second Peter contains a number of possible allusions to Paul's letters, which the author knows from a collection (3:16).[210] The key passage is 2 Pet. 3:15-16:

> *15* and regard the patience of our Lord as salvation. So also our beloved brother Paul wrote to you according to the wisdom given him, *16* speaking of this as he does in all his letters. There are some things in them hard to understand, which the ignorant and unstable twist to their own destruction, as they do the other scriptures.

For the author, Paul is a fellow apostle ("brother"), whose letters are known to the audience, that is, the corpus continues to be circulated. The claim that Paul wrote "to you" (v. 15) is another witness to the Deutero-Pauline program. Paul's words are directed to all believers.[211]

Accompanying this view is a sort of hermeneutical corollary: the apostle said the same thing in each and all of his letters. Romans 2:4 (cf. 9:22) is the closest specific allusion to "patience," but that is not essential, for all apostles taught the same, as, for that matter, do all the authoritative writings.[212]

It is nonetheless true that some of what his brother said is difficult to understand and subject to various misinterpretations. This observation is valid, for Paul has supplied exegetes with almost two millennia of employment, and his actual and putative comments have without doubt been twisted by many persons, not all of them to be numbered among the ignorant or unstable. One example of that vast company is, in the view of modern interpreters, the author of 2 Peter, since Paul does not share his view of the time of the end.[213]

Second Peter knows of some interpretations of Paul with which he does not agree, and extends this alleged misinterpretation to other authoritative early Christian texts. The extension is a partial answer to the question of why, given his controversial and problematic writings, 2 Peter mentions Paul at all. To patronize or denigrate Paul would damage his value as proof. For this reason, as Lindemann argues,[214] the difficulty of understanding is not, in the author's eyes, absolute, but the result of subjective exegesis. Paul is *not* difficult for the true believer. Invocation of Paul is the climactic argument of the letter, scarcely an afterthought. Heretics—Marcion and early "Gnostics" come to mind, but not exclusively—misuse authoritative texts. Proto-orthodoxy and incipient heresy divide over the methods of interpretation. For 2 Peter Paul remains a hero of the faith. These two apostles are pillars of orthodoxy. His opponents may use—abuse, by his lights— Paul, but there is no suggestion that they identify themselves as followers of Paul.[215] Today's scholars are more likely to say that the problem is that 2 Peter misinterprets Paul, but that is not how the author understood it. All apostles taught the true faith. With this view *1 Clement* agreed in principle and Acts in practice. In this letter, Paul is an apostle equal in rank to Peter, whose writings are viewed as an authoritative body applicable to all Christians in their various circumstances. The Pauline corpus is a good book, on a smooth path toward admission into the Good Book.

Second Peter is the first work to introduce inspiration as a category that bears upon interpretation. Valid interpretation requires possession of the Spirit, which is first and foremost a possession of the community, rather than of the individual. That community stands in succession to Jesus and the leaders he had chosen. Spirit is associated with both tradition and office.[216] This is an essential feature of the emerging catholic church, one that has been widely accepted—the concept of the *consensus fidelium*, a matter upon which all believers concur—and also the target of attack by various reformers in most eras of church history.

DIONYSIUS OF CORINTH

This chapter closes with a glance at another collection of letters that reveals the continued vitality of the Pauline model in an era of complex ecclesiastical politics, as well as information on the reception of Pauline and other letters. Bishop Dionysius of Corinth was active in the middle of the reign of Marcus (161–180), a period marked by a number of local persecutions.[217] Dionysius' known literary activity was in good part a response to these actions against Christians.[218]

All that is known of this correspondence derives from Eusebius (*H.E.* 2.25.8; 4.23, who doubtless summarized what he found most edifying. The historian preserves four quotes from Dionysius' letter to the Roman bishop Soter. As after the great persecutions of the mid-third and early fourth century, Christians had at that time to deal with numerous pastoral problems, in particular the issue of how to handle those who had fallen away but wished reinstatement. Dionysius took a moderate position on this question, as well as on the issue of moral rigor, particularly as it applied to sexual activity and marriage.

The dossier utilized by Eusebius included seven letters to churches,[219] one to an individual, and a copy of a letter sent Dionysius by Pinytos, Bishop of Knossos in Crete, who was himself an active writer. The numeration, seven to communities, followed by a letter to an individual, corresponds to one form of the Pauline corpus.[220] Dionysius may well have composed other letters. These eight he selected and sent to Soter in response to questions raised.[221] The letters of Dionysius are thus another example of a collection generated by its author. In this instance, the collection sought to address specific issues, but it survived because of its general value. Dionysius' goal was apologetic, that is, defense of his own views.

With one exception (Amastris, *H.E.* 4.23.6), Dionysius apparently wrote upon his own initiative.[222] His goal was pastoral, but he was also interested in promoting the power of Corinth. Although he can appeal to apostolic origins (see below), the key position of Corinth in communications between Rome (and the West) and Asia Minor (and the East) made the Roman church sensitive to circumstances in Corinth, as *1 Clement* also indicated earlier. Soter demonstrated his care for Corinth by sending money for the poor (*H.E.* 4.23.10). Dionysius promptly replied. A fragment cited provides interesting information about the use of letters. He states that Soter's letter had been read to the community that Sunday, adding that this practice would recur, and went on to observe that *1 Clement* was still read at worship (*H.E.* 4.23.12). The action required in 1 Thess. 5:27 remained in effect: the reception of a letter was a community event.[223] Dionysius' language indicates that the implied author of such letters was the church at Rome, among others, the actual author its agent.[224]

One may ask whether Dionysius read the entirety of Soter's letter to his community or whether he offered some comments upon it, for the Bishop of Rome had made some critical observations about Dionysius' theology.[225] Soter evidently bolstered his authority by appealing to Peter and Paul as founders of the Roman church, but Dionysius aptly parried this claim by noting that Peter and Paul were also the founders of the church at Corinth, activity that, he need not mention, predated their arrival in Rome (*H.E.* 4.25.8). Rather than subordinate Corinth to Rome, Soter had placed them on an equal level. The source of his claim is 1 Corinthians (1:12; 3:22; 9:5), which does not state that Peter came to Corinth, but could be so interpreted. Dionysius sought to uphold and promote the authority of his see against that of the imperial capitol.[226]

First Corinthians constituted a battleground in the controversies Dionyius addressed. His (and Corinth's) interaction with Soter (and Rome) evidently came about because of a complaint, probably lodged by Pinytos of Knossos, about Dionysius' pastoral laxity. Just before taking up the correspondence with Soter, Eusebius (*H.E.* 4.23.6-8) summarized correspondence with Amastris and other churches in Pontus as well as a letter exchange with Knossos and its bishop, Pinytos. The former was evidently in response to issues raised by Baccylides and Elpistus, persons of unknown status who had evidently visited Corinth and requested support. Dionysius' letter discussed marriage and demanded that genuine penitents who had erred in theology or behavior be restored to the communion of the church. An underlying issue is the question of celibacy, within or without marriage, as a requirement for full membership in the Christian church.[227] The debate shows the continuing vitality of Paul's preference for celibacy, vigorously maintained by Marcion, whose views enabled Dionysius to introduce the innuendo that staunch support for enforced celibacy was Marcionite.[228] The Amastris letter indicates that those who opposed marriage ("encratites") also opposed any softness toward sinners and apostates (presumably including both those who had succumbed to opposed teachings and those who had fallen away during local persecutions). In short, Dionysius attempted to classify encratism as a Marcionite deviation and linked opposition to marriage to rigorous refusal of readmission. Soter was not likely to have been an encratite, but he did favor strict discipline.[229]

Celibacy was the theme of the epistle to Pinytos, whom Dionysius exhorted toward pastoral sensitivity in this matter. In his reply, Pinytos flattered Dionysius—as the latter would Soter—but requested that he write again, including more hearty spiritual nurture. This is a clear allusion to 1 Cor. 3:1.[230] Both parties must have drawn from 1 Corinthians 7, Dionysius stressing "better to marry than to burn" (1 Cor. 7:9; cf. v. 7b), and the proponents of celibacy evoking 1 Cor. 7:1-7a.[231] Pinytos (and, possibly, others) evidently complained to Soter about Dionysius' theology or about his interference, probably both. For Pinytos, 1 Cor. 7:9 was a concession for spiritual neophytes that did not befit the mature.[232] Pinytos probably did not require celibacy, but viewed it as a higher vocation. In reply, Dionysius wrote to Soter in self-defense, including copies of his correspondence, which, he claimed had been falsified (4.23.12), and evidently throwing in for good measure a letter to one Chrysophora, filled with appropriate spiritual rations. The most likely explanation of this addition to the dossier was that Chrysophora was celibate. Dionysius was demonstrating that he was quite supportive of *voluntary* chastity.[233]

Dionysius' complaint that his letters had been corrupted by additions and deletions offers insight into the fate of letters: others could produce modified copies through interpolation of new material and removal of objectionable items. He may have had justice; the letters of Paul were likewise edited. The best-known radical revision was that of Marcion, and Dionysius does not hesitate to suggest that he has been the victim of similar sharp practice,[234] unworthy as he is of the comparison with Paul. Another implication of this approach is that anyone whose letters experience tampering must be on the right side.

In the history of the reception of Paul, Dionysius is not a major figure. He is included here because his writings show the continuation of Paul's practice in different circumstances. Letters continue to be a favored means for communicating church policy, but, rather than missives from an itinerant missionary who was (at least in theory) unable to visit, letters stem from communities in the person of their bishops, who are interested in increasing their power as well as in assisting other communities. The story of Dionysius shows that the practice of reading epistles aloud at the Sunday eucharist remained, and that at least one (*1 Clement*) continued to be so honored many decades after their composition.

The case of Dionysius illustrates one way by which an epistolary corpus could be formed: at the initiative of its author who (presumably) selected and (presumably) edited letters as a means of defending his own views. They further illuminate "the battle for Paul,"[235] in which different sides of an issue appeal to the Pauline corpus in support of their views. The apostle is an authority invoked to settle debates. Paul's preference for celibacy can be supported by proto-orthodox leaders, followers of Marcion, and some who did not ground their views in Pauline thought. Positions are becoming firmer.

This chapter has shown the continued vitality of Paul's techniques and views in the second century. For some, including *1 Clement*, Ignatius, Polycarp, and Dionysius of Corinth, the apostle is an important authority whose statements retain their value. Others, such as James and 2 Peter, engage in dialogue with Paul. The former criticizes him in the traditional manner,[236] without mentioning his name. Second Peter cannot praise Paul too much, but acknowledges that interpretation is not uniform. Heretics, alas, can utilize Paul. For the author of 1 Peter, evocations of Paul lend power to his message. Hebrews survived and gained power because it was incorporated into the collection of Paul's letters.

For *1 Clement*, Paul is first and foremost a proponent of good order. This is the line that will characterize the Pastoral Epistles and Polycarp, among others. Ignatius does not disagree, but he also reflects on theological constructs advanced by Paul, developing these in fresh directions. Theologians will award him the only "A" given to any of these authors. Dionysius opens the door to an intra-Pauline debate that will be characteristic of later periods, in which contending parties hurl Pauline quotes against one another as spears, weapons in a conflict. Both 2 Peter and Dionysius show that Paul was becoming an object of interpretation. Liked or not, Paul was always there, a basis of power, a target to attack, a literary model to imitate. The next chapter, the last of those oriented around generic categories, will investigate various narratives about Paul, stories dealing with his actions.

4. Paul in Narrative

This chapter will take up stories about Paul, in particular the various acts. Like most divisions, this is somewhat artificial, for, as has been shown,[1] letters also relate an implied story. The first area of investigation is the canonical Acts (hereafter Acts). The traditional title "Acts of the Apostles" is not original, for its principal character, Paul, is not an apostle.[2] That fact serves as an immediate introduction to controversy.

Since c. 1840, a struggle about the sources for a life of the "real Paul" has been active, sometimes simmering, sometimes at a boil.[3] The acute criticism of Ferdinand Christian Baur (1792–1860) and his followers in the "Tübingen School" posited Acts as a late—close to mid-second century —text dominated by unhistorical tendencies. Efforts to refute Baur propelled New Testament study into modern maturity. Leaders of those investigations included Theodor Zahn (1838–1933) in Germany and Joseph B. Lightfoot (1828–1889) in the United Kingdom.[4] When the great Berlin church historian Adolph von Harnack (1851–1930) shifted his position to embrace an early date for Acts, it seemed that Baur's views had been completely refuted. The twentieth century saw a gradual erosion of confidence in the historical value of Acts, a tendency strongly reinforced by the commentary of Ernst Haenchen (1896–1975), first published in 1956.[5]

A major impetus for Haenchen's literary analysis (focus upon what Luke wrote rather than his sources) was Martin Dibelius, who, in fact, occupied a middle position between the extremes.[6] Still, conservative exegetes in both the U.K. and Germany, among other countries, continue to defend the reliability of Acts. The dominant trend in the U.S. at present is to treat Acts as literature. This has a corrosive effect (often unacknowledged) upon arguments for its historical reliability. Most would agree that

Acts *contains* history, whatever the author's purpose. The extent of that history is a matter for debate. The present tendency is to view Acts not simply as material to be compared to the letters, but as one element in the reception of Paul.[7]

The major difficulties with accepting Acts as a historical record are, in fact, literary. These include a proclivity toward symmetry, most notably in the various "parallels" among characters. Similar deeds and experiences mark the lives of Moses, Elijah, Elisha, Jesus, Peter, and Paul.[8] No critical historian will believe that history repeats itself quite so frequently and conveniently. Repetition, such as three accounts of the conversions of Cornelius and Paul, is a means of emphasis. Another element is consistent reliance upon stereotyped scenes. Paul, for example, routinely begins his mission in a synagogue. This leads to opposition from Jews, sparking a persecution that propels the missionary onward to a new site. Finally, one may note the uses of some narrative techniques more suitable to fiction than to historiography.[9] Luke's portrait of Paul is best viewed as a response to contemporary issues[10] rather than as an attempt to extract historical data from various sources.[11] The object of this exploration is not to compare these "two Pauls" but to set forth the characterization and actions of Paul in Luke's sequel to his gospel.[12] Contrasts between the "Paul of the letters" and the "Paul of Acts" do exist. The following table identifies a number of them:

Table 8: Paul: Letters vs. Acts

Undisputed Letters	Acts
Paul imitates Christ by suffering.	Paul imitates Christ by working miracles
Paul is an apostle.	Saul/Paul is not an apostle.
Paul is a missionary to gentiles.	Paul is a missionary to Jews first.
Paul has conflicts with his communities.	Paul has no conflicts with his communiti
Paul's theological opponents are other believers.	Paul's opponents are primarily Jews.
Paul had difficult relations with other leaders; he was not subordinate to Jerusalem.	Paul and other leaders had no conflicts; he was subordinate to Jerusalem.
Paul engaged in conflict over Torah.	Conflict with Jews involves resurrection.
Paul's colleagues were important figures in his mission.	Paul's colleagues were very junior assistai
Natural theology shows that everyone is without excuse.	Natural theology levels playing field between Jews and gentiles.[13]
Paul does not claim benefits pertinent to his worldly status.	Paul is a Roman citizen of high status wh makes use of his privileges.
Paul is known as a letter-writer.	Paul does not write letters.

Other items of divergence could be identified. Some of these contrasts are strongly stated. Debate is possible. The major issue is not the extent to which each can be minimized or as indications of how Luke traduced Paul, but what they reveal about the agenda of Acts.

Luke possessed sources for his depiction of Paul, probably including a published collection of nine or ten letters.[14] In addition, based upon the hypothesis that Luke worked (or spent a good deal of time) in Ephesus,[15] is the possibility that he had access to administrative or other correspondence not deemed worthy of inclusion in the collected letters. A written source traditionally designated "the Antioch source," which I call "the gentile mission source," mentioned Paul (in connection with Barnabas). A written source dealing with "the pre-Christian Paul," as it were, can be detected in Acts 8:1-3; 9:1-19a. Finally, it is reasonable to suspect that Luke had access to some oral traditions about Paul. It is also apparent that Luke utilized other material, including stories derived from the LXX and the Jewish historian Josephus. With these final items the task has shifted from identification of possibly historical material to composition. Luke was the master of all his sources, selecting what he wished and molding the material into the shape desired.

Use of the letters—including pseudonymous pieces—and the introduction of post-Pauline narrative material establish Acts as a Deutero-Pauline text. A major contrast is that, whereas the Deutero-Pauline letters often present Paul as effectively the only apostle and universalize his message, Acts universalizes the church, a body that includes Paul and James, neither of whom is an apostle, as well as the Twelve (especially Peter) and representatives of the Seven (Stephen and Philip). Unity is Luke's object. His universal church of the apostolic age, so to speak, was headed by the Jerusalem community, itself under successive single leaders, first Peter then James.[16] Paul therefore had no independent mission, did not break with Peter and Antioch, and repeatedly returned to Jerusalem for consultation, as he had done shortly after he went over to the Jesus movement (9:26-30). All leaders share the same theology, a theology that shows at least as much influence from the historical Paul as from any conjectural reconstructions of the views of Peter and James.

Luke's task was to support the legitimacy of the gentile mission without cutting the links to the ancestral religion of Israel. His major challenge was not from those who wished to impose Torah observance upon all Christians. In the Aegean world, that was no longer a vital controversy—in so far as extant evidence indicates. A greater problem came from those who were willing to kiss that heritage goodbye. This is quite apparent in Luke's Gospel, which revises Mark along the lines of continuity with the Israelite heritage.[17] With this are associated several apologetic goals: Paul is no renegade Jew, but remained faithful and observant to the end. He was not the originator of the gentile mission. That honor belonged to Peter (10:1—11:18), followed by anonymous missionaries in Antioch, who were supported by the Jerusalem community, which sent Barnabas to their aid. Barnabas recruited Paul (11:19-25). Paul was not a rebel against duly constituted authority. All claims of this nature were the fraudulent concoctions of devious enemies. These controversies are already apparent in Paul's correspondence.

Paul (introduced in the narrative with the name Saul, used until 13:9 and never thereafter, except in retrospect) sets out to convince Jews that their hopes have been fulfilled by what God did through Jesus. Most Israelites disagreed, justifying his subsequent turns to gentiles.[18] Paul's Jewish credentials are superior to those of any other believer in Acts. He was reared and educated in Jerusalem, a Pharisee taught by the eminent Gamaliel, rising eventually to become a member of the Israelite high court (the Sanhedrin) and a prominent persecutor of the partisans of Jesus, authorized by the high priests to arrest and incarcerate the same, for whose executions he dutifully voted (Acts 22:3-5; 26:10). The historical Paul affirmed that he had been a Pharisee; in Acts Paul remains a Pharisee, still an adherent of that strictly observant sect (23:6).[19] Indeed, Paul is the only Christian in Acts depicted as participating in the temple cult (21:26). His Jewish résumé is therefore utterly unimpeachable.

This is not to suggest that he was a "barbarian," lacking Hellenic attributes. Paul was a citizen of no less prestigious a citadel of Greek culture than Tarsus (21:37). Showing is Luke's major means for establishing his hero's Hellenism. Paul is a gifted orator who can dissuade "barbarians" from sacrificing to him (14:8-18), quiet a riotous crowd with a gesture (21:40), engage the philosophers of Athens (17:22-33), and entertain Hellenistic monarchs and provincial officials with his erudition (24:24-26; 26:1-32). These worthies may not agree with Paul, but they respect his character and learning. The character of Paul manifests some development. The youthful Saul had many good qualities, but, like the typical tyrannical persecutor, his temper was out of control (8:3; 9:1-2). In the Greco-Roman world, uncontrolled rage was among the most deprecated of vices. After conversion Paul gave up his fanatical rage. Thereafter his anger found appropriate channels (e.g., 17:16). He became an example of the classical virtues of prudence, moderation, courage, and justice.[20] Virtuous people allowed reason to regulate their conduct, manifested a courageous temper, and never lost control of their emotions.

Those who were considered eligible to lead the virtuous life were wealthy and well educated. Paul enjoyed a high social status. He was wealthy (24:26), but willing to engage in a craft and live the rigorous life of an itinerant teacher of wisdom. This status is most apparent in the ease with which he can move in high society, although he has no difficulty in associating with those further down the social scale.[21] To his Jewish and Greek credentials Paul adds Roman citizenship, inherited, not acquired (e.g., 22:25-28), high, not low. Such is the force of his character and bearing that no one challenges his claim to be a citizen of Rome. Roman officials and military officers repeatedly declare that he is innocent.[22] One result of his fulsome *curriculum vitae* is that Paul exhibits in person the universality of the Christian faith and mission. Paul is a highly placed and learned Jew, embodying the Israelite heritage, a capable and cultured Hellene fully equipped to evangelize Greek-speaking gentiles, and a Roman of excellent standing, embodying the official virtues of the ruling political power.

Paul does not lack the charismatic qualities of speaking, healing, and leading. His hands bestow the Spirit, his voice curses the wayward, his cast-off clothing cures the afflicted (19:1-7; 13:6-12; 19:11-12).[23] The one-time Saul is also a hero of the traditional sort, manifest in courage before mobs (14:14-17; 21:39b-40) and judges (e.g., 23:1-10), his ability to act vigorously despite severe injuries (14:19-20; 21:25-40), and his resourceful courage aboard a storm-battered ship (27:21-43). Paul in Acts does not work with true colleagues. His historical associates, such as Timothy, are low-level assistants who perform errands. This is one means for demonstrating Paul's superiority and self-sufficiency.[24] One reason that Paul does not write letters in Acts is that he does not need to do so. His communities have no problems and evidently do not require friendly, pastoral support beyond what visits convey.

Because of the numerous parallels between and among Jesus, Peter, and Paul, the care taken by Luke to conform Paul's biography to that of Jesus is easily overlooked. Since the former began as a violent enemy of God's people while the latter was the Son of God by birth, the task was not easy.[25] Nonetheless, the story of Paul begins with a baptism and receipt of the Spirit (Acts 9:17-18; cf. Luke 3:20-21), accompanied by prophecies about his destiny (e.g., Acts 9:15-16; Luke 1:30-33). Both had forerunners.[26] Both preached an inaugural sermon in a synagogue that generated contention (Luke 4:16-30; Acts 13:14-50).[27] Each is a teacher engaged in an itinerant mission, that is, journeys. Both are "chosen vessels" (Luke 9:35; Acts 9:15). An important thematic similarity is that each pursues courses that lead to the center of his mission—Jerusalem and Rome, respectively—missions that conform to the will and plan of God.[28] Peter and others are appointed as witnesses, but they do not have a mission explicitly characterized as fulfillment of God's will. The final part of Paul's story (Acts 20:1—28:16) closely conforms to that of Jesus.

▨ Table 9: The "Passions" of Jesus in Luke and Paul in Acts[29]

Jesus (in Luke)	Paul (in Acts)
1. "Passion Predictions": 9:22, 34; 18:31	1. "Passion Predictions": 20:23-25; 21:4, 11-13
2. Final Address: 22:14-38	2. Final Address: 20:17-35
3. Argument with Sadducees over Resurrection: 20:27-39	3. Argument with Sadducees over Resurrection: 23:6-10
4. Agents of High Priest Slap: 22:63-64	4. Agents of High Priest Slap: 23:1-2
5. Four "Trials":	5. Four "Trials":
A. Sanhedrin: 22:66-71	A. Sanhedrin: 22:30—23:10
B. Roman Governor (Pilate): 23:1-5	B. Roman Governor (Felix): 24:1-22
C. Herodian King (Antipas): 23:6-12	C. Herodian King (Agrippa): 26
D. Roman Governor (Pilate): 23:13-25	D. Roman Governor (Festus): 25:6-12
6. Officials Declare Innocent: Pilate: 23:14 (cf. 23:4, 22); Herod: 23:14; centurion: 23:47	6. Officials Declare Innocent: Lysias (Tribune): 23:29; Festus: 25:25; Agrippa: 26:31
7. Mob Demands Death: 23:18	7. Mob Demands Death: Acts 22:22

This symmetry demanded substantial labor (and the sacrifice of much historical credibility). Luke indubitably wishes to make the legal experiences of Paul replicate those of his master. This compels raising the question of why Luke does not narrate the martyrdom of Paul, as the *Acts of Paul* would do. In the same structural place where Luke's Gospel records the conviction, crucifixion, and resurrection of Jesus (Luke 23:24—24:49), Acts describes Paul's journey to Rome (Acts 27:1—28:16). This narrative is a symbolic death and resurrection.[30] Acts presents the story of Paul as a kind of "gospel," a life pressed into the mold of myth, that is, the creed. In Acts Paul is not just a bearer of the saving message; he is also a savior figure. This is clearly depicted on the voyage to Rome, where all are saved because of Paul, who promises deliverance, echoing the words of Jesus (Acts 27:34; cf. Luke 21:18). Cast, like Jonah, alive onto dry land, he shows himself invulnerable to poison and is therewith vindicated, as comments of the local "natives" confirm.[31] For Luke, a major function of the resurrection of Jesus was likewise the vindication of one wrongly executed. The "risen" Paul then engages in a ministry that echoes Jesus' early activity (Acts 28:7-9; Luke 4:38-41) A. J. Mattill observes, "It is almost as if Paul were Jesus *redivivus*..."[32] He is. The theme of Paul the savior is one component of the Deutero-Pauline portrait.[33] Paul does not replace Christ, whose servant he is, but he does bring redemption to others, light for those who live in darkness. Both can be characterized as "light for the nations" (Luke 1:32; Acts 13:47).

This high "paulology" is congruent with Lucan soteriology and anthropology, which do better service to the cause of continuity in salvation history than to the status of Jesus as a unique redeemer.[34] In the realm of anthropology, Colossians and Ephesians are more akin to Luke and Acts than to Paul, for, despite the affirmations of newness of life, there is a tendency to replace the indicative/imperative model with ethical instruction, in other words, to regard moral capacity as a natural endowment for which grace is a kind of "booster shot."

The canonical Acts plays quite successfully with both sides of divinization: Paul is received as a god by those who know no better. The most famous incidents take place in Lystra (14:8-20)[35] and on the island of Malta (28:3-6).[36] Another text worthy of examination is the telling (and humorous[37]) Acts 19:13-17:

> *13* Then some itinerant Jewish exorcists tried to use the name of the Lord Jesus over those who had evil spirits, saying, "I adjure you by the Jesus whom Paul proclaims." *14* Seven sons of a Jewish high priest named Sceva were doing this. *15* But the evil spirit said to them in reply, "Jesus I know, and Paul I know; but who are you?" *16* Then the man with the evil spirit leaped on them, mastered them all, and so overpowered them that they fled out of the house naked and wounded. *17* When this became known to all residents of Ephesus, both Jews and Greeks, everyone was awestruck; and the name of the Lord Jesus was praised.

The phrase "Jesus...and Paul I know" evokes the supernatural knowledge of demons confronted by the Jesus in Mark 1:24: "and he cried out, 'What have you to do with us, Jesus of Nazareth? Have you come to destroy us? *I know who you are*, the Holy One of God.'"[38]

In summary, the heroization of Paul in Acts is not highly restrained. Paul has it all and does it all. His story and his accomplishments rival that of Jesus in some important respects. Luke did not construct his portrait of the heroic Paul simply to glorify him. Every element of his extraordinary character served his mission, namely, Luke's theological and other goals. The Paul of Acts is both the agent and symbol of the worldwide mission to create a universal church, the legitimate heir of Israel and a tent under which all people could experience the salvation of God. One of the ironies of history is that Luke, who did not fully embrace Paul's theology and did not acknowledge the existence of his letters, did much to establish a framework in which the letters of Paul were received by the emerging orthodox church.[39]

Paul is without doubt Luke's hero, but Luke does not present the leading features of Paul's theology, nor does he reveal some of the more salient elements of his biography. For the author of Acts, the heritage of gentile Christianity pioneered by Paul was under attack, and Paul could only be defended through some major modifications. One of these concerns the title "apostle," a title used routinely by Paul of his vocation and authority. Paul is Luke's hero, but Luke cannot assign him the title of apostle, which was restricted to the followers of Jesus. As far as Luke's circumstances went, the opponents of Paul in Galatians and 2 Corinthians had triumphed! Luke's was not, despite its ultimate success, the only resolution to the problem of the Pauline heritage and to the issue of church unity.

THE ACTS OF PAUL

The *Acts of Paul* appeared in the second half of the second century, between c. 160 and c. 190, probably c. 170–175.[40] The works now designated "apocryphal acts of the apostles" are a disparate group united by a biographical frame that follows an apostolic missionary from his original commission to his death, usually by martyrdom. Five of these books—those featuring Andrew, John, Paul, Peter, and Thomas—are called "major," although a case can now be made for adding the *Acts of Philip* to that category. Only the *Acts of Thomas* is complete, and all of these acts were subjected to editing.[41] Of the major Acts the piece devoted to Paul was the most acceptable in catholic circles, particularly on doctrinal grounds, and was ultimately condemned because of its use by heretics, notably the Manichees as well as followers of Priscillian.[42] Nonetheless, the *Acts of Paul* continued to be read and utilized as an historical and edifying source throughout the Middle Ages.[43]

Perhaps two-thirds of the entire work survives, and several sections exist in scanty fragments. The existence of some scenes can be identified or outlined by reference to the sixth-century *Acts of Titus* and two Byzantine authors, Nicetas of Paphlagonia (tenth century) and Nicephorus Callistus (c. 1256–c. 1335).[44] Although the work was composed in the late second century, the edition now reconstructed is not earlier than c. 300. Three components of the *Acts of Paul* enjoyed a separate existence. One, the martyrdom, was used liturgically on the appropriate feast, and was thus subject to considerable editing.[45] Another, *3 Corinthians*, was not an original part of the *Acts of Paul*.[46] The third is the material featuring Thecla (or Thekla) of Iconium, who became an immensely popular saint in antiquity and later eras, as well as a more recent feminist heroine.[47] The residue of the work must be reconstructed from incomplete papyrus texts.

As is the case with all of the apocryphal acts of the apostles except those of Thomas, the opening of the *Acts of Paul* is not extant. The logical and standard place to begin was the call of the particular apostle. In the case of Paul that means his "conversion" in the vicinity of Damascus. The span of *Acts of Paul* thus extended from that event to his martyrdom in Rome under Nero.[48] The intervening material relates visits to various sites. In the more complete passages, these visits are not explicitly initial, church-founding visits. The emphasis is upon the apostle's pastoral role. This is in keeping with much of the Deutero-Pauline tradition, which honored Paul as a great missionary, but focused upon his role as a teacher for the extant church, as, most notably, in the Pastoral Epistles.

This orientation has helped to promote a hypothesis that *Acts of Paul* is a *sequel* to the canonical Acts.[49] One should note, however, that a number of Paul's visits could have been foundational, as the data are incomplete (see below). In order to support his argument that *Acts of Paul* is a sequel, Richard Bauckham has to posit that the *Acts of Paul* did not begin with an account of his conversion.[50] In response to Bauckham, Richard Pervo proposed that *Acts of Paul* sought to revise the story of Paul in the canonical Acts, while Daniel Marguerat argues that it should be considered as a "Rereading."[51] All three of these approaches argue that *Acts of Paul* knew and utilized the canonical Acts.

Willy Rordorf, a distinguished authority on the *Acts of Paul*, has long dissented from this view, holding that *Acts of Paul* is quite independent of Acts.[52] He therefore rejects all of the above-mentioned theories. The evidence for use of Acts by the *Acts of Paul* is, however, quite strong, including not only its general plan and content—a journey from Damascus to Rome, from conversion to martyrdom—but also specific examples of linguistic borrowing, as emphasized by Julian Hills, as well as imitation/revision of particular episodes.[53] The use of Paul's letters is undisputed.[54] Equally manifest is the use of gospel traditions. (See below.) The stories about Thecla contain some marks of an earlier, possibly first-century, origin.[55]

The question of intertextual relationships among the various apocryphal acts of the apostles is vexing.[56] Because these works exist in multiple editions, none original, separation of initial borrowing (such as the use of Mark by Matthew) from later contamination is difficult.[57] The question is most acute in comparison of the *Acts of John*, *Peter*, and *Paul*. The use of a form of the *Quo Vadis* story in *Acts of Paul* 13 probably derives from the *Acts of Peter* 35 (Passion 6).[58] This is quite possibly a secondary improvement to the *Acts of Paul* rather than the imitation by the author of one scene from the extant *Acts of Peter*, but certainty is not possible. If *Acts of Paul* utilized the Petrine acts, it is not to be dated before c. 175. Other sources, possibly oral in origin, are probable, especially for the story of Thecla.[59] In its present form, the episodes featuring Thecla are an integral portion of the work, as numerous intratextual allusions indicate. The most notable of these is the encounter each has with a friendly lion (4.3; 9.23).[60] This intratextual parallelism indicates that, despite the ravages of editors, condemnation, and the varied fate and state of manuscripts, *Acts of Paul* is a literary work executed by an author in control of his sources.[61] The following table reveals the evident plan of the original work, in so far as surviving sources indicate.

Table 10: Synopsis of the *Acts of Paul*

Locality	Section[62]	Source	First Visit/Revisit[68]	NT Data
Damascus	1[63]	2, 5, [6][65]	First	Galatians, Acts
Jericho	9, 7	1, 6	First	___
Jerusalem	1	2	?	Acts (Gal)
Syrian (?) Antioch	2	1a, 2, 7, 8	First[69]	Galatians, Acts
Iconium	3	2, 3, 8	First[70]	Acts 14:1-6[73]
Pisidian Antioch	4[64]	2, 3, 8	First	Acts 13
Myra	5	2, 8	Unknown[71]	Acts 27:5-6[74]
Sidon	6	2, 7[66]	Unknown	Acts 27:3
Tyre	7	7[67]	Unknown	Acts 21:3, 7
Jerusalem-Cilicia-Smyrna	8	6	Unknown	Galatians, Acts
Ephesus	9	1, 6, 7, 8, 9	First	Acts 19, letters
Philippi	10-11	1a, 2, 7	Unknown	Acts 16
Corinth	12	1, 2	Re-visit (?)[72]	Acts, letters
Voyage	13	1, 1a	___	Acts 27
Rome	14	1, 2, 4, 7	First	Acts, PE

Source Key:

1. Greek papyrus of third-fourth century (P. Hamb.). Eleven leaves.[75]

1a. P. Michigan 1317, 3788, P. Berlin 13893, P. Oxy. 6, 1602, P. Bodmer 10, fourth century, mostly overlapping with P. Hamb.[76]

2. Coptic papyrus of fifth-sixth century (P. Heid.). 2000 fragments of parts of the entire work.[77]

3. Acts of Paul and Thecla, available in over forty Greek mss. and various versions.[78]

4. The Martyrdom, available in several Greek mss. and various versions.

5. P. Rylands inv. 44. A short but valuable Coptic papyrus.[79]

6. Coptic P. Bodmer XLI.

7. The *Acts of Titus.*

8. Nicetas of Paphlagonia.

9. Nicephorus Callistus.

Observations: (1) Although substantial portions of some episodes are missing, the general plan of the book and of its contents is clear. This is apparent from the overlap among the larger sources, which link the various sections, and from the multiple attestations for many of the episodes. The beginning is the most obscure, but it is most likely that the story included an account of Paul's conversion, modeled more upon Galatians than upon Acts 9. The *Acts of Paul* knows nothing of a release in Rome, followed by a mission to Spain.

(2) The chief plank in Richard Bauckham's argument that *Acts of Paul* is a sequel to the canonical Acts is the contention that it features return visits to sites already evangelized by Paul.[80] The text itself is silent on this matter, and, more often than not, implies, or at least is open to, the interpretation that this is Paul's first stay at a site.[81] Residence in the house of a

believer does not prove that he has been at a city previously. The house-church of Onesiphorus (3), for example, was evidently founded by Titus. Paul was unknown to Onesiphorus (3:2) His stay with Prisca and Aquila at Ephesus (9) is a logical inference from Acts 18–19 (cf. 1 Cor. 16:19). *Acts of Paul* is not interested in the question of initial or repeat visits, and the inference that Paul has been to many of these communities on a previous occasion is generally unwarranted.[82] Paul is a wandering preacher supported by household patrons in almost every place.[83]

The chief inspiration for the portrayal of Paul in the *Acts of Paul* is the canonical gospel type, from opening epiphany to post-mortem appearance.[84] The author took pains to make the story, both in its general plan and in many details, an echo of that of Jesus. The following list does not seek to be exhaustive; it is demonstrative:

1. Initial epiphany. Commission of Paul in a vision of Christ. (referred to in *APl* 9:5-6). Compare the baptism of Jesus.

2. "Temptation." Paul goes to the desert and is "with the wild beasts" (cf. *APl* 9:7). Compare Mark 1:12-13. On his journey to Jericho (in the desert region) Paul encounters and baptizes a lion (1).[85]

3. A ministry of proclamation, wonderworking, and persecution. Note, for example, *Acts of Paul* 2, where the apostle preaches, raises a dead person, and is thrown out of town (cf. Luke 4:16-30). In Ephesus, Paul's antagonist, Hieronymus, loses an ear, but is healed through the intervention of an angel deputizing for Paul (*APl* 9:27-28; cf. Luke 22:50-51). Like Jesus, Paul had forerunners (e.g., Titus, *APl* 3:2[86]).

4. Paul recruits a disciple who follows his path of preaching (baptizing) and persecution (*APl* 3–4; cf. Mark 6:6b-13; 30). The apostle begins his mission in Iconium by preaching a sermon that opens with beatitudes (3:6; cf. Matt. 5:3-12). This leads to the conversion of Thecla, who gives up all to follow him.[87] Her fiancé came to arrest Paul with an armed crowd (4:15; cf. Mark 14:43).[88] The offical before whom Paul is tried hears him gladly (cf. Mark 6:20 [John the Baptizer and Antipas]). Thecla is like a sheep without a shepherd (cf. Mark 6:34). In a vision she sees the Lord in the form of Paul (*APl* 3:21). Paul arranges to feed the household of Onesiphorus, which has given up all to follow him,[89] by selling his cloak for five loaves (*APl* 3:23; 25; cf. Mark 6:35-44).[90] Thecla offers to give up

her sexual identity (gender) and follow Paul wherever he goes (*APl* 3:25; cf. Luke 9:57-58). When condemned to the beasts, she has an inscription describing her crime (*APl* 4:28; cf. John 19:19). The traditional name "Acts of Paul and Thecla" is no less appropriate than the "Acts of God and the Apostles" would be for the canonical book. Paul is the master, the shepherd, Thecla the lamb and pupil. He is, in some sense, Christ to her. In the episodes centering upon Thecla, Paul is like the "absent" Christ, to whom one prays and from whom consolation is sought:

But as a lamb in the wilderness looks around for the shepherd, so Thecla [condemned to burn in the arena] kept searching for Paul. And having looked into the crowd she saw the Lord sitting in the likeness of Paul and said, "As if I were unable to endure, Paul has come to look after me." And she gazed upon him with great earnestness, but he went up to heaven.[91]

These images speak for themselves.[92] Paul is a celestial shepherd who comes to succor his sheep. He also finds means for meeting their bodily needs: In the *Acts of Paul* 3:23-25, the apostle has his cloak[93] sold to buy bread for his starving followers. The yield was five loaves. One doubts that the number was pulled out of a hat.[94] The capacity for such sacrifice is miraculous.

At Myra no kinder fate lay in store:

...He saw Hermippus coming with a drawn sword in his hand, and with him many other young men with their cudgels. Paul said to them, "I am not a robber,[95] nor am I a murderer..."[96]

Such repeated reminiscences point out that Paul did indeed take up his cross daily and suffer not one but many passions. One might argue that he had accomplished greater things than Jesus.[97] The text just cited is a case in point, for the apostle thwarted this attack. His assailant was struck blind and broke down into confession. Presently he is, of course, healed.

5. Paul undergoes a passion (*APl.* 14:4-7).[98] On the voyage to Rome, (*APl* 13) Paul (who, 13:1, like Jesus [Mark 4:38] has fallen asleep) meets the risen Lord, walking on the water (cf. Mark 6:45-52), who announces that he is about to be crucified again. This—probably

secondary—"passion prediction"[99] indicates that Paul's death will have a saving effect.[100] Condemned, like Jesus, by the ruling authority (Nero in this case), Paul was beheaded. From his neck flowed milk. This parallel to John 19:34 is followed by admiration from the soldier and bystanders (cf. Mark 15:39 and parallels). Following the execution Paul appears to the emperor and makes a speech. The soldiers, Longus and Cestus (the latter a centurion), come "very early" (cf. Mark 16:1) to the grave, find two men praying with Paul, and flee in fear. The two, Titus and Luke, likewise flee in fear of the soldiers, but all works out for the best.

> And, as Paul had told them, Longus and Cestus, the centurion, came in fear very early[101] to the grave of Paul. And when they drew near they found two men in prayer and Paul with them, and they became frightened when they saw the unexpected miracle, but Titus and Luke, being afraid at the sight of Longus and Cestus, turned to run away.[102]
>
> But they followed and said to them, "We follow you not in order to kill you, blessed men of God, as you imagine, but in order to live, that you may do to us as Paul promised us. We have just seen him in prayer beside you." Upon hearing this Titus and Luke gave them joyfully the seal[103] in the Lord, glorifying God and the Father of our Lord Jesus Christ to whom be glory for ever and ever. Amen.[104]

This report is a recasting of the empty tomb story in Mark 16:1-8. It includes several "improvements" upon the original. Paul appeared to Nero rather than to his own followers.[105] Moreover, his (male) disciples, in contrast to those of Jesus, remained with him. Unlike the women, they did not flee. The attendant soldiers (cf. Matt. 27:62-66; *Gospel of Peter* 35; 38, are converted and initiated. Paul's death (and resurrection) epitomizes the soteriological character of his ministry. Paul does not replace Christ, whose messenger he remains, but he recruits disciples, as had Jesus. These followers view Paul as their master and savior. The story follows the model of the canonical Gospel, arguably that of Mark. Although the same shape can be seen, in more subtle fashion, in the canonical Acts,[106] and this could have inspired the author, his particular model was apparently Mark, whose political orientation was more congenial to the author than was that of the Gospel of Luke.[107]

The *Acts of Paul* promotes the most radical—next to Marcion—form of Paulinism yet witnessed. Its views represent a nearly diametrically opposite view to those of the Pastoral Epistles on such matters as authority, church and society, and ethics.[108] The roots of its theology do not derive from Paul alone. This Paul does turn "mother against daughter and daughter against mother" (Luke 12:53).[109] Rejection of marriage sets the mission against the fundamental institution of Greco-Roman society—the household.[110] Although married couples can be found (e.g., Onesiphorus and Lectra, ch. 3; Aquila and Priscilla, 9:1), there is no suggestion that they procreate, and Paul, like the heroes of other Acts, certainly disrupts marriages (e.g. those of the affianced Thecla, 3; Eubula and Diophantes; Artemilla and Hieronymus, ch. 9; and Stratonike, the wife of Apollophanes[111]). In the apocryphal acts of the apostles conflict over sex replaces, as it were, the conflicts with Jews that motivate much persecution in the canonical Acts. In the *Acts of Paul,* the apostle continues the tradition of the radical, alienated, penniless itinerant, now active in the Greek-speaking urban world rather than in Syria and Palestine.[112]

The *Acts of Paul* brooks no compromise with the world. In response to harassment by the highly placed Alexander, Thecla "...attacked Alexander and rent his raiment, and tore off the golden crown of the figure of Caesar, which he had on his head, and dashed it to the ground, and left him naked, destitute and full of shame." (This follows the Armenian version,[113] as the Greek text has been bowdlerized.[114]) Alexander was a priest of the imperial cult, and his crown bore the image of Caesar. Thecla's action was a crime against the emperor.[115] The *Acts of Paul* uses the image of holy war—Christian warfare—in opposition to the Empire. Christians are soldiers of the eternal monarch (*APl* 14:2-3). This declaration of war survives even in the martyrdom, where one would reasonably expect eventual editorial mollification.[116]

Moral rigorism, vigorous eschatology, embrace of ecstatic prophecy, and acceptance of women prophets have led to the reasonable conclusion that *Acts of Paul*, which emerged in central Asia Minor at about the same time as the "New Prophecy," known after its founder as Montanism, represents and/or advocates this movement. At the very least, *Acts of Paul* reflects the strong interest in spiritual renewal characteristic of the region at that time. If the *Acts of Paul* is a specimen of outright Montanist propaganda, it is quite subtle. No "new"—in the sense of post-apostolic—revelations are delivered. Such pronouncements were characteristic of the New Prophecy, which saw itself as the recipient of the promised

"Paraclete" (John 14:16). Thecla is an ideal Montanist icon because of her celibacy and ardor, but it is remarkable that the portion of the work devoted to her (*APl* 3–4) does not refer to the Spirit (although she does have a vision, 3:21). The safest conclusion is that the *Acts of Paul* and the New Prophecy come from a similar environment, but that *Acts of Paul* is not a direct representative of it.[117]

This work displays modest theological sophistication; it propounds a popular theology with charismatic elements that is not without parallels in many eras of Christian history. In this regard, the author was not utterly unlike his canonical predecessor, although his theology was both more popular and more charismatic. Literarily, however, the author displayed more than a little sophistication by placing his story of Paul within the gospel shape. Those who received Paul (and Thecla) received Christ. Salvation history is a tool for opposing heretics, but it does not play the vital role that it does for Luke.[118]

The Paul of these non-canonical Acts, like the Paul of Acts, is a wandering missionary, who works wonders and converts large numbers to the faith. Differently from the Paul of Acts, his message has a strongly anti-establishment edge, rejecting the established forms of authority, notably the emperor, and its institutions, particularly the family. He is, like the Paul of the Deutero-Pauline letters, but unlike the Paul of Acts, a "loner," with no apparent connections to a community in Jerusalem or to other leaders, such as Peter and James.[119]

THE EPISTULA APOSTOLORUM

This text,[120] the title[121] of which derives from its content, was probably composed in Egypt during the last quarter of the second century.[122] The *Epistula* survives fully in very late Ethiopic manuscripts, probably translated from an Arabic version of a presumed Greek original.[123] *Epistula Apostolorum* itself is a revelation dialogue, a post-resurrection conversation between Jesus and the apostles that is embedded within a communication itself embedded within a narrative introduction. The text is, in structure, a double Chinese box. No epistolary conclusion is provided. The revelation dialogue flourished in the world of Gnosis. The generally "orthodox" *Epistula Apostolorum* was an attempt to capture this genre for catholic Christianity. This suggests that the form—a distant descendant of Plato's brilliant dialogues—had some appeal.[124] These conversations are also testaments of Jesus, with roots in that genre also.[125] The quasi-epistolary framework is additional evidence for the importance of the letter as a medium of communication among Christians. Behind this framework stands, at some remove, the impact of Paul.

This is the most "catholic" of "epistles," addressed to churches in East and West, North, and South (ch. 2). It therefore pretends both that the apostles had gone out to the four corners of the earth to evangelize the world and yet were evidently together at the time of its composition. It also draws upon a wide range of early Christian literature, including many of the texts that would find their way into the eventual New Testament canon, and the Apostolic Fathers, as well as a number of Christian apocrypha. Allusions to the Pauline corpus are frequent.[126] The author was also familiar with Acts and, possibly, with the *Acts of Paul*.

In retrospect, it is likely that the concept of a document from the apostolic college was inspired by Acts 15:23-29. For the author, Acts was no sacred or inviolable source. In ch. 15, the Lord predicts that one of the group will be in prison at Passover, experience an angelic delivery and miraculously opened door, then spend time with believers. This reflects the adventure of Peter in Acts 12:1-17, which has, in its complexity, the marks of a Lucan composition. The most probable explanation is that the author utilized and modified Acts 12, clarifying somewhat the enigmatic conclusion of v. 17.[127]

After a command to preach to Jews and gentiles throughout the world in ch. 30, chs. 31–32 turn to a new subject. The Twelve will meet a man named Saul, "which being interpreted means Paul."[128] The Lord then narrates the conversion, following the D-Text, and/or, possibly, the *Acts of Paul*.[129] The apostles themselves will heal his blinded eyes. After an expanded account of the prophecy about Paul's future in Acts 9:10-16, the Lord tells his hearers to instruct Paul in all matters of the faith, with particular reference to prophetic scripture. According to ch. 33, Paul will come to them "quickly," presumably in Jerusalem, per Acts 9:26-30. This account, which is at considerable variance with Galatians 1, goes beyond Acts in its efforts to integrate Paul into the early Jerusalem community and the company of Jesus' immediate followers. Like Luke, this author stresses the continuity of salvation history and places Paul within it as a subordinate of the Jerusalem authorities.

Polemical and controversial issues cannot be directly detected.[130] If, however, any spoke of conflict between Paul and the Jerusalem leaders, either positively, as did Marcion, or negatively, as in the Clementines, one could point to the *Epistula Apostolorum* to correct these views. Although quite different from the roughly contemporary Irenaeus, this text likewise assumes Paul's regularity and legitimacy. Paul teaches nothing that Peter does not teach. False teachers and doctrine exist,[131] but Paul cannot be linked to any of them. Unlike Irenaeus, *Epistula Apostolorum* is utterly innocent of Pauline theology.[132] Although Pauline letters are cited by allusion, *Epistula Apostolorum* says nothing about Paul as an author. In balance, it is likely that the insertion of Paul into the *Epistula Apostolorum* was deemed important[133] and that its purpose was to assure the readers that Paul belongs to what it views as, and eventually became, the mainstream. Otherwise stated: this report will correct opposing views of Paul. *Epistula Apostolorum* may be a rare voice of an Egyptian "popular" Christianity that lacked the sophistication of such Alexandrians as Clement and various "Gnostics."[134] Egypt also contained some for whom Paul was primarily a teacher of righteousness.[135] The *Epistula Apostolorum* shows the utilization of Pauline narratives within another narrative for purposes not unlike those of the canonical Acts, in a different and later context.

THE ACTS OF PETER

The *Acts of Peter* exists, like the *Acts of Paul*, only in fragments.[136] The martyrdom section, used, like that of Paul, in worship, alone survives in complete Greek witnesses. The subject of this section is the *Actus Vercellenses* (*Verc.*), a sixth- or seventh-century Latin piece derived from a translation made in the third or fourth century.[137] The earliest certain attestation of the work is Eusebius (*H.E.* 3.3.1-2), who places it among rejected Petrine writings.[138] Third-century writers made use of the work, without attribution,[139] and the thicket of intertextual relationships among the *Acts of Peter*, *Paul*, and *John* make it quite certain that the work existed in the last quarter of the second century.[140] The general perspective of the *Acts of Peter* is quite unlike that of the *Acts of Paul*, for it opposes rigorism.[141] Lapsed believers who repent are to be restored to communion, martyrdom is to be accepted but not pursued, and money may be received from those of questionable character.

Two-thirds of the original work survives, although not in its original state. The original evidently had two foci: Jerusalem and Rome. This is to say that travel was not a major focus of the *Acts of Peter*. Its hero was the leader of the church in two "capitals," the Holy City of the biblical tradition and the imperial center. The shift in his location represents the movement from Jewish to gentile Christianity. Probably because of its combination with the Pseudo-Clementines,[142] this section was removed and the book re-edited to account for gaps. The Pauline material (*Verc.* 1-3) is a later addition to the *Acts of Peter*; it now begins the major surviving section. Two pieces from the earlier Jerusalem component survive, each edited in a strongly misogynist fashion to support celibacy.[143] Both of these stories use miracle as a symbol and evidently sought, in their earlier form, to reinforce the view that God's ways may seem cruel but work out for the best. Other episodes may be implied.

Actus Vercellenses begins with Paul in Rome. After he leaves for Spain, Simon (the magician of Acts 8) makes substantial inroads into the community. A vision summons Peter to Rome, where he engages in a lengthy contest with Simon, whom he utterly masters in a duel of miracles. Forestalled by Peter in an attempt to fly, Simon was injured and eventually died. Disruption of partnerships and marriages brought about by Peter's preaching lead to persecution. Advised of the plot, Peter leaves Rome but experiences an appearance of Christ (the *Quo Vadis* episode) and returns to Rome, where, at his request, he is crucified upside down, delivering a moving oration to his followers.[144] Peter's death brought the persecution to a close.

Actus Vercellenses opens, in effect, where Acts left off, with the exception that Paul seems to be in prison, rather than in a private house,[145] although he has regular contact with the faithful. Among his converts was Candida, the warden Quartus' wife. She, in turn, brought her husband into the fold.[146] That worthy, without making any reference to legal issues, instructs Paul to leave Rome and travel at his own discretion.[147] Paul leaves the matter in God's hand. At the end of a three-day fast, he prayed and received a vision with an oracle directing him to become a physician to the Spaniards.[148] The balance of the unit is an extended farewell scene.[149] The faithful lament and recall, somewhat gratuitously, his arguments with Jewish leaders (cf. Acts 28:17-31), whom he refuted by saying that Christ, whom *their* fathers killed, had abrogated the "ritual" law. The people entreated Paul to restrict his Spanish mission to a year, at most, comparing the apostle to a mother who abandons her children. A public voice from heaven squelches their petitions. Paul will be executed by Nero. This silences the protests and augments faith.

The narrative is aware of the tradition that Paul fulfilled his plans to visit Spain,[150] but does not adopt the theory that Paul was acquitted at trial and later returned to Rome and re-arrest. The public voice from heaven is superior to private revelations received, for example, in Acts

9:15-16. Paul's commission comes from Christ. The immediate object of this divine intervention is pastoral: believers must not resist the will of God. The first paragraph has established three qualities of Paul: he is a missionary who can convert influential people,[151] a pastor who nourishes the faithful, and a disputant who can rout rivals.[152] He is, moreover, a privileged agent of God, one who communicates privately with the deity and publicly on God's behalf.

Chapter 2 describes the farewell liturgy,[153] also set in a pastoral context. Paul celebrates a (bread and water[154]) eucharist. Spiritual insight led him to rebuff one communicant, Rufina, who was involved in an adulterous relationship.[155] She may be saved if she repents. In punishment, Rufina was paralyzed on one side and lost her speech.[156] This incident panics the other believers, who wonder if they can be forgiven. The apostle responds with a brief address promising that those who abide in the moral requirements of their faith will be forgiven sins committed in ignorance.[157] As in the epistles (e.g., Col. 3:5-17), his exhortations take the form of contrasting catalogues of virtues and vices.

In his subsequent prayer, Paul utilizes the Deutero-Pauline "once... now" frame[158] to characterize himself as a former blasphemer, persecutor, and enemy of Christ. This prayer makes the pastoral purpose of such passages as 1 Tim. 1:12-17 (an apparent model)[159] explicit: if God forgave the abominable Paul, he can also forgive the likes of me. The faithful, recognizing their vulnerability, pray that Paul may return as soon as possible. This foreshadows the difficulty that will soon arise. *Acts of Peter* represents the venerable view that heresy could gain no foothold so long as the original apostles were present.[160]

The final Pauline unit (ch. 3) draws out the farewell through retardation. Among those conducting him to the harbor are representatives of all sorts and conditions, headed by a Senator, Demetrius.[161] Unfavorable weather prevents an immediate departure. Paul sends messengers with this news, motivating large numbers to come by various means to be with Paul, who edifies them for three days before he finally departs. This unit reinforces the great love of the entire community for Paul.

The Paul of these secondary chapters is very much the Deutero-Paul found elsewhere: a gentile, to all intents and purposes, a sinner turned around by God; the chosen vessel; and a great spiritual leader. Grace stands at the center of his theology. "He" understands that grace is power, the source of faith, which equips believers. Even egregious sinners can repent and return.[162] The purpose of the addition is clear: to place Paul on an equal footing with Peter (who also advocates reception of the penitent) in Rome, where both will lead in turn and in turn be martyred. The tendency to strengthen the relationship between the two apostles, first concelebrated in *1 Clement*, will continue to develop.[163]

Related texts include the *Passion of Peter and Paul* and the *Acts of Peter and Paul*. Sources of the *Passion* included the *Acts of Peter*, Pseudo-Marcellus (below), the Clementines, and the *Acts of Paul*.[164] The longer edition of the *Passion* opens with Paul's return from Spain to Rome, where he assists Peter, whose theology he shares, in debate with some Jews and in the conflict with Simon. Their joint prayers send the airborne Simon to his just doom.[165] This event, rather than recalcitrant wives and concubines,[166] led to the condemnation of both, who die in the respective manners.[167] Nero, too, soon dies.[168] Paul's role is relatively minor in this account, but his link to Peter, which extended to their deaths, is clear. In that sense the *Passion* resolves matters that the *Acts of Peter* anticipated.

The *Acts of Peter and Paul*, known as "Ps.-Marcellus" from the putative author (a companion of Peter in the *Acts of Peter*), is a sixth- or seventh-century Greek text also available in various versions.[169] Elaborations of Paul's travels and martyrdom give Paul a role more nearly equal to that of Peter. They are the "two great lights."[170] A remarkable feature of this work is that it begins with data derived from Acts 28:10-15: Paul departs from Malta ("Gaudomeleta") and stops at Syracuse, Rhegium [Messina, Didymus],[171] Puteoli, Three Taverns, and the Forum of Appius. He follows this itinerary as a free man who can choose his own destination. Ps.-Marcellus thus uses data from Acts while adopting the view of the *Acts of Paul* that Paul was not a prisoner.[172]

After a number of adventures, Paul arrives in Rome, after which the story blends into the tradition of the *Acts of Peter*.[173] This text was the most successful attempt to unify the ministries of Peter and Paul. As de Santos Otero observes, it amounted to a rejection of the earlier acts of the two apostles.[174] One might add that this program also rejects the spirit of the major apocryphal acts of the apostles, each of which presented its hero in near isolation from the other apostles. Like some other later Acts, this book was summoned to the aid of ecclesiastical politics. In its rivalry with the "New Rome" of Constantinople, the old Rome could invoke the bones of the two greatest apostles of the faith. One example of that tendency is the *Acts of Titus*. Another is the *Acts of Barnabas*.

THE ACTS OF BARNABAS

The *Journeys and Witness of St Barnabas the Apostle*, as it is entitled barely qualifies for a place in Lipsius-Bonnet's standard edition of apocryphal Acts, where it constitutes an Appendix.[175] The work derives from the late fifth century. Its major purpose was to defend the autonomous character of the Church of Cyprus.[176] The leading interest here is its treatment of the conflict between Paul and Barnabas (Acts 15:36-39), which was quite troubling to patristic authorities and has influenced the text of this work.[177] Both the purpose of the text and its geographical information indicate that *Acts of Barnabas* was composed in Crete. Probable sources include, in addition to Acts and Galatians, an old edition of the *Acts of Mark*, and the *Acts of Paul*.

Mark, the point of contention in Acts 15:36-39, narrates the work in the first person singular. In contrast to Acts 12, Mark was of polytheist origin, a former servant of Cyrillus, high priest of Zeus, who was baptized by Paul, Barnabas, and Silas in Iconium.[178] His story frames the account (chs. 1–6; 24–26). The mission focuses upon the conflict with polytheism, the feasts and temples of which play a prominent role.[179] This may well represent the continuance of popular festivals that even the baptized were reluctant to abandon.[180] The agent who brings about the martyrdom of Barnabas is none other than Paul's old adversary Barjesus (Acts 13:6-12). He foments the Jews to arrest and eventually lynch Barnabas (chs. 8 and 23). Pursued by a Jewish mob, Mark and his companions were able to escape, arriving eventually in Alexandria, where Mark launched his mission.[181] The narrative leaves no room for Mark to meet with Peter and compose his Gospel, nor was he an eyewitness to Jesus' ministry. The focus of the central section is upon Mark's relations with Barnabas and Paul.

After Mark's baptism, Mark and Barnabas had paired visions, the content of which Barnabas commanded him to disclose to no one (chs. 2–3). This establishes a link between the two and a distance from Paul, who is kept ignorant of God's plan for Mark. The mission to Cyprus had its point of origin in Iconium (ch. 5).[182] The Antiochene commission of Acts 13:1-3 is implicitly contradicted, perhaps because that made no mention of John Mark. Chapter 5 reports that Mark spent two months in Perga, hoping to sail west, but was forbidden by the Spirit to do so. Learning that "the apostles" were in Antioch, he went there. Once again, the account expands and contradicts Acts (13:14;

cf. 15:38), which implies that Mark deserted Paul and Barnabas on his own initiative.

The portrait of Paul in chs. 6–10 is neither heroic nor edifying; to the modern reader, at least, it is amusing. Mark found the apostle sick in bed[183] and furious with him because of his "delay" in Pamphylia. Mark avoided Paul for some time and finally begged his forgiveness by kneeling before him for several weeks, but to no avail. It transpires that Mark had retained some parchments while at Perga.[184] Their work at Antioch completed, the two decided to evangelize the East and then return to Cyprus for a pastoral visit. Barnabas wanted to go to Cyprus first (while Lucius proposed Cyrene[185]). Paul received a vision directing him to Jerusalem. Barnabas nonetheless continued to press the case of Cyrpus. The result was a big fight, one not ameliorated by Barnabas' proposal that he and Paul take Mark with them. The other believers supported this plan. In the end, Paul—who is clearly Barnabas' superior rather than a colleague whom Barnabas had recruited—said that, if Barnabas were to take Mark, he should go on his own. The two then made up, with a full ration of tears and prayers. Barnabas affirmed that they would not meet again, as he was to die in Cyprus. Paul, for his part, reported a vision of the Lord who told him not to resist Barnabas' plans, while he was to go to Jerusalem and learn of his own fate. The situation in view is more like that of Acts 20–21 (Paul's final journey to Jerusalem) than to Acts 15.

Although *Acts of Barnabas* seeks to justify Mark's action and Barnabas' continuing support of him, it does so by portraying Paul as stubborn and irascible, slow to forgive and unwilling to forget. The narrator obviously relied upon evidence and intimations from the epistles suggesting that the great apostle could be difficult. With that view many modern readers will agree. It is the most "candid" and unflattering portrait of Paul in early Christian literature, *ad hoc* but not without some careful exploration of the tradition. In the end, the whole controversy is patched up with mutual good wishes and visions, which are shared, if at all, after matters had been decided. God decided the outcome, to be sure, but with support from Paul that came too little and too late. Those who write laudatory biographies of the apostle to the gentiles will not invoke these Acts as evidence. Barnabas could not, evidently, be the patron of Cyprus without establishing his reasons for separating from Paul.[186] Even more importantly, the founder and patron of the Alexandrian church could not be portrayed as a Pauline reject.[187] It was necessary to show, with or without delicacy and divine intervention, that Paul was wrong about Mark.

The Acts of Titus

The *Acts of Titus*[188] is very similar to the work just discussed. Probably written c. 550–600, it focuses upon ecclesiastical issues and conflicts with polytheism. The form of the work is, unlike most of the various Acts, biographical, following the subject from birth to death and covering most of the standard topics.[189] Like the correspondence between Seneca and Paul,[190] this story deals with the problems of well-educated people faced with the poor literary quality of the Christian scriptures. Titus himself was a Hellene of high social standing. Paul did not convert him—in fact, Titus was a very early believer. The information about Paul is unremarkable. He did authorize Titus to engage in missionary work. Titus preceded Paul to every missionary site (ch. 4). Paul's status can be taken for granted. His character requires no defense or exposition. The Pauline itinerary is, of necessity, different, including a foray to Crete, which was evangelized before Ephesus (ch. 5).[191]

Xanthippe

The Life and Conduct of the Holy Women Xanthippe, Polyxena, and Rebecca,[192] commonly known as the *Acts of Xanthippe and Polyxena (Xan)*, makes rich use of various apocryphal acts of the apostles, as well as the canonical book, in the construction of a short Christian novel. The date is difficult to determine. M. R. James suggested the middle of the third century. Stefan Davies proposes 190–250,[193] though the language of the extant edition cannot be earlier than c. 400.[194] Note also the apparent use of the *Acts of Philip*. An Eastern provenance is likely. Spain is a closed book for the author, who cannot identify a single place in the Iberian Peninsula. All of the characters except Probus have Greek names. Greece, the other scene of action, may be a likely place of composition, but the geography of Greece is no less vague than that of Spain. *Xanthippe* is closer in content to the ancient romantic novels than any of the other works surveyed in this chapter. The work falls into two parts, rather like the Jewish novel *Aseneth*, with a conversion story in the first part and adventures in the second. Chapters 1–21 relate the initiation of Xanthippe by Paul during his mission to Spain, with the normal consequent marital difficulties, all happily resolved by the eventual baptism of her husband.[195]

Xanthippe came equipped with a beautiful younger sister, Polyxena. Chapters 22–42 relate her story, beginning with her kidnapping by a rival of her suitor, assisted by a gang of bandits. They set sail for Babylonia.[196]

Cast upon the Greek shore by a storm, she was rescued by Philip, who had been warned of her arrival in a vision.[197] Polyxena fled in the face of an attack by the bandits. Through the assistance of a lioness and the apostle Andrew (apostles were thick on the ground in Greece just then[198]), she and a Jewish slave named Rebecca received baptism, after which Andrew left them to their own devices.[199] An official presently kidnapped the ravishing Polyxena, while a private soldier had to be content with the possession of Rebecca. The non-compliant Polyxena is condemned but, like Thecla, finds a friendly lion. Eventually she makes her way back to Spain. A barbarian assault and her attempt to do away with herself rather than face a fate worse than death enlivened this voyage. *Xanthippe* conforms to the popular convention of "There and back." In structure and plot, it is a Christian alternative to romantic novels such as *An Ephesian Story*. Even by the standards of that terse production, *Xanthippe* is so brief that the second part reads like an outline that would serve a narrator as an *aide-mémoire*.[200] Paul is the chief religious authority, the equal, at least, of other apostles, but he enjoys no adventures.[201] All of those are experienced by women, as the title aptly indicates. This is not an Acts of Paul, Xanthippe, and others.

The story opens in Spain. Probus, an official, sent his slave to Rome with messages. While there the slave happened to hear the message of Paul, "the truly golden and beautiful nightingale." This purple patch effectively characterizes the preaching of the apostle.[202] The slave is smitten, but must return. The theme of a cult diffused through a slave illustrates a famous thesis of historians of religion.[203] Both this slave and Mme. Probus, our very own Xanthippe, fall sick with longing for the faith. Their symbolic language about illness (clearly intelligible to the Christian reader) leads Probus to believe that the sickness is physical and that Paul is a conventional physician (chs. 1–2).[204] Physician was applied metaphorically to Christ.[205]

In due course, "The preacher and teacher and illuminator of the world" arrived in Spain. The circumstances conform to the *Actus Vercellenses* (of Peter).[206] The epithets conform to the Deutero-Pauline portrait of the apostle. Xanthippe is sick with (religious) love, and longs to touch his garments (ch. 7).[207] When the poor Probus learns of Paul's presence, he rushes into the street and beseeches him to come to his house. Xanthippe's spiritual insight reveals that upon his forehead are the words "Paul the herald of God." She washes Paul's feet with her hair (cf. Luke 7:38). These parallels to interactions between Jesus and women help nurture the implicit paulology of this story. Paul is Christ to Xanthippe. The success of Paul's mission is described in terms reminiscent of the gospel.[208] The apostle has the power to remit sins.[209] His suffering is vicarious.[210] After a normal series of adventures she is rewarded by a christophany, when the savior appears in the form of Paul (ch. 15).[211]

Chapter 22 introduces Polyxena. She had a threatening dream, in which Christ appeared in the form of Paul. Xanthippe advised her to receive baptism the very next day, then left to hear Paul. Kidnappers disrupted this plan. As she was finally preparing, following her diverse adventures (narrated above), to return home, Onesimus[212] breaks into the narrative in the first person (ch. 38[213]). While en route to Paul in Spain, with letters (ch. 41), Onesimus received a vision directing him to pick up the two women and convey them to Paul. Weather prevented their departure. This was providential, for it gave "Lucius" (probably Luke[214]) opportunity to convert the entire city. Upon their return, they are welcomed by Paul. Both Polyxena's kidnapper (who has returned by some unreported route and means)[215] and her former suitor abandon their schemes upon receipt of baptism. Just as in romantic novels, the entire populace celebrates the return of a heroine.[216] Polyxena, however, will remain a virgin and never let Paul (rather than a husband) out of her sight. Nothing is said of Paul's eventual return to Rome.

The text is not clear about marital sex. Although Paul appears to endorse lawful marriage for those who burn, his subsequent words to Probus imply that sex is best avoided, and readers may conclude that the two will live in chastity, since Xanthippe had withdrawn from his bed after baptism. Polyxena will never marry. The surface interpretation is that baptism precludes marriage and that baptism after marriage should preclude sex, but this is not certain. The evident ambiguity may be due to subsequent editing of an earlier anti-sexual text.[217]

The apostle of *Xan* is the typical hero of later Paulinism. He possesses all of the qualities—universal missionary, divinely guided hero, surrogate savior—of the tradition, and evidently works alone, with the support of various colleagues, but Paul is not the only or an isolated apostle.[218] This image is taken for granted in this little novel, in which Paul's chief function is to ignite the plot. Many Christian authorities would have found Xanthippe and company preferable heroines to Thecla, for they do not challenge valid authority acting correctly in its proper sphere.

Apocalypses

In so far as they relate the content of visions, apocalypses are narratives. A popular type in early Judaism and Christianity featured tours of heaven and hell.[219] One of the most widespread and influential examples of this type was the *Apocalypse of Paul* (*Visio Pauli*).[220] The original was probably composed in Greek, possibly in Egypt, c. 250. The most familiar form of the piece is a Latin text of the fifth and sixth centuries. This is incomplete and not well organized. So many editions in various languages exist that Richard Bauckham characterized the remnants as a "collection of literature."[221] The *ApocPl* became the most popular apocalypse of its type and exercised a vast influence upon Christian art and literature, culminating in the great achievement of Dante. The extent of its popularity is manifest in the number of editions and translations into ancient and later vernacular languages, although its relatively thin attestation by theologians might lead one to conclude that *ApocPl* was an obscure text.[222] The present form of the edition can be dated to c. 390, as it reports the discovery of the long-hidden book in Tarsus at that time.[223] The work is orthodox, meting out stringent penalties for those who deny the virgin birth and the resurrection (chs. 41–42). A monastic, ascetic interest is patent. Clergy who commit sexual sins or neglect the poor also receive harsh treatment (chs. 34–36). Virgins of either sex receive a seven-fold greater reward than the married (ch. 22). Still and all, the focus of the piece is upon God's love and mercy.

Although apocalypses were attributed to other apostles, Paul was a natural, since he reported that he had received a heavenly vision (2 Cor. 12:2-4).[224] For the figures of salvation history, from Adam to Abraham, the Patriarchs to Moses, and the prophets, Paul is *the* apostolic missionary (e.g., ch. 20) and the recipient of considerable praise as a guide to souls and for his powers of persuasion (e.g., ch. 51). He is often hailed as the "beloved of God" (e.g., chs. 20, 47, 48), and is the recipient of macarisms ("blessed are you...," for example, chs. 49–50). At the close (available only in Coptic), Paul returned from his tour of the other worlds to the Mount of Olives where he joins the other apostles. The heavenly world had salutations for Peter and John, but especially for Paul: "Greetings, Paul, honored letter-writer [or 'bearer']. Greetings Paul, mediator of the covenant! Greetings, Paul, roof and foundation of the church." This is the most complete integration of Paul into the apostolic college known from the ancient world. It silently refutes both the Paul of the letters and the Paul of Acts, who had a post-resurrection career as a persecutor of the church.

Through his intercession, those suffering in hell will receive a doubt-less welcome day off each Sunday (ch. 44). Paul is, readers may safely conclude, a rather important and influential person. An angel predicts that he will defeat the accuser in the underworld.[225] This makes him an agent rather than simply a herald of salvation, and sets the stage for the next work to be considered. In this once-famous apocalypse Paul is the apostle *par excellence*, recognized as such by God, implicitly, the heavenly Lord, and every prominent figure from the Hebrew Bible. Things do not get much better than this.

The Coptic *Apocalypse of Paul*, which probably dates from the second century,[226] is preserved in the Nag Hammadi Library (V, 2; 17,19—24,9).[227] It stands first in a group of four writings designated as "apocalypses." The classification is based upon the title rather than upon its apparent genre.[228] A Greek original is presumed. This book is among the earliest efforts to asso-ciate the vision report of 2 Cor. 12:2-4 with Paul's conversion experience related in Gal. 1:15-17. It therefore contradicts Acts 9:1-19a. The author may not have known—or honored—Acts. Knowledge of epistles is certain, as there are citations of or allusions to 2 Corinthians, Galatians, and Ephesians. The text has one undisputedly Gnostic passage (19, 1-7), and represents the creator god, who resides in the seventh heaven, as inferior to higher beings (22,24—23,30). Murdock and MacRae believe that it represents the Valen-tinian reception and estimation of Paul in the second century.[229] If Paul is not superior to the other apostles, he is certainly their full peer (19, 14-19).

Some of the opening is lost. Paul has encountered a little child (the *puer speciosus*, one form taken by the Savior[230]). It transpires that he is upon a mountain (a favored site for epiphanies), "the mountain of Jeri-cho." That site evokes the apparent initial scene of the *Acts of Paul*.[231] Paul asks the youth for directions to Jerusalem—a feature not in harmony with Galatians, although it could fit the *Acts of Paul*. The child says, "I know who you are Paul. You are he who was blessed from his mother's womb. For I have [come] to you so that you may [go up to Jerusalem] to your fellow [apostles."][232]

"I know who you are" is reasonable enough, but it also evokes demonic recognitions of Jesus (Mark 1:24). The macarism transforms Gal. 1:15 into a statement like that made about Jesus in Luke 1:42. When caught up to the third heaven (cf. 2 Cor. 12:2), Paul sees the twelve beneath him. (At 21:30 it is not clear whether they are ahead of him; in 22:14-15 Paul leads them. In the Ogdoad [eighth heaven, 23,29—24,3] the apostles greet Paul and accompany him upward.)

In the seventh heaven, the apostle responds to a question of the elderly, enthroned, resplendent figure (the Demiurge, inferior creator god) by saying: "I am going down to the world of the dead in order to lead captive the captivity that was led captive in the captivity of Babylon."[233] The immediate source of this saying is Eph. 4:8: "Therefore it is said, 'When he ascended on high he made captivity itself a captive; he gave gifts to his people.'" The author of Ephesians had applied Ps. 68:19 to the victory of Christ. In the Coptic *ApocPl*, the apostle applies it to himself. He is a redeemer in his own right. One may argue that this is a transformation of Paul's own view that the preaching of the message is an eschatological event (2 Cor. 6:1-2). This is the most remarkable and dramatic presentation of Paul as a redeemer, because he is the *source* of redemption. No less remarkable is its basis: a Pauline citation about the work of Christ.

Several features of these two apocalypses coincide. Each applies macarisms to the apostle; each fully aligns him with the Twelve, and that not to his disadvantage; and each describes his descent as a means of salvation.[234] The two apocalypses are evidently connected by a no longer readily recoverable intertextual web. The simplest solution is to posit that a Greek edition of the text now extant in Coptic served as a source for the theologically purified Latin edition, but this is not the sole possibility. These apocalypses show the continuation of the Deutero-Pauline efforts to magnify Paul's role in salvation history, with the concomitant shift from portraying him as the sole apostle (the letters) or as a non-apostle who is the great witness to the ends of the earth (Acts) to making him a peer, perhaps *primus inter pares*, of the original twelve.

The Pseudo-Clementines

Among the writings purporting to stem from Clement of Rome is a work based upon, or using as a model, a novel of the "family" type. It probably appeared in west Syria c. 250.[235] From extensive revisions there remain the *Homilies* (*Hom.*), which exhibit Arian sympathies, and the *Recognitions* (*Rec.*), which survives in Latin and Syriac translations.[236] The Clementines[237] are difficult to characterize.[238] They are rather rationalistic, like the Apologists, although with speculative tinges, but display a stridently anti-Pauline, "Judeo-Christian" orientation. From a literary perspective, the Pseudo-Clementines may be compared to the apocryphal acts of the apostles, in so far as they treat Peter's travels, conflicts, and message, but this dimension, like the novel framework, is in danger of being swamped by the concentration upon sermons. For a summary of the complex plot, it is difficult to improve upon that of the late Bishop of Durham, Joseph Barber Lightfoot[239]:

Clement, a noble Roman citizen, was connected by birth with the family of the Caesars. His father Faustus was a near relation and a foster brother of the reigning emperor, and had married one Mattidia, likewise Caesar's kinswoman. From this union had sprung two elder sons, Faustinus and Faustianus,[240] who were twins, and our hero Clement, who was born many years after his brothers. At the time when Clement first comes before our notice, he is alone in the world. Many years ago, when he was still an infant, his mother had left home to escape dishonourable overtures from her husband's brother, and had taken her two elder sons with her. Not wishing to reveal his brother's turpitude to Faustus, she feigned a dream which warned her to leave home for a time with her twin children. Accordingly she set sail for Athens. After her departure her brother-in-law accused her to her husband of infidelity to her marriage vows. A storm arose at sea, the vessel was wrecked on the shores of Palestine, and she was separated from her children, whom she supposed to have been drowned. Thus she was left a lone woman dependent on the charity of others. The two sons were captured by pirates and sold[241] to Justa the Syrophoenician woman mentioned in the Gospels,[242] who educated them as her own children, giving them the names Aquila and Nicetes. As they grew up they became fellow-disciples of Simon Magus, whose doctrines they imbibed. Eventually however they were brought to a better mind by the teaching of Zacchaeus,[243] then a visitor to those parts; and through his influence they attached themselves to S. Peter, whom they accompanied from that time forward on his missionary circuits. They were so engaged at the moment when the narrative, to which we owe this account of their career, presents them to our notice.

Their father Faustus, as the years rolled on and he obtained no tidings of his wife and two elder children, determined after many fruitless enquiries to go in search of them himself. Accordingly he set sail for the east, leaving at home under the charge of guardians his youngest son Clement, then a boy of twelve years. From that time forward Clement heard nothing more of his father and suspected that he had died of grief or been drowned in the sea.

Thus Clement grew up to man's estate a lonely orphan. From his childhood he had pondered the deep questions of philosophy, till they took such hold on his mind that he could not shake them off. On the immortality of the soul more especially he had spent much anxious thought to no purpose. The prevailing philosophical systems had all failed to give him the satisfaction which his heart craved. At length—it was during the reign of Tiberius Caesar—a rumour reached the imperial capital, that an inspired teacher had appeared in Judaea, working miracles and enlisting recruits for the kingdom of God. This report determined him to sail to Judaea. Driven by stress of wind to Alexandria[244] and landing there, he fell in with one Barnabas, a Hebrew[245] and a disciple of the divine teacher, and from him received his first lessons in the Gospel. From Alexandria he sailed to Caesarea, where he found Peter,[246] to whom he had been commended by Barnabas.[247] By S. Peter he was further instructed in the faith, and from him he received baptism. He attached himself to his company, and attended him on his subsequent journeys.

At the moment when Clement makes the acquaintance of S. Peter, the Apostle has arranged to hold a public discussion with Simon Magus. Clement desires to know something about this false teacher, and is referred to Aquila and Nicetes, who give him an account of Simon's antecedents and of their own previous connexion with him. The public discussion commences, but is broken off abruptly by Simon, who escapes from Caesarea by stealth.[248] Saint Peter follows him from city to city, providing the antidote to his baneful teaching. On the shores of the island of Aradus,[249] Peter falls in with a beggar woman, who had lost the use of her hands. In answer to his enquiries she tells him that she was the wife of a powerful nobleman, that she left home with her two elder sons for reasons which she explains, and that she was shipwrecked and has lost her children at sea. Peter is put off the right scent for the time by her giving feigned names from shame.[250] But the recognition is only delayed. Clement finds in this beggar woman his long-lost mother, and the Apostle heals her ailment.

Aquila and Nicetes had preceded the Apostle to Laodicea. When he arrives there, they are surprised to find a strange woman in his company. He relates her story. They are astounded and overjoyed. They declare themselves to be the lost Faustinus and Faustinianus, and she is their mother. It is needless to add that she is converted and baptised. After her baptism they betake themselves to prayer. While they are returning, Peter enters into conversation with an old man whom he had observed watching the proceedings by stealth. The old man denies the power of prayer. Everything, he says, depends on a man's nativity. A friend of his, a noble Roman, had had the horoscope of his wife cast. It foretold that she would prove unfaithful to him and be drowned at sea. Everything had come to pass in accordance with the prediction. Peter's suspicions are roused by the story; he asks this friend's name, and finds that he was none other than Faustus the husband of Mattidia. The reader's penetration will probably by this time have gone a step farther and divined the truth, which appears shortly afterwards. The narrator is himself Faustus, and he had represented the circumstances as happening to a friend, in order to conceal his identity. Thus Clement has recovered the last of his lost relatives, and the 'recognitions' are complete. One other incident however is necessary to crown the story. Faustus is still a heathen. But the failure of Mattidia's horoscope has made a breach in the citadel of his fatalism, and it is stormed by S. Peter. He yields to the assault and is baptised.

This survey must acknowledge the issue of the sources of the Pseudo-Clementines, the numerous and thorny problems regarding which it will not engage. Scholarly consensus agrees that the anti-Pauline texts to be examined, *Recognitions* (1.27-71); the *Epistula Petri* (2), and *Homilies* (17.13-19), derive from sources.[251] In the Pseudo-Clementines, Peter is closely allied with and subordinate to James, who is the Bishop of Jerusalem and effectively the "ecumenical patriarch." The primacy of James suggests an anti-Pauline orientation. F. Stanley Jones has studied the question of a source behind *Rec.* 1.27-71 (specifically, 1.27.1-44.1, 53.4-71.6).[252] He identifies "Matthew" as the name of the putative author of this text, which he dates c. 200.[253] Sources included the LXX, *Jubilees*, Matthew, Luke, Acts, Hegesippus, Justin, and (possibly) the *Gospel of the Ebionites*. Gerd Lüdemann characterizes this material as "...virtually...a competitor with Acts... [that] intentionally sets out to correct a section of Luke's Acts with its own version of the story."[254] The thesis of this material is that Paul was to blame for the failure of James to convert his fellow Jews.[255]

Recognitions 1.27-39[256] present a review of salvation history, with certain particular features.[257] Chapter 39 describes the appearance of the prophet announced by Moses.[258] He demanded the cessation of animal sacrifice, which was to be replaced with water baptism as a means of forgiveness. The people rejected him and had him crucified. This deed was changed to good (ch. 40). Rejection by the people authorized the conversion of gentiles (42.1). Under the leadership of James, the Jerusalem community prospered. At the climax of a series of disputes between the apostles and the priestly leadership, James goes to the temple with the entire community of believers (ch. 66). Gamaliel, a secret believer and a spy within the Council, spoke first. James was then invited to say his piece—and quite a piece it was. After seven days everyone, including the high priest, was on the verge of baptism. At this point (70.1), a hostile person entered to disrupt proceedings[259] and throw James down the temple steps, leaving him for dead.[260]

This "enemy" is Paul. The epithet comes from the Parable of the Wheat and the Weeds (Matt. 13:24-30), in which an "enemy" secretly planted wheat-like weeds in the crop (vv. 25, 28). The originator of this interpretation understood the parable as an allegory of salvation history and assigned to Paul the role most readers would attribute to a satanic adversary. Paul is thus portrayed as an agent of the evil one.[261] *Recognitions* 1.71 confirms this when Gamaliel reports that the enemy had been sent to Damascus to attack the believers.[262] These incidents portray in narrative form the author's thesis: Paul halted James' mission when it was on the verge of complete success.

Introducing the Pseudo-Clementines are several authenticating texts. The *Letter of Peter to James* (*Epistula Petri*) accompanies Peter's "Preachings" (*kērygmata*). James is Peter's brother in the faith, but also "lord and bishop of the holy church" (1.1). The writer's goal is the proper protection and dissemination of James' thought. The model for this activity is the Jewish practice of guarding tradition. Following this is the *Contestatio*, a narrative of a covenant ceremony, somewhat reminiscent of the ceremony of the Qumran community,[263] in which the presbyters solemnly engage to follow the regulations for the protection of these books. Finally comes a letter from Clement to James, "the lord and bishop of bishops, who governs the holy church of the Hebrews at Jerusalem and those which by the providence of God have been well founded everywhere, together with the presbyters and deacons and all the other believers."[264] After considerable praise of Peter, Clement describes his ordination by Peter as his successor, including a homily on the duties of a bishop (chs. 3–19). The Pseudo-Clementines extend their claims from Jerusalem to Rome. This letter serves to introduce the novel, a copy of which accompanies it. The use of letters is probably a distant reflection of the Pauline practice.[265]

Warnings in 1.2-5 and 3.1-2 frame the *EpPetri*. The reason for stringent precautions emerges in 2.3: "For some from among the gentiles have rejected my lawful preaching and have preferred a lawless and absurd doctrine *of the man who is my enemy.* 2.4. And indeed some have attempted, whilst I am still alive, to distort my words by interpretations of many sorts, as if I taught the dissolution of the law and, although I was of this opinion, did not express it openly. But that may God forbid!"[266] Galatians 2 is in mind, in particular 2:11-14, 17. Peter borrows the words of Gal. 2:17 to rob Paul's gospel of validity.[267] The author reinforces the permanence of the Torah with citations from Matt. 5:18 and 24:35. The enemy of James is also the enemy of Peter.

Peter's principal enemy in the apocryphal tradition was Simon of Samaria ("the magician"). In contrast to the proto-orthodox tradition, the Pseudo-Clementines hold that the false always precedes the true. The result is a series of "syzygies," pairs of representatives of one and the other. This pattern can be traced throughout salvation history (*Hom.* 2.15-18). Simon therefore preceded Peter. *Homilies* 2.17.2-3 reads:

> There came as the first the one who was among those that are born of women,[268] and after that there appeared the one who was among the sons of men. Whoever follows this order can discern by whom Simon, who as the first came before me to the gentiles, was sent forth, and to whom I [Peter] belong who appeared later than he did and came in upon him as light upon darkness, as knowledge upon ignorance, as healing upon sickness.[269]

Although Simon is given the traditional "Gnostic" biography (*Hom.* 2.22-26), he represents Paul. The Pseudo-Clementines slandered Paul's views by placing them in the mouth of one of early Christianity's great villains. All that Paul said and did can be dismissed via this *ad hominem* claim.

Homilies 2.17.13-19 are part of a debate between Peter and Simon. The former claims that association with Jesus and instruction by him are superior to visions and dreams. Peter knows that sinners can experience dreams, while visions can be conjured by demons. Proper discourse among friends is oral and clear, not involving enigmatic speech or appeals to visions, for they entail uncertainty. The issue is the question of whether someone like Paul could offer a message of equal validity with the associates of the historical Jesus.[270] There is at least one clear allusion to 1 Cor. 15:1-8. Peter's case rests upon his confession (Matt. 16:13-20).[271] If "Simon's" commission by way of a vision were valid, his message would be the same as that of Peter and James.[272] On two grounds his doctrine cannot stand: it does not harmonize with that of the acknowledged leaders, and its basis is untrustworthy. As even a casual reading of the epistles will confirm, these conflicts go back to Paul's own lifetime. The Pseudo-Clementines show that they remained alive at the close of the second century.[273] In the end, it is difficult to understand the persistence of these views beyond affirmation that Paul was an early "bad guy," for, if the Pseudo-Clementines reflect the requirement that Jewish males by birth be circumcised—and this may be a residue from the past—they exhibit a hostility to the cult that surpasses anything in Paul and retain only the so-called "moral law," with which Paul was in essential agreement. All in all, the chief surprise is that the overt anti-Paulinism was not more thoroughly expurgated from the tradition.

Another text that plays an important role in the debate over the sources of the Pseudo-Clementines is the *Ascents* (or *Steps*) *of James.*[274] The title comes from the speech and fate of James on the temple steps (e.g., *Rec.* 1.65-70). The work is mentioned by the arduous, if a notch or two below brilliant, fourth-century Bishop of Salamis, Epiphanius, who collected many descriptions of heretical sects in his *Panarion*, a heresiological pharmacology. In that he states:

> They [Jewish Christians] call other acts 'of the apostles.' In these there is much that is full of impiety. There they armed themselves against the truth in no minor way. 7 Now they set out certain steps and guides in the *Steps of James* as if he expounds against the temple and sacrifices and against the fire on the altar and many other things full of babble. 8 Hence, they are not ashamed of denouncing even Paul here through certain contrived falsehoods of their pseudoapostles' villainy and deceit. They say, on the one hand, that he was a Tarsian, as he himself declares and does not deny. On the other hand, they assert that he was from the Greeks by taking a pretext in the passage spoken by him through love of the truth, 'I am a Tarsian, a citizen of no ignoble city' [Acts 21:39]. 9 Then they say that he was a Greek, the child of both a Greek mother and a Greek father, that he went to Jerusalem and remained there a while, that he desired to marry a priest's daughter,[275] that for this reason he became a proselyte and was circumcised, that when he still did not receive such a girl[276] he became angry and wrote against circumcision and against the Sabbath and the law.[277]

The claim that Paul was inspired by a worldly motive is typical of religious polemic. Asserting that Paul was a gentile contradicts Phil. 3:4-6. The basis is Acts, which is cited. The exegesis is not without justice, for it recognizes that it would have been difficult for a practicing Jew to obtain full citizenship at Tarsus, which required not only participation in polytheist worship, but two citizen parents. The characterization also builds upon the image of Paul as a man who could not manage his anger.[278] It is also interesting that Epiphanius (rightly) rejects the claim that James opposed the temple cult, although this would have been congenial to the theme of perfect harmony among the apostles. The thesis that Paul was a gentile is also in harmony with the Deutero-Pauline tradition, which often makes him effectively such in the interest of encouraging gentile converts.[279] This venomous legend attests to the depths of anti-Paulinism in certain Jewish-Christian circles.[280] That subject will continue to receive attention in the subsequent chapter.

CONCLUSION

The portraits in these narratives vary considerably, from the hero portrayed in the canonical Acts to the villain of the Pseudo-Clementine tradition. Among the pro-Pauline writings, the *Acts of Paul* presents the most distinct portrait. There an "anti-establishment" Paul survives. Otherwise, the Deutero-Pauline tradition tends to yield to the understanding of Paul among the apostles. Rather than the subordinate of Jerusalem who ran his own mission, Paul is accepted into the apostolic college and granted his own sphere(s) of labor. His ultimate close association with Peter came to stand as a symbol of church unity and as a powerful argument for the claims of the church in the imperial capital.

From the outset Christians at Rome were not shy about their two most distinguished local martyrs: Peter and Paul. The historical Paul focused upon his relations with Peter. These ended in disappointment (Gal. 1–2). In 1 Peter and *1 Clement* Paul is the more important of the two.[281] By the height of the Patristic era, Peter had become the more prominent, because he was the leader of the others and thus earthly head of the church. Up to the middle of the fifth century, the two apostolic martyrs held an equal place as founders of the Roman community. That this was not true is demonstrated by Paul's letter to the Romans, but few sought to challenge the claim.[282] The (edited) *Acts of Peter* (*Verc.* 23) portrays them as a tag team: Peter goes to Rome to replace the absent Paul.

By c. 170, Dionysius of Corinth could depict the two as teaching together in Italy and as martyred in close temporal proximity.[283] He was not motivated by a desire to augment the prestige of Rome. The culmination of this process, which can be seen in a number of the later acts, amounted to replacement of the earlier *Acts of Paul* and the *Acts of Peter*. The two worked together and died together.[284] Its liturgical symbol is the selection of a single day (29 June) to mark their joint martyrdom. The *Decretum Gelasianum*, of the early sixth century and probably of Italian origin, assigns to "heretics" the view that the two did not work and die as a pair.[285] In due course, Peter and Paul would oust Romulus and Remus as patrons of Rome.[286] This was not unrelated to ecclesiastical politics and was stimulated by the rise of Constantinople as a new and Christian Rome.[287] In the end, in poetry rather than mere fact, Peter and Paul joined hands in God's service. This is the eschatological conclusion to Paul in early Christian narrative.[288]

Narratives about Paul confirm the opening claim of this book that Paul has long been both a great hero and a nefarious villain within Christian circles. The data and portrait set forth in the canonical Acts exercised substantial influence over subsequent accounts, including those that had no interest in exalting Paul. The narratives (excepting the *Acts of Paul*) do not follow the Deutero-Pauline letters in portraying Paul as the only apostle worth mentioning. Integration of him into the apostolic circle is either assumed or demonstrated. In some cases, this involves subordination (e.g., *Epistula Apostolorum*; *3 Corinthians*), a major object of which is to show congruity between his teaching and that of the other apostles. The *Coptic Apocalypse of Paul* evidently places him in a superior position.

Another noteworthy component of the narrative tradition is the representation of Paul as a savior figure in his own right. The means for this vary considerably. It is most notable in the close of the *Acts of Paul* and the Coptic *Apocalypse*, but it can be observed in the canonical Acts and in such a relatively late orthodox work as *Xanthippe and Polyxena*. Here continuity with the Deutero-Pauline letters is present, for Colossians already elevated Paul's trials to a soteriological level.

Identification of trajectories and common threads should not obscure the wealth of variety and creativity displayed by these disparate authors over several centuries. The narrative established by Luke continued to exercise a potent influence, already apparent in the *Acts of Paul*, which sought to modify its content, and even in the Pseudo-Clementines, which do Acts the honor of rewriting it to reflect a thoroughly contrary viewpoint. Beginning with Acts, Christians of various orientations sought to make Paul the subject of biographical narrative and thus, to complete the circle, a figure resembling Jesus.

5. Other Representatives of Anti-Paulinism

Silence regarding Paul

Opposition to Paul began during his own lifetime and has probably never ceased to exist, in one form or another.[1] The previous chapters have taken a generic rather than chronological approach to the legacy and reception of Paul. This has led to the consideration of two anti-Pauline texts, the Letter of James, and some sources of the Pseudo-Clementines.[2] At this point the method shifts toward the thematic, beginning with the consideration of various anti-Pauline texts and movements, followed by a survey of writers and documents that, for various and often not readily discernible reasons, do not mention Paul. Much of the information about explicit anti-Paulinism comes from brief, second-hand patristic reports.[3] These materials usually offer few details about Paul but provide much cumulative evidence for the view that hostility toward the apostle was a definitive characteristic of "Jewish Christianity."[4] The previous chapter's examination of the Pseudo-Clementines is sufficiently illustrative of this orientation.

Silence is, in general, not a valid ground for assuming animosity toward Paul, unless it is supported by other factors. Those who neither name Paul nor appropriate aspects of his theology *may* have had negative views of the apostle, but this thesis cannot be assumed. Silence is nonetheless worthy of attention, particularly so as the date advances, as it becomes increasingly difficult by the mid-second century to assume that an author had never heard of the apostle to the gentiles. The survey begins with a narrative text: the First Gospel.

MATTHEW

Matthew probably appeared toward the end of the first century, quite possibly in Antioch.[5] Because its major source, Mark, is known, and its other chief source, Q, can be reconstructed with general certainty, Matthew's own views—the name is used for convenience—are readily identified. The question of Torah is one of these issues. This evangelist supported the value of both the "old" and the "new" (13:52). This leads to some apparently contradictory elements, evidently intended to honor, but not to enthrone, the old.[6] The Gospel's final words enjoin the evangelization of gentiles, who are to be baptized rather than (in the case of males) circumcised, and instruction in the words of Jesus, rather than the Torah.

For more than a millennium, Matthew was the most popular canonical Gospel in the West.[7] Its didactic presentation and accessible structure contributed to this popularity. Matthew presents the teaching of Jesus in five major speeches, each of which has a particular theme, such as ethics (chs. 5–7). This organization shows that the first evangelist has produced a gospel with features of a church order, in which such topics as community discipline and behavioral expectations are placed under one head.[8] The popularity of Matthew is another indicator of the emphasis placed upon righteous behavior during the post-Apostolic era.

In the period from c. 30 to c. 50, believers engaged in such issues discussed the question of the relation of Jesus to Torah. By the time and circumstances of Matthew, the issue was: What is the relevance of Mosaic Law to Jesus, Messiah, Lord, and Son of God? For Paul, of course, the matter had been resolved: Jesus was the goal or end of Torah (Rom. 10:4).

Matthew deemed that the matter required further discussion.[9] Like Paul (1 Cor. 1:24), Matthew identified Christ with heavenly Wisdom.[10] (Contrast, for example, Matt. 11:2, 19 to Luke 7:18, 35). Israelite theologians had earlier identified heavenly Wisdom with Torah (e.g., Sir. 24). As Wisdom/Torah itself, Jesus could both interpret and revise Torah. This is manifest in the famous antitheses of the Sermon on the Mount ("You have heard...but I say...," Matt. 5:21-48), which reject the divine words transmitted to Moses in favor of radical reinterpretations. Paul utilized a rather pessimistic anthropology; Matthew's anthropology is "high." For example, whereas the high christology of the Fourth Gospel is reflected in Jesus' statement, "I am the light of the world" (John 8:12), Matthew has Jesus proclaim to his followers, "You are the light of the world" (Matt. 5:14). When the Sermon on the Mount is read from a Pauline/Western Christian perspective, its demands seem intolerable. For the first evangelist, the moral life involves the pursuit of excellence. It is consonant with and grounded in the Jewish belief that the faithful *can* obey God's commandments. The object is hortatory; everyone knows that failures will occur. For Matthew, these failures are not the basis for reflection on law, that is, one does not start with the certainty of failure, but with the call to holiness.

Matthew, in accordance with ancient practice, does not mention Paul's name.[11] His views emerge in 5:17-20, a complex passage:

> *17* "Do not think that I have come to abolish the law or the prophets; I have come not to abolish but to fulfill. *18* For truly I tell you, until heaven and earth pass away, not one letter, not one stroke of a letter, will pass from the law until all is accomplished. *19* Therefore, whoever breaks one of the least of these commandments, and teaches others to do the same, will be called least in the kingdom of heaven; but whoever does them and teaches them will be called great in the kingdom of heaven. *20* For I tell you, unless your righteousness exceeds that of the scribes and Pharisees, you will never enter the kingdom of heaven."

Verses 17 and 20 constitute a frame: Jesus summons believers to a higher form of "righteousness" (which is behavior, not status).[12] Verse 17 uses the language of retrospection ("I have come") about the mission of Jesus. This form derives from the tradition. These sayings refer to the significance of Christ rather than to the historical utterances of Jesus of Nazareth. Verse 20 is a prophetic utterance about the conditions for entering the kingdom of heaven.[13] Verse 19 is an antithetical, casuistic statement of the same type, from the milieu of early Judaism, in which contrasts between large and small, least and greatest, are common.

Verse 18 is the core. This is a traditional prophetic utterance, characterizing that which is eternal and utmost in value, in this case Torah. The saying was probably formulated in conservative circles in opposition to the Q saying at Luke 21:33//Matt. 24:35, which grants the sayings of Jesus eternal validity. Matthew includes two qualifications. The final clause, "until all is accomplished," allows the understanding that "all" refers to the crucifixion–resurrection narrative. The victory of Christ will abrogate Torah. Verse 19 is a moderate corrective of this claim. Those who "break"[14] the law are not excluded from the kingdom, but they have limited honor within it. Paul was guilty of breaking the law and teaching others to do the same. The adjective "least" is probably a reference to Paul's self-deprecation.[15] For Matthew "doing" (v. 19) is fundamental. The close of the sermon returns to the thought of 5:20 in 7:21-23: "Not everyone who says to me, 'Lord, Lord,' will enter the kingdom of heaven, but only the one who *does* the will of my Father in heaven." Contrast this with Rom. 10:9: "because if you confess with your lips that Jesus is Lord and believe in your heart that God raised him from the dead, you will be saved."[16] Matthew's soteriology was quite different from that of Paul, which he regarded as a dangerous invitation to antinomianism (cf. Matt. 7:23). Unlike James, Matthew does not allude to a specific letter, but he is a critic of Pauline theology and not simply of a radical form of Paulinism, although he may have known of such.

This Gospel also rigorously opposes the Pauline model of leadership, in particular the Deutero-Pauline image of Paul as a teacher. In addition to 5:19, cited above, is the rejection of the title of "Rabbi," just emerging in Judaism, and "instructor" in Matt. 23:8, 10. Contrast this with Eph. 4:11; 1 Tim. 1:11; 2:7, and so on.[17] Matthew rejects the assumption of the *magisterium* by community leaders. Between those two comments (23:8) Matthew rejects the title "father." Paul portrayed himself as the parent of his foundations (e.g., 1 Cor. 4:14-15). Matthew's views of leadership and community organization may have involved more wish than reality. The *Didache*, which has much in common with Matthew, recognizes both the charismatic prophet and the resident "bishop."[18] The First Gospel stands on the proto-orthodox divide of "Jewish Christianity." Although the name "Matthew" would appear in a number of "Jewish-Christian" works,[19] the Gospel did not suffer because of its anti-Pauline orientation and positive view of law. From the end of the first century (e.g., *1 Clement*), Paul was viewed as a teacher of righteousness and thus in harmony with the Jesus of the First Gospel.

Leading characteristics of Jewish Christian writings and movements were the elevation of James, with Peter at his side, and the condemnation of Paul.[20] The Ebionites described by Irenaeus (*A.H.* 1.26.2; 3.15.1) accepted only the Gospel of Matthew and rejected the letters of Paul because of his apostasy from Torah.[21] It is not clear whether "Ebionite" (which means "poor," a term found in the Qumran texts that stands in the background of Luke 1–2) constituted a distinct sect or were just one name for Jewish Christians. Epiphanius (*Panarion* 28.5.3) lists a number of sects, the Encratites, the Severians,[22] the Cerinthians, who reject Paul's letters (and, in some cases Acts).[23] The Elkasites (or Elchasaites) developed Jewish Christianity in a gnosticizing direction.[24] Their possible influence upon the Pseudo-Clementines has been a subject for scholarly debate.[25] Mani was reared in an Elkasite community.[26] His interest in Paul, upon whom he modeled himself, came from distinctly Christian circles.

The *Acts of John* merit brief mention in the thrust and counter-thrust of claims of apostolic foundation. Acts does not claim that Paul was the founder of the Jesus-movement in Ephesus, although he effectively functions in that role (as he does also in Rome.)[27] H. J. Klauck says that parts of *Acts of John* "read like a counterfoil to the image of Paul in the Acts of the Apostles."[28] John, like Paul, was blinded as an element of his divine call. He definitely established the faith in Ephesus, destroyed the temple and cult of Artemis rather than remaining on the sidelines (Acts 19:23-40), and like Paul, experienced divine guidance through visions. This book is not hostile to Pauline theology, but it takes some pains to show that John "owns" Ephesus and was generally superior to Paul.

HEGESIPPUS

Hegesippus (c. 130–c. 190) traveled in the last quarter of the second century from some point in the East to Rome, stopping at Corinth, among other places.[29] His work, the *Memoirs of Ecclesiastical Acts*, survives in fragments preserved by Eusebius (*H.E.* 2.23.4-18, parts of 3.5.2-3; 3.11.1-12.1; 3.16.1; 3.20.1-6; 3.32.1-8; 4.8.2; and 4.22.1-9). Eusebius was primarily interested in Hegesippus as a source of episcopal succession lists in major sees.[30] Hegesippus may have been a "Jewish-Christian" of sorts. Eusebius would not highlight any deviant views of this valuable source. It is arguable that Hegesippus was anti-Pauline.[31] A fragment from a Byzantine author, Stephanus Gobarus, preserved in Photius' *Bibliotheca* (cod. 232), evidently discusses an attack upon 1 Cor. 2:9. This saying was widely disseminated in various forms throughout Jewish and Christian circles.[32] Gobarus understood this as a rejection of the passage, but evidence that Hegesippus mentioned either Paul or 1 Corinthians is lacking. He may have had *1 Clement* 24:8 in mind. Since Hegesippus knew *1 Clement* (Eusebius, *H.E.* 4.22.1), it is not possible that he had never heard of Paul. This is not sufficient to rank Hegesippus among the ardent anti-Paulinists, but it is very likely that Paul was not an authority for him.[33] The LXX, and "the Lord" (that is, traditions of Jesus' teaching, possibly as written gospels), sufficed. To this extent he was somewhat old-fashioned for his era. Hegesippus is thus to be numbered among those who knew of Paul but either ignored or rejected his writings.

OTHERS WHO ARE SILENT ABOUT PAUL

Although the once-prevalent theory that Paul suffered neglect (*altum silentium*, profound silence) in orthodox circles from the period 140–180 has been refuted,[34] there were authors who either ignored Paul or made use of him without mentioning his name. When date or locale make ignorance of Paul unlikely, these authors should be considered. Among these is Papias of Hierapolis.

Papias came from Hierapolis, a city in the Lykos Valley that was part of the Pauline mission (Col. 4:13).[35] One would therefore expect Papias to have been aware of Paul and his labors. He was familiar with other letters: 1 John and 1 Peter. Lindemann argues that for Papias the valid authorities were disciples of Jesus (or their followers).[36] He therefore omits Luke, and would not have valued Acts or Paul. This is the safest conclusion: Papias ignored Paul because he focused upon the Jesus tradition and those linked to it, but one must also ask why he took this position. Papias did not regard even the Pauline heritage of his own community as worthy of preservation. That fact does not justify elaborate theories of hostility to Paul,[37] but a fact it remains.

The *Shepherd of Hermas* is very difficult to date. It appeared between c. 110 and c. 145. *Hermas* does not quote written authorities. Paul is no exception. The author of this apocalyptically oriented exhortation to conversion (*metanoia*) lived in Rome. Knowledge of 1 Corinthians is relatively certain.[38] John Muddiman has recently argued that the ecclesiology of *Hermas* is influenced by Ephesians.[39] Given his techniques, both his silence about Paul and some use of his letters are unremarkable.

The so-called *Epistle of Barnabas*, a treatise with an epistolary frame,[40] is of obscure date and provenance. Although often assigned to Alexandria on the grounds of its "spiritual exegesis" of the LXX, Asia Minor should not be excluded from consideration. Syria and Palestine are also possible. This treatise was evidently composed between c. 100 and c. 130.[41] In general, *Barnabas* has a thoroughly non-Pauline view of Christianity's ancestral religion. Judaism is illegitimate because it failed to comprehend its own sacred texts, which now belong to believers in Christ. Contact with Pauline tradition is highly likely. The understanding of Abraham (13:7) exhibits Pauline influence.[42] Since the author was aware of Pauline thought but obviously preferred to go another way, the work is to that degree anti-Pauline, although "non-Pauline" might be a more apt characterization. *Barnabas* is not explicitly opposed to Paul, and should be ranked with those texts that knew of Paul but did not embrace his theology.[43]

The work known as *2 Clement*, which may be the earliest extant Christian sermon actually delivered to a community,[44] is extremely difficult to pin down in time and space. A date range of c. 120 and c. 160 is possible, and a number of places have been proposed for its provenance.[45] *Second Clement*'s theology is decidedly non-Pauline.[46] The author knew of Paul, for he had read *1 Clement*, but he does not mention the apostle's name. The question of allusions to Pauline texts has received careful scrutiny, without any general agreement or fully convincing proposals.[47] The author's moralism and futuristic eschatology may be due to the dangers he saw in opposing theological movements. If this is true, his opponents quite probably appealed to Paul. *Second Clement* falls into the category of silence about Paul quite possibly grounded in opposition.

Although it is not justifiable to identify all who ignored Paul as opponents, it is quite apparent that many Christian authors of the second quarter of the second century did not regard him as a normative authority. Reasons for this varied. The chief are belief that the LXX and "the Lord" (written or oral teachings of Jesus) are the major, if not the only Christian authoritative texts, as well as different theological orientations from that of Paul. These factors become more acute when attention turns to Justin and other apologists.

The Greek apologists of the second century attempted to justify Christianity by interpreting the movement in philosophical terms and categories.[48] The beginnings of this effort can be seen in Acts, probably inspired by Josephus.[49] Apologetics belongs formally to the realm of juridical rhetoric, a legal defense, but symboleutic (persuasive) rhetoric also plays a prominent role. A more minimal definition is that the apologists sought to show that Christianity was reasonable. The ostensible purpose of the apologetic enterprise was to persuade the authorities to refrain from persecution of Christians. Although the implied readers of apologies belonged to the polytheist ruling class, the actual audience came from the Jewish or Christian circles being defended. These texts provided moral support, and may also have supplied arguments to be used in conversation with unbelievers. Advocacy of the reasonableness of Christianity is apparent in *Diognetus*.[50]

This treatise, available in but a single (now lost) ms., is incomplete, as indicated by the copyist. The final two chapters (11 and 12) derive from another text, which is evidently a sermon. No convincing arguments have been made regarding possible authors, provenance, or date. The range for the last extends from before 70 to the sixteenth century. A date between 150 and 200, perhaps closer to the latter, is reasonable, but not demonstrable.[51] The addressee, "most excellent Diognetus," cannot be identified with any certainty.[52] *Diognetus* is one of the most attractive Christian short writings to survive from antiquity, but it had no detectable influence upon the early Church.[53] It filled no niche, lacking the heft of the major apologetic works, especially those issued by known and notable authors.[54]

Despite the brevity of the surviving text, *Diognetus* shows more signs of Pauline influence than any other Greek apologist.[55] Tatian alone is somewhat comparable. In addition to a number of possible and probable allusions, vigorous imitation of Paul's paradoxical style, the writer engages major Pauline themes. *Diognetus* 5.12-16 (with a supplement in v. 17) imitates the catalogue of hardships of 2 Cor. 6:8b-10, "democratizing" the Pauline description of apostolic existence.[56] The author takes up Paul's soteriology and bases his ethics upon that doctrine. *Diognetus* 5.7 utilizes Paul's understanding of "flesh": "They are found in the flesh but do not live according to the flesh" (ἐν σαρκὶ τυγχάνουσιν, ἀλλ᾽ οὐ κατὰ σάρκα ζῶσιν). Compare, for example, 2 Cor. 10:3.[57] *Diognetus* 9.1-5 is indebted to Romans.[58] Andreas Lindemann says, "*Diognetus* 9 is the author's attempt to express the substance of Pauline soteriology in the categories of the Greco-Roman milieu and religiosity without consequently abandoning the Pauline conception."[59] These examples suffice to show that *Diognetus* does not simply allude to Paul as an authority but that it makes creative use of essential features of Pauline theology.

The *Apology of Aristides* may have been written relatively early.[60] Indubitable allusions to Pauline letters are lacking, as is the influence of Pauline thought.[61] Similar comments may be made about Athenagoras, who issued his apology in the late 170s.[62] Theophilus of Antioch, active in the 180s, did include and cite Pauline texts as authoritative writings, but Theophilus was in no sense a "Pauline theologian."[63] Interest rises when the discussion turns to the martyred theologian Justin, born in Samaria but active in Rome in the middle of the second century.[64]

Justin's surviving genuine works include two apologies, perhaps better seen as an apology with an appendix, or as a composite work,[65] and a lengthy *Dialogue with Trypho*, a Jew.[66] Justin also wrote a critique of various heresies, including the doctrine of Marcion. This work has been lost, perhaps because it was subsumed by Irenaeus and other heresiologists. Justin was therefore not unaware of Paul's place in Marcion's theology. This has created considerable interest.[67] It is likely that Justin did not view Paul as an authority. He knows Luke, but does not betray any knowledge of Acts.[68] Nonetheless, in the context of the apologetic tradition summarized above, Justin's failure to mention Paul requires no appeal to conspiracy theories or characterization of Justin as an opponent of Pauline theology. His theology was based upon different presuppositions and, like other Christian apologists, Justin did not cite Christian authorities, other than Jesus, by name. Justin makes no reference to any letters. This contrasts with the known tradition of the Roman community, which made its debut on the early Christian state with a letter (*1 Clement*) and is associated with or mentioned in others (Hebrews, 1 Peter, *Ptolemy to Flora*[69]). Those who argue for a growing collection of authoritative texts that will contain much of the eventual text of the New Testament find no support in Justin. For him, a harmony of Synoptic texts, essentially Matthew and Luke, are central. These are his "apostolic" authorities.[70] The impact of Marcion may account for this relatively narrow base.[71]

Although allusions to Pauline letters are few and debatable in the *Apology*,[72] the *Dialogue* shows that Justin had access to the Pauline corpus.[73] As might be expected in conversation with Jewish adversaries, Romans and Galatians are not ignored. Justin does not make casual allusions to the epistles; he takes up their arguments and revises them for his own purposes.[74] For example, Justin appropriated from Paul the thesis that Abraham was acceptable to God without circumcision:

> We have been led to God through this crucified Christ, and we are the true spiritual Israel, and the descendants of Juda, Jacob, Isaac, and Abraham, who, though uncircumcised, was approved and blessed by God because of his faith and was called the father of many nations.[75]
>
> Furthermore,[76] the Scriptures and the facts of the case force us to admit that Abraham received circumcision for a sign, not for justification itself. Thus was it justly said of your people: "That soul which shall not be circumcised on the eighth day shall be destroyed out of his people." [Gen 17:14] Moreover, the fact that females cannot receive circumcision of the flesh shows that circumcision was given as a sign, not as an act of justification. For God also bestowed upon women the capability of performing every good and virtuous act...[77]

Justin makes use of Paul's view that "true circumcision" is "spiritual" (Rom. 2:28-29). His claim that circumcision was a "sign" for Abraham derives from Rom. 4:1-12. The language of "justification" is also Pauline in background. Justin alludes to the same texts earlier utilized by Paul: Gen 12:3; 15:6; 17:24.[78] After citing a catalogue of gifts based upon 1 Cor. 12:8-10, Justin proceeds to cite Ps. 69:19 with reference to the Ascension, quite like Eph. 4:7-16, which is its certain source (39.2-5).[79] *Dialogue with Trypho* 95–96 introduce Paul's proofs from scripture in Gal. 3:6-14 about covenantal blessing and curse, utilizing the same passages (Deut. 27:26; 21:23) about curses for the disobedient and any who is crucified, in the service of his claims that the Jews are cursed for putting Jesus to death.

In his summary, Albert E. Barnett found fifteen highly probable allusions, as well as a number of less probable possibilities.[80] Justin arguably belongs among the interpreters of Paul, with the important qualification that he cites neither author nor text.[81] He is, as Werline argues, a "transformer" of Pauline theology, which is to say an interpreter. Justin may have been familiar with earlier, for example, Valentinian, interpreters of Paul, and, as noted, knew the work of Marcion. His borrowings demonstrate that Justin cannot be called a representative of a vigorously anti-Pauline tradition.[82] His pupil Tatian marks the evident transition to a new era.

Tatian, like Justin, came to Rome from the East, probably from a region east of the Euphrates.[83] After an education in Greek culture, he went, like many prospective philosophers and sophists, to Rome,[84] where he became a convert to Christianity, probably under Justin—despite his claim that he was converted by reading the Bible.[85] His link to Justin is evident in his *Diatessaron*, a single gospel produced by weaving together four (or five) gospel texts. Tatian, however, eventually went his own way, returning to the East, where he was associated with a stringently ascetic movement.[86]

Tatian became a bitter opponent of the Greek culture that he had once embraced. His apology, *Address to the Greeks*, written c. 179,[87] is not so much a defense of Christianity as it is an assault upon Greek culture.[88] Robert M. Grant concludes: "It will be plain that Tatian knows Paul well and that in part, at least, his theology is based on the Pauline epistles, including Hebrews."[89] Specific use of Romans, 1 and 2 Corinthians, Galatians, Ephesians, Philippians, Colossians, and Hebrews can be posited. All of his New Testament quotes contained no attribution.

Since Tatian was prepared to compose a single new gospel, continuing a process that began with Matthew, if not earlier,[90] it is not surprising that he would paraphrase Paul. These texts were authoritative, but they were not "sacred Scripture." Since he was a contemporary of Irenaeus, Tatian shows that Irenaeus' views about authoritative texts were not a matter of general consensus in the last quarter of the second century. The two held diametrically opposing views on the problem of the plurality of the gospels and about the integration of Paul into Christian theology. Eusebius took umbrage at Tatian's improvements of Paul's grammar (*H.E.* 4.29.6). In an extant fragment of a later work, *On Perfection according to the Savior*,[91] Tatian revised/interpreted 1 Cor. 7:2-5 in a direction hostile to conjugal intercourse.

> I believe Tatian the Syrian made bold to teach these doctrines [*that marriage is a diabolic invention*]. At any rate he writes these words in his book *On Perfection according to the Saviour*: "While agreement to be continent makes prayer possible [cf. 1 Cor. 7:5], intercourse of corruption destroys it. By the very disparaging way in which he allows it, he forbids it. For although he allowed them to come together again because of Satan and the temptation to incontinence, he indicated that the man who takes advantage of this position will be serving two masters, God if there is 'agreement,' but, if there is no such agreement, incontinence, fornication, and the devil." This he says in expounding the apostle.[92]

The use of "he" indicates that Tatian had identified Paul by name, as the final comment of Clement (Eusebius' source) indicates.[93] Tatian was, like the near contemporary Dionysius of Corinth and his correspondents, engaged in a battle over Paul's views of marriage.[94] The apostle was an important authority for all concerned in this controversy. His teachings could not be ignored. Jerome claimed that Tatian rejected some epistles, specifically, 1 Timothy.[95] Robert M. Grant explains this on the grounds of 1 Timothy's acceptance of marriage, meat, and wine, for that letter, while Titus' use of "celibate" and its attack upon "Jewish myths and genealogies" would make that epistle more acceptable.[96] Tatian perceived that 1 Timothy had revised Paul's views of marriage from a less desirable option to a positive requirement. He is the first known Pauline critic to question the authenticity of the Pastoral Epistles on the grounds of conflict with other letters.

Like his teacher Justin, Tatian made use of Paul without specification of a source in his "apology." Unlike Justin, for whom Paul served mainly as a resource for anti-Jewish polemic, Tatian regarded Paul as a major source of theological inspiration. This deviation indicates that, in the environment of Justin, Paul's epistles were known, read, and utilized. One may suspect that Tatian had a good deal more admiration for the perspective of Marcion than had his teacher. Eusebius, typically, says that all of Tatian's deviations (which he associates with the Valentinians, Marcion, and Saturninus) emerged after the death of his mentor (*H.E.* 4.29.1-3).

Silence about Paul is not, in and of itself, grounds for proposing anti-Paulinism. In the case of the apologists, it belongs to the standard procedure of not introducing Christian writers by name. Tatian provides a clear illustration. In a non-apologetic work, he was prepared to cite and interpret Paul. Failure to mention Paul cannot be attributed to ignorance in every case, as the use of the apostle can, as exemplified by Justin, often be demonstrated. The discussion has, however, shown that there were a number of authorities during the period c. 125–c. 175 who based their theological arguments upon "the Prophets" and "the Lord," without any recourse to the Pauline epistles. Although a certain reserve toward, even opposition to, Paul can be suspected in some cases, the more important question is judgment about authoritative texts. It is clear that Paul was widely known, but not universally accepted into this category. Marcion and other "heretics" may have influenced this position, but that conclusion is rarely certain. Marcion did not put Paul under a cloud in the middle third of the second century. The clouds were scattered. The following chapter will show that one source of these scattered clouds was the popularity of Paul among those who were eventually assigned to the "heretical" side of the emerging division between proto-orthodoxy and its rivals.

6. Paul as an Object of Interpretation: Marcion to Irenaeus

THE FOCUS OF this chapter is upon Paul as a writer of authoritative texts for exegesis. The distinction is clear in the case of explicit *commentaries* upon various epistles, a practice that can be identified in Clement of Alexandria (although only fragments of his *Hypotyposeis* survive), and authors of subsequent centuries. Implicit commentary upon the undisputed epistles begins with Colossians and extends throughout the Deutero-Pauline letters. Ignatius and Polycarp, already considered, commented upon Paul, as did others, such as *1 Clement* and Dionysius of Corinth. The distinction is therefore somewhat artificial. Three categories are clear. The first is the application of ancient critical methods to the Pauline corpus. A second is the use of Paul as a proof text and/or for explication of some passage or issue. Both of these methods first emerged in the "heretical" use of Paul. Heretical practice constitutes the third area of examination. The chapter concludes with the work of Irenaeus of Lyons, who achieved the integration of Pauline thought into a synthesis of most of the Christian movements of the period. He represents a major point in the reception of Pauline thought and provides a logical conclusion to the survey.[1]

Robert M. Grant has demonstrated that the critical study of Christian texts first emerged in "heretical" circles and that proto-orthodox believers were driven to make use of the same methods in order to attempt to refute their opponents.[2] The best-educated followers of Christ were speculative theologians whose views appeared unsound to later Christians. This state of affairs obtained through Clement of Alexandria, many of whose works disappeared, and Origen, whose views also fell out of official favor and were ultimately condemned.

The term *hairesis* referred to a party, faction, or philosophical "school" or movement. Just as formative Judaism rejected the existence of sects, so Christianity also officially rejected various movements as "sects," in distinction from the truth of the catholic faith.[3] This redefinition is apparent in Justin. Without "orthodoxy" "heresy" is impossible, and vice-versa. What was denounced in Rome or Alexandria as heresy might in some region be viewed as "normative," or at least as normal, Christianity.[4] The transmission of literature via manuscript (or, for that matter, oral tradition) raised questions of authenticity. Pseudonymous literature could be produced as readily as authentic texts, leading to quarrels among critics and partisans of philosophical sects.[5] Readers and copyists could readily introduce interpolations.[6] Christians did not produce a standardized copy of their scriptures until the Byzantine era. This edition of the New Testament, which remained dominant until the late nineteenth century and still has its partisans, was, in terms of its Greek text, somewhat corrupt.[7]

Among texts corrupted by Christians was the LXX. In Justin's *Dialogue with Trypho* (70–71),[8] the narrator (Justin) claims both that the LXX is accurate (*vis-à-vis* the Hebrew text) and that Jewish teachers have removed some christological passages from the original. The first issue is Isa 7:14, which Justin's opponents claim (correctly) should be rendered "young woman" rather than "virgin" and which Justin says does not refer to Hezekiah, but to Jesus. Another example of a "better" text is Esdras' explication of the Passover:[9]

> This Passover is our savior and refuge. And if you have understood, and it has entered into your hearts, that we are about to humiliate him on a cross, and afterwards hope in Him, then this place will never be forsaken, says the Lord of hosts. But if you will not believe Him, nor listen to His teaching, you shall be the laughing-stock of the gentiles.[10]

This is obviously a Christian interpolation based upon a typological interpretation of the Passover as the passion of Jesus.[11] The normal LXX text of Jer 11:19 introduces the word "wood" (ξύλον), used by Christians as a trope for the cross (72.2). This phrase is not part of the MT. Its removal was defensible as a valid correction on the grounds that the Hebrew text was more original. Another alleged deletion from Jeremiah spoke of the Lord's descent to preach salvation to those in the underworld (72.4).[12]

This is an attempt to prophesy the descent of Christ into Hell. A final example is the claim that Jewish critics have excised the final words of Ps. 96:10: "The Lord reigns [from a tree]" (73:1). These bracketed words are indubitably Christian.[13] Justin's confidence has no rhetorical or intellectual basis. Its grounds are dogmatic.[14] Christian and Jewish scholars of today would agree with Justin's opponents. His LXX was corrupt, based upon Christian efforts to substantiate prophecies of the future messiah by creating additional examples of the phenomenon.

These illustrations from Justin Martyr serve to show that when critics like Marcion claimed that Christian writings had been tampered with, he was not making utterly improbable claims. Justin himself had engaged in producing harmonized gospel texts, and the publication of the Pastoral Epistles show that the apostle Paul was also the object of supplementation. Marcion understood himself as, like Justin, restoring the original text on dogmatic grounds.

Ancient scholars had to develop criteria for the criticism of extant texts, the identification of pseudonymous productions, and other literary problems.[15] The text-critical judgments of Alexandrian scholars regarding the Homeric epics survive in the comments known as *scholia*. Origen followed their methods in his own approach to textual criticism. The nature of basic rhetorical education can be found in the surviving textbooks known as *Progymnasmata*. In his treatment of the *chreia* ("anecdote, saying"), the author of one such text, Theon, advances these grounds for refutation: the "...unclear, pleonastic, deficient, impossible, incredible, false, inexpedient, useless, or shameful."[16] Some of these involve logic, but the last three are moral. Theon gives examples of each type.[17]

Another author, Hermogenes, provides a similar list for refutation: the "...unclear, implausible, impossible; from the inconsistent, also called the contrary; from what is inappropriate, and from what is not advantageous."[18] His example of the impossible comes from Herodotus 1.24, in refutation of which one will say that Arion could not have been saved by a dolphin. The inappropriate is illustrated by the claim that Apollo, a god, would not have sex with a woman. The mixture of such categories as the implausible or the impossible and the inconsistent, which remain in use, and moral grounds for objection illuminate the gap between ancient and more recent criticism. Critics of today would agree with the principle that it is inappropriate for teachers to have sexual relationships with their students, but that is not a ground for saying that Professor *X* did not have an affair with *N. N.* The claims that some commandments were unworthy of God or Jesus would have held an accepted—which is not to say undisputed—place in ancient criticism. Rhetorically based criticism moves from the "should not" to the "did not."[19]

Marcion of Sinope

The traditional dates for Marcion are c. 85–c. 160.[20] He may have been born a decade earlier. Marcion came from Sinope, on the south coast of the Black Sea. It is possible that he was a Christian from birth.[21] When he developed his distinctive understanding of the Christian message is not clear; equally unclear are how much his ideas evolved and the nature of various influences upon them.[22] As a wealthy shipowner, according to tradition,[23] Marcion would have traveled a great deal. His travels took him to eastern Asia Minor, where his message provoked hostility from Polycarp and, evidently, the Pastor. This suggests that he actively shared his views there during the 120s.[24] In due course, Marcion went to Rome, as had many teachers,[25] where he eventually fell out with the major Christian community (which returned a large donation he had made). The conventional date of his activity in Rome, 137–144, is probably a bit late.[26] The claim that Marcion was excommunicated by the Roman community is unsupported.[27] He evidently "excommunicated" them and proceeded to establish his own community.[28] Marcion was, like his hero Paul, a missionary and organizer.[29] He built up a church that lasted for centuries in the East. Marcion evidently made use of his business and organizational skills in his missionary enterprise. He died c. 160.

Marcion's background is to be sought in the Pauline missionary orbit of the early second century. His home community evidently made use of a collection of Pauline letters and may have reflected a relatively radical form of Paulinism that did not make much use of the LXX.[30] He was a follower of Paul, who, for him, was the only true apostle. Support of this thesis can be found in Colossians and Ephesians,[31] for example.[32] Marcion was not a philosophical theologian, nor was he a profound thinker. Like many energetic proponents of uncomplicated ideas, he admitted no gray into his palette. All is either black or white.

The question with which the classic Gnostic thinkers wrestled, the problem of the origin of evil, did not particularly trouble Marcion, nor did he view humans as possessing a spark or particle of the divine. He did not, like Paul in E. P. Sanders' famous formulation,[33] argue from solution to problem, but from the solution, period: redemption through Jesus

Christ. Marcion defended simple, if not perfectly consistent, answers to complex questions. For those who like cinematic analogies, Marcion's creator god is like the god of Woody Allen, an underachiever. Creation is not an altogether happy place. Marcion's unknown god is, to continue the analogy, like the superior beings who come from outer space—as they often did in 1950s films—to deliver humanity.

What did trouble Marcion was the contrast he saw between the just, angry, and vengeful god of the Hebrew Bible and the goodness, love, and mercy of the god proclaimed by Jesus. Like many other ancient theologians, Marcion did not consider the possibility that religious thought and revelation had evolved. Most Jewish and Christian theologians dealt with these matters via allegorical and symbolic interpretation. Marcion, the good businessman who focused upon the concrete, regarded such techniques as unacceptable dodges. Only texts that were explicitly figurative could be so interpreted.[34] He took the Jewish scriptures at face value and did not find them despicable.[35] If Paul tended to stress—albeit it not exclusively (cf. Rom. 9–11)—the discontinuity between old and new, nature and grace, for Marcion discontinuity was everything. This has earned him the epithet of "hyperpauline." With some support from Paul, Marcion posited a sharp divide between creation and redemption. The standard view is that Marcion posited the existence of two different gods, the just god of the Israelite scriptures, and the loving god revealed by Jesus.[36] This may overstate the matter, for, as in the Platonist tradition, it is possible to distinguish a "demiurge," the active agent in creation, from the one God.[37] What seems clear is that, whereas the Pauline tradition began with the alienation of the human race from god, Marcion began with an alien god, wholly unknown until revealed by Jesus.[38]

Marcion issued three notable works, evidently intended as a trilogy. The first, the *Antitheses*, utilized the principle of contradiction. Specifically, Jesus contradicted many of the claims of the Hebrew Bible.[39] Marcion's *Gospel* (a term he may have introduced) presented the mission and message of Jesus in a restored form, while his *Apostle* was a purified edition of the genuine letters of Paul. Marcion held that both the original gospel and the letters of Paul had been the victim of Judaizing interpolations.[40] The *Gospel* and *Apostle* constituted something like a Christian scripture, effectively superseding the Jewish Law and Prophets. Adolph von Harnack argued that the very existence of a Christian "New Testament" (rather than, for example, a Bible composed of Law, Prophets, Writings, and Good News) was due to the influence of Marcion's "canon."

His claim, developed by Hans von Campenhausen, is not without merit, even if it is somewhat exaggerated.[41] This discussion does emphasize that Marcion's Paul was a book, the author of the letters collected in his *Apostle*. No data survive about claims to have possessed oral traditions about Paul's teaching.

Although his church included the orders of bishops, presbyters, and deacons (indicating their prevalence by his time), he retained a "lay" suspicion of hierarchy and ecclesiastical authority.[42] Marcion was, at heart, more than a bit of a rebel, and he viewed his hero Paul as a rebel against the "establishment" of Jerusalem. Marcion's view of Paul is, ironically, somewhat like that of Acts, except that his Paul was harassed by Christian "Judaizers," whereas the enemies of the Lucan Paul were "Jews."

Marcion's conviction that he had grasped the center of Pauline theology led him to posit contamination in the textual tradition. Paul, as could be determined from Galatians and elsewhere, had battled with those who supported observance of Jewish practices, notably male circumcision, which served as a symbol of observance. These "Judaizers" had achieved a number of victories, in good part because of their willingness to sow deceptive tares in the pure wheat of Paul's field. On the grounds of his theological presuppositions, Marcion undertook to correct the text of the *Gospel* and the *Apostle*. In critical terms, he expunged the "false," which he characterized as that which was at variance with his presuppositions.[43]

The basis for the *Gospel* was an edition of Luke. Since for Marcion this was still an anonymous book,[44] it is not likely that Marcion associated it with a companion of Paul.[45] The claim that Marcion knew Acts but rejected it cannot be sustained.[46] Marcion, with justification from the opening verses of Galatians, objected to the plurality of gospels, a question that still troubled Irenaeus.[47] This edition of Luke may have been the Gospel used in his home community at Pontus. The question is complicated by uncertainty about whether Marcion edited a copy of canonical Luke or made use of a different, earlier edition.[48] The opening words, at any rate, are the product of editing: "In the fifteenth year of the Emperor Tiberius, Jesus came down to Capernaum."[49] Marcion removed all but the first member of the elaborate synchronism of Luke 3:1 and jumped to 4:31, deleting the ministry of the Baptizer, the baptism of Jesus, his genealogy, and the temptation narrative.[50]

For his *Apostle* Marcion utilized an extant edition of ten letters, opening with Galatians. That placement may have been Marcion's own contribution. If not, it was certainly convenient,[51] for Galatians set forth the

Paul Marcion viewed as original and characteristic. Marcion's Pauline text is a continual object of scholarly study, for behind it stood a very early edition of the corpus.[52] Tertullian sought to refute Marcion by using his opponent's text of Paul.[53] This method provides many clues to the contents. Marcion's deletions are more or less predictable. He suspected any passages that affirmed the continuity of salvation history. Romans 9, for example, was almost obliterated, and little of chs. 10–11 was retained.[54] An important principle is that one cannot demand perfect consistency of Marcion or any other editor, particularly those of ancient times, who had to work in poor light with handwritten scrolls.[55]

Adolph von Harnack summarized his appreciative study of Marcion in words that have echoed and re-echoed throughout hundreds of lecture halls: "It may be said that in the second century only one Christian—Marcion—took the trouble to understand Paul; but it must be added that he misunderstood him."[56] Harnack, it should be noted, did not claim that Paul was largely unknown throughout the second century; he asserted that he was not properly understood. The statement presumes that Paul is "properly" grasped by heirs of the Lutheran Reformation. Such assumptions no longer stand.[57] Harnack merits approval for his desire to treat with sympathy a religious leader rejected by orthodox Christianity, but one can no longer deal with Marcion by means of a footnote to Harnack.[58]

Harnack was correct in that Marcion rejected the view of Paul as essentially a teacher of righteousness. He was first and foremost a messenger of God's righteousness. His Paul was both exaggerated and limited, but Marcion did understand the apostle as a proclaimer of salvation freely offered to all. His "doctrine of justification," to use later terminology, did not visibly upset his Christian opponents, for Marcion did not have a drop of libertine blood. He ran a tight ship that included a vigorous morality that required strict celibacy and a rigorous diet and code of conduct. His followers did not attempt to evade martyrdom. Marcion built a widespread church rather than circles of followers within the "Great Church" or a patently deviant and effervescent sect.

Two major disputed matters regarding Marcion are the relationship of his system to ancient thought, philosophy in general and Gnosis in particular, and the dates of his activity. The two are related in that, if Marcion's system was created at Rome in the fourth decade of the second century, Gnostic influence is more probable. Recognizing the possibility that his thought may well have undergone development, it is very probable that he was active in Asia Minor in the 120s, possibly earlier. Both the Pastor and Polycarp, the former mainly by inference, the latter more directly, were concerned about his teachings.[59] As noted above, the 137–144 dates for his Roman ministry can be questioned.[60]

The debate about Marcion's relationship to "Gnostic" thought reveals almost as much about the debate regarding Gnosticism as it does about Marcion. The patristic tradition, represented by Irenaeus (*A.H.* 1.27.1; cf. 4.17.11), was clear: Marcion was a disciple of Cerdo, who is remembered for saying that the God of whom the Law and the Prophets spoke was not the Father of Jesus Christ, but unknown.[61] Cerdo may have provided Marcion with some notions, but heresiologists were no less fond of chains of heretical succession than of apostolic succession.[62] This assertion gains but limited credence. Kurt Rudolph, who sought to comprehend a wide range of phenomena under the rubric of Gnosis, argued that "Gnostic" thought was central to Marcion.[63] Von Harnack, who wanted to put as much distance between Marcion and Gnosticism as possible, countered that Marcion could have reached his conclusions through study of the lxx.[64]

Several features of Marcion's thought are typical of systems associated with Gnosis. Marcion was a dualist, but it is not possible to discover an underlying metaphysical dualism in his thought. Marcion's dualism may have been more dialectical than ontological, that is, a reflection of the tension between the realms of creation and redemption. Marcion was also a docetist—Christ did not have an earthly body. Once again, however, in contrast to other docetic constructions,[65] the non-earthly body of Jesus really suffered and died on the cross.[66] As previously observed, Marcion's creator cannot be attributed to Gnostic thought.[67] Marcion did not claim that humans contained a spark of the divine, a key feature of systems categorized as "Gnostic."[68] Links to contemporary philosophy have been explored without definite results.[69] In conclusion, Marcion's thought can be compared to Gnosticism and related to philosophical concepts, but in its fundamentals it was independent. Marcion was not a student of systematic thought, but it would be foolish to imagine that he had never been in contact with contemporary ideas.

Marcion's successors sought to bring more system to his theology. Among their concerns were Marcion's separation of redemption from creation and his total disavowal of the Israelite heritage and continuity within salvation history. His patristic opponents took issue, again and again, with Marcion's unknown God.[70] This was a weak point in his system, but his critics were not just exploiting a logical shortcoming. They, too, may have regretted much about "the flesh," but they were not prepared to pitch all of creation into the dustbin, and, anti-Jewish as so many of them were, they accepted the complex burden of maintaining that the God revealed in Jesus was also the God of Abraham, Isaac, and Jacob. Marcion took both too much of Paul and too little. He was old-fashioned in that he was a late representative of a radical gentile Christianity founded almost entirely upon the message of Paul. Marcion insisted upon taking his Paul neat. The most successful tool for refuting his understanding was, as F. C. Baur perceived, the book of Acts. This may not have been unintentional.[71] Marcion, together with the "Gnostics," compelled emergent orthodoxy to adopt critical methods, to refine systematic thought, and to reach for a comprehensive synthesis. This last Irenaeus was able to do without sacrificing key features of Pauline thought. Both Marcion and his rivals sought consistency. Marcion derived consistency from within Pauline thought, whereas proto-orthodox theologians achieved consistency by assimilating Paul to others. Both, of course, dealt selectively with Pauline texts, advancing those that favored their particular cause. In effect, Marcion compelled emergent catholic Christianity either to accept Paul's contribution or to exclude it. Many followed the latter path, either covertly, like Justin, or more explicitly, as in the sources of the Clementines, but the dominant majority did not. One implication of the inclusion of Paul is that his letters (and thought) had already gained a firm foothold among believers. Exclusion (setting aside the considerable merits of Paul's contribution) was not an option for the "Great Church." Marcion's contributions to catholic Christianity were therefore considerable. He forced serious reflection upon Pauline soteriology and gave considerable impetus to the formation of a collection of Christian sacred writings.

Paul among the "Gnostics"

Viewed historically from a broad phenomenological perspective, Gnosticism was a radical movement of alienation relative to factors deeply rooted within the culture of the Roman Imperial and succeeding eras. Gnosis, a more general term favored by German scholarship, can be identified as a type (or types) of deviance, a "heresy," within Judaism, Christianity, and Platonism, with related developments in Islam. Gnosticism also characterizes distinct religions. One of these was Manichaeism, now extinct, but once a missionary movement that extended from Spain to China.[72] Another, the Mandaean religion, still survives in Iraq and a diaspora.[73]

Modern discussion of "the Gnostic Problem" proceeds from the attempts to devise a definition at Messina, Italy in 1966.[74] There a distinction between gnosis and Gnosticism was formalized. "Gnosis" refers to the knowledge of divine mysteries reserved for an elite group. "Gnosticism" proper was reserved for the developed systems of the second century. Gnosticism was characterized as a dualistic, acosmic religion of salvation communicated by a heavenly redeemer, whose message is to inform all that they contain within themselves a spark of the divine. This is a typical compromise definition, one that evades the fundamental issue at stake: the origins of Gnosis.

Dissatisfied with the high level of generalization utilized in such definitions, scholars nurtured by immersion in the Nag Hammadi Library have begun to question whether "Gnosticism" is a useful term.[75] Primary texts cannot fully be synthesized with the summaries of Christian heresiologists, whose motives were not friendly and who sought to demonstrate links between and among various teachers and movements. One is left with a number of quite divergent texts. The movements characterized as "Gnostic" were mainly unregulated and speculative; they tended to revel in diversity and disdain for ecclesiastical authority. These objections are useful qualifications. They warn against introducing presuppositions based upon particular systems into discussions of texts that may not bear out those presuppositions.

For the context of the present study the model presented by Bentley Layton is valuable, provided that it is viewed as no more than a model.[76] Layton begins with a sect that called itself "Gnostics," which emerged sometime in the period c. 50 CE–c. 150. This "classic Gnosis" is characterized by a strong sectarian identity, including the use of specialized jargon, a complex myth of origins, and a baptismal ritual (or rituals).[77] Groups representing this basic type acquired different names as the movement proliferated into various sects: "Archontics," "Barbelites," and "Sethians." The last is often used generically for the movement. Philosophers of the first and second centuries liked, following the example of Plato, to express important issues in the form of narrative myth. The classic Gnostic myth deals with the problem of the existence of evil. It reads like the typical plot of a Greek romantic novel,[78] beginning with original perfection, the theft or loss of perfect, celestial material, resulting in a most imperfect world, and the ultimate recovery and reunion of the divine substance.

Excursus: Primary Sources of Gnosis

Primary sources for the study of Gnosis include both actual primary sources, written by Gnostics, most of which have been recovered in the past two centuries, and descriptions of Gnosis from its opponents, in patristic sources. The first includes:

(1) Material of a Gnostic orientation is found within the collection known as the *Corpus Hermeticum*, particularly in Tractates 1 and 13 (*Poimandres* and *Asclepius*). These have been known to scholars since the Renaissance. Christian influence[79] is absent from these originally Greek texts.[80]

(2) The Mandaean texts, first made widely known to the West in the opening decades of the twentieth century. Although late, they contain some early traditions. These too are non-Christian. They are written in an Aramaic dialect.[81]

(3) The Nag Hammadi Library (*NHL*) is a very well preserved ancient collection of codices (that is, books), buried or hidden in the fourth century and discovered in 1945, but not fully published until the late 1970s.[82] These texts are written in dialects of Coptic, the latest form of the ancient Egyptian language. All are probably translations from Greek. Within this eclectic collection are fragments of Plato and the *Corpus Hermeticum*, as well as some products of Christian Gnosis, others only slightly christianized, and a few with no taints of Christianity. The library contains thirteen volumes, about 90 per cent (1153 of 1257 pages) of which is preserved. There are fifty-one texts in total, forty-one of which were previously unknown. Ten are fragmentary, with the balance in good and sometimes excellent condition. No consensus yet exists as to how and why this body of literature was collected.

(4) In addition, there are some Coptic documents with Gnostic properties that exist apart from the Nag Hammadi Library, such as the *Pistis Sophia* and other texts mainly recovered from other Egyptian sites.

(5) Manichaean writings are found in a number of languages, including Greek, Coptic, and dialects of the further Orient. These include an autobiography of Mani in Greek, and Coptic translations of the *Kephalaia*, his principle doctrines, sermons, and a Psalter.[83]

(6) Among the major surviving refutations of Gnosis from Christian hands are, in particular, Irenaeus' *Adversus Haereses*, Hippolytus' *Refutatio Omnium Haeresium*, various works of Tertullian (c. 150– c. 225), and the *Panarion* of Epiphanius (315–403). These represent the major surviving heresiologists.

If there is one general characteristic of the treatment of Paul in Gnosis, it is concentration upon him as a theologian rather than a missionary, community organizer, or teacher of morality.[84] This quality, shared in part by Marcion (who did not ignore mission and organization), is relatively distinct in the reception of Paul between Ignatius and Irenaeus. The ordinary Christian reader of today will often attend to the eccentricity of Gnostic use of Paul. This perception is correct, but many proto-orthodox writers were equally unequal in their approach to Paul. Historically, the emergence of gnosticizing Christianity apparently blunted, in emergent proto-orthodox circles, that line of Deutero-Pauline theology interested in cosmic speculation (Colossians, Ephesians, Ignatius).[85]

Although Basilides was the first Gnostic to use as text from which proofs can be cited,[86] the most fruitful line for investigation of the Gnostic reception of Paul in a general survey like this lies in exploration of Valentinus and the movements that arose from his system.[87] Valentinus (c. 100–c. 175) appeals to historians of theology because he was one of the most brilliant and creative Christian theologians of the second century. He was the founder of a school, in the philosophical sense,[88] that produced "Western" (Italic) and "Eastern" (mainly Alexandrian) wings. The former is represented by Heracleon, Ptolemy, and others. Eastern Valentinians of the second century included a man named Mark and Theodotus. Brilliance also characterized many of these successors. Valentinus and his immediate followers regarded themselves as elite members of the "Great Church."[89] Not until the early third century—and not everywhere then—did distinctively Valentinian communities, with their own sacramental systems, emerge. This schism was in good part the result of efforts of leaders like Irenaeus to root them out.[90] The Valentinians held that Jewish and Christian writings could not be understood without resource to a secret tradition.[91] Later Valentinians claimed that their master had been instructed at Alexandria by one Theudas, a pupil of Paul. More than one party, it transpired, could play at the game of succession.[92] The proto-orthodox also held that a hermeneutical key was necessary for understanding the Hebrew Bible, but this claim that the LXX referred to the messiah Jesus through prophecy and typology was public rather than the secret possession of an elite.

Born in Egypt, Valentinus had the benefit of an education in Alexandria. This included philosophical studies in the Middle Platonic tradition.[93] While in Alexandria, Valentinus may have become a Christian. He may also have come into contact there with the teachings of Basilides.[94] At any rate, Valentinus went, like so many others, to Rome, c. 135–140. There he sought to build a synthesis between the more ebullient expressions of Christian Gnosis and the broader Christian community.[95] He developed his own form of the Gnostic myth of origins and made frequent use of "normal" Christian texts, including the Gospels of Matthew and John, 1 John, and, from the Pauline corpus, Romans, 1 and 2 Corinthians, Ephesians, Colossians, and Hebrews. In the course of time, Valentinians cite Romans, 1 and 2 Corinthians, Galatians, Ephesians, Philippians, Colossians, 1 Thessalonians, and Hebrews. They tended to ignore the Pastoral Epistles, the very texts used against them by Irenaeus and others.[96] As Pagels notes, their studies were apparently based upon an edition of the letters known in Alexandria.[97]

Valentinus' language sounds more orthodox than it probably is. This leaves him open to the charge, also leveled against Ptolemy,[98] that his true agenda was masked. This is debatable.[99] The ancient philosophical tradition distinguished between esoteric and exoteric teaching, with official priority to the private. Use of this principle allowed Gnostics and others to generate a great deal of secret teaching. Valentinus was an active and admired teacher and leader at Rome. Tertullian claims that he expected to be elected bishop.[100] Because the Valentinians saw in Gnosticism a tool for the interpretation of the Christian message, they provide useful examples for examining the reception of Paul in speculative circles.

One will rarely err (in appropriate contexts) by opening with a prayer. The first item in the *NHL* is "*A Prayer of Paul.*"[101] This short text was inscribed on the flyleaf of the first codex. It is not certainly Valentinian.[102] The attribution to Paul comes in an appended note, "A Prayer of Paul the Apostle. In peace. Holy is the Christ."[103] The prayer is framed, in the conventional fashion, by a (lost) opening address and a concluding doxology. The residue consists of petitions, the first six of which derive from predications that serve as motives, in effect, "because you are my treasure, give to me."[104] The title is something of a misnomer, for the prayer is a petition for Pauline power and authority:

> [Give] me your unregretted gifts through the child of the human being,[105] [by the] spirit, the intercessor, of [truth]. Give me authority, [I] request of you. Give me [healing] for my body, as I request [of] you through the preacher of the gospel[106] [and] redeem my luminous soul [for] ever, and my spirit. And [disclose] unto my intellect the [firstborn] of the fullness of grace.

Bestow what eyes of angels have not [seen], what ears of rulers have
not heard, what [has not] come upon the hearts of human beings...[107]

The last lines cited echo 1 Cor. 2:9. Line 12 refers to Phil. 2:9.[108] More
important than these intertextual connections is the prominence assigned
to Paul, the agent through whom the subject prays. Compare the standard
conclusion to Christian prayers: "through Jesus Christ our Lord..." The
Prayer shows that Gnostics—like others—could view Paul as a powerful,
inspiring model for theological reflection. It is also a subtle evocation of
his authority for the entire subsequent book. Paul has power that Valentinians (and others) found worthy of appropriation.

The *Gospel of Truth* (*GTr*) may well be a composition of Valentinus.[109]
This is a sermon or meditation that seeks to persuade through evocation rather than logic. The author works by association and trope rather
than through the conventional rhetorical techniques. "He [Christ] was
nailed to a tree and became fruit of the father's acquaintance"[110] This kind
of metonymy (tree = cross; trees yield fruit) would be characteristic of
patristic and later composition.[111] Shortly thereafter the text associates
Christ with the heavenly "living book": "Jesus appeared, wrapped himself in that document, was nailed to a piece of wood, and published the
father's edict upon the cross."[112] Writing of this sort is difficult for those
who require logical progression, but welcome to people who respond
happily to associative and meditative techniques. Prose poetry like this
would find a home in the liturgical prayers of the Greek Christian East.
Valentinus possessed considerable stylistic gifts in addition to his brilliant
mind.[113]

Jacqueline A. Williams studied seventy-three possible allusions to
what would become Christian scripture in the *Gospel of Truth*.[114] Williams found that 33.3 per cent of these derive from the Pauline corpus.
She also commented upon the author's presuppositions[115] and methods.[116]
Many of the latter will become dominant, including typology and allegorical interpretation. The latter was developed in Hellenistic philosophical
schools as a tool for the interpretation of myth.[117] Although Valentinus
(or the author) made use of the LXX, the *Gospel of Truth* indicates a shift
toward the utilization of Christian texts. Johannine influence is strong,
but allusions to Pauline texts are frequent. Paul does not enjoy a special
status in the *Gospel of Truth*.[118] The following table summarizes William's
findings:

Table 11. Allusions to Paul's Letters in the Gospel of Truth

Source[119]	Probable	Possible	Dubious
Romans	4	1	2
1 Corinthians	1	2	2
2 Corinthians	1	2	-
Ephesians	1	1	1
Philippians	-	3	-
Colossians	3	1	1
2 Timothy	-	1	-
Hebrews	1	3	-
Total	**11**	**14**	**6**

About half (fifteen) of the identified allusions come from the generally oft-cited Romans and 1 and 2 Corinthians. Galatians and the Thessalonian correspondence are absent. The letters with cosmological features (Colossians, Ephesians, Hebrews) are well represented (twelve allusions). The *Gospel of Truth* does not present Paul as an authority, either by name or by direct use as a proof-text; it does show a writer who is thoroughly familiar with the corpus and permeates the language of his address with Pauline phrases. This practice may also intimate that the author believed that his audience would grasp some of these allusions, that is, that they were familiar with the letters.

The Valentinians began, in so far as is known, the practice of writing commentaries upon Christian books. This practice was less an acknowledgment of their sacred, "canonical," standing than an indicator of the movement's philosophical self-understanding, since the practice of writing commentaries upon acknowledged classics, such as the *Timaeus* of Plato, was a characteristic activity of philosophers in the Roman era.[120] Ptolemy was a pupil of Valentinus and one of the founders of the Western, "Italic" branch of the Valentinian movement. He revised Valentinus' form of the myth of origins the specifics of which have been preserved by Irenaeus (*A.H.* 1.1.1–1.8.5).[121]

An exoteric philosophical letter of Ptolemy is extant in the original Greek.[122] The style of *Ptolemy to Flora* has received enthusiastic praise from that esteemed connoisseur of Greek prose, Eduard Norden.[123] Since Ptolemy undoubtedly hoped for—and received—attention from a wide audience for this composition, it is not material whether "Flora" refers to an actual person or is symbolic.[124] The major subject of this letter was the meaning and application of the Torah. This was a problem for all Christians save Marcion, since the Hebrew Bible contains contradictions and alleged improprieties and stands at occasional variance with the teachings of Jesus and the statements of Paul (and others). Most early Christians agreed, implicitly if not otherwise, that the "ritual law," that is, the cult, had been abolished.[125]

Like some other thinkers of the second century, Ptolemy has a tripartite approach to the law.[126] One division derives from God, another from Moses, the third from elders of the people. Proofs are adduced from Matt. 15:1-20 and 19:3-12.[127] From these sayings on marriage one can determine the will of God (union of man and woman), Moses' reasonable alteration of that principle, and, thirdly, changes derived from tradition. The law thus has three divisions: (1) that which is pure but imperfect, an example of which is the Decalogue, the imperfections of which had to be fulfilled by the Savior; (2) that which is contaminated with injustice, such as the *Lex talionis* (eye for an eye), which is just but incongruous with the will of God; and (3) that which is purely symbolic, that is, the "ritual law." Logic leads to the conclusion that the law cannot come from a perfect god and must therefore stem from the creator (demiurge), who, like the god of Marcion, is just—and therefore not an evil entity.

Justin, by comparison, also advocates a tripartite division: some commandments serve piety and just actions, others appertain to the mystery of Christ, and some arose because of the hardness of human hearts.[128] The difference is that Ptolemy, in typically Gnostic (and philosophical) fashion, focuses upon origins, whereas Justin is concerned with the purpose of the commandments. Ptolemy's approach may have been inspired by Jewish and Jewish-Christian traditions, probably encountered in Alexandria.[129] His method is also more "scholarly," in that it seeks to distinguish layers of tradition.

Ptolemy clearly states what would become a basic Christian principle: "Now, once the truth had been manifested, the referent of all these ordinances was changed, inasmuch as they are images and allegories."[130] The criterion is the contrast between promise and fulfillment. The method is allegorism.[131] He supports this with one allusion to Rom. 2:29 (spiritual circumcision, *PtolFlor* 5.11) and an explicit reference: "Likewise, the apostle Paul makes it clear that Passover and the Feast of Unleavened Bread were images, for he says that 'Christ, our paschal lamb, has been sacrificed' and, he says, be without leaven...by 'leaven' he means evil..." (1 Cor. 5:7)[132]

Ptolemy to Flora 6.6 builds upon the foregoing: "His (Jesus') disciples made these teachings known, and so did the apostle Paul...[*then follows a summary of Passover imagery*]... The part consisting of a law interwoven with injustice he made known by speaking of 'abolishing the law of commandments and ordinances'; and the part not interwoven with the inferior, when he says, 'the law is holy, and the commandment is holy and just and good.'"[133] The relevant citations derive from Eph. 2:15 and Rom. 7:12. This is one means for resolving apparent conflicts within the Pauline corpus. The principle is that Paul does not contradict himself. When he appears to do so, he is referring to different matters. *Ptolemy to Flora* 7.6 cites 1 Cor. 8:6, with a modification: "There is one unengendered father, from whom are all things."[134] ("Unengendered father" replaces "one God the father.")

The apostle Paul and the savior are the two authorities named by Ptolemy. He does not have to convince "Flora," who belongs to the catholic circle, of the value of Paul and his letters. Since the composition belongs to the era of Justin (c. 150), this letter is another important witness to the authority of Paul at Rome at the time of Justin. That Ptolemy would quote Paul is not surprising, for the apostle was esteemed as the chief source of Valentinian tradition,[135] but he can assume that his non-Valentinian readers also viewed Paul as an apostolic authority. Ptolemy claims that his views are part of the apostolic tradition that those of his school have received in succession (7.9). This is the first known Christian use of the view that valid tradition is authenticated by apostolic succession—that is, by a line of teachers holding and transmitting these views.[136]

Robert M. Grant holds that Ptolemy had a "hidden agenda" and that he "...is leading Flora down the garden path toward Gnostic Cosmology."[137] This is not quite fair, for Ptolemy was quite explicit about his agenda. In *PtolFlor* 7.9-10, Ptolemy states that Flora's next lesson will treat "both the first principle and the generation of these two other gods..."[138] In short, if she proves herself worthy, Flora will be eligible to learn "Gnostic Cosmology." The flowers lining the subsequent section of the garden path are clearly identified.

Although the idea that human beings might have an immortal component ("the soul") was widespread in the ancient world, the notion of a corporeal restoration ("resurrection") was either unwelcome or confusing to many. Even early Christian authors who sought to defend resurrection could confound it with immortality.[139] Misunderstanding of resurrection and its consequences is a central theme of 1 Corinthians.[140] Symbolic approaches to resurrection were characteristic of much Gnostic thought, and Paul's apparent opposition to this notion occasioned no great embarrassment to them. One reason for this was that Paul did not view the resurrection "body" as a replication of flesh and blood existence (1 Cor. 15:50),[141] but as a "spiritual body" (σῶμα πνευματικόν, 1 Cor. 15:44). In the course of the second century, proto-orthodox believers argued, not least because of their controversies with Gnostics and other dualists, for resurrection of the *flesh*.[142]

The *Treatise on the Resurrection* (*TRs*) is a Valentinian work probably of the later second century that defends this spiritual understanding of resurrection, which must be understood as a present possession of the informed believer. The author is familiar with the Middle Platonic themes incorporated into the Valentinian system, as well as with Ptolemy's form of the basic myth.[143] Formally, it represents an introductory philosophical treatise, less likely a philosophical letter,[144] addressed to one Rheginus, a seeker.

The text utilizes Pauline language. Christ "swallowed death" (*TRs* 45.14-18), that is, exchanged the corruptible for the incorruptible (1 Cor. 15:53-54). The conclusion is "So then, as the apostle said of him, 'we have suffered with him, and arisen with him, and ascended with him'" (*TRs* 45.23-27).[145] The language is (Deutero-)Pauline (cf. Rom. 8:17; Eph. 2:4-6; Col. 2:12; 3:1-3). After an analogy from the then popular "solar theology" that compares believers to rays of the sun,[146] the author states that belief in the resurrection resides in the domain of faith (*TRs* 46.3-7; cf. 1 Cor. 15:54; 2 Cor. 5:4). Paul would not disagree. *Treatise on the Resurrection* 46.14-18 propounds a creed: "For we are acquainted with the child of the human being [*Son of Man*] and have come to believe that he arose from the dead. And he is the one of whom we say, 'He became death's undoing.'"[147] With this affirmation the proto-orthodox could not quibble.

The treatise proceeds, in due course (47.1—48.18), to argue that resurrection of the flesh is undesirable, that salvation is immediate, and that resurrection is genuine (that is, not an apparition or ghost). The language evokes Colossians and conforms to Deutero-Pauline theology. At this point (48.19-32), the narrator claims that the material world lacks "reality." That statement would have offended Paul and aroused objections from the author of Colossians. After a poetic passage recalling both the "solar language" used earlier and the Pauline concept of "swallowing up" "corruption" (48.33—49.8), 49.9-25 affirms that resurrection is a present possession. This, like Col. 3:1-4, is the indicative that grounds an imperative. Resurrection is not life at ease in Zion; it requires discipline.[148]

The argument of this treatise is thoroughly Pauline and, for the most part, is no less defensible as valid exegesis than the counter claims that Paul spoke about resurrection of the flesh. Resurrection is a present possession, but the need for intellectual (and, presumably, ascetic) exercise attests to a "not yet." The author has substituted a Gnostic myth of origins for Paul's apocalyptically oriented mythology. Modern critics will disapprove, with justice, but in the second century apocalyptic mythology was often handled as a realistic description of the coming millennium and the material benefactions of heaven.[149]

Not since Colossians and Ephesians had believers made such insightful use of the Pauline corpus. Even Irenaeus conceded that Gnostics interpreted Paul intelligently.[150] The essential criterion was not exegetical method, but the different theological presuppositions. For Irenaeus, that factor was the "rule of faith," the assertions of the creed.[151] The Gnostic creed was their myth of origins, in various forms. Against this elaborate development, the proto-orthodox needed to set forth a few short words: belief in "God the Father Almighty, maker of heaven and earth." Difficulty in refuting the interpretations of the Valentinians, and others, led emergent catholicism to focus upon Paul's role in the chain of tradition, as a witness to Christ, rather than to his specific theological arguments. As a corollary of their insistence that Paul taught secretly, the Valentinians held that, just as Jesus taught mysteries in parables, so the teaching of Paul was parabolic. Such texts as Rom. 2:28-29 (e.g., *PtolFlor* 5.11) justified this method.[152] Many people of different eras (including the present) have found the idea that conventional texts contained encoded forms of great mysteries attractive. That impulse was strong in the second century, and Gnostics were among those who made use of its appeal.

The final example in this section will illuminate a pastoral and ecclesiological dimension of the Valentinian tradition: *The Interpretation of Knowledge* (NHC XI, 11-21, 35).[153] This text deals explicitly with a subject that is not without contemporary relevance: conflict over spiritual gifts. The treatise has a homiletic quality. Its final third (14:15—21:43) takes up a number of Pauline texts, 1 Corinthians, Romans (probably), Colossians, Ephesians, and Philippians, to present a synthesis of Pauline ecclesiology, focused upon the image of the body of Christ.[154] The author seeks to build up the community by an appeal to unity based upon the equality of believers with different gifts. Since the situation envisioned includes both "spiritual" and "psychic" persons, *Interpretation of Knowledge* probably stems from the middle of the second century, when Valentinians sought to remain a part of the broader church. The following extracts indicate this Pauline grounding:[155]

14.28 [After affirming that the Son] "...removed the old bond[156] of debt [against] those condemned in Adam [who] have been [brought] from death, received forgiveness for their sins and been redeemed...Christ loves [his members] with all his heart. [One who is jealous sets] his members against [one another. If] he is [not] jealous, [he will not] be removed from (the [other members]... 15.35 Does someone have a prophetic gift? Share it without hesitation... 16.18 [Now] your brother [also has his] grace... 16.24 So do not consider [him foreign] to you... 16.28 By [loving] the Head who possesses them, you also possess the one from whom it is that these outpourings of gifts exist among your brethren.

16.32 But is someone making progress in the Word? Do not be hindered by this; do not say: "Why does he speak while I do not?" for what he says is (also) yours... 17.14 eye or a [hand only, although they are] a [single] body... 17.35 For the Word is rich, generous, and kind. Here he gives away gifts to his mortals without jealousy... 18.17 [Rather] by laboring with [one another they will] work with one another, [and if] one of them [suffers, they will] suffer with him... 18.28 Do not accuse your Head because it has not appointed you as an eye but rather as a finger. And do not [be] jealous of that which has been put in the class of an eye or a hand or a foot...

Although *Interpretation of Knowledge* does not lack Valentinian jargon, much of which is utilized to reinforce the central message, the author's passion for unity in diversity indicates a sound grasp of Paul's arguments in 1 Corinthians 12–14 and elsewhere. At least one Valentinian preacher possessed pastoral insight and skill. His/her theology of the Body of Christ is Deutero-Pauline, interpreting the body image through Colossians' and Ephesians' portrait of Christ as "head of the body" (14.28; for example, Col. 1:18//Eph. 1:22), and the distribution of gifts in 1 Cor. 12:28-29 via Eph. 4:11. Spiritual gifts make community life possible. An important feature of this exposition is its demonstration that the Valentinians did not always claim that their elite, "spiritual" status justified overlooking and demeaning those with different gifts.[157] The author is quite silent on the question of ecclesiastical offices and their role. From this one might infer a survival (or revival) of the "charismatic" model against the early catholic emphasis upon structure.

From the documents surveyed above one can understand why Valentinian exegesis of Paul has attracted admiration from modern scholars. A quite different impression would arise if attention focused upon their mythological presuppositions. In part this is because the Jewish and Christian myths (e.g., Genesis) in their apocalyptic manifestation are familiar. In the second and third centuries various efforts to explicate the "great chain of being," as ultimately represented in Neo-Platonism, were part of the intellectual enterprise.

Irenaeus vigorously attacked this mythological enterprise. One would love to peruse his review of *Interpretation of Knowledge*, among other writings. The late Bishop of Lyons was one of many who benefited from Valentinian thought.[158] In ways often different from Marcion, the Valentinian interpreters of the Apostle displayed genuine insight into his thought. Tertullian's claim that Paul is "the apostle of the heretics" (*Adv. Marc.* 3.5.4) should be ranked among that author's frequent exaggerations, but his frustration indicates that rivals to emergent orthodoxy could make substantial use of the epistles in their literary productions.[159]

Before taking up Irenaeus, it is appropriate to provide a final instance of the Gnostic appropriation of Paul. The time is later, in the mid-third century, and the subject is Mani, who provides the most forthright evocation of Galatians 1 surviving from the ancient world. The source is the Manichean confession contained in the Cologne Mani Codex, *Concerning the Origin of His Body* 64.1-19. This is the only primary text of the Manichean religion extant in Greek. Elements of it go back to Mani, himself:

[We acknowledge] that he has received it neither from mortals, nor from the reading of books, just as our father (Mani) himself says in the letter which he sent to Edessa. For he says thus: "The truth and the secrets which I speak about—and the laying on of hands which is in my possession—not from mortals have I received it nor from fleshly creatures, not even from studies in the Scriptures. But when [my] most blessed [father], who called me into his grace...[160]

Compare Gal. 1:1, 11-12:

1 Paul an apostle—sent neither by human commission nor from human authorities, but through Jesus Christ and God the Father, who raised him from the dead—*11* For I want you to know, brothers and sisters, that the gospel that was proclaimed by me is not of human origin; *12* for I did not receive it from a human source, nor was I taught it, but I received it through a revelation of Jesus Christ.[161]

For Mani, in all probability, and for his followers certainly, the opening verses of Galatians were a ringing declaration of the revelation of a new religion, in words of such power that they deserved the most sincere form of flattery. Marcion was not unique in his appropriation of the opening of Paul's epistle to the Galatians. That sense of newness has never ceased to thrill believers, including Matthew, who endorsed it no less than the old. Matthew pressed for compromise and synthesis. The early Christian master of these activities was the pastor of a community in second-century France.

Irenaeus of Lyons

The Refutation and Overthrow of the Gnosis Falsely So Called, vulgarly known as *Adversus Haereses* (*Against Heresies*), is the earliest surviving work of orthodox anti-heretical writing.[162] Irenaeus marks a transition from "proto-orthodoxy" to early orthodox Christianity. Although considered a relic of by-gone days in the late fourth century, leading to the nearly complete disappearance of the Greek original texts of his writings, today Irenaeus is widely admired in Christian circles. Born c. 135–140, in Asia Minor, and reared as a Christian, he claims to have sat at the feet of Polycarp.[163] At some point Irenaeus evidently relocated to Lyons, a major city in Gaul, where he was made a presbyter.[164] An embassy to Rome fortunately removed him from the persecution that fell upon that city in 177. Irenaeus succeeded the martyred bishop Pothinus. It is probable that he was no longer alive at the close of the century. Irenaeus' literary output is to be viewed in the light of his episcopal task. Ecclesial unity and peace were major objects of his ministry. He writes as a pastor and a teacher, not as a Christian philosopher like Justin (whose works he uses and with whom he may have studied[165]). When the Bishop of Rome, Victor, moved to take action against the Asian Christians in Rome who celebrated Easter in accordance with the Jewish Calendar (the "Quartodeciman Controversy"), Irenaeus intervened on the Easterners' behalf.[166] He also pleaded for sympathy with the Montanist "new prophecy."[167]

Against Heresies, most of which survives only in a rather wooden Latin translation,[168] is the larger of his two extant works.[169] The first of its five books traces the origins of Gnosis from Simon Magus. Book 2 consists of rational arguments against Gnostic systems. Books 3 and 4 take up the traditions about the apostles and Jesus, respectively, demonstrating the continuity and congruity of their teachings, as well as the unity of Israelite and Christian scripture. Book 5 contributed to the later neglect of Irenaeus, for it promotes a millenarian eschatology that later theologians found crude. Irenaeus' principal target is the western Valentinian system of Ptolemy. His tools are rhetoric and reason, as well as claims for support from scripture and the succession of right-thinking teachers. Irenaeus' model is therefore derived from a philosophical principle: we belong to the valid line of leaders and the fundamental texts uphold our views. His polemic is rather conventional, valuable because of his citation of primary sources.

Irenaeus' positive theology proceeds from a tradition first developed in outline by the author of Luke and Acts: the continuity of salvation history. This continuity extends to other spheres, including those between nature and grace, redemption and creation. In constructing his arguments, Irenaeus was obviously motivated by Marcion and the Gnostics, who stressed discontinuity between creation and redemption and a severe rupture between grace and nature. His theology is similar to the biblical writers, in particular Paul, in that his thought is expressed in dynamic rather than essentialist terms—that is, Irenaeus speaks of what God has done and does rather than what God is or concerning the nature of the divine. The elements of Pauline (and Johannine) thought that he does not develop were those that had made these works so useful for the Gnostics.

In opposition to rival cosmologies, Irenaeus sets forth a doctrine of *creatio ex nihilo* (creation out of nothing).[170] He not only asserts that the creator and the redeemer are one and the same God, but also develops a theological scheme that correlates the two functions. God is in charge of the world. A major difference from Paul is that for Irenaeus, God redeems nature by nature and through nature. Irenaeus presents, against the Gnostics, who viewed the world in negative terms, a world-affirming "natural theology." The unity Irenaeus sees in creation and redemption leads him toward an evolutionary model. Creation is a process. God put Adam and Eve in the garden with the intention that they would mature. They were not perfect, but they were capable of growth. The "Fall" was an obstacle to growth rather than a catastrophic decline from perfection. God had taken it into account.[171] Mistakes can lead to learning. In God's plan, Christ is the ground where creation and redemption meet. A key soteriological term is "recapitulation." This is a development of the Deutero-Pauline view of Christ as the leader of a new humanity (cf. Eph. 1:10). The goal of both creation and redemption is to gather all things in Christ. "Recapitulation" is the process through which Satan is defeated. In the incarnation, God became human to make humans divine.[172] This theology is a response to Gnostic speculation that is probably partly indebted to it, but, in sum, Irenaeus' theology is like Paul's in that its basis is the originally apocalyptic concept of God's ultimate victory.

Irenaeus' anthropology can be summarized in the phrase "image of God." The genuine image is the son, in and by whom humans are created and whose image humans bear.[173] He understood this concept dynamically. Like some other early (and later) Christians,[174] Irenaeus viewed creation as a process. The divine image is the object of our growth and development. For Irenaeus, the initial victory was not in the resurrection, but in the incarnation, by which the image of God was united with that of human beings.

Irenaeus presents the essence of what would become the Christian Bible: four Gospels, Acts, a full Pauline corpus and other apostolic writings, together with the "Old Testament." These are foundational texts, the final and irrevocable deposit of apostolic doctrine. They do not constitute a "canon," but they are Christian scriptures. Irenaeus produced a culminating great synthesis of various strands within early Christianity, including most of those found within the later New Testament (Gospels, Paul) and the Apologists. (The major exception is the Egyptian theology represented by such persons as Clement of Alexandria. This was apparently suspect to Irenaeus, in so far as he may have known it.[175]) This compelling synthesis of various trends gave formal place to a rational understanding of scripture and tradition, as well as voice to an explicitly "orthodox" interpretation of John and Paul.

The Bishop of Lyons is the first explicit witness to Acts, and the first person known to link Acts with the Third Gospel, the author of which he names as Luke, an "inseparable companion" of Paul.[176] This concept was central for Irenaeus, since, if the author of Luke—an edition of which constituted Marcion's *Gospel*—also wrote Acts, which portrays Paul as at one with Peter and James, Marcion's thesis could not stand, for Acts portrays Paul as a colleague of the Jerusalem leaders rather than their opponent. The Valentinian claim to possess secret traditions handed down from Paul was refuted by Acts, which made no mention of a Pauline accomplice by the name of Theudas and excluded esoteric instruction.[177]

Irenaeus' comprehensiveness is apparent in his argument for a plurality of gospels. In distinction from his contemporary Tatian, who still sought to produce one grand gospel, Irenaeus argues that there must be four.[178] Like modern interpreters, he views the differences among them as a gift, rather than a deficit. The four-gospel collection quickly developed into a four-gospel canon. Irenaeus probably did not invent this collection, but he made a positive argument for it.

From the perspective of his positions pertaining to authority and tradition, Irenaeus represents the latest levels of the Pauline texts included within the Christian scripture, that is, Acts and the Pastorals. His Paul is sometimes regarded as Acts plus the Pastor, but Irenaeus' citations reveal a different picture. According to the calculations of Harvey,[179] Irenaeus cited the LXX 629 times and Christian scripture 1,065 times. Of these citations, 324, or about 30 percent, come from the *Corpus Paulinum* (Romans = 84, 1 Corinthians = 102, 2 Corinthians = 18, Galatians = 27, Ephesians = 37, Philippians = 13, Colossians= 18, 1 Thessalonians = 2, 2 Thessalonians = 9, the Pastoral Epistles = 14).[180] A quarter of his citations and allusions are to Romans (which he knew in the fourteen-chapter edition); nearly 30 percent come from 1 Corinthians.

The contrast with earlier writers is remarkable. Irenaeus propounds a collection of authoritative Christian writings in which John and Paul have prominent places. The pillars of his edifice are law, prophets, gospels, and apostles. Irenaeus had close ties to communities in both Asia and at Rome (where the church was then still predominantly Greek-speaking, although Latin was gaining ground). Although he may have sat at the feet of Justin (above), Irenaeus made extensive and prominent use of John, Acts, and the Pauline epistles, none of which Justin acknowledged. Justin knew Paul's letters and may have known the Fourth Gospel, but he betrays no specific knowledge of Acts.[181] Irenaeus' views of sacred and inspired[182] writings therefore probably came from the East rather than from Rome.[183]

Until c. 1975, the tendency in Protestant circles was to judge Irenaeus' view of Paul as one-sided, at best. Reference to Johannes Werner was often deemed sufficient[184] to exclude him from the circle of serious Pauline exegetes. The judgment of Wilhelm Bousset (c. 1920) is characteristic.[185] Bousset admired Irenaeus, but viewed his Paulinism as a mere semblance, for he brought creation and redemption together. "[Irenaeus]...is the first representative of that exegetically tempered Paulinism which since then has been so widely dominant."[186] He claimed, not without insight, that Irenaeus stood on the ground of the apologists in his distinction from Paul and Gnosticism. Bousset also credited the Bishop of Lyons with delivering Paul from the Gnostics. The price was high. Marcion, the Gnostics, and Irenaeus all offered one-sided views of Paul, and the dullest of these was Irenaeus.

Behind such views stood the assumption that the Lutheran and Reformed interpretation of Paul was *not* one-sided. In the last decades of the twentieth century this assumption collapsed, leading to a quest for the "center" of Pauline theology. From that point of view, Irenaeus would be characterized as working from/identifying a "center" other than justification by faith. If, to take the approach of one Reformed theologian, Ralph P. Martin,[187] "reconciliation" were regarded as the Pauline center, one could trace a trajectory from 2 Corinthians through Colossians, Ephesians, and Ignatius to Irenaeus. Not all constructions of Paul are equal, but all deserve evaluation upon their merits and consistency. Toward the close of the last century, the way lay open for a re-examination of the Paulinism of Irenaeus. Just as one cannot understand the context of such Lutheran slogans as *sola scriptura* (by Scripture alone) without awareness of an ecclesiological context in which church authorities claimed to be the arbiters of tradition and thus interpretation, so one cannot evaluate Irenaeus apart from his circumstances.[188] Valentinian anthropology and cosmology were primary issues,[189] and his appropriation of Paul reflects those concerns.

Irenaeus' understanding of Pauline "natural theology" (Rom. 1:18-32) is quite similar to that of Luke.[190] In support of his view of the divine origin of the world he cites the addresses of Paul at Lystra and Athens (Acts 14:14-18; 17:22-31).[191] The texts utilized to demonstrate the unity of God and the identity of "Jesus" and "Christ" (e.g., 1 Cor. 8:4-6), may seem strained, but they are no less valid for all that.[192] In the same manner Irenaeus makes use of the "plain sense" of statements about Jesus' birth, death, and resurrection to argue that Jesus was a genuine human being. Paul provides Irenaeus with strong evidence for his claims that God is one, Christ is one, and that the course of human history follows divine will. The last point was the most complex and difficult. Gnosis, like polytheism, had ready explanations for the presence of misfortune. Those who can write off history and nature need not wrestle unduly with the problem of evil.

The problem of the continuity between the covenants was an issue used by Marcion to drive a wedge between law and grace and gave Gnostics a tool for discovering layers in the Hebrew Bible.[193] Paul's developmental model (Torah as pedagogue) was music to Irenaeus' ears. He was also able to make good use of Paul's discussion of Abraham in Galatians, treating the patriarch as both type and source of the church.[194] Irenaeus discovers another source of continuity by describing the prophets as "members" of Christ's body.[195]

Recapitulation serves the same purpose. Based upon Col. 1:15-20 and Eph. 1:10, Irenaeus views Christ as the one who gathers up all human experience and in whom the invisible God and God's visible creation coincide:

> There is therefore, as I have pointed out, one God the Father, and one Christ Jesus, who came by means of the whole dispensational arrangements [connected with Him], and gathered together all things in Himself. But in every respect, too, He is man, the formation of God; and thus He took up man into Himself, the invisible becoming visible, the incomprehensible being made comprehensible, the impassible becoming capable of suffering, and the Word being made man, thus summing up all things in Himself: so that as in super-celestial, spiritual, and invisible things, the Word of God is supreme, so also in things visible and corporeal He might possess the supremacy, and, taking to Himself the pre-eminence, as well as constituting Himself Head of the Church, He might draw all things to Himself at the proper time.[196]

His fondness for paradox and the collision of opposites evokes Ignatius. Paul also used such language (e.g., 2 Cor. 6:3-10); for Irenaeus it serves ontological ends. He could nonetheless have claimed the apostle as a model. Paul's comparison of Christ and Adam was for Irenaeus solid justification of his method.[197] He develops Rom. 5:19 in the following manner:

> For as by one man's disobedience sin entered, and death obtained [a place] through sin; so also by the obedience of one man, righteousness having been introduced, shall cause life to fructify in those persons who in times past were dead. And as the protoplast himself Adam, had his substance from untilled and as yet virgin soil ("for God had not yet sent rain, and man had not tilled the ground"), and was formed by the hand of God, that is, by the Word of God, for "all things were made by Him," [John 1:3] and the Lord took dust from the earth and formed man; so

did He who is the Word, recapitulating Adam in Himself, rightly receive a birth, enabling Him to gather up Adam [into Himself], from Mary, who was as yet a virgin. If, then, the first Adam had a man for his father, and was born of human seed, it were reasonable to say that the second Adam was begotten of Joseph. But if the former was taken from the dust, and God was his Maker, it was incumbent that the latter also, making a recapitulation in Himself, should be formed as man by God, to have an analogy with the former as respects His origin. Why, then, did not God again take dust, but wrought so that the formation should be made of Mary? It was that there might not be another formation called into being, nor any other which should [require to] be saved, but that the very same formation should be summed up [in Christ as had existed in Adam], the analogy having been preserved.[198]

On the Pauline basis of Christ as second Adam (1 Cor. 15:22, 45), Irenaeus could present Mary as a new Eve. New creation does not contradict the old; it fulfills it. Analogy and typology[199] were his weapons against discontinuity. Paul would not have followed the same path, but Irenaeus' method does not betray his Pauline authority. History "repeats itself" and thus demonstrates its unity, continuity, and divine impulse. Paul was somewhat less inclined toward the celebration of continuity, but in Irenaeus' circumstances such emphases were required, and he could always appeal to Romans 9–11, for example.[200] It is difficult to argue that an author who devoted so much attention to Romans and Galatians was interested in Paul only for defensive purposes.

As can be seen from the preceding citation, Irenaeus blended Pauline and Johannine theology. If Paul is the single standard, one can, like Bousset, accuse him of adulterating the apostle. If one is seeking to create a theological synthesis, the practice is commendable. One basis for this is the identification by both John and Paul of Christ with Divine Wisdom.[201] Irenaeus read both John and Paul as strongly incarnational, in staunch opposition to docetic interpretations.[202] By so doing, he established a norm in orthodox Christian theology that remains to the present day. Galatians 4:4-6 was central to this argument. Irenaeus cites that passage thirteen times in *A.H.* 3–4.[203] Romans was, however, Irenaeus' principal source for Pauline theology. He utilized Romans 4–8 to argue for soteriological continuity and for the ultimate restoration of creation in its original glory.[204]

The Bishop of Lyons had no particular interest in Paul's biography or portrait. Paul was first and foremost a theologian. As an apostle he taught what the other apostles taught. Individuality and particularity were neither sought nor found. He could, nonetheless, speak of "the apostle," and use "Peter and Paul" as a synecdoche for all the apostles.[205] Although Acts makes some important contributions to Irenaeus' understanding of Pauline theology, particularly in the realm of natural theology, his exposition of the epistles focuses upon major letters—Romans, 1 Corinthians, and Galatians. These are viewed through a Deutero-Pauline lens (Colossians, Ephesians, with some contributions from the Pastoral Epistles, where useful), but Irenaeus does not stop to ask whether his arguments from Romans, for example, are consonant with Acts.[206] His neglect of justification by faith[207] is in full conformity with most second-century interpreters of Paul other than Marcion.[208] Irenaeus' view of grace was synthetic and complex, but in the end he arrived at a place not far from Paul. Deliverance is the result of God's love for the human race God had created.

For Irenaeus, Paul was one important authority for explication of the Christian message. His letters were arguably the most important, certainly the most prominent, of these authorities. The view of Irenaeus as primarily a domesticator and leveler of the apostle to the gentiles is not sound. Irenaeus was, in important ways, a Pauline theologian. Like every other interpreter of Paul, he brought to his construction presuppositions and goals that differed from those of the historical Paul, but these do not automatically amount to a betrayal. Irenaeus should be ranked among the creative and insightful exponents of Pauline theology. He provided stimulus for the subsequent Greek interpretation of Paul. Irenaeus did not "rescue" Paul from the clutches of the heretics, but he did show one path to a positive theological use of the apostle's words. Subsequent to Irenaeus, Paul was not only a teacher of morals and missionary of the gospel; he was also, and more importantly, a foundational theologian for Christian orthodoxy.

An additional contribution, important in its time but not always beneficial thereafter, was his linkage of the epistles to Luke and Acts. In so far as evidence is available, Irenaeus created the unity of Luke and Acts.[209] He appealed to Acts to legitimize Paul, but, as the foregoing has argued, the heart of his interpretation of Paul's theology derives from the epistles. Irenaeus invoked Acts to place Paul among the apostles and used the apostle's letters in the development of his own theology.

The unifying theme of this diverse chapter is a description of how Paul became a theologian in the formal sense. The *altum silentium* (deep silence) about Paul in proto-orthodox circles can be characterized as silence about his theology.[210] As in the case of critical methods, attention to Pauline theology (with the qualified exception of Ignatius) in the second century arose first in circles ultimately deemed heretical. Marcion and various Gnostics, notably the Valentinians, regarded Paul as a source of and stimulus toward speculative, systematic theology. Two generations later Irenaeus, utilizing various intellectual and rhetorical methods, shaped the portrait of Paul as an orthodox theologian within the framework of emerging Christian Bible, creed, and methodology

CONCLUSION

THE OPERATING PRINCIPLE of this book has been that disappointment with some interpretations of Paul, although quite valid, does not constitute proper evaluation. A major contribution of historical criticism is the demand that assessments take place with attention to particular historical environments and with recognition of the priority of questions that motivated various theologians rather than with the questions generated by the concerns of our own era and cultures.[1] Before assigning old answers an "A" or an "F," it is necessary to seek the consistency and relevance of those answers within the generating contexts. Then the possibility of more general assessments acquire legitimacy.

Paul's ethical exhortations were soundly grounded upon his apocalyptically oriented thought, but often their content appears to be prudent moral sense. He did not set out ethical recommendations that always found a firm basis in his theology. Various groups and individuals received aspects of Paul's rich inheritance and erected upon them more consistent systems of their own.[2] This is a common fate of original thinkers. A leading danger of the post-Pauline era was the adoption of a "sectarian" morality (whether puritanical or permissive) that devalued the church as a body of the political sort and could quickly give Christianity a bad reputation.

The post-Pauline texts surveyed in the foregoing chapters confront readers with the frail nature of the Pauline inheritance and the problems its transmission to subsequent generations raised. Paul had not attempted to present an immutable gospel carved upon stone tablets. His writings were occasional, models for dealing theologically with pastoral problems rather than catchall solutions. These letters were often obscure, especially to those who were not part of the generating discussion. They were provocative and stimulating documents with a proclivity to increase speculation through their incentive to reflection. The communities Paul had organized were vulnerable. It can be argued that this vulnerability was not completely unintentional.

A major task of those who wished to promulgate the authority of Paul as a means for helping to stabilize the communities he had formed was to fashion from his diverse correspondence a book. Paul may have played a role in the project of sharing his letters with others, but it should be noted that he was quite aware of their occasional character and that such sharing could make him appear opportunistic and inconsistent. Romans was his final and most irenic missive, and 1 Corinthians had a great deal to offer. These two letters enjoyed independent circulation, albeit not without some modification. Romans could be read as a kind of summary of Paul's thought. Both Romans and Ephesians look back upon Paul's letters as givens. Ephesians had the advantage of explicit generality.

The evidence suggests that by the close of the first century, a substantial collection of probably ten letters had begun to circulate. Paul thereafter became not a writer of letters that may be found here and there, but the source of a book. The apostle known to subsequent generations was to be found in this book. Ephesus was the most probable site for the first edition of the collected letters. Various editions existed, including one of seven letters to seven churches, the very form of which intimated universality. Preparation of this book was motivated by that very challenge: to fashion the particular and occasional epistles of Paul into a universal message. That task motivated editors to "departicularize" the letters, through changes in their addresses and removal of extraneous material, including data that was pertinent to the immediate situation but of limited use to later readers.

Since historical and chronological concerns were of limited use, amalgamations of multiple letters into one, as well as the decision to omit much administrative and personal material, should occasion no surprise. The issuance of a book also facilitated the inclusion of pseudonymous letters, since these texts were first encountered by most as elements of the collection, rather than as items that suddenly popped up in the communities to which they were allegedly directed. The author of Luke and Acts knew Paul's letters as a group, probably as a collection. The existence of a collection as such is demonstrated in the period c. 110–125 by Marcion, who utilized an existing edition, and by the Pastoral Epistles, a small collection inspired by the larger one, of which it would eventually form a part.

Whatever one thought of Paul, his technique of utilizing letters as a means for community-building and management was eminently successful. Some wrote letters in Paul's name. Ardent admirers, such as Ignatius and Polycarp, as well as less ardent admirers, including the author of *1 Clement*, imitated his practice. First Peter does not mention Paul, but does seek the authority of his network and his literary technique. The author of James was no unqualified admirer of the apostle to the gentiles, whom he criticizes through the medium of a universal letter. Others continued the practice, which still survives in the pastoral letters of bishops (and other ecclesial leaders) to their communities.

Paul used letters both to deal with communities that he could not then visit and also to help build relations among communities. A primary instrument and goal of this effort to link groups of believers was his collection for Jerusalem. For Paul, the idea of a single united church bound together by intercommunication was somewhat inchoate, but it quickly caught on. By the close of the first century, *1 Clement* attests to the interests of believers at Rome in the experiences of their coreligionists in Corinth. This practice is almost without parallel in ancient religion and absolutely unparalleled in quantity. Ancient cults in various localities were essentially independent, unless linked to a mother site, from which they did not expect to receive much in the way of direction. Paul helped to create[3] and provided a medium for what would become the catholic church, local communities connected to one another by a variety of means, including spiritual and material assistance.[4]

A fundamental feature of the post-mortem Paul was the transformation of his concept of "righteousness." As conflicts about Torah-observance receded into the past, Pauline statements about "law" and "works" appeared dangerously antinomian, a denial of any ethical norms. "Righteousness" regained—better, retained—its general meaning of "doing the right thing." Those who did not reject his language as ethically irresponsible and conducive to lawlessness presented him as a "teacher of righteousness," a guide to and proponent of the ethical life. This understanding dominated the understanding of Paul in proto-orthodox circles for a good half (c. 120–c. 180) of the second century.

That century gave birth to several contrasting narrative portraits of Paul. The canonical Acts integrated the missionary known from the epistles with the Jerusalem leadership and presented a more conventional biographical portrait. Paul was a great leader, an astonishing miracle worker, and a powerful speaker. The latter two are at considerable variance from what is found in the letters (especially 2 Corinthians). The Paul of Acts cannot be an apostle. Luke accepted a definition of that title that excluded his hero.[5] It is difficult to imagine that he did this willingly. In Acts Paul does not write letters. Since he has no problems with his communities—all his problems come from outsiders—he does not need to compose epistles. Still, Luke thought it best to overlook this practice, although he knew and used those very letters. The Paul of Acts was a great success. From the late second century to the mid-nineteenth—and still today for some—Acts provides the framework for interpreting those sometimes perplexing epistles. Not all of those in the second century endorsed Acts or its Paul. Two who did not issued narratives of their own: the *Acts of Paul* and some of the sources of the Clementines.

The *Acts of Paul* are a primary witness for an apocalyptic Paul, who took a strong stand against the standards and values of this inferior and transitory age. A major resource for this portrait was certain elements of 1 Corinthians. The Paul of these Acts is a true disciple of the Jesus embodied in the sayings tradition (Q), a homeless, itinerant prophet who denounced the social, political, and economic establishment. A merit of this approach was its recognition that the historical Paul did not find in this world a true home. The *Acts of Paul* achieved consistency by working out this principle in social terms. In some ways, this was the most successful synthesis of the teachings of Jesus and those of Paul. One contemporary standard for which the *Acts of Paul* had no use was the subordination of women. Paul knew and accepted women missionaries and leaders. The trajectory of Deutero-Pauline letters reveals increasing restriction and subjugation of female believers, culminating in the Pastoral Epistles. These two texts frame the historical Paul's views of women, each more extreme than the original, although the non-canonical *Acts of Paul* are closer to the historical figure than are the Pastoral Epistles in some important ways. Otherwise, *Acts of Paul* was relatively orthodox, a position strengthened by the subsequent interpolation of *3 Corinthians*.

So-called "Jewish Christianity," a movement prominent in East Syria, can be defined, in part, through its rejection of Paul. Vicious hatred of the apostle is prominent in some of the sources later incorporated into the Clementine *Recognitions* and *Homilies*, books preserved because of their stories about Peter and his links with Clement of Rome. This hatred was essentially historical, recollection of an ancient enemy. These texts identified Paul with Simon Magus and produced a slanderous account of his conversion. Although the Clementines were open to gentiles and rejected the Israelite cult, they clung to animosity for the apostle to the gentiles. Behind this tradition lay disappointment for the failure of the Jewish mission in Judea, a failure attributed, not without some justice, to Paul's labors in the Diaspora and his rejection of Torah as a prerequisite for membership in the communities of those who viewed Christ as a heavenly Lord. Jewish Christianity appears to have manifested little vitality after the third century. The future belonged to Pauline, urban Christianity, as the contents and shape of the New Testament indicates. Not all early Christian literature was composed in Greek, but no text in another language found a place in the Christian canon, and that which did survive is almost entirely urban in its setting.[6]

Apart from the essentially unique position of Luke, who could not designate Paul as an apostle, the tradition shows a clear development. In the Deutero-Pauline letters Paul is essentially the only apostle, at least the only one deserving specific mention. Marcion, who otherwise had little in common with the Pastoral Epistles, shared this understanding. In the course of time, Paul is gradually integrated into the apostolic circle, perhaps as one instructed by them, but essentially as one of the company. A separate tendency, already apparent in *1 Clement*, is to pair him with Peter at the head of the apostolic college. By the end of antiquity, this portrait of the "heavenly twins" had begun to erode the separate stories of the two. Peter and Paul together served the ancient capital of Rome in its claims for ecclesiastical prominence.

By the middle of the second century, it is clear that there were several Pauls competing for Christian attention or rejection. One is the Paul of the Gnostic interpreters, who seized upon his dialectic of spirit and flesh in a strongly dualistic manner, opposing inferior matter to the higher level of spirit. This was congenial to many and found root in that suspicion of the human body that became characteristic of early Christianity in general. Their interpretation built upon tendencies visible in Colossians and Ephesians, with roots in 1 Corinthians. One may with justice claim that these interpreters read Paul from their presuppositions—and also claim that so does everyone else. The merit of their approach was the achievement of a consistent reading. They also continued the Pauline tradition of speculative theology, which, like Gnosis, had its origin and roots in the Jewish wisdom and apocalyptic traditions.

In that same period some ignored Paul, although malice is rarely certain, and the shadow cast by Marcion had a limited influence. Those such as Papias, who preferred to limit authoritative status to "the prophets" (Israelite scripture) and "the Lord" (sayings of/writings about Jesus) were not able to maintain their position. For whatever reason, authoritative Christian texts would include an apostolic component. In the end, this would include a full edition of Paul's letters, including Hebrews, and a number of works associated with other apostles.

The synthesis that became normative, however, is that of the canonical Acts, which follow a line reflected in different ways by Romans, Ephesians, and the Pastoral Epistles. Paul is a universal apostle and a heroic figure. Building upon thoughts such as those expressed in Romans, as well as Ephesians, the Paul of Acts stands in continuity with the tradition and faith of Israel, which has reached its fullest and most proper expression in the message of Jesus. Jesus and Paul are wandering teachers and social critics, but their message is milder and less antithetical to all of the roots of the social order. Paul, like Luke's Jesus, is more a reformer than a revolutionary.[7]

The Pastoral Epistles present a similar teacher, although one even less critical of the social order. In them the conventional ethical advice of Paul lacks any critical edges. Neither Acts nor the Pastoral Epistles place any emphasis upon the dialectical elements of Pauline theology, its method of discourse and persuasion, its recognition of different views. The Pastoral Epistles try to carve out a sphere of Christian existence within the world. They seek to make possible a kind of social life that will be Christian without scandalizing the pagans, but yet will not sell out to them. The Pastorals aim at the existence of an enduring body that will "whip the world into shape." From the apocalyptic perspective, the world is transitory and provisional. Grace will soon eradicate nature. In a Gnostic worldview nature is both evil and unreal. Only the divine world of grace really deserves the label of "existent." Emerging catholic Christianity sought to convert the world through the modification of nature by grace.

For Marcion dialectic took a central place. He relegated conventional apocalyptic to the periphery of worldly, Jewish expectation, while the opposition between old and new, creation and redemption, law and gospel, determines all. Marcion grasped much of the heart of Paul's thought, but he attempted to create a consistent system and thus expunged some of Paul's major paradoxes and dilemmas, notably the relation of Christ to

Israel, the tension between now and not yet, and the view of God as creator in the face of imperfect, sin-scarred creation.

Each of these movements gave primary emphasis to aspects of Paul's own thought and work, usually at the expense of other aspects. None of this is surprising. Such is, as noted, the typical fate of important thinkers, whose systems are both incomplete and possibly a bit inconsistent. Each successor focused upon particular dimensions of Paul's thought. So have other and later thinkers, including Augustine and Luther, not to mention more recent theologians. The battle for the center of Pauline theology has a long, fruitful but unfinished history.

By the end of the second century, the dominant line will appear, in the writings of Irenaeus, who is an even more comprehensive synthesizer than was the author of Luke and Acts. Like Luke—and Marcion and the author of the *Acts of Paul*—Irenaeus provides a synthesis of the messages of Jesus and of the apostles, including Paul, but his scope is much broader, including four gospels, thirteen/fourteen Pauline epistles, and other apostolic writings. His synthesis endured, more or less, until at least the nineteenth century. That is, by any standards, a pretty good run—and Irenaeus continues to spark theological thought and admiration.

The End: In the Beginning

That the letters of Paul have somehow found their way into the Christian Bible is rather remarkable. People have found them useful, as well as frustrating. It is far simpler either to denounce Paul as a villain or to set him up as a pillar of right thinking than it is to become entangled with the questions Paul raises and his methods for answering them. In his life and work we catch glimpses of some of the varieties of early Christianity, whose members were already engaged in conflict and in pursuit of varied goals. No other known early Christian leader so skillfully brought so many voices, including scripture and tradition, old and knew, as well as conventional moral insight applied with a shrewd political sense, into the conversation. Paul was a master of polyphony. In him and his heritage the emergence of Christianity as a religion of gentiles distinct from that Judaism which was still rather diverse ("Judaisms") becomes apparent. Paul was a major impetus to this manifestation of two distinct world religions, but was himself a Jew. Therein the tension is symbolized.

Paul was a complex, difficult, and often exasperating individual. When viewed as a writer of letters, Paul is a pastor continually engaged in seeking to get his converts to keep learning what it means to be the people of God, the Church. Why is this so? Why did Paul not pursue some other angle? His heritage proclaimed the one God of the one people. In attempting to create this sense of belonging to the community of God's own, Paul took up the language of apocalyptic to describe the decisive turning point of the ages, as well as vocabulary, concepts, and structures from a vast repertory, including politics, mystery religions, wisdom and philosophical schools, and popular teaching, but even after one has established the relevance of each possible background, one has not nailed this apostle down. All of these sets and tools have been transposed into a different key or translated into a different language by fundamental presuppositions.

Paul saw the action of God, typified for him in the event we call his conversion, as a demand to re-evaluate everything—at least in theory. God's act is a declaration of divine freedom, freedom to be loyal to commitments made by God to the human race. Paul does not construe creation as a limit imposed upon God's being, nor as a concatenation of forces and powers to be appeased. Because old creation has been invaded by newness, it stands as opportunity rather than obstacle. All of the dualistic, anti-creation, interpretations of Paul have missed this basic understanding, misled, in part, by Paul's rather down to earth recognition of earthly limits and dangers.

Because of this positive attitude toward creation as transformable, Paul thus portrays salvation in the rather old-fashioned and dangerous (to many Greco-Roman ears) language of freedom, rather than, for example, as afterlife or as relief for troubled souls, as good feeling, or as enrichment of existence, certainly as anything other than the smooth road to riches, power, and success. Paul did understand that God's freedom was larger than Paul was. Because of this conviction, he continually urged his converts to think, to work out their own issues in accordance with the grace they had received, even when he knows what they will probably do and the difficulties that will almost certainly ensue. He, too, had difficulties, and he did not labor strenuously to conceal them.

Subsequent believers took up his challenge. The various roads taken may, as noted, produce some disappointment. A number of his successors produced solo works or concertos in response to, or in place of, his symphonies. To shift the metaphor, the tree that he planted generated many branches and more than a few hybrids.[8] What might he say of the various answers and programs based upon his work? Much would appall him, pardon the pun, not in the least the use of his name as an instrument of persecution and oppression—but he, too, I should like to believe, would be pleased that people continued, and continue, to engage the issues that drove his passion.

The Pauline tree is an often untidy growth, but the miracle is that it sprang from what was, in the perspective of c. 60 CE, a mustard seed. Paul was executed in the wake of the failure of his effort to find grounds for unity among followers of Christ. The most important conclusion to take from this review of the Pauline legacy is its multiple successes. He was too important to be ignored. The legacy of Paul is not a list of dismal appreciations and misunderstandings, but of inspiration to generate fresh understandings of his message for the service of the church and the world. Paul deserves honor as the principal founder of catholic Christianity, a body in, but not of, for, not against, the world, possessing both the flexibility needed to survive successive historical upheavals and the fallibility required to demand both modesty and recognition of failure. An old and popular cliché designates Paul as "the inventor of Christianity," the anti-alchemist who transformed the golden teachings of Jesus into the leaden dross of escapist myth. Historians of religion find this shallow. In so far, however, as the growing Christian church was urban, Greek-speaking, and more oriented to the ethics of Paul and Paulinism than to the challenges of Jesus, the claim has value. Paul may, with considerable justice, be called the foundational figure of what would become normative Christianity.

This book has presented some reasons to explain why traditions about Paul were collected, edited, and published. The parallels with traditions about Jesus are patent. Similar motives underlie each. The Gospels seek to legitimate Jesus as Messiah, Son of God, and Savior. Stories about and letters of Paul seek to legitimate the gentile mission, to answer the difficult question: Why, if Jesus is God's fulfillment of the promises to Abraham and the Covenants, has most of Israel declined the offer? The Christian riposte was to appeal to a universalism they found in the promises to Abraham. Universal claims demanded a universal and inclusive organization. Such an organization the Christian church developed, largely through working out the plans and ideas of Paul, which, of course, they understood as the plan of God.

There are a number of ways in which the formation and proliferation of traditions about Jesus and Paul are similar. In both cases, followers set out to preserve the heritage by producing texts from oral and written traditions. The process included the amalgamation of different genres, the editing of multiple texts into one, experiments with different sorts of editions, and the production of "apocrypha."[9] Universalism was another interest. In this matter Paul had a head start, as it were, through his explicitly gentile and ecumenical mission, but followers took pains to make his occasional letters to specific communities applicable to believers everywhere. Matthew, John, Luke (and the composer of Mark 16:9-20) seek to establish the worldwide, inclusive character of the Jesus movement. Universalism is not simply a missionary ideal. It serves also to make the particular Galilean and Judean teachings of Jesus and the occasional instructions of Paul to particular communities general.[10] Paul came to have an advantage that Jesus lacked: a sinful past that in itself exemplified the benefits of conversion. He was a figure in whom gentile converts could find identification as well as inspiration. Both Jesus and Paul gathered disciples or followers to whom they delivered their message and over whom they exercised spiritual and pastoral care. For both Jesus and Paul, heroic suffering came to play a decisive role. The gospels that achieved normative status among mainstream believers were those based upon the "creedal" shape introduced by Mark. What validated Jesus' message and delivered his followers was not the specific content of his ethical teaching, nor his great deeds, but the offering of his own life on the cross. In the course of time, Paul's suffering not only acquires romantic hues; it also comes to have redemptive significance. The bringer of salvation is also a savior. It need not be said that a rather full repertory of saving deeds, exorcisms, healings, and resurrections, accompanied that emphasis.

Scholars do not doubt that traditions about Jesus came into the written forms now available in the second and third generations. We do not call this "Deutero-Jesusism," although during the past two centuries there has been no lack of allegations that the tradition has suffered corruption. So also in the case of Paul most of the extant material, whether narrative or epistolary, legendary, pseudonymous, edited or collected, is the result of efforts to keep Paul and the faith he proclaimed alive. The followers of Paul cannot be accused of utter betrayal simply because they attempted to make his message catholic. There is a line, however unsteady and occasionally dotted, between Paul's letters to Corinth in the 50s and the first ecumenical council of Christian bishops that met at Nicea in 325—and all subsequent councils, synods, conventions, and assemblies. This line is a bit less apparent than the linkage between Paul's letters and the pastoral letters of bishops today, but it can be traced.

A major contrast between the traditions about Jesus and those about Paul is that the Jesus tradition is intensely anti-urban, while Paul is more or less always associated with cities. The large and important city of Sepphoris, but three miles from Nazareth, is never mentioned in the Gospels. In the parallel to the oracles against the nations (Isa. 14:13-15), Jesus denounces these "cities": Chorazin, Bethsaida, and Capernaum (Luke 10:13-15)! The one large city in the Jesus tradition is Jerusalem, a wicked place.[11] Christianity long remained a religion of the cities, an "urban phenomenon," as reflected in the terms later used for the unconverted: "pagans" (people who live in the country; cf. "heathen," those out in the heather). Paul was not the pioneer of this urban mission, but he was its most successful agent.

Paul gave his life, in the end, to the pursuit of unity. The emergent catholic church was due, in some part, to his vision. The theological problem was resolved through the claim, already promulgated in the book of Acts, that all of the leaders, including Peter, Paul, and James, taught the same thing and enjoyed a nearly perfect harmony. Scholars can deconstruct and explode this hypothesis with the tip of a learned finger, to be sure, but the *function* of this perspective is important. Unity among believers has been an ever present and always elusive goal from the earliest times. All early Christians agreed that unity did not mean complete uniformity; problems arose in the identification of those matters in which agreement, let alone uniformity, was paramount. In this discussion Paul has always been a, if not the, pivotal figure, the apostle who died in an attempt to achieve some kind of unity. The paradox is that it is no less true that Paul has often been the apostle of disunity. He was complex; the complexity of his legacy is no more than a fitting tribute.

Appendix: A Pauline Family Tree

N O T E : No diagram of this type can begin to comprehend the complexity of the situation. The "left-wing" gradient reflects (usually hostile) attitudes toward Judaism, dualism, gnosis, and radical asceticism. The right gradient indicates stances in the direction of "bourgeois ethics," justification by faith, and traditional apocalypticism. Documents may be "right-wing" in some regards, leftish in others. Ephesians and Ignatius are examples—and note Revelation! A better approach would portray a number of "trajectories" intersecting at varied points, but this diagram may nevertheless provide helpful orientation to early understandings of Paul.

Date (approx.)	"Left" (hyper Paul)	"Center"	"Right"	Anti-Pau[l]
180	Clement of Alexandria			
170		Irenaeus		
		Acts of Peter		
160				
	Opponents of Dionysius of Corinth;	Dionysius of Corinth		Sources of Clementi[ne]
			3 Corinthians	
150	Valentinians;			
	Acts of Paul;			2 Peter
140	*De Resurrectione*			
			Polycarp of Smyrna	
130	Marcion		1 and 2 Timothy, Titus	
120	"pre-Marcionites"			
		Ignatius of Antioch		
110			Luke and Acts	Matthew
			1 Clement	Revelatio[n]
100				
	Corinthian rebels (Revelation!)			
90				
		Ephesians	1 Peter	James
80		Hebrews		2 Thessal[onians]
70	Opponents of 2 Thessalonians			
60	Mark	Colossians		
55		Romans Philemon		
50		2 Corinthians Philippians Galatians 1 Corinthians 1 Thessalonians		

Comments on the Pauline Family Tree

Acts of Paul. One of the five major "apocryphal acts of the apostles," centering upon Paul's mission, apparently from conversion to martyrdom at Rome. Around two-thirds of the work survives. The most famous portion focuses upon Thecla, a young woman of Iconium.

Acts of Peter. One of the five major "apocryphal acts of the apostles." The surviving portions center in Rome, where Peter defeats Simon "the Magician" (*magus*) and is martyred under Nero.

First Clement. A letter written by the Church at Rome to that at Corinth, c. 100, criticizing the latter's removal of duly appointed leaders.

Clement of Alexandria. Clement of Alexandria was a Christian theologian (c. 200). Well-educated, he was a practitioner of "allegorical" interpretation.

Colossians. This letter is apparently the earliest surviving product of a "Pauline school."

Third Corinthians. A Pauline pseudepigraph that came to be incorporated in the *Acts of Paul.* The letter refutes Gnostic teaching.

Corinthian Rebels. The Corinthian rebels were those opposed in *1 Clement.* Some scholars attribute to them particular theological ideas.

De Resurrectione. "*On the Resurrection*" is a gnostic work of the mid-second century that makes use of Pauline letters.

Dionysius. Dionysius was the bishop of Corinth, c. 160–175. He wrote a number of important letters to other churches and persons. His *opponents* included radical Paulinists.

Ephesians. A product of the Pauline school, Ephesians was probably written at Ephesus. Colossians is a major source.

Gnosis, Gnosticism. A highly dualistic religion or religious orientation that influenced many late antique systems of thought, including Christianity. Most Gnostics relate the creation of matter to evil.

Hebrews. A treatise, with some epistolary features that reflects affinities with as well as tensions with paulinism.

Ignatius. Ignatius was the bishop of Antioch, executed in Rome c. 130. He knew of traditions like those found in the Gospels of Matthew and John and referred to Paul's letters in his own.

Irenaeus. Bishop of Lyons in France c. 180, Irenaeus wrote several books, including a five volume critique of teachers regarded as false (*Against Heresies*). Irenaeus produced a major synthesis.

James. A letter found in the New Testament, linked to the brother of Jesus, James/Jacob. James is hostile to some forms of Paulinism.

Luke/Acts. Two anonymous books now found in the New Testament. The first is one of the "Synoptic Gospels" (Matthew and Mark are the others). The second tells the story of the growth of gentile Christianity. These works may have been written at Ephesus, perhaps c. 100.

Marcion. A Christian theologian who came to Rome. Marcion maintained that Christian writings had been contaminated by pro-Jewish believers. He produced his own sacred text, a gospel (based upon Luke) and an Apostle (ten letters of Paul). Marcion strongly distinguished the God of Israel from the savior revealed in Christ.

Mark. The earliest canonical Gospel. Mark appears to reflect radical pauline ideas, in part.

Matthew. A Synoptic Gospel, c. 90, that is apparently inimical to pauline Christianity. It may emanate from western Syria.

Pastorals. First and Second Timothy and Titus are a short collection of letters written in Paul's name by a later follower.

First Peter. A New Testament letter attributed to Peter that derives from Asia Minor or, perhaps, from Rome. First Peter reflects pauline method and thought.

Second Peter. A New Testament letter attributed to Peter. This is quite late, probably from the early second half of the second century. The author views Paul as something of a problem.

Polycarp. The bishop of Smyrna, in Asia Minor, martyred c. 155, Polycarp made use of Paul (and 1 John) in his surviving letters.

Pre-Marcionites. A hypothetical group or groups of radical paulinists who did not make much use of Jewish scripture and revered the apostle's heritage.

Pseudo-Clementines. The "Pseudo-Clementine" writings (*Homilies* and *Recognitions*) use the framework of a novel to present a particular form of Christianity, often called "Judeo-Christianity." Peter is the hero, Paul the (falsely named or anonymous) villain. These survive only in later editions.

Revelation. An apocalypse written by a Christian prophet John c. 90. This text addresses the pauline orbit (cities of Asia Minor) and uses letters, but is quite distinct in viewpoint from Luke–Acts and Paul.

Second Thessalonians. A post-pauline letter that imitates 1 Thessalonians and asserts a strongly apocalyptic theology. Quite unlike Colossians and Ephesians. The opponents appear to have been paulinists.

Valentinians. Valentinus was a mid-second-century Christian who developed one of the most enduring Gnostic interpretations of Christianity.

ABBREVIATIONS

AB	Anchor Bible
ABD	*The Anchor Bible Dictionary*, ed. David Noel Freedman; 6 vols.; New York: Doubleday, 1992. *ABD on CD-ROM*. Version 2.0c., 1995, 1996.
ABRL	The Anchor Bible Reference Library
ACNT	Augsburg Commentary on the New Testament
AAndr.	*Acts of Andrew*
ABarn.	*Acts of Barnabas*
AJn	*Acts of John*
APet.	*Acts of Peter*
APhil.	*Acts of Philip*
APl	*Acts of Paul*
ApocPl	*Apocalypse of Paul*
AThom.	*Acts of Thomas*
ACW	Ancient Christian Writers
ANF	Ante-Nicene Fathers, eds. Alexander Roberts and James Donaldson.
ANRW	*Aufstieg und Niedergang der römischen Welt,* ed. Hildegard Temporini and Wolfgang Haase
Aristides	
Apol.	*Apology*
AThANTBS	Abhandlungen zur Theologie des Alten und Neuen Testaments
ATLA	American Theological Library Association Biblical Series
ATR	*Anglican Theological Review*
Barn.	*Epistle of Barnabas*
BBET	Beiträge zur biblischen Exegese und Theologie
BDAG	Walter Bauer, *A Greek-English Lexicon of the New Testament and Other Early Christian Literature*, ed. William F. Arndt, F. Wilbur Gingrich; 3rd ed. rev. by Frederick W. Danker; Chicago: University of Chicago Press, 2000.
BETL	Bibliotheca Ephemeridum Theologicarum Lovaniensium
BHT	Beiträge zur historischen Theologie
BIFCS	*The Book of Acts in Its First Century Setting*, 5 vols., ed. Bruce W. Winter. Grand Rapids: Eerdmans, 1993–96.
Bib	*Biblica*

BIS	Biblical Interpretation Series
BJRL	*Bulletin of the John Rylands Library*
BJS	Brown Judaic Studies
BK	Bibel und Kirche
BR	*Biblical Research*
BTB	*Biblical Theology Bulletin*
BZ	*Biblische Zeitschrift*
BZNW	Beihefte zur ZNW, Supplements to ZNW
c.	circa, approximately
CBQ	*Catholic Biblical Quarterly*
CBQMS	Catholic Biblical Quarterly Monograph Series
CCSA	Corpus Christianorum, Series Apocryphorum
CCSL	Corpus Christianorum, Series latina
CD	Cairo (Genizah) text of the Damascus Document
CE	Common era
ch.	Chapter
CHJ	*Cambridge History of Judaism*
Cicero	
Ad Att.	Letters to Atticus
1, 2 Clem.	*First, Second Epistle of Clement*
Clement of Alexandria	
Paed.	*Paedagogus*
Protrep.	*Protrepticus*
Strom.	*Stromata*
Corp. Herm.	*Corpus Hermeticum*
CSEL	Corpus Scriptorum Ecclesiastorum Latinorum
DAC	*Dictionary of the Apostolic Church*
DBI	*Dictionary of Biblical Imagery*
DDD	*Dictionary of Deities and Demons in the Bible*, ed. Karel van der Toorn et al.; 2nd rev. ed.; Leiden: Brill; Grand Rapids, Mich.: Eerdmans, 1999.
Did.	Didache
Dio of Prusa	
Or.	Oration
Diogn.	*Epistle to Diognetus*
DPL	*Dictionary of Paul and His Letters*, ed. G. F. Hawthorne, R. P. Martin, and Daniel G. Reid. Downers Grove, IL: Intervarsity, 1993.
EB	Études bibliques
ed(s).	editor, edition or edited by
EKK	Evangelisch-Katholischer Kommentar zum Neuen Testament
Ep.	*Epistle*
Epictetus	
Diss.	*Discourses*
Epiphanius	
Pan.	*Panarion, Medicine Chest against the Heresies*
ERE	*Encyclopedia of Religion and Ethics*
esp.	especially
et al.	at alii, and others
EThL	*Ephemerides theologicae Lovanienses*

EThR	*Études théologiques et religieuses*
Eusebius	
H.E.	*Ecclesiastical History*
Prep. Ev.	*Preparation for the Gospel*
EvTh	*Evangelical Theology*
Exp.	*Expositor*
ExpTim	*Expository Times*
FilolNT	*Filologia Neotestamentaria*
frg(s).	fragment(s)
FRLANT	Forschungen zur Religion und Literatur des Alten und Neuen Testaments
FS	Festschrift
GBS	Guides to Biblical Scholarship
Gos. Jas.	*Gospel of James*
Gos. Pet.	*Gospel of Peter*
HDR	Harvard Dissertations in Religion
Hermas	*The Shepherd of Hermas*
Man.	*Mandates*
Sim.	*Similitudes*
Vis.	*Visions*
Hippolytus	
Ref.	*Refutatio Omnium Haeresium, Refutation of all Heresies*
HNT	Handbuch zum Neuen Testament
HTKNT	Herders theologischer Kommentar zum Neuen Testament
HTR	*Harvard Theological Review*
HUT	Hermeneutische Untersuchungen zur Theologie
ibid.	ibidem, in the same place
ICC	International Critical Commentary
IDB	*Interpreter's Dictionary of the Bible*
Idem	the same, the same as previously mentioned
Ignatius	
Eph.	Letter to the Ephesians
Magn.	Letter to the Magnesians
Phld.	Letter to the Philadelphians
Polyc.	Letter to Polycarp
Rom.	Letter to the Romans
Smyrn.	Letter to the Smyrneans
Trall.	Letter to the Trallians
Int.	*Interpretation*
Irenaeus	
A. H.	*Against the Heresies*
IRT	*Issues in Religion and Theology*
JAAR	*Journal of the American Academy of Religion*
JAC	*Jahrbuch für Antike und Christentum*
JBL	*Journal of Biblical Literature*
JECS	*Journal of Early Christian Studies*
JEH	*Journal of Ecclesiastical History*
JFSR	*Journal for the Feminist Study of Religion*
JHC	*Journal of Higher Criticism*

Josephus	
Ant.	*Antiquities of the Jews*
Ap.	*Against Apion*
Bell.	*The Jewish War*
Vit.	*Life*
JQR	Jewish Quarterly Review
JSNT	Journal for the Study of the New Testament
JSNTSS	Journal for the Study of the New Testament Supplement Series
JTS	*Journal of Theological Studies*
Justin	Justin Martyr
1, 2 Apol.	*First, Second Apology*
Dial.	*Dialogue with Trypho*
Epit.	
KAV	Kommentare zum Apostolischen Väter
Lampe	*Patristic Greek Lexicon*, ed. G.W.H. Lampe. Oxford, 1961.
LCC	Library of Christian Classics
LCL	Loeb Classical Library
LD	Lectio divina
LEC	Library of Early Christianity
lit.	literally
LNTS	Library of New Testament Studies
LSJ	Henry George Liddell, Robert Scott, and Henry Stuart Jones, Greek-English Lexicon; 9th ed.; Oxford: Clarendon, 1940; reprinted 1966.
LTQ	*Lexington Theological Quarterly*
LXX	The Septuagint
m.	*Mishna tractate*
Mart. Perp.	*Martyrdom of Perpetua*
Mart. Pol.	*Martyrdom of Polycarp*
MT	Masoretic Text
NAC	New American Commentary
NCB	New Century Bible
NHC	Nag Hammadi Codex
NICNT	New International Commentary on the New Testament
NPF	Nicene and Post-Nicene Fathers
NovT	*Novum Testamentum*
NovTSup	Novum Testament Supplements
NRSV	New Revised Standard Version
N.S.	New Series
NTApoc	*New Testament Apocrypha*, ed. Wilhelm Schneemelcher; 2 vols.; rev. ed.; Cambridge, UK: James Clarke; Louisville: Westminster John Knox, 1991, 1992.
NTM	New Testament Message
NTOA	Novum Testamentum et Orbis Antiquus
NTS	*New Testament Studies*
OBO	Orbis Biblicus et Orientalis
OBT	Overtures to Biblical Theology
Od. Sol.	*Odes of Solomon*

Origen
C. Cels.	*Against Celsus*
Comm. in Ioh.	Commentary on John
Hom. in Jer.	Homilies on Jeremiah
OTP	James H. Charlesworth, ed., *Old Testament Pseudepigrapha*
par(r).	parallel(s)
PerspRelStud	*Perspectives in Religious Studies*
PE	The Pastoral Epistles (1-2 Timothy, Titus
PG	Migne, Patrologia Graeca

Pliny
Ep.	Letters

Plutarch
PNF	*Post-Nicene Fathers*

Polycarp
Phil.	*Letter to the Philippians*
Ps. Clem.	Pseudo Clementine
Hom.	*Homilies*
Rec.	*Recognitions*
PTS	Patristische Texte und Studien
QD	Quaestiones Disputatae
RAC	Reallexikon für Antike und Christentum
RB	*Revue biblique*
RSPhTh	*Revue des sciences philosophiques et théologiques*
RSR	*Religious Studies Review*
RThPh	*Revue de théologie et philosophie*
SacPag	Sacra Pagina
SAAA	Studies on the Apocryphal Acts of the Apostles
SANT	Studien zum Alten und Neuen Testament
SBL	Society of Biblical Literature
SBLDS	SBL Dissertation Series
SBLEJL	SBL Early Judaism and Its Literature
SBLMS	SBL Monograph Series
SBLSBS	SBL Sources for Biblical Study
SBLSP	SBL Seminar Papers
SBLSS	SBL Semeia Studies
SBLSymS	SBL Symposium Series
SBLTT	SBL Texts and Translations
SBLWGRW	SBL Writings of the Greco-Roman World
SBS	Stuttgarter Bibelstudien
SBT	Studies in Biblical Theology
SC	Sources chrétiennnes. Paris: Cerf: 1943–
SCHNT	Studia ad Corpus Hellenisticum Novi Testamenti
SciEsp	*Science et Esprit*
SEÅ	*Svensk exegetisk årsbok*
SecCent	*Second Century*
Sem	*Semeia*
SNTSMS	Studiorum Novi Testamenti Societas Monograph Series
ST	*Studia Theologica*
StudDoc	Studies and Documents
StNT	Studien zum Neuen Testament

StudNTUmwelt	*Studien zum Neuen Testament und seiner Umwelt*
SUNT	Studien zur Umwelt des Neuen Testament
Syb. Or.	*Sybilline Oracles*
Tacitus	
Ann.	*Annals of Imperial Rome*
TDNT	*Theological Dictionary of the New Testamen,* ed. G. Kittel and G. Friedrich; trans. and ed. Geoffrey W. Bromiley; 10 vols.; Grand Rapids, MI: 1964–1976.
Tertullian	
Adv. Marc.	*Against Marcion*
Adv. Val.	*Against Valentinus*
Apol.	*Apology*
De Bapt.	*On Baptism*
De res. carn.	*On the Resurrection of the Flesh*
TextsS	Texts and Studies
Theophilus	
Autolyc.	*To Autolycus*
ThQ	*Theologische Quartalschrift*
TRE	*Theologische Realenzyklopadie.* Ed. G. Krause and G. Müller, Berlin, 1977–
ThRu	*Theologische Rundschau*
trans.	translator, translation
TRev	*Theologische Revue*
TSAJ	Texte und Studien zum antiken Judentum/Texts and Studies in Ancient Judaism
TU	Texte und Untersuchungen zur Geschichte der altchristlichen Literatur
TynBul	*Tyndale Bulletin*
VC	*Vigiliae Christianae*
v. l.	*varia lectio,* variant reading
VT	*Vetus Testamentum*
WMANT	Wissenschaftliche Monographien zum Alten und Neuen Testament
WUNT	Wissenschaftliche Untersuchungen zum Neuen Testament
ZBK	Zürcher Bibelkommentare
ZNW	*Zeitschrift für die neutestamentliche Wissenschaft*
ZWTh	*Zeitschrift für Wissenschaftliche Theologie*

Bibliography

Aageson, James W. "The Pastoral Epistles and the *Acts of Paul*: A Multiplex Approach to Authority in Paul's Legacy." *LTQ* 40 (2005): 237–48.

_____. *Paul, the Pastoral Epistles, and the Early Church*. Peabody, Mass.: Hendrickson, 2008.

Abbott, T. K. *Ephesians and Colossians*. ICC. Edinburgh: T. & T. Clark, n.d.

Aejmelaeus, Lars. *Die Rezeption der Paulusbriefe in der Miletrede*. Helsinki: Suomalienen Tiedeakatemia, 1987.

Agrell, Goran. *Work, Toil and Sustenance: An Examination of the View of Work in the New Testament*. Lund: Verbum Hakan Ohlssons, 1976.

Aland, Barbara. "Marcion/Marcioniten." *TRE* 22 (1992): 89–101.

_____. "Marcion—Versuch einer neuen Interpretation." *ZTK* 70 (1973): 420–47.

_____. "Sünde und Erlösung bei Marcion und die Konsequenz für die sogennante beiden Götter Marcions." In May and Greschat, eds., *Marcion*, 147–58.

Aland, Kurt. "Die Enstehung des Corpus Paulinum." In *Neutestamentliche Entwürfe*, 302–50. Munich: Kaiser, 1979.

_____. "Der Schluss und die Ursprüngliche Gestalt des Römerbriefes." In *Neutestamentliche Entwürfe*, 284–301. Munich: Kaiser, 1979.

_____. *Synopsis Quattuor Evangeliorum*. Stuttgart: Württembergische Bibelanstalt, 1964.

Aleith, Eva. *Paulusverständnis in der alten Kirche*. BZNW 18. Berlin: Töpelmann, 1937.

Anderson, C. P. "The Epistles to the Hebrews and the Pauline Letter Collection." *HTR* 59 (1966): 429–38.

_____. "Hebrews among the Letters of Paul." *Studies in Religion* 5 (1975–76): 258–66.

Andriessen, P. "The Authorship of the Epistula ad Diognetum." *VC* 1 (1947): 129–36.

Anger, Rudolph. *Ueber den Laodicenerbrief: Eine biblisch-kritische Untersuchung*. Leipzig: Gebhardt & Reisland, 1843.

Ascough, Richard S. *The Formation of Pauline Churches*. New York: Paulist, 1998.

_____. "On Becoming an Angel: Rival Baptismal Theologies at Colossae." In *Religious Propaganda and Missionary Competition in the New Testament World*, edited by L. Bormann et al., 481–98. FS Dieter Georgi. NovTSup 74. Leiden: Brill, 1994.

_____, ed. *Nag Hammadi Codex I*. 2 vols. Nag Hammadi Studies 22–23. Leiden: Brill, 1985.

Attridge, Harold W. *The Epistle to the Hebrews*. Edited by Helmut Koester. Hermeneia. Philadelphia: Fortress Press, 1989.

Auwers, J. M., and H. J. de Jonge, eds. *The Biblical Canons*. BETL 153. Leuven: Peeters, 2003.

Baasland, Ernst. "Der 2. Klemensbrief und frühchristliche Rhetorik: 'Die erste christliche Predigt' im Lichte der neueren Forschung." *ANRW* II.27.1 (1993): 78–157.

Babcock, William S., ed. *Paul and the Legacies of Paul*. Dallas: Southern Methodist University Press, 1990.

Bakke, Odd Magne. *"Concord and Peace."* WUNT 143. Tübingen: Mohr Siebeck, 2001.

Balás, David L. "Marcion Revisited: A 'Post-Harnack' Perspective." In *Texts and Testaments: Critical Essays on the Bible and Early Church Fathers*, edited by W. E. March, 95–108. San Antonio: Trinity University Press, 1980.

_____. "The Use and Interpretation of Paul in Irenaeus' Five Books *Adversus Haereses*. *SecCent* 9 (1992): 27–39.

Balch, David. *Let Wives Be Submissive: The Domestic Code in 1 Peter*. SBLMS 26. Chico, Calif.: Scholars, 1981.

Barlow, C. W. *Epistolae Senecae ad Paulum et Pauli ad Senecam quae vocantur*. Papers and Monographs of the American Academy in Rome 10. Rome: American Academy, 1938.

Barnard, Leslie W. "The Epistle of Barnabas and Its Contemporary Setting." *ANRW* II.27.1 (1993): 159–207.

_____. *Justin Martyr: His Life and Thought*. Cambridge: Cambridge University Press, 1967.

Barnes, Timothy D. "The Date of Ignatius." *ExpTim* 120 (2009): 119–30.

_____. *Tertullian: A Historical and Literary Study*. Oxford: Clarendon, 1971.

Barnett, Albert E. *Paul Becomes a Literary Influence*. Chicago: University of Chicago Press, 1941.

Barr, David L. *New Testament Story: An Introduction*. 2nd ed. Belmont, Calif.: Wadsworth, 1995.

Barrett, Charles K. *Acts*. Vol. 2. ICC. Edinburgh: T. & T. Clark, 1998.

_____. "Acts and the Pauline Corpus." *ExpTim* 88 (1976–77): 2–5.

_____. *New Testament Essays*. London: SPCK, 1972.

_____. "Pauline Controversies in the Post-Pauline Period." *NTS* 20 (1973–74): 229–45.

Barth, C. *Die Interpretation des Neuen Testaments in der valentinianischen Gnosis.* TU 37/3. Leipzig: Hinrichs, 1911.

Barton, J. "Marcion Revisited." In *The Canon Debate*, edited by L. M. McDonald and J. A. Sanders, 295–320. Peabody, Mass.: Hendrickson, 2002.

Bassler, Jouette M. "Limits and Differentiation: The Calculus of Widows in 1 Timothy 5:3-16." In Levine, ed., *Feminist Companion*, 122–46.

_____. "Peace in All Ways: Theology in the Thessalonian Letters. A Response to R. Jewett, E. Krentz, and E. Richard." In Bassler, ed., *Pauline Theology*, 1:71–85.

_____. "The Widow's Tale: A Fresh Look at 1 Tim. 5:3-16." *JBL* 103 (1984): 23–41.

_____, ed. *Pauline Theology.* Vol. 1, *Thessalonians, Philippians, Galatians, Philemon.* Minneapolis: Fortress Press, 1991.

Bauckham, Richard. "2 Peter: An Account of Research." *ANRW* II.25.5 (1988): 3713–52.

_____. "The Acts of Paul as a Sequel to Acts." In Winter and Clarke, eds., *The Book of Acts in Its First Century Setting*, 1:105–52.

_____. "The *Acts of Paul*: Replacement of Acts or Sequel to Acts?" *Semeia* 80 (1997): 159–68.

_____. "Pseudo-Apostolic Letters." *JBL* 107 (1986): 469–94.

Bauer, Walter. "Accounts." In Schneemelcher, ed., *New Testament Apocrypha*, 2:35–74.

_____. *Orthodoxy and Heresy in Earliest Christianity.* Translated and edited by Robert A. Kraft and Gerhard Krodel. Philadelphia: Fortress Press, 1971.

Bauer, Walter, and Henning Paulsen. *Die Briefe des Ignatius von Antiochia und der Polykarperbrief.* HNT 18. Tübingen: Mohr/Siebeck, 1985.

Baur, Ferdinand Christian. *Ausgewählte Werke.* 5 vols. Stuttgart: Fromman, 1963–75.

Beard, Mary. *The Roman Triumph.* Cambridge, Mass.: Harvard University Press, 2007.

Beavis, Mary Ann. "'If Anyone Will Not Work, Let Them Not Eat': 2 Thessalonians 3.10 and the Social Support of Women." In Levine, ed., *Feminist Companion*, 29–36.

Becker, Eve-Marie. "Marcion und die Korintherbrief nach Tertullian, Adversus Marcionem V." In May and Geschrat, eds., *Marcion*, 95–109.

Beker, J. Christiaan. *Heirs of Paul: Paul's Legacy in the New Testament and in the Church Today.* Minneapolis: Fortress Press, 1991.

Berger, Klaus. "Apostelbrief und Apostolische Rede: Zum Formular frühchristlicher Briefe." *ZNW* 64 (1974): 190–231.

Berry, Paul. *Correspondence between Paul and Seneca.* New York: Mellen, 1999.

Best, Ernest. "Recipients and Title of the Letter to the Ephesians: Why and When the Designation 'Ephesians'?" *ANRW* 2.25.4 (1987): 3247–79.

_____. "Who Used Whom? The Relationship of Ephesians and Colossians." *NTS* 43 (1997): 72–96.

Betz, Hans Dieter. *2 Corinthians 8 and 9.* Hermeneia. Philadelphia: Fortress Press, 1985.

_____. "2 Cor. 6:14—7:1: An Anti-Pauline Fragment?" *JBL* 92 (1972): 88–108.

Bianchi, Ugo, ed. *The Origins of Gnosticism: The Colloquium of Messina.* Studies in the History of Religions. 2nd ed. Leiden: Brill, 1970.

Bieler, Ludwig. ΘΕΙΟΣ ΑΝΗΡ: *Das Bild des "Göttlichen Menschen" in Spätantike und Früchristentum.* 2 vols. Darmstadt: Wissenschaftliche Buchgesellschaft, 1967. Original 1935–36.

Bienert, Wolfgang A. "Marcion und der Antijudäismus." In May and Greschat, eds., *Marcion,* 191–205.

_____. "The Picture of an Apostle in Early Christian Tradition." In Schneemelcher, *New Testament Apocrypha,* 2:5–25.

Beyschlag, Karlmann. *Clemens Romanus und der Frühkatholizismus.* BHT 35. Tübingen: Mohr/Siebeck, 1966.

Biblia Patristica I. *Des origins à Clément d'Alexandrie et Tertullien. Centre d'analyse et de documentation patristiques.* Paris: Éditions du center national de la recherché scientifique, 1975.

Bingham, D. Jeffrey. "Irenaeus Reads Romans 8: Resurrection and Renovation." In Gaca and Welborn, eds., *Romans,* 114–32.

Blackman, E. C. *Marcion and His Influence.* London: SPCK, 1948.

Blassi, Anthony J. *Making Charisma: The Social Construction of Paul's Public Image.* New Brunswick: Transaction, 1991.

_____. "Which Paul?" In Babcock, ed., *Paul,* 45–54.

Boccioline Palagi, Laura. *Il carteggio apocrifo di Seneca e San Paolo.* Accademia Toscana di scienze lettere La Colombaria 46. Florence: Olschki, 1978.

_____. *Epistolario apocrifo di Seneca e san Paolo.* Biblioteca Patristica. Florence: Nardini, 1985.

de Boer, Martinus C. "Images of Paul in the Post-Apostolic Period." *CBQ* 42 (1980): 359–80.

Boismard, Marc-Émile. "Paul's Letter to the Laodiceans." In Porter, ed., *The Pauline Canon,* 45–57.

Bonner, Gerald. "The Scillitan Saints and the Pauline Epistles." *JEH* 7 (1956): 141–46.

Borgen, Peder. *Philo, John and Paul: New Perspectives on Judaism and Early Christianity.* BJS 131. Atlanta: Scholars, 1987.

Bornkamm, Gunther. "Der Philipperbrief als paulinische Briefsammlung." In van Unnik, ed., *Neotestamentica et Patristica,* 192–202.

_____. "Die Vorgeschichte des sogenannten Zweiten Korintherbriefes." In *Geschichte und Glaube,* 162–94. Gesammelte Aufsätze IV. Munich: Kaiser, 1971.

Bousset, Wilhelm. *Kyrios Christos: A History of the Belief in Christ from the Beginnings of Christianity to Irenaeus.* Translated by John Steely. Nashville: Abingdon, 1970.

Bovon, François. "Le Saint-Esprit, l'Église et les relations humaines selon Actes 20,36—21,16." In *Les Actes des Apôtres: Traditions, redaction, théolgies*, edited by Jacob Kremer, 339–58. BETL 43. Leuven: Leuven University Press, 1979.

———. "The Synoptic Gospels and the Non-Canonical Acts of the Apostles." *HTR* 81 (1988): 19–36.

Bovon, F., and P. Geoltrain, eds. *Écrits apocryphes chrétiens 1*. Paris: Gallimard, 1997.

Bowe, Barbara E. *A Church in Crisis*. HDR 23. Minneapolis: Fortress Press, 1988.

Brändle, R. *Die Ethik der "Schrift and Diognet": Eine Wiederaufnahme paulinischer und johanneischer Theologie am Ausgang des zweiten Jahrhunderts*. AThANT 64. Zurich: Theologischer, 1975.

Bremmer, Jan N., ed. *The Apocryphal Acts of Paul and Thecla*. SAAA 2. Kampen: Kok Pharos, 1996.

——— *The Apocryphal Acts of Peter: Magic, Miracles and Gnosticism*. SAAA 3. Leuven: Peeters, 1998.

Brennecke, H.-C. "Die Anfänge einer Paulusverehrung." In *Biographie und Persönlichkeit des Paulus*, edited by E.-M. Becker and P. Pilhofer, 295–305. WUNT 187. Tubingen, 2005.

Brock, Ann G. "The Genre of the *Acts of Paul*: One Tradition Enhancing Another." *Apocrypha* 5 (1994): 119–36.

Brodie, Thomas L., Dennis R. MacDonald, and Stanley E. Porter, eds. *The Intertextuality of the Epistles: Explorations of Theory and Practice*. Sheffield: Sheffield Phoenix, 2006.

Brown, Michael J. "Jewish Salvation in Romans according to Clement of Alexandria in *Stromateis 2*." In Gaca and Welborn, eds., *Romans*, 42–62.

Brown, Peter. *The Body and Society: Men, Women, and Sexual Renunciation in Early Christianity*. New York: Columbia University Press, 1994.

Brown, Raymond E. *An Introduction to the New Testament*. ABRL. New York: Doubleday, 1997.

Brown, Raymond E., and John P. Meier. *Antioch and Rome: New Testament Cradles of Catholic Christianity*. New York: Paulist, 1983.

Brox, Norbert. "Lukas als Verfasser der Pastoralbriefe?" *JAC* 13 (1970) 61–77.

———. *Pseudepigraphie in der heidnischen und jüdisch-christlichen Antike*. Wege der Forschung 484. Darmstadt: Wissenschaftliche Buchgesellschaft, 1977.

Bruce, Frederick F. *Paul: Apostle of the Heart Set Free*. Grand Rapids: Eerdmans, 1977.

———. *The Pauline Circle*. Grand Rapids: Eerdmans, 1985.

Bujard, Walter. *Stilanalytische Untersuchungen zum Kolosserbrief als Beitrag zur Methodik von Sprachvergleichen*. SUNT 11. Göttingen: Vandenhoeck & Ruprecht, 1973.

Bultmann, Rudolph. *Exegetica*. Edited by Erich Dinkler. Tübingen: J. C. B. Mohr, 1967.

_____. *Theology of the New Testament.* Translated by K. Grobel. 2 vols. New York: Scribner's, 1951–55.

Burchard, Christoph. *Der dreizehnte Zeuge.* FRLANT 103. Göttingen: Vandenhoeck & Ruprecht, 1970.

Cameron, Ron, and Arthur J. Dewey. *The Cologne Mani Codex (P. Colon. Inv. Nr. 4780) "Concerning the Origin of His Body."* SBLTT 15. Missoula, Mont.: Scholars, 1979.

Campbell, William S., Peter S. Hawkins, and Brenda D. Schlingen, eds. *Medieval Readings of Romans.* London: T&T Clark International, 2002.

Von Campenhausen, Hans. *Ecclesiastical Authority and Spiritual Power.* Translated by J. A. Baker. Stanford: Stanford University Press, 1969.

_____. *The Formation of the Christian Bible.* Translated by J. A. Baker. Philadelphia: Fortress Press, 1972.

_____. "Polykarp von Smyrna und die Pastoralbriefe." In *Aus der Frühzeit des Christentums: Studien zur Kirchengeschichte des ersten und zweiten Jahrhunderts,* 197–252. Tübingen: Mohr/Siebeck, 1963.

Cannon, George E. *The Use of Traditional Materials in Colossians.* Macon, Ga.: Mercer University Press, 1983.

Carleton-Paget, James. "The *Epistle of Barnabas* and the Writings That Later Formed the New Testament." In Gregory and Tuckett, eds., *Reception,* 229–49.

_____. "Paul and the Epistle of Barnabas." *NovT* 38 (1996): 359–81.

Carrington, Philip. *The Early Christian Church.* 2 vols. Cambridge: Cambridge University Press, 1957.

Carroll, Kenneth L. "The Expansion of the Pauline Corpus." *JBL* 72 (1953): 230–37.

Charlesworth, James H. *The New Testament Apocrypha and Pseudepigrapha: A Guide to Publications, with Excursuses on Apocalypses.* ATLA BibSer 17. Metuchen, N.J.: Scarecrow, 1987.

Childs, Brevard. *The New Testament as Canon.* Philadelphia: Fortress Press, 1985.

Cirillo, Luigi. *Elchasai e gli elchasaiti: Un contributo all storia delle communità giudeo-cristiane.* Università degli studi della Calabria. Centro interdipartimentale di scienze religiose. Studi e Ricerche 1. Cosenza: Marra, 1984.

Clabeaux, John J. *A Lost Edition of the Letters of Paul: A Reassessment of the Text of the Pauline Corpus Attested by Marcion.* CBQMS 21. Washington, D.C.: Catholic Biblical Association, 1989.

Clark, David J. "Structural Similarities in 1 and 2 Thessalonians: Comparative Discourse Anatomy." In Brodie et al., eds., *Intertextuality,* 196–207.

Collins, Raymond F. *1 and 2 Timothy and Titus: A Commentary.* New Testament Library. Louisville: Westminster John Knox, 2002.

_____. "The Image of Paul in the Pastorals." *Laval thélogique et philosophique* 31/2 (1975): 147–73.

_____. "'The Gospel of Our Lord Jesus' (2 Thes 1,8): A Symbolic Shift of Paradigm." In Collins, ed., *Thessalonian Correspondence,* 426–40.

_____. *Letters That Paul Did Not Write.* Wilmington: Michael Glazier, 1988.

_____, ed. *The Thessalonian Correspondence*. BETL 87. Leuven: Leuven University Press, 1990.

Connolly, R. H. "The Date and Authorship of the Epistle to Diognetus." *JTS* 36 (1935): 347–53.

Constable, George. *Letters and Letter Collections*. Typologie des sources du Moyen Age occidental 17. Turnhout: Brepols, 1976.

Conybeare, Francis C. *The Apology and Acts of Appolonius and Other Monuments of Early Christianity*. London: Swan Sonnenschein, 1894.

Conzelmann, Hans. "Die Schule des Paulus." In *Theologia Crucis—Signum Crucis*, edited by Carl Andresen and Günter Klein, 85–96. FS Erich Dinkler. Tübingen: Mohr (Siebeck), 1979.

Crum, W. E. "New Coptic Manuscripts in the John Rylands Library." *BJRL* 5 (1920): 497–503.

Czachesz, István. "The Acts of Paul and the Western Text of Luke's Acts: Paul between Canon and Apocrypha." In Bremmer, ed., *The Apocryphal Acts of Paul and Thecla*, 107–25.

_____. *Commission Narratives: A Comparative Study of the Canonical and Apocryphal Acts*. SAAA 8. Leuven: Peeters, 2007.

Dahl, Nils A. "A Fragment and Its Content: 2 Corinthians 6:14—7:1." In *Studies in Paul*, 62–91. Minneapolis: Augsburg, 1977.

_____. "The Origin of the Earliest Prologues to the Pauline Letters." *Semeia* 12 (1978): 233–77.

_____. "The Particularity of the Pauline Epistles as a Problem in the Ancient Church." In van Unnik, ed., *Neotestamentica et Patristica*, 261–72.

Danker, Frederick W. "2 Peter 1: A Solemn Decree." *CBQ* 40 (1978): 64–82.

Dassmann, Ernst. "Archeological Traces of Early Christian Veneration of Paul." In Babcock, ed., *Legacies*, 281–306.

_____. *Der Stachel im Fleisch: Paulus in der frühchristlichen Literatur bis Irenäus*. Münster: Aschendorff, 1979.

Dautzenberg, Gerhard. "Der Zweite Korintherbrief als Briefsammlung: Zur Frage der literarischen Einheitlichkeit und des theologischen Gefüges von 2 Kor 1–8." *ANRW* 2.25.4 (1987): 3045–66.

Davies, Stevan L. *The Revolt of the Widows: The Social World of the Apocryphal Acts*. Carbondale, Ill.: Southern Illinois University Press, 1980.

Deakle, David W. "Harnack & Cerdo: A Reexamination of the Patristic Evidence for Marcion's Mentor." In May and Greschat, eds., *Marcion*, 177–90.

Dehandschutter, Boudewijn. "Polycarp's Epistle to the Philippians: An Early Example of Reception." In *The New Testament in Early Christianity*, edited by Jean-Marie Sevrin, 275–91. Leuven: Leuven University Press, 1989.

Dibelius, Martin. *Studies in the Acts of the Apostles*. Translated by M. Ling and P. Schubert. Edited by H. Greeven. New York: Charles Scribner's Sons, 1956.

Dibelius, Martin, and H. Conzelmann. *The Pastoral Epistles*. Translated by P. Buttolph and A. Yarbro. Hermeneia. Philadelphia: Fortress Press, 1972.

Dillon, John. *The Middle Platonists*. London: Duckworth, 1977.

Donelson, Lewis R. *Pseudepigraphy and Ethical Argument in the Pastoral Epistles.* HUT 22. Tübingen: Mohr Siebeck, 1986.

Donfried, Karl P. "The Theology of Second Clement." *HTR* 66 (1973): 487–501.

Drijivers, Han J. W. "Marcionism in Syria: Principles, Problems, Polemics. *Sec-Cent* 6 (1987–88): 153–72.

Dubowy, Ernst. *Klemens von Rom über die Reise Pauli nach Spanien.* Freiburg: Herder, 1914.

Duensing, Hugo, and Aurelio de Santos Otero. "Apocalypse of Paul." In Schneemelcher, ed., *New Testament Apocrypha*, 2:712–52.

Duff, P. B. "The March of the Divine Warrior and the Advent of the Greco-Roman King: Mark's Account of Jesus' Entry into Jerusalem." *JBL* 111 (1992): 55–71.

Dunn, Peter W. "The Influence of 1 Corinthians on the *Acts of Paul*." In *SBL 1996 Seminar Papers*, 438–54. SBLSP 35. Atlanta: Scholars, 1996.

Ebner, Martin, ed. *Aus Liebe zu Paulus? Die Akte Thekla neu aufgerollt.* Stuttgarter Bibelstudien 206. Stuttgart: Katholisches Bibelwerk, 2005.

Ehrman, Bart D. *The Apostolic Fathers.* LCL. 2 vols. Cambridge, Mass.: Harvard University Press, 2003.

Elliott, James Keith. *The Apocryphal New Testament.* Oxford: Clarendon, 1993.

Elliott, John H. *1 Peter.* AB 37B. New York: Doubleday, 2000.

_____. *The Elect and the Holy. An Exegetical Examination of 1 Peter.* NovTSup 12. Leiden: Brill, 1966.

Elze, M. "Härisie und Einheit der Kirche im 2. Jahrhundert." *ZTK* 71 (1974): 389–409.

Epp, Eldon Jay. "Text-Critical, Exegetical, and Socio-Cultural Factors Affecting the Junia/Junias Variation in Romans 16,7." In *New Testament Textual Criticism and Exegesis*, edited by A. Denaux, 227–91. FS J. Delobel. BETL 161. Leuven: Leuven University Press/Peeters, 2002.

Esch-Wermeling, Elisabeth. *Thekla—Paulusschülerin wider Willen? Strategien der Leserlenkung in den Theklaakten.* Neutestamentliche Abhandlungen. n.f. 53. Münster: Aschendorff, 2008.

Evans, Ernest. *Tertullian's Treatise on the Resurrection.* London: SPCK 1960.

Evans, Ernest, ed. and trans. *Tertullian Adversus Marcionem.* 2 vols. Oxford: Clarendon, 1972.

Fee, Gordon D. *The First Epistle to the Corinthians.* NICNT. Grand Rapids: Eerdmans, 1987.

Feuillet, André, "La doctrine des Epîtres Pastorales et leurs affinities avec l'oeuvre lucanienne," *RevThom* 78 (1978) 181–225.

Finegan, Jack. "The Original Form of the Pauline Collection." *HTR* 49 (1956): 85–103.

Finlan, Stephen. *The Apostle Paul and the Pauline Tradition.* Collegeville, Minn.: Liturgical, 2008.

Fiore, Benjamin J. *The Pastoral Epistles: 1 Timothy, 2 Timothy, Titus.* SP 12. Collegeville, Minn.: Liturgical, 2007.

Fiorenza, Elisabeth Schüssler. *In Memory of Her: A Feminist Theological Reconstruction of Christian Origins.* New York: Crossroads, 1983.

Fitzmyer, Joseph. *Acts of the Apostles.* AB 31. New York: Doubleday, 1998.

_____. "Qumran and the Interpolated Paragraph in 2 Corinthians 6:14—7:1." *CBQ* 23 (1961): 273-80.

_____. "The Structured Ministry of the Church in the Pastoral Epistles." *CBQ* 66 (2004): 582-96.

Foakes Jackson, F. J., and Kirsopp Lake, eds. *The Beginnings of Christianity.* Part I. 5 vols. New York: Macmillan, 1920-33.

Foerster, Werner. *Gnosis: A Selection of Gnostic Texts.* Translated by R. McL. Wilson. 2 vols. Oxford: Clarendon, 1972.

Fohlen, J. "Un apocryphe de Sénèque mal connu: le De verborum copia." *Medieval Studies* 42 (1980): 139-91.

Foster, Paul. "The Epistles of Ignatius of Antioch." *ExpTim* 117 (2005-2006): 487-95; 118 (2007-2008): 2-11.

_____. "The Epistles of Ignatius of Antioch and the Writings That Later Formed the New Testament." In Gregory and Tuckett, eds., *Reception,* 159-86.

Frede, Hermann Josef. *Altlateinische Paulus-Handschriften.* Freiburg: Herder, 1964.

_____. "Die Ordnung des Paulusbriefe und der Platz des Kolosserbrief im Corpus Paulinum." In *Vetus Latina. Die Reste der altlateinischen Bibel, 24.2,* 290-303. Epistulae ad Philippenses et Collosenses. Freiburg: Herder, 1969.

Funk, Robert W. *Parables and Presence: Forms of the New Testament Tradition.* Philadelphia: Fortress Press, 1982.

Funk, Wolf-Peter. "The Coptic Gnostic Apocalypse of Paul." In Schneemelcher, ed., *New Testament Apocrypha,* 2:695-700.

Furnish, Victor P. *II Corinthians.* AB 32A. Garden City: Doubleday, 1984.

_____. "On Putting Paul in His Place." *JBL* 113 (1994): 3-17.

Fürst, A. "Pseudepigraphie und Apostolizität im apokryphen Briefwechsel zwischen Seneca und Paulus." *JAC* 41 (1999): 41-67.

Gaca, Kathy L. "Paul's Uncommon Declaration in Romans 1:18-32 and Its Problematic Legacy for Pagan and Christian Relations." In Gaca and Welborn, eds., *Romans,* 1-33.

Gaca, Kathy L., and Larry L. Welborn, eds. *Early Patristic Readings of Romans.* Romans through History and Cultures. New York: T&T Clark International, 2005.

Gager, John G. "Marcion and Philosophy." *VC* 26 (1973): 53-59.

Gamba, Giovanni. "Il carteggio tra Seneca e San Paiol. Il 'problema' della sua autenticità." *Salesianum* 60 (1998): 209-50.

Gamble, Harry. *The New Testament Canon: Its Making and Meaning.* GBS. Philadelphia: Fortress Press, 1985.

_____. *The Textual History of the Letter to the Romans.* StudDoc 42. Grand Rapids: Eerdmans, 1977.

Gardner, Iain, and Samuel N. C. Lieu. *Manichaean Texts from the Roman Empire.* Cambridge: Cambridge University Press, 2004.

Gaventa, Beverly R. "The Overthrown Enemy: Luke's Portrait of Paul." In *SBL 1985 Seminar Papers,* edited by K. H. Richards, 439-49. SBLSP 24. Atlanta: Scholars, 1985.

Georgi, Dieter. "Irenaeus's and Origen's Treatment of Paul's Epistle to the Romans: An Assessment." In Gaca and Welborn, eds., *Romans*, 206–12.

Gielen, Marlis. "Zur Interpretation der paulinischen Formel *he kat'oikon ekklesia*." *ZNW* 77 (1986): 109–25.

Gilchrist, J. Michael. "Intertextuality and the Pseudonymity of 2 Thessalonians." In Brodie et al., eds., *Intertextuality*, 152–75.

Gillman, Florence M. *Women Who Knew Paul.* Zacchaeus Studies. Collegeville, Minn.: Liturgical, 1992.

Glaser, Timo. *Paulus als Briefroman erzählt: Studien zum antiken Briefroman und seiner christlichen Rezeption in den Pastoralbriefen.* SUNT Göttingen: Vandenveck & Ruprecht, 2009.

Gnilka, Joachim. *Der Epheserbrief.* HTKNT 10. Freiburg: Herder, 1971.

_____. *Der Kolosserbrief.* HTKNT 10. Freiburg: Herder, 1980.

_____. "Das Paulusbild im Kolosser-und-Epheserbrief." In *Kontinuität und Einheit,* edited by P.-G. Müller and W. Stenger, 179–93. FS Franz Mussner. Freiburg im B: Herder, 1981.

Goodenough, Erwin R. *The Theology of Justin Martyr: An Investigation into the Conceptions of Early Christian Literature and Its Hellenistic and Judaistic Influences.* Amsterdam: Philo, 1968.

Goodspeed, Edgar J. *New Solutions to New Testament Problems.* Chicago: University of Chicago Press, 1927.

Gorman, Jill C. "Sexual Defence by Proxy: Interpreting Women's Fasting in the *Acts of Xanthippe and Polyxena*." In Levine, ed., *Feminist Companion*, 206–15.

_____. "Thinking with and about 'Same-sex Desire': Producing and Policing Female Sexuality in the *Acts of Xanthippe and Polyxena*." *Journal of the History of Sexuality* 10 (2001): 416–41.

Goulder, Michael D. *Type and History in Acts.* London: SPCK, 1964.

Graham, Susan L. "Irenaeus as Reader of Romans 9–11: Olive Branches." In Gaca and Welborn, eds., *Romans*, 87–113.

Grant, Robert M., ed. *The Apostolic Fathers: A New Translation and Commentary.* 6 vols. Camden, N.J.: Nelson, 1964–67.

_____. "The Bible of Theophilus of Antioch." *JBL* 66 (1947): 173–96.

_____. *Greek Apologists of the Second Century.* Philadelphia: Westminster, 1988.

_____. *Heresy and Criticism.* Louisville: Westminster John Knox, 1993.

_____. *Irenaeus of Lyons.* London: Routledge, 1997.

_____. *Miracle and Natural Law in Greco-Roman and Early Christian Thought.* Amsterdam: North-Holland, 1952.

_____. "Tatian and the Bible." In *Studia Patristica*, vol. 1, edited by K. Aland and F. L. Cross, 297–306. Berlin: Akademie-Verlag, 1957.

_____. "A Woman of Rome: The Matron in Justin, *2 Apology* 2.1-9." *Church History* 54 (1985): 461–72.

Gregg, J. A. F. "The Commentary of Origen upon the Epistle to the Ephesians." *JTS* 3 (1902): 233–44, 398–420, 551–76.

Gregory, Andrew. "*2 Clement* and the Writings That Later Formed the New Testament." In Gregory and Tuckett, eds., *Reception*, 251–92.

_____. *The Reception of Luke and Acts in the Period before Irenaeus.* WUNT 169. Tübingen: Mohr Siebeck, 2003.

Gregory, Andrew, and Christopher Tuckett, eds. *The Reception of the New Testament in the Apostolic Fathers.* The New Testament and the Apostolic Fathers 1. Oxford: Oxford University Press, 2005.

_____. *Trajectories through the New Testament and the Apostolic Fathers.* The New Testament and the Apostolic Fathers 2. Oxford: Oxford University Press, 2005.

Grosheide, F. W., ed. *Some Early Lists of the Books of the New Testament.* Textus Minores I. Leiden: Brill, 1948.

Gunther, John J. *Paul: Messenger and Exile; A Study in the Chronology of His Life and Letters.* Valley Forge, Penn.: Judson, 1972.

Haenchen, Ernst. *The Acts of the Apostles.* Translated and edited by B. Noble et al. Philadelphia: Westminster, 1971.

Hahneman, Geoffrey M. *The Muratorian Fragment and the Development of the Canon.* OTM. Clarendon: Oxford, 1992.

Haight, Elizabeth. *More Essays on Greek Romances.* New York: Longmans, 1945.

Halkin, F. "La légende crétoise de saint Tite." *Analecta Bollandia* 79 (1961): 241–56.

Harnack, Adolph v. "Der apokryphe Brief des Apostel Paulus an die Laodicener: Eine marcionitische Fälschung aus der 2. Hälfte des 2. Jahrhunderts." In *Sitzungsberichte der Preussischen Akademie der Wissenschaften*, 235–45. Berlin: Akademie Verlag, 1923.

_____. *Geschichte der altchristlichen Literatur bis Eusebius.* Teil 2, *Die Chronologie.* 2 vols. 2nd ed. Leipzig: Hinrichs, 1904.

_____. *Marcion: Das Evangelium vom fremden Gott.* 2nd ed. Leipzig: Hinrichs, 1924.

_____. *Marcion: The Gospel of the Alien God.* Translated by J. E. Steely and L. Bierma. Durham, N.C.: Labyrinth, 1990.

Harrill, J. Albert. *Manumission of Slaves in Early Christianity.* HUT 32. Tübingen: Mohr Siebeck, 1995.

Harrison, P. N. *Polycarp's Two Epistles to the Philippians.* Cambridge: Cambridge University Press, 1936.

_____. *The Problem of the Pastoral Epistles.* Oxford: Oxford University Press, 1921.

Harvey, William W. *Sancti Irenaei Episcopi Lugdunensis.* Cambridge: Typis Academicis, 1857.

Hatch, William H. P. "The Position of Hebrews in the Canon of the New Testament." *HTR* 29 (1936): 135–51.

Hawthorne, Gerald W., and Ralph P. Martin, eds. *Dictionary of Paul and His Letters.* Downers Grove, Ill.: InterVarsity, 1993.

Hedrick, Charles W., ed. *Nag Hammadi Codices XI, XII, XIII.* NHS 27. Leiden: Brill, 1990.

Heinrici, C. F. Georg. *Die Valentinianische Gnosis und die heilige Schrift.* Berlin: Wiegandt & Grieben, 1871.

Hennecke, Edgar, ed. *Neutestamentlichen Apokryphen.* 2nd ed. Tübingen: Mohr Siebeck, 1924.

Henrichs, Albert. "Pagan Ritual and the Alleged Crimes of the Early Christians: A Reconsideration." In *Kyriakon*, edited by P. Granfield and J. A. Jungmann, 1:18–35. FS Johannes Quasten. 2 vols. Munich: Kössel, 1970.

Hering, J. P. *The Colossian and Ephesian Haustafeln in Theological Context: An Analysis of Their Origins, Relationship, and Message*. American University Studies 7. Theology and Religion 260. New York: Lang, 2007.

Hillhorst, A. "Tertullian on the Acts of Paul." In Bremmer, ed., *Acts of Paul*, 150–63.

Hills, Julian V. "The *Acts of Paul* and the Legacy of the Lukan Acts." *Semeia* 80 (1997): 145–58.

_____. "The Acts of the Apostles in the *Acts of Paul*." *SBL 1994 Seminar Papers*, edited by Eugene H. Lovering, 24–54. SBLSP 33. Atlanta: Scholars, 1994.

_____. *The Epistle of the Apostles*. Santa Rosa, CA: Polebridge, 2009.

_____. *Tradition and Composition in the Epistula Apostolorum*. Harvard Theological Studies 57. Minneapolis: Fortress Press, 2008.

Himmelfarb, Martha. *Ascents to Heaven in Jewish and Christian Apocalypses*. New York: Oxford University Press, 1993.

_____. *Tours of Hell: An Apocalyptic Form in Jewish and Christian Literature*. Philadelphia: Fortress Press, 1985.

Hoffmann, R. Joseph. "How Then Know This Troublous Teacher? Further Reflections on Marcion and His Church." *SecCent* 6 (1977–78): 173–91.

_____. *Marcion: On the Restitution of Christianity*. AARAS 46. Chico, Calif.: Scholars, 1984.

Holland, Glenn S. " 'A Letter Supposedly from Us': A Contribution to the Discussion about the Authorship of 2 Thessalonians." In Collins, ed., *Thessalonian Correspondence*, 394–402.

_____. *The Tradition That You Received from Us: 2 Thessalonians in the Pauline Tradition*. HUT 24. Tübingen: Mohr Siebeck, 1988.

Holloway, P. A. "The Apocryphal *Epistle to the Laodiceans* and the Partitioning of Philippians." *HTR* 91 (1998): 321–25.

Holmberg, Bengt. *Paul and Power: The Structure of Authority in the Primitive Church as Reflected in the Pauline Epistles*. Philadelphia: Fortress Press, 1980.

Holmes, Michael W. "Polycarp's *Letter to the Philippians* and the Writings That Later Formed the New Testament." In Gregory and Tuckett, eds., *Reception*, 187–227.

Holzberg, Niklas, ed. *Der griechische Briefroman: Gattungstypologie und Textanalyse*. Classica Monacensia 8. Tübingen: Narr, 1994.

_____. "Letters: *Chion*." In *The Novel in the Ancient World*, edited by Gareth Schmeling, 645–53. Rev. ed. Leiden: Brill, 2003.

Horn, Friedrich Wilhelm, ed. *Das Ende des Paulus. Historische, theologische und literaturgeschichtliche Aspekte*. BZNW 106. Berlin: de Gruyter, 2001.

Hornschuh, Manfred. *Studien zur Epistula Apostolorum*. PTS 5. Berlin: de Gruyter, 1965.

Horrell, David G. "The Product of a Petrine Circle? A Reassessment of the Origin and Character of 1 Peter." *JSNT* 86 (2002): 29–60.

_____. *The Social Ethos of the Corinthian Correspondence: Interests and Ideology from 1 Corinthians to 1 Clement.* Edinburgh: T. & T. Clark, 1996.

Houlden, John L. *Paul's Letters from Prison.* Baltimore: Penguin, 1970.

Hovhanessian, Vahan. *Third Corinthians: Reclaiming Paul for Christian Orthodoxy.* Studies in Biblical Literature 18. New York: Lang, 2000.

Hughes, Frank W. *Early Christian Rhetoric and 2 Thessalonians.* JSNTS 30. Sheffield: JSOT, 1989.

Hultgren, Arland J. *1–II Timothy, Titus.* ACNT. Minneapolis: Augsburg, 1984.

Hultgren, S. J. "2 Cor 6.14—7.1 and Rev 21.3-8: Evidence for the Ephesian Redaction of 2 Corinthians." *NTS* 49 (2002): 267–82.

Hunt, Emily J. *Christianity in the Second Century: The Case of Tatian.* London: Routledge, 2003.

Hurtado, Larry W. "The Doxology at the End of Romans." In *New Testament Textual Criticism: Essays in Honour of Bruce M. Metzger,* edited by E. J. Epp and G. D. Fee, 185–99. Oxford: Clarendon, 1981.

Hyldahl, Niels. "The Reception of Paul in the Acts of the Apostles." In *The New Testament as Reception,* edited by M. Müller and H. Tronier, 101–19. JSNTS 230. London: Sheffield Academic Press, 2002.

St. Irenaeus of Lyons Against the Heresies. Translated and annotated by D. J. Unger, O.F.M. Further Revisions by J. J. Dillon. ACW 55. Mahwah, N.J.: Paulist, 1992.

Jacobson, Glen R. "Paul in Luke–Acts: The Savior Who Is Present." In *SBL 1983 Seminar Papers,* edited by K. H. Richards, 131–46. SBLSP 22. Chico, Calif.: Scholars.

James, Montague Rhodes. "The Acts of Titus and the Acts of Paul." *JTS* 6 (1905): 549–56.

_____. *Apocrypha Anecdota 2.* Texts and Studies 2. Cambridge: Cambridge University Press, 1893.

_____. *The Apocryphal New Testament.* Oxford: Clarendon, 1924.

Jeffers, James S. *Conflict at Rome.* Minneapolis: Fortress Press, 1991.

Jefford, Clayton N. "Household Codes and Conflict in the Early Church." *Studia Patristica* 31 (1997): 121–27.

_____. *Reading the Apostolic Fathers: An Introduction.* Peabody, Mass.: Hendrickson, 1996.

Jewett, Robert. *A Chronology of Paul's Life.* Philadelphia: Fortress Press, 1979.

_____. "A Matrix of Grace: The Theology of 2 Thessalonians as a Pauline Letter." In Bassler, ed., *Pauline Theology,* 1:61–70.

_____. "Paul, Phoebe, and the Spanish Mission." In *The Social World of Formative Christianity and Judaism: Essays in Tribute to Howard Clark Kee,* edited by Jacob Neusner et al., 142–61. Philadelphia: Fortress Press, 1988.

_____. "The Redaction of 1 Corinthians and the Trajectory of the Pauline School." *JAARSup* 44 (1978): 389–444.

_____. *Romans*. Assisted by Roy Kotansky. Hermeneia. Minneapolis: Fortress Press, 2007.

Johnson, Luke T. *The First and Second Letters to Timothy*. AB 35A. New York: Doubleday, 2001.

_____. *The Writings of the New Testament: An Interpretation*. Philadelphia: Fortress Press, 1986.

Johnson, Scott F. *The Life and Miracles of Thekla: A Literary Study*. Washington, D.C.: Center for Hellenic Studies, 2006.

Johnston S., and P.-H. Poirier. "Nouvelles citations chez Éphrem et Aphraate de la correspondence entre Paul et les corinthiens." *Apocrypha* 16 (2005): 137–47.

Jones, F. Stanley. *An Ancient Jewish Christian Source on the History of Christianity: Pseudo-Clementine Recognitions 1.21-71*. SBLTT 37. Atlanta: Scholars, 1995.

_____. "Eros and Astrology in the Περίοδοι Πέτρου: The Sense of the Pseudo-Clementine Novel." *Apoc* 12 (2001): 53–78.

_____. "A Jewish Christian Reads Luke's Acts of the Apostles: The Use of the Canonical Acts in the Ancient Jewish Christian Source behind Pseudo-Clementine *Recognitions* 1.27-71." In *SBL 1995 Seminar Papers*, edited by Eugene H. Lovering, 617–35. SBLSP 34. Atlanta: Scholars, 1995.

_____. "The Pseudo-Clementines: A History of Research." *SecCent* 2 (1982): 1–33, 63–96.

Junod, Eric. "Vie et conduite des saintes femmes Xanthippe, Polyxène et Rébecca (BHG 1977)." In Papandreou, Bienert, and Schäferdiek, eds., *Oecumenica et Patristica*, 83–106.

Kaestli, Jean-Daniel. "Luke-Acts and the Pastoral Epistles: The Thesis of a Common Authorship," in C. M. Tuckett, ed., *Luke's Literary Achievement: Collected Essays*. JSNTSupp 116. Sheffield: Sheffield Academic Press, 1995, 110–26

Kapler, René. "Correspondance de Paul et de Sénèque," in F. Bovon and P. Geoltrain, eds., *Écrits apocryphes chrétiens 1*. Paris: Gallimard, 1997, 1581–94.

Kasser, Rodolphe. "Acta Pauli 1959." *RHPR* 40 (1960): 45–57.

Kasser, Rodolphe, and Philippe Luisier. "Le Papyrus Bodmer XLI en Édition Princeps: l'Épisode d'Éphèse des *Acta Pauli* en Copte et en Traduction." *Le Muséon* 117 (2004): 281–384.

Kelley, Nicole. *Knowledge and Authority in the Pseudo-Clementines: Situating the Recognitions in 4th Century Syria*. WUNT 213. Tübingen: Mohr Siebeck, 2006.

Kennedy, George A. *Progymnasmata: Greek Textbooks of Prose Composition and Rhetoric*. SBLWGRW 10. Atlanta: SBL, 2003.

Kertelge, Karl, ed. *Paulus in den Neutestamentlichen Spätschriften: Zur Paulusrezeption im Neuen Testament*. QD 89. Freiburg: Herder, 1981.

Kidd, R. M. *Wealth and Beneficence in the Pastoral Epistles: A "Bourgeois" Form of Early Christianity?* SBLDS 122. Atlanta: Scholars, 1990.

Kiley, Mark. *Colossians as Pseudepigraphy*. The Biblical Seminar 4. Sheffield: JSOT, 1986.

King, Karen L. *What is Gnosticism?* Cambridge, Mass.: Belknap, 2003.

Kinzig, Wolfram. "Ein Ketzer und sein Konstrukteur. Harnacks Marcion." In May and Geschrat, eds., *Marcion*, 253–74.

Kitchen, Martin. *Ephesians.* New Testament Readings. London: Routledge, 1994.

Klauck, Hans-Josef (with D. R. Bailey). *Ancient Letters and the New Testament.* Waco, Tex.: Baylor University Press, 2006.

_____. *The Apocryphal Acts of the Apostles: An Introduction.* Translated by Brian McNeil. Waco, Tex.: Baylor University Press, 2008.

Klijn, Albertus F. J. "The Apocryphal Correspondence between Paul and the Corinthians. *VC* 17 (1963): 2–23.

Klijn, Albertus F. J., and G. J. Reinink, eds. *Patristic Evidence for Jewish-Christian Sects.* NovTSup 36. Leiden: Brill, 1973.

Knox, John. *Marcion and the New Testament.* Chicago: University of Chicago Press, 1942.

_____. *Philemon among the Letters of Paul.* 2nd ed. Nashville: Abingdon, 1959.

Knust, Jennifer W. "2 Thessalonians and the Discipline of Work." In Vaage and Wimbush, eds., *Asceticism*, 255–67.

Koch, H. "Petrus und Paulus im zweiten Osterfeierstreit." *ZNW* 19 (1919–20): 178–79.

Koester, Helmut. *Ancient Christian Gospels: Their History and Development.* Philadelphia: Trinity Press International, 1990.

_____. "From Paul's Eschatology to the Apocalyptic Schemata of 2 Thessalonians." In Collins, ed., *Thessalonian Correspondence*, 441–58.

_____. "Gospels and Gospel Traditions in the Second Century." In Gregory and Tuckett, eds., *Trajectories*, 27–44.

_____. *Introduction to the New Testament.* 2 vols. New York: de Gruyter, 1995–2000.

_____, ed. *Ephesos: Metropolis of Asia.* HTS 41. Valley Forge: Trinity Press International, 1995.

Koschorke, Klaus. "Paulus in den Nag-Hammadi Texten: Ein Beitrag zur Geschichte der Paulusrezeption im frühen Christentum." *ZTK* 78 (1981): 177–205.

_____. *Die Polemik der Gnostiker gegen das kirchliche Christentum.* NHS 12. Leiden: Brill, 1978.

Krentz, Edgar. "Traditions Held Fast: Theology and Fidelity in 2 Thessalonians." In Collins, ed., *Thessalonian Correspondence*, 505–15.

Kuhn, Karl Georg. "Der Epherserbrief im Lichte der Qumran Texte." *NTS* 7 (1960–61): 334–46.

Kümmel, Werner Georg. *The New Testament: The History of the Investigation of Its Problems.* Translated by S. Mclean Gilmour and Howard C. Kee. Nashville: Abingdon, 1970.

Kurz, William S. *Farewell Addresses in the New Testament.* Collegeville, Minn.: Liturgical, 1990.

Kürzinger, J. *Papias von Hierapolis und die Evangelien des Neuen Testaments.* Regensburg: Pustet, 1983.

Lambrecht, Jan. *Second Corinthians.* SP 8. Collegeville, Minn.: Liturgical, 2000.

Lampe, G. W. H. *A Patristic Greek Lexicon.* Oxford: Clarendon, 1961.

Lampe, Peter. *From Paul to Valentinus: Christians at Rome in the First Two Centuries.* Translated by Michael Steinhauser. Edited by Marshall D. Johnson. Minneapolis: Fortress Press, 2003.

———. "The Roman Christians of Romans 16." In *The Romans Debate,* edited by Karl P. Donfried, 216–30. Peabody, Mass.: Hendrickson, 1991.

———. "Zur Textgeschichte des Römerbriefes." *NovT* 27 (1985): 273–77.

Lapham, Fred. *An Introduction to the New Testament Apocrypha.* London: T&T Clark International, 2003.

Laub, Franz. "Paulinische Autorität in nachpaulinischer Zeit (2 Thes)." In Collins, ed., *Thessalonian Correspondence,* 403–17.

Lawson, John. *The Biblical Theology of Saint Irenaeus.* London: Epworth, 1948.

Layton, Bentley. *The Gnostic Scriptures.* Garden City, N.Y.: Doubleday, 1987.

Lee, Michelle V. *Christ, the Stoics and the Body of Christ.* SNTSMS 137. New York: Cambridge University Press, 2006.

Leloir, Louis. *Apocrypha Apostolorum Armeniaca II.* CCSA 4. Turnhout: Brepols, 1992.

Lentz, John C. Jr. *Luke's Portrait of Paul.* SNTSM 77. Cambridge: Cambridge University Press, 1993.

Leppä, Outi. "2 Thessalonians among the Pauline Letters: Tracing the Literary Links between 2 Thessalonians and Other Pauline Epistles." In Brodie et al., eds., *Intertextuality,* 176–95.

Levine, Amy-Jill, ed. *Feminist Companion to the New Testament Apocrypha.* New York: T&T Clark International, 2006.

Levine, Amy-Jill, with Marianne Blickenstaff, ed. *A Feminist Companion to the Deutero-Pauline Epistles.* Cleveland: Pilgrim, 2003.

Liénard, E. "Sur la Correspondance apocryphe de Sénèque et de Saint-Paul." *Revue Belge de Philologie et d'Histoire* 11 (1932): 5–23.

Lienhard, Joseph T. "The Christology of the Epistle to Diognetus." *VC* 24 (1968): 280–89.

Lietzmann, Hans. *An die Korinther I–II.* HNT 9. 4th expd. ed. by W. G. Kümmel. Tübingen: Mohr Siebeck, 1949.

Lieu, Samuel N. C. *Manichaeism in the Later Roman Empire and Medieval China.* 2nd ed. Tübingen: J. C. B. Mohr, 1992.

Lightfoot, Joseph B. *The Apostolic Fathers.* 5 vols. in two parts. New York: Macmillan, 1889–90.

———. *Saint Paul's Epistle to the Philippians.* 4th alt. ed. London: Macmillan, 1898.

———. *Saint Paul's Epistles to the Colossians and to Philemon: A Revised Text.* 1879. Grand Rapids: Zondervan, 1959.

———. "St Paul's History after the Close of the Acts." In *Biblical Essays,* 421–37. 1893. Reprint, Grand Rapids: Baker Book House, 1979.

Lincoln, Andrew T. "The Household Code and Wisdom Mode of Colossians." *JSNT* 74 (1999): 93–112.

Lindemann, Andreas. *Die Clemensbriefe.* HNT 17. Tübingen: Mohr/Siebeck, 1992.

_____. *Der Kolosserbrief.* ZBK. Zürich: Theologischer Verlag, 1983.

_____. "Paulinische Theologie im Brief an Diognet." In *Kerygma und Logos,* edited by A. M. Ritter, 337–50. FS C. Andresen. Göttingen: Vandenhoeck & Ruprecht, 1979.

_____. "Paul in the Writings of the Apostolic Fathers." In Babcock, ed., *Paul,* 25–45.

_____. "Paul's Influence on 'Clement' and Ignatius." In Gregory and Tuckett, eds., *Trajectories,* 9–24.

_____. *Paulus, Apostel und Lehrer der Kirche.* Tübingen: Mohr Siebeck, 1999.

_____. *Paulus im ältesten Christentum.* BHT 58. Tübingen: Mohr Siebeck, 1979.

_____. "Die Sammlung der Paulusbriefe im 1. und 2. Jahrhundert." In Auwers and de Jonge, eds., *The Biblical Canons,* 321–51.

Linton, Olaf. "The Third Aspect." *StudTheol* 3 (1951): 79–95.

Lipsius, Richard A., and Maximilian Bonnet. *Acta Apostolorum Apocrypha.* 2 vols. Leipzig: Hermann Mendelssohn, 1891–1903.

Lohfink, Gerd. "Paulinische Theologie in der Rezeption der Pastoralbriefe." In Kertelge, ed., *Paulus,* 70–121.

Lohse, Eduard. *Colossians and Philemon.* Translated by William R. Poehlmann and Robert J. Karris. Hermeneia. Philadelphia: Fortress Press, 1971.

Lona, Horacio E. *Der erste Clemensbrief.* KAV. Göttingen: Vandenhoeck & Ruprecht, 1998.

Long, William R. "The *Paulusbild* in the Trial of Paul in Acts." In *SBL 1983 Seminar Papers,* edited by K. H. Richards, 87–105. SBLSP 22. Chico, Calif.: Scholars.

Löning, Karl. "Paulinismus in der Apostelgeschichte." In Kertlege, ed., *Paulus,* 202–34.

Lüdemann, Gerd. *Opposition to Paul in Jewish Christianity.* Translated by M. E. Boring. Minneapolis: Fortress Press, 1989.

Lupieri, Edmondo. *The Mandaeans: The Last Gnostics.* Grand Rapids: Eerdmans, 2002.

Luttikhuizen, Gerard. "The Apocryphal Correspondence with the Corinthians and the Acts of Paul." In Bremmer, ed., *The Apocryphal Acts of Paul and Thecla,* 75–91.

_____. *The Revelation of Elchasai.* TSAJ 8. Tübingen: Mohr Siebeck, 1985.

MacDonald, Dennis R. "Apocryphal and Canonical Narratives about Paul." In Babcock, ed., *Legacies,* 55–70.

_____. "A Conjectural Emendation of 1 Cor 15:31-32: Or the Case of the Misplaced Lion Fight." *HTR* 73 (1980): 265–76.

_____. *The Legend and the Apostle: The Battle for Paul in Story and Canon.* Philadelphia: Westminster, 1983.

MacDonald, Margaret Y. "Citizens of Heaven and Earth: Asceticism and Social Integration in Colossians and Ephesians." In Vaage and Wimbush, eds., *Asceticism,* 269–98.

_____. *Colossians and Ephesians.* SP 17. Collegeville, Minn.: Liturgical, 2000.

_____. *Early Christian Women and Pagan Opinion: The Power of the Hysterical Woman*. Cambridge: Cambridge University Press, 1996.

_____. "Early Christian Women Married to Unbelievers." In Levine, ed., *Feminist Companion*, 14–28.

_____. *The Pauline Churches*. SNTSMS 60. Cambridge: Cambridge University Press, 1988.

Mackay, T. W. "Content and Style in Two Pseudo-Pauline Epistles." In *Apocryphal Writings and the Latter-Day Saints*, edited by C. W. Griggs, 215–40. Provo, Utah: Religious Studies Center, Brigham Young University.

Maier, Harry O. "The Politics and Rhetoric of Discord and Concord in Paul and Ignatius." In Gregory and Tuckett, eds., *Trajectories*, 304–24.

_____. "Purity and Danger in Polycarp's Epistle to the Philippians: The Sin of Valens in Social Perspective." *Journal of Early Christian Studies* 1 (1993): 229–47.

Malherbe, Abraham. *Ancient Epistolary Theorists*. SBLSBS 19. Atlanta: Scholars, 1988.

_____. *The Cynic Epistles*. SBS 12. Missoula, Mont.: Scholars, 1977.

_____. "Hellenistic Moralists and the New Testament." *ANRW* II 26.3 (1992): 267–333.

_____. *Paul and the Popular Philosophers*. Minneapolis: Fortress Press, 1989.

_____. "'Seneca' on Paul as Letter Writer." In *The Future of Early Christianity: Essays in Honor of Helmut Koester*, edited by Birger A. Pearson, 414–21. Minneapolis: Fortress Press, 1991.

Manns, F. "Les pseudo-clementines (*Homélies et Reconnaisances*): État de la Question." *Studii Biblici Franciscani Liber Annuus* 53 (2003): 157–84.

Marguerat, Daniel. "The *Acts of Paul* and the Canonical Acts: A Phenomenon of Rereading." *Semeia* 80 (1997): 169–83.

_____. "L'image de Paul dans les Actes des Apôtres." In *Les Actes des Apôtres: Histoire, récit, théologie. XXᵉ congrès de l'Association catholique française pour l'étude de la Bible (Angers, 2003)*, edited by M. Berder, 121–54. LD 199. Paris: Cerf, 2005.

_____. "Paul après Paul: une histoire de reception." *NTS* 54 (2008): 317–37.

Markschies, Christoph. "Die valentianische Gnosis und Marcion—einige neue Perspektiven." In May and Greschat, eds., *Marcion*, 159–75.

Marrou, Henri-I. *A Diognète*. SC 33. 2nd ed. Paris, 1965.

Martin, J. Louis. "Clementine Recognitions 1, 33-71, Jewish Christianity, and the Fourth Gospel." In *God's Christ and His People: Studies in Honour of Nils Alstrup Dahl*, edited by Jacob Jervell and Wayne A. Meeks, 265–95. Oslo: Universitetsforlaget, 1977.

Martin, Ralph P. *Reconciliation: A Study of Paul's Theology*. Rev. ed. Grand Rapids: Zondervan, 1990.

Masson, Charles. *L'épître de Saint Paul aux Colossiens*. Commentaire du Nouveau Testament X. Neuchatel: Delachaux & Niestlé, 1950.

Matthews, Shelly. "Thinking of Thecla: Issues in Feminist Historiography." *Journal of Feminist Studies in Religion* 17 (2002): 39–65.

Mattill, Andrew J., Jr. "The Paul-Jesus Parallels and the Purpose of Luke–Acts: H. H. Evans Reconsidered." *NovT* 17 (1975): 15–47.

May, Gerhard. "Marcion in Contemporary Views: Results and Open Questions." *SecCent* 6 (1987–88): 129–51.

———. "Der 'Schiffsreder' Markion." *StPatr.* 21 (1989): 142–53.

May, Gerhard, and Katharinia Greschat, eds. *Marcion und seine kirchengechichtliche Wirkung.* TU 150. Berlin: de Gruyter, 2002.

McGowan, Andrew. *Ascetic Eucharists: Food and Drink in Early Christian Ritual Meals.* Oxford: Oxford University Press, 1999.

———. "Marcion's Love of Creation." *JECS* 9 (2001): 295–311.

Meade, D. G. *Pseudonymity and Canon.* Grand Rapids: Eerdmans, 1987.

Meecham, H. G. *The Epistle to Diognetus: The Greek Text with Introduction, Translation and Notes.* Manchester, 1949.

Meeks, Wayne A. "The Divine Agent and His Counterfeit." In *Aspects of Religious Propaganda in Judaism and Early Christianity,* edited by E. Schüssler Fiorenza, 43–67. Notre Dame: University of Notre Dame Press, 1976.

———. *The Origins of Christian Morality: The First Two Centuries.* New Haven: Yale University Press, 1993.

Meijering, E. P. "Bemerkungen zu Tertullian's Polemik gegen Marcion (Adversus Marcionem 1.1-25)." *VC* 32 (1976): 81–108.

———. *Tertullian contra Marcionem. Gotteslehre in der Polemik. Adversus Marcionem I–II.* Leiden: Brill, 1977.

Meinardus, Otto F. A. "Cretan Traditions about St Paul's Mission to the Island." *Ostkirchliche Studien* 22 (1973): 172–83.

Merkel, Helmut. "Die Epheserbrief in der neueren exegetischen Diskussion." *ANRW* II.25.4 (1987): 3156–246.

Merklein, Helmut. "Paulinische Theologie in der Rezeption des Kolosser- und Epheserbriefes." In Kertelge, ed., *Paulus,* 25–69.

Merz, Annette, "The Fictitious Self-Exposition of Paul," in D. R. MacDonald, S. E. Porter and T. L. Brodie, eds., *Intertextuality of the Epistles: Explorations of Theory and Practice.* Sheffield: Sheffield Phoenix, 2006.

———, *Die fiktive Selbstauslegung des Paulus. Intertextuelle Studien zur Intention und Rezeption der Pastoralbriefe.* NTOA 52. Göttingen, 2004.

Metzger, Bruce M. *The Canon of the New Testament. Its Origin, Development, and Significance.* Oxford: Clarendon, 1989.

———. *A Textual Commentary on the Greek New Testament.* 2nd ed. New York: American Bible Society, 1994.

———. *The Text of the New Testament. Its Transmission, Corruption, and Restoration.* 3rd ed. New York: Oxford University Press, 1992.

Miller, James D. *The Pastoral Letters as Composite Documents.* SNTSMS 93. Cambridge: Cambridge University Press, 1997.

Mitchell, Margaret M. "The Letter of James as a Document of Paulinism?" In *Reading James with New Eyes: Methodological Reassessments of the Letter of James,* edited by Robert L. Webb and John S. Kloppenborg, 75–98. New York: T&T Clark International, 2007.

_____. *Paul and the Rhetoric of Reconciliation*. Louisville: Westminster John Knox, 1991.

Mitton, C. Leslie. *The Epistle to the Ephesians: Its Authorship, Origin and Purpose*. Oxford: Clarendon, 1951.

_____. *The Formation of the Pauline Corpus of Letters*. London: Epworth, 1955.

Mollenkott, Virginia Ramey. "Emancipative Elements in Ephesians 5.21-33: Why Feminist Scholarship Has (Often) Left Them Unmentioned, and Why They Should Be Emphasized." In Levine, ed., *Feminist Companion*, 37–58.

Momigliano, Arnaldo. "Note sulla leggenda del cristianesimo di Seneca." *Rivista storica italiana* 62 (1950): 325–44.

Moreschini, Claudio, and Enrico Norelli. *Early Christian Greek and Latin Literature*. Translated by Matthew J. O'Connell. 2 vols. Peabody, Mass.: Hendrickson, 2005.

Mount, Christopher. "1 Corinthians 11:3-16: Spirit Possession and Authority in a Non-Pauline Interpolation." *JBL* (2005): 313–40.

Mouton, Elna. "(Re)Describing Reality? The Transformative Potential of Ephesians across Times and Cultures." In Levine, ed., *Feminist Companion*, 59–87.

Mowry, Lucetta. "The Early Circulation of Paul's Letters." *JBL* 63 (1964): 73–86.

Muddiman, John. "The Church in Ephesians, 2 Clement, and the Shepherd of Hermas." In Gregory and Tuckett, eds., *Trajectories*, 107–21.

_____. *A Commentary on the Epistle to the Ephesians*. London: Continuum, 2001.

Mühlenberg, E. "Marcion's Jealous God." In *Disciplina Nostra: Essays in Memory of Robert F. Evans*, edited by D. F. Winslow, 93–113. Philadelphia: Philadelphia Patristic Foundation, 1979.

Müller, Dieter. "Prayer of the Apostle Paul." In *Nag Hammadi Codex I*, edited by H. Attridge, 1:5–11. 2 vols. Nag Hammadi Studies 22-23. Leiden: Brill, 1985.

Müller, Paul-Gerhard. *Anfänge der Paulusschule: Dargestellt am zweiten Thessalonicherbrief und am Kolosserbrief*. Abhandlungen zur Theologie des Alten und Neuen Testaments 74. Zürich: Theologischer, 1988.

_____. "Der 'Paulinismus' in der Apostelgeschichte. Ein Forschungsgeschichtlicher Überblick." In Kertelge, ed., *Paulus*, 157–201.

Munck, Johannes. "Discours d'adieu dans le Nouveau Testament et dans la literature biblique." In *Aux sources de la tradition chrétienne: Mélanges offerts à Maurice Goguel*, 155–70. Bibliothèque théologique. Neuchatel: Delachaux, 1950.

Munier, Charles. "A propos d'Ignace d'Antioche: Observations sur la liste épiscopal d'Antioche." *RSR* 55 (1981): 126–31.

_____. "Où en est la question d'Ignace d'Antioche? Bilan d'un siècle de recherches 1870-1988." *ANRW* 2.27.1 (1993): 359–484.

Murdock, William R., and George W. MacRae. "The Apocalypse of Paul." In *Nag Hammadi Codices V 2-5 and VI with Papyrus Berolensis 8502, 1 and 4*, edited by Douglas M. Parrott, 47–63. Nag Hammadi Studies 11. Leiden: Brill, 1979.

Musurillo, Herbert. *The Acts of the Christian Martyrs*. Oxford: Clarendon, 1972.

Nautin, Pierre. *Lettres et écrivains chrétiens des IIe et IIIe siècles*. Patristica II. Paris: Cerf, 1961.

Neyrey, Jerome H. *2 Peter, Jude*. AB 37 C. New York: Doubleday, 1993.

Nielsen, C. M. "The Epistle to Diognetus: Its Date and Relationship to Marcion." *ATR* 52 (1970): 77–91.

_____. "The Status of Paul and His Letters in Colossians." *Perspectives in Religious Studies* 12 (1985): 103–22.

Nielsen, J. T. *Adam and Christ in the Theology of Irenaeus of Lyons*. Assen: Van Gorcum, 1968.

Nienhuis, David R. *Not by Paul Alone: The Formation of the Catholic Epistle Collection and the Christian Canon*. Waco, Tex.: Baylor University Press, 2007.

Nock, Arthur Darby. *Conversion: The Old and the New in Religion from Alexander the Great to Augustine of Hippo*. Oxford: Oxford University Press, 1933.

Noormann, Rolf. *Irenäus als Paulusinterpret: Zur Rezeption und Wirkung der paulinischen und deuteropaulinischen Briefe im Werk des Irenäus von Lyon*. WUNT 66. Tübingen: Mohr Siebeck, 1994.

Norden, Eduard. *Die antike Kunstprosa*. 2 vols. 1915. Reprint, Stuttgart: Teubner, 1995.

Norelli, Enrico. "Marcion: ein christlicher Philosoph oder ein Christ gegen die Philosophie?" In May and Greschat, eds., *Marcion*, 113–30.

Norris, Richard A. "Irenaeus' Use of Paul in His Polemic against the Gnostics." In Babcock, ed., *Paul*, 79–98.

Oakes, Peter. "Leadership and Suffering in the Letters of Polycarp and Paul to the Philippians." In Gregory and Tuckett, eds., *Trajectories*, 353–73.

Ogg, George. *The Chronology of the Life of Paul*. London: Epworth, 1968.

O'Neill, John C. "Paul Wrote Some of All, but Not All of Any." In Porter, ed., *The Pauline Canon*, 169–88.

Origen. *Contra Celsum*. Translated by Henry Chadwick. Cambridge: Cambridge University Press, 1953.

Osiek, Carolyn, and David L. Balch. *Families in the New Testament World*. Louisville: Westminster John Knox, 1997.

Padovese, L. "L'antipaulinisme chrétien au IIe siècle." *Recherches de science religieuse* (2002): 390–422.

Pagels, Elaine H. *The Gnostic Paul: Gnostic Exegesis of the Pauline Letters*. Philadelphia: Fortress Press, 1975.

_____. "The Valentinian Claim to Esoteric Exegesis of Romans as Basis for Anthropological Theory." *VC* 26 (1972): 241–58.

Painter, John. *Just James: The Brother of Jesus in History and Tradition*. Columbia: University of South Carolina Press, 1997.

Papandreou, Damaskinos, Wolfgang A. Bienert, and Knut Schäferdiek, eds. *Oecumenica et Patristica*. FS W. Schneemelcher. Stuttgart: Teubner, 1989.

Parsons, Mikeal C., and Richard I. Pervo. *Rethinking the Unity of Luke and Acts*. Minneapolis: Fortress Press, 1993.

Payne, Philip B. "Fuldensis, Sigla for Variants in Vaticanus, and 1 Cor 14:34-35." *NTS* 41 (1995): 240-50.

_____. "Ms. 88 as Evidence for a Text without 1 Cor 14.34-35." *NTS* 44 (1998): 152-58.

Pearson, Birger. "I Thessalonians 2:13-16: A Deutero-Pauline Interpolation." *HTR* 64 (1971): 79-94.

Penny, Donald N. "The Pseudo-Pauline Letters of the First Two Centuries." Ph.D. diss., Emory University, 1979.

Pérès, Jacques-Noël. "Epître des apôtres." In Bovon et Geoltrain, eds., *Ecrits apocryphes chrétiens*, 357-92.

_____. *L'Epître des apôtres et le Testament de notre Seigneur et notre Sauveur Jésus-Christ*. Turnhout: Brepols, 1994.

Peretto, E. *La Lettera ai Romani cc. 1-8 nell' Adversus Haereses d'Ireneo*. Bari: Istitutio di Letteratura Cristiano Antica, 1971.

Perkins, Pheme. *The Gnostic Dialogue: The Early Church and the Crisis of Gnosticism*. New York: Paulist, 1980.

_____. "Philippians: Theology for the Heavenly Politeuma." In Bassler, ed., *Pauline Theology*, 1:89-104.

Perry, Ben Edwin. *The Ancient Romances: A Literary Historical Account of the Origins*. Sather Lectures 1951. Berkeley: University of California Press, 1967.

Pervo, Richard I. *Acts*. Hermeneia. Minneapolis: Fortress Press, 2009.

_____. "The Acts of Titus: A Preliminary Translation, with an Introduction and Notes." In *SBL 1996 Seminar Papers*, 455-82. SBLSP 35. Atlanta: Scholars, 1996.

_____. "The Ancient Novel Becomes Christian." In *The Novel in the Ancient World*, edited by G. Schmeling, 685-711. Mnemosyne Supplementum 159. Leiden: Brill, 1996.

_____. "Aseneth and Her Sisters: Women in Jewish Narrative and in the Greek Novels." In *"Women like This." New Perspectives on Jewish Women in the Greco-Roman World*, edited by Amy-Jill Levine, 145-60. SBLEJL 1. Atlanta: Scholars, 1991.

_____. *Dating Acts: Between the Evangelists and the Apologists*. Santa Rosa, Calif.: Polebridge, 2006.

_____. "Egging on the Chickens: A Cowardly Response to Dennis MacDonald and Then Some." *Semeia* 80 (1997): 43-56.

_____. "The Gates Have Been Closed (Acts 21:30): The Jews in Acts." *Journal of Higher Criticism* 11 (2005): 128-49.

_____. "A Hard Act to Follow: The Acts of Paul and the Canonical Acts." *Journal of Higher Criticism* 2/2 (1995): 3-32.

_____. "Johannine Trajectories in the Acts of John." *Apoc* 3 (1992): 47-68.

_____. "Meet Right—and Our Bounden Duty: Meetings and Assemblies in Acts." *Forum* n.s. 4/1 (2001): 45-62.

_____. "The Paul of Acts and the Paul of the Letters: Luke as an Interpreter of the Corpus Paulinum." In D. Marguerat, ed., *Réception du paulinisme dans les Actes des Apôtres* (Leuven: Pecters, 2009), 141-55.

_____. *Profit with Delight: The Literary Genre of the Acts of the Apostles*. Philadelphia: Fortress Press, 1987.

_____. "Romancing an Oft-neglected Stone: The Pastoral Epistles and the Epistolary Novel." *Journal of Higher Criticism* 1 (1994): 25–47.

_____. "Social and Religious Aspects of the Western Text." In *The Living Text*, edited by D. Groh and R. Jewett, 229–41. FS E.W. Saunders. Ann Arbor: University Press of America, 1985.

_____. "With Lucian: Who Needs Friends? Friendship in the Toxaris." In *Greco-Roman Perspectives on Friendship*, edited by J. Fitzgerald, 163–80. Atlanta: Scholars, 1997.

Pesthy, Monika. "Thecla in the Fathers of the Church." In Bremmer, ed., *The Apocryphal Acts of Paul and Thecla*, 164–78.

Pfister, Franz. "Die zweimalige römische Gefangenschaft und die spanische Reise des Apostels Paulus und der Schluss der Apostelgeschichte." *ZNW* 14 (1913): 216–21.

Pfleiderer, Otto. *Paulinism: A Contribution to the History of Primitive Christian Theology*. Translated by E. Peters. 2 vols. London: Williams & Norgate, 1891.

Pherigo, Lindsey P. "Paul's Life after the Close of Acts." *JBL* 70 (1951): 277–84.

Pietersen, Lloyd K. *The Polemic of the Pastorals: A Sociological Examination of the Development of Pauline Christianity*. JSNTS 264. London: T&T Clark International, 2004.

Pink, Karl. "Die pseudo-paulinischen Briefe I." *Bib* 6 (1925): 68–91.

_____. "Die pseudo-paulinischen Briefe II." *Bib* 6 (1925): 179–200.

Plank, Karl A. *Paul and the Irony of Affliction*. Atlanta: Scholars, 1987.

Pomeroy, Sarah B., ed. *Plutarch's Advice to the Bride and Groom and a Consolation to His Wife*. Oxford: Oxford University Press, 1999.

Portefaix, Lilian. " 'Good Citizenship' in the Household of God: Women's Position in the Pastorals Reconsidered in the Light of Roman Rule." In Levine, ed., *Feminist Companion*, 147–58.

Porter, Stanley E. "When and How was the Pauline Canon Compiled? An Assessment of Theories." In Porter, ed., *The Pauline Canon*, 95–127.

Porter, Stanley E., ed. *The Pauline Canon*. Pauline Studies 1. Leiden: Brill, 2004.

Poupon, Gérard. "Les 'Actes de Pierre' et leur remaniement." *ANRW* II.25.6 (1988): 4363–83.

_____. "L'Origine africaine des Actus Vercellenses." In Bremmer, ed., *Acts of Peter*, 192–99.

Praeder, Susan Marie. "Jesus-Paul, Peter-Paul, and Jesus-Peter Parallelisms." In *SBL 1984 Seminar Papers*, edited by K. H. Richards. SBLSP 23. Chico, Calif.: Scholars, 1984.

Prieur, J.-M. "L'étique sexuelle et conjugale des chrétiens des premiers siècles et ses justifications." *Revue d'histoire et de philosophie religieuses* 82 (2002): 267–82.

Quinn, Jerome D. "The Last Volume of Luke: The Relation of Luke–Acts to the Pastoral Epistles." In *Perspectives on Luke-Acts*, edited by C. H. Talbert, 62–75. Edinburgh: T. & T. Clark, 1978.

_____. *The Letter to Titus.* AB 35. New York: Doubleday, 1990.

_____. "P46—the Pauline Canon?" *CBQ* 36 (1974): 379–85.

_____. " 'Seven Times He Wore Chains' (1 Clem 5.6)." *JBL* 97 (1978): 574–76.

Quispel, Gilles. "De Brief aan die Laodicensen—ein Marcionistische vervalsing." *Nederlands Theologisch Tijdschrift* 5 (1950): 43–46.

_____. "Marcion and the Text of the New Testament." *VC* 52 (1998): 349–60.

_____. *Ptolémée: Lettre à Flora.* SC 24. 2nd ed. Paris: Cerf, 1966.

Radl, Walter. *Paulus und Jesus im Lukanischen Doppelwerk: Untersuchungen zu Parallelmotiven im Lukasevangelium und in der Apostelgeschichte.* Europäische Hochschulschriften 23/49. Bern: Lang, 1975.

Ramelli, Ilaria. "L'epistolario apocrifo Seneca–san Paolo: alcune osservazioni." *Vetera Christiana* 34 (1997): 299–310.

Ramsay, William M. *The Church in the Roman Empire.* London: Hodder & Stoughton, 1897.

_____. *The Letters to the Seven Churches of Asia and Their Place in the Plan of the Apocalypse.* New York: Armstrong, 1904.

Rathke, H. *Ignatius von Antiochen und die Paulusbriefe.* TU XCIX. Berlin: de Gruyter, 1967.

Redalié, Yann. *Paul après Paul. Le temps, le salut, la morale selon les êptires à Timothée et à Tite.* Monde de la Bible 31. Geneva: Labor et Fides, 1994.

Reis, David M. "Following in Paul's Footsteps: Mimesis and Power in Paul and Ignatius." In Gregory and Tuckett, eds., *Trajectories*, 287–305.

Rensberger, David K. "As the Apostle Teaches: The Development of the Use of Paul's Letters in Second-Century Christianity." Ph.D. diss., Yale University, 1981.

Reumann, John. *Variety and Unity in New Testament Thought.* Oxford: Oxford University Press, 1991.

Richard, Earl J. *First and Second Thessalonians.* SP 11. Collegeville, Minn.: Liturgical, 1995.

Richards, W. A. *Difference and Distance in Post-Pauline Christianity: An Epistolary Analysis of the Pastorals.* Studies in Biblical Literature 44. New York: Lang, 2002.

Rigaux, Beda. *Saint Paul. Les épîtres aux Thessaloniciens.* EB. Paris: Gabalda, 1956.

Robertson, Archibald, and Alfred Plummer. *A Critical and Exegetical Commentary on the First Epistle of St Paul to the Corinthians.* ICC. 2nd ed. Edinburgh: T. & T. Clark, 1914.

Robinson, James M. "The Historicality of Biblical Language." In *The Old Testament and Christian Faith*, edited by B. W. Anderson, 124–58. New York: Harper & Row, 1963.

_____, ed. *The Nag Hammadi Library in English.* Rev. ed. San Francisco: Harper & Row, 1988.

Robinson, James M., et al. *The Critical Edition of Q.* Hermeneia. Minneapolis: Fortress Press, 2000.

Robinson, James M., and Helmut Koester. *Trajectories through Early Christianity.* Philadelphia: Fortress Press, 1971.

Rohde, Joachim. "Pastoralbriefe und Acta Pauli." *Studia Evangelica* V (*TU* 103) (1968): 303–10.

Roloff, Jürgen. "Die Paulus-Darstellung des Lukas: Ihre geschichtlichen Voraussetzungen und ihr theologisches Ziel." *EvTh* 39 (1979): 510–31.

Roose, Hanna. "2 Thessalonians as Pseudepigraphic 'Reading Instruction' for 1 Thessalonians: Methodological Implications and Exemplary Illustration of an Intertextual Concept." In Brodie et al., eds., *Intertextuality*, 133–51.

Rordorf, Willy. "Actes de Paul." In Bovon and Geoltrain, eds., *Écrits apocryphes chrétiens*, 1115–77.

_____. "Hérésie et Orthodoxie selon la Correspondance apocryphe entre les Corinthiens et l'apôtre Paul." In *Lex Orandi, Lex Credendi. Gesammelte Aufsätze zum 60. Geburtstag (Paradosis)*, 380–431. Fribourg: Universitätsverlag, 1993.

_____. "In welchem Verhältnis stehen die apokryphen Paulusakten zur kanonischen Apostelgeschichte und zu den Pastoralbriefen?" In *Text and Testimony: Essays on New Testament and Apocryphal Literature in Honour of A. F. J. Klijn*, edited by T. Baarda et al., 225–41. Kampen: Uitgeversmaatschappij J. H. Kok, 1988.

_____. "Nochmals: Paulusakten und Pastoralbriefe." In *Tradition and Interpretation in the New Testament*, edited by G. F. Hawthorne and O. Betz, 319–27. FS E. E. Ellis. Grand Rapids: Eerdmans, 1987.

_____. "Paul's Conversion in the Canonical Acts and in the Acts of Paul." *Semeia* 80 (1997): 137–44.

_____. "Was wissen wir über Plan und Absicht der Paulusakten?" In Papandreou, Bienert, and Schäferdiek, eds., *Oecumenica et Patristica*, 71–82.

Rosenmeyer, Patricia A. *Ancient Epistolary Fictions. The Letter in Greek Literature*. Cambridge: Cambridge University Press, 2001.

Rothschild, Clare K. *Hebrews as Pseudepigraphon: The History and Significance of the Pauline Attribution of Hebrews*. WUNT 235. Tübingen: Mohr, 2009.

Rudolph, Kurt. *Gnosis: The Nature and History of Gnosticism*. Translated and edited by R. McL. Wilson. San Francisco: Harper & Row, 1983.

Runciman, Steven. *The Medieval Manichee: A Study of the Christian Dualist Heresy*. Cambridge: Cambridge University Press, 1947. Reissued 1982.

Salles, A. "La diatribe anti-pauliniene dans le 'le roman pseudo-clémentin' et l'origine des 'kérygmes de Pierre.'" *RB* 64 (1957): 516–51.

Sand, Alexander. "Überlieferung und Sammlung der Paulusbriefe." In Kertelge, ed., *Paulus*, 11–24.

Sanders, E. P. *Paul and Palestinian Judaism*. Philadelphia: Fortress Press, 1977.

Sappington, Thomas J. *Revelation and Redemption at Colossae*. JSNTSup 53. Sheffield: JSOT, 1991.

Schenke, Hans-Martin. "Das Weiterwirken des Paulus und die Pflege seines Erbes durch die Paulus-Schule." *NTS* 21 (1975): 505–18.

Schmeller, T. *Schulen im Neuen Testament? Zur Stellung des Urchristentums in der Bildungswelt seiner Zeit*. Herders biblische Studien 30. Freiburg: Herder, 2001.

Schmid, Ulrich. *Marcion und sein Apostolos. Rekonstruktion und historische Einordnung der marcionitschen Paulusbriefausgabe*. ANTF 25. Berlin: de Gruyter, 1995.

_____. "Marcions Evangelium und die neutestamentlichen Evangelien. Rückfragen zur Geschichte und Kanonisierung der Evangelienüberlieferung." In May and Geschrat, eds., *Marcion*, 67–77.

Schmidt, Carl. *Acti Pauli: Aus der heidelberger koptischen Papyrushandschrift nr. 1.* 2 vols. Leipzig: Hinrichs, 1905. Reprint, Hildesheim: Georg Olms, 1965.

Schmidt, Carl, with Wilhelm Schubart. ΠΡΑΞΕΙΣ ΠΑΥΛΟΥ. *Acta Pauli.* Glückstadt: J. J. Augustin, 1936.

Schmidt, Darryl. "1 Thess 2:13-16: Linguistic Evidence for an Interpolation." *JBL* 102 (1983): 269–79.

Schmithals, Walter. *Paul and the Gnostics.* Translated by John E. Steely. Nashville: Abingdon, 1972.

_____. *Der Römerbrief als Historisches Problem.* SNT 9. Gütersloh: Mohn, 1975.

_____. *Der Römerbrief. Ein Kommentar.* Gütersloh: Mohn, 1988.

Schnackenburg, Rudolf. *Ephesians: A Commentary.* Translated by H. Heron. Edinburgh: T. & T. Clark, 1991.

Schneemelcher, Wilhelm, "The Epistle to the Laodiceans." In Schneemelcher, ed., *New Testament Apocrypha*, 2:42–46.

_____. "Paulus in der griechischen Kirche des zweiten Jahrhunderts." *Zeitschrift für Kirchengeschichte* 75 (1964): 1–20.

_____, ed. *New Testament Apocrypha.* 2 vols. Translated and edited by R. McL. Wilson. Louisville: Westminster John Knox, 1991–92.

Schoedel, William R. "Ignatius and the Reception of Matthew in Antioch." In *Social History of the Matthean Community*, edited by D. Balch, 129–86. Minneapolis: Fortress Press, 1991.

_____. *Ignatius of Antioch: A Commentary on the Letters.* Hermeneia. Philadelphia: Fortress Press, 1985.

_____. "Papias." *ANRW* 2.27.1 (1993): 235–70.

_____. *Polycarp, Martyrdom of Polycarp, Fragments of Papias: The Apostolic Fathers. A New Translation and Commentary*, vol. 5. Edited by R. M. Grant. Camden, N.J.: Nelson, 1967.

_____. "Polycarp of Smyrna and Ignatius of Antioch." *ANRW* 2.27.1 (1993): 272–358.

Schrage, Wolfgang. *The Ethics of the New Testament.* Translated by David E. Green. Philadelphia: Fortress Press, 1988.

Schröter, Jens. "Kirche im Anschluss an Paulus. Aspekte der Paulusrezeption in der Apostelgeschichte und in den Pastoralbriefen." *ZNW* 98 (2007): 77–104.

Schwartz, Daniel. "The End of the Line: Paul in the Canonical Book of Acts." In Babcock, ed., *Paul*, 3–24.

Segal, Alan F. *Two Powers in Heaven: Early Rabbinic Reports about Christianity and Gnosticism.* Leiden: Brill, 1977.

Sellen, Gerhard. "Hauptprobleme des Ersten Korintherbriefes." *ANRW* 1.25.4 (1987): 2940–3044.

Sellew, Philip. "*Laodiceans* and the Philippians Fragments Hypothesis." *HTR* 87 (1994): 17–28.

Selwyn, Edward Gordon. *The First Epistle of St. Peter*. 2nd ed. London: Macmillan, 1947.

Skarsaune, Oskar. *The Proof from Prophecy: A Study in Justin Martyr's Proof-text Tradition: Text-Type, Provenance, Theological Profile*. NovTSup 56. Leiden: Brill, 1987.

Souter, Alexander. *Earliest Latin Commentaries on the Epistles of St Paul*. Oxford: Clarendon, 1927.

Speyer, Wolfgang. *Bücherfunde in der Glaubenswerbung der Antike*. Göttingen: Vandenhoeck & Ruprecht, 1970.

_____. *Die literarische Fälschung im heidnischen und christlichen Altertum: Ein Versuch ihrer Deutung*. Handbuch der Altertumswissenchaft I/2. Munich: Beck, 1971.

Spicq, Ceslas. *Les épîtres pastorales*. 4th ed. 2 vols. Paris: Galbalda, 1969.

_____. "L'imitation de Jésus-Christ durant les dernier jours de l'Apôtre Paul." In *Mélanges bibliques: en hommage au R. P. Béda Rigaux*. Gembloux: Duculot, 1970.

Standhartinger, Angela. "Colossians and the Pauline School." *NTS* 50 (2004): 572–93.

_____. "The Epistle to the Congregation in Colossae and the Invention of the 'Household Code.'" in Levine, ed., *Feminist Companion*, 88–97.

_____. *Studien zur Entstehunggeschichte und Intention des Kolosserbriefs*. NovTSup 94. Leiden: Brill, 1999.

Staniforth, Maxwell. *Early Christian Writings: The Apostolic Fathers*. Baltimore: Penguin, 1968.

Stenger, W. "Timotheus und Titus als literarische Gestalten." *Kairos* 16 (1974): 252–67.

Sterling, Gregory E. "'Athletes of Virtue': An Analysis of the Summaries in Acts (2:41-47; 4:32-34; 5:12-16)." *JBL* 113 (1994): 679–96.

_____. "From Apostle to the Gentiles to Apostle of the Church: Images of Paul at the End of the First Century." *ZNW* 98 (2007): 74–98.

Stewart-Sykes, Alistair. "Bread and Fish, Water and Wine: The Marcionite Menu and the Maintenance of Purity." In May and Greschat, eds., *Marcion*, 207–20.

Stone, Michael, and John Strugnell, ed. and trans. *The Books of Elijah*, parts 1–2. SBLTT 18. Missoula, Mont.: Scholars, 1979.

Stowers, Stanley K. "Friends and Enemies in the Politics of Heaven: Reading Theology in Philippians." In Bassler, ed., *Pauline Theology*, 1:105–21.

_____. *Letter Writing in Greco-Roman Antiquity*. LEC 5. Philadelphia: Westminster, 1986.

Strecker, Georg. "Paulus in nachpaulinischer Zeit." *Kairos* 12 (1970): 208–16.

Streete, Gail Corrington. "Askesis and Resistance in the Pastoral Letters." In Vaage and Wimbush, eds., *Asceticism*, 299–316.

Strugnell, John. "A Plea for Conjectural Emendation in the New Testament, with a Coda on 1 Cor 4:6." *CBQ* 34 (1974): 543–58.

Stylianopoulos, Theodore. *Justin Martyr and the Mosaic Law.* Missoula, Mont.: Scholars, 1975.

Suggs, M. Jack. *Wisdom, Christology, and Law in Matthew's Gospel.* Cambridge, Mass.: Harvard University Press, 1970.

Sundberg, Albert C. "Canon Muratori: A Fourth-Century List." *HTR* 66 (1973): 1–41.

Svenster, J. N. *Paul and Seneca.* NovTSup 4. Leiden: Brill, 1961.

Swain, Simon. *Hellenism and Empire: Language, Classicism, and Power in the Greek World, AD 50–250.* Oxford: Clarendon, 1996.

Szepessy, Tomas. "The Ancient Family Novel (A Typological Proposal)." *Acta Antiqua Acadamiae Scientiarum Hungaricae* 31 (1985–88): 357–65.

Tajra, Harry W. *The Martyrdom of St. Paul: Historical and Judicial Context, Traditions, and Legends.* WUNT 67. Tübingen: Mohr (Siebeck), 1994.

Talbert, Charles H. *Literary Patterns, Theological Themes, and the Genre of Luke-Acts.* SBLMS 20. Missoula, Mont.: Scholars, 1974.

_____. *Luke and the Gnostics.* New York: Abingdon, 1966.

Testuz, Michel. *Papyrus Bodmer X–XII.* Cologny-Geneve: Bibliotheque Bodmer, 1959.

_____. "La correspondance apocryphe de Saint Paul et des Corinthiens." In *Litterature et Theologie Paulinienes,* 217–23. Paris: Desclee de Brouwer, 1960.

Theissen, Gerd. *The Social Setting of Pauline Christianity: Essays on Corinth.* Edited and translated by John H. Schütz. Philadelphia: Fortress Press, 1982.

_____. *Sociology of Early Palestinian Christianity.* Translated by John Bowden. Philadelphia: Fortress Press, 1978.

Thoma, Albrecht. "Justins literarisches Verhältnis zu Paulus und zum Johannes-Evangelium." *ZWTh* 18 (1875): 385–412.

Thomas, Christine M. *The Acts of Peter, Gospel Literature, and the Ancient Novel: Rewriting the Past.* New York: Oxford University Press, 2003.

_____. "The 'Prehistory' of the *Acts of Peter.*" In *The Apocryphal Acts of the Apostles,* edited by François Bovon et al., 41–62. Harvard Divinity School Studies. Cambridge, Mass.: Harvard University Press, 1999.

Thomassen, Einar. "Orthodoxy and Heresy in Second-Century Rome." *HTR* 97 (2004): 241–56.

Thurston, Bonnie Bowman. *The Widows: A Women's Ministry in the Early Church.* Minneapolis: Fortress Press, 1989.

Tobin, Thomas H. *The Creation of Man: Philo and the History of Interpretation.* CBQMS 14. Washington: Catholic Biblical Association of America, 1983.

Trenkner, Sophie. *The Greek Novella in the Classical Period.* Cambridge: Cambridge University Press, 1958.

Trilling, Wolfgang. "Literarische Paulusimitation im 2. Thessalonicherbrief." In Kertelge, ed., *Paulus,* 146–56.

_____. *Untersuchungen zum zweiten Thessalonicherbrief.* Leipzig: St. Benno, 1972.

Trobisch, David. *Die Entstehung der Paulusbriefsammlung: Studien zu den Anfängen christlicher Publizistik.* Novum Testamentum et Orbis Antiquus 10. Freiburg: Editions universitaires, 1989.

_____. *The First Edition of the New Testament.* Oxford: Oxford University Press, 2000.

_____. *Paul's Letter Collection: Tracing the Origins.* Minneapolis: Fortress Press, 1994.

Troeltsch, Ernst. *The Social Teaching of the Christian Churches,* vol. 1. Translated by O. Wyon. 1911. Reprint, New York: Harper & Brothers, 1960.

Trummer, Peter. "Corpus Paulinum—Corpus Pastorale: Zur Ortung der Paulustradition in den Pastoralbriefen." In Kertelge, ed., *Paulus,* 122–45.

_____. *Die Paulus Tradition der Pastoralbriefe.* BBET 8. Frankfurt: Lang, 1978.

Turner, Nigel. *Style.* Vol. 4 of *A Grammar of New Testament Greek,* by James H. Moulton. 3rd ed. Edinburgh: T. & T. Clark, 1976.

Tyson, Joseph B. *The Death of Jesus in Luke–Acts.* Columbia: University of South Carolina Press, 1986.

_____. *Marcion and Luke-Acts: A Defining Struggle.* Columbia: University of South Carolina Press, 2006.

Vaage, Lief E., and Vincent L. Wimbush, eds. *Asceticism and the New Testament.* London: Routledge, 1999.

van Unnik, W. C. "Die Rücksicht auf die Reaktion der Nicht-Christen als Motiv in der altchristlichen Paränese." In *Judentum, Urchristentum, Kirche,* edited by Walther Eltester, 221–34. FS J. Jeremias. BZNW 26. Berlin: Töpelmann, 1960.

van Unnik, W. C., ed. *Neotestamentica et Patristica.* FS Oscar Cullmann. NovTSup 6. Leiden: Brill, 1962.

van Voorst, Robert E. *The Ascents of James: History and Theology of a Jewish-Christian Community.* SBLDS 112. Atlanta: Scholars, 1989.

Verheyden, Josef. "The Canon Muratori: A Matter of Dispute." In Auwers and de Jonge, eds., *The Biblical Canons,* 487–556.

_____. "The *Shepherd of Hermas* and the Writings That Later Formed the New Testament." In Gregory and Tuckett, eds., *Reception,* 293–329.

Verner, David. *The Household of God: The Social World of the Pastoral Epistles.* SBLDS 71. Chico, Calif.: Scholars, 1983.

Versnell, H. S. *Triumphus: An Inquiry into the Origin, Development and Meaning of the Roman Triumph.* Leiden: Brill, 1970.

Vinzent, Markus. "Der Schluß des Lukasevangeliums bei Marcion." In May and Geschrat, eds., *Marcion,* 79–93.

Voelker, Walter. "Paulus bei Origenes." *Th. St. Kr.* 102 (1930): 258–79.

Vouaux, Léon. *Les Actes de Paul et ses letters apocryphes.* ANT. Paris: Letouzey, 1913.

_____. *Les Actes de Pierre.* ANT. Paris: Letouzey, 1922.

Walker, William O. Jr. "1 Cor 15:29-34 as a non-Pauline Interpolation." *CBQ* 69 (2007): 84–103.

_____. *Interpolations in the Pauline Letters.* JSNTS 213. London: Sheffield Academic Press, 2001.

_____. "Interpolations in the Pauline Letters." In Porter, ed., *The Pauline Canon,* 189–235.

Weinfeld, Moshe. *The Organizational Pattern and the Penal Code of the Qumran Sect: A Comparison with Guilds and Religious Associations of the Hellenistic–Roman Period.* Novum Testamentum et Orbis Antiquus. Göttingen: Vandenhoeck & Ruprecht, 1986.

Weiss, Johannes. *Earliest Christianity: A History of the Period A. D. 30–150.* Translated by F. C. Grant et al. 2 vols. 1914. New ed. New York: Harper & Bros., 1959.

Welborn, Larry L. "The Soteriology of Romans in Clement of Alexandria, *Stromateis 2:* Faith, Fear, and Assimilation to God." In Gaca and Welborn, eds., *Romans,* 66–83.

Wengst, Klaus. *Tradition und Theologie des Barnabasbriefes.* Arbeiten zur Kirchengeschichte 42. Berlin: de Gruyter, 1971.

Werline, Rodney. "The Transformation of Pauline Arguments in Justin Martyr's *Dialogue with Trypho.*" HTR 92 (1999): 79–93.

Werner, Johannes. *Der Paulinismus des Irenaeus.* TU 6/2. Leipzig: Teubner, 1889.

Westcott, Brooke F. *A General Survey of the History of the Canon of the New Testament.* 6th ed. London: Macmillan, 1889.

White, John L. *The Form and Structure of The Official Petition.* SBLDS 5. Missoula, Mont.: University of Montana Press, 1972.

Whittaker, Molly, ed. and trans. *Tatian:* Oratio ad Graecos. Oxford: Clarendon, 1982.

Wild, Robert A. "The Image of Paul in the Pastoral Letters." *The Bible Today* 23 (1985): 239–45.

_____. "The Warrior and the Prisoner: Some Reflections on Ephesians 6:10-20." *CBQ* 46 (1984): 284–98.

Wilder, T. L. *Pseudonymity, the New Testament, and Deception: An Inquiry Into Intention and Reception.* Lanham, Md.: University Press of America, 2004.

Wiles, Maurice F. *The Divine Apostle: The Interpretation of St. Paul's Epistles in the Early Church.* Cambridge: Cambridge University Press, 1967.

Williams, D. S. "Reconsidering Marcion's Gospel." *JBL* 108 (1989): 477–96.

Williams, Jacqueline A. *Biblical Interpretation in the Gnostic Gospel of Truth from Nag Hammadi.* SBLDS 79. Atlanta: Scholars, 1988.

Williams, Michael A. *Rethinking Gnosticism: An Argument for Dismantling a Dubious Category.* 2d ed. Princeton: Princeton University Press, 1999.

Wilson, Bryan. *Magic and the Millenium.* New York: Harper & Row, 1973.

Wilson, Robert McL. *Gnosis and the New Testament.* Philadelphia: Fortress Press, 1968.

Wilson, R. S. *Marcion: A Study of a Second Century Heretic.* London: Clarke, 1933.

Wilson, Stephen G. *Leaving the Fold: Apostates and Defectors in Antiquity.* Minneapolis: Fortress Press, 2006.

_____. "The Portrait of Paul in Acts and the Pastorals." In *SBL 1976 Seminar Papers*, edited by George MacRae, 397–411. SBLSP 10. Missoula, Mont.: Scholars.

_____. *Related Strangers: Jews and Christians 70–170 CE*. Minneapolis: Fortress Press, 1995.

Winter, Bruce W., and A. D. Clarke, eds. *The Book of Acts in Its First Century Setting*. Vol. 1, *The Book of Acts in Its Ancient Literary Setting*. Grand Rapids: Eerdmans, 1993.

Witherington, Ben E., III. *The Acts of the Apostles: A Socio-Rhetorical Commentary*. Grand Rapids: Eerdmans, 1998.

Wolter, Michel. *Die Pastoralbriefe als Paulustradition*. FRLANT 146. Göttingen: Vandenhoeck & Ruprecht, 1988.

Wright, W. *Apocryphal Acts of the Apostles: Edited from Syriac Manuscripts in the British Museum and Other Libraries*. 2 vols. London: Williams & Norgate, 1871.

Young, Frances. *The Theology of the Pastoral Letters*. Cambridge: Cambridge University Press, 1994.

_____. "Wisdom in the Apostolic Fathers and the New Testament." In Gregory and Tuckett, eds., *Trajectories*, 85–104.

Zahn, Theodor. *Geschichte des neutestamentlichen Kanons*. 3 vols. Erlangen: Deicher, 1890–92.

Zuntz, Gunther. *The Text of the Epistles: A Disquisition upon the* Corpus Paulinum. London: Oxford University Press, 1953.

NOTES

Preface

1. To cite but one example: Acts 16:1-3, which relates the circumcision of Timothy, in apparent opposition to Galatians (esp. 5:11), is defended by appeal to 1 Cor. 9, by, for example, Ben E. Witherington III, *The Acts of the Apostles: A Socio-Rhetorical Commentary* (Grand Rapids: Eerdmans, 1998), 476. Joseph Fitzmyer (*Acts of the Apostles*, AB 31 [New York: Doubleday, 1998], 575-76) inclines to accept the story, but avoids appeal to 1 Corinthians, while C. K. Barrett (*Acts*, ICC; 2 vols. [Edinburgh: T. & T. Clark, 1998], 2:760-61) prefers to reject the account.

2. Paul does not say that he "became a Greek to the Greeks," nor "strong to the strong."

3. An example lying near to hand is 1 Cor. 8:13: "Therefore, if food is a cause of their falling, I will never eat meat, so that I may not cause one of them to fall."

4. See, for example, the *Damascus Document* 1.18. The scriptural authority is Isa. 30:10.

5. Andreas Lindemann, *Paulus im Ältesten Christentum*, BHT 58 (Tübingen: Mohr Siebeck, 1979), 15.

6. See Chapter 1.

7. See Chapter 6.

8. The more sophisticated will say "the Renaissance" and point to the work of Erasmus and such figures as John Colet, the Dean of St Paul's, both of whom focused upon the text of Paul's epistles rather than the history of their interpretation.

9. The Jesuit scholar Richard Simon (1638-1712) had earlier made this case, with strong critical arguments. He found no warm reception in his own communion and was rebuffed by many Protestants. Semler showed that the New Testament canon was the result of a historical process rather than a unified entity. Baur took up Semler's thesis and identified a number of competing schools of thought within nascent Christianity. He stressed that historians had to look at sources in terms of the leading questions and understandings of their time of origin.

10. See Table 2.

11. One exception is the traditional popular history of the American Civil War. See Richard I. Pervo, *Dating Acts* (Santa Rosa, Calif.: Polebridge, 2006), 56-57.

12. See p. 232.

13. "Current" is important. Prior to printed editions of the New Testament (c. 1450), the place of Acts varied.

14. See Table 9.

15. See Table 5.

Introduction

1. The Latin text of the *Acts of the Scillitan Martyrs*, with a facing English translation, can be found in Herbert Musurillo, *The Acts of the Christian Martyrs* (Oxford: Clarendon, 1972), 86–88. The full list of names appears in §17.

2. If taken in this strict sense, it would be one of the very few examples of the use of scrolls (as opposed to codices, books) for Christian scripture.

3. Gerald Bonner, "The Scillitan Saints and the Pauline Epistles," *JEH* 7 (1956): 141–46, is confident that "books" refers to "gospels." From a later perspective this is probable. The grammatical difficulty is the absence of a modifier, such as "some" (*aliqui*), with books.

4. The major question is whether this is an account from c. 180. It evidently presumes the existence of a Latin translation of Paul's letters. The proconsul has the believers executed in a manner appropriate for Roman citizens, without torture and other abuse. The brief statement about Paul is unlikely to be a later invention, however.

5. On the *Acts of Paul*, see Chapter 4.

6. See above, p. ix.

7. For an inventory of these texts, see Tables 1 and 2.

8. The subsequent chapters will flesh out details of these assertions.

9. An excellent recent study is H.-J. Klauck (with D. R. Bailey), *Ancient Letters and the New Testament* (Waco, Tex.: Baylor University Press, 2006).

10. For the distinction between Lucan and "Q" material here, see James M. Robinson *et al.*, *The Critical Edition of Q*, Hermeneia (Minneapolis: Fortress Press, 2000), 376–87. (Q is a hypothetical gospel, composed of sayings, that was used by both Matthew and Luke.)

11. This citation from Colossians is part of the earliest surviving Christian example of the Household Code, brief summaries of duties for various pairs: owner/slave, husband/wife, parent/children. The impact of this standard for contemporary "family values" is ubiquitous in Christian texts from c. 80–140 CE (Colossians, Ephesians, 1 Peter, *1 Clement*, the Pastoral Epistles, Ignatius of Antioch, and Polycarp of Smyrna). See David Balch, *Let Wives Be Submissive: The Domestic Code in 1 Peter*, SBLMS 26 (Chico, Calif.: Scholars, 1981); David Verner, *The Household of God: The Social World of the Pastoral Epistles*, SBLDS 71 (Chico, Calif.: Scholars, 1983); Elisabeth Schüssler Fiorenza, *In Memory of Her: A Feminist Theological Reconstruction of Christian Origins* (New York: Crossroads, 1983), 251–79; Clayton N. Jefford, "Household Codes and Conflict in the Early Church," *Studia Patristica* 31 (1997): 121–27; Andrew T. Lincoln, "The Household Code and Wisdom Mode of Colossians," *JSNT* 74 (1999): 93–112; and Angela Standhartinger, "The Epistle to the Congregation in Colossae and the Invention of the 'Household Code,'" in *A Feminist Companion to the Deutero-Pauline Epistles*, ed. A.-J. Levine (Cleveland: Pilgrim, 2003), 88–97.

12. The interpretation of Paul proffered by Augustine of Hippo (354–430) gained the admiration of most Reformation theologians and their successors.

13. An outstanding example of this tendency is Johannes Werner, *Der Paulinismus des Irenaeus*. TU 6.2 (Leipzig: Hinrichs, 1889). Slightly more nuanced, but still largely negative, is Eva Aleith, *Paulusverständnis in der alten Kirche*, BZNW 18 (Berlin: Töpelmann, 1937). See n. 30.

14. See, for example, William S. Campbell, Peter S. Hawkins, and Brenda D. Schlingen, eds., *Medieval Readings of Romans* (New York: T&T Clark International, 2002), followed by Kathy L. Gaca and Larry L. Welborn, *Early Patristic Readings of Romans* (New York: T&T Clark International, 2005).

15. On Mani and his mission, see Samuel N. C. Lieu, *Manichaeism in the Later Roman Empire and Medieval China*, 2nd ed. (Tübingen: Mohr, 1992).

16. This movement sparked the reforms of the Fourth Lateran Council (1215), the formation of the Dominicans, and the development of the Inquisition. An accessible survey is Steven Runciman, *The Medieval Manichee: A Study of the Christian Dualist Heresy* (Cambridge: Cambridge University Press, 1947 [reissued in 1982]). The Cathari furnished the German word for "heretic," *Ketzer*.

17. This was his conflict with Pelagius, an English monk who had a less pessimistic view of human nature than Augustine.

18. Traditional orthodoxy was also discredited by the wars of religion, including the Thirty Years' War (1618–48). By the dawn of the eighteenth century, many believed that religious differences did

not justify the killing of some Christians by others. The last third of the eighteenth century saw a challenge to religio-political authority. The newly formed United States of America prohibited established religion and essentially guaranteed freedom of religious belief. In its early phases, the leaders of the French Revolution felt obliged to outlaw the Roman Catholic Church.

19. Criticism existed before the eighteenth century. Patristic authorities, notably Eusebius, recorded divergent opinions about the suitability of certain books. In the first edition of his German New Testament (1522), Martin Luther (1483-1546) rendered negative judgments about Hebrews, James, 2 Peter, and Revelation. These theological conclusions led to historical observations, such as the distance of the narrator of Jude from the time of the apostles. See Werner Georg Kümmel, *The New Testament: The History of the Investigation of Its Problems*, trans S. McLean Gilmour and Howard C. Kee (Nashville: Abingdon, 1970), 23-26.

20. To complicate the problems, different bodies had different canonical lists and practices. Anglicans, for example, excluded the "Deutero-Canonical"/"Apocryphal" books, but read them in church (one criterion of canonicity), while Lutherans declined to issue a canonical list. Eastern Christians have a larger Old Testament than Western believers.

21. F. C. Baur rejected the Pauline authorship of the Pastoral Epistles in 1835 and found this grounds for expelling them from the canon. See his *Ausgewählte Werke* (Stuttgart: Fromman, 1963-75), 3:296.

22. The complex question of pseudepigraphy will not be discussed here, as its function in the Deutero-Pauline tradition is clear. For bibliography on the subject, see Stanley E. Porter, "When and How Was the Pauline Canon Compiled? An Assessment of Theories," in *The Pauline Canon*, ed. Stanley E. Porter; Pauline Studies 1 (Leiden: Brill, 2004), 95-127 (112 n. 58). Note, in particular, Wolfgang Speyer, *Die literarische Fälschung im heidnischen und christlichen Altertum: Ein Versuch ihrer Deutung*, Handbuch der Altertumswissenchaft I/2 (Munich: Beck, 1971); Norbert Brox, *Pseudepigraphie in der heidnischen und jüdisch-christlichen Antike*, Wege der Forschung 484 (Darmstadt: Wissenschaftliche Buchgesellschaft, 1977); Lewis R. Donelson, *Pseudepigraphy and Ethical Argument in the Pastoral Epistles*, HUT 22 (Tübingen: Mohr Siebeck, 1986); T. L. Wilder, *Pseudonymity, the New Testament, and Deception: An Inquiry into Intention and Reception* (Lanham, Md.: University Press of America, 2004); and Clare K. Rothschild, *Hebrews as Pseudepigraphon: The History and Significance of the Pauline Attribution of Hebrews*, WUNT 235 (Tübingen: Mohr, 2009), 121-39. For a compact summary of the question, see Martin Kitchen, *Ephesians*, New Testament Readings (London: Routledge, 1994), 22-28. Note also the bibliography in Klauck, *Ancient Letters*, 399-402.

23. The last work to claim that title was Otto Pfleiderer's *Paulinism: A Contribution to the History of Primitive Christian Theology*, trans. E. Peters; 2 vols. (London: Williams & Norgate, 1891). Pfleiderer (2:51-253) dealt with Pauline influence upon Hebrews, Colossians, *Barnabas*, *1 Clement*, 1 Peter, Ephesians, the Pastoral Epistles, Ignatius, and Acts. Aleith's *Paulusverständnis* is succinct to the point of superficiality and driven by the assumption that no one understood Paul.

24. Ernst Dassmann, *Der Stachel im Fleisch: Paulus in der frühchristlichen Literatur bis Irenäus* (Münster: Aschendorff, 1979).

25. Notably William S. Babcock, ed., *Paul and the Legacies of Paul* (Dallas: Southern Methodist University Press, 1990). See also Andrew Gregory and Christopher Tuckett, eds., *The Reception of the New Testament in the Apostolic Fathers*. The New Testament and the Apostolic Fathers 1 (Oxford: Oxford University Press, 2005), and *Trajectories through the New Testament and the Apostolic Fathers*, The New Testament and the Apostolic Fathers 2 (Oxford: Oxford University Press, 2005), both of which treat Pauline texts, among others.

26. Acts 24:17 shows that Luke knew about the collection.

27. No evidence for *Petros* ("rock") as a proper name prior to the apostle has come to light.

28. On the deaths of Peter and Paul, see p. 169 (Chapter 4). The first accounts of their Roman martyrdoms are in the respective Apocryphal Acts. Josephus reports that James was stoned in Jerusalem in 62 (*Ant.* 20.200). This is somewhat more probable than the date of 66/7 or 69 proposed by Eusebius (*H.E.* 2.23.18).

29. Eusebius (*H.E.* 3.5.3) reports that the Christians of Jerusalem fled to Pella. This is probably not historical.

30. The gentile Christian mission began within two years of the first Easter. Missions of the "Jewish-Christian" (an unsatisfactory term) type continued for many years, eventually giving birth to what is often called "Judeo-Christianity," represented, for example in the Pseudo-Clementine literature and other east Syrian texts issued under the authority of Peter or James.

31. See pp. 220-26.

32. Appeal to the guidance of the Spirit/Paraclete is characteristic of the Johannine tradition (John 13-17). First John shows some of its dangers. The perceived threat of Montanism (a second century movement of spiritual revival) laid this approach to a temporary rest.

33. That is, written gospels and their predecessors. See Helmut Koester, *Ancient Christian Gospels: Their History and Development* (Philadelphia: Trinity Press International, 1990).

34. The sayings to which Paul occasionally appeals (e.g., 1 Cor 7:10; 1 Thess 4:15) are those of the heavenly Lord.

35. Bauer (*Orthodoxy and Heresy in Earliest Christianity*, trans. and ed. Robert A. Kraft and Gerhard Krodel [Philadelphia: Fortress Press, 1971], 233) may, not for the first time, overstate the case: "What he held together by virtue of his own personality fell to pieces, was fought over, and was divided up after his death."

36. Although there is probably some consensus about the existence of one or more "Pauline schools," their origin, nature, and scope are a matter of considerable debate and speculation. At present I should prefer to have this term understood in the broadest sense. For a good discussion of the models proposed, see Andreas Lindemann, *Paulus im ältesten Christentum*, BHT 58 (Tübingen: Mohr Siebeck, 1979), 36-38; Paul-Gerhard Müller, *Anfänge der Paulusschule: Dargestellt am zweiten Thessalonicherbrief und am Kolosserbrief*, Abhandlungen zur Theologie des Alten und Neuen Testamens 74 (Zurich: Theologischer, 1988); and, more recently, Angela Standhartinger, *Studien zur Entstehungsgeschichte und Intention des Kolosserbriefs*, NovTSup 94 (Leiden: Brill, 1999), 277-89. In "Colossians and the Pauline School," NTS 50 (2004): 572-93, Standhartinger seeks to show a "school" at work by identifying the revision of Pauline tradition. In order to accomplish this goal, she allows for only limited intertextuality, essentially Philemon. Two seminal studies of the subject are H.-M. Schenke, "Das Weiterwirken des Paulus und die Pflege seines Erbes durch die Paulus-Schule," NTS 21 (1974-75): 505-18, and Hans Conzelmann, "Die Schule des Paulus," in *Theologia Crucis—Signum Crucis: Festschrift E. Dinkler*, ed. E. Dinkler, C. Andresen, and G. Klein (Tübingen: Mohr Siebeck, 1979), 85-96. Schenke and Conzelmann take different approaches to the subject. For a critique of "school-theories" as explanations of pseudonymity and references to literature, see D. G. Meade, *Pseudonymity and Canon* (Grand Rapids: Eerdmans, 1987), 6-9. For a specific critique of Schenke and Lindemann, see Alexander Sand, "Überlieferung und Sammlung der Paulusbriefe," in *Paulus in den Neutestamentlichen Spätschriften: Zur Paulusrezeption im Neuen Testament*, ed. K. Kertlege; QD 89 (Freiburg: Herder, 1981), 11-24. See also Birger A. Pearson, "Hellenistic-Jewish Wisdom Speculation and Paul," in *Aspects of Wisdom in Judaism and Early Christianity*, ed. Robert L. Wilken (Notre Dame: University of Notre Dame Press, 1975), 43-66. A favorable judgment of the school model is propounded by Richard S. Ascough, *The Formation of Pauline Churches* (New York: Paulist, 1998). T. Schmeller, *Schulen im Neuen Testament? Zur Stellung des Urchristentums in der Bildungswelt seiner Zeit*. Herders biblische Studien 30 (Freiburg: Herder, 2001), raises a number of important questions relating to the disparities between early Christian communities and ancient philosophical schools.

37. See p. 24.

38. Cf. also 1 Tim. 3:14.

39. See, for example, the various manifestations of the Parable of the Great Banquet (Luke 14:25-34 parr.).

40. Attitudes toward Jewish scripture vary from the wholesale approval and appropriation—represented, for example, in Luke and Acts—to the total rejection of Marcion. Although it is often assumed that Paul encouraged gentile converts to "search the scriptures," this is far from certain.

41. First Corinthians 1-4 shows that there were debates about personal sources of authority: Peter, Paul, Apollos, or no human authority (Christ) already within Paul's lifetime. On Ephesus as a probable site for an edition of Paul's letters, see pp. 55-61.

42. A different, but not unrelated, approach is taken by Daniel Marguerat ("Paul après Paul: une histoire de reception," NTS 54 [2008]: 317-37), who distinguishes among three different types

of reception: "documentary" (the letters), "biographical" (e.g., Acts, *Acts of Paul*), and "doctoral" (e.g., pseudo-Pauline letters). It is appropriate to identify leading characteristics of each type. Contamination occurs as early as *1 Clement*, which evokes 1 Corinthians (ch. 47), summarizes a biography (5:6), and identifies Paul as a universal teacher of righteousness (5:7). Colossians, Ephesians, and 2 Timothy utilize biographical detail to support Paul's teachings, while continuing the epistolary tradition. These categories are *means* for developing the Pauline tradition.

43. See Table 1.

44. Comparison between Acts 9 and Gal. 1–2 (see also Gal. 5:11 vs. Acts 16:1-3) indicates that stories about Paul circulated during his lifetime continued to attract credence, despite his denials. It is most interesting that Acts can repeat these stories in *support* of Paul. O. Linton stressed the existence of such stories in "The Third Aspect," *ST* 3 (1951): 79–95.

45. I have gained some comfort from learning that Robert A. Wild, S.J., President of Marquette University, is willing to use the same expression ("The Warrior and the Prisoner: Some Reflections on Ephesians 6:10-20," *CBQ* 46 [1984]: 284–98).

46. This outline is quite indebted to the classroom teaching of Helmut Koester at Harvard (1972–74), to Lindemann, *Paulus*, as well as to C. K. Barrett, "Pauline Controversies in the Post-Pauline Period," *NTS* 20 (1973–74): 229–45; M. C. de Boer, "Images of Paul in the Post-Apostolic Period," *CBQ* 42 (1980): 359–80, and Beker, *Heirs*, 93–94.

47. Note, in addition to texts discussed below: *1 Clem.* 47.1; Ignatius, *Eph.* 12.2; *Rom.* 4.3; Polycarp, *Phil.* 9:11; 11:2-3. The title "The Divine Apostle" is first attested in Clement of Alexandria (*Strom.* 1.94.4; 5.5.1 et al.). "The apostle" is ubiquitous.

48. V. Furnish, "Colossians, Letter to," *ABD* 1:1094.

49. To a degree the title "apostle" and the relation of Paul to "the Twelve" can be a bit of a red herring here. Second Thessalonians does not use the term "apostle," but authority revolves around the interpretation of Paul's letters, which are so weighty that they inspire forgeries. Colossians likewise uses the title only in the prescript. Nonetheless, Paul is practically the sole apostle. See Col. 1:23.

50. In terms of Jewish tradition, the model is that of the succession of prophets, followed most explicitly in Luke and Acts: Moses, Elijah–Elisha, Jesus, Peter, Paul.

51. Cf. also Col. 1:6: "that has come to you. Just as it is bearing fruit and growing in the whole world, so it has been bearing fruit among yourselves from the day you heard it and truly comprehended the grace of God." Contrast the popular legend of the "Apostolic Lottery," in which the Twelve drew lots to determine which of twelve sections of the world was to be their missionary field. It is described in *The Acts of Thomas* 1, *The Acts of Andrew and Matthias*, and *Acts of Philip* 8 1. The use of lots in Acts 1 provides good grounds for seeing direct conflict between the canonical and later Acts. Note also Justin, *1 Apology* 39.2-3: "For a band of twelve men went forth from Jerusalem, and they were common men, not trained in speaking, but by the power of God they testified to every race of mankind that they were sent by Christ to teach to all the word of God" (trans. Edward R. Hardy in Cyril C. Richardson, ed., *Early Christian Fathers* ([LCC 1, Philadelphia: Westminster, 1953]), 266. This is significant because of Justin's well-known silence regarding Paul and in light of arguments that Justin knew and valued Acts. Justin does not wish to yield universal mission to one apostle, certainly not Paul.

52. This is the important thesis of C. Burchard, *Der dreizehnte Zeuge*, FRLANT 103 (Göttingen: Vandenhoeck & Ruprecht, 1970).

53. Examples include 1 Tim. 2:1 and 2 Tim. 1:11. *First Clement* 5:6 hails Paul as "herald in both east and west," that is, everywhere. *First Clement* 9:4 shows that this is traditional (cf. also 7:6). Second Peter 2:5 describes Noah as a herald to all those of his generation. The *Acts of Xanthippe and Polyxena* 7 apostrophizes him as "the blessed Paul, herald, teacher, and illuminator of the world." In ch. 8 of the same work, the phrase "Paul the Herald of God" appears on his forehead. The term was avoided in earlier writings because heralds were sacred personages. The term's usage in the Pastoral Epistles testifies to Paul's exalted status. See also the Greek papyrus of the *Acts of Phileas*, Herbert Musurillo, *The Acts of the Christian Martyrs* (Oxford: Clarendon, 1972), 336. It is used of the philosopher by Epictetus, *Diss.* 3.21.13-16. See Gerhard Friedrich, "κῆρυξ," *TDNT* 3:683–97, and Ceslas Spicq, *Les épitres pastorales*, 4th ed.; 2 vols. (Paris: Galbalda, 1969), 1:319.

54. Cf. Eph. 2:20; 3:5; and 4:11.

55. For example, 3.4: "For I delivered to you first of all what I had received [cf. 1 Cor. 15:3] from the apostles before me [cf. Gal. 1:17] who were always with Jesus Christ [cf. Acts 1:21]" (J. K. Elliott, trans., *The Apocryphal New Testament* [Oxford: Clarendon, 1993], 381).

56. See *Epist. Apost.* 31-33.

57. This quality of collegiality is made explicit by the addition of *3 Corinthians* to the *Acts of Paul.* See 3.1, and the letter of the Corinthians to Paul (1.4-5). Paul is also a major figure in the later text of The *Acts of Peter,* where he labors in harmonious tandem with its hero. See pp. 162-69.

58. The length of the Ephesian mission (19:10) is (correctly) attributed to the use of Ephesus as a base for wide-ranging activities.

59. For further references to Acts 1:8; 13:47, see below.

60. "All, every" occurs fifty times in Ephesians, thirty-nine in Colossians, of 460 appearances in the corpus (111 of which are in 1 Corinthians).

61. Philemon 23-24 is the apparent source of the list of greetings in Col. 4:10-14. For Colossians' major Pauline sources (including Philippians), see Mark Kiley, *Colossians as Pseudepigraphy* (Sheffield: JSOT, 1986).

62. Cf. the process of editing, p. 31.

63. Cf., for example, Phil. 3:3-8.

64. See Gal. 1:13, 23; Phil. 3:6. On the meaning of "persecution," see p. 17. The term used for "persecutor" also appears in *Did.* 5:2 and *Barn.* 20:2.

65. On these terms, see M. Dibelius and H. Conzelmann, *The Pastoral Epistles,* trans. P. Buttolph and A. Yarbro; ed. H. Koester; Hermeneia (Philadelphia: Fortress Press, 1972), 27–28; G. Bertram, "ὕβρις," *TDNT* 8:295–307 (306); H. W. Beyer, "βλασφημέω," *TDNT* 1:621–25 (624); and, most fully, Spicq, *Les épitres pastorales,* 1:341–42. Spicq can support his acceptance of the applicability of these terms by reference to Acts.

66. On ἀγνοία, see Spicq, *Les épitres pastorales,* 1:342.

67. See 1 Tim. 1:16, cited above.

68. See Richard I. Pervo, *Acts: A Commentary,* Hermeneia (Minneapolis: Fortress Press, 2009), 241.

69. Paul's Jewish past is an issue about which the writer of the Pastoral Epistles is silent.

70. Note, in particular, Acts 8:3; 9:1-2.

71. See John C. Lentz, Jr., *Luke's Portrait of Paul,* SNTSMS 77 (Cambridge: Cambridge University Press, 1993).

72. Spicq, *Les épitres pastorales,* 1:342.

73. Cf. 1 Tim. 1:15 (above), where Paul ranks himself "first," that is, chief among sinners. The writer of Ephesians is not content with a mere superlative, but must add to this a(n elative) comparative suffix: "very leastest."

74. The *Acts of Peter* 2 shares the same perspective in line with the Deutero-Pauline metamorphosis of the "once...now" pattern. Paul, about to depart to Spain, addresses the Roman believers with these words: "Once I was a blasphemer, but now I am blasphemed; Once I was a persecutor, Now I suffer persecution from others; Once I was an enemy of Christ, now I pray to be his friend" (Elliott, trans., *The Apocryphal New Testament,* 400).

75. Eph. 2:3 may have helped to inspire the speech in *The Acts of Peter* 2, cited in the previous note.

76. If one associates Ephesians, Acts, and the Pastoral Epistles with Ephesus, as is likely, it is possible to suggest Ephesus as a locale for the development of Pauline legends stressing his wicked and essentially "pagan" past. Revelation indicates conflict between "Jewish" Christians and those of a more "gentile" (Pauline?) orientation. That Revelation also has some "Pauline" characteristics (use of letters, authority derived from the heavenly Christ rather than teachings of earthly Jesus transmitted by "original disciples") indicates the complexity of the problem.

77. Scholars (e.g., Furnish, "Paul in His Place," 4–5) tend to stress the gap between Paul's use of himself as an example of life conformed to the cross and the moralism of the Deutero-Paulines. Patristic interpreters of Paul tend to be no less moralizing, to the disgust of many recent exegetes. For a rather general survey of this material, see Maurice F. Wiles, *The Divine Apostle: The Interpretation of St. Paul's Epistles in the Early Church* (Cambridge: Cambridge University Press, 1967).

78. Cf., for example, 1 Cor. 4:7-15; 2 Cor. 10–13.

79. See, for example, Richard I. Pervo, *Profit with Delight* (Philadelphia: Fortress Press, 1987), 14–24, et passim.

80. For these imprisonments, see, in addition to the commentaries, J. D. Quinn, " 'Seven Times He Wore Chains' (*1 Clem* 5.6)," *JBL* 97 (1978): 574–76, and Richard Bauckham, "The Acts of Paul as a Sequel to Acts," in *The Book of Acts in Its First Century Setting*, vol. 1, *The Book of Acts in Its Ancient Literary Setting*, ed. B. W. Winter and A. D. Clarke (Grand Rapids: Eerdmans, 1993), 105–52. For a response, see Richard I. Pervo, "A Hard Act to Follow: The *Acts of Paul* and the Canonical Acts," *Journal of Higher Criticism* 2, no. 2 (1995): 3–32.

81. *Acts of Paul* 3.17-18.

82. *Acts of Paul* 9/7. (When two chapter numbers for the *Acts of Paul* are cited, the former is that of the forthcoming critical edition of Willy Rordorf. The smaller numbers refer to the standard translations.)

83. *Acts of Paul* 10/8.

84. *Acts of Paul* 14/11.3. One of the *cruces* for the understanding of *Acts of Paul* in relation to other texts (especially canonical Acts) is that Paul goes to Rome as a free person.

85. M. Staniforth, trans., *Early Christian Writings* (London: Penguin, 1968), 145 (modified).

86. See Pervo, *Acts*, 309.

87. Ephesus is a likely provenance for Luke and Acts. See Pervo, *Acts*, 5–6.

88. For a possible source of v. 24, compare and contrast Phil. 1:29.

89. First Thessalonians 2:17—3:5 give one Pauline view of suffering as hindrance to mission.

90. See, for example, Pervo, *Profit*, 18–21.

91. At this point, witnesses (K^mg, 181^mg, Sy^hmg) add a marginal gloss referring readers to both *Acts of Paul* (Thecla) and canonical Acts (Jews do not play a role in the Thecla story). At 2 Tim. 4:19, 181 and a few MSS fill out the names of the household of Onesiphorus on the basis of *Acts of Paul* 2. These show that the *Acts of Paul* was long viewed as a source for historical information. Narrative implications of the Pastorals are discussed in Richard I. Pervo, "Romancing an Oft-neglected Stone: The Pastoral Epistles and the Epistolary Novel," *Journal of Higher Criticism* 1 (1994): 25–47.

92. Note, in particular, Col. 1:24; 4:3, 18; Eph. 3:1, 13; 4:1.

93. See Phil. 2:12; 1 Thess. 2:17-20.

94. First Corinthians 5:3 reads: "For though absent in body, I am present in spirit; and as if present I have already pronounced judgment."

95. Major recent discussions include M. D. Goulder, *Type and History in Acts* (London: SPCK, 1964); C. Talbert, *Literary Patterns, Theological Themes, and the Genre of Luke-Acts*, SBLMS 20 (Missoula, Mont.: Scholars, 1974); W. Radl, *Paulus und Jesus im Lukanischen Doppelwerk* (Bern: Lang, 1975); and G. R. Jacobson, "Paul in Luke-Acts: The Savior Who Is Present," in *SBLSP 1983*, ed. K. H. Richards (Chico, Calif.: Scholars, 1983), 131–46. Note also the useful cautions in Susan M. Praeder, "Jesus-Paul, Peter-Paul, and Jesus-Peter Parallelisms," in *SBLSP 1984*, ed. K. H. Richards (Chico, Calif.: Scholars, 1984), 23–39.

96. See Goulder, *Type and History in Acts*, 60.

97. The "farewell address" of Acts 20:17-38, like 2 Timothy, to which it bears strong resemblances, depends for its effectiveness upon the fact of Paul's death.

98. See Pervo, *Acts*, 647–54.

99. See p. 169 (Chapter 4).

100. Cf. Eph. 2:6. Note also such admonitions as Col. 2:20-23.

101. Cf. 2 Thess. 1:7: "and to give relief to the afflicted as well as to us, when the Lord Jesus is revealed from heaven with his mighty angels." The "rest" in question is compared by R. Bultmann ("ἀνίημι," *TDNT* 1:367) and B. Rigaux (*Saint Paul. Les épitres aux Thessaloniciens*, EB [Paris: Gabalda, 1956], 623), with eschatological rest (Acts 3:20, Matt. 11:25-30). Μεθ᾽ ἡμῶν is readily construed as sociative, but Paul could be seen, like Jesus, as the source of rest. With this comes an understanding of the "earthly" Paul as a figure of the past; cf. 1:10: "when he comes to be glorified by his saints and to be marveled at on that day among all who have believed, because our testimony to you was believed."

102. See p. 130 (Chapter 4).

103. See p. 75.

104. See p. 68.

105. The preference for spatial imagery in Colossians and Ephesians is widely noted, usually from the theological perspective of a shift from eschatology to cosmology and from christology to ecclesiology. The ecclesiological thrust has a social dimension also.

106. Amalgamation of genres: Mark (parables, miracles, pronouncement stories, passion narrative, and so on), Matthew (Mark, Q, a church order[?]); use of multiple texts: Matthew, Luke (Justin[?]), Tatian; varying editions: Q[?], *Gospel of Thomas*, Marcion. "Apocrypha": the various non-canonical gospel texts.

107. Mark 16:9-20 is a later addition to the text.

108. See Matt. 28:19-20 and Luke 24:49-53 exemplify this object.

109. The *Acts of Paul* and the so-called *Acts of Titus* (on which see Richard I. Pervo, "The Acts of Titus: A Preliminary Translation, with an Introduction and Notes," in *SBLSP, 1996* [Atlanta: Scholars, 1996], 555–82) provide Paul with a John the Baptist-like forerunner: Titus. (This is a role that Titus does not play in Acts, for the very good reason that the book takes no account of his existence.)

110. Ephesians circulated under different names, notably "Laodiceans" (Marcion).

111. Hebrews is anonymous, but was circulated as a part of the Pauline Corpus.

112. Armenian Canon Lists and Latin Bibles often include *3 Corinthians*, which is embedded in the *Acts of Paul* and also attested independently.

113. *Laodiceans* was in general a part of the Western Bible until the Renaissance.

114. This is a collection of fourteen letters, six of which are assigned to Paul.

115. A pseudonymous Letter to the Alexandrians is mentioned in the so-called Muratorian List, but no traces of it have been found.

116. The Muratorian List refers to other forged letters. Clement of Alexandria (*Prot.* 9.87.4) speaks of a letter to the Macedonians, which may be Philippians.

117. Although Paul did not write *Laodiceans*, nearly every word is from Philippians, Galatians, or another letter.

118. Some view Rom. 16 as a once-distinct letter. Those who regard it as integral are likely to view 16:17-20 as an interpolation. Few consider Rom. 16:24-27 as original. (Most Christians of the first two centuries or more who had access to Romans encountered it in an edition of fourteen or fifteen chapters.) The text evidently contains some glosses, and larger interpolations have been argued.

119. Interpolations are likely. Some see 1 Corinthians as a compilation of various letters.

120. See p. 39.

121. See p. 43.

122. Some propose that an authentic letter is embedded in Colossians.

123. Some propose to partition 1 Thessalonians; 2:13-16, or part thereof, is unlikely to be original.

124. Some find pieces of genuine correspondence in 2 Thessalonians. (Since much of it is based upon 1 Thessalonians, this must, in part, be true.)

125. The conclusion of 1 Timothy presents minor questions.

126. See p. 105.

Chapter 1: Paul Becomes a Book

1. The philosophical tradition was fond of gossip, as can be seen from a survey of Diogenes Laertius' *Lives of the Philosophers* 7.183. For example, he reports the useful datum that the pioneer Stoic Chrysippus tended, when in his cups, toward silence, but that he walked unsteadily.

2. See 2 Cor. 10:10.

3. For basic literature on ancient epistolary theory and practice see the various bibliographies in H.-J. Klauck (with D. R. Bailey), *Ancient Letters and the New Testament* (Waco, Tex.: Baylor University Press, 2006), 1–65. See also Stanley K. Stowers, *Letter Writing in Greco-Roman Antiquity*, LEC 5 (Philadelphia: Westminster, 1986). For primary texts and valuable discussion, see Abraham J. Malherbe, *Ancient Epistolary Theorists*, SBLSBS 19 (Atlanta: Scholars, 1988).

4. The letters to Trajan constitute the tenth, final, book of Pliny's collected letters.

5. Nils A. Dahl, "The Particularity of the Pauline Epistles as a Problem in the Ancient Church," in *Neotestamentica et Patristica*, ed. W. C. van Unnik; FS Oscar Cullmann; NovTSup 6 (Leiden: Brill, 1962), 261–72.

6. See p. 110 (Paulsen).

7. For an edition of Pauline letters evidently arranged on perceived chronological grounds, see below, p. 58.

8. See Niklas Holzberg, ed., *Der griechische Briefroman: Gattungstypologie und Textanalyse*, Classica Monacensia 8 (Tübingen: Narr, 1994), 1–52, and, *idem*, "Letters: *Chion*," in *The Novel in the Ancient World*, ed. Gareth Schmeling; rev. ed. (Leiden: Brill, 2003), 645–53.

9. On these see Richard I. Pervo, "Romancing an Oft-neglected Stone: The Pastoral Epistles and the Epistolary Novel," *Journal of Higher Criticism* 1 (1994): 25–47, and below, p. 312n179.

10. For a survey of literary letters, see Klauck, *Ancient Letters*, 103–82.

11. See Klauck, *Ancient Letters*, 149–55.

12. See the summary in D. Trobisch, *Paul's Letter Collection: Tracing the Origins* (Minneapolis: Fortress Press, 1994), 47–51. For details, see his *Die Entstehung der Paulusbriefsammlung: Studien zu den Anfängen christlicher Publizistik*, Novum Testamentum et Orbis Antiquus 10 (Freiburg: Editions universitaires, 1989).

13. Trobisch, *Letter Collection*, 55–95. His arguments are based in part upon the signs of removal of personal data, removal of names, and the like.

14. See below, p. 39.

15. On the question of Paul's personal involvement, see "When and How Was the Pauline Canon Compiled? An Assessment of Theories," in *The Pauline Canon*, ed. Stanley E. Porter; Pauline Studies 1 (Leiden: Brill, 2004), 95–127, 109–18.

16. Trobisch does not claim that Paul was familiar with the literary tradition. His theory rests upon the perceived practices of a variety of authors. See the review by Stanley K. Stowers (*CBQ* 53 [1991]: 721–23), who raises the question of comparing Paul with persons like Cicero and Pliny.

17. See p. 45.

18. "Lists" is a comprehensive term including data derived from various sources. See Table 3.

19. Ibid.

20. Another explanation is that Hebrews was associated with Rome (cf. Heb. 13:24).

21. The symbolic value of fourteen (ten commandments and four gospels) was of great importance to Gregory the Great, *Mor. in Job* 35.20.

22. On this corpus, see David R. Nienhuis, *Not by Paul Alone: The Formation of the Catholic Epistle Collection and the Christian Canon* (Waco, Tex.: Baylor University Press, 2007).

23. The specific notion of biblical inspiration arose in response to the translation of the Hebrew Bible into Greek. Israelites regarded the Torah and other scriptures as the word of God. Was this word still authoritative when rendered into another language? To meet this challenge, proponents of the Greek translation developed a theory of inspiration and reported an appropriate legend: King Ptolemy of Egypt (or his librarian, Demetrius of Phalerum) sent to Jerusalem requesting suitable translators. Seventy arrived (whence the title *Septuagint* [LXX] for the Greek Old Testament). Their individual versions were identical. This story appears in the so-called *Letter to Aristeas*, and is subsequently repeated by Philo, who attributed the agreement to verbal inspiration (*Mos.* 2.31-44), and Josephus (*Ant.* 1.10-12; 12.11-16, 34-57, 89-118; cf. *C. Ap.* 2.45-46). The story was picked up by Christians, beginning with Justin (*Apology* 1.31), and elaborated over time with miraculous additions. For a claim that the entire Hebrew Bible is inspired, see Josephus, *C. Ap.* 1.37-42. Philo describes inspiration in *Spec.* 1.65; 4.49 and *Her.* 263–66.

24. Hebrews is, in the canonical text, addressed to a group rather than to a community.

25. Much of the evidence for this editorial work can be found in or deduced from ancient manuscripts, lists of writings, and discussions by ancient writers. Items 4 and 9, in particular, are determined by historical-critical research and reconstruction.

26. Marcion was active in the second century. He edited a known edition of the Pauline epistles that did not include the Pastorals (which had probably not yet been written). This order is reconstructed from several sources; some details are unclear.

27. That is, Ephesians.

28. This papyrus edition of the Pauline corpus was written c. 200–225. It is complete for none of the epistles, but probably contained 2 Thessalonians and Philemon.

29. The end of this MS is lost. It almost certainly included 2 Thessalonians and Philemon.

30. The so-called "Muratorian Canon" is a fragmentary Latin document incompetently translated from Greek. Serious challenges have been made to its traditional date of c. 200. For arguments

against an early date, see Geoffrey M. Hahneman, *The Muratorian Fragment and the Development of the Canon*, OTM (Oxford: Clarendon, 1992). Josef Verheyden, "The Canon Muratori: A Matter of Dispute," in *The Biblical Canons*, ed. J. M. Auwers and H. J. de Jonge; BETL 153 (Leuven: Peeters, 2003), 487–556, seeks to defend an early date without particularly cogent or cohesive arguments. For a transcription of the MS printed *en face* with Hans Lietzmann's edition, see *Some Early Lists of the Books of the New Testament*, ed. F. W. Grosheide; Textus Minores 1 (Leiden: Brill, 1948), 7–11.

31. This catalogue is found between Philemon and Hebrews in a sixth-century MS (D 06). See Grosheide, *Early Lists*, 16–17.

32. The list closes, after Jude, with *Barnabas*, Revelation, Acts, *Hermas*, the *Acts of Paul*, and the *Revelation of Peter*.

33. The so-called *Decretum Gelasianum* probably arose in southern Gaul (France) during the sixth century

34. "Ambrosiaster" is the name, coined by Erasmus, used for a commentary on the Pauline epistles written the final third of the fourth century. The commentary of Pelagius (c. 350–c. 425) followed the same order, indicating that it was not unique. A general introduction to these authors is Alexander Souter, *Earliest Latin Commentaries on the Epistles of St Paul* (Oxford: Clarendon, 1927), 39–95, 205–30. For a general overview, see Claudio Moreschini, and Enrico Norelli, *Early Christian Greek and Latin Literature*, trans. Matthew J. O'Connell; 2 vols. (Peabody, Mass.: Hendrickson, 2005), 2:296–98 (Ambrosiaster) and 326–28 (Pelagius).

35. The order of Ephesians and Philippians varies in the MSS of Ambrosiaster.

36. Victorinus (d. c. 304) was an early Latin exegete who worked in Pannonia (Bosnia).

37. Augustine of Hippo (354–430) was from North Africa. On his commentaries, see Souter, *Earliest Latin Commentaries*, 139–204. For a general survey, see Moreschini and Norelli, *Literature*, 2:362–409.

38. The sources are the *Catologus Sinaiticus* and Ephrem (c. 306–373), a theologian who wrote in Syriac. For details, see John J. Clabeaux, *A Lost Edition of the Letters of Paul: A Reassessment of the Text of the Pauline Corpus Attested by Marcion*, CBQMS 21 (Washington, D.C.: Catholic Biblical Association, 1989), 2 n. 3.

39. The absence of 1 Timothy from this list is probably an oversight, although it could have been omitted, as by Tatian (p. 194), because of its presumption of marriage.

40. See below (p. 49).

41. The earliest attestation of Hebrews is in the West (Rome). See *1 Clement*, for example, 36:2-6, which does not acknowledge that it is citing a text (in contrast to 1 Cor. 47:1-2).

42. See William H. P. Hatch, "The Position of Hebrews in the Canon of the New Testament," *HTR* 29 (1936): 135–51, and Bruce M. Metzger, *A Textual Commentary on the Greek New Testament*, 2nd ed. (New York: American Bible Society, 1994), 661–62.

43. C. P. Anderson, "The Epistles to the Hebrews and the Pauline Letter Collection," *HTR* 59 (1966): 429–38.

44. On this question, see Hermann J. Frede, "Die Ordnung des Paulusbriefe und der Platz des Kolosserbrief im Corpus Paulinum," in *Vetus Latina. Die Reste der altlateinischen Bibel* 24.2. Epistulae ad Philippenses et Collosenses (Freiburg: Herder, 1969), 290–303.

45. Walter Bauer (*Orthodoxy and Heresy in Earliest Christianity*, trans. and ed. Robert A. Kraft and Gerhard Krodel [Philadelphia: Fortress Press, 1971]) argued for the strong influence of Marcion upon Christian origins in eastern Syria. Helmut Koester (in James M. Robinson and Helmut Koester, *Trajectories through Early Christianity* [Philadelphia: Fortress Press, 1971], 127) modifies this claim. It is quite possible, however, that the first Christians who utilized Paul's epistles in eastern Syria were followers of Marcion, since the Thomas tradition, which had an early and strong influence there, does not seem to promote Paul.

46. Joseph B. Lightfoot, *Saint Paul's Epistles to the Colossians and to Philemon: A Revised Text*, repr. (Grand Rapids: Zondervan, 1959 [1879]), 278. The hypothesis that Rom. 16 was sent to Ephesus as a letter of recommendation has fallen out of favor.

47. On these, see below.

48. Knox wrote a short book on the subject: *Philemon among the Letters of Paul*, 2nd ed. (Nashville: Abingdon, 1959). Knox's romantic theory is charming, but it is more likely that Philemon survived

because of its association with Colossians, possibly because it was considered the letter mentioned in Col. 4:16.

49. Those who do not believe that Philippians and Philemon—the only undisputed "imprisonment epistles"—are from Rome may ask why nothing survives of Paul's writing after his arrest in Jerusalem. One hypothetical source used by the writer of Acts was a letter, with which Paul may have been associated, reporting on the result of the collection. See Richard I. Pervo, *Dating Acts: Between the Evangelists and the Apologists* (Santa Rosa, Calif.: Polebridge, 2006), x, 358. It is possible that Paul was not at liberty to write, or that his writings from this period were not deemed suitable for preservation.

50. Acts shows a similar understanding of the delivery of letters; see 15:30; cf. 16:4.

51. Probable recipients were believers in the cities of Ancyra, Pessinus, Tavium, and Gordium.

52. Cf. 3 John.

53. *Polycarp (Phil.* 13) indicates some of the difficulties, as well as the desirability, of sharing correspondence c. 130: "Both you and Ignatius have written to me that if anyone is going to Syria he should take along your letter. I will do so if I have the opportunity—either I or someone I send as a representative on your behalf and mine. the letters of Ignatius that he sent to us, along with all the others we had with us, just as you directed us to do. These accompany this letter; you will be able to profit greatly from them, for they deal with faith and endurance and all edification that is suitable in our Lord. And let us know what you have learned more definitely about Ignatius himself and those who are with him." (Bart D. Ehrman, trans., *The Apostolic Fathers,* LCL; 2 vols. (Cambridge, Mass.: Harvard University Press, 2003), 1:351.

54. On Colossae, see p. 66.

55. Marcion's text probably was blank in the letter itself. "Laodiceans" was the superscript. The title reflects no Marcionite proclivities, and probably stems from the Laodicean letter mentioned in Col. 4:16 (cited above). In light of the similarities between these two letters, the choice was intelligent. It also shows that the title was probably associated with a collection, since the person responsible for it knew Colossians.

56. P46, a*, B*, 6, 424^c 1739, Marcion(?), Origen. See Ernest Best, "Recipients and Title of the Letter to the Ephesians: Why and When the Designation 'Ephesians'?," *ANRW* 2.25.4 (1987): 3247–79, and Clabeaux, *Lost Edition,* 94–98.

57. G, 1739mg, Origen, some others.

58. G, old Latin, mss of the Vulgate, Ambrosiaster.

59. G and Origen in Latin. (Another type of variant reading lends support to this reading.)

60. Ephesians is a general letter, despite the address.

61. Although reference to "chapters" is convenient, the chapter divisions in the New Testament stem from the Middle Ages (while verse divisions were made in the middle of the sixteenth century). The oldest known divisions, called *kephalaia* ("chapters"), mark a new unit at 15:1.

62. Harry Gamble, *The Textual History of the Letter to the Romans,* SD 42 (Grand Rapids: Eerdmans), 1977), 16–33, 96–124. The evidence is mainly indirect but it is imposing. The bilingual mss indicate that the mss that omitted "Rome" in 1:7, 15 also ended with ch. 14. See also Nils A. Dahl, "The Particularity of the Pauline Epistles as a Problem in the Ancient Church," in van Unnik, ed., *Neotestamentica et Patristica,* 261–72, and idem, "The Origin of the Earliest Prologues of the Pauline Letters," *Semeia* 12 (1978): 233–77. For a concise review of the forms of Romans, see Robert Jewett (assisted by Roy Kotansky), *Romans,* Hermeneia, ed. Eldon J. Epp (Minneapolis: Fortress Press, 2007), 4–9.

63. The evidence, which, as in all cases, is based upon the position of the doxology (Rom. 16:25-27), comes only from 1506 (dated to 1320), and P46. Unlike the case of the fourteen-chapter edition, patristic evidence for this edition is meager. Gamble (*Textual History,* 33–34, 124–26), however, presents arguments based upon 1739 in support of the view that Origen commented upon a fifteen-chapter edition.

64. See, for example, Gamble, *Textual History,* 36–55; Kurt Aland, "Der Schluss und die Ursprüngliche Gestalt des Römerbriefes," in *Neutestamentliche Entwürfe* (Munich: Kaiser Verlag, 1979), 284–301; Peter Lampe, "Zur Textgeschichte des Römerbriefes," *NovT* 27 (1985): 273–77, and "The Roman Christians of Romans 16," in *The Romans Debate,* ed. Karl P. Donfried (Peabody, Mass.: Hendrickson, 1991), 216–30, and Robert Jewett, "Paul, Phoebe, and the Spanish Mission," in *The Social*

World of Formative Christianity and Judaism: Essays in Tribute to Howard Clark Kee, ed. Jacob Neusner et al. (Philadelphia: Fortress Press, 1988), 142–61.

65. Lampe, "Roman Christians," 217, and "Textgeschichte," 273–77. See also *From Paul to Valentinus: Christians at Rome in the First Two Centuries*, trans. Michael Steinhauser; ed. Marshall D. Johnson (Minneapolis: Fortress Press, 2003), 153–65. Lampe's goal is to argue for the integrity of Rom. 1–16. He wishes to disprove the theory that Rom. 1–15 was the original letter.

66. Aland, "Schluss," 296–97; Gamble, *Textual History*, 124. Romans 15:33 is not unlike the close of 2 Corinthians and Galatians.

67. More conservative second-century Christians would have taken ready exception to the designations of Phoebe as a διάκονος (a technical term for an order of ministry by the second century) and patron of the church at Cenchreae (16:1-2) or of Junia as a distinguished apostle (16:7).

68. Marcion would scarcely have found this material amenable and one might be inclined, with Origen, to assign him responsibility for deleting these verses, had Tertullian been willing to lay the blame at his feet, yet he does not do so, for his text also ends at chap. 14, and Marcion probably utilized an already abbreviated text of Romans. So Gamble, *Textual History*, 100–106.

69. See, for example, the personal instructions in 2 Tim. 4:9-13; Titus 3:12-13, and the list of greetings in 2 Tim. 4:19-21. Note also Eph. 6:21; Col. 4:7-18.

70. See Pervo, *Dating Acts*, 79, 134, and *Acts*, 507–8.

71. In so far as I have yet learned, the second century passes over Paul's Collection in silence.

72. The view of a release, followed by a second trial, is a scholarly construct designed to account for the Deutero-Paulines. The idea is at least as old as Eusebius (*H.E.* 2.22.1-2). These letters do not, in any case, envision a trip to Spain, but return Paul's focus to the Aegean. Church history in Spain begins in the second century, without reference to Pauline missionary work. See Jewett, *Chronology*, 45. F. F. Bruce, *Paul: Apostle of the Heart Set Free* (Grand Rapids: Eerdmans, 1977), 447–48, provides a list of modern authorities with views on both sides of the question. On the theory that Paul was exiled to Spain, see p. 330n112 (Chapter 3).

73. See F. Pfister, "Die zweimalige römische Gefangenschaft und die spanische Reise des Apostels Paulus und der Schluss der Apostelgeschichte," *ZNW* 14 (1913): 216–21, who notes (216) similar tendencies operative in legendary accounts of the travels of such figures as Heracles and Alexander the Great. Justin (*1 Apology* 39.3) states that the apostles dispersed throughout the entire world. Irenaeus (*Adv. Haer.* 3.1.1) echoes this sentiment. For varying accounts and perceptions, see Walter Bauer, "Accounts," in *New Testament Apocrypha*, ed. E. Hennecke and W. Schneemelcher; trans. and ed. R. M. Wilson; 2 vols. (Philadelphia: Westminster, 1965), 2:35–74 (43–44). Bauer cites, in addition to the aforementioned, Matt. 28:19-20; Luke 24:47-48; Acts 1:8; *Pseudo-Mark* 16:16; the *Kerygma Petrou* frg. 4; the *Epistle of the Apostles* 30 (41); the *Diatessaron*; Aristides; Irenaeus; and the *Ascension of Isaiah*. Eusebius (*H.E.* 3.1) asserts that "the holy Apostles and disciples" dispersed over the entire world, referring to a lottery. (Eusebius appeals to Book 3 of Origen's commentary on Genesis, but the scope of this reference is not clear.) On this lottery, see p. 219n51.

74. For a discussion, with references, see, for example, J. B. Lightfoot, "St Paul's History after the Close of the Acts," in *Biblical Essays*, repr. (Grand Rapids: Baker Book House, 1979 [1893]), 421–37, and Harry W. Tajra, *The Martyrdom of St. Paul: Historical and Judicial Context, Traditions, and Legends*, WUNT 2/67 (Tübingen: Mohr [Siebeck], 1994), 102–17. The Muratorian Fragment, lines 38-40, says, after noting that Acts did not relate the death of Peter, that Paul went from Rome to Spain. This reflects the view of the *Acts of Peter* (*Verc.*) 1-3. Cyril of Jerusalem (*Mystagogical Catecheses* 17.26) notes that Paul visited Spain, as do Jerome (*Ep.* 65.12; *De vir. Ill.* 5; *Comm. in Isa.* 2:10), Chrysostom (*In Epistolam ad Hebraeos* arg. 1.1; *Comm. in epistolam secundam ad Tim.* 10.3), and Epiphanius (*Pan.* 7.9). Lightfoot ("St Paul's History," 426–27) takes note of Theodore of Mopsuestia, Pelagius, and Theodoret. To these one may add the *Acts of Xanthippe and Polyxena*, part of which is set in Spain.

75. See L. W. Hurtado, "The Doxology at the End of Romans," in *New Testament Textual Criticism: Essays in Honour of Bruce M. Metzger*, ed. E. J. Epp and G. D. Fee (Oxford: Clarendon, 1981), 185–99 (197–98), and Jewett, *Romans*, 997–1011. See also below.

76. For lists (presumably based on chronological order) that place Romans last, see Jack Finegan, "The Original Form of the Pauline Collection," *HTR* 49 (1956): 85–103. The doxology (16:25-27) may have specific reference to Romans, but it could also serve as a solemn and resonant conclusion to the

corpus. (In this connection, one may compare Jude 24-25, which serves to conclude the epistolary literature of the eventual canon, or at least to close the catholic epistles.) In support of a collection concluding with Romans, see Walter Schmithals, *Der Römerbrief als Historisches Problem*, StNT 9 (Gütersloh: Mohn, 1975), 117-22. Gamble, *Textual History*, 121-22, argues against this theory.

77. David Trobisch, *Paul's Letter Collection: Tracing the Origins* (Minneapolis: Fortress Press, 1994), 86.

78. The same phrase appears in Gal. 1:2.

79. P⁴⁶, B, D*, F, G, b, m, Ambrosiaster.

80. On the fluctuating place of "which is in Corinth," as evidence for the secondary character of v. 2b, see Dahl, "Particularity," 270; Gunther Zuntz, *The Text of the Epistles: A Disquisition upon the Corpus Paulinum* (London: Oxford University Press, 1953), 91-92; and Gamble, *Textual History*, 117 n. 109.

81. A and a few others.

82. P46, 69 and a few.

83. See p. 36.

84. "Old Latin" refers to Latin translations that preceded that of Jerome (the Vulgate), which became standard.

85. Translated by Wilhelm Schneemelcher, in *New Testament Apocrypha*, ed. Wilhelm Schneemelcher; trans. and ed. R. McL. Wilson; 2 vols. (Louisville: Westminster John Knox, 1991-92), 1:35-36.

86. The claim that John wrote Revelation before Paul wrote letters is one of the most astonishing statements in this list. (The letters of Rev. 2-3 are in view.)

87. The list then proceeds to discuss spurious letters.

88. On the possibility of Romans as the final element in a collection, see n.76 above.

89. See the Excursus on the number seven.

90. John Knox, *Marcion and the New Testament* (Chicago: University of Chicago Press, 1942), 62-70.

91. See Gamble, *Textual History*, 118, and *The New Testament Canon: Its Making and Meaning*, GBS (Philadelphia: Fortress Press, 1985), 41-42. Tertullian (*Adv. Marcionem* 4.5) also places Corinthians first (followed by Galatians, Philippians, 1 and 2 Thessalonians, Ephesians, Romans). For additional bibliography on the seven-letter edition, see Albert C. Sundberg, "Canon Muratori: A Fourth-Century List," *HTR* 66 (1973): 1-41 (20 n. 63).

92. "Seven," *DBI* 774-75. See also Walter Schmithals, *Paul and the Gnostics*, trans. John E. Steely (Nashville: Abingdon, 1972), 26a n. 2, and John Reumann, *Variety and Unity in New Testament Thought* (Oxford: Oxford University Press, 1991), 101.

93. The multiples seventy and seventy-seven participate in this symbolism, as in the table of nations of Gen. 10. Cf. also the seventy disciples of Jesus (Luke 10:1; seventy-two is a variant).

94. As the solar week, this temporal unit became general in the West during the Roman imperial period. (Names of the English weekdays reflect the adoption of this calendric unit prior to Christianization.)

95. Philo, *Op. mun.* 99-100; *Rev div. Her.* 170; *Spec. leg.* 2.64. Angeology enumerated seven classes of angels, led by seven archangels.

96. See also William M. Ramsay, *The Letters to the Seven Churches of Asia and Their Place in the Plan of the Apocalypse* (New York: Armstrong, 1904), 177.

97. On Ignatius and Dionysius, see p. 133/144.

98. These are probably not Marcionite in origin or theology. See Nils Dahl, "The Origin of the Earliest Prologues to the Pauline Letters, *Semeia* 12 (1978): 233-77, and the summary of John J. Clabeaux, "Marcionite Prologues to Paul," *ABD on CD-ROM*. Version 2.0c., 1995, 1996.

99. The adverb *similiter* ("similarly") looks back to the opening words of the prologue to Galatians.

100. The Thessalonian preface states that the recipients had not been seduced by false apostles. This claim is vaguely applicable to 2 Thessalonians, which mentions no apostles, but not to the first letter.

101. Examples from early Christian literature include (possibly) the correspondence of Polycarp, the so-called *Letter of Diognetus*, the transmission of Justin's *Apologies*, items in the corpus of

Tertullian and evidently in other cases. The Syriac epitome of Ignatius' letters also contains some combinations.

102. See p. 32.

103. For varied hypotheses on the partition of 1 Corinthians, see Hans Dieter Betz and Margaret Mitchell, "Corinthians, First Epistle to the," ABD on CD-ROM. Version 2.0c., 1995, 1996. Note in particular Robert Jewett, "The Redaction of 1 Corinthians and the Trajectory of the Pauline School," JAARSup 44 (1978): 389-444.

104. See Earl J. Richard, First and Second Thessalonians, SP 11 (Collegeville, Minn.: Liturgical, 1995), 11-16.

105. For example, Charles Masson, L'épitre de Saint Paul aux Colossiens, Commentaire du Nouveau Testament X (Neuchatel: Delachaux & Niestlé, 1950), 86, who revived a theory advanced by H. J. Holtzmann in 1872. Some envision the letter to the Laodiceans as embedded in the current canonical Colossians: Marc-Emile Boismard, "Paul's Letter to the Laodiceans," in The Pauline Canon: Pauline Studies 1, ed. S. E. Porter (Leiden: Brill, 2004), 45-57. Note also A. Lindemann, Der Kolosserbrief, ZBK (Zurich: Theologische Verlag, 1983), 76-77. In support of this hypothesis are the presence of doublets and the inclusion of polemical material within a parenetic letter.

106. P. N. Harrison, The Problem of the Pastoral Epistles (Oxford: Oxford University Press/ Humphrey Milford, 1921), 87-135. A recent exploration of this thesis is James D. Miller, The Pastoral Letters as Composite Documents, SNTSMS 93 (Cambridge: Cambridge University Press, 1997).

107. First Clement knows Romans, but this can be attributed to the Roman origin of this post-apostolic text.

108. See Pervo, Dating Acts, 60-64, 101, 116-17.

109. See Gunther Bornkamm, "Die Vorgeschichte des sogenannten Zweiten Korintherbriefes," in Geschichte und Glaube, Gesammelte Aufsätze IV (Munich: Kaiser, 1971), 162-94; Gerhard Dautzenberg, "Der Zweite Korintherbrief als Briefsammlung: Zur Frage der literarischen Einheitlichkeit und des theologischen Gefüges von 2 Kor 1-8," ANRW 2.25.4 (1987): 3045-66, and, for a general survey, Hans Dieter Betz, "Corinthians, Second Epistle to," ABD on CD-ROM. Version 2.0c., 1995, 1996. A dissenter from the consensus is Jan Lambrecht, Second Corinthians, SP 8 (Collegeville, Minn.: Liturgical, 2000), 7-9. He states that there is no manuscript evidence for partition and that hypotheses should be avoided. Manuscript evidence is not relevant, since 2 Corinthians never circulated in other than its present form. Furthermore, every view, including that which holds that it is an integral letter, is a hypothesis.

110. A representative of this position is Victor P. Furnish, II Corinthians, AB 32a (Garden City, N.Y.: Doubleday, 1984), 35-41.

111. Since recommendations for anonymous individuals are without value, it is apparent that the proper name of "the brother" in 2 Cor. 8:18-22 has been deleted. This may be because, although Titus was an important figure, the other person was not. Another possibility is that the unnamed individual fell into disfavor.

112. Note that 2 Cor. 7:2 follows 6:13 rather smoothly.

113. "Beliar" or "Belial" (a variant in 2 Cor. 6:15) is a common name for the Devil in the Qumran literature and the Pseudepigrapha. This is its only occurrence in early Christian literature. See S. D. Sperling, "Belial," DDD 169-71.

114. See Hans Dieter Betz, "2 Cor. 6:14—7:1: An Anti-Pauline Fragment?" JBL 92 (1972): 88-108; Nils A. Dahl, "A Fragment and Its Content: 2 Corinthians 6:14—7:1," in Studies in Paul (Minneapolis: Augsburg, 1977), 62-91; and Joseph A. Fitzmyer, "Qumran and the Interpolated Paragraph in 2 Corinthians 6:14—7:1," CBQ 23 (1961): 273-80.

115. The Roman letters are conventional symbols for the various fragments.

116. Some regard this as the "tearful letter" of 2:4 and 7:8.

117. This is often called "The Letter of Reconciliation."

118. Revelation 2:1-7; Acts 20:17-35, and the Pastorals Epistles indicate major problems and conflicts in Ephesus at the conclusion of the first century and the first decades of the second. See also S. J. Hultgren, "2 Cor 6.14—7.1 and Rev 21.3-8: Evidence for the Ephesian Redaction of 2 Corinthians," NTS 49 (2002): 267-82.

119. The reference to Tychicus in Eph. 6:21 is borrowed from Col. 4:7. Tychicus is associated with Ephesus (Acts 20:4; 2 Tim. 4:12; Tit. 3:12). Second Corinthians refers, outside of Timothy in the

opening (1:1), which is suspect (see below), only to Titus, who is mentioned nine times. Titus has become Paul's most important colleague in his later relations with Corinth. Acts does not mention Titus. This may be compared to the Roman practice of *damnatio memoriae*. The names of those who had become "non-persons" were erased from public inscriptions. See David Trobisch, *Paul's Letter Collection: Tracing the Origins* (Minneapolis: Fortress Press, 1994), 57–62. On 2 Cor. 8:18, see Hans Lietzmann and Werner G. Kümmel, *An die Korinther I–II*, HNT 9; 4th ed. (Tübingen: Mohr Siebeck, 1949), 136–37.

120. The address may have been altered when the Corinthian correspondence was treated as a single letter and re-created at the time of separation (above).

121. On these forms, see James M. Robinson, "The Historicity of Biblical Language," in *The Old Testament and Christian Faith*, ed. B. W. Anderson (New York: Harper & Row, 1963), 124–58, 131–50. On the standard thanksgiving form, see above.

122. See Andreas Lindemann, *Paulus im ältesten Christentum*, BHT 58 (Tübingen: Mohr Siebeck, 1979), 122 n. 50.

123. See Lohse, *Colossians and Philemon*, 70–72.

124. The phrase comes from Karl A. Plank, *Paul and the Irony of Affliction* (Atlanta: Scholars, 1987).

125. Undisputed Pauline texts also make reference to his sufferings and correlate them with the experience of Jesus, and not without rhetorical purpose. A difference is that in later times Paul was a famous martyr whose sufferings redound to his glory, whereas the historical Paul frequently had to defend himself—not least in 2 Corinthians. Cf. Phil. 1 and 1 Cor. 4, which also deal with charges that his afflictions demonstrated his inadequacy and/or illegitimacy. For the later view of Paul's sufferings, see Acts 20:17-38.

126. The verb *parakalō* ("beseech") appears twenty-eight times in the undisputed letters, eighteen of which are in 2 Corinthians. The noun *paraklēsis* ("consolation") occurs seventeen times in the undisputed texts. Eleven of these come from 2 Corinthians. Note also four uses of *thlipsis* ("affliction"), four of *pathēma* ("suffering"), and two uses of *perisseuō* ("abound").

127. In support of the view that the author of Ephesians used 2 Corinthians are, for example, Alfred E. Barnett, *Paul Becomes a Literary Influence* (Chicago: University of Chicago Press, 1941), 1–40; C. L. Mitton, *The Epistle to the Ephesians: Its Authorship, Origin and Purpose* (Oxford: Clarendon, 1951), 137; and Joachim Gnilka, *Der Epheserbrief*, HTK 10 (Freiburg: Herder & Herder, 1971), 22.

128. Cf. *Acts of Paul* 9/7 (Ephesus): "[Paul] was dragged in, saying nothing but bowed down and groaning because he was led in triumph (*ethriambeueto*) by the city" (citing from *The Apocryphal New Testament*, trans. James K. Elliott [Oxford: Clarendon, 1993], 378).

129. Ancient (and some modern) authors often marked their return to a source that they had expanded by repeating the final words of that source. This is called "resumptive repetition."

130. See *1 Clem.* 5:5-7 and, in general, Acts. Colossians 2:14-15 also utilizes the theme to illustrate the defeat of the hostile powers. See Angela Standhartinger, "Colossians and the Pauline School," *NTS* 50 (2004): 572–93 (590).

131. See Rudolf Schnackenburg, *Ephesians: A Commentary*, trans. H. Heron (Edinburgh: T. & T. Clark, 1991), 348 (index, under "Qumran").

132. See n. 133 (on Ephesians)

133. Examples include the synoptic speeches in Mark 13 parr.; Acts 20:17-35; Jude 14-19; *Did.* 16. Such warnings are a common feature of the "Farewell address." A seminal study of this genre is Johannes Munck, "Discours d'adieu dans le Nouveau Testament et dans la littérature biblique," in *Aux sources de la tradition chrétienne: Mélanges offerts à Maurice Goguel*, Bibliothèque théologique (Neuchâtel: Delachaux, 1950), 155–70. William S. Kurz (*Farewell Addresses in the New Testament* [Collegeville: Liturgical, 1990]) provides a good overview of the form. Cf. also the addition of vv. 17-20 in Rom. 16.

134. See 2 Cor. 13:11-13, which probably did not conclude Letter B. It may have concluded Letter C or been drawn from other sources.

135. Money is an important issue in *1 Clement* and Acts 20:17-35 (esp. v. 33). See also Rev. 2:5.

136. See Pervo, *Acts*.

137. For a review of the discussion, see John T. Fitzgerald, "Philippians, Letter to the," *ABD on CD-ROM*. Version 2.0c., 1995, 1996. For the solution adopted here, see Gunther Bornkamm, "Der

Philipperbrief als paulinische Briefsammlung," in *Neotestamentica et Patristica*, FS O. Cullmann; NovTSup 6 (Leiden: E. J. Brill, 1962), 192–202, and Helmut Koester, *Introduction to the New Testament*, 2 vols. (New York: de Gruyter, 1995–2000), 2:136–40.

138. Lindemann, *Paulus*, 23.

139. On the genre of the farewell speech, see above, n.133.

140. Perhaps 4:21-23 belongs with Letter A.

141. Philippians 4:2-7 appear to belong to Letter B; 4:21-23 may have come from this letter.

142. Philippians 4:8-9 may have been part of Letter C.

143. A number of attempts have been made to sort out the components of ch. 4 (especially vv. 10-20).

144. None of the "bishops and deacons" (a phrase that has often been challenged on the grounds that it is a later addition) are named, nor are greetings from or to specific individuals given. Those named are Timothy, Epaphroditus, and the somewhat mysterious group in 4:2-3, all of whom are described as co-workers. The "loyal companion" of v. 3 could be a Philippian believer, but this person is described only with a nickname, somewhat evocative of the famous "brother" of 2 Cor. 8:18.

145. Greed: Eph 4:19; 5:3; Acts 20:33-35; 1 Tim. 3:3 (bishops), 8 (deacons); 6:10; Titus 1:12. cf. 2 Pet 2:3, 14.

146. Biblical examples include Isa. 24:22; Jonah 2:6; Ps. 107:10-14; 1 Pet 3:19. See also Pervo, *Acts* II.

147. Of the various letters from prison, only Philemon is undisputed in authenticity and integrity. Philippians is composite, Colossians and Ephesians are not authentic, while the Pastoral Epistles, which were to be taken as a group, end with Paul imprisoned and facing death (2 Timothy). Second Thessalonians alone is not a "captivity epistle."

148. On Colossians' use of Philippians, see Mark Kiley, *Colossians as Pseudepigraphy*. The Biblical Seminar 4 (Sheffield: JSOT, 1986). One need not presume that the author of Colossians made use of canonical Philippians.

149. Those without facility in ancient languages can apprehend the situation by leafing through the six volumes of Euripides' plays produced by David Kovacs for the Loeb Classical Library (Cambridge, Mass.: Harvard University Press, 1994–2002), noting the passages marked with [ ] as interpolations. Many of these suspect sections, which can range from a few words to long passages, are pedantic, moralistic, or of otherwise questionable character. (This edition also includes one play, *Rhesus*, which was not written by Euripides but composed and preserved to compensate for a lost play of the same name; cf. the pseudo-Pauline *Laodiceans*, p. 146.) Selection was also a factor. Ten of Euripides' plays come from "Selected Works," not unlike those of the surviving plays of Aeschylus and Sophocles. The other nine come from an edition of his complete works, arranged in alphabetical order. A parallel closer to Paul in theme and form is the letters of Euripides. Stanley F. Stowers ("Greek and Latin Letters," *ABD on CD-ROM*. Version 2.0c., 1995, 1996) notes changes in his teachings added to fit later situations. See also Robert M. Grant, *Heresy and Criticism* (Louisville: Westminster John Knox, 1993), 12, 33–47, 111. Note also the changes introduced into Acts by the D ("Western")-Text.

150. William O. Walker, *Interpolations in the Pauline Letters*, JSNTS 213 (London: Sheffield Academic Press, 2001), 21–24, distinguishes between glosses and interpolations and differentiates between editing and interpolation.

151. Examples of obvious interpolations include such practices as adding "Jesus" to "Christ" and vice-versa.

152. See, among many studies, William O. Walker, Jr., "Interpolations in the Pauline Letters," in *The Pauline Canon*, ed. Stanley E. Porter; Pauline Studies 1 (Leiden: Brill, 2004), 189–235 (228–35).

153. Cf. Dennis R. MacDonald, *The Legend and the Apostle: The Battle for Paul in Story and Canon* (Philadelphia: Westminster, 1983), 86–89.

154. ἐπιτρέπεται.

155. ὑποτασσέσθωσαν.

156. Ἐν πάσῃ ὑποταγῇ.

157. ἐπιτρέπω.

158. See the thorough discussion, with bibliography, of Eldon J. Epp, "Text-Critical, Exegetical, and Socio-Cultural Factors Affecting the Junia/Junias Variation in Romans 16,7," in *New Testament Textual Criticism and Exegesis*, ed. A. Denaux; FS J. Delobel; BEThL 161 (Leuven: Leuven University

Press/Peeters, 2002), 227–91 (237–42). See also Philip B. Payne, "Ms. 88 as Evidence for a Text without 1 Cor 14.34-35," *NTS* 44 (1998): 152–58, and "Fuldensis, Sigla for Variants in Vaticanus, and 1 Cor 14:34-35," *NTS* 41 (1995): 240–50; Gordon D. Fee, *The First Epistle to the Corinthians*, NICNT (Grand Rapids: Eerdmans, 1987), 699–708, and *God's Empowering Presence: The Holy Spirit in the Letters of Paul* (Peabody, Mass.: Hendrickson, 1994), 272–81.

159. See MacDonald, *Legend*. Note also Richard I. Pervo, "Social and Religious Aspects of the Western Text," in *The Living Text*, ed. Dennis Groh and Robert Jewett; FS Earnest W. Saunders (Lanham, Md.: University Press of America, 1985), 229–41.

160. MacDonald, *Legend*, 88.

161. See also Peter Dunn, "The Influence of 1 Corinthians on the *Acts of Paul*," in *SBLSP, 1996* (Atlanta: Scholars, 1996), 438–54 (452).

162. The communities founded by Marcion allowed women to serve as bishops, presbyters, and deacons.

163. This view was first stated in recent times by Birger Pearson, "I Thessalonians 2:13-16: A Deutero-Pauline Interpolation," *HTR* 64 (1971): 79–94, and developed by others. See Richard, *First and Second Thessalonians*, 119–27, with further bibliography.

164. Those (e.g., E. Richard) who mark the beginning of the interpolation at v. 14 explain this repetition differently.

165. For other data, see Darryl Schmidt, "1 Thess 2:13-16: Linguistic Evidence for an Interpolation," *JBL* 102 (1983): 269–79.

166. First Thessalonians 2:16c probably refers to the destruction of Jerusalem. Very similar language occurs in *T. Levi* 6.11: ἔφθασε δὲ ἡ ὀργὴ κυρίου ἐπ᾽ αὐτοὺς εἰς τέλος ("but the wrath of God came upon them with ultimate effect"). The context is punishment for mistreatment and persecution of Abraham and others. Note also 2 Chr. 36:16. For enduring wrath, see John 3:36.

167. The repetition of "we ought to give thanks" in 2 Thess. 1:3 and 2:13 could be invoked by those who do not regard 1 Thess. 2:13 as part of the interpolation.

168. The charge of hatred of the human race was lodged by Tacitus (early second century) in his *Hist.* 5.5 and *Ann.* 15.44. Cf. also Greek Esth. 3:13d; Philostratus, *Apollonius of Tyana* 5.33; Juvenal, *Satire* 14.103-4.

169. See Jewett, *Romans*, 985–96.

170. On this phenomenon, see the Excursus on the integrity of 2 Corinthians, above, p. 38.

171. This phenomenon is especially prominent in the Pastorals, but is also characteristic of Ignatius and Polycarp, among others.

172. It is uncharacteristic for Paul to refer to believers in general with such patronizing terms as ἄκακοι ("innocent").

173. Note also how various mss transfer greetings from "all the churches" to the section following the warnings against false teachers (16:22-23). Affinities with Phil. 3 and 2 Cor. 10–13 suggest that the composer of Rom. 16:17-20a was familiar with a collection of Pauline epistles. The reference to trampling upon Satan evokes the milieu of 2 Thessalonians and may indicate identification of the serpent of Gen. 3 with the Devil. (Note that those who regard Rom. 16 as a separate letter incline to view vv. 17-20 as original.)

174. D G mss of the old Latin, Sedulius Scotus.

175. P 33. 104. 365 *pc* Syᴾ Boᵐˢˢ Ambst.

176. See above, p. 294n63.

177. See above, p. 32.

178. See above.

179. See, in addition to Hurtado, "The Doxology," Bruce M. Metzger, *A Textual Commentary on the Greek New Testament*. 2nd ed. (New York: American Bible Society, 1994), 470–73.

180. See, in addition to Jude 24-25; *1 Clem.* 20:12; *Mart Poly.* 20:2; and, in particular, *2 Clem.* 20:5.

181. William O. Walker, *Interpolations in the Pauline Letters*, JSNTS 213 (London: Sheffield Academic Press, 2001), 190–99.

182. The phrase "*my* Gospel" is suspect, probably derived from 2 Tim. 2:8. Paul prefers to say "the Gospel of God" (e.g., Rom. 1:1; 15:16; 1 Thess. 2:2, 8, 9).

183. Rudolph Bultmann, "Glossen im Römerbrief," in *Exegetica*, ed. E. Dinkler (Tübingen: Mohr, 1967), 278–84.

184. Walker, *Interpolations*, 17–19, with a list of references.

185. Cf. 1 Cor. 1–4; 1 Cor 8; 1 Cor 10; 9:19-23; 2 Cor. 10; Acts 20:20 (and 20:17-35 in general).

186. First Corinthians 11:16 is different and less likely to have been added. See Gerhard Sellin, "Hauptprobleme des Ersten Korintherbriefes," *ANRW* 1.25.4 (1987): 2940–3044.

187. John Strugnell, "A Plea for Conjectural Emendation in the New Testament, with a Coda on 1 Cor 4:6," *CBQ* 34 (1974): 543–58, sees the present text as a third stage in the transmission.

188. For a survey, with references, see Walker, *Interpolations*, 199–209.

189. First Corinthians 11:3-16 has come under increasing suspicion; see, for example, Christopher Mount, "1 Corinthians 11:3-16: Spirit Possession and Authority in a Non-Pauline Interpolation," *JBL* (2005): 313–40.

190. William O. Walker, Jr., "1 Cor 15:29-34 as a Non-Pauline Interpolation," *CBQ* 69 (2007): 84–103.

191. Other proposed interpolations in the corpus include: Gal. 2:7-8; Phil 1:1c; 2:6-7; 1 Thess. 4:1-8, 10b-12, 18; 5:1-11, 12-22, 27. See Walker, "1 Cor 15:29-34 as a Non-Pauline Interpolation."

192. First Corinthians 10:1-22 is an example. For some (e.g., R. Jewett, W. Schmithals) the conflict between this and 1 Cor. 8 supports claims that 1 Corinthians is a compilation. Others (e.g., Walker) argue that it is a post-Pauline composition. The former are obliged to show why Paul said one thing on one occasion and its near opposite on another. For the latter it is a matter of showing that 10:1-22 conforms Paul to the views of a later era, since proto-orthodox believers firmly rejected the eating of food offered to polytheist gods under any circumstances (e.g., Acts 15:29). Both have merit, although the placement of both sections within 1 Corinthians can also be defended.

193. Large numbers of manuscript lectionaries from the Middle Ages survive. They are valuable in determining the evolution of the Byzantine type of the Greek text.

194. Initial lectionary changes for clarification, for example, "*Jesus* said to *the disciples*" instead of "he said to them" (a practice still followed in printed lectionaries) are less common in the epistles.

195. See p. 32.

196. See, for example, 1 Cor. 16:24. One MS, G, offers a Greek equivalent: "So be it! So be it!" (γενεθήτω γενεθήτω).

197. See the discussion of the editions of Romans and of the partition of 2 Corinthians, pp. 32/38.

198. Data for Marcion's editing of Paul comes from his opponents, in particular, Tertullian, who wrote a lengthy work *Against Marcion*. The pioneer study of this edition of Paul is Adolf von Harnack, *Marcion: Das Evangelium vom fremden Gott* (Leipzig: Hinrichs, 1921), translated in part by J. E. Steely and L. Bierma, *Marcion: The Gospel of the Alien God* (Durham, N.C.: Labyrinth, 1990). For recent discussions, see Markus Vinzent, "Der Schluß des Lukasevangeliums bei Marcion," in *Marcion und seine kirchengeschichtliche Wirkung*, ed. Gerhard May and Katharina Greschat; TU 150 (Berlin: de Gruyter, 2002), 79–150, and Joseph B. Tyson, *Marcion and Luke-Acts: A Defining Struggle* (Columbia: University of South Carolina Press, 2006), 79–120.

199. See J. Albert Harrill, *Manumission of Slaves in Early Christianity*, HUT 32 (Tübingen: Mohr Siebeck, 1995), and the review in *JECS* 4 (1996): 546–47.

200. The various prologues can be found in critical editions of the Latin Bible, for example, J. Wordsworth and H. J. White, *Novum Testamentum Domini Nostri Jesu Christi, Latine* (Oxford: Clarendon, 1889–98). Biblical books were also supplied with *hypotheses* or *argumenta*, formally similar to the synopses provided in program booklets for plays and operas. On these, see Bruce M. Metzger, *The Text of the New Testament: Its Transmission, Corruption, and Restoration*, 3rd ed. (New York: Oxford University Press, 1992), 25–26.

201. So the old MSS preface the four Gospels with "the Gospel," marking each item with "according to Matthew," and so on. The Gospel is one, to which each evangelist makes a contribution.

202. For examples of such titles, see Constantin Tischendorf, *Novum Testamentum Graece*, Editio Octava Critica Maior; 2 vols. (Leipzig: Hinrichs, 1869), 2:363.

203. Some of these subscripts show careful reading. The Byzantine text of 2 Corinthians states that it was written from Philippi "through Titus and Luke." This associates the text with the collection

(2 Cor. 8–9) and Acts 20:1-6 (where the first-person plural evidently implies the author's [Luke's] presence).

204. The chapter divisions in Codex Vaticanus, a fourth-century MS, show that the letters of Paul were treated as one book. They are not original to this MS, for they indicate the use of a prototype in which Hebrews followed Galatians.

205. See Chapter 4.

206. "Herald" (κῆρυξ) appears as a variant reading at Col. 1:23. On the term, see p. 13 [intro].

207. Book 11 of Apuleius' *Metamorphoses* (or *The Golden Ass*) reports the hero's conversion to the worship of Isis. After he moves to Rome, a new initiation is required because the robes in which he had been initiated remained in Corinth (11.29). This book is a novel, but it is realistic. An early Christian who had been properly been baptized in Corinth would not require rebaptism if s/he moved to Rome.

208. For reviews of research, see Porter, "When and How," and Arthur G. Patzia, "Canon," in *Dictionary of Paul and His Letters*, ed. Gerald F. Hawthorne and Ralph P. Martin (Downers Grove, Ill.: InterVarsity, 1993), 85–92. Contributions include Leslie C. Mitton, *The Formation of the Pauline Corpus of Letters* (London: Epworth, 1955); Kurt Aland, "Die Enstehung des Corpus Paulinum," in *Neutestamentliche Entwürfe* (Munich: Kaiser, 1979), 302–50; Alexander Sand, "Überlieferung und Sammlung der Paulusbriefe," in *Paulus in den Neutestamentlichen Spätschriften: Zur Paulusrezeption im Neuen Testament*, ed. Karl Kertlege; QD 89 (Freiburg: Herder, 1981), 11–24; and Andreas Lindemann, "Die Sammlung der Paulusbriefe im 1. und 2. Jahrhundert," in *The Biblical Canons*, ed. J. M. Auwers and H. J. de Jonge; BETL 153 (Leuven: Peeters, 2003), 321–51.

209. Ref to John Knox, p. 30.

210. See p. 43.

211. See David R. Nienhaus, *Not by Paul Alone: The Formation of the Catholic Epistle Collection and the Christian Canon* (Waco, Texas: Baylor University Press, 2007).

212. See p. 83.

213. Johannes Weiss anticipated Goodspeed's thesis: *Earliest Christianity. A History of the Period A D 30–150*. trans. F. C. Grant et al.; 2 vols.; new ed. (New York: Harper & Bros, 1959 [original 1914]), 2:684.

214. E. J. Goodspeed, *New Solutions to New Testament Problems* (Chicago: University of Chicago Press, 1927), 1–64, and many subsequent publications. See Pervo, *Dating Acts*, 386 n. 5. Raymond F. Collins, *Letters That Paul Did Not Write* (Wilmington: Michael Glazier, 1988), 132–70. 134.

215. See p. 218.

216. W. Schmithals, *Paul and the Gnostics*, trans. John E. Steely (Nashville: Abingdon, 1972), 239–74.

217. Lindemann, "Die Sammlung," 22–23.

218. See p. 218.

219. Aland, "Die Enstehung des Corpus Paulinum," 302–50.

220. For information on the practical details of letter writing and delivery/circulation, see Klauck, *Ancient Letters*, 43–66.

221. For data, see the next chapter.

222. Acts, probably issued between 110 and 120, shows familiarity with at least seven letters, probably eight (Romans, 1 Corinthians, 2 Corinthians [perhaps only a fragment], Galatians, Ephesians, Philippians, Colossians, and 1 Thessalonians); see Pervo, *Dating Acts*, 51–147. The quantity indicates that Luke utilized a collection.

223. The theology of 2 Thessalonians, in which salvation is essentially entirely future, would not have been congenial to Luke.

224. The NRSV differs from the RSV, which, in turn, differs from the ASV, which differs from the AV, while the AV differed from the Bishop's Bible and other predecessors. Each of these has appeared in different formats, with or without notes, and so on. The foregoing covers only one line in the history of English editions. The most widely used Greek New Testament (Nestle-Aland) is in its twenty-seventh edition. That edition has been revised several times.

225. See p. 55.

226. Philemon presents difficulties. See p. 30.

227. Note, however, the prominent position of Hebrews in P46.

228. The basis is Tertullian, *Adv. Marcionem* 5. Epiphanius, however, placed Philemon after Colossians, leading to the inference that it may have been embedded in that letter (*Panarion* 49.9.4), or treated as a companion to it.

229. Gamble, *Textual History*, 112. Even more hypothetical is an edition in chronological order that ended with Romans (see p. 38).

230. Marcion, may, however, have relocated Galatians to the head of the list. See p. 30.

231. See p. 66.

232. See above, p. 33.

233. Jude is notoriously difficult to date, 90–100 being a reasonable range.

234. Revelation reflects the use of letters, a practice pioneered by Paul, for commendation and criticism of local churches. Like Paul, its authority does not rest upon direct or indirect links to the authority of the earthly Jesus but to revelation from the heavenly Christ. Note also the rather distinctly Pauline salutation "Grace to you and peace" (1:4).

235. See below.

236. In fact, this practice is explicitly attested only in 1 Cor. 16:21 and Phlm. 19, among the undisputed letters. Cf. also Col. 4:18.

237. Helmut Koester, "Ephesos in Early Christian Literature," in idem, ed., *Ephesos: Metropolis of Asia*, HTS 41 (Valley Forge: Trinity Press International, 1995), 119–40.

238. See Richard I. Pervo, "Johannine Trajectories in the *Acts of John*," *Apocrypha* 3 (1992): 47–68.

239. John 13:23-26; 20:2; 21; 21:20-23.

240. According to Irenaeus (*A.H.* 5.30.3), Revelation appeared at the end of the principate of Domitian (81–96). Since Irenaeus seeks to date Christian writings as early as possible, most accept this date. Domitian had the reputation of a persecuting emperor, leaving the possibility that Revelation appeared under Trajan (98–117). Irenaeus claims that the seer John was still alive during Trajan's reign (*A.H.* 2.22.5).

241. Barnett, *Literary Influence*, 41, takes Revelation as a "certain witness" to the existence of the Pauline Corpus. For possible links between Revelation and Pauline epistles, especially Ephesians, see 41–51.

242. See, for example, Ignatius, *Ephesians* 3-5.

243. On the argument for 2 Cor. 6:14—7:1 as grounds for Ephesus as the location of the editing of canonical 2 Corinthians, see S. J. Hultgren, "2 Cor 6.14—7.1 and Rev 21.3-8: Evidence for the Ephesian Redaction of 2 Corinthians," *NTS* 49 (2002): 267–82.

244. Not even Acts quite claims that Paul was the founder of Christianity in Ephesus.

245. The model is Corinth, where (1 Corinthians) various groups reached divergent positions on a number of issues. The most progressive believed that they were doing what Paul wanted them to do, while the most conservative doubtless saw themselves as defending views with which the apostle would agree.

246. Note also Acts 21:25, which also universalizes the regulations.

247. Tertullian, *Adv. Marcionem* 5.17, in discussing the addressees of Ephesians. Examples of the subsequent assertion of this view include Victorinus of Pettau's commentary on Rev. 1:20 (Migne Patrologia Latina Suppl. I, 109–10); Cyprian, *De Exhort. Martyr.* 11; *Testim. Adv. Jud.* 1.20, and Jerome, *Epist. II. Ad Paulinum*, wrote to seven churches. Note also Irenaeus, *A.H.* 5.20.2, who refers to the church as preaching truth in all places, as the seven-branched candlestick showing the light of Christ.

Chapter 2: The Pseudepigraphic Pauline Letters

1. Some scholars defend the authenticity of some of these epistles, as the discussion of each will indicate. The purpose of the present study is less to demonstrate their Deutero-Pauline character than to develop the implications of it.

2. Margaret Y. MacDonald, *The Pauline Churches*, SNTSMS 60 (Cambridge: Cambridge University Press, 1988). Her survey is limited to Colossians, Ephesians, and the Pastorals—that is, I am responsible for judgments about the other texts noted.

3. "Religion" is in quotes because no movement in the period prior to c. 250 meets the modern Western understanding of a religion, which, particularly in the United States, is viewed as a matter of personal conviction and individual practice and belief and therefore does not provide a proper constructive framework for the study of ancient phenomena.

4. For basic bibliography on Colossians, see H.-J. Klauck (with D. R. Bailey), *Ancient Letters and the New Testament* (Waco, Tex.: Baylor University Press, 2006), 320-21.

5. Eduard Lohse, *Colossians and Philemon*, trans. William R. Poehlmann and Robert J. Karris; ed. Helmut Koester; Hermeneia (Philadelphia: Fortress Press, 1971), 84-91.

6. Walter Bujard, *Stilanalytische Untersuchungen zum Kolosserbrief als Beitrag zur Methodik von Sprachvergleichen*, SUNT 11 (Göttingen: Vandenhoeck & Ruprecht, 1973).

7. Raymond E. Brown, *An Introduction to the New Testament*, ABRL (New York: Doubleday, 1997), 610.

8. Most Roman believers were strangers to Paul.

9. Compare *1 Clement*, the speeches in Acts, the Pastoral Epistles (in part), and Ignatius (in part).

10. These are mainly Greek particles.

11. See, for example, George E. Cannon, *The Use of Traditional Materials in Colossians* (Macon, Ga.: Mercer University Press, 1983).

12. Other identifiable sources include Pauline letters. It is possible to argue for Romans, but this is far from conclusive. Philemon is certain, as the greeting lists in Phlm. 23-24 and Col. 4:10-14 demonstrate. The major epistolary source is Philippians, which also stresses the exaltation of Christ and his sovereignty over the created order, including the invisible powers (Phil. 2:10-11; 3:21). See Mark Kiley, *Colossians as Pseudepigraphy*, The Biblical Seminar 4 (Sheffield: JSOT, 1986).

13. Ephesians seeks to reverse this view.

14. See, for example, Lohse, *Colossians and Philemon*, 177-83.

15. Tychicus (Col. 4:7) is also associated with Ephesus: Acts 20:4; Eph. 6:21; 2 Tim. 4:12; Titus 3:12. On the list, see Angela Standhartinger, "Colossians and the Pauline School," *NTS* 50 (2004): 572-93 (574-75).

16. For examples of the developmental hypothesis, see Lohse, *Colossians and Philemon*, 90 n. 170.

17. Similarity to canonical Philippians is apparent. This may reflect a Deutero-Pauline tendency to include some critique of false teaching in every letter. Cf. Rom. 16:17-20. Standhartinger, "Colossians and the Pauline School," 587-88, argues that the critique of practices is internal in thrust, related to experiences at worship. One value of this solution is that it resolves the tension between pastoral letter and conflict with false teachers.

18. Tacitus, *Ann.* 14:27. Standhartinger, "Colossians and the Pauline School," 586, disputes this. The town, small to begin with, doubtless recovered in time, at least to a degree, and was probably never deserted, but it probably remained "off the map" for a good decade or two. Her point, that the selection of a small city in rural Asia Minor shows the worldwide diffusion of Christianity, is valid.

19. Cf. the letter to Laodicea in Rev. 3:14-22. For an argument that Laodicea is the actual destination of Colossians, see A. Lindemann, *Paulus, Apostel und Lehrer der Kirche* (Tübingen: Mohr Siebeck, 1999), 187-210.

20. Note Acts 20:25.

21. Note Martinus de Boer, "Images of Paul in the Post-Apostolic Period," *CBQ* 42 (1980): 359-80 (360-63), who attributes this to the predominance of gentiles in the communities.

22. J. Christiaan Beker, *Heirs of Paul: Paul's Legacy in the New Testament and in the Church Today* (Minneapolis: Fortress Press, 1991), 68.

23. On this principle, see Tertullian, *Adv. Marc.* 5.17.

24. 1 Cor. 12:12-27; Rom. 12:4-8.

25. The Pastorals develop this image by propounding a christology modeled in part upon the imperial cult. (See below.) In keeping with spatial imagery, "kingdom" in Colossians (and Ephesians) is generally spatial in reference. See Col. 1:13 (4:11 is ambiguous).

26. The ecclesiology of the Pastorals shows some affinity with a corporate (that is, household) model.

27. Contrast Rom. 3:24 with Eph. 2:5.

28. See Helmut Merklein, "Paulinische Theologie in der Rezeption des Kolosser- und Epheserbriefes," in *Paulus in den Neutestamentlichen Spätschriften: Zur Paulusrezeption im Neuen Testament*, ed. Karl Kertlege; QD 89 (Freiburg: Herder, 1981), 25–69 (47–50).

29. Compare Luke and Acts. Cf. Mikeal C. Parsons and Richard I. Pervo, *Rethinking the Unity of Luke and Acts* (Minneapolis: Fortress Press, 1993), 84–114.

30. Colossians does not contain a single reference to the Holy Spirit. Cf. 1:8. Ephesians corrects this.

31. The author of Colossians does not push this view to the limit. The new life of believers is hidden with Christ in God (3:3).

32. Angela Standhartinger, *Studien zur Entstehungsgeschichte und Intention des Kolosserbriefs*, NovTSup 94 (Leiden: Brill, 1999), 285–86.

33. See Table 1.

34. This conventional view is set forth in a speech of Creon (Sophocles, *Antigone* 639-80). Creon was addressing the disobedience of Antigone, whom he had reared and espoused to his son.

35. Aristotle, *Politics* 1.2. On the relation of household and *polis* (city) to the formation of early Christian ethics, see Wayne A. Meeks, *The Origins of Christian Morality: The First Two Centuries* (New Haven: Yale University Press, 1993), 37–51.

36. Ethics was (as it still is) a branch of philosophy and not linked to theology—distinct from piety or religious practice. In Jewish and Christian thought, ethics was (and is) closely tied to theology.

37. On the Household Codes, see David Balch, *Let Wives Be Submissive: The Domestic Code in 1 Peter*, SBLMS 26 (Chico, Calif.: Scholars, 1981); David Verner, *The Household of God: The Social World of the Pastoral Epistles*, SBLDS 71 (Chico, Calif.: Scholars, 1983), Helmut Koester, *Introduction to the New Testament*, 2 vols. (New York: de Gruyter, 1995–2000); 2:270, 294–95, 304, 309; and Elisabeth Schüssler Fiorenza, *In Memory of Her: A Feminist Theological Reconstruction of Christian Origins* (New York: Crossroads), 251–79. For a recent study, with copious bibliography, see J. P. Hering, *The Colossian and Ephesian Haustafeln in Theological Context: An Analysis of Their Origins, Relationship, and Message*, American University Studies Series 7; Theology and Religion 260 (New York: Lang, 2007).

38. Examples of the Household Code in various permutations include: Col. 3:18—4:1; Eph. 5:22—6:9; 1 Pet. 2:18—3:7; *1 Clem.* 1:3; 21:6-9; *Did.* 4:9-11; 1 Tim. 2:8-15; Titus 2:1-10; Ignatius, *Polyc.* 4:1—5:1; Polycarp, *Phil.* 4:2—6:3. Contrast 1 John 2:12-14.

39. Chattel slavery has no responsible defenders in the Western world. Obedience of children to parents and parental care for their offspring are widely viewed as desirable. Modern discussion focuses upon the definition of marriage as an unequal relationship. In U.S. society, only extreme conservatives advocate the subordination of wives. (These comments do not relate to actual practice. Slavery continues to exist, and many wives are subordinate partners.)

40. In his famous letter about procedures against Christians to the Emperor Trajan, the Younger Pliny notes that he uncovered no evidence of moral aberration (*Epist.* 10.96.8; c. 110). For allegations against Christians, see Albert Henrichs, "Pagan Ritual and the Alleged Crimes of the Early Christians: A Reconsideration," in *Kyriakon*, ed. P. Granfield and J. A. Jungmann; FS Johannes Quasten; 2 vols. (Munich: Kössel, 1970), 1:18–35.

41. Angela Standhartinger, "The Epistle to the Congregation in Colossae and the Invention of the 'Household Code,' " in *A Feminist Companion to the New Testament Apocrypha*, ed. A.-J. Levine (New York: T&T Clark International, 2006), 88–97, highlights the tensions between the Code and other passages in Colossians. She argues from a perspective that views the letter as written by a woman ("Pauline") that the context subverts the surface meaning. It is equally possible that the author overlooked the implications of this mixture of "genuine" and Deutero-Pauline elements.

42. B. Wilson, *Magic and the Millennium* (New York: Harper & Row, 1973), 9–30.

43. Wives are to be subordinate to their husbands because it is "fitting." This is the essence of "bourgeois morality": doing what is viewed as socially appropriate.

44. Contrast the Pastorals.

45. A number of Greco-Roman cults and voluntary associations admitted both free people and slaves. That is, this was not, in a religious context, radical.

46. Similar concerns may have motivated the preservation of Philemon. Paul does not argue for general emancipation of slaves. Only the owner, Philemon, can do that.

47. Nympha was probably viewed as the leader of this church. Some editors changed her into a man, Nymphas: D (F G) Y M [syp.hmg]. For speculation about her, see Florence M. Gillman, *Women Who Knew Paul*, Zacchaeus Studies (Collegeville, Minn.: Liturgical, 1992), 39–42, and Marlis Gielen, "Zur Interpretation der paulinischen Formel *he kat 'oikon ekklesia*," *ZNW* 77 (1986): 109–25.

48. On the Ephesian code, see below.

49. Other writings, including (Luke and) Acts and the *Acts of Paul*, continue the original Pauline distrust of marriage.

50. On asceticism in Colossians and Ephesians, see Margaret Y. MacDonald, "Citizens of Heaven and Earth: Asceticism and Social Integration in Colossians and Ephesians," in *Asceticism and the New Testament*, ed. Lief E. Vaage and Vincent L. Wimbush (London: Routledge, 1999), 269–98.

51. Anti-Judaism may have been another factor. The Flavian dynasty's (69–96) propaganda to support its position magnified the extent of the danger posed by the Judean revolt (66–73/4) and contributed to the development of anti-Semitism, prompting some followers of Jesus to minimize their links to observant Jews. See Richard I. Pervo, *Dating Acts: Between the Evangelists and the Apologists* (Santa Rosa, Calif.: Polebridge, 2006), 324–27.

52. For pathos related to Paul in Acts, see Richard I. Pervo, *Profit with Delight* (Philadelphia: Fortress Press, 1987), 66–69. Second Timothy is the most egregious example of this quality.

53. The Mark of Phlm. 24 need not be the individual described in Acts (12:12, 25; 13:5, 13; 15:37-39). In Colossians, however, he is the same person.

54. In Colossians, Luke sends greetings to the community. Acts says nothing about a mission in the Lykos Valley region.

55. See proclaimer/proclaimed, p. 205.

56. This is a more or less eternal cliché of letter writing: "having a great time, wish you were here," developed in particular ways by Paul. See Robert W. Funk, *Parables and Presence: Forms of the New Testament Tradition* (Philadelphia: Fortress Press, 1982), 81–102.

57. Most notably the christological hymn of Col. 1:15-20. Colossians exhibits use of the dualistic "wing" of the Wisdom tradition. See Standhartinger, *Studien*, 280, and "Colossians and the Pauline School." Frances Young compares and contrasts the wisdom christology of Colossians and Ephesians in "Wisdom in the Apostolic Fathers and the New Testament," in *Trajectories through the New Testament and the Apostolic Fathers*, ed. Andrew Gregory and Christopher Tuckett; The New Testament and the Apostolic Fathers 2 (Oxford: Oxford University Press, 2005), 85–104 (99–100). Ephesians, following a Jewish tradition, identifies Wisdom with revelation.

58. Note, however, the reference to Jewish colleagues in 4:10-11. True circumcision is, nonetheless, a spiritual act: removal of vices (2:11-16).

59. The rival theology (2:8) also focuses upon "traditions."

60. See John Muddiman, "The Church in Ephesians, 2 Clement, and the Shepherd of Hermas," in Gregory and Tuckett, eds., *Trajectories*, 107–21, for the link between universalism and ecclesiology in Ephesians.

61. On Colossians as a testament, see Standhartinger, "Colossians and the Pauline School," 588 n. 71.

62. For basic bibliography on Ephesians, see Klauck, *Ancient Letters*, 315–16. Helmut Merkel, "Die Epheserbrief in der neueren exegetischen Diskussion," *ANRW* II.25.4 (1987): 3156–246, reviews Ephesians research. For a theological comparison, see Merklein, "Paulinische Theologie."

63. If accepted, this hypothesis would be a telling argument against Goodspeed's proposal that the author of Ephesians was the editor of the first corpus of Paul's letters, since that author would not have included a text he wished to replace.

64. On the use of the opening "blessing" rather than a thanksgiving, as well as its significance, see p. 126. (Ephesians also contains a thanksgiving: 1:15-23).

65. David L. Barr provides a convenient comparative outline: *New Testament Story: An Introduction*, 2nd ed. (Belmont, Calif.: Wadsworth, 1995), 165.

66. For details, see Rudolf Schnackenburg, *Ephesians: A Commentary*, trans. H. Heron (Edinburgh: T. & T. Clark, 1991), 30–32. Earnest Best has attempted to show that Colossians imitates Ephesians: "Who Used Whom? The Relationship of Ephesians and Colossians," *NTS* 43 (1997): 72–96.

67. For a summary of the issues and arguments, see Schnackenburg, *Ephesians*, 24–29. Erasmus (1519) observed that the style deviated from that of other letters.

68. Pervo adduces nineteen possible instances of Acts' use of Ephesians. See the summary in *Dating*, 141.

69. Schnackenburg, *Ephesians*, 26 n. 19, lists nine examples. T. K. Abbott, *Ephesians and Colossians*, ICC (Edinburgh: T. & T. Clark, 1946), xxxii, lists a number of words not found in the undisputed Paulines that appear in later New Testament (Luke–Acts, 1 Peter, Hebrews, and the Pastorals).

70. See Muddiman, "The Church in Ephesians."

71. For example, John Reumann, *Variety and Unity in New Testament Thought* (Oxford: Oxford University Press, 1991), 117; MacDonald, *Pauline Churches*, 93–94.

72. See Schnackenburg, *Ephesians*, 21–23.

73. Contrast Col. 1:1 (Timothy).

74. According to Schnackenburg (*Ephesians*, 40 n. 4), Theodore of Mopsuestia noted the author's lack of personal knowledge of the church he addressed and compared this to Romans.

75. Two studies that relate the address to broader questions are Earnest Best, "Recipients and Title of the Letter to the Ephesians: Why and When the Designation 'Ephesians'?," *ANRW* II.25.4 (1987): 3247–79, and Lindemann, *Paulus, Apostel*, 211–27.

76. Cf. Eph. 1:15; 3:2.

77. Astute patristic commentators, such as Theodore of Mopsuestia and Jerome, recognized this problem, which they associated with the problem of the addressee. See Schnackenburg, *Ephesians*, 24.

78. Compare also Col. 4:16 and 1 Thess. 5:27 (above).

79. See also Gregory Sterling, "From Apostle to the Gentiles to Apostle of the Church: Images of Paul at the End of the First Century," *ZNW* 98 (2007): 74–98 (88–89).

80. Schnackenburg, *Ephesians*, 36, states that Romans, 1 and 2 Corinthians, Galatians, and Philemon are certain. See also Alfred E. Barnett, *Paul Becomes a Literary Influence* (Chicago: University of Chicago Press, 1941), 40.

81. Here, too, comparison with Romans is possible, although modern critics rightly reject Melanchthon's description of that letter as a theological compendium. (Melanchthon was a humanist colleague of Luther.)

82. On the theme of unity Ephesians is also a precursor of Ignatius, who developed the theme to a remarkable degree, on which see Schnackenburg, *Ephesians*, 164. Ignatius is discussed in the following chapter, p. 133.

83. See p. 71.

84. See above p. 305n63.

85. Contrast Matthew and Luke to Mark. John also reflects a milieu permeated by conflict with Jews.

86. See Pervo, *Dating Acts*, 325–26.

87. See Pervo, *Dating Acts*, 293–99.

88. Strong influence was posited by Karl Georg Kuhn, "Der Epherserbrief im Lichte der Qumran Texte," *NTS* 7 (1960–61): 334–46 (published in English translation as "The Epistle to the Ephesians in the Light of the Qumran Texts," in *Paul and the Dead Sea Scrolls*, ed. J. Murphy O'Connor and James H. Charlesworth [New York: Crossroads, 1990 (original 1968)], 115–31). See also Schnackenburg, *Ephesians*, index *s.v.* "Qumran Texts," 348. Attention to these important parallels should not obscure the changes in meaning that take place when such terms as "mystery" are rendered into Greek.

89. See p. 40.

90. Such phrases as "man of power" = "powerful man" are characteristic of Semitic languages, which are not rich in adjectives. The New Testament has many such expressions, but their volume in Ephesians is notable.

91. Similar observations could be made about *1 Clement*.

92. Such sentiments would have been unthinkable at Qumran. The writings from Qumran are quite anti-gentile.

93. See Richard I. Pervo, "The Gates Have Been Closed (Acts 21:30): The Jews in Acts," *Journal of Higher Criticism* 11 (2005): 128–49.

94. The adjective "one" appears at Eph. 2:14, 15, 16, 18; 4:4 (3x); 5:4 (3x), 6, 7 16; 31, 33, the noun "unity" (ἑνότης) at 4:3, 13, 17. Seven uses of compounds using *syn*-("with," "together") support this understanding: 2:5, 6 (× 2), 21, 22; 4:3, 16. In short: "Let's do this *together!*"

95. Appeals for unity (ὁμονοία) based upon subordination are a common theme of political oratory in the second century. See Richard I. Pervo, "Meet Right—and Our Bounden Duty: Meetings and Assemblies in Acts," *Forum* NS 4.1 (2001): 45–62. Note also Simon Swain, *Hellenism and Empire: Language, Classicism, and Power in the Greek World*, AD *50–250* (Oxford: Clarendon, 1996), 173–83.

96. Ephesians 2:19 places believers in God's household. This theme is not developed, as it will be in the Pastorals.

97. Ephesians 6:2-3 cite the commandment "thou shalt love thy father..."

98. Galatians 5:13 may have provided inspiration.

99. Virginia Ramey Mollenkott ("Emancipative Elements in Ephesians 5.21-33: Why Feminist Scholarship Has [Often] Left Them Unmentioned, and Why They Should Be Emphasized," in Levine, ed., *Feminist Companion*, 37–58) makes a strong argument for the positive aspects of Ephesians' presentation of marriage. See also, in the same volume, Elna Mouton, "(Re)Describing Reality? The Transformative Potential of Ephesians across Times and Cultures," 59–87.

100. The comparison runs into difficulty, since men are not asked to die for their wives and Christ did not cherish his own body (cf. Eph. 5:28-29). The model of Christ is valid only in terms of present, heavenly realities. The author does not have the historical Jesus in mind.

101. Note, in particular, Plato, *Symposium* 192E. For a study of the use of philosophical concepts in the Hellenistic Jewish interpretation of Gen. 1-3, see Thomas H. Tobin, *The Creation of Man: Philo and the History of Interpretation*, CBQMS 14 (Washington: Catholic Biblical Association of America, 1983).

102. The basis for this speculation in a Jewish milieu was the two accounts of the creation of humanity in Gen. 1:27 and 2:7. See Tobin, *Creation of Man*.

103. The position is positive in the sense of favoring marriage, rather than the contemporary view of an equal partnership.

104. Note 2:11-22, particularly 2:15, which speaks of making the two (Jews and gentiles) one. The mythology of marriage extends into ecclesiology.

105. This shift from poetry to reality has led to substantial abuse of women. The author should not be assigned complete responsibility for this misuse. Another unintended effect of this language of the union of pairs, "syzigies," was its congeniality to later Gnostic systems.

106. Cf. Rev. 21:2; *Did.* 11:1; Ignatius, *Polyc.* 5:1; Hermas, Vis. 1.1.6; 3.4; 2.4.1; *2 Clem.* 14:1-4; 2:1; Papias, *Frg.* 6; Irenaeus, *A.H.* 1.11.1. For Paul, this was still a trope (2 Cor. 11:2; and note 11:3, which introduces the seduction of Eve).

107. Schüssler Fiorenza, *In Memory of Her*, 270.

108. Ignatius (*Polyc.* 5), however, cites Eph. 5:22-23 in apparent support of endogamy. On the subject of exogamy, see Margaret Y. MacDonald, "Early Christian Women Married to Unbelievers," in Levine, ed., *Feminist Companion*, 14–28.

109. Ernst Troeltsch, *The Social Teaching of the Christian Churches*, trans. O. Wyon (New York: Harper & Brothers, 1960 [original 1911]), vol. 1.

110. Behind this is the Greek philosophical view (see above) of the household as a microcosm. The author was familiar not just with the details of the Household Code, but also with its intellectual roots.

111. MacDonald, "Citizens of Heaven," 287.

112. One result of the ecclesiology of Ephesians is the potential danger of viewing the church as invisible.

113. Eph. 2:9 shifts from Paul's expression "works of the Law" (e.g., Gal. 2:16) to "works." This was a fundamental change that has had important implications for church history, since sixteenth-century and later theologians have often understood "salvation by works" in terms of Ephesians.

114. Compare Luke 10:21-24//Matt. 11:25-27.

115. Contrast Eph. 3:1-13 with 1 Cor. 3:1-10.

116. Cf. p. 288n73 (intro, elative).

117. *Barnabas* 5:9 views all of the apostles as sinners prior to their conversion by Jesus.

118. See chapter 4.

119. See Robert A. Wild, S.J., "The Warrior and the Prisoner: Some Reflections on Ephesians 6:10-20," *CBQ* 46 (1984): 284-98.

120. Wild, "Warrior and Prisoner," 294.

121. Acts may have been inspired by the close of Ephesians, presenting its sentiment in narrative form. Cf. also Merklein, "Paulinische Theologie," 32.

122. Another possibility is that the author does not approve of governance by presbyters (or bishops).

123. Contrast resides in the difference between "mystery" and "deposit." The latter amounts to the elements of Christian doctrine.

124. This anachronism refers to Christians of the third and fourth centuries who suffered for the faith and were willing to accept martyrdom, but were not executed.

125. Schnackenburg, *Ephesians*, 28.

126. Neither "Jew" nor "gentile" appears in 2 Thessalonians.

127. For an argument of familiarity with other letters, see Outi Leppä, "2 Thessalonians among the Pauline Letters: Tracing the Literary Links between 2 Thessalonians and Other Pauline Epistles," in *The Intertextuality of the Epistles: Explorations of Theory and Practice*, ed. Thomas L. Brodie, Dennis R. MacDonald, and Stanley E. Porter (Sheffield: Sheffield Phoenix Press, 2006), 176-95.

128. For studies of this subject and summaries of the discussion, see Brown, *Introduction*, 591-92, and Klauck, *Ancient Letters*, 395-99. For a detailed but accessible account, see Raymond Collins, *Letters That Paul Did Not Write* (Wilmington: Michael Glazier, 1988), 209-41.

129. This quality makes 2 Thessalonians an ideal text for the exploration of the relationship between pseudonymity and intertextuality. See the following studies in Brodie, MacDonald, and Porter, eds., *Intertextuality*: David J. Clark, "Structural Similarities in 1 and 2 Thessalonians: Comparative Discourse Anatomy," 196-207; J. Michael Gilchrist, "Intertextuality and the Pseudonymity of 2 Thessalonians," 152-75; and Hanna Roose, "2 Thessalonians as Pseudepigraphic 'Reading Instruction' for 1 Thessalonians: Methodological Implications and Exemplary Illustration of an Intertextual Concept," 133-51.

130. 1 Thess. 1:1; 5:28; 2 Thess. 1:1-2; 3:18. The opening of 2 Thessalonians may reflect a restoration of two distinct letters from the combined seven-letter edition, as noted above, p. 36.

131. See the comparative table in Earl J. Richard, *First and Second Thessalonians*, SP 11 (Collegeville, Minn.: Liturgical, 1995), 21, with comments on pp. 20 and 22.

132. Particles are Greek adverbs and conjunctions that often convey delicate nuance.

133. Krentz, "Thessalonians," 520.

134. Krentz, "Thessalonians," provides a catalogue of these features.

135. See the list of Wolfgang Trilling, *Untersuchungen zum zweiten Thessalonicherbrief* (Leipzig: St. Benno, 1972), 52-53.

136. A recent attempt to defend the theology of 2 Thessalonians as Pauline is Robert K. Jewett, "A Matrix of Grace: The Theology of 2 Thessalonians as a Pauline Letter," in *Pauline Theology*, vol. 1, *Thessalonians, Philippians, Galatians, Philemon*, ed. Jouette M. Bassler (Minneapolis: Fortress Press, 1991), 61-70. For a convincing refutation, see Helmut Koester, "From Paul's Eschatology to the Apocalyptic Schemata of 2 Thessalonians," in *The Thessalonian Correspondence*, ed. Raymond F. Collins; BETL 87 (Leuven: Leuven University Press, 1990), 441-58.

137. Collins, *Letters*, 237.

138. This hypothesis presumes that Paul did not write church letters prior to 1 Thessalonians. Even had he done so, there is no evidence within the correspondence that Paul was known as a writer of letters prior to 2 Cor. 10, several years later than 1 Thessalonians.

139. 2 Thess. 1:7 speaks of "relief" from difficulties.

140. Moralizing results from juxtaposing ethics and eschatology rather than deriving ethics *from* eschatology, as in 1 Thess. 4-5.

141. See Goran Agrell, *Work, Toil and Sustenance: An Examination of the View of Work in the New Testament* (Lund: Verbum Hakan Ohlssons, 1976). The orientation of 2 Thessalonians is quite similar to Acts 20:33-35. Note also Eph. 4:28, which may refer to slaves, but could also apply to those who, as in 2 Thess. 3:10, "sponge" from the community.

142. See the comments of Koester, *Introduction*, 2:250. Contrast 1 Thess. 4:11-12 to 2 Thess. 3:7-13.

143. "Once" is to be underlined, for more recent American evangelicalism, including the revivalist tradition, prefers to speak of God's love and the human need for acceptance. The irony, as Reumann (*Variety and Unity in New Testament*, 126) observes, is that a letter intended to dampen eschatological anxiety has often been used to exacerbate it.

144. Koester, *Introduction*, 2:247-66.

145. Cf. the fragment 2 Cor. 6:14—7:1, which places Christ and Beliar upon an effectively equal footing (above).

146. E.g., 1 Tim. 6:20; 2 Tim. 1:12, 14.

147. See Lindemann, *Paulus, Apostel*, 228-40.

148. The only other use of this phrase in the period is Ignatius, *Eph.* 12, where it certainly refers to a collection of Paul's epistles.

149. But see 2 Thess. 2:15, which refers to writing, arguably to 1 Thessalonians.

150. The co-senders, Sylvanus and Timothy (1:1), play no role in the narrative. They are borrowings from 1 Thess. 1:1.

151. This is one inference from 2 Thess. 2:13.

152. The logical interpretation of 2 Thess. 3:10 is not that the unemployed ought to refrain from eating, but that the community should not support them from its common purse (and, probably, welcome them at community meals).

153. The nature of these difficulties is unknown. It is not likely that they involved formal "persecution" by the authorities.

154. Possibilities for this letter include: 1 Thessalonians, Colossians, Ephesians, or a lost pseudepigraph.

155. The opposite of the "agitation" mentioned in 2:2.

156. Condemnation of those with different views as trouble-makers, "disorderly," is evocative of the Pastorals (e.g., Titus 1:10-11). "Idle" is not a good translation of α[τακτοι. See Jennifer W. Knust, "2 Thessalonians and the Discipline of Work," in *Asceticism and the New Testament*, ed. Lief E. Vaage and Vincent L. Wimbush (London: Routledge, 1999), 255-67 (258).

157. See, however, the argument of Mary Ann Beavis, " 'If Anyone Will Not Work, Let Them Not Eat': 2 Thessalonians 3.10 and the Social Support of Women," in Levine, ed., *Feminist Companion*, 29-36, relates this issue to support of "clergy," including widows who serve the church. This is possible, but one may ask whether the author might have been more direct.

158. For a somewhat different narrative analysis, see Jouette M. Bassler, "Peace in All Ways: Theology in the Thessalonian Letters. A Response to R. Jewett, E. Krentz, and E. Richard," in Bassler, ed., *Pauline Theology*, vol. 1, 71-85 (72-81). Her emphasis upon the epistolary frame (1:1-2; 3:18) is somewhat vitiated by these verses' wooden imitation of 1 Thessalonians.

159. See Frank W. Hughes, *Early Christian Rhetoric and 2 Thessalonians*, JSNTSS 30 (Sheffield: JSOT, 1989), 99-104.

160. Second Thessalonians lacks any independent attestation. When cited, from the middle of the second century onward, it is as part of the corpus.

161. This conflict is strong evidence against the notion that the author of Ephesians fashioned the corpus (unless 2 Thessalonians is viewed as a subsequent addition, a hypothesis for which evidence is lacking).

162. According to Reumann (*Variety and Unity*, 129), the label "Pastoral Epistles" was first used by Paul Anton, a professor at Halle, in 1726-27. For basic bibliography, see Klauck, *Ancient Letters*, 322-24. Note in particular, Andreas Lindemann, *Paulus im ältesten Christentum*, BHT 58 (Tübingen: Mohr Siebeck, 1979), 44-49, 134-49; Ernst Dassmann, *Der Stachel im Fleisch: Paulus in der frühchristlichen Literatur bis Irenäus* (Münster: Aschendorff, 1979), 158-73; Gerd Lohfink, "Paulinische Theologie in der Rezeption der Pastoralbriefe," in Kertlege, ed., *Paulus*, 70-121, and in the same volume, Peter Trummer, "Corpus Paulinum—Corpus Pastorale: Zur Ortung des Paulustradition in den Pastoralbriefen," 122-45; and Richard I. Pervo, "The Pastoral Epistles," in *Eerdmans Dictionary of the Bible*, 1014-15. Recent studies include James W. Aageson, *Paul, the Pastoral Epistles, and the Early Church* (Peabody, Mass.: Hendrickson, 2008); Benjamin Fiore,

The Pastoral Epistles: 1 Timothy, 2 Timothy, Titus, SP 12 (Collegeville, Minn.: Liturgical, 2007); and Raymond F. Collins, *1 and 2 Timothy and Titus: A Commentary,* New Testament Library (Louisville: Westminster John Knox, 2002), and Annette Merz, *Fiktive Selbstauslegung des Paulus: Intertextuelle Studien zur Intention und Rezeption der Pastoralbriefe* (Göttingen: Vandenhoeck & Ruprecht, 2004). (See also her "The Fictitious Self-Exposition of Paul," in D. R. MacDonald, S. E. Porter and T. L. Brodie, eds., *Intertextuality of the Epistles: Explorations of Theory and Practice* [Sheffield: Sheffield Phoenix, 2006], 113–32.) Aageson allows the possibility that 2 Timothy has a different author from the other two letters. Merz argues that the pastoral epistles serve as guides for reading the other Pauline letters.

163. Brown (*Introduction,* 668) estimates that between 80 and 90 per cent of scholars view the Pastoral Epistles as non-Pauline.

164. Barnett, *Literary Influence,* 251. On the Pastoral Epistles' use of Pauline letters, see pp. 252–77. Note also Aageson, *Pastoral Epistles,* 72–86. He relates each to a primary Pauline source or model.

165. On the vocabulary and style of the Pastoral Epistles, see Nigel Turner, vol. 4, *Style,* in James H. Moulton, *A Grammar of New Testament Greek.* 3rd ed.; 4 vols. (Edinburgh: T. & T. Clark, 1906–76, 1976), 101–5, and his references. Turner classifies the style as belonging to "the higher *koine*" and judges it as "...the least Semitic, most secular, and least exciting" in the New Testament. He concludes (105): "It is commonplace." See also Quinn, "The Pastoral Epistles," *ABD* 6:663.

166. 1 Tim. 5:18 cites Luke 10:7 (Matt. 10:10 differs) as taken from a "writing."

167. Some of the distinctive theological elements of the Pastoral Epistles are treated below.

168. See Koester, *Introduction,* 2:305–6. Irenaeus cites the Pastoral Epistles in his refutation of Gnosis. Irenaeus, *A.H.* 1 pref. 1 cites 1 Tim. 1:4, in the opening words of his treatise; *A.H.* 1.3.7 invokes 2 Tim. 3:6; 1.24.3 applies 2 Tim. 6:20 to the Simonians; Preface to Book 2, 1 to those refuted in book 1; cf. 2.14.7; 2.21.2 applies 2 Tim. 4:3 to the Valentinians. At the least, Irenaeus views Paul as arguing against teachings similar to those he is seeking to overthrow.

169. See Pervo, *Dating Acts,* 301–7. Although the parallels with Polycarp's *Philippians* are extensive, the Pastoral Epistles also have much in common with *1 Clement,* including the view of order, Christian life-style, and theology in general.

170. See Arland J. Hultgren, *1–II Timothy, Titus,* ACNT (Minneapolis: Augsburg, 1984), 21–29, for detailed evidence on Ephesus as the location of the Pastoral Epistles.

171. The Pastoral Epistles were not part of Marcion's collection and were not in P46. Tertullian's claim that Marcion rejected the Pastoral Epistles (*Adv. Marc.* 5.21) is not supported by other witnesses and lacks credibility. (*Third Corinthians* and *Laodiceans* appear in many mss. [see below], but are not included in the major canon lists.) The earliest ms. evidence for the Pastoral Epistles is p³², which contains fragments of Titus 1–2. This is dated c. 200, or slightly earlier. The full contents of the original ms. cannot be determined.

172. Three is often a minimum number for narrative, as in many jokes. The first two establish normality and expectations, for example, the foot that will fit the shoe found by the prince is not typical, while the last brings surprise or difference.

173. See Peter Trummer, "Corpus Paulinum—Corpus Pastorale: Zur Ortung der Paulustradition in den Pastoralbriefen," in Kertlege, ed., *Paulus,* 122–45 (126), who uses the term "triptych."

174. The canonical sequence is based upon length.

175. The Muratorian List and Codex Claromontanus (table 3).

176. On the priority of Titus, see Jerome D. Quinn, *The Letter to Titus,* AB 35 (New York: Doubleday, 1990), 19–20.

177. Ready comparison may be found in the letters of Pliny, who corresponded with friends, social inferiors, and the emperor.

178. On these similarities, see Lewis R. Donelson, *Pseudepigraphy and Ethical Argument in the Pastoral Epistles,* HUT 22 (Tübingen: Mohr Siebeck, 1986). For relevant examples, see Abraham Malherbe, *The Cynic Epistles,* SBS 12 (Missoula, Mont.: Scholars Press, 1977).

179. For a survey, see Niklas Holzberg, "Letters: Chion," in *The Novel in the Ancient World,* ed. Gareth Schmeling; rev. ed. (Leiden: Brill, 2003), 645–53. On the specific comparison, see Richard Pervo, "Romancing an Oft-neglected Stone: The Pastoral Epistles and the Epistolary Novel," *Journal of Higher Criticism* 1 (1994): 25–47. See also the discussion of the Seneca–Paul correspondence, p. 172.

180. Titus 2:7, 15b; 1 Tim. 4:12.

181. This advice extends even to matters of diet. Witness the oft-quoted exhortation that Timothy utilize wine—in moderation, of course—as an aid to digestion (1 Tim. 5:23). (Wine was a staple of the Mediterranean diet.)

182. Titus 3:4-5. The *Acts of Titus* will develop this theme.

183. Second Timothy 1:3-14; 3:15.

184. In business terms they are "managers."

185. 1 Tim. 1:3 (Ephesus); Titus 1:5 (Crete).

186. Titus is, for example, to appoint presbyters (1:5), whereas these officers are already in place in 1 Tim. 5.

187. My reading has much in common with the observations of Luke T. Johnson, *The Writings of the New Testament: An Interpretation* (Philadelphia: Fortress Press, 1986), 381-406.

188. The compass of travel envisioned in the Pastoral Epistles is essentially that of what we are wont to call the "Third Missionary Journey," a concept derived from, but not used in, the book of Acts.

189. As Robert A. Wild ("The Image of Paul in the Pastoral Letters," *The Bible Today* 23 [1985]: 239-45) observes, the emphasis is upon Paul's "departures," probably a reference to his departure from this world.

190. Lloyd K. Pietersen, *The Polemic of the Pastorals: A Sociological Examination of the Development of Pauline Christianity*, JSNTS 264 (London: T & T Clark International, 2004) utilizes social-scientific method to determine the nature of views attacked by the Pastoral Epistles, concluding that the Pastor rejects a thaumaturgic (miracle-working) view of Paul. This sets the collection against the canonical Acts no less than the *Acts of Paul*.

191. Barr (*New Testament Story*, 172) says that the author "chooses order over ardor."

192. See p. 142 on code.

193. So Hymenaeus, 1 Tim. 1:20; 2 Tim. 2:17; Alexander, 1 Tim. 1:20; 2 Tim. 4:14; Phygelus and Hermogenes, 2 Tim. 1:15; and Philetus, 2 Tim. 2:17.

194. Cf. 2 Cor. 2:5-11; Gal. 1:7.

195. Ignatius, *Smyrn.* 5.3 (trans. W. R. Schoedel): "their names, which are faithless, it did not seem right to me to record; indeed, I would rather not even remember them until they repent in regard to the passion, which is our resurrection" (*Ignatius of Antioch*, ed. H. Koester; Hermeneia [Philadelphia: Fortress Press, 1985], 230). See his n. 28 on p. 235, and, in general, the Roman penchant for *damnatio memoriae* (the practice of deleting all references from inscriptions, an so on to those who had been condemned, made into "unpersons"). The Gospels and Acts also prefer to refer to members of groups or to "some people" (τινες), as in Acts 15:1. (One may compare the old political tradition of "my opponent" or to the advertising use "rule" against naming competitors, both now in abeyance.)

196. Quinn (*ABD* 6:565, 567) notes the unusual nature of this practice.

197. Personal references and details are especially prominent in 2 Timothy. Note, for example, 2 Tim. 1:15-18.

198. 2 Tim. 4:13. These may well have a wider significance. Apostles are to be self-sufficient. One cloak is all that is needed, but it is better to have than to beg or borrow. "Parchments" may refer to scriptures required for the pious activity of study.

199. 2 Tim. 4:9-18.

200. 2 Tim. 4:19-22 provide an effective upbeat that drives the pathos home. Even at the point of death, Paul sends greetings and hopes that Timothy will be able to visit.

201. See Pervo, *Profit*, 66-68, and *Dating*, 111-33, 299-301.

202. 2 Tim. 1:3.

203. See p. 15 on 1 Tim. 1:12-17.

204. Second Timothy can without difficulty, unlike Acts, avoid narrating Paul's death. In both cases, the absence of the final scene strengthens the force of the story.

205. So, to quote a sample: Lindemann, *Paulus*, 46, and Quinn, *ABD* 6:564.

206. Paul is certainly the only apostle of whom the Pastoral Epistles take note, he being a unique agent of God, but this need not imply allegations that he was not a true apostle. It can equally stem from a milieu in which Paul is *the* missionary and authority. That is, in fact, the normative model of the Deutero-Pauline world, with the important exception of Acts.

207. Note especially 2 Tim. 3:10-14.

208. This approach reduces the tension Brevard S. Childs (*The New Testament as Canon* [Philadelphia: Fortress Press, 1985], 383) finds in interpretations of the Pastoral Epistles based upon pseudonymity: that they make Paul the *object* rather than the *subject* of the collection.

209. See p. 74.

210. First Timothy takes up Paul's early career in a retrospective; see 1:12-17 (the thanksgiving period). Acts deals with Paul's death prospectively (20:17-38). The *Acts of Paul* views the conversion in a retrospective speech (ch. 9), as does Acts (chs. 22 and 26). The *Acts of Paul* differs in that it narrates his martyrdom (ch. 14).

211. Conversions to philosophy could be of the same sort. See the story of the conversion of Polemo from absolute dissipation to the philosophy of the Academy; see also Lucian, *The Double Indictment* 17; Diogenes Laertius, *Lives of the Philosophers* 4. On the subject, see István Czachesz, *Commission Narratives: A Comparative Study of the Canonical and Apocryphal Acts*, Studies on Early Christian Apocrypha 8 (Leuven: Peeters, 2007), 44–52.

212. See pp. 59-60.

213. For many interesting observations on parallels between Acts and the Pastoral Epistles, see also Jens Schröter, "Kirche im Anschluss an Paulus. Aspekte der Paulusrezeption in der Apostelgeschichte und in den Pastoralbriefen," *ZNW* 98 (2007): 77–104.

214. The technique all but advertises the fictitious character of the Pastoral Epistles, for it is inconceivable that Timothy was quite unaware of Paul's method of organizing churches, to which one must add that the ecclesiastical organization depicted here had almost no resemblance to the apostle's actual practice.

215. On the use of sports metaphors in Judaism and Christianity, see Pervo, *Dating Acts*, 300 and 446 n. 278.

216. On Ephesians, see Pervo, *Dating Acts*, 293–99. For 2 Timothy, see Schröter, "Kirche im Anschluss," 87.

217. Ancient games always had a religious component. (For an analogy, think of the association of American civil religion with football.) Contests honored one or more gods and included sacrifice (of which a libation was a component). Victors received a crown, awarded by judges. Vows could be involved. "I have kept the faith" has a military ring, the maintenance of one's oath of service. Athletic training was related, in the ancient Greek city, to military service. ("The battle of Waterloo was one on the playing fields of Eton.") Pindar's odes for the victors in athletic contest often feature epiphanies of relevant gods. Ceslas Spicq examines the range of meanings in 2 Tim. 4:6-8 in his *Les épitres pastorales*, 4th ed.; 2 vols. (Paris: Galbalda, 1969), 2:803–8.

218. Examples include *4 Macc.* 17:10, 12, 17. A notable Christian example is the *Martyrdom of Perpetua and Felicity* 10. The noun or verb occurs more than 500 times in hagiographic literature. Particularly relevant to the case of Paul is *1 Clem.* 6:2.

219. The lion is a symbol of death. See *NewDocuments* 3 (1983): 50-51. The Psalter is familiar with this image (Ps. 22:21). The *Acts of Paul* 9 uses it literally and also symbolically.

220. See Pervo, *Acts*, 529-30.

221. For edifying advice compare the *Testaments of the Twelve Patriarchs*.

222. Two memorable symbols are his request for "books and parchments," intimating his ongoing study and literary activity (v. 12), and his request for a cloak. Paul faces death without a coat on his back. This is a touching bit of pathos. It also suggests that his missionary career has ended, as missionaries were not allowed a cloak (Mark 6:9). Cynics famously avoided an outer garment. With the passage compare *Socratic Epistle* 9.2 (Aristippus to Antisthenes): "Put away some dried figs so that you might have some for the winter, and get some Cretan bread, for these things seem to be better than money, and both bathe and drink from the Nine Spouts, and wear the same threadbare cloak summer and winter, as is fitting for a free man living democratically in Athens" (trans. Malherbe, *The Cynic Epistle*, 257, *altered*.

223. See Pervo, *Dating Acts*, 51-147.

224. The closest analogy among the undisputed letters is Philippians. Paul does not use pathos to manipulate his readers.

225. For recent discussion of the view that the author of Luke and Acts composed the Pastorals, see Jean-Daniel Kaestli, "Luke-Acts and the Pastoral Epistles: The Thesis of a Common Authorship," in C. M. Tuckett, ed., *Luke's Literary Achievement: Collected Essays; JSNTSupp* 116. (Sheffield:

Sheffield Academic Press, 1995), 110-26. 112. Note also André Feuillet, "La doctrine des Epîtres Pastorales et leurs affinities avec l'oeuvre lucanienne," *RevThom* 78 (1978) 181-225, and Norbert Brox, "Lukas als Verfasser der Pastoralbriefe?" *JAC* 13 (1970) 61-77.

226. See p. 60, and Verner, *Household of God*.

227. Bishop: 1 Tim. 3:4-5; Titus 1:6; Deacon: 1 Tim. 3:12. Note Sophocles, *Antigone* 661-62 (n. 29): "The man who is useful in family affairs will also be shown to do the right thing in civic affairs" (author's paraphrase).

228. A full-fledged Church Order can be seen in the *Apostolic Tradition* once attributed to Hippolytus. Church orders deal with the various offices in the community, including moral and other qualifications, rites and ceremonies, and the various duties and obligations incumbent upon all.

229. The *Didache* includes features of the Church Order in its nascent form. *First Clement* assumes church order and contains Household Code material. There were analogies, including the rules for various cult organizations, such as the Rules of the Qumran community. See Moshe Weinfeld, *The Organizational Pattern and the Penal Code of the Qumran Sect: A Comparison with Guilds and Religious Associations of the Hellenistic-Roman Period*, Novum Testamentum et Orbis Antiquus (Göttingen: Vandenhoeck & Ruprecht, 1986).

230. The term εὐσέβεια ("religion, piety, godliness") appears ten times in the Pastoral Epistles, four times in 1 Peter, and once in Acts in the New Testament.

231. For the significance of the term "sound, healthy" (ὑγιής) in the Pastoral Epistles (1 Tim. 1:10; 6:3; 2 Tim. 1:13; 4:3; Titus 1:9; 2:1, 8), see Abraham Malherbe, *Paul and the Popular Philosophers* (Minneapolis: Fortress Press, 1989), 121-36.

232. In Rom. 1:26-27 and 1 Cor. 11:14 Paul utilizes what he presumed would be undisputed examples based upon "human nature," but he generally relies upon conventional and rational tenets (e.g., 1 Cor. 7).

233. Cf. 1 Cor. 8.

234. See M. Dibelius and H. Conzelmann, *The Pastoral Epistles*, trans. P. Buttolph and A. Yarbro; ed. H. Koester; Hermeneia (Philadelphia: Fortress Press, 1972), 105, and the study by Lilian Portefaix, " 'Good Citizenship' in the Household of God: Women's Position in the Pastorals Reconsidered in the Light of Roman Rule," in Levine, ed., *Feminist Companion*, 147-58. Portefaix provides a good deal of social context, although it should be noted that Roman law did not apply in the area addressed by the Pastoral Epistles (Asia Minor).

235. The exception is Titus 1:6: children are to be believers.

236. Note that women occupy the office of deacon and, possibly, presbyter (1 Tim. 3:11; Titus 2:3). Since the same word (γυνή) may mean "woman" or "wife," one cannot be certain. It is more probable that women served as deacons.

237. This is the thesis of Dennis R. MacDonald, *The Legend and the Apostle: The Battle for Paul in Story and Canon* (Philadelphia: Westminster, 1983). Features of MacDonald's reconstruction may be questioned, but he shows that the Pastoral Epistles and the *Acts of Paul* must be set against one another. See also Aageson, *Pastoral Epistles*, 198-206.

238. In so far as many women were denied education and most of their time was spent secluded at home, the dogma was self-fulfilling.

239. See Margaret Y. MacDonald, *Early Christian Women and Pagan Opinion: The Power of the Hysterical Woman* (Cambridge: Cambridge University Press, 1996).

240. See Brown, *Introduction*, 660.

241. Note that spiritual components are also necessary (1 Tim. 2:15).

242. "Self-control" (σωφροσύνη), which soon comes to mean "celibacy" rather than simply "chastity," frames 1 Tim. 2:9-15.

243. For Jewish usage, see Philo, *Spec. leg.* 1.102; 3.51. A Greek example can be seen in Plutarch's *Marital Precepts* 9-10, *Mor.* 139C. On the latter, see Sarah B. Pomeroy, ed., *Plutarch's Advice to the Bride and Groom and a Consolation to His Wife* (Oxford: Oxford University Press, 1999), 48.

244. On enrollment, see 1 Tim. 5:9. On widows as an order, see Bonnie Bowman Thurston, *The Widows: A Women's Ministry in the Early Church* (Minneapolis: Fortress Press, 1989), 36-75.

245. Cf. Ignatius, *Smyrn.* 13:1, "the virgins called widows." Note also Tertullian, *On the Veiling of Virgins* 9.

246. Chrysostom (*Homily on Acts* 14) remarks that the management of widows requires a great deal of "philosophy." He was not referring to their ability to argue about the finer points of ontology.

247. 1 Tim. 5:16 envisions women like Tabitha.

248. Eligibility began at age sixty (1 Tim. 5:9), a milestone that few women then attained.

249. See Jouette M. Bassler, "Limits and Differentiation: The Calculus of Widows in 1 Timothy 5:3-16," in Levine, ed., *Feminist Companion*, 122–46.

250. Anna (Luke 2:37) is the model widow. Fasting is not prescribed. The Pastor has reservations about ascetic activity.

251. For treatments of widows in ancient literature, see Richard I. Pervo, "Aseneth and her Sisters: Women in Jewish Narrative and in the Greek Novels," in *"Women like This": New Perspectives on Jewish Women in the Greco-Roman World*, ed. Amy-Jill Levine; BLEJL 1 (Atlanta: Scholars Press, 1991), 145–60 (155–59).

252. See the judicious study of Frances Young, *The Theology of the Pastoral Letters* (Cambridge: Cambridge University Press, 1994). Polycarp shares a number of ideas and values with the Pastoral Epistles.

253. The single charisma noted is that associated with ordination (1 Tim. 4:14; 2 Tim. 1:6).

254. Dibelius and Conzelmann, *The Pastoral Epistles*, 104; Young, *Theology*, 64–65. Six of the eight New Testament uses of the word "Savior" are found in the Pastoral Epistles. See Pervo, *Dating Acts*, 287–88.

255. Two brief surveys of the ethics of the Pastoral Epistles are Wolfgang Schrage, *The Ethics of the New Testament*, trans. David E. Green (Philadelphia: Fortress Press, 1988), 257–68, and Young, *Theology*, 32–39.

256. See p. 83.

257. See Table 1.

258. See p. 83.

259. Beker, *Heirs of Paul*, 108.

260. See p. 12.

261. See 2 Tim. 1:5.

262. Bishops: 1 Tim. 3:1-6; Titus 1:7-9; deacons: 1 Tim. 3:8-13; presbyters: 1 Tim. 5:17-22; Titus 1:5-6. Note that bishops are closely associated with deacons in 1 Tim. 3, while presbyters and the bishop seem interchangeable in Titus 1.

263. See Pervo, *Dating Acts*, 204–18, 269, 301–5.

264. Joseph Fitzmyer presents a recent discussion of the issues: "The Structured Ministry of the Church in the Pastoral Epistles," *CBQ* 66 (2004): 582–96.

265. See Lohfink, "Paulinische Theologie," 71.

266. Examples include military leaders, as illustrated from Onosander, *On the Office of a General* 1 (in Dibelius and Conzelmann, *The Pastoral Epistles*, 158–60), and the astrologer: "Study and pursue all the distinguishing marks of virtue... Be modest, upright, sober, eat little, be content with few goods, so that the shameful love of money may not defile the glory of this divine science... See that you give your responses publicly in a clear voice, so that nothing may be asked of you which is not allowed either to ask or to answer... Have a wife, a home, many sincere friends; be constantly available to the public; keep away from all quarrels; do not undertake any harmful business; do not at any time be tempted by an increase in income; keep away from all passions of cruelty; never take pleasure in others' quarrels... Employ peaceful moderation in your dealings with other people; avoid plots; at all times shun disturbances and violence... Therefore be pure and chaste..." (Firmicus Maternus, *Mathesis* 2.30, trans. Jean Rhys Bram, *Ancient Astrology: Theory and Practice* [Park Ridge: N.J., Noyes, 1975], 68–70).

267. The Pastoral Epistles do assume, like most of the Deutero-Pauline literature, a static world.

268. The farewell phrases in 1 Tim. 6:21; 2 Tim. 4:22, and Titus 3:15 are all in the plural, letting the cat out of the bag. (The singular variants in 1 and 2 Timothy are secondary corrections.)

269. On "herald," see Introduction.

270. Collins, *Letters*, 168.

271. Harry W. Tajra, *The Martyrdom of St. Paul: Historical and Judicial Context, Traditions, and Legends*, WUNT 2/67 (Tübingen: Mohr [Siebeck], 1994), 85.

272. Author's translation. Consult also the versions of Wilhelm Schneemelcher, in *New Testament Apocrypha*, ed. Wilhelm Schneemelcher; 2 vols.; trans. and ed. Robert McL. Wilson (Louisville: Westminster John Knox, 1992), 213-70 (254-57); J. K. Elliott, *The Apocryphal New Testament* (Oxford: Clarendon Press, 1993), 379-82; Vahan Hovhanessian, *Third Corinthians: Reclaiming Paul for Christian Orthodoxy*, Studies in Biblical Literature 18 (New York: Peter Lang, 2000), 76-79 (letters only, based upon the Greek text); and Willy Rordorf, "Actes de Paul," in *Ecrits apocryphes chrétiens* 1, ed. F. Bovon and P. Geoltrain (Paris: Gallimard, 1997), 1115-77, 1161-66. The variants are conveniently displayed in Hovhanessian, *Third Corinthians*, 138-45; for a bibliography of published texts, see pp. 179-81. The textual problems are acute. Other important studies of the past fifty years are M. Testuz, *Papyrus Bodmer X-XII* (Cologny-Geneve: Bibliotheque Bodmer, 1959), 9-45; A. F. J. Klijn, "The Apocryphal Correspondence between Paul and the Corinthians," *VC* 17 (1963): 2-23; Donald N. Penny, "The Pseudo-Pauline Letters of the First Two Centuries" (Ph.D. diss., Emory University, 1979), 288-319; and Willy Rordorf, "Hérésie et Orthodoxie selon la Correspondance apocryphe entre les Corinthiens et l'apôtre Paul," in *Lex Orandi, Lex Credendi. Gesammelte Aufsätze zum 60. Geburtstag (Paradosis)* (Fribourg: Universitätsverlag, 1993), 380-431. Note also Donelson, *Pseudepigraphy*, 43-45. For other bibliography, see James H. Charlesworth, *The New Testament Apocrypha and Pseudepigrapha: A Guide to Publications, with Excursuses on Apocalypses*, ATLABS 17 (Metuchen, N.J.: Scarecrow, 1987), 299-302, supplemented by Hovhanessian.

273. The Coptic word reconstructed as *C[MA]T*. This term has many meanings (W. E. Crum, *A Coptic Dictionary* [Oxford: Clarendon, 1939], 340-42, *s.v.* CMOT). See the discussion of Gerard Luttikhuizen, "The Apocryphal Correspondence with the Corinthians and the Acts of Paul," in *The Apocryphal Acts of Paul and Thecla*, ed. Jan Bremmer; SAAA 2 (Kampen: Kok Pharos, 1996), 75-91 (83 n. 16).

274. The items in [ ] are restored from the data in section III.

275. The short title derives from *P.Bod.* X. For others, see Hovhanessian, *Third Corinthians*, 139.

276. *V.l.* "Stephanus." The versions obscure the difference between "Stephanas" (1 Cor. 1:16, etc.) and "Stephen." The question is whether "Stephanas" is a correction to bring the narrative into the orbit of 1 Corinthians. Since the text displays other efforts to coordinate with the authentic Corinthian correspondence, "Stephanas" has a stronger claim to originality.

277. For variants in this list, see Hovhanessian, *Third Corinthians*, 139.

278. Cf. 2 Tim. 2:18, from which this is borrowed.

279. The masculine relative pronoun could refer to Simon and Cleobius or to their "words." The latter is grammatically logical.

280. *Papyrus Bodmer* does not mention "apostles." Most variants do so.

281. The Armenian (mss. and Ephraem) make her a man: Theonas, Etheonas. In part of the Latin tradition she is Atheona(e).

282. This section is not in *Papyrus Bodmer*.

283. *Papyrus Bodmer* adds this sub-title. One strand of the Latin tradition (Hovhanessian, *Third Corinthians*, 141) reads, "The third epistle to the Corinthians, which is not authentic."

284. The Armenian tradition elaborates this verse. Latin M refers to Gabriel (Hovhanessian, *Third Corinthians*, 141).

285. *Perhaps*: to serve his pleasure.

286. Latin mss. include v. 14: "Who believed with all her heart and conceived by the Holy Spirit that Jesus could come into the world."

287. The relative could refer to "Christ," "temple," or "body." The last is chosen as it is the most proximate.

288. Some authorities omit vv. 22-23. Two Latin mss. and the Armenian read: "22. For you are not children of disobedience but of the beloved church. 23. Therefore is the time of the resurrection preached to all."

289. This verse is elaborated to explain denial of the resurrection in the Armenian tradition (Hovhanessian, *Third Corinthians*, 144).

290. The Armenian tradition makes this eucharistic—"supported by the body and the blood" (Hovhanessian, *Third Corinthians*, 144).

291. Av. 33 appears in the Armenian and Latin ms. M: Also Elijah the prophet: he raised up the widow's son from death: how much more shall the Lord Jesus raise you up from death at the sound of the trumpet, in the twinkling of an eye? For he has shown us an example in his own body (Latin). See Hovhanessian, *Third Corinthians*, 145.

292. Some mss. add: "And when he is raised from the dead shall obtain eternal life."

293. Verses 37-38 are defective in Greek.

294. This brief closure is expanded in Armenian and Latin M (Hovhanessian, *Third Corinthians*, 145).

295. The Greek text is found in *P.Bod.* X, which precedes *3 Corinthians* with the *Nativity of Mary* and follows it with the Eleventh *Ode of Solomon*, omitting sections I and III.

296. See S. Johnston and P.-H. Poirier, "Nouvelles citations chez Éphrem et Aphraate de la correspondence entre Paul et les corinthiens," *Apocrypha* 16 (2005): 137-47.

297. See Hovhanessian, *Third Corinthians*, 3-16. Testuz, *Papyrus Bodmer X-XII*, 23-24, notes that *3 Corinthians* remained in favor in the diocese of Milan until as late as the thirteenth century.

298. The essentials of a petition are the background motivating the request and the request itself, framed within an opening and closing. On official petitions, see John L. White, *The Form and Structure of the Official Petition*, SBLDS 5 (Missoula, Mont.: University of Montana Press, 1972), esp. 1-19. White briefly discusses private letters of request (2-3 n. 2).

299. See Luttikhuizen, "Apocryphal Correspondence," 86-91.

300. Later tradition expanded this with v. 33. See n. 291.

301. Discussion of the fine points of rhetorical organization would be superfluous. The letters are not fine specimens of rhetorical craft.

302. An exception is the crucifixion, which, however, was mentioned only in the narrative introduction (I). The author of I evidently found this a deficit. In fact, neither letter discusses the death of Jesus explicitly. The death may be implicit in IV.16, but it is not necessary to the argumentation, which is that God saved flesh by assuming flesh. On that theme, see, for example, *1 Clem.* 49:1; *2 Clem.* 9:4; *Barn.* 5:6.

303. Cf. Acts 15:29; Ignatius, *Rom.* 10; *Smyrn.* 13.

304. The *Acts of Paul* does not say whether these were initial visits. On the stay at Philippi, see also Richard I. Pervo, "The Acts of Titus: A Preliminary Translation, with an Introduction and Notes," in *SBLSP, 1996* (Atlanta: Scholars, 1996), 555-82.

305. Rordorf's argument ("Actes de Paul," 1166) that this represents a second visit to Philippi is improbable. See Schneemelcher, "Acts of Paul," 227 (who, 256-57, includes this with the Philippi chapter).

306. In his commentary, Ephraem attempted to fit these events into the framework of Acts 16:19-34 (according to Léon Vouaux, *Les Actes de Paul et ses letters apocryphes*, ANT [Paris: Letouzey, 1913], 253-54). Although Ephraem knew more of the *Acts of Paul* than is now extant, it is unlikely that he found those details there.

307. Cf. Acts 20:38.

308. On the thesis that the church was free of heretical inroads until the deaths of the apostles, see Pervo, *Dating Acts*, 315-16.

309. See the arguments of Gerard Luttikhuizen, "Apocryphal Correspondence," 76-81, and Hovhanessian, *Third Corinthians*, 50-56.

310. The text could have identified him as a different person of the same name or taken note of his rehabilitation. Characters bearing this name also appear in the *Acts of John* 18, etc., and in the *Acts of Peter* (*Verc.*) 3.

311. Plans could have changed following Paul's delivery at Philippi, but the extant narrative does not state this.

312. See p. 156 on the *Acts of Paul*.

313. The reference to those apostles "who were always with Jesus Christ" has the viewpoint of Acts (1:22), upon which it may depend.

314. See Penny, "Pseudo-Pauline Letters," 303-5.

315. As translated by Elliott, *New Testament Apocrypha*, 384 (following a review of salvation history): "...*God* sent them in addition prophets to proclaim our Lord Jesus Christ; and these in succession received a share and portion of the Spirit of Christ..." The Greek text is in Carl Schmidt,

with Wilhelm Schubart, PRAXEIS PAULOU. *Acta Pauli* (Glückstadt: J. J. Augustin, 1936), 56, 58, attested also by *P.Mich.* 1317.

316. The view of Christ as Spirit dwelling in flesh appears in other texts of the second century, for example, *2 Clem.* 9; *Hermas Sim.* 5:6. Redemption is the liberation of the flesh from bondage to the devil, developed by Irenaeus, *A.H.* 5.21.2-3. The language of IV.13, "...sent Spirit through fire into Mary the Galilean," suggests that the author may have known an apocryphon about the conception of Jesus. Fire is often associated with epiphanies (e.g., Acts 2:3), while the link between "spirit"/"wind" appears in the message of John the Baptizer (e.g., Luke 3:16). Fire may have been regarded as the element that purified Mary's womb. For references to fire in association with the pregnant virgin, see Klijn, "Apocryphal Correspondence," 16 n. 27.

317. Because IV.10 is present in *P.Bod.* X, the hypothesis of an interpolation would require the assumption that the text in that papyrus derives (at some point) from the *Acts of Paul*. This is possible.

318. See 1 Pet. 1:10-12; Ignatius, *Magn.* 8; Justin, *1 Apol.* 32-39; Irenaeus, *A.H.* 4.20.4, 33.9; Tertullian, *Prescription of Heretics* 13.

319. The surviving components of the *Acts of Paul* derive from different mss., that is to say, different editions. The work manifests "textual fluidity," on which see Christine M. Thomas, *The Acts of Peter, Gospel Literature, and the Ancient Novel: Rewriting the Past* (New York: Oxford University Press, 2003). One cannot presume that *3 Corinthians* was interpolated into the *Acts of Paul* as we have it, and that the text of both remained stable.

320. IV.18 describes the body of Christ as "a temple of righteousness." With this one may compare 3.5 (Thecla), which characterizes the celibate as "a temple of God." The latter is based upon 1 Cor. 3:16, whereas the former views Christ as a (new) temple.

321. Hovhanessian, *Third Corinthians*, 50-55, argues for theological differences between the letters and the narrative. Most of these are disputable, but they suggest, at the least, an indifferent editor.

322. The Armenian tradition includes III, suggesting derivation from the *Acts of Paul*. *P.Bod.* X lacks any narrative and is thus a witness for the letters alone. Other parts of the acts also circulated independently: the episodes featuring Paul and Thecla and the Martyrdom chapter.

323. Tertullian, *De baptismo* 17.5. See the discussion by A. Hilhorst, "Tertullian on the Acts of Paul," in Bremmer, ed., *Acts of Paul*, 150-63.

324. See below.

325. *P.Bod.* X, dated to the third century, precludes a date more than two decades later than 200, at most.

326. In II.1, Stephanas joins his fellow presbyters. He is the leader. "Fellow presbyter" was often used by bishops in relation to priests, probably inspired by 1 Pet. 5:1. See Geoffrey W. H. Lampe, *Patristic Greek Lexicon* (Oxford: Clarendon, 1961), 1260 *s.v.* συμπρεσβύτερος. Note also the prescript of the letter of Polycarp, Bishop of Smyrna, to the Philippians.

327. See p. 138.

328. Hovhanessian, *3 Corinthians*, 103.

329. Vouaux (*Actes de Paul*, 249 n. 1) says that "Daphnus" and "Zeno" are "arbitrary."

330. On the various names in *3 Corinthians*, see C. Schmidt, *Acti Pauli: Aus der heidelberger koptischen Papyrushandschrift nr. 1.*, 2 vols. (Leipzig: Hinrichs, 1905), 1:98-107.

331. See Penny, "Pseudo-Pauline Letters," 295.

332. See also the comments on the *Epistula Apostolorum*, p. 164.

333. See Hovhanessian, *Third Corinthians*, 122-24.

334. This is attested by Tertullian's vigorous arguments against a literal interpretation of this verse. See *De res. carn.* 48 (and below).

335. Penny, *Pseudo-Pauline Letters*, 301-2. On "flesh" as the substance of the post-mortem body, see, for example, *2 Clem.* 2:9; Justin, *Dial.* 80.4; Irenaeus, *A.H.* 1.22.4; 1.27.3.

336. For some examples, see Hovhanessian, *Third Corinthians*, 116-19. Two Nag Hammadi texts, The *Treatise on the Resurrection* (I,4) and the *Gospel of Philip* (II,3), are cogent examples. The *Treatise on the Resurrection* makes use of a number of Pauline epistles, while the *Gospel of Philip* (which probably dates from c. 250) takes up the question of whether the risen are clothed (56.27—57.9), on which cf. *3 Cor.* IV.26.

337. Note *1 Clem.* 24-25, which proposes several arguments for resurrection: day dies and rises (24.3; cf. also Theophilus, *Ad Autolycum* 1.13; Tertullian, *De res. carn* 12), seeds are buried and rise (24.4-5), and (25) the case of the Phoenix. These arguments arose in Stoicism; see Robert M. Grant, *Miracle and Natural Law in Greco-Roman and Early Christian Thought* (Amsterdam: North-Holland, 1952), 235-45.

338. Cf. also John 12:24.

339. For some examples, see Hovhanessian, *Third Corinthians*, 124. Note also the Stoic conception of "seeds," utilized in *PaulSen* 14.1-6.

340. See also Tertullian, *De res. carn.* 32.

341. Pervo, *Acts*, 15. The *Apostolic Constitutions* (6.30.5) also mentions the potency of Elisha's grave. Saints' graves and their relics were a continuing source of healing throughout the Middle Ages (and beyond).

342. The names Simon and Cleobius may derive from tradition. See Eusebius, *H.E.* 4.22.5 (from Hegesippus), and the *Apostolic Constitutions* 6.8, 16. Simon ("Magus") was viewed as the originator of all heresies. It is also possible that the tradition derives from this passage.

343. *Third Corinthians* III.5 seems to be based upon 2 Cor. 1:4-11.

344. *Third Corinthians* IV.21.

345. Young notes this similarity, *Theology*, 130-32.

346. For example, "children of wrath" in IV.19 evokes Eph. 2:3. III.3 imitates Phil. 1:23. See M. Testuz, *Papyrus Bodmer X-XII*, 14. For a number of references to New Testament texts, see Penny, "Pseudo-Pauline Letters," 292-94, including allusions to the Gospels and Acts.

347. This is the reasonable conclusion of Luttikhuizen, "Apocryphal Correspondence," 91, and, with more detail, of Hovhanessian, *Third Corinthians*, 126-31.

348. As Penny ("Pseudo-Pauline Letters," 310) suggests, "angels" may be popular terminology for the lower points in the chain of emanations, the "aeons" of various dualistic systems. Simon and Basilides spoke of the angels that made the world: Irenaeus, *A.H.* 1.23.3; 1.24.

349. Note that the crucifixion, which for Irenaeus was the means by which Jesus died, plays no major role in his theology. The only reference to the crucifixion in *3 Corinthians* is in the introductory narrative (I).

350. It would be even more interesting if *3 Corinthians* was familiar with antecedents of Irenaeus, but this raises the bar of speculation beyond reasonable limits.

351. See Young, *Theology*, 130.

352. D. G. Meade, *Pseudonymity and Canon* (Grand Rapids: Eerdmans, 1987), 159.

353. Author's translation of Lightfoot's Latin text.

354. Cf. Gal. 1:1.

355. Cf. Gal. 1:3; Phil. 1:2; Rom. 1:7; 1 Cor. 1:2, etc.

356. Cf. Phil. 1:3-4; 2:30; 2 Thess. 1:3; Rom. 2:7.

357. Cf. Gal. 5:5.

358. Cf. Phil. 1:6, 10; 1 Cor. 1:8; 2 Pet 2:9; 3:7.

359. Cf. Gal. 1:11 (and 1:8).

360. Cf. 2 Tim. 4:4; Col. 1:5; Gal. 2:5; 5:14.

361. Cf. Phil. 1:12.

362. Cf. Eph. 2:10.

363. The text of v. 5 is corrupt.

364. Cf. Phil. 1:13.

365. Cf. Matt. 5:12; Phil. 1:18.

366. Cf. Phil. 1:19.

367. Cf. Phil. 1:19-20.

368. Cf. Phil. 1:21.

369. Cf. Phil. 2:2.

370. Cf. Phil. 2:12.

371. Cf. Rom. 2:7; 5:21; 6:22-23; Gal. 6:8; 2 Thess. 2:5; cf. Vulgate.

372. Cf. Phil. 2:13.

373. Cf. Col. 3:17, 23.

374. Cf. Phil. 2:14.

375. Cf. Phil. 3:1.

376. Cf. Phil. 3:2; 1 Tim. 3:8; Tit. 1:7

377. Cf. Phil. 4:6

378. Cf. 1 Cor. 15:58.

379. Latin *sensu*.

380. Cf. Phil. 4:7; 1 Cor. 2:16.

381. Cf. Phil. 4:8-9.

382. Verse 17 appears in a few witnesses.

383. Cf. Phil. 4:22.

384. Cf. Phil. 4:23.

385. "To the Colossians" is omitted by some witnesses.

386. Brooke F. Westcott, *A General Survey of the History of the Canon of the New Testament*, 6th ed. (London: Macmillan, 1889), 458. On pp. 457–66 he discusses the place of this text in the medieval West.

387. For bibliography on *Laodiceans*, which does not seem to have attracted much recent attention, see Charlesworth, *The New Testament Apocrypha and Pseudepigrapha*, 302–5, and Charles P. Anderson, "The Apocryphal Letter to the Laodiceans," *ABD on CD-ROM*. Version 2.0c., 1995, 1996. Studies include Joseph B. Lightfoot, *Saint Paul's Epistles to the Colossians and to Philemon: A Revised Text* (Grand Rapids: Zondervan, 1959 [repr. of 1879]), 274–300; Theodor Zahn, *Geschichte des neutestamentlichen Kanons*, 3 vols. (Erlangen: Deicher, 1890–92), 2:566–85; Vouaux, *Actes de Paul*, 315–26; Penny, "Pseudo-Pauline Letters," 320–30; and the brief but cogent remarks of Donelson, *Pseudepigraphy*, 42–43.

388. Lightfoot's arguments for a Greek original (*Colossians*, 291–92) stand. He attributes the style to over-literal rendition of Greek phrases and, more importantly, shows that neither the extant Old Latin nor the Vulgate versions were employed, as would befit a Latin composition. For data on the ms., see Elliott, *Apocrypha*, 543–44.

389. Lightfoot's survey of the data (*Colossians*, 282–86) is not complete, but it provides an adequate indication of the widespread presence of *Laodiceans* in the Latin West. See also K. Pink, "Die pseudo-paulinischen Briefe II," *Bib* 6 (1925): 179–200 (179–82).

390. *Act.* VI, *Tomus* 5 of the Council of Nicea II (787), which acknowledged the presence of the epistle in some (almost certainly Greek) mss. The text is cited by Lightfoot, *Colossians*, 293 n. 6.

391. Westcott (*Canon*, 459–60) thinks that the views of Gregory the Great were of importance for the medieval Western estimation of *Laodiceans*.

392. Erasmus was contemptuous of *Laodiceans* and quite aware of its absence from Greek mss. See Lightfoot, *Colossians*, 291 n. 1. Erasmus' New Testament became the basis of all early modern versions. None of the sixteenth-century lists of canonical books included it.

393. The Friends ("Quakers") long accepted and admired this text, a testament to its character.

394. Wilhelm Schneemelcher, "The Epistle to the Laodiceans," in Schneemelcher, ed., *New Testament* Apocrypha, 2:42–46 (43), citing R. Knopf and G. Krüger, "Laodicenerbrief," in *Neutestamentlichen Apokryphen*, ed. Edgar Hennecke; 2nd ed. (Tübingen: Mohr Siebeck, 1924), 150–51 (150).

395. For example, Penny, "Pseudo-Pauline Letters," 324. The characterization is at least as old as Lightfoot, *Colossians*, 281: "...a cento of Pauline phrases strung together without any definite connexion or any clear object..."

396. Various opinions were offered in the Patristic and Medieval period about the meaning of Col. 4:16. See Lightfoot, *Colossians*, 274–76, and Vouaux, *Actes de Paul*, 315–16. Antiochene interpreters, including Theodore of Mopsuestia and Theodoret, favored the position that a letter to Paul was in view. This was a weapon against the authenticity of *Laodiceans*.

397. Theories about the partition of 1 Corinthians can attempt to account for 1 Cor. 5:9 by presuming that the letter is incorporated into the canonical conglomerate. On 2 Cor. 6:14—7:1, see already Archibald Robertson and Alfred Plummer, *A Critical and Exegetical Commentary on the First Epistle of St Paul to the Corinthians*; ICC; 2nd ed. (Edinburgh: T. & T. Clark, 1914), 104. For discussion of 2 Cor. 10–13 as the "tearful letter," see Hans Dieter Betz, *2 Corinthians 8 and 9*, ed. George W. MacRae; Hermeneia (Philadelphia: Fortress Press, 1985), 21 n. 190.

398. Cf. the *Acts of Paul*.

399. Philip Sellew, "*Laodiceans* and the Philippians Fragments Hypothesis," *HTR* 87 (1994): 17–28. For a critique of his hypothesis, see P. A. Holloway, "The Apocryphal *Epistle to the Laodiceans* and the Partioning of Philippians," *HTR* 91 (1998): 321-25.

400. Vouaux, *Actes de Paul*, 321, describes the work as "*aussi anodine que possible.*"

401. Those who wish to assign "worst" to Marcion and "best" to worthless are free to do so.

402. "Day of judgment" (v. 3) is not Pauline terminology.

403. Adolf von Harnack, "Der apokryphe Brief des Apostel Paulus an die Laodicener: Eine marcionitische Fälschung aus der 2. Hälfte des 2. Jahrhunderts," in *Sitzungsberichte der Preussischen Akademie der Wissenschaften* (Berlin: Akademie, 1923), 235-45. See also *Marcion*, *134-*49.

404. G. Quispel, "De Brief aan die Laodicensen—ein Marcionistische vervalsing," *Nederlands Theologisch Tijdschrift* 5 (1950): 43-46.

405. If the author had access to canonical Philippians and were a Marcionite, elements of the polemic of Phil. 3:2-21 would have been useful.

406. *Fertur etiam ad Laodicensses, alia ad Alexandrinos, Pauli nomine finctae ad haeresem Marcionis et alia plura, quae in catholicam ecclesiam recipi non potest.*

407. There was nothing tendentious in this title, which served to help "correct" Colossians by suggesting that one should read this letter, as recommended in Col. 4:16, in conjunction with it. A hypothesis that followers of Marcion promptly corrected the title to "Ephesians" in response to criticism, leaving a blank spot for "Laodiceans," is without merit.

408. Tertullian, *Adv. Marc.* 5.11.

409. See Vouaux, *Actes de Paul*, 316-20.

410. Gregory the Great, *Moralia on Job* 35.20. Cf. also the addition of a fourteenth letter (Letter 11) to the *Correspondence of Paul and Seneca*.

411. For bibliography, see Charlesworth, *New Testament Apocrypha*, 298-99.

412. Zahn, *Geschichte*, 2:586-92.

413. *Epistola Pauli apostolic ad Colos.*

414. For an English translation, see M. R. James, *The Apocryphal New Testament* (Oxford: Clarendon, 1924), 479-80.

415. So James, *The Apocryphal New Testament*, 480, and, in more detail, Vouaux, *Actes de Paul*, 327-32. Note also Elliott, *Apocryphal New Testament*, 553-54.

416. For earlier bibliography, see Charlesworth, *New Testament Apocrypha*, 294-93. Major publications include the now-preferred edition of Laura Boccioline Palagi, *Epistolario apocrifo di Seneca e san Paolo*, Biblioteca Patristica (Florence: Nardini, 1985); E. Liénard, "Sur la Correspondance apocryphe de Sénèque et de Saint-Paul," *Revue Belge de Philologie et d'Histoire* 11 (1932): 5-23; C. W. Barlow, *Epistolae Senecae ad Paulum et Pauli ad Senecam quae vocantur*, Papers and Monographs of the American Academy in Rome 10 (Rome: American Academy, 1938); A. Momigliano, "Note sulla leggenda del cristianesimo di Seneca," *Rivista storica italiana* 62 (1950): 325-44; J. N. Svenster, *Paul and Seneca*, NovTSup 4 (Leiden: Brill, 1961); A. Fürst, "Pseudepigraphie und Apostolizität im apokryphen Briefwechsel zwischen Seneca und Paulus," *JAC* 41 (1999): 41-67; and P. Berry, *Correspondence between Paul and Seneca*, ANETS 12 (New York: Mellen, 1999). Introductions and translations are available in the standard handbooks, notably: Elliott, *Apocryphal New Testament*, 547-54; Cornelia Römer, "The Correspondence between Seneca and Paul," in Schneemelcher, ed., *New Testament Apocrypha*,2:46-53; and René Kappler, "Correspondance de Paul et de Sénèque," in Bovon et Geoltrain, eds., *Ecrits apocryphes chrétiens*, 1579-94, whose translation is based upon the best available text; A. J. Malherbe, " 'Seneca' on Paul as Letter Writer," in *The Future of Early Christianity: Essays in Honor of Helmut Koester*, ed. Birger A. Pearson (Minneapolis: Fortress Press, 1991), 414-21, and Donelson, *Pseudepigraphy*, 45-47.

417. The collection often appeared as a preface to the works of Seneca.

418. Römer's comment ("Correspondence," 46), "In general the content of the letters may be described as meagre," is typical.

419. Acts 19:31 describes Paul as enjoying friendly relations with those at the apex of provincial society.

420. Luke 1:1 refers to him as "most excellent," an adjective suitable for governors of lesser provinces (e.g., Acts 23:26).

421. The evidence from Lactantius is not decisive, for it proves no more than that the work had not reached his attention, but it establishes a probable date. Jerome's comments are normally prefixed to the collection in the ms. tradition. This collection was also known to the author of the *Passio Sancti Pauli Apostoli* (known as "Pseudo-Linus") 1. This work belongs to the fourth or fifth century. See Harry W. Tajra, *The Martyrdom of St. Paul: Historical and Judicial Context, Traditions, and Legends*, WUNT 67 (Tübingen: Mohr Siebeck, 1994), 138–42 (139).

422. E.g., J. B. Lightfoot, *Saint Paul's Epistle to the Philippians*, 4th ed., *altered* (London: Macmillan, 1898), 330–31; Vouaux, *Actes de Paul*, 336–37. Zahn (*Geschichte*, 2:614–18) believes that the collection known to Jerome was contaminated with later material.

423. J. N. Svenster, *Paul and Seneca*, NovTSup 4 (Leiden: Brill, 1961), concludes that Jerome knew the extant correspondence.

424. The work of E. Liénard, "Sur la Correspondance apocryphe de Sénèque et de Saint-Paul," *Revue Belge de Philologie et d'Histoire* 11 (1932): 5–23, is regarded as decisive. Attempts to envision a first-century background occasionally appear. See I. Ramelli, "L'epistolario apocrifo Seneca–san Paolo: alcune osservazioni," *Vetera Christiana* 34 (1997): 299–310, and G. Gamba, "Il carteggio tra Seneca e San Paiol. Il 'problema' della sua autenticità," *Salesianum* 60 (1998): 209–50.

425. Erasmus (*Seneca* 1529, p. 679) had nothing but contempt for these letters.

426. Tertullian, *On the Soul* 20.1 (c. 200). Jerome (*Adv. Jovin.* 1.49) was able to delete the adverb: "our Seneca."

427. This tradition has been ably illustrated by Abraham Malherbe, in, among other works, *Paul and the Popular Philosophers* (Minneapolis: Fortress Press, 1989), and "Hellenistic Moralists and the New Testament," *ANRW* II 26.3 (1992), 267–333.

428. Vouaux, *Actes de Paul*, 337.

429. Malherbe ("Seneca") illustrates a number of clichés (including "wish you were here" [1]) with examples from extant correspondence, ancient handbooks, and modern secondary literature (418–19). An example suggesting familiarity with published letters occurs in Letter 2, where Paul apologizes for delay in answering by stating that he did not have a reliable messenger on hand. See, for example, Cicero, *Ad Att.* 6.72; 8.14.2; Pliny, *Ep.* 2.12.6 (from Malherbe, "Seneca," 419 n. 32, who adds other references). On pp. 420–21, Malherbe shows that the discussion on the order of names ("Paul" usually reverses the normal order, placing Seneca's name first) also relates to theory and Christian epistolary practice.

430. Vouaux (*Actes de Paul*, 344) says that *Paul and Seneca* looks like a literary exercise. A similar judgment was made by Barlow, *Epistolae*, 91–92.

431. That education contained no Greek. The narrator presumes that Paul's letters were composed in Latin and read in that language by Seneca (13), while 14 shows some awareness of philosophical jargon.

432. Alexander ("the Macedonian, the son of Philip" [356–323 BCE]) is followed by "the Cyruses, Darius, and Dionysius." The narrator then leaps to Gaius Caesar (37–41 CE). Cyrus I ruled Persia in the mid-sixth century BCE Cyrus II was the late fifth-century rebel who features in Xenophon's *Anabasis*. Darius I was defeated at Marathon (490). Dionysius I ruled Syracuse in the late fifth and early fourth century. The author's intent was to produce a list of tyrants, more or less from the viewpoint of the philosophical tradition.

433. "One will die for many" (*Aen.* 5.815).

434. 132 *domus* (mansions), 4000 *insulae* (apartment blocks) burned in six days.

435. Popular texts are not loath to represent rapid changes of character. See Pervo, *Profit*, 33, with its references. The portrait of Nero in Letter 11 derives from Christian tradition, notably the *Acts of Paul* 11/14.

436. René Kapler, "Correspondance de Paul et de Sénèque," in F. Bovon and P. Geoltrain, eds., *Écrits apocryphes chrétiens* 1 (Paris: Gallimard, 1997), 1581–94, 1582. Failure to attach dates to all of the correspondence is inexplicable. Dating contributes to verisimilitude.

437. Other rearrangements are proposed. See Laura Boccioline Palagi, *Il carteggio apocrifo di Seneca e San Paolo*, Accademia Toscana di scienze lettere La Colombaria 46 (Florence: Olschki, 1978). If Letter 11 is set aside, the order is intelligible.

438. Perhaps a subsequent editor misplaced Letter 11. A shrewd interpolator may have been aware that the final items in a collection tend to attract suspicion, but such critical acumen was wanting during the period when *Paul and Seneca* was transmitted.

439. For examples, see Table 3, and Westcott, *General Survey*, 539–80.

440. Another possibility is that a letter from Paul has been suppressed, as 12 and 13 both stem from Seneca. See below.

441. The Greek loan word *apocryphus* would not have appeared in first-century Latin. Its technical meaning, "non-canonical scripture," is most unlikely here.

442. The school of Epicurus, for example, was known as "the garden," from its original meeting place. On religious dialogue in gardens, see also Clementine, *Homily* 4.10.

443. Distinguishing sycophants from friends was a leading theme of ancient friendship literature. Plutarch wrote a treatise on the subject (*Mor.* 48E-74E). See the comments in Richard I. Pervo, "With Lucian: Who Needs Friends? Friendship in the *Toxaris*," in *Greco-Roman Perspectives on Friendship*, ed. J. Fitzgerald (Atlanta: Scholars, 1997), 163–80.

444. *Quaedam volumina ordinavi et divisionibus suis statum eis dedi.*

445. Poppaea Sabina was a political supporter of Jews, not a religious sympathizer.

446. The triangle of monarch/wicked queen/prophet is widespread in folklore and gossipy history. In the biblical tradition, the model is "Jezebel" (1 Kings). See also Mark 6:14–29, and Pervo, *Dating Acts*, 42–43.

447. The terminology is a typical: "Galatians, the Corinthians, and the Achaeans." This is a touch of realism. Rather than cite the later published edition, Seneca takes his titles from the opening verse of each letter. Cf. 2 Cor. 1:1.

448. The immediate source was probably Lactantius, *Div. Inst.* 2.7.10; cf. Cicero, *De nat. deorum* 2.2.6, and Valerius Maximus 1.8.1.

449. For examples of these arguments from Origen and others, see Malherbe, "Seneca," 414 nn. 3 and 4, and Maurice F. Wiles, *The Divine Apostle: The Interpretation of St. Paul's Epistles in the Early Church* (Cambridge: Cambridge University Press, 1967), 14–17.

450. Letter 8 closes with the observation that Poppaea, *si est regina, non indignabitur; si mulier est, offendetur*, the meaning of which is that, if Poppaea is a proper queen, she will not take umbrage at any implied rebuke; yet, if she acts in accordance with her female nature, she will find the subject offensive. The implication of this misogynistic observation is that Poppaea will act like a woman and manifest all the fury of hell.

451. The correspondence influenced the *Passio Sancti Pauli* (see Richard A. Lipsius and Maximilian Bonnet, *Acta Apostolorum Apocrypha*, 2 vols. [Leipzig: Hermann Mendelssohn, 1891–1903], 1:24), known as "Ps. Linus," which reports that one of Paul's supporters in the imperial court was Nero's teacher. *Paul and Seneca* took part of its inspiration from the *Acts of Paul* and eventually came to have a place within it.

452. A book under Seneca's name with this title appeared in the Middle Ages. See J. Fohlen, "Un apocryphe de Sénèque mal connu: le De verborum copia," *Medieval Studies* 42 (1980): 139–91.

453. See above, p. 38.

454. Note the description of the Word as *stabile dei derivamentum crescentis et manentis in aeternum* ("unmoved...the emanation from God that continues to increase and abides for ever," 14.4-5). This word creates a new person "without corruption." This phrase (*sine corruptela*) derives from the Old Latin of 1 Cor. 15:42, "an ever moving creature" (*perpetuum animal*), borrowed from Plato, *Phaedrus* 245C.

455. The author has astutely limited Seneca's admiration to Paul's ethics.

456. The terms are *allegorice* and *aenigmatice*. As Malherbe shows ("Seneca," 420), epistolary theorists discussed precisely these terms. "Allegorical" letters had meaning only for their addressees, while the "enigmatic" (of which *Paul and Seneca* has examples) left some matters unsaid. Both terms apply to the Pauline corpus, as nearly two millennia of exegesis demonstrate. This criticism is an inevitable result of the position that Paul wrote to all believers of every era.

457. See Momigliano, "Note sulla leggenda."

458. For a concise introduction to the subject, see Holzberg, "Letters: *Chion*," and Holzberg, ed., *Der griechische Briefroman: Gattungstypologie und Textanalyse*, Classica Monacensia 8 (Tübingen: Narr, 1994).

459. A classical model of this technique survives the final six letters (16-21) of Ovid's *Heroides*, which present an exchange of letters between three different couples.

460. Letter 10 contains an allusion to 1 Cor. 9:22.

461. Letter 1.7: *libellus*.

462. Universality is presumed in the discussion. The text does not say, as would a modern critic, that these letters were addressed to small bands of adherents to a fresh sect, but takes them as addressed to all the inhabitants of these places.

463. On the partition of 2 Corinthians, see p. 38.

464. See n. 54.

465. This has a geographic component. Depiction of Paul as *the* apostle was prominent in Asia Minor (Colossians, Ephesians, the Pastoral Epistles, Polycarp), whereas *1 Clement* (Rome) already links Paul to Peter. Acts is, although probably from Ephesus, an early representative of the association of Paul with the apostles. Ignatius (with an eye to Rome), does likewise.

466. Desire to make texts contemporary is also visible in the manuscript tradition of biblical texts. A notable example is the D ("Western") text of Acts. See Pervo, *Acts*, 3-4.

467. The same may be said of the edited Philippians and of the interpolated edition of Romans (16:17-20).

Chapter 3: Paul and the Epistolary Tradition in Early Christianity

1. See Introduction, x.

2. See the appendix. The tradition of letter writing continued. For examples from the early church, see H.-J. Klauck (with D. R. Bailey), *Ancient Letters and the New Testament* (Waco, Tex.: Baylor University Press, 2006), 438-39.

3. In standard English: "If you cannot defeat them, join them."

4. For a current, basic bibliography to Hebrews, see Klauck, *Letters*, 334-35. On the subject, see now Clare K. Rothschild, *Hebrews as Pseudepigraphon: The History and Significance of the Pauline Attribution of Hebrews*, WUNT 235 (Tübingen: Mohr, 2009). Note also C. P. Anderson, "The Epistle to the Hebrews and the Pauline Letter Collection," *HTR* 73 (1966): 429-38, and "Hebrews among the Letters of Paul," *Studies in Religion* 5 (1975-76): 258-66.

5. See H. W. Attridge, *The Epistle to the Hebrews*, Hermeneia (Philadelphia: Fortress Press, 1989), 2 n. 7.

6. Attridge, *Hebrews*, 2-5.

7. The title "to [the] Hebrews" is characteristic of the Pauline corpus, which identifies letters by destination, in contrast to the catholic epistles, identified by putative author ("James," etc.). Even Tertullian, who attributes Hebrews to Barnabas, identifies it in this Pauline manner (*De Pud.* 20).

8. They are thus the forerunners of more recent attempts to resolve critical problems in the Pauline corpus by postulating the use of an amanuensis, the equivalent of a modern person with a reliable secretary to whom s/he can say, "Write Jones a letter indicating that I am interested in his proposal."

9. In his *Hypotyposes* Clement's "canon" was broad, including *Barnabas* and the *Apocalypse of Peter*.

10. This claim shows that Clement, like Irenaeus, viewed Luke as the author of Acts (to which he compares the style of Hebrews) and the companion of Paul.

11. See Salvatore Lilla, "Pantaenus," in *Encyclopedia of the Early Church*, ed. Angelo Di Beradino; trans. Adrian Walford; 2 vols. (New York: Oxford University Press, 1992), 2:639.

12. This title, like other items in the Pauline corpus, identifies the addressees, rather than, as in the catholic epistles, the putative author.

13. See p. 6.

14. Eusebius' own view was that Clement of Rome translated Hebrews into Greek (*H.E.* 3.38.2). His disagreement with Origen reflects the assurance of Eastern Christianity about its authorship.

15. The most indisputable evidence for dependence is in *1 Clem.* 36.2-6. Other illusions are probable. See Attridge, *Hebrews*, 6-7. The first to postulate use of Hebrews in *1 Clement* was Eusebius (*H.E.* 3.38.1).

16. Hebrews 13:20-25 evidently implies that Rome was the work's destination. This does not rule out the possibility that it was also written at Rome. Peter Lampe (*From Paul to Valentinus: Christians at Rome in the First Two Centuries*, trans. Michael Steinhauser; ed. Marshall D. Johnson [Minneapolis: Fortress Press, 2003], 76–78) discusses the Roman associations of Hebrews.

17. An example is Valentinus (fl. c. 120–160) came from Alexandria to Rome. The *Gospel of Truth* is attributed to him (Bentley Layton, *The Gnostic Scriptures* [Garden City, N.Y.: Doubleday, 1987], 251). This meditation contains two clear references to Hebrews (1:5 at 38.10; 2:17 at 20.11) and two that are possible: 4:12 at 25.1-3 and 9:17 at 20.15-16.

18. See Rothschild, *Hebrews*, 163–213.

19. Attridge, *Hebrews*, 14. Acts 13:15 uses the expression "consoling message" (λόγος παρακλήσεως) for a sermon by Paul in Pisidian Antioch; Hebrews describes itself with the same words: 13:22.

20. Andreas Lindemann, *Paulus im ältesten Christentum*, BHT 58 (Tübingen: Mohr Siebeck, 1979), 233–40; Attridge, *Hebrews*, 13, 384–85; and, in full detail, Rothschild, *Hebrews*, 67–81.

21. Writers often began addresses with some form of *pol-* ("much, many"). See, for example, Isocrates, *Panegyricus* 1.1. The practice was also common in prefaces, as in Luke 1:1.

22. Attridge, *Hebrews*, 13.

23. Anthony J. Blassi, *Making Charisma: The Social Construction of Paul's Public Image* (New Brunswick: Transaction, 1991), 101.

24. Good Greek prose favored lengthy sentences, called "periods." These often approximate the modern paragraph. For comments on Hebrews' style, see Eduard Norden, *Die antike Kunstprosa*, 2 vols. (Stuttgart: Teubner, 1915), 2:499–500.

25. Until the fourth century, Latin-speaking theologians often lacked a rich philosophical education—Tertullian is only a partial exception. The dominant Western tradition opposed rigorism in the treatment of sinners; Hebrews (6:2-4) lent support to the rigorists. This may have influenced its reception in the Latin world.

26. For a general introduction to James, see Raymond E. Brown, *An Introduction to the New Testament*, ABRL (New York: Doubleday, 1997), 725–47. Klauck, *Ancient Letters*, 337–38, has a current bibliography.

27. See chapter 4.

28. On traditions relating to James, see Helmut Koester, *Introduction to the New Testament*, 2 vols. (New York: de Gruyter, 1995–2000), 2:156–57.

29. See Brown, *Introduction*, 254–55.

30. On the approach to law in early interpretation of Paul, see Maurice F. Wiles, *The Divine Apostle: The Interpretation of St. Paul's Epistles in the Early Church* (Cambridge: Cambridge University Press, 1967), 49–65 (49), who observes, "Marcion stands off stage and casts shadow upon every player on it." The ambivalence of Paul's views was manifest.

31. The environment reflected in James is not dissimilar to that of the Syrian Christians who collected the sayings found in Q and the *Gospel of Thomas*, for example. Wisdom, with a lower-case "w," is prominent. This refers to the content of traditional oral wisdom, as found in the Jewish Wisdom tradition (Proverbs, Sirach, etc.). One observes many close parallels to the sayings of the Jesus-tradition, such as a critique of the wealthy. The environment is, however, urban. Similar use of wisdom is found elsewhere, as in *1 Clem*, for example.

32. In this context it is worth observing that, whereas Colossians and Ephesians tilt toward support of persons of means, notably slave-owners, James heaps scorn upon the rich and demands care for the poor (e.g. 1:27—2:13).

33. David R. Nienhuis, *Not by Paul Alone: The Formation of the Catholic Epistle Collection and the Christian Canon* (Waco, Tex.: Baylor University Press, 2007), dates James in the mid-second century and assigns it a pivotal place in the generation of the corpus of catholic epistles. Margaret M. Mitchell, "The Letter of James as a Document of Paulinism?," in *Reading James with New Eyes: Methodological Reassessments of the Letter of James*, ed. Robert L. Webb and John S. Kloppenborg (New York: T&T Clark International, 2007), 75–98 (88–93), offers evidence for knowledge of 1 Corinthians as well as Galatians, supporting the possibility that the author had a collection.

34. On reservations about James, see Brown, *Introduction*, 743, who observes that one old Latin ms., Codex Corbeiensis (ninth century) placed James among the extracanonical writings. See also John Painter, *Just James: The Brother of Jesus in History and Tradition* (Columbia: University of South Carolina Press, 1997), 234. Erasmus also questioned the traditional authorship. For a translation of Luther's comments about James in the first edition of his German New Testament, see Werner Georg Kümmel, *The New Testament: This History of the Investigation of Its Problems*, trans. S. McLean Gilmour and Howard C. Kee (Nashville: Abingdon, 1972), 24–25. Luther recognized that James cites Paul and made many cogent objections to the assignment of the epistle to James of Jerusalem.

35. Luther understood the Pauline opposition between works and faith much as did James, for he equated works with human activity designed to please God rather than Torah piety. (Luther, to be sure, was engaged in debate with some persons who defended a rather crude understanding of the relationship between works and faith.)

36. See Lindemann, *Paulus*, 240–52; Gerd Lüdemann, *Opposition to Paul in Jewish Christianity*, trans. M. E. Boring (Minneapolis: Fortress Press, 1989), 140–47, and Ernst Dassmann, *Der Stachel im Fleisch: Paulus in der frühchristlichen Literatur bis Irenäus* (Münster: Aschendorff, 1979), 108-18.

37. The LXX begins, in Hebraizing language, with "and." Romans and James replace this with the particle dev, which amounts to a punctuation mark.

38. See p. 296n119 (damnatio).

39. This is a traditional means by which Jews refer to Jesus.

40. See Mitchell, "A Document of Paulinism?"

41. Brown, *Introduction*, 707.

42. Brown, *Introduction* 296.

43. Brown's "largely" allows for a substantial amount of non-independent material, while Koester's statement could, in theory, assign a strong majority of the text to the category of "general Christian tradition."

44. John H. Elliott devoted four decades to this enterprise, beginning with his dissertation (published as *The Elect and the Holy: An Exegetical Examination of 1 Peter*, NovTSup 12 [Leiden: Brill, 1966]), and culminating with his contribution to the Anchor Bible (*1 Peter*, AB 37B [New York: Doubleday, 2000]). For a convenient summary of his views, see his "Peter, First Epistle of," *ABD on CD-ROM*. Version 2.0c., 1995, 1996.

45. The extent of early Christian tradition reflected in 1 Peter was demonstrated by E. G. Selwyn, *The First Epistle of St. Peter*, 2nd ed. (London: Macmillan, 1947). For a list of possible links to Paul, see Elliott, "Peter, First Epistle of," D. 1, with the common tradition listed in D. 2.

46. In fact, 1 Peter was widely known in early Christianity. A likely early witness is 2 Pet. 3:1. Irenaeus was the first to mention this letter by name (*A.H.* 4.9.2, 16.5; 5.7.2), followed by Clement of Alexandria and Tertullian in North Africa. It was generally accepted without reservation in both East and West, and listed by Eusebius as a writing that had achieved universal approval (*H.E.* 3.25.2). On the relationship of 1 Peter to Paulinism, see Dassmann, *Stachel*, 68–76.

47. See p. 184.

48. David G. Horrell, "The Product of a Petrine Circle? A Reassessment of the Origin and Character of 1 Peter," *JSNT* 86 (2002): 29–60, finds no basis for the identification of a "Petrine circle" in this letter.

49. In the Pauline corpus the best texts read "Christ Jesus," although the reverse order is also attested.

50. First Peter includes the optative "be multiplied" (πληθυνθείη), at home in the Deutero-Pauline sphere: *1 Clem.* 1:5; Poly. *Phil.* 1:1; *Mart. Poly.* 1:5; as well as Jude and 2 Peter.

51. See Albert E. Barnett, *Paul Becomes a Literary Influence* (Chicago: University of Chicago Press, 1941), 54, for comparison of this passage with Ephesians.

52. Romans 16:16a; 1 Cor. 16:20; 2 Cor. 13:12; cf. 1 Thess. 5:26.

53. See Barnett, *Literary Influence*, 51–69.

54. See the balanced discussion of Lindemann, *Paulus*, 252–61.

55. The preposition diav with the genitive can refer to the letter carrier, as in Ignatius, *Rom.* 10:1; *Phld* 11:2; *Smyrn.* 12:1, but it may also refer to a role in composition: *BDAG* 225 A. 4 *s.v.* Silas, usually equated with Sylvanus, is the bearer of the letter from Jerusalem in Acts 15:27.

56. This hypothesis would assume that Paul wrote from imprisonment in Rome (cf. 2 Tim. 4:11). First Peter 5:13 is thus the apparent fountainhead of the view that Mark was Peter's penman and the author of the Second Gospel.

57. The actual provenance of 1 Peter is disputable, since pseudonymous letters most often originated in the area to which they are directed. First Peter claims to originate from Rome, as is consonant with Petrine tradition and with the letter itself. ("Babylon" is a code name for Rome, 5:13.) Affinities with Hebrews, 1 Clement, and Romans suggest that the letter was composed at Rome.

58. Lindemann, *Paulus*, 260-61.

59. Two recent commentaries on 1 Clement are: Andreas Lindemann, *Die Clemensbriefe*, HNT 17 (Tübingen: Mohr/Siebeck, 1992), and Horacio E. Lona, *Der erste Clemensbrief*, KAV (Göttingen: Vandenhoeck & Ruprecht, 1998). J. B. Lightfoot's *The Apostolic Fathers*, 5 vols. in two parts (New York: Macmillan, 1889-90), Part 1, is a classic. Two American studies of recent decades are Barbara E. Bowe, *A Church in Crisis*, HDR 23 (Minneapolis: Fortress Press, 1988), and James S. Jeffers, *Conflict at Rome* (Minneapolis: Fortress Press, 1991). Note also Odd Magne Bakke, *"Concord and Peace,"* WUNT 143 (Tübingen: Mohr Siebeck, 2001). For other recent bibliography as well as a modern translation, see Bart D. Ehrman, ed. and trans., *The Apostolic Fathers*, LCL; 2 vols. (Cambridge, Mass.: Harvard University Press, 2003), 1:17-51. On the portrait of Paul and the use of Pauline letters, see Lindemann, *Paulus*, 72-82; 177-99, as well as "Paul's Influence on 'Clement' and Ignatius," in *Trajectories through the New Testament and the Apostolic Fathers*, ed. Andrew Gregory and Christopher Tuckett; The New Testament and the Apostolic Fathers 2 (Oxford: Oxford University Press, 2005), 9-24; and Dassmann, *Stachel*, 77-98, 231-36.

60. The prescript of 1 Clement resembles that of 1 Peter and is followed by the *Martyrdom of Polycarp*. The participle παροικοῦσα ("temporary resident, sojourner") is found in adjectival form in 1 Pet. 2:11.

61. See Lawrence Welborn, "Clement, First Epistle of," *ABD on CD-ROM*. Version 2.0c., 1995, 1996. Some of this popularity may have been due to the name of the traditional author, Clement of Rome, regarded as an early bishop of that community and, in time, assigned authorship of a range of writings, including the Clementines and the *Apostolic Constitutions*, but its popularity in the second century, at least, was due to its presumed merits. The second century saw the production of a Latin translation, continued reading at Corinth (Dionysius of Corinth, according to Eusebius, *H.E.* 4.23; cf. also 3.16). Polycarp borrows from it without attribution. Irenaeus praised it (*A.H.* 3.3.3), and Clement of Alexandria cited it often. See Richard I. Pervo, *Dating Acts: Between the Evangelists and the Apologists* (Santa Rosa, Calif.: Polebridge, 2006), 243-45.

62. An indication of this change is the commentary of Lindemann.

63. See Pervo, *Dating Acts*, 203-10, 213-18, 249-56.

64. Note 1 Clem. 2:2, which speaks of the Spirit being poured out upon all, and 63:2, in which the text states that it has been written "through the Holy Spirit," that is, with inspiration.

65. Peter Lampe, *Paul to Valentinus*, 206-17, studies the author. He questions attempts to describe him as a product of the chancery. "Clement's" education did not advance beyond the level of grammar school. Lampe shows that, although it is not possible to prove that 1 Clement has taken *all* of his moral and religious material from Diaspora Judaism, the opposite is also true. The author was a person of modest education steeped in traditions derived from Hellenistic Judaism and early Christianity. He concludes (217) that the work is "genuinely communal," exhibiting little individuality. See also the important research of Karlmann Beyschlag, *Clemens Romanus und der Frühkatholizismus*, BHT 35 (Tübingen: Mohr/Siebeck, 1966).

66. David G. Horrell perceives links and continuities among these texts; see his *The Social Ethos of the Corinthian Correspondence: Interests and Ideology from 1 Corinthians to 1 Clement* (Edinburgh: T. & T. Clark, 1996).

67. See Dassmann, *Stachel*, 89.

68. See n. 69.

69. See Richard I. Pervo, "The Paul of Acts and the Paul of the Letters: Luke as an Interpreter of the *Corpus Paulinum*," for the conference at Lausanne, "Le paulinisme de Luc-Actes," 25-26 April, 2008 (forthcoming).

70. The best example of such use of Romans is *1 Clem.* 35:5-6, which is arguably based upon memory rather than consultation. See Barnett, *Literary Influence*, 85-86; Dassmann, *Stachel*, 82; and Lindemann, *Clemensbriefe*, 18, 109-10. Barnett (88-104) finds five possible but only this virtually certain reference to the use of Romans. For possible uses of the Pauline corpus, see Lindemann, *Paulus*, 177-79.

71. On this structure, see p. 68.

72. See Pervo, *Dating Acts*, 266-68.

73. See above.

74. Hospitality is an important theme for *1 Clement* (four uses). This relates to the letter's political purposes. If believers at Corinth denied hospitality to allies of the Roman community, they would effectively block, or at least strongly inhibit, communication between Rome and the eastern Mediterranean.

75. For the traditional use of the image, see the fable of Menenius Agrippa in Livy 2.32-33; Dionysius of Halicarnassus, *Ant. Rom.* 6.86. On the philosophical background, see Michelle V. Lee, *Christ, the Stoics and the Body of Christ*, SNTSMS 137 (New York: Cambridge University Press, 2006). *1 Clement* exhibits a Pauline background by referring to mutual subjection as a "gift" (cavrisma, 38.1), but, as the previous verse (37:5) indicates, "subjection" is primarily subordination to leadership.

76. See p. 284n11.

77. See below.

78. Hans von Campenhausen, *Ecclesiastical Authority and Spiritual Power*, trans. J. A. Baker (Stanford: Stanford University Press, 1969), 87, puts it rather sharply: "The miracle of the new life is now understood as the fulfillment of order and law... That everything should be done 'decently and in order' is, indeed, an idea which Paul himself could express at the appropriate moment' [1 Cor. 14:40]. In Paul, however, it occurs only as a peripheral comment... For Clement it has turned into a piece of sacred knowledge which touches the essence of the Church..."

79. Following the model of M. MacDonald (p. 63), *1 Clement* stands on the border of the transition from the "community stabilizing" to the "community protecting" orientation. Wiles (*The Divine Apostle*, 137-38) relates the moralistic emphasis of early interpretation of Paul to missionary history in general.

80. Such arguments intimate the apologists. Cf. Theophilus, *Ad Autolycum* 1.12, where the monthly "resurrection" of the moon is a "proof" of resurrection.

81. 1 Cor. 15:20-23 is utilized in *1 Clem.* 24:1, although with different theological grounds.

82. The reference is to the creeds, the first part of which deals with creation and the role of the first person of the Trinity.

83. See p. 83.

84. This assertion presumes that Rome would have been among the first localities to which the published collection was sent. (Copies of *1 Clement* may well have been sent to other places, such as Ephesus, which might add their weight to the argument.)

85. See Margaret M. Mitchell, *Paul and the Rhetoric of Reconciliation* (Louisville: Westminster/ John Knox, 1991), and Harry O. Maier, "The Politics and Rhetoric of Discord and Concord in Paul and Ignatius," in Gregory and Tuckett, eds., *Trajectories*, 304-24. A notable example comes in *1 Clem.* 9:4, where it is stated that God, through Noah, saved the animals that entered the ark "in harmony" (ἐν ὁμονοίᾳ). A negative example is Mme. Lot, who "fell out of harmony" and became an enduring pillar of salt. For data on *homonoia* and related terms, see Jeffers, *Conflict*, 136-37.

86. Contrast Acts, in which the title "apostle" is not granted to Paul.

87. See Pervo, *Dating Acts*, 302-3.

88. On the stylistic, rhetorical, liturgical, and parenetic conventions in *1 Clement*, see Welborn, "Clement," and Lampe, *Paul to Valentinus*, 215-17.

89. Trans. Bart D. Ehrman, *The Apostolic Fathers*, LCL; 2 vols.; Cambridge: Harvard University Press, 2003), 43-45.

90. This term, στῦλοι ("pillars"), is applied to Peter, James, and John in Gal 2:9. Here it is an attribute of Paul (who did view himself as the equal of Peter et al.). In the background of this metaphor is the mythological conception of the earth as God's house, erected upon pillars, and the subsequent view of temples as models of the cosmos, applied also to the church as God's building. Cf. Matt 16:16-18; 1 Cor 3:16; Eph 2:20; Rev 3:12. See Ulrich Wilckens, στῦλος, *TDNT* 7:734-36.

91. The verbal form of "athlete."

92. The verb, λάβωμεν, is that rendered "we should consider" in v. 1.

93. In this context "good" (ἀγαθός) means "noble" or "victorious."

94. "Witness," in the noun form, is the operative word for proclamation of the message in Acts (1:8, etc.). Here it has the sense of "martyr," a witness to the death.

95. On "place" in the sense of one's ultimate destiny see Pervo, *Dating*, 289. Note Acts 1:20 (fate of Judas) and the enigmatic statement about Peter in Acts 12:17.

96. "Syncrisis is parallel scrutiny of goods or evils or persons or things, by which we try to show that the subjects under discussion are both equal to each other or that one is greater than the other." Nicolaus, *Progymnasmata* 9 (trans. George A. Kennedy, *Progymnasmata: Greek Textbooks of Prose Composition and Rhetoric*, SBLWGRW 10 [Atlanta: SBL; Leiden: Brill, 2003], 162). (This attestation is indirect. See Kennedy's note.) On the comparison of equals, see also Hermogenes 8.

97. See Gregory E. Sterling, "'Athletes of Virtue': An Analysis of the Summaries in Acts (2:41-47; 4:32-34; 5:12-16)," *JBL* 113 (1994): 679–96. Philo's chief example was Moses (*Vit. Mos.* 1.158; cf. 1.289). See also Wayne A. Meeks, "The Divine Agent and His Counterfeit," in *Aspects of Religious Propaganda in Judaism and Early Christianity*, ed. E. Schüssler Fiorenza (Notre Dame: University of Notre Dame Press, 1976), 43–67 (50). For specific examples from Greco-Roman philosophy of the themes, see Lampe, *Paul to Valentinus*, 213, and Lindemann, *Clemensbriefe*, 40.

98. The term "labors" (πόνοι) is applied to Peter, *1 Clem.* 5:4.

99. See Franz Pfister, "Die zweimalige römische Gefangenschaft und die spanische Reise des Apostels Paulus und der Schluss der Apostelgeschichte," *ZNW* 14 (1913): 216–21.

100. For Paul, see Pervo, *Acts, passion*.

101. This is not a particularly mature claim.

102. Even the *Acts of Peter* reports few "hardships" outside of the martyrdom.

103. See chapter 1.

104. See p. 37.

105. J. D. Quinn, "'Seven Times He Wore Chains' (1 Clem 5.6)," *JBL* 97 (1978): 574–76, entertains, but rejects, a symbolic approach. Richard Bauckham, "The Acts of Paul as a Sequel to Acts," in *The Book of Acts in Its First Century Setting*. Vol. 1, *The Book of Acts in Its Ancient Literary Setting*, ed. B. W. Winter and A. D. Clarke (Grand Rapids: Eerdmans, 1993), 105–52 (114–15), proposes that the *Acts of Paul* uses this as grounds for completing the number in Acts.

106. The straits of Gibraltar were known as "the pillars of Heracles."

107. The opening chapters of the *Acts of Peter*, a later addition, know of but one arrest, as do the *Acts of Paul*.

108. See p. 294n73.

109. Cf. Ignatius, *Rom.* 2:2, cited below.

110. E.g., 9:23, 30.

111. See, for example, Dio of Prusa, *Or.* 8.11-13; Epictetus, *Diss.* 1.11.33; 2.1.10. Since 1 Clement's proposed solution to the conflict is that those responsible go into voluntary exile (ch. 54), Paul's willingness to endure exile is for them an example of appropriate humility.

112. See J. B. Lightfoot, "St Paul's History after the Close of the Acts," in *Biblical Essays* (Grand Rapids: Baker, 1979 [repr. of 1893]), 421–37; Pfister, "Zweimalige"; Lindsey P. Pherigo, "Paul's Life after the Close of Acts," *JBL* 70 (1951): 277–84; John J. Gunther, *Paul: Messenger and Exile. A Study in the Chronology of His Life and Letters* (Valley Forge, Pa.: Judson, 1972), 144–48; F. F. Bruce, *Paul: Apostle of the Heart Set Free* (Grand Rapids: Eerdmans, 1977), 445–48; and Lindemann, *Clemensbriefe*, 39.

113. E.g. Epictetus, *Diss.* 3.22.69.

114. See Pervo, *Dating Acts*, 60-62.

115. See p. 13.

116. See above.

117. See below on Dionysius of Corinth.

118. For research and bibliography on Ignatius, see William R. Schoedel, "Polycarp of Smyrna and Ignatius of Antioch," *ANRW* 2.27.1 (1993): 272–358, and *Ignatius of Antioch: A Commentary on the Letters*, Hermeneia (Philadelphia: Fortress Press, 1985); Charles Munier, "Où en est la question d'Ignace d'Antioche? Bilan d'un siècle de recherches 1870–1988," *ANRW* 2.27.1 (1993): 359–484. On his use of Paul, see also Lindemann, *Paulus*, 199–201.

119. Schoedel, *Ignatius of Antioch*, 11, thinks it likely "that the secular authorities of Antioch chose to try to frighten Christians into conformity or maintenance of a lower profile (cf. *Eph.* 10) by removing their leader."

120. Four of the letters were written from Smyrna; three from Troas.

121. On the impact of emotion upon Ignatius' style, see Eduard Norden, *Die antike Kunstprosa*, 2 vols. (Stuttgart: Teubner, 1995 [reprint of 1915]), 2:511. Ignatius' rhetoric is associated—notably in Romans—with the florid style known as "Asianism," opposed by the promoters of Attic purity: Greek composition should follow the great Athenian authors of the fifth century B.C.E.

122. See Lindemann, *Paulus*, 200–201.

123. See, for example, the handbook of Clayton N. Jefford, *Reading the Apostolic Fathers: An Introduction* (Peabody, Mass.: Hendrickson, 1996), 57–58.

124. Schoedel, *Ignatius of Antioch*; Walter Bauer and Henning Paulsen, *Die Briefe des Ignatius von Antiochia und der Polykarperbrief*, HNT 18 (Tübingen: Mohr/Siebeck, 1985).

125. On the following, see W. R. Schoedel, "Ignatius and the Reception of Matthew in Antioch," in *Social History of the Matthean Community*, ed. David Balch (Minneapolis: Fortress Press, 1991), 129–86 (130–31), and, with considerably more detail, Shoedel's "Polycarp of Smyrna and Ignatius of Antioch," *ANRW* 2.27.1 (1993): 272–358 (347–49).

126. Eusebius, *H.E.* 3.21-22, 36.

127. John lived in the sixth century. On Ignatius, see his *Chronographia* 11 (PG 97.417b).

128. Eusebius dates the martyrdom of Polycarp as simultaneous with that of the martyrs of Lyons, in 177; his date for Polycarp's death was the seventh year of the Emperor Marcus (167). This date is later than is now thought to be the case. (See below, under "Polycarp of Smyrna.") Eusebius viewed Marcus as a persecuting emperor, like Trajan. This may have been the result of his own experience of empire-wide persecutions, which he projected onto the past.

129. For additional critique of Eusebius' dating, see now Timothy D. Barnes, "The Date of Ignatius," *ExpTim* 120 (2009): 119–30 (126–28).

130. See Pervo, *Dating Acts*, 20. W. R. Schoedel, "Papias," *ANRW* 2.27.1 (1993): 235–70 (236–37, 261–62), proposes c. 110. His arguments are largely negative: "Gnosticism does not yet seem to loom large, Papias can still ignore Paul, and he can deal freely with the gospels and the gospel tradition" (237). Justin could still ignore Paul, and free handling of the gospel tradition was still a possibility for Tatian. The identification of the human authors of two gospels (Matthew and Mark) would be remarkable as early as 110. Fragment 16 (according to the enumeration of J. Kürzinger, *Papias von Hierapolis und die Evangelien des Neuen Testaments* [Regensburg: Pustet, 1983]) refers to the reign of Hadrian. Fragments 20 and 21 associate Papias with the composition of the Fourth Gospel. The picture these remains present is confused and not always reliable, but the data associating him with Ignatius and Polycarp are unlikely to have placed him too late, and a date under Hadrian (117–38) is less likely to be concocted than assertions that he was associated with apostles.

131. This argument is not based upon the partition of Polycarp's *Philippians*.

132. The early end of this range would mean that scarcely a decade has past since John, the author of Revelation, wrote to three of the same churches (Ephesus, Smyrna, and Philadelphia). Granting different purposes and genres, the differences are more than ten years can account for.

133. Ignatius presumes a three-fold ministry in Ephesus, Magnesia, Tralles, Philadelphia, and Smyrna. Rome is the exception.

134. See Introduction.

135. Adolph von Harnack (*Geschichte der altchristlichen Literatur bis Eusebius. Teil 2, Die Chronologie*, 2 vols.; 2nd ed [Leipzig: Hinrichs, 1904], 1:388–406, allowed a date as late as 125. See also Charles Munier, "A propos d'Ignace d'Antioche: Observations sur la liste épiscopale d'Antioche," *RSR* 55 (1981): 126–31; Andreas Lindemann, "Paul's Influence on 'Clement' and Ignatius," in Gregory and Tuckett, eds., *Trajectories*, 9–24 (17); Paul Foster, "The Epistles of Ignatius of Antioch," *ExpTim* 117 (2005-2006): 487–95; 118 (2007-2008): 2–11 (c. 125–150); and Barnes, "Date of Ignatius," who dates the Bishop's martyrdom under Pius (138–161) close to that of Polycarp.

136. The scheme of Ignatius' itinerary was worked out by Lightfoot, *Apostolic Fathers, Ignatius*, 1:1–37.

137. See Schoedel, *Ignatius*, 12.

138. The situation of Judaism is complicated by national and ethnic features. Diaspora Jews who provided help for the needy in Palestine were not necessarily offering aid to coreligionists. Nationality would have been the principal motivator. Religion was generally associated with geography and ethnicity in the ancient world.

139. For details, see Schoedel, *Ignatius*, 1–7. Eusebius (*H.E.* 3.36) provides a useful starting point, for he lists and cites from the seven letters belonging to the "Middle Recension."

140. See Schoedel, *Ignatius*, 7, et passim, as well as Munier, "Où en est la question d'Ignace d'Antioche?" 380–88.

141. Barnett (*Literary Influence*, 152) recognizes this fact, which is often neglected in research.

142. See John P. Meier's comments in Raymond E. Brown and John P. Meier, *Antioch and Rome: New Testament Cradles of Catholic Christianity* (New York: Paulist, 1983), 24 nn. 57–58.

143. Ignatius shares the Johannine focus upon revelation.

144. For a brief review of possibilities, see Schoedel, *Ignatius*, 15–17.

145. Meier in Brown and Meier, *Antioch and Rome*, 78–79. For similarities with the Johannine tradition, see R. Bultmann, *Theology of the New Testament*, trans. K. Grobel; 2 vols. (New York: Scribner's, 1951–55), 2:191–92.

146. For a survey of literature on the subject, see Munier, "Question," 391–93, and, in particular, Lindemann, *Paulus*, 199–221; Dassmann, *Stachel*, 126–49; Paul Foster, "The Epistles of Ignatius of Antioch and the Writings That Later Formed the New Testament," in *The Reception of the New Testament in the Apostolic Fathers*, ed. Andrew Gregory and Christopher Tuckett; The New Testament and the Apostolic Fathers 1 (Oxford: Oxford University Press, 2005), 159–86; and David M. Reis, "Following in Paul's Footsteps: *Mimesis* and Power in Paul and Ignatius," in Gregory and Tuckett, eds., *Trajectories*, 287–305.

147. See *Eph.* 12:2. The expression "in every letter" may intimate a collection. It also supports the belief that Paul said the same thing in every letter, a corollary of the principle that what he said to one community he said to all. Compare Luke's use of the term "all the prophets" (e.g. Acts 3:18), which boils down to "the prophetic tradition, as interpreted by followers of Jesus."

148. Ignatius links the names of Peter and Paul in connection with Rome (*Rom.* 4:3).

149. Cf. Phil. 1:1 (which may stem from the editor of the compilation).

150. See Pervo, *Dating Acts*, 203–29.

151. Ignatius does not restrict charismatic gifts like prophecy to leaders (*Phld.* 7).

152. "Concord" (ὁμόνοια) appears eight times (e.g. *Eph.* 4:1-2; 13:1). Paul stressed the theme, but did not use this political term. See above on *1 Clement*. Note Maier, "Politics and Rhetoric," who shows that 1 Corinthians was a model for Ignatius' views on the subject.

153. See, for example, *Eph.* 14; *Magn.* 1.

154. See Lindemann, *Paulus*, 218–19.

155. Bultmann, *Theology*, 2:187 and 198, respectively. See also his essay, "Ignatius und Paulus," in *Exegetica*, ed. E. Dinkler (Tübingen: Mohr/Siebeck, 1967), 400–11.

156. On the subject, see, for example, Schoedel, *Ignatius*, 23-24, and Dassmann, *Stachel*, 140–42.

157. Docetism sought not to deny the divinity of Christ but to affirm and protect it. See also the sage comment of R. Joseph Hoffmann, *Marcion: On the Restitution of Christianity*, AARAS 46 (Chico, Calif.: Scholars Press, 1984), 159 n. 50: "Docetism was also an expression at that time for the belief that Christ was not a product of his time and that genius and divinity do not develop from nature."

158. Opposition to Docetism is general, but especially prominent in the letters to Tralles and Smyrna (*Trall.* 10; *Smyrn.* 4.2).

159. See, for example, *Trall.* 11:1.

160. Much as he prized martyrdom as fulfillment of his vocation, Ignatius did not view it as the only path to Christian perfection. All believers are "fellow-initiates" (συμμύσται) of Paul (*Eph.* 12:2). His view of imitation differed somewhat from that of Paul; see Schoedel, *Ignatius*, 29–30. For Ignatius' imitation was first and foremost obedience.

161. See p. 15.

162. Trans. Ehrman, *Apostolic Fathers*, 1:273.

163. Cf. Melito (Frg. 8b 2-4) for adaptation of the imagery of the course of the sun to baptism ("dying" in the waters of the west; "rising" again in the east).

164. See Robert M. Grant, ed., *The Apostolic Fathers: A New Translation and Commentary*, 6 vols. (London: Nelson, 1966), 4:90, and Dassmann, *Stachel*, 135–36.

165. Trans. Bart D. Ehrman, *The Apostolic Fathers* 1:273.

166. The chorus refers to the hymns often sung at the occasion of sacrifices.

167. See P. B. Duff, "The March of the Divine Warrior and the Advent of the Greco-Roman King: Mark's Account of Jesus' Entry into Jerusalem," *JBL* 111 (1992): 55–71. On the Roman triumph, see H. S. Versnell, *Triumphus: An Inquiry into the Origin, Development and Meaning of the Roman Triumph* (Leiden: Brill, 1970), and Mary Beard, *The Roman Triumph* (Cambridge, Mass.: Harvard University Press, 2007).

168. Among the best known, because of their depictions in art and literature, are the processions to the Parthenon (temple of Athena) at Athens and the procession to the Temple of Artemis of Ephesus. For descriptions, see the account of a procession in honor of Dionysus sponsored by Ptolemy II Philadelphus in Alexandria (Athenaeus *Deipnosophistae* 5.196A-203A), and the Isaic procession at Corinth (Apuleius, *Metamorphoses* 11.8-17). A good sense of the content of such procession can be seen in saint's day procession in Europe, as well as in ethnic neighborhoods in the U.S.

169. See Schoedel, *Ignatius*, 67.

170. Schoedel, *Ignatius*, 190; cf. also *Smyrn* Inscr (Schoedel, 219) and the comments on 2 Cor. 14–17 (p. 42).

171. Cf. *Rom.* 4:3 (in which Ignatius distinguishes himself from the apostles), which implies that Ignatius believed that both Peter and Paul had preached and taught, perhaps together, in Rome. The widely disseminated *1 Clement* may have been the source of this view.

172. On Polycarp, see W. Schoedel, *Polycarp, Martyrdom of Polycarp, Fragments of Papias*, in Grant, ed., *The Apostolic Fathers*, vol. 5, and "Polycarp of Smyrna and Ignatius of Antioch," *ANRW* 2.27.1 (1993): 272–358 (272–85), and Bauer and Paulsen, *Briefe*, 111–26.

173. Tertullian, *Praescription of Heretics* 32, states that Polycarp was consecrated by the apostle John.

174. Polycarp evidently knows 1 John (Polycarp, *Phil.* 7:1; see n. **x**), but he does not identify an author of the text or state that he is citing a document. For doubts about Polycarp as a link to the initial Christian generation, see Schoedel, "Polycarp," 275 n. 8.

175. See above, p. 138.

176. Cf. P. N. Harrison, *Polycarp's Two Epistles to the Philippians* (Cambridge: Cambridge University Press, 1936), 3.

177. Although a witness to the importance of Polycarp as a figure of early church history, the *Life* attributed to Pionius dates from the fifth century and is more or less utterly fictitious.

178. Harrison, *Polycarp's Two Epistles*.

179. For a review of research, see Schoedel, "Polycarp," 279–81. (Schoedel supports unity.)

180. The argument is important for the history of the New Testament canon. If, c. 110, Polycarp in Smyrna had access to two written Gospels (Matthew and Luke), the letters of Paul, including the Pastoral Epistles, 1 Peter, and 1 John, it could be maintained that the "core" (Gospels, Paul, catholic epistles) of the canon was in place in the early second century. If true, this would make Polycarp an anomaly. Moreover, this conclusion overlooks Polycarp's use of the material (below).

181. For a summary, see Koester, *Introduction*, 2:308–10. For more detail, see Koester's *Ancient Christian Gospels: Their History and Development* (Philadelphia: Trinity Press International, 1990), 19–20.

182. Cf. Ignatius, *Magn.* 10:3; Acts 3:18, 24. Polycarp may have known Acts (Pervo, *Dating Acts*, 17–20); he knew Ignatius.

183. See Bauer and Paulsen, *Briefe*, 125.

184. Polycarp, *Phil.* 6:1 is reminiscent of Prov. 3:4, but 2 Cor. 8:21 is equally possible.

185. The statement that Paul wrote letters to the Philippians (3:2) probably reflects the notion that what Paul wrote to one community he wrote to all. Cf. A. Lindemann, "Paul in the Writings of the Apostolic Fathers," in *Paul and the Legacies of Paul*, ed. William S. Babcock (Dallas: Southern Methodist University Press, 1990), 25–45 (41). (This essay has been updated and published in German in Lindemann's *Paulus, Apostel und Lehrer der Kirche* [Tübingen: Mohr Siebeck, 1999], 252–79; Polycarp is the subject of pp. 273–78). On the general question of Polycarp's use of early Christian

literature, see Barnett, *Literary Influence*, 170–85; B. Dehandschutter, "Polycarp's Epistle to the Philippians: An Early Example of Reception," in *The New Testament in Early Christianity*, ed. Jean-Marie Sevrin (Leuven: Leuven University Press, 1989), 275–91; and, for a recent review, Michael W. Holmes, "Polycarp's *Letter to the Philippians* and the Writings That Later Formed the New Testament," in Gregory and Tuckett, eds., *Reception*, 187–227.

186. *Sicut Paulus docet.* Lindemann (*Paulus*, 90, 227) notes that this statement may derive from the Latin translator.

187. Hans von Campenhausen, "Polykarp von Smyrna und die Pastoralbriefe," in *Aus der Frühzeit des Christentums: Studien zur Kirchengeschichte des ersten und zweiten Jahrhunderts* (Tübingen: Mohr/Siebeck, 1963), 197–252. This essay first appeared in 1951. Polycarp's letter, although regarded as mediocre, has inspired two of the most brilliant and beguiling studies of the apostolic fathers of the twentieth century: Harrison's *Two Epistles*, and von Campenhausen's essay on its authorship.

188. On the use of 1 John by Polycarp, see Paulsen, *Die Briefe*, 120.

189. This is not a Pauline "theology of the cross" (although Polycarp affirms in 1:2 that Christ died for human sins); see Lindemann, *Paulus*, 230.

190. On this see J. M. Robinson's comments in J. M. Robinson and H. Koester, *Trajectories through Early Christianity* (Philadelphia: Fortress Press, 1971), 37–38.

191. Polycarp (*Phil.* 2:1) rejects verbal argument as worthless.

192. See Schoedel, *Polycarp*, 23–24, and Paulsen, *Die Briefe*, 120–21, on the possibilities and problems of associating *Phil.* 7 with Marcion.

193. Schoedel, "Polycarp," 284.

194. See below, under "Marcion."

195. On the Pauline features of Polycarp's theology, see Bultmann, *Theology*, 2:171–73; Lindemann, *Paulus*, 221–32; and Dassmann, *Stachel*, 149–58.

196. Cf. *1 Clem.* 5:5, where Paul takes first prize in "endurance." On the importance of suffering as a quality of genuine leadership, see Peter Oakes, "Leadership and Suffering in the Letters of Polycarp and Paul to the Philippians," in Gregory and Tuckett, eds., *Trajectories*, 353–73.

197. Contrast his sources: Rom. 6:13; 13:12; 2 Cor. 6:7; 10:4; 1 Thess. 5:8; cf. Eph. 6:11. In Polycarp, as in the Pastoral Epistles, the injunctions of the codes involve only duties and are addressed to adult males.

198. M. Staniforth, *Early Christian Writings: The Apostolic Fathers* (Baltimore: Penguin, 1968).

199. For such a reading, see Schoedel, *Polycarp*.

200. See the analysis of Harry O. Maier, "Purity and Danger in Polycarp's Epistle to the Philippians: The Sin of Valens in Social Perspective," *Journal of Early Christian Studies* 1 (1993): 229–47.

201. Cf. also *1 Clem.* 47:1.

202. For current bibliography, see Klauck, *Letters*, 408–9, with a useful survey, as well as Elliott (see the following note). A relatively recent commentary is Jerome H. Neyrey, *2 Peter, Jude*, AB 37C (New York: Doubleday, 1993). Note also the survey of Richard Bauckham, "2 Peter: An Account of Research," *ANRW* II.25.5 (1988): 3713–52.

203. See John H. Elliott, "Peter, Second Epistle of," *ABD on CD-ROM*. Version 2.0c, 1995, 1996.

204. C. Detlef G. Müller, "Apocalypse of Peter," in Schneemelcher, ed., *New Testament Apocrypha*, 2:620–38 (622).

205. See the partial synopsis in Klauck, *Letters*, 416–18. Second Peter improves Jude's references by placing them in the biblical order and omitting citations of extracanonical texts.

206. Note the utilization of the Transfiguration (1:16-18), a popular episode in the *Acts of Peter* and the *Acts of John*, on which see, for example, Richard I. Pervo, "Egging on the Chickens: A Cowardly Response to Dennis MacDonald and Then Some," *Semeia* 80 (1997): 43–56.

207. See Frederick W. Danker, "2 Peter 1: A Solemn Decree," *CBQ* 40 (1978): 64–82.

208. Koester, *Introduction*, 2:295–96.

209. On this passage, see, in particular, Lindemann, *Paulus*, 91–97.

210. On the expression "every letter"/"all the letters," see p. 332n147. For allusions to the corpus, see Barnett, *Literary Influence*, 222–28; Lindemann, *Paulus*, 261–63; and Neyrey, *2 Peter*, 134, 250.

211. Cf. Lindemann, *Paulus*, 92 n. 4.

212. Translation of γραφαί (v. 16) as "scriptures," even in the lower case, may be misleading. A canon is not in view. The writings in question probably include gospels and other letters, certainly 1 Peter (3:1-2), and, judging by the modification of Jude and the various examples, the LXX (cf. 3:2).

213. Second Peter has no positive view of the end as a source of hope or consolation. It is a doctrine to which Christians must, at peril, subscribe.

214. Lindemann, *Paulus*, 93–94.

215. They may have done so, but 2 Peter gives no evidence.

216. See Lüdemann, *Opposition*, 118–25.

217. When the empire experienced great difficulties (war against Persia, barbarians, Bubonic plague in this period), the cry went up that these misfortunes were punishment for neglecting the gods. Modern analogies will come to mind.

218. This account relies upon Pierre Nautin, *Lettres et écrivains chrétiens des IIᵉ et IIIᵉ siècles*, Patristica II (Paris: Cerf, 1961), 13–22, a model of sound historical reconstruction. See also Philip Carrington, *The Early Christian Church*, 2 vols. (Cambridge: Cambridge University Press, 1957), 2:192–206.

219. Eusebius calls these letters to churches "catholic," evidently promoting the notion that they were of value for all believers.

220. Cf. also the Ignatian corpus.

221. Dionysius may well have sent this collection to other communities, but Rome generated its formation.

222. Dionysius protests in his letter to Soter that he wrote at the request of others (*H.E.* 4.23.12), but this may be part of his defense.

223. The practice remains in that pastoral letters from the bishop are read on a Sunday in each community.

224. Eusebius (*H.E.* 4.23.1) calls *1 Clement* "the former letter, sent *through* (διά) Clement." The source of this statement is unknown. The most probable solution is that those who delivered the letter stated that a certain Clement was its material composer.

225. This is a logical inference from Dionysius' reply and action. Eusebius does not mention the reproof.

226. As in the case of *1 Clement*, Soter's concern was partly motivated by the importance of Corinth as a maritime nexus between Rome and the Aegean area.

227. On the subject, see J.-M. Prieur, "L'étique sexuelle et conjugale des chrétiens des premiers siecles et ses justifications," *Revue d'histoire et de philosophie religieuses* 82 (2002): 267–82.

228. See Nautin, *Lettres*, 17.

229. Later systems demanded that penitents remain celibate for life. This condition may already have been current.

230. Eusebius admires the sentiments of Pinytos more than those of Dionysius (*H.E.* 4.23.8). For other possible allusions to Paul's epistles in this correspondence, see David K. Rensberger, "As the Apostle Teaches: The Development of the Use of Paul's Letters in Second-Century Christianity" (Ph.D. diss., Yale, 1981), 83.

231. Opponents of re-admission of those who had committed serious sins would probably appeal to 1 Cor. 5:1-5.

232. Eusebius (*H.E.* 4.23.8) uses the expression τελειοτέροις γράμμασιν ("more mature letter"). This play upon Paul's language (1 Cor. 2:6; 13:10; 14:20) probably comes from Pinytos' letter.

233. Nautin, *Lettres*, 32.

234. It is also possible that Dionysius revised his letters before sending them to Soter and claimed that he suffered from hostile editing. Alternatively, Pinytos could have sent bishop Soter only those portions of Dionysius' communication that he deemed relevant.

235. The phrase is an *hommage* to Dennis R. MacDonald, *The Legend and the Apostle: The Battle for Paul in Story and Canon* (Philadelphia: Westminster, 1983).

236. See p. 87.

Chapter 4: Paul in Narrative

1. See chapter 7.

2. On the term πράξεις ("acts, deeds") as a title, see Richard I. Pervo, *Acts*, Hermeneia (Minneapolis: Fortress Press, 2009), 29–30. The original title of Acts, if one existed, is unknown.

3. For a survey of research, see Paul-Gerhard Müller, "Der 'Paulinismus' in der Apostelgeschichte. Ein Forschungsgeschichtlicher Überblick," in *Paulus in den Neutestamentlichen Spätschriften: Zur Paulusrezeption im Neuen Testament*, ed. Karl Kertelge; QD 89 (Freiburg: Herder, 1981), 157–201.

4. Zahn's work remains valuable because of his monumental erudition and unflagging energy. He was not immune to excesses of speculation. Lightfoot also remains valuable, particularly because of the clarity, honesty, and logic with which he addressed questions.

5. The English translation, *The Acts of the Apostles*, trans. and ed. B. Noble et al. (Philadelphia: Westminster, 1971), was based upon the 1965 edition.

6. M. Dibelius, *Studies in the Acts of the Apostles*, trans. M. Ling and P. Schubert; ed. H. Greeven (New York: Scribner's, 1956).

7. See Karl Löning, "Paulinismus in der Apostelgeschichte," in Kertelge, ed., *Paulus*, 202–34; Daniel Marguerat, "L'image de Paul dans les Actes des Apôtres," in *Les Actes des Apôtres: Histoire, récit, théologie. XXᵉ congrès de l'Association catholique française pour l'étude de la Bible (Angers, 2003)*, ed. M. Berder; LD 199 (Paris: Cerf, 2005), 121–54. See Marguerat, ed., *La Réception du paulinsime dans les Actes des Apôtres*.

8. See Table 6.

9. See Pervo, *Acts*, 14–18.

10. So Andreas Lindemann, *Paulus im ältesten Christentum*, BHT 58 (Tübingen: Mohr Siebeck, 1979), 49–50.

11. The same observation may be made about many, perhaps most, modern historians. Many books about the "founding fathers" of the U.S., for example, are explicit or implicit programs or tracts about how contemporary problems should be addressed. The difference is, however, clear. A biography of Thomas Jefferson that had him addressing same-sex marriage or arms-reduction treaties would be the object of laughter. Luke's Paul is anachronistic.

12. Ernst Haenchen (*The Acts of the Apostles*, trans. and ed. B. Noble et al. [Philadelphia: Westminster, 1971], 904) says: "The Lucan Paul lacks much that the real Paul possessed, perhaps the best. But again the Lucan Paul also possesses much that was lacking from the real Paul, and yet was necessary if he was to be portrayed as *the* Christian witness to the truth in his time."

13. In effect, both Paul and Luke see natural theology as an equalizer. See Richard I. Pervo, "The Paul of Acts.

14. See Richard I. Pervo, *Dating Acts: Between the Evangelists and the Apologists* (Santa Rosa, Calif.: Polebridge, 2006), 51–147. Evidence for the use of 2 Thessalonians is lacking.

15. Pervo, *Acts*, 5–7.

16. Acts 15 is the pivot. Peter gives the first speech, supporting the mission to convert gentiles without requiring them to observe Torah. In a short speech of his own, James agrees, then announces the decision (vv. 7-21). The torch has been passed on.

17. Compare Ephesians' revision of Colossians.

18. Paul stated (Gal. 1:16-17) that his call included the commission to convert gentiles.

19. In Acts (unlike Luke), the important quality of the Pharisaic party is its affirmation of resurrection (23:6-12).

20. On Paul and the virtues, see John C. Lentz, Jr., *Luke's Portrait of Paul*, SNTSM, 77 (Cambridge: Cambridge University Press, 1993), 62–104.

21. See Richard I. Pervo, *Profit with Delight* (Philadelphia: Fortress Press, 1987), 77–81. Lentz, *Luke's Portrait of Paul*, 66, contrasts this model of discipleship to that of the Gospel of Luke.

22. See Table 6.

23. It is inappropriate to distinguish between "miraculous" and "non-miraculous" in constructing such lists. Speaking can be no less inspired than exorcizing (cf. Acts 6:8-15; Luke 12:11-12).

24. Note also Titus, the memory of whom is expunged from Acts.

25. Much of the data for this section is well summarized by Glen R. Jacobson, "Paul in Luke-Acts: The Savior Who Is Present," in *SBLSP, 1983* (Chico, Calif.: Scholars, 1983), 131–46. Note also

A. J. Mattill, Jr., "The Paul–Jesus Parallels and the Purpose of Luke–Acts: H. H. Evans Reconsidered," *NovT* 17 (1975): 15–47.

26. In Luke the forerunners of Jesus are "all the prophets," who predicted his advent and mission. The specific forerunner is John the Baptizer. Paul's forerunners include Peter, Stephen, Philip, and Barnabas. Apollos is also a forerunner like the Baptizer (18:24-28).

27. The narrator shows both Jesus and Paul as frequently preaching in synagogues: Luke 4:15, 16, 33, 44; 6:6; 7:5; 13:10; Acts 9:20; 13:5, 14; 14:1; 17:1, 10, 17; 18:4, 19, 26; 19:18. Doubts can be raised about the frequency with which Paul was welcomed to share his message in synagogues, and the same may be said about Jesus.

28. Note the frequently mentioned parallel between Luke 9:50 and Acts 19:21.

29. For additional data, see Walter Radl, *Paulus and Jesus im Lukanischen Doppelwerk: Untersuchungen zu Parallelmotiven im Lukasevangelium und in der Apostelgeschichte*, Europäische Hochschulschriften 23/49 (Bern: Lang, 1975), 169–251, and, with emphasis upon the trial of Jesus as a Lucan composition, Joseph B. Tyson, *The Death of Jesus in Luke–Acts* (Columbia: University of South Carolina Press, 1986), 114–41.

30. For arguments supporting this, see Pervo, *Acts*, 644–54.

31. Antiquity related stories about evil persons who escaped one tragedy only to be cut down by a snake. See Pervo, *Acts*, 673–75.

32. Mattill, "Paul–Jesus Parallels," 145.

33. Cf. p. 41 on Col. 1:24.

34. The death of Jesus in Luke and Acts is not just the death of another martyred prophet, although the account in Luke more closely resembles a martyrdom than do the other canonical passions. One effect of this presentation is to facilitate comparison of the respective "passions" of Luke and Paul. See, among many studies, Tyson, *The Death of Jesus*, and M. Parsons and Richard I. Pervo *Rethinking the Unity of Luke and Acts* (Minneapolis: Fortress Press, 1993), Chapter 3.

35. See Pervo, *Profit*, 64–65, and Parsons and Pervo, *Rethinking*, 90–94.

36. See Pervo, *Profit*, 65.

37. Pervo, *Profit*, 63.

38. Cf. also the exorcism of Acts 16:16-18 with Luke 4:34, 41.

39. See the discussion of Irenaeus, p. 220.

40. For an introduction, see W. Schneemelcher, "The Acts of Paul," in *New Testament Apocrypha*, ed. W. Schneemelcher; 2 vols.; trans. and ed. R. McL. Wilson (Louisville: Westminster John Knox, 1991–92), 2:213–37, and Hans-Josef Klauck, *The Apocryphal Acts of the Apostles: An Introduction*, trans. Brian McNeil (Waco, Tex.: Baylor University Press, 2008), 47–79. The fullest translation is that of W. Rordorf, "Actes de Paul," in *Ecrits apocryphes chrétiens* 1, ed. F. Bovon and P. Geoltrain (Paris: Gallimard, 1997), 1115–77. Recent English versions are found in Schneemelcher, ed., *New Testament Apocrypha*, 2:237–70, and J. K. Elliott, trans., *The Apocryphal New Testament* (Oxford: Clarendon, 1993), 364–88.

41. For a brief description of the various Acts in their literary context, see Richard I. Pervo, "The Ancient Novel Becomes Christian," in *The Novel in the Ancient World*, ed. G. Schmeling; *Mnemosyne* Supplementum 159 (Leiden: E. J. Brill, 1996), 685–711. Note the important new introduction by Klauck, *Apocryphal Acts*.

42. For early attestation and opinion, see Elliott, *Apocrypha*, 350–52. In *H.E.* 3.3.4-6, Eusebius discusses "his" Acts, after noting the debate about Hebrews, as if Paul were the author. He did not accept the *Acts of Paul* as "undisputed," which appears to place it in the category of "disputed" books, like Hebrews, and then discusses *Hermas*, also left in the middle ground. At 3.25.4, however, the *Acts of Paul* are lodged with *Hermas*, the *Apocalypse of Peter*, and others as "not genuine." Nonetheless, it does not receive the opprobrium assigned to other apocroyphal acts of the apostles (3.25.6). These not entirely harmonious views are indicative of the mixed reception of the *Acts of Paul*, which were not condemned on doctrinal grounds.

43. On the use of the work through the twelfth century, see Léon Vouaux, *Les Actes de Paul et ses letters apocryphes*, ANT (Paris: Letouzey, 1913), 24–69.

44. See Richard I. Pervo, "The Acts of Titus: A Preliminary Translation, with an Introduction and Notes," in *SBLSP, 1996* (Atlanta: Scholars, 1996), 455–82.

45. Such editing included both expansion and abbreviation as well as conformity with accepted theological views and historical traditions.

46. See the discussion of *3 Corinthians*, p. 96.

47. On the popularity of Thecla, see M. Pesthy, "Thecla in the Fathers of the Church," in *The Apocryphal Acts of Paul and Thecla*, ed. Jan Bremmer; SAAA 2 (Kampen: Kok Pharos, 1996), 164–78, and S. F. Johnson, *The Life and Miracles of Thekla: A Literary Study* (Washington: Center for Hellenic Studies, 2006), 1–14. Johnson's study focuses upon a fifth-century paraphrase of her life, which was issued with a collection of miracles worked at her shrine. For a review of recent thought, see Shelly Matthews, "Thinking of Thecla: Issues in Feminist Historiography," *Journal of Feminist Studies in Religion* 17 (2002): 39–65; Elisabeth Esch-Wermeling, *Thekla—Paulusschülerin wider Willen? Strategien der Leserlenkung in den Theklaakten*, Neutestamentliche Abhandlungen. Neue Folge 53 (Münster: Aschendorff, 2008), and the collection edited by Martin Ebner, *Aus Liebe zu Paulus? Die Akte Thekla neu aufgerollt*, Stuttgarter Bibelstudien 206 (Stuttgart: Katholisches Bibelwerk, 2005).

48. As noted earlier, this is the same span covered in Acts and the Pastoral Epistles, although neither narrate Paul's death.

49. The most forceful promoter of this interpretation has been Richard Bauckham, "The Acts of Paul as a Sequel," in *The Book of Acts in its First Century Setting*, vol. 1, *The Book of Acts in Its Ancient Literary Setting*, ed. B. W. Winter and A. D. Clarke (Grand Rapids: Eerdmans, 1993), 105–52, with additional discussion in "'The Acts of Paul*: Replacement of Acts or Sequel to Acts?" *Semeia* 80 (1997): 159–68.

50. For evidence that the *Acts of Paul* did begin with the conversion, see W. Rordorf, "Paul's Conversion in the Canonical Acts and in the *Acts of Paul*," *Semeia* 80 (1997): 137–44.

51. Richard I. Pervo, "A Hard Act to Follow: *The Acts of Paul* and the Canonical Acts," *Journal of Higher Criticism* 2, no. 2 (1995): 3–32; D. Marguerat, "The *Acts of Paul* and the Canonical Acts: A Phenomenon of Rereading," *Semeia* 80 (1997): 169–83. Both Bauckham (previous n.) and Marguerat utilize a model of revision. Bauckham appeals to the analogy of the "Rewritten Bible," while Marguerat utilizes the intertextual theory of R. Genette. This model dictates a certain admiration for the text being rewritten, an assumption that is not fully supported by the text of the *Acts of Paul*.

52. For example, Willy Rordorf, "In welchem Verhältnis stehen die apokryphen Paulusakten zur kanonischen Apostelgeschichte und zu den Pastoralbriefen?" in *Text and Testimony: Essays on New Testament and Apocryphal Literature in Honour of A. F. J. Klijn*, ed. T. Baarda et al. (Kampen: Uitgeversmaatschappij J.H. Kok, 1988), 225–41.

53. See Julian Hills, "The Acts of the Apostles in the *Acts of Paul*," in *SBLSP, 1994* (Atlanta: Scholars, 1994), 24–54, and "The *Acts of Paul* and the Legacy of the Lukan Acts," *Semeia* 80 (1997): 145–58. For imitation of particular episodes, see, for example, Pervo, "Hard Act," 10–17.

54. For examples from 1 Corinthians, see P. Dunn, "The Influence of 1 Corinthians on the *Acts of Paul*," in *SBLSP, 1996* (Atlanta, Scholars Press, 1996), 438–54. For other certain and possible allusions to early Christian writings, see Schneemelcher, "Acts of Paul," 265–70.

55. See W. M. Ramsay, *The Church in the Roman Empire* (London: Hodder & Stoughton, 1897), 375–428. In his notes, Ramsay attended to the differences in the Syriac and Armenian traditions. On the latter, see F. C. Conybeare, *The Apology and Acts of Apollonius and Other Monuments of Early Christianity* (London: Swan Sonnenschein, 1894). Lipsius recognized the value of the Syriac version; see Richard A. Lipsius and Maximilian Bonnet, *Acta Apostolorum Apocrypha*, 2 vols. (Leipzig: Hermann Mendelssohn, 1891–1903), 1:cv-cvi.

56. See the studies appearing in Robert F. Stoops, ed., *The Apocryphal Acts of the Apostles in Intertextual Perspectives, Semeia* 80 (1997).

57. Determination that Mark was the major source for Matthew and Luke required the establishment of a sound text, since the Byzantine tradition had resulted in a great deal of contamination, for example, of Mark and Luke by Matthew. This achievement was based upon a large number of complete mss. In the case of the apocroyphal acts of the apostles, complete mss. are, except for the *Acts of Thomas*, lacking.

58. The criterion of appropriateness gives priority to the *Acts of Peter* in that the *Quo Vadis* story is an anecdote that is typical of stories told about Peter. Cf. Mark 14:29-31. In the *Acts of Peter*, this is a lesson about martyrdom and discipleship; for the *Acts of Paul*, it amounts to a prophecy. Moreover, Peter is crucified, whereas Paul is beheaded.

59. See E. Esch-Wermeling, *Thekla—Paulusschülerin wider Willen? Strategien der Leserlenkung in den Theklaakten*, Neutestamentliche Abhandlungen. Neue Folge 53 (Münster: Aschendorff, 2008).

60. For others, see C. Schmidt, with Wilhelm Schubart, PRAXEIS PAULOU. *Acta Pauli* (Glückstadt: J. J. Augustin, 1936), 120–22.

61. An example of literary skill not easily recognized because of the fragmentary state of the evidence is that the narrator withholds description of Paul until 3.3.

62. The numberings follow those of Rordorf, which will appear in his forthcoming edition, the first full edition of the *APl* in original languages (Greek and Coptic).

63. For the possibility that the *APl* reported Paul's journey as beginning in Tarsus, see the following discussion of the *Epistula Apostolorum*.

64. Rordorf divides the story of Paul and Thecla into two chapters, based upon stations. The division is at par. 26 of the conventional numeration.

65. For interesting proposals that Ephrem made use of the *APl* in his commentary on Acts, see I. Czachesz, "Between Canon and Apocrypha," 109–11.

66. *ATit* 3 mentions, in inverse order, the exorcism of Amphia, wife of Chrysippus and the destruction of the temple, following a summary of Paul's conversion.

67. See Rordoff, *Actes*, 1149–50.

68. "Revisit" is a presumption based upon the presence of an organized community of believers who acknowledge Paul as their leader.

69. According to *ATit* 4, this was an initial visit.

70. According to 3.2, Titus had evangelized Iconium before Paul's visit.

71. From the fragmentary material of P.Heid., one might conclude that this was an initial visit. Hermocrates (and his family) had, however, come to the faith, but had not received baptism.

72. When *3 Corinthians* is taken out of consideration, it is not clear that Paul has previously been to Corinth.

73. *Contra* Acts 14:1-6.

74. *V. l.* at 21:1. Myra is an example of "filling in" stations at which no mission work is described in Acts. This tendency can be observed (without details) in the D-Text, as in Acts 21:1.

75. C. Schmidt, with Wilhelm Schubart, PRAXEIS PAULOU.

76. For other small fragments, see Elliott, *Apocrypha* 352, with bibliography, 357–58.

77. C. Schmidt, *Acti Pauli: Aus der heidelberger koptischen Papyrushandschrift nr. 1.* (2 vols. Leipzig: Hinrichs, 1905).

78. F. C. Conybeare, *Apology*, 49–88, judges (59) that the Latin tradition is superior to the Greek, the Syriac to the Latin, and the Armenian to Syriac. His arguments, 49–60, are still worth consulting. For a translation of the Syriac, see W. Wright, *Apocryphal Acts of the Apostles, Edited from Syriac Manuscripts in the British Museum and Other Libraries,* 2 vols. (London: Williams and Norgate, 1871) 2:116–45. The variant traditions indicate, at the very least, that this story experienced considerable editing. Additional bibliography on various versions can be found in Elliott, *Apocrypha*, 358–59.

79. W. E. Crum, "New Coptic Manuscripts in the John Rylands Library," *BJRL* 5 (1920), 497–503, 501.

80. Bauckham, "Sequel."

81. *Third Corinthians* is an exception, but this is a subsequent addition.

82. The canonical Acts tends to locate most of the information about a site at the report of the first visit.

83. The exception is Rome, where he rents a large building (14:1). This was because the people at Corinth raised a collection for Paul (14:6), a subject not unrelated to controversy about Paul's collection for Jerusalem.

84. See, in general, F. Bovon, "The Synoptic Gospels and the Non-Canonical Acts of the Apostles," *HTR* 81 (1988): 19–36. In particular, see Dennis R. MacDonald, "Apocryphal and Canonical Narratives about Paul," in *Paul and the Legacies of Paul*, ed. William S. Babcock (Dallas: Southern Methodist University Press, 1990), 55–70 (63–68), and Ann G. Brock, "Genre of the *Acts of Paul*: One Tradition Enhancing Another," *Apocrypha* 5 (1994): 119–36. Apparent knowledge of all the canonical Gospels suggests a date near 170, as proposed above.

85. The episode is symbolic in meaning. Ability to subdue the animal kingdom is one attribute of a "divine person"; see Ludwig Bieler, EIOS ANHR: *Das Bild des "Göttlichen Menschen" in Spätantike*

und Frühchristentum, 2 vols. (Darmstadt: Wissenschaftliche Buchgesellschaft, 1967 [original 1935–36]), 1:103–10, provides examples). That baptism led a lion to elect a celibate life is an example *a maiore ad minus* for human beings.

86. *Acts of Titus* 4 proudly reports that Titus was Paul's forerunner in every city. This is probably not derived from the *Acts of Paul*. He, with Luke, also anticipated Paul's arrival in Rome (14.1).

87. Onesiphorus and his household also abandoned all ties and possessions to follow Paul (3.23).

88. This arrest is repeated in Myra (*APl* 5), where Paul shouts that he is not a robber (cf. Mark 14:48).

89. Onesiphorus illustrates the tension between the ideal wandering believer and the household patron. The one-time patron can no longer support himself. In short, the ideal that all should give up their possessions is just that, for enactment would all but destroy the movement.

90. Note that this action in Mark follows the statement about the shepherdless crowd, applied in the *Acts of Paul* to Thecla.

91. *Acts of Paul* 3:21 (trans. Elliott, *Apocrypha*, 368).

92. Polymorphy is also a characteristic of Paul (3.3). Transfiguration was a common (Acts 6:15; 7:55) and controversial (2 Cor. 3:7-18) item of the repertory of holy persons.

93. On the cloak, cf. 2 Tim. 4:3, and Richard I. Pervo, "Romancing an Oft-neglected Stone: The Pastoral Epistles and the Epistolary Novel," *Journal of Higher Criticism* 1 (1994): 25–47 (42 n. 94), as well as Spicq, *Les épitres pastorales*, 814–16.

94. Cf. Mark 6:41; John 6:9.

95. Cf. Mark 14:48.

96. *Acts of Paul* 6/4. *P.Heid.* 31 (trans. Elliott, *Apocrypha*, 375).

97. Cf. John 14:12.

98. On the later developments of this tradition, which included the integration of Paul's martyrdom with Peter's, see Harry W. Tajra, *The Martyrdom of St. Paul: Historical and Judicial Context, Traditions, and Legends*, WUNT 67 (Tübingen: Mohr Siebeck, 1994), 118–65. Paul is the prototypical martyr for Ignatius (*Eph.* 12:2) and Polycarp (*Phil.* 11:3).

99. See above.

100. Even if this episode was taken by the author or a subsequent editor from the *Acts of Peter* (*Verc.* 36/Passion 5), as is likely, its function in the *Acts of Paul* is clear.

101. cf. Mark 16:2.

102. Cf. Mark 16:8.

103. That is, baptism.

104. *Acts of Paul. Martyrdom* 7 (trans. Elliott, *Apocrypha*, 388).

105. This appearance refuted the claim of Celsus, who wondered why Jesus elected to appear to Galilean fishermen and what he was pleased to call "hysterical women" (Origen, *Contra Celsum* 2.63).

106. Pervo, *Acts*, pp. 20–21.

107. For argument and evidence, see MacDonald, "Apocryphal and Canonical," 66–67.

108. See, for example, Dennis R. MacDonald, *The Legend and the Apostle: The Battle for Paul in Story and Canon* (Philadelphia: Westminster, 1983).

109. See Table 1.

110. See p. 286n11.

111. This is preserved in *3 Corinthians* II, but is unlikely to have been invented by the interpolator. Note also Frontina, who has been alienated from her parents (10-11). Paul also alienates Patroclus from the affections of Nero (14.2-3). Those who read printed editions of the apocroyphal acts of the apostles are accustomed to episodes in which the conversion of a woman of high status leads to persecution. These are undoubtedly original, but the majority of mss. censor them. In the case of the *Acts of Paul* this censorship has been quite successful.

112. On the subject, see Gerd Theissen, *The Social Setting of Pauline Christianity: Essays on Corinth*, ed. and trans. John H. Schütz (Philadelphia: Fortress Press, 1982), 27–54, and *Sociology of Early Palestinian Christianity*, trans. John Bowden (Philadelphia: Fortress Press, 1978).

113. Conybeare, *Apology*, 76–77, and his note on p. 88.

114. "And taking hold of Alexander, she tore his cloak and pulled off his crown and made him a laughing-stock" (trans. Elliott, *Apocrypha*, 369). Since Syrian and Armenian Christians opposed the theology of the current emperors, they left the text unaltered.

115. Note the *v.l.* συριάρχης (Imperial Priest of Syria), which, despite the objections of Vouaux (*Actes de Paul*, 195), is probably original.

116. One might speculate that some of the most exuberant anti-imperial rhetoric ended up on the cutting room floor.

117. MacDonald (*Legend*, 78–85) locates the author in a Montanist milieu.

118. For examples from Israelite history, see *APl* 13. Use of such examples is not equivalent to a theology of salvation history.

119. *Third Corinthians*, not an original component of the *Acts of Paul*, differs.

120. For introduction and a translation, see C. Detlef G. Muller, "Epistula Apostolorum," in Schneemelcher, ed., *New Testament Apocrypha*, 1:249–78. See also Jacques-Noël Pérès, "Epître des apôtres," in Bovon et Geoltrain, eds., *Ecrits apocryphes chrétiens*, 357–92, and *L'Epître des apôtres et le Testament de notre Seigneur et notre Sauveur Jésus-Christ* (Turnhout: Brepols, 1994); Julian V. Hills, *Tradition and Composition in the Epistula Apostolorum*, HDR 24 (Minneapolis: Fortress Press, 1990). On its view of Paul, see also Manfred Hornschuh, *Studien zur Epistula Apostolorum*, PTS 5 (Berlin: de Gruyter, 1965), 84–91. On the *Epistula's* relation to Pauline traditions, see Lindemann, *Paulus*, 109–12, and Dassmann, *Stachel*, esp. 261–66.

121. Pérès ("Epître des apôtres") prefers to entitle the work "the book that Jesus Christ revealed to his disciples" (360) and uses the equivalent of "book" in ch. 1 (365) where the German version speaks of the equivalent of a "letter." ("Book" is also used in the translation of Julian Hills (*The Epistle of the Apostles*. Santa Rosa, CA: Polebridge, 2009), who kindly supplied an advance draft.)

122. Arguments for c. 150 derive from ch. 17, which says that the end will come after the 150th year (Ethiopic) or the 120th "part" (Coptic). Based upon our knowledge that the crucifixion took place c. 30, this would indicate that the work was composed c. 150. It is not certain that the author knew the date of the crucifixion, and numbers could be symbolic. Familiarity with a range of early Christian literature makes a date c. 175–200 more likely.

123. A substantial portion of a Coptic edition, from a ms. of the fourth or fifth century, also survives.

124. The dialogue tradition became a framework for speeches rather than genuine conversation, as can be seen in Cicero's philosophical dialogues. In the Christian revelation dialogues, the disciples' questions tend to be little more than titles for lengthy speeches. For a survey, see Pheme Perkins, *The Gnostic Dialogue: The Early Church and the Crisis of Gnosticism* (New York: Paulist, 1980).

125. The "churchly" character of *Epistula Apostolorum* is apparent in that, at the close, it becomes, with substantial influence from Matthew, a church order of sorts.

126. Of the more than 230 notes devoted to intertextual references identified by Muller ("Epistula Apostolorum"), 47 refer to Pauline epistles (including Hebrews). Not all of these are certain by any criterion. See the conservative evaluation of Lindemann, *Paulus*, 391–93. David K. Rensberger, "As the Apostle Teaches: The Development of the Use of Paul's Letters in Second-Century Christianity" (Ph.D. diss., Yale, 1981), 89–90, is dubious, but familiarity with the corpus is almost certain.

127. The narrator reports that Peter went to an unspecified "another place." See Pervo, *Acts*, 299–312. Reference to the cockcrow indicates that *Epistula Apostolorum* understood Acts 12:1-17 as a kind of "Passion of Peter."

128. Trans. Muller, "Epistula Apostolorum," 267. This passage is available only in Ethiopic. The formula treats "Paul" as the Greek translation of "Saul."

129. See Czachesz, "The Acts of Paul." In ch. 32, the Lord states that Paul's journey to Damascus began in Cilicia. This could be based upon Acts' claim that Paul came from Tarsus, but it contradicts Acts 9:1, where Paul departs from Jerusalem with written authorization from the high priests. A possible source for this statement is the *Acts of Paul*.

130. Hornschuh, however, (n. 120) argues for an anti-gnostic context of the Pauline material.

131. Chapter 1 mentions Simon and Cerinthus.

132. Johannine features are most prominent, as are themes from the Synoptics, but the work is not, on balance, a model of systematic theology.

133. Hornschuh, *Studien*, 84, says that the attention devoted to Paul is "astonishing."

134. *Epistula Apostolorum* contains some syncretistic features, including notions utilized by "Gnostic" theologians. See Muller, "Epistula Apostolorum," 251.

135. On the view of Paul in *Epistula Apostolorum*, see also Lindemann, *Paulus*, 109–12.

136. On the state of the question, see Gérard Poupon, "Les 'Actes de Pierre' et leur remaniement," *ANRW* II.25.6 (1988): 4363–83, and Christine M. Thomas, "The 'Prehistory' of the *Acts of Peter*," in *The Apocryphal Acts of the Apostles*, ed. François Bovon et al.; Harvard Divinity School Studies (Cambridge, Mass.: Harvard University Press, 1999), 41–62. Note her full-length study, *The Acts of Peter, Gospel Literature, and the Ancient Novel: Rewriting the Past* (New York: Oxford University Press, 2003). See also the essays in Jan Bremmer, ed., *The Apocryphal Acts of Peter: Magic, Miracles and Gnosticism*, SAAA 3 (Leuven: Peeters, 1998), as well as Klauck, *Apocryphal Acts*, 81–112.

137. G. Poupon ("L'Origine africaine des *Actus Vercellenses*," in Bremmer, ed., *The Apocryphal Acts of Peter*, 192–99) argues for an African provenance of this translation.

138. This classification does not prevent Eusebius from drawing historical data from the *Acts of Peter (H.E. 2.14).*

139. Origen (probably), the *Didascalia* 6.7-9 (highly probable), and Commodian, *Carmen Apologeticum* 625–630 (probably c. 250 CE).

140. See the various essays in Stoops, ed., *The Apocryphal Acts of the Apostles in Intertextual Perspectives*, and Jan N. Bremmer, "Aspects of the Acts of Peter: Women, Magic, Place and Date," in Bremmer, ed., *The Apocryphal Acts of Peter*, 1–20 (14–20).

141. See also the discussion of Dionysius of Corinth, p. 144.

142. See below.

143. *Actus Vercellenses* 17, a flashback, was evidently transferred from the original Jerusalem ministry to provide context for Peter's conflict with Simon.

144. This speech provides Peter with the opportunity for a formal farewell address, an item lacking in the canonical book.

145. This may be due to the influence of 2 Timothy.

146. The model is evidently Acts 16:25-40 (Philippi).

147. Conversion of women takes one of two narrative directions in the apocroyphal acts of the apostles. Either the husband also converts, enhancing the mission, or strongly resists her new-found continence, and launches a persecution. The choice lies more or less entirely in the hands of the narrator. A persecution could also have propelled Paul to Spain. The choice made in *Verc.* 1 portrays the apostle as enjoying good standing with a Roman official.

148. The image of physician is developed in the *Acts of Xanthippe and Polyxena*, p. 173.

149. On the farewell scene, see n. 153.

150. See chapters 1 and 3.

151. The narrative does not state explicitly that Paul founded the Roman community, but he is its undisputed leader.

152. The narrator is blissfully unaware that Paul's christological message, as summarized, would have been utterly unconvincing to faithful Jews.

153. On the types of farewell scene, see François Bovon, "Le Saint-Esprit, l'Église et les relations humaines selon Actes 20,36—21,16," in *Les Actes des Apôtres: Traditions, redaction, théolgies*, ed. Jacob Kremer; BETL 43 (Leuven: Leuven University Press,1979), 339–58.

154. The use of water instead of wine may be a secondary emendation. This is evidence for the ascetic character of *Actus Vercellenses*. On the subject, see Andrew McGowan, *Ascetic Eucharists: Food and Drink in Early Christian Ritual Meals* (Oxford: Oxford University Press, 1999).

155. His words evoke Acts 13:10-11 (Paul and Elymas), as well as 8:20-23 (Peter and Simon).

156. This is an improvement upon the episode of Peter's daughter (from the no longer extant Jerusalem section), who was paralyzed to prevent her from serving as an object of temptation for men.

157. On this motif, see p. 15.

158. E.g., Col. 1:21-22; 3:7-8.

159. See p. 14.

160. The text reinforces this thesis. In ch. 4, Simon gains adherents because Paul, as well as Timothy and Barnabas, were not on the scene. This comment may be part of the earlier text, since it says nothing about Spain. The faithful pray for Paul's return. In ch. 6, the faithful Ariston laments

the absence of Paul. The power of Satan has overcome all those entrusted to the leadership by Paul. The apostle appeared to Ariston in a vision (like Christ!) advising him to flee. Chapter 40 (*Mart.* 12) contains a reference to the expected return of Paul. With the possible exception of the first, all of these are later additions.

161. The author was evidently unaware that no first-century Roman Senator would bear the Greek name Demetrius.

162. Allusions to and borrowings from the Pauline epistles are especially prominent in the later additions to *Acts of Peter*. See Vouaux, *Actes de Pierre*, 47.

163. See the excursus, p. 184.

164. On this text, see Aurelio de Santos Otero, "Later Acts of Apostles," in Schneemelcher, ed., *New Testament Apocrypha*, 2:426–82 (443), and Tajra, *Martyrdom*, 154–57.

165. In *Acts of Peter* 32, Paul is absent when Peter prays Simon out of the sky.

166. This shift conforms to the tendency of later editors to remove episodes in which apostles break up lawful marriages.

167. The *Passion* takes pains to authenticate the traditional burial sites of the two apostles.

168. The shorter edition has Peter and Paul arrive in Rome together and does not narrate their deaths.

169. See de Santos Otero, "Later Acts," 440–42. The text is found in Lipsius and Bonnet, *Acta Apostolorum Apocrypha*, 1:178–222.

170. *Acts of Peter and Paul* 5.

171. The two added stations (Messina, Didymus) probably represent the interest of later Christian communities in possessing an apostolic foundation.

172. Dioscurus, captain of the vessel on which Paul sailed to Italy, becomes a Christian and martyr. His name derives from the name of the ship (an Alexandrian ship with the Twin Brothers as its figurehead, Acts 28:11).

173. See Tajra's summary, *Martyrdom*, 144–50. An example of its historical reliability is the claim that Peter converted Livia, the wife of Nero (ch. 31). Its novelistic propensity is illustrated by the story of Perpetua (ch. 80 [Plautilla in accounts of Paul's martyrdom]). She, blind in one eye, gave Paul her handkerchief for a blindfold, as he is led out to execution. When it was returned, she put it back on, whereupon her eye was healed. This corresponds to Paul's healing scarves (Acts 19:11-12) and to the legend of Veronica, who, having been healed by touching Jesus' garment (Mark 5:25-34), wiped his face with a cloth while he was on the way to the cross.

174. De Santos Otero, "Later Acts," 440. The *Gelasian Decree* III.2 attributed the claim that the two died separately to heretics, that is, it utilized the repudiation of the apocroyphal acts of the apostles to support the claim that both were martyred on the same day.

175. Lipsius and Bonnet, eds., *Acta Apostolorum Apocrypha*, 2:292–302. An old English version can be found in *ANF* 8:493–96.

176. See de Santos Otero, "Later Acts," 465–66, and István Czachesz, *Commission Narratives: A Comparative Study of the Canonical and Apocryphal Acts*, Studies on Early Christian Apocrypha 8 (Leuven: Peeters, 2007), 184–207, with bibliography 184 n. 1. Note also Klauck, *Apocryphal Acts*, 247.

177. See de Santos Otero, "Later Acts," 466. Chapters 6 and 7, which deal with Mark's elaborate and extended penance of Mark, are omitted in various witnesses, including Cod. Vat. gr. 1667.

178. In Acts Silas "replaces" Barnabas. Perhaps readers will think that John, whose Hebrew (!) name was changed to Mark in a vision, was associated with the cult of Zeus at Lystra (Acts 14:8-18).

179. Chapters 16, 19–22.

180. Chapter 19 reports an athletic event in which a multitude of naked men and women participated. Men did compete naked, and a few examples of competitions involving girls and women are recorded, but a joint contest would have been unusual. The narrator's knowledge appears imperfect. For a similar situation, see the Armenian version of the *Martyrdom of Bartholomew* 3 (Louis Leloir, *Apocrypha Apostolorum Armeniaca* II, CCSA 4 [Brepols: Turnhout, 1992], 495). One technique was to "baptize" old festivals by transforming them into Christian holidays.

181. Mark is the traditional "apostolic" founder of the church in Alexandria.

182. An anonymous host there may be the Onesiphorus of *APl* 3.

183. This probably derives from Gal. 4:13. The author had read Galatians with care.

184. Cf. 2 Tim. 4:13, the evident inspiration.

185. Cf. Acts 13:1-3.

186. The pair nonetheless took pains (ch. 11) to prevent people from discovering that Paul and Barnabas had separated.

187. The claim that Mark founded the church at Alexandria is reported in Eusebius, *H.E.* 2.16.1. The statement follows the reference to Mark in 1 Pet. 5:12; its authority is anonymous ("they say"). The historian then proceeds to describe the life of Mark's converts, which was so "philosophical" that Philo wrote about them (the *Vita contemplativa*). This chapter inspires little confidence. It is, however, true that Clement of Alexandria did make use of the Gospel of Mark, which was generally ignored.

188. Cf. O. F. A. Meinardus, "Cretan Traditions about St Paul's Mission to the Island," *Ostkirchliche Studien* 22 (1973): 172–83; Pervo, "Acts of Titus"; Czachesz, *Commission Narratives*, 208–23; and Klauck, *Apocryphal Acts*, 77–78.

189. Czachesz, *Commission Narratives*, 210–15.

190. See p. 110.

191. On Paul's itinerary in *ATit*, see Pervo, "Acts of Titus," 462.

192. Βίος καὶ πολιτεία (Life and Conduct) is a conventional title for saints' lives. On this text, see M. R. James, *Apocrypha Anecdota*, Texts and Studies 2 (Cambridge: Cambridge University Press, 1893), 43–57 (introduction), 59–85 (text); E. Haight, *More Essays on Greek Romances* (New York: Longmans, 1945), 66–80; S. L. Davies, *The Revolt of the Widows: The Social World of the Apocryphal Acts* (Carbondale, Ill.: Southern Illinois University Press, 1980), 8–10, 64–69; for a translation, see *ANF* 10:205–17. Note E. Junod, "Vie et conduite des saintes femmes Xanthippe, Polyxène et Rébecca (BHG 1977)," in *Oecumenica et Patristica*, FS W. Schneemelcher (Stuttgart: Teubner, 1989), 83–106. A recent study is J. Gorman, "Thinking with and about 'Same-sex Desire': Producing and Policing Female Sexuality in the *Acts of Xanthippe and Polyxena*," *Journal of the History of Sexuality* 10 (2001): 416–41. See also Klauck, *Apocryphal Acts*, 250–51.

193. James, *Apocrypha Anecdota*, 67; Davies, *Revolt*, 8–10.

194. See Junod, "Vie et conduite," and Richard I. Pervo, review of S. Davies, *Revolt of the Widows*, *ATR* 63 (1981): 329–30.

195. Evidently the couple will live in a celibate partnership.

196. Babylonia is part of the geography of romantic novels. If this requires a seacost, it will, like Shakespeare's Bohemia (*A Winter's Tale*), receive one.

197. Shipwreck is a normal mode of travel in the Greek romantic novels, and kidnapping, bandits, and pirates are staples of the genre.

198. In their respective *Acts*, both Philip and Andrew spend time in Greece.

199. On the relations between female characters in *Xan*, see the possibilities explored by Gorman, "Thinking with and about 'Same-sex Desire.' "

200. One speculation is that *Xan* is a later abbreviation of an earlier narrative.

201. The ship bearing Peter to Rome also plays a part in the narrative (*Xan.* 24).

202. The first part of the book is characterized by flowery rhetoric, much of it from the mouth of Xanthippe.

203. Slaves, along with soldiers and merchants, are groups identified by A. D. Nock as primary agents of cultic diffusion; see Nock's *Conversion: The Old and the New in Religion from Alexander the Great to Augustine of Hippo* (Oxford: Oxford University Press, 1933), 66–67. Slaves are distinct because they could bring about upward diffusion of ideas and other matters.

204. See above.

205. Mark 2:17. For later use, see G. W. H. Lampe, *A Patristic Greek Lexicon* (Oxford: Clarendon, 1961), 662, *s.v.* ἰατρός 3.

206. Chapter 24 also reflects *Actus Vercellenses*.

207. Cf. Mark 5:27-28; 6:56.

208. Cf. Matt. 9:26; Luke 4:14.

209. Cf. Mark 2:1-12. In this case authority resides with Paul; Xanthippe lacks this power (ch. 19).

210. Chapter 9: "*Paul* said to *Xanthippe*, 'Believe me, daughter, that by the *Devil's* suggestion and working I have not passed a single hour without chains and blows.' Xanthippe said to him, 'But

you suffer these things by your own free will, since you have not neglected your preaching even to scourging, but this again I tell you, that your bonds shall be the defeat of the prompter, and your humiliation their overthrow' " (trans. W. A. Craigie, in Allan Menzie, ed., *The Ante-Nicene Fathers, vol. X.* (Grand Rapids: Eerdmans, 1978), 207, alt.

211. Cf. *APl* 3.21 (Thecla).

212. Undoubtedly the subject of Philemon. Onesimus also appears in the Deutero-Pauline tradition (Col. 4:7). A person with the same name was Bishop of Ephesus in the time of Ignatius (*Eph.* 1:3).

213. First-person narration continues into ch. 41, where, in the fashion of Acts (e.g., 16:18), the narrative suddenly reverts to the third-person.

214. Another possibility is Lucius of Cyrene (Acts 13:1), but note the tradition of the old Gospel prologue that Luke died at 84 in Boeotia; see K. Aland, *Synopsis Quattuor Evangeliorum* (Stuttgart: Württembergische Bibelanstalt, 1964), 353.

215. This could be the result of textual abbreviation.

216. Cf. *Callirhoe* 8.6-8; *Ephesian Tale* 5.13.

217. Note also ch. 31 (Jas 80.9-10), also ambiguous and possibly edited. This interest in celibacy, an ascetic reference in ch. 31 (no wine), and the occasionally monarchian character of its theology (e.g., ch. 12) might lead one to suspect a Priscillianist background, but the work shows no knowledge of Spain, and the (presumably) original Greek language also tells against this hypothesis.

218. Note the expression "god of Paul" (20 [× 2], 26, 27 [× 3], and 31).

219. On the genre, see M. Himmelfarb, *Ascents to Heaven in Jewish and Christian Apocalypses* (New York: Oxford University Press, 1993), and *Tours of Hell: An Apocalyptic Form in Jewish and Christian Literature* (Philadelphia: Fortress Press, 1985).

220. Surveys, with introduction, bibliography, and translation may be found in Hugo Duensing and Aurelio de Santos Otero, "Apocalypse of Paul," in Schneemelcher, ed., *New Testament Apocrypha,* 2:712-52, and Elliott, *Apocrypha*, 616-44.

221. Richard Bauckham, "Apocryphal Pauline Literature," *DPL*, 35–37 (37) Dictionary. Consult abbreviations..

222. On attestation, see Elliott, *Apocrypha*, 620; Duensing and de Santos Otero, "Apocalypse of Paul," 712. This is a good caution against deriving conclusions about popularity from patristic discussions.

223. On this technique, see Wolfgang Speyer, *Bücherfunde in der Glaubenswerbung der Antike* (Göttingen: Vandenhoeck & Ruprecht, 1970).

224. On this probable parody of a vision report, see p. 176.

225. Duensing and de Santos Otero, "Apocalypse of Paul," 741.

226. More strictly, at some time from 150–350.

227. Nag Hammadi texts are referred to by codex in Roman, the document, and the page and line numbers. On this text, see W. R. Murdock and G. W. MacRae, eds., "The Apocalypse of Paul," in *Nag Hammadi Codices V 2-5 and VI with Papyrus Berolensis 8502, 1 and 4*, ed. Douglas M. Parrott; Nag Hammadi Studies 11 (Leiden: Brill, 1979), 47-63, and Wolf-Peter Funk, "The Coptic Gnostic Apocalypse of Paul," in Schneemelcher, *New Testament Apocrypha*, 2:695-700, both with bibliography. On its relation to Paul, see also Lindemann, *Paulus*, 332–34.

228. The others include two works entitled "'The Apocalypse of James" and "'The Apocalypse of Adam."

229. Lindemann, *Paulus*, 332, does not agree.

230. See, for example, *APl* 12; *Acts of John* 88; *Apocryphon of John* 20.19—21.4.

231. See above.

232. *Apocalypse of Paul* 18.14-19, trans. MacRae and Murdock, 257.

233. *Apocalypse of Paul* 23.13-17 (trans. Murdock and MacRae, 61). In a note, Funk ("Coptic Gnostic Apocalypse," 700 n. 12) offers an alternate rendition: "I will go into the world of the dead in order to become a (fellow-) prisoner in the captivity which was led captive in the captivity of Babylon." This is barely possible, grammatically, but the version cited is preferable.

234. This is additional evidence against Funk's alternate translation.

235. On this genre, see Tomas Szepessy, "The Ancient Family Novel (A Typological Proposal)," *Acta Antiqua Acadamiae Scientiarum Hungaricae* 31 (1985–88): 357-65. The use of a previous novel

as a source is widely accepted in scholarship. See S. Trenkner, *The Greek Novella in the Classical Period* (Cambridge: Cambridge University Press, 1958), 101-2, and B. E. Perry, *The Ancient Romances: A Literary Historical Account of the Origins*, Sather Lectures, 1951 (Berkeley: University of California Press, 1967), 285–93. F. Stanley Jones rejects this view: "Eros and Astrology in the Περίοδοι Πέτρου: The Sense of the Pseudo-Clementine Novel," *Apoc* 12 (2001): 53–78.

236. See N. Kelley, *Knowledge and Authority in the Pseudo-Clementines: Situating the Recognitions in 4ᵗʰ Century Syria*, WUNT 213 (Tübingen: Mohr Siebeck, 2006).

237. The designation "Pseudo-Clementines" is otiose.

238. A standard introduction is Johannes Irmscher and Georg Strecker, "The Pseudo-Clementines," in Schneemelcher, ed., *New Testament Apocrypha*, 2:483–541, with excerpts. No complete English version exists. For a survey of earlier research, see F. Stanley Jones, "The Pseudo-Clementines: A History of Research," *SecCent* 2 (1982): 1–33, 63–96; F. Manns, "Les pseudo-clementines (*Homélies et Reconnaisances*): Etat de la Question," *Studii Biblici Franciscani Liber Annuus* 53 (2003): 157–84; and Klauck, *Apocryphal Acts*, 193–229. See also Lüdemann, *Opposition to Paul in Jewish Christianity*, 169–94; Lindemann, *Paulus*, 101–9; and Dassmann, *Stachel*, 279–86.

239. J. B. Lightfoot, *The Apostolic Fathers*. Part One. *Clement*. Vol. 1 (Grand Rapids: Baker Book House, 1981 [reprint of 1890]), 14–16. (The notes are mine.)

240. In the *Recognitions*, the father is named Faustinianus, the brothers Faustinus and Faustus.

241. Shipwreck, pirates, and enslavement are standard motifs of ancient popular literature.

242. Mark 7:24-30; Matt. 15:21-28.

243. Luke 19:1-10.

244. The motif is novelistic.

245. Note that Barnabas is regarded as a disciple of Jesus.

246. The source is Acts 9:32—11:18.

247. This presumes (correctly) that Barnabas had sided with Peter.

248. Cf. Paul's escape from Damascus in Acts 9:23-25.

249. This island was also the site of the recognition scene in the novel *Callirhoe* (7.5—8.1).

250. Obstacles to recognition are a common and often not highly credible feature of popular literature.

251. See Klauck, *Apocryphal Acts*, 196–98.

252. F. S. Jones, *An Ancient Jewish Christian Source on the History of Christianity: Pseudo-Clementine Recognitions 1.21-71*, SBLTT 37 (Atlanta: Scholars Press, 1995), 111–55.

253. Jones, *An Ancient Jewish Christian Source*, 157–67.

254. Lüdemann, *Opposition*, 183. (Lüdemann's own source theory differs from that of Jones.) For similar views, see J. L. Martyn, "Clementine Recognitions 1,33-71, Jewish Christianity, and the Fourth Gospel," in *God's Christ and His People: Studies in Honour of Nils Alstrup Dahl*, ed. Jacob Jervell and Wayne A. Meeks (Oslo: Universitetsforlaget, 1977), 265–95 (273), and F. S. Jones, "A Jewish Christian Reads Luke's Acts of the Apostles: The Use of the Canonical Acts in the Ancient Jewish Christian Source behind Pseudo-Clementine *Recognitions 1.27-71*," in *SBLSP, 1995* (Atlanta: Scholars Press, 1995), 617–35.

255. This thesis is quite defensible. See John Painter, *Just James: The Brother of Jesus in History and Tradition* (Columbia: University of South Carolina Press, 1997). The thesis is valid in that success of the gentile, Torah-free, mission placed grave obstacles upon the mission to observant Jews.

256. This section follows Jones' translation of the Syriac, Armenian, and Latin editions of *Recognitions* (*An Ancient Jewish Christian Source*, 51–109).

257. The inspiration comes from Acts 7 and makes use of *Jubilees*. See Jones, "Jewish Christian," 632.

258. This corresponds to the Christian belief that Jesus was the prophet promised in Deut. 18:15-18 (e.g., Matt. 17:5; Luke 24:25; John 1:21; Acts 3:22; 7:37).

259. This is the pre-conversion of Paul in Acts, a person with no control of his temper and a penchant for violence. See p. 15 (lentz).

260. Cf. Acts 14:19-20. The motif of apparent death is common in popular fiction. See Pervo, *Profit*, 148 n. 42.

261. A marginal note in a ms. makes the identification explicit.

262. By adding that the enemy believed that Peter had fled to Damascus, *Rec* provides justification for the odd mission of Acts 9:1.

263. The *contestation* is one of the preliminary documents to the *Homilies*.

264. *Epistula Clementis* 1.1 (trans. Irmscher and Strecker, "The Pseudo-Clementines," 2:496–97).

265. Formally, they use the Semitic greeting of "peace," rather than the Pauline blend of "grace and peace."

266. Trans. Irmscher and Strecker, "The Pseudo-Clementines," 2:494.

267. The specific subject need not be the description of the controversy at Antioch in Gal. 2. Paul there portrayed Peter as liberal on Torah observance, willing to remain observant rather than offend the "people from James."

268. Matt. 11:11. In the scheme of syzygies the first, wicked prophet represents the female.

269. Trans. Irmscher and Strecker, "The Pseudo-Clementines," 2:535–36.

270. This criterion disqualifies Paul from being an apostle in Acts (1:21-22).

271. The confession of Peter is a popular theme in the Pseudo-Clementines.

272. One could cause difficulties by asking how James' teaching is correct, since he was not among the followers of Jesus, according to the gospel tradition.

273. For other examples, see Lüdemann, *Opposition*, 185–91.

274. See Robert E. Van Voorst, *The Ascents of James: History and Theology of a Jewish-Christian Community*, SBLDS 112 (Atlanta: Scholars Press, 1989). Note also the comments in Jones, *An Ancient Jewish Christian Source*, index p. 190 *s.v. Anabathmoi Jakobou*.

275. The Greek reads "of the priest," allowing the interpretation that the high priest's daughter was the object of his affection.

276. Members of priestly families could not marry proselytes.

277. Trans. Jones, "Jewish Christian," 617–18 n. 2. For another version, see Lüdemann, *Opposition*, 180. Jones believes that this text drew upon both the *Steps of James* and *Rec.* 1.27-71.

278. See p. 288n71.

279. Acts 9; 1 Tim. 1.

280. Compare the story that Jesus was the illegitimate child of a Roman soldier: Origen, *C. Cels* 1.32. Origen, *C.Cels* 1.32. See *Contra Celsum*, trans. Henry Chadwick (Cambridge: Cambridge University Press, 1953), 31 n. 3.

281. See pp. 124 and 127.

282. For this view of coordination, see, for example, Ignatius, *Rom.* 4:3; Irenaeus, *A.H.* 3.1.1; Tertullian, *Adv. Marcion* 4.5; *Praescription of Heretics* 36.

283. Eusebius, *H.E.* 2.25.5-7, cites Gaius, a second-/third-century presbyter, and opponent of Montanism, on the tombs of Peter and Paul at Rome. The next paragraph (8) cites Dionysius.

284. For the traditions, see Tajra, *Martyrdom*, 183–97. Note also de Santos Otero, "Later Acts," 440–42.

285. *Decretum Gelasianum* III 2. Note also Arator's mid-sixth-century epic based on Acts, which, in the end (at 2:1218), abandons the plot of Acts to report the joint martyrdom of Peter and Paul.

286. E.g., Leo the Great, *Sermon* 82.

287. A by-product of this relationship is that the patron saints of the Episcopal Cathedral in Washington, D.C. (intended from the beginning to be a "national Cathedral"), are Peter and Paul.

288. For an early synthesis of the various traditions regarding Peter and Paul, see Eusebius, *H.E.* 2.22.1-3.

Chapter 5: Other Representatives of Anti-Paulinism

1. On opposition to Paul in the course of his career, see Gerd Lüdemann, *Opposition to Paul in Jewish Christianity*, trans. M. E. Boring (Minneapolis: Fortress Press, 1989), 35–115. For a survey of the second century, see L. Padovese, "L'antipaulinisme chrétien au IIᵉ siècle," *Recherches de science religieuse* (2002): 390–422. Padovese includes a detailed discussion of Polycrates of Ephesus.

2. See pp. 122 and 127.

3. These texts are conveniently collected and edited by A. F. J. Klijn and G. J. Reinink, *Patristic Evidence for Jewish-Christian Sects*, NovTSup 36 (Leiden: Brill, 1973).

4. Cf. Irenaeus, *A.H.* 1.26.2; 3.15.1; Origen, *C. Cels.* 5.65; *Hom. XIX.12 in Jerem.* (Sermon on Jeremiah); Eusebius, *H.E.* 3.27.4; Epiphanius, *Pan.* 38.5.

5. For a general introduction, see Raymond E. Brown, *An Introduction to the New Testament,* ABRL (New York: Doubleday, 1997), 171–224.

6. Cf. Matt. 23:2, which endorses the scribes and Pharisees as interpreters of the Torah.

7. One can see this by observing the prominence of Matthew in the pre-Vatican Roman lectionary for Sundays and major feasts, which was also the source of Lutheran and Anglican lectionaries.

8. A notable omission is worship, as comparison with the *Didache* and the *Apostolic Tradition,* full-fledged Church Orders, will indicate.

9. On Paul and Matthew, see Andreas Lindemann, *Paulus im ältesten Christentum,* BHT 58 (Tübingen: Mohr Siebeck, 1979), 154–58, and Ernst Dassmann, *Der Stachel im Fleisch: Paulus in der frühchristlichen Literatur bis Irenäus* (Münster: Aschendorff, 1979), 102–7.

10. See M. Jack Suggs, *Wisdom, Christology, and Law in Matthew's Gospel* (Cambridge, Mass.: Harvard University Press, 1970).

11. Cf. the Pseudo-Clementines. On the technique, see p. 310n195.

12. See p. 231.

13. Cf. Matt. 7:21; 18:3; 19:23-24; Mark 9:47; John 3:5; Acts 14:22.

14. Literally, "loose." Loose and bind are legal terms referring to authority. Judges and magistrates bind people over to courts or loose them from activity. Cf. Matt. 16:19 and 18:18, where the term refers to forgiveness.

15. Cf. 1 Cor. 4:3; 15:9; cf. Eph. 3:8.

16. "Doing" is also emphasized as the closing parable: Matt. 7:24-27.

17. The Deutero-Pauline tradition stresses Paul's role as teacher.

18. On the absence of Pauline theological influences upon the *Didache,* see Lindemann, *Paulus,* 174–77.

19. See p. 180 (Pseudo-Clementines).

20. Note Dassmann, *Stachel,* 279–86, who makes the important observation that the Jewish revolts of the era 66–135 also radicalized Jewish Christian movements. The staunch opposition of the Pseudo-Clementines to animal sacrifice is probably one indication of this radical orientation.

21. Se also Origen, *C. Cels.* 5.65; *Hom. in Jer.*] 20.1-7.

22. See Eusebius *H.E.* 4.29.5, who says that the Severians use both the Hebrew Bible and the Gospels, but blaspheme Paul, rejecting both his letters and Acts.

23. Although earlier writers, such as Irenaeus (*A.H.* 1.26), describe Cerinthus in Gnostic terms, those of a later era tend to align him with the Ebionites as a Jewish Christian. For example, Epiphanius (*Pan.* 28.1–8) credits him with accepting the heavenly origin of both the Law and the Prophets, that is, the creator, promoting circumcision and denouncing Paul.

24. Georg Strecker, "Elchasaites," *ABD on CD-ROM.* Version 2.0c., 1995, 1996. Studies include Luigi Cirillo, *Elchasai e gli elchasaiti: Un contributo all storia delle comunità giudeo-cristiane,* Università degli studi della Calabria. Centro interdipartimentale di scienze religiose. Studi e Ricerche 1 (Cosenza: Marra, 1984), and G. P. Luttikhuizen, *The Revelation of Elchasai,* TSAJ 8 (Tübingen: Mohr Siebeck, 1985).

25. See Lüdemann, *Opposition,* 191–92. Points of contact suggest a common background of Elkasites and the sources of the Pseudo-Clementines.

26. Iain Gardner and Samuel N. C. Lieu, *Manichaean Texts from the Roman Empire* (Cambridge: Cambridge University Press, 2004), 3–5.

27. See Pervo, *Acts,* 457.

28. Hans-Josef Klauck, *The Apocryphal Acts of the Apostles: An Introduction,* trans. Brian McNeil (Waco, Tex.: Baylor University Press, 2008), 40. See further, pp. 40–41. Klauck refers to a paper by one of his students, T. W. Thompson. See also Richard I. Pervo, "Johannine Trajectories in the *Acts of John,*" *Apocrypha* 3 (1992): 47–68.

29. See Glenn F. Chestnut, "Hegessipus," *ABD on CD-ROM.* Version 2.0c., 1995, 1996.

30. Christians (and Jews) took up from the scholastic philosophical tradition the practice of determining the valid representatives of a movement by providing lists of successive heads of "schools," which, for Christians, meant bishops.

31. This argument is advanced by Lüdemann, *Opposition*, 155–68. See also David K. Rensberger, "As the Apostle Teaches: The Development of the Use of Paul's Letters in Second-Century Christianity" (Ph.D. diss., Yale, 1981), 202–3; Lindemann, *Paulus*, 293–96; and Dassmann, *Stachel*, 240–43.

32. See M. E. Stone and J. Strugnell, eds. and trans., *The Books of Elijah*, Parts 1-2; SBLTT 18 (Missoula: Montana: Scholars, 1979), 41–73.

33. Had Hegesippus made favorable comments about Paul, Eusebius might well have noted them. Had he provided negative judgments, Eusebius would not have included them. Silence does not prove anti-Paulinism, but it makes favorable reports less probable.

34. The theory was strongly supported by Walter Bauer (*Orthodoxy and Heresy in Earliest Christianity*, trans. and ed. Robert A. Kraft and Gerhard Krodel [Philadelphia: Fortress Press, 1971]) whose use of arguments from silence has received substantial criticism. Refutation of this claim was one of the major achievements of Rensberger, "As the Apostle Teaches"; Lindemann, *Paulus*; and Dassmann, *Stachel*. Note the last scholar's survey of silence about Paul (222–44).

35. On Papias, see also p. 192.

36. Lindemann, *Paulus*, 290–92.

37. Lindemann, *Paulus*, 291. See also Dassmann, *Stachel*, 237–40. Rensberger, "As the Apostle Teaches," 199–201, who allows the possibility that Papias did refer to Paul.

38. Lüdemann, *Paulus*, 282–90, discusses the various possibilities. Note also Rensberger, "As the Apostle Teaches," 39–40; Dassmann, *Stachel*, 226–31; and J. Verheyden, "The *Shepherd of Hermas* and the Writings That Later Formed the New Testament," in *The Reception of the New Testament in the Apostolic Fathers*, ed. Andrew Gregory and Christopher Tuckett; The New Testament and the Apostolic Fathers 1 (Oxford: Oxford University Press, 2005), 293–329.

39. J. Muddiman, "The Church in Ephesians, 2 Clement, and the *Sherpherd of Hermas*, in *Trajectories through the New Testament and the Apostolic Fathers*, ed. Andrew Gregory and Christopher Tuckett; The New Testament and the Apostolic Fathers 2 (Oxford: Oxford University Press, 2005), 107–21 (116–21).

40. The letter frame is a distant *hommage* to the Pauline practice.

41. For a survey, see Leslie W. Barnard, "The Epistle of Barnabas and Its Contemporary Setting," *ANRW* II.27.1 (1993): 159–207. Barnard is a staunch advocate of an Egyptian origin. For Asia Minor as the provenance, see Klaus Wengst, *Tradition und Theologie des Barnabasbriefes*, Arbeiten zur Kirchengeschichte 42 (Berlin: de Gruyter, 1971).

42. See Lindemann, *Paulus*, 279–80, and James Carleton-Paget, "The *Epistle of Barnabas* and the Writings That Later Formed the New Testament," in Gregory and Tuckett, eds. *Reception*, 229–49 (245). On Abraham, see the comments about Justin, below.

43. Rensberger, "As the Apostle Teaches," 77–78 n. 40, strongly rejects idea that Barnabas is anti-Pauline.

44. Ernst Baasland, "Der 2. Klemensbrief und frühchristliche Rhetorik: 'Die erste christliche Predigt' im Lichte der neueren Forschung," *ANRW* II.27.1 (1993): 78–157. Another candidate is the *Gospel of Truth*.

45. Neither Rome nor Corinth command general support. See the summary statement of Andreas Lindemann, *Die Clemensbriefe*, HNT 17 (Tübingen: Mohr/Siebeck, 1992), 195.

46. K. P. Donfried, "The Theology of Second Clement," *HTR* 66 (1973): 487–501.

47. Lindemann, *Paulus*, 263–72; Rensberger, "As the Apostle Teaches," 83; and Andrew Gregory, "2 Clement and the Writings That Later Formed the New Testament," in Gregory and Tuckett, eds., *Reception*, 251–92. On p. 279, Gregory concludes the author did not use Paul in a deliberate manner.

48. A useful survey is Robert M. Grant, *Greek Apologists of the Second Century* (Philadelphia: Westminster, 1988). Justin was acquainted with the Middle Platonic school and makes substantial use of their terminology.

49. Richard I. Pervo, *Dating Acts: Between the Evangelists and the Apologists* (Santa Rosa, Calif.: Polebridge, 2006), 149–99.

50. Although entitled "Epistle to Diognetus," the work is not a letter.

51. Grant, *Greek Apologists*, 178–79.

52. Similar questions arise about the "most excellent Theophilus" of Luke 1:3. In both cases, the name may be a symbolic fiction. See Pervo, *Acts*, 35.

53. Portions of ch. 7, rendered into meter by F. Bland Tucker, serve as the lovely hymn "Great Creator of the Worlds."

54. Dassmann, *Stachel*, 257, observes that the work is more parenetic than apologetic.

55. See Lindemann, *Paulus*, 343–50, and *Paulus, Apostel*, 280–93; Rensberger, "As the Apostle Teaches," 286–91; and Dassmann, *Stachel*, 254–59.

56. Cf. 1 Cor. 4:12, also.

57.' Ἐν σαρκὶ γὰρ περιπατοῦντε" οὐ κατὰ σάρκα στρατευόμεθα (Indeed, we live as human beings, but we do not wage war according to human standards).

58. Lindemann, *Paulus*, 347.

59. Lindemann, *Paulus*, 348.

60. Grant, *Greek Apologists*, 36–39.

61. Lindemann, *Stachel*, 350–52.

62. Grant, *Greek Apologists*, 100–111. On his possible use of Paul, see Albert E. Barnett, *Paul Becomes a Literary Influence* (Chicago: University of Chicago Press, 1941), 248–51, and Dassmann, *Stachel*, 250–51.

63. See Grant, *Greek Apologists*, 140–201, et passim, and Dassmann, *Stachel*, 251–54.

64. Peter Lampe provides a sympathetic sketch of Justin's life and its social context in his *From Paul to Valentinus: Christians at Rome in the First Two Centuries*, trans. Michael Steinhauser; ed. Marshall D. Johnson (Minneapolis: Fortress Press, 2003), 257–84. Justin does not seem to have engaged rhetoric or literature at the higher levels. His education in philosophy may have been informal, that is, he heard lectures of various philosophers and engaged in reading.

65. Lampe, *From Paul to Valentinus*, 54–55.

66. On Justin, see Lampe, *From Paul to Valentinus*, 46–73, et passim; Lindemann, *Paulus*, 353–67; and Oskar Skarsaune, *The Proof from Prophecy: A Study in Justin Martyr's Proof-text Tradition: Text-Type, Provenance, Theological Profile*, NovTSup 56 (Leiden: Brill, 1987), 115–18.

67. Lindemann, *Paulus*, 353, lists four proposals.

68. Pervo, *Dating Acts*, 20–22; Andrew Gregory, *The Reception of Luke and Acts in the Period before Irenaeus*, WUNT 169 (Tübingen: Mohr Siebeck, 2003), 317–21.

69. On Ptolemy to Flora, see the following chapter.

70. On Justin's use of gospel material, see Helmut Koester, *Ancient Christian Gospels: Their History and Development* (Philadelphia: Trinity Press International, 1990), 360–402. On his "Bible," see Grant, *Greek Apologists*, 57–59. Justin did not appear to endorse the notion of a single Gospel (*1 Apol.* 66.3), but the evidence that he used John is scanty, at best.

71. Justin also assigns the worldwide mission to the Jerusalem apostles who were present with Jesus during his ministry (*1 Apol.* 39.3). This leaves no room for Paul.

72. Lindemann, *Paulus*, 355–58.

73. In addition to Lindemann, *Paulus*, 358–67, see Albrecht Thoma, "Justins literarisches Verhältnis zu Paulus und zum Johannes-Evangelium," *ZWTh* 18 (1875): 385–412; Rodney Werline, "The Transformation of Pauline Arguments in Justin Martyr's *Dialogue with Trypho*," *HTR* 92 (1999): 79–93; Leslie W. Barnard, *Justin Martyr: His Life and Thought* (Cambridge: Cambridge University Press, 1967), 62–63; Theodore Stylianopoulos, *Justin Martyr and the Mosac Law* (Missoula, Mont.: Scholars, 1975), 70, 104–8; Erwin R. Goodenough, *The Theology of Justin Martyr: An Investigation into the Conceptions of Early Christian Literature and Its Hellenistic and Judaistic Influences* (Amsterdam: Philo Press, 1968), 96.

74. Bauer, *Orthodoxy*, 215–16, argues for the necessity of minimizing claims of Pauline reminiscence in Justin. His thesis drove him to incorrect conclusions.

75. Justin, *Dial.* 11.5, trans. Thomas B. Falls, *Saint Justin Martyr* (New York: Christian Heritage, 1948), 165.

76. Justin had just repeated the argument of 11.5.

77. *Dial.* 23.4-5, trans. Falls, 183.

78. Cf. also *Dial.* 92; 119.5.

79. Both exhibit the same important deviation from the LXX. Justin follows Ephesians in altering the text from second person to third, the verb "you took" to "he gave," and the obscure ἐν ἀνθρώπῳ ("for a mortal") [?] to the plural: "for mortals."

80. Barnett, *Literary Influence*, 231–47. Eight are from Romans, one from 1 Corinthians, and two each from Galatians, Ephesians, and Colossians.

81. See the following chapter.

82. Lindemann, *Paulus*, 366–67.

83. See Grant, *Greek Apologists*, 113–32; M. Whittaker, *Tatian: Oratio ad Graecos* (Oxford: Clarendon, 1982); Lampe, *From Paul*, 285–91; and Emily J. Hunt, *Christianity in the Second Century: The Case of Tatian* (London: Routledge, 2003). Note also O. C. Edwards, "Tatian," *ABD on CD-ROM.* Version 2.0c., 1995, 1996.

84. Lucian of Samosata had a similar background. He too came from a Syriac-speaking region, and opted for a Hellenic education. Both display a biting temperament, but Lucian's Greek culture was superior to that of Tatian, and he rejected neither the empire nor Hellenism.

85. On Tatian's conversion, see Whittaker, *Tatian*, 55, and Hunt, *Christianity*, 36–38.

86. The *Diatessaron* may have been issued in Syriac, or in both Greek and Syriac.

87. Grant, *Greek Apologists*, 113–14. "Against the Greeks" is a better title.

88. On its genre, see Grant, *Greek Apologists*, 115–17.

89. Robert M. Grant, "Tatian and the Bible," *Studia Patristica*. Vol. 1, ed. K. Aland and F. L. Cross (Berlin: Akademie-Verlag, 1957), 297–306 (303). Note also Hunt, *Christianity*, 36–45.

90. Matthew and Luke composed a new gospel based upon Mark and Q.

91. Fragment 5 (Whittaker), from Clement of Alexandria, *Stromata* 3.80.3–81.3.

92. Clement of Alexandria, *Stromata*, 3.80.1-3 (trans. John E. L. Oulton, *Alexandrian Christianity*, LCC [Philadelphia: Westminster, 1954], 77–78).

93. For discussion, see Grant, *Greek Apologists*, 127–28.

94. See p. 144.

95. See Jerome's Preface to his commentary *In Ep. ad Tit.* (*Commentary on the Epistle to Titus.*)

96. Grant, "Tatian and the Bible," 301. *Oratio* 27.1-2 may refer to Titus 1:2 on the credibility of Cretans. See also Hunt, *Christianity*, 44–45, who finds no certain allusions to the Pastoral Epistles in Tatian's *Oration*.

Chapter 6: Paul as an Object of Interpretation

1. Maurice F. Wiles (*The Divine Apostle: The Interpretation of St. Paul's Epistles in the Early Church* [Cambridge: Cambridge University Press, 1967], 4–5) puts it this way: "Throughout the second century the great majority of Christians and would-be Christians were concerned to find in Paul's writings support for their particular understanding of Christian truth." The third century witnessed a shift to a more systematic approach, although it was some time before fully "orthodox" commentaries appeared, since both Clement and Origen were, in part, successors to the Valentinian tradition.

2. R. M. Grant, *Heresy and Criticism* (Louisville: Westminster/John Knox, 1993). The following section is indebted to his exposition and analysis.

3. See Richard I. Pervo, *Dating Acts: Between the Evangelists and the Apologists* (Santa Rosa, Calif.: Polebridge, 2006), 261–62.

4. This is apparent in a later period, when Nestorian or Monophysite Christianity dominated entire regions. The achievement of Walter Bauer (*Orthodoxy and Heresy in Earliest Christianity*, trans. and ed. Robert A. Kraft and Gerhard Krodel [Philadelphia: Fortress Press, 1971]) was to emphasize the particularities of regional forms of Christianity and the persistence of groups viewed as heretical by the emergent mainstream.

5. See Chapter 1.

6. See Chapter 1, n. 143

7. The process was further stimulated by Erasmus, whose Greek New Testament was produced in haste on the basis of bad mss. and often conformed to the dominant Latin Vulgate.

8. On this work, see p. 40.

9. Cf. Ezra 6:19-23; 1 Esd. 1.

10. *Dialogue with Trypho* 72.1, trans. Falls, 263.

11. Lactantius also cites it, *Inst. Div.* 4.18.

12. Irenaeus attribute this to either Isaiah or Jeremiah (*A.H.* 3.20; 4.20; *Demonstratio* 78).

13. Justin cites them in *1 Apol.* 41.4. The interpolation is common in Latin Christian writers.

14. The debate shows that Jews were still making use of (and revising, evidently) the LXX in the second half of the second century.

15. See Grant, *Heresy*, 15–32.

16. Aelius Theon 3, from George A. Kennedy, ed. and trans., *Progymnasmata: Greek Textbooks of Prose Composition and Rhetoric*, SBLWGRW 10 (Atlanta: Society of Biblical Literature, 2003), 22–23.

17. His example of the false is "that Bion did not truthfully say that love of money was the mother city of all evil; for intemperance is more so" is a value judgment. (For the sentiment, see 1 Tim. 6:10.)

18. Hermogenes, *Progymnasmata* 5 (see Kennedy, *Progymnasmata*, 79).

19. This survives in claims that X "would not have said Y." The argument gains validity when one cites a number of examples in which X clearly opposed Y, but it proves no more than the improbability of the argument. People change and are not always inconsistent.

20. See Barbara Aland, "Marcion/Marcioniten," *TRE* 22 (1992): 89–101.

21. Literature on Marcion includes: Adolf von Harnack, *Marcion, Marcion: Das Evangelium vom fremden Gott*, 2nd ed. (Leipzig: Hinrichs, 1924); R. S. Wilson, *Marcion: A Study of a Second Century Heretic* (London: Clarke, 1933); John Knox, *Marcion and the New Testament* (Chicago: University of Chicago Press, 1942); E. C. Blackman, *Marcion and His Influence* (London: SPCK, 1948); R. Joseph Hoffmann, *Marcion: On the Restitution of Christianity*, AARAS 46 (Chico, Calif.: Scholars Press, 1984); U. Schmid, *Marcion und sein Apostolos. Rekonstruktion und historische Einordnung der marcionitischen Paulusbriefausgabe*, ANTF 25 (Berlin: de Gruyter, 1995); J. B. Tyson, *Marcion and Luke-Acts: A Defining Struggle* (Columbia: University of South Carolina Press, 2006); Gerhard May, "Marcion in Contemporary Views: Results and Open Questions," *SecCent* 6 (1987–88): 129–51; Gerhard May and Katharinia Greschat, eds., *Marcion und seine kirchengechichtliche Wirkung*, TU 150 (Berlin: de Gruyter, 2002), and, in the same volume, H. J. W. Drijivers, "Marcionism in Syria: Principles, Problems, Polemics," 153–72; R. J. Hoffmann, "How then Know This Troublous Teacher? Further Reflections on Marcion and his Church," 173–91; D. J. Balás, "Marcion Revisited: A 'Post-Harnack' Perspective," in *Texts and Testaments: Critical Essays on the Bible and Early Church Fathers*, ed. W. E. March (San Antonio: Trinity University Press, 1980), 95–108. On Marcion as an interpreter of Paul, see also Andreas Lindemann, *Paulus, Apostel und Lehrer der Kirche* (Tübingen: Mohr Siebeck, 1999), 379–95, and Ernst Dassmann, *Der Stachel im Fleisch: Paulus in der frühchristlichen Literatur bis Irenäus* (Münster: Aschendorff, 1979), 176–92.

22. See the Excursus below.

23. Tertullian, *Prescription of Heretics* 30.1; *Adv. Marc.* 1.18.4, among others. On the possible meanings of this term, see May, "Marcion," 136–37. Lampe, *From Paul to Valentinus: Christians at Rome in the First Two Centuries*, trans. Michael Steinhauser; ed. Marshall D. Johnson (Minneapolis: Fortress Press, 2003), 241–52, is quite useful, particularly in his attention to Marcion's trade. Note also Gerhard May, "Der 'Schiffsreder' Markion," *StPatr* 21 (1989): 142–53.

24. Hoffmann, *Marcion*, 31–74, shows the weakness of dating based upon inconsistent and tendentious patristic data. Cf. also Tyson, *Defining Struggle*. Since patristic writers prefer to date heretics as late as possible, Clement of Alexandria's claim (*Strom.* 7.17.106-7) that Marcion appeared under Hadrian (117–138) is credible, and is supported by other witnesses. Grant (*Heresy*, 34) attributes some of Marcion's impetus to the anti-Jewish feelings sparked by the Second Revolt (132–135). One should also consider the strong impact of the Diaspora revolt under Trajan. See Pervo, *Dating Acts*, Appendix IV, 369–72, and now Miriam Pucci Ben Zeev, "The Uprisings in the Jewish Diaspora, 116–117," in *The Cambridge History of Judaism*, vol. 4, ed. S. Katz (Cambridge: Cambridge University Press, 2006), 93–104. If Marcion played upon the sentiment aroused by the revolts, the earlier period is at least as likely a candidate as the events under Hadrian. See also Wolfgang A. Bienert, "Marcion und der Antijudaismus," in May and Greschat, eds., *Marcion*, 191–205.

25. Pervo, *Acts*, 482–83.

26. The basis for this is Tertullian's reference to the date when Marcion claimed to have become an apostle: 115 years and six and a half months after Christ appeared in 29 (*Adv. Marc.* 1.19.2).

27. See Epiphanius, *Pan.* 42.1-2.

28. See Einar Thomassen, "Orthodoxy and Heresy in Second-Century Rome," *HTR* 97 (2004): 241–56. Not until the end of the second century did the Roman church develop an organization capable of expelling those viewed as "heretics."

29. Tertullian complained that the followers of Marcion built churches as wasps build nests (*Adv. Marc.* 4.5).

30. This was the hypothesis of Knox, *Marcion*. Colossians shows that a Paulinism that did not require Israelite scriptures emerged relatively early.

31. Marcion knew our Ephesians as "Laodiceans."

32. See p. 66.

33. E. P. Sanders, *Paul and Palestinian Judaism* (Philadelphia: Fortress Press, 1977).

34. For example, Tertullian claimed that Marcion debated with Roman Christian leaders about the sayings regarding old and new wineskins (Mark 2:21-22 parr.; Tertullian, *Adv. Marc.* 3.16.5; 4.11.9) and good and bad trees (Luke 6:43-44 parr.; Tertullian, *Adv. Marc.* 1.2.1). Both sides doubtless accepted the figurative meaning of these "parables." The issue was their specific application.

35. Tertullian, *Adv. Marc.* 4.6.3.

36. Marcion may have taken up distinctions based upon the major names of God in the LXX: *kyrios* and *theos* ("Lord," that is, "Yahweh") and "God" (*Elohim*).

37. On the question, see Barbara Aland, "Marcion—Versuch einer neuen Interpretation," *ZTK* 70 (1973): 420–47 (445–47), and "Sünde und Erlösung bei Marcion und die Konsequenz für die sog. Beiden Götter Marcions," in May and Geschat, eds., *Marcion*, 147–57; and Andrew McGowan, "Marcion's Love of Creation," *JECS* 9 (2001): 295–311.

38. Marcion did not, evidently, ask why this god had remained out of the picture for all of antecedent human history.

39. For this Marcion relied upon the antitheses of Matt. 5:21-49, indicating that this book was probably issued (or revised) in Rome.

40. Lampe, *Paul to Valentinus*, 252–56, relates Marcion's techniques and philosophical commonplaces to the grammatical level of education, as well his undue use of dogmatic presuppositions.

41. Adolf von Harnack, *Marcion: The Gospel of the Alien God*, trans. J. E. Steely and L. Bierma (Durham, N.C.: Labyrinth, 1990), 128–32 (the translation unfortunately omits the appendices); Hans von Campenhausen, *The Formation of the Christian Bible*, trans. J. A. Baker (Philadelphia: Fortress Press, 1972), 148–67. More recent studies of the Christian Canon have wrestled with details, ambiguities, and differences. Campenhausen attempted to identify the dynamics behind the process. See also the following essays in May and Geschrat, eds., *Marcion*: U. Schmid, "Marcions Evangelium und die neutestamentlichen Evangelien. Rückfragen zur Geschichte und Kanonisierung der Evangelienüberlieferung," 67–77; M. Vinzent, "Der Schluß des Lukasevangeliums bei Marcion," 79–93; and Eve-Marie Becker, "Marcion und die Korintherbriefe nach Tertullian, Adversus Marcionem V," 95–109.

42. For evidence of Marcion's use of traditional liturgical practices, see Alistair Stewart-Sykes, "Bread and Fish, Water and Wine: The Marcionite Menu and the Maintenance of Purity," in May and Greschat, eds., *Marcion*, 207–20 (207–11).

43. For contemporary analogies, see Grant, *Heresy*, 34–36.

44. Tertullian's claim that Marcion's *Gospel* was anonymous and that this represented a falsification (*Adv. Marc.* 4.3.5) is erroneous. In this matter, Marcion was truly more "primitive" than his later opponent.

45. Marcion evidently identified Luke as the book referred to as "my gospel" (Rom. 2:16; cf. 16:25; 2 Tim. 2:8). Rom. 2:16 is suspect. If Marcion appealed to this verse, it was already present in his text of Romans.

46. See Pervo, *Dating Acts*, 25. Acts was not an authoritative text in Marcion's time.

47. Cf. Origen, *Comm. In Ioh.* 5.7 (*Griechische christlichen Schriftsteller* 10, 104.26).

48. A recent argument for the use of a different edition can be found in Tyson, *Defining Struggle*. For a summary of the view that Marcion could have begun with canonical Luke, see Grant, *Heresy*, 33–47. The major source for Marcion's *Gospel* is Tertullian, *Adv. Marc.* IV. The classic reconstruction is von Harnack's *Marcion*, *159-*237.

49. Tertullian, *Adv. Marc.* 4.33.7.

50. The main verb of Luke 3:1-3 is ἦλθεν εἰς. Luke 4:31 reads κατῆλθεν εἰς ("came to...came down to"). Marcion evidently looked for a logical continuation.

51. See Chapter 1.

52. The foundational study is von Harnack, *Marcion*, *39–*156. See also John J. Clabeaux, *A Lost Edition of the Letters of Paul: A Reassessment of the Text of the Pauline Corpus Attested by Marcion*, CBQMS 21 (Washington: Catholic Biblical Association, 1989), and Ulrich Schmid, *Marcion und sein Apostolos. Rekonstruktion und historische Einordnung der marcionitschen Paulusbriefausgabe*, ANTF 25 (Berlin: de Gruyter, 1995).

53. It is not clear whether this was a Latin edition, which could have deviated from the Greek original. On the question, see Balás, "Marcion Revisited," 102-3.

54. See von Harnack, *Marcion*, *106–*107.

55. See Grant's comments in *Heresy*, 34, with a citation from Morton Smith.

56. "Marcion," *The Encyclopaedia Britannica*, 11th ed. (New York: Encyclopaedia Britannica, 1911), 17:691-93, 692. (It is said that von Harnack picked up this phrase from Franz Overbeck.)

57. The most enduring component of the view of Paul propounded by E. P. Sanders and J. D. G. Dunn is the rejection of the view that the Protestant Reformation established the normative understanding of Pauline theology.

58. For examples of recent thinking about Marcion, see the essays in May and Greschat, eds., *Marcion*. Gerhard May opens this collection with an essay entitled "Marcion ohne Harnack," 1–7. See also, in the same volume, W. Kinzig, "Ein Ketzer und sein Konstrukteur. Harnacks Marcion," 253-74. Barbara Aland's earlier essays helped generate the revision of von Harnack's construction.

59. Pastoral Epistles: 1 Tim. 6:20; on Polycarp, see Irenaeus, AH 3.3.4. Polycarp visited Rome, according to Irenaeus, *A.H.* 3.3-4 (c. 155). This visit was a good twenty-five years after his correspondence with Philippi.

60. See n. 26 above.

61. Cf. also Tertullian, *Adv. Marc.*1.2; 2.24.

62. David W. Deakle, "Harnack & Cerdo: A Reexamination of the Patristic Evidence for Marcion's Mentor," in May and Greschrat, eds., *Marcion*, 177–90, shows that too little is known of Cerdo to make the alleged link between him and Marcion useful.

63. Kurt Rudolph, *Gnosis: The Nature and History of Gnosticism*, trans. and ed. R. McL. Wilson (San Francisco: Harper & Row, 1983), 313-17. Synthetic approaches to Gnosis are under fire, as the subsequent section will note. Examples of the difficulties on both Marcionite and Gnostic sides are provided by Christoph Markschies, "Die valentianische Gnosis und Marcion—einige neue Perspektiven," in May and Greschat, eds., *Marcion*, 159-75.

64. Von Harnack, *Marcion*, *28–*36.

65. Strongly docetic constructions of the crucifixion appear, for example, in the *Acts of John* 97-102, and the *Second Treatise of the Great Seth* (NHC VII, 2) 55.1—56.20.

66. Marcion may have found justification for his view in 1 Cor. 15:44 ("spiritual body").

67. See Aland, "Marcion—Versuch einer neuen Interpretation," 423, 444-46.

68. See Michael A. Williams, *Rethinking Gnosticism: An Argument for Dismantling a Dubious Category*, 2nd ed. (Princeton: Princeton University Press, 1999), 25 and n. 37.

69. See John G. Gager, "Marcion and Philosophy," VC 26 (1973): 53-59, who notes affinities with the Epicurean tradition, and Enrico Norelli, "Marcion: ein christlicher Philosoph oder ein Christ gegen die Philosophie?" in May and Greschat, eds., *Marcion*, 113-30, who is largely negative on the question of direct philosophical influence.

70. Marcion did speak of the "Harrowing of Hell." After his death, Jesus descended to Hades and preached salvation to all the departed. His message was welcomed by various sinners but rejected by the righteous, who therefore remained in Hades (Irenaeus, *A.H.* 1.27.3).

71. See Tyson, *Defining Struggle*, who links the appearance of canonical Luke and Acts to the impetus generated by Marcion.

72. The extent of this enterprise was rivaled—in part surpassed—only by Islam in the Middle Ages. Not until the sixteenth century did the Christian mission encompass a similar area.

73. See Edmondo Lupieri, *The Mandaeans: The Last Gnostics* (Grand Rapids: Eerdmans, 2002). The date of Mandaean origins is disputed. They can be traced back to the third century, at the

latest. (The matter was complicated by Rudolph Bultmann's use of Mandaean texts to illuminate the background of the Fourth Gospel in the 1920s. They were the current "hot discoveries," though they came to be largely superseded, from the perspective of Christian origins, by the Dead Sea Scrolls and the Nag Hammadi Library.) Lupieri (*Mandaeans*, 61–126) shows the extent of contact with Western Christians prior to nineteenth-century Protestant research. The Mandaeans' tangled understanding of their own history indicates that, along with Christians and Manichaeans, they experienced persecution under the Sassanid Persian state, which emerged in 224 CE and, under Bahram I (274–277), undertook persecution of dissident religions. Second-century existence of the body is not probable, but data for earlier origins are lacking.

74. See Ugo Bianchi, ed., *The Origins of Gnosticism: The Colloquium of Messina*, Studies in the History of Religions; 2nd ed. (Leiden: Brill, 1970).

75. Williams, *Rethinking Gnosticism*, and Karen L. King, *What is Gnosticism?* (Cambridge: Belknap, 2003).

76. Bentley Layton, *The Gnostic Scriptures* (Garden City, N.Y.: Doubleday, 1987).

77. Layton, *Gnostic Scriptures*, 5–21. On pp. 23–214 he translates a number of texts emanating from this sect or descriptions of them. (Layton's translations are recommended because of their readability.)

78. For use of a novelistic plot in the Nag Hammadi Library, see *The Exegesis on the Soul* (NHC I, 6).

79. The influence of the LXX is, however, clear.

80. One of the tractates exists only in a Latin version and some of the fragments also survive only in Latin.

81. See n. 73.

82. For a brief overview of the library, its origin, discovery, and publication, see James M. Robinson, ed., *The Nag Hammadi Library in English*, rev. ed. (San Francisco: Harper & Row, 1988), 10–26.

83. See Iain Gardner and Samuel N. C. Lieu, *Manichean Texts from the Roman Empire* (Cambridge: Cambridge University Press, 2004).

84. For more general surveys of the use of Paul in Gnosis, see Lindemann, *Paulus im ältesten Christentum*, BHT 58 (Tübingen: Mohr Siebeck, 1979), 297–343, and *Paulus, Apostel*, 306–15; Dassmann, *Stachel*, 192–222; David K. Rensberger, "As the Apostle Teaches: The Development of the Use of Paul's Letters in Second-Century Christianity" (Ph.D. diss., Yale, 1981), 214–49; and Klaus Koschorke, "Paulus in den Nag-Hammadi Texten: Ein Beitrag zur Geschichte der Paulusrezeption im frühen Christentum," *ZTK* 78 (1981): 177–205.

85. See John Muddiman, "The Church in Ephesians, 2 Clement, and the *Shepherd of Hermas*," in Gregory and Tuckett, eds., *Trajectories*, 107–21 (121).

86. Rensberger, "As the Apostle Teaches," 346. See also Lindemann, *Paulus*, 306–8.

87. In *The Gnostic Paul: Gnostic Exegesis of the Pauline Letters* (Philadelphia: Fortress Press, 1975), Elaine H. Pagels approaches the material on a letter-by-letter basis. Readers should note that, apparently by some accident, many of her references to ancient texts are erroneous.

88. See p. 10.

89. Valentinians called themselves *pneumatikoi* and *teleioi*, "the Spiritual" and "the Perfect" (1 Cor. 2:6; 2:15, etc.; 14:20). "Ordinary" Christians were viewed as "Psychics" (cf. 1 Cor. 2:14). These persons were educable, targets for Valentinian evangelism. Unbelievers were "Hylics," beings consigned to the material realm and beyond the pale. The name "Valentinians" derives originally from their opponents. These designations may eventually be accepted by the members, as was the case, for example, with "Christians," "Lutherans," and "Wesleyans."

90. For inscriptional material that may relate to Valentinian sacramental practice, see Lampe, *Paul to Valentinus*, 298–313.

91. Irenaeus, *A.H.* 3.2.2. Clement of Alexandria agrees (*Strom.* 6.7.61).

92. On Gnostic claims to "apostolic tradition," see also *Ptolemy to Flora* 7.9 (discussed below); *Gospel of Philip* 74.16-17. The claim that Paul taught his followers in secret was old enough to have been denied in Acts 20:27. Jesus is depicted as instructing his disciples privately on the meaning of his parables in Mark 4:20-32.

93. A useful survey is John Dillon, *The Middle Platonists* (London: Duckworth, 1977).

94. Basilides was active at Alexandria in the first half of the second century. According to Hippolytus (*Ref.* 7.20.2-3), he posited the most "wholly other," "negative" description imaginable." "There was a time when there was nothing; not even the nothing was there, but simply, clearly, and without any sophistry there was nothing at all..." (trans. W. Foerster, *Gnosis: A Selection of Gnostic Texts*, 2 vols.; Engl. trans. R. McL. Wilson [Oxford: Clarendon, 1972], 1:64). On Basilides' links with Paulinism, see Lindemann, *Paulus*, 306-8, and Rensberger, "As the Apostle Teaches," 134-35. According to Clement of Alexandria (*Strom.* 3.2.1), Basilides called Paul "the apostle." He was reportedly the first to use the *Corpus Paulinum* as an authoritative text for comment.

95. On the conflict among various Christians at Rome in that period, see Thomassen, "Orthodoxy and Heresy."

96. Irenaeus opens his famous treatise by pitting Paul against Gnostic claims, with citations of 1 Tim. 1:4 and Tit. 3:9 (*A.H.* preface). Tertullian (*Prescription of Heretics* 6) insists that the same person wrote both Galatians and Titus.

97. Pagels, *Gnostic Paul*, 5.

98. See below.

99. Cf. Richard I. Pervo's review of Horton Harris, *The Tuebingen School*, ATR 60 (1978): 222-23, which objects to Harris' efforts to rule out the sermons of F. C. Baur on the grounds that they lacked candor.

100. Tertullian, *Adv. Val.* 4. Such claims must be treated with reserve, but this one is not impossible.

101. Layton, *Gnostic Scriptures*, 303-5. For detailed study, see Dieter Müller, "Prayer of the Apostle Paul," in H. Attridge, ed., *Nag Hammadi Codex I*, Nag Hammadi Studies 22-23; 2 vols. (Leiden: Brill, 1985), 1:5-11 (2 nn. 1-5).

102. The date is uncertain. Müller ("Prayer of the Apostle Paul,") points to similarities with prayers in the *Corpus Hermeticum*, magical, and other documents from the *NHL*.

103. Titles are often found at the end of treatises in the *NHL*.

104. Cf. A 7.

105. Better: "Son of Man."

106. Namely, Paul.

107. A 15-29, trans. Layton, *Gnostic Scriptures*, 305. (The ellipsis does not mark a lacuna in the text, but the close of the citation.)

108. Other lines allude to John (A 16, 23-24) and to Gen. 1-2 (A 30-32).

109. Layton, *Gnostic Scriptures*, 251.

110. *Gospel of Truth* 18.25, trans. Layton, *Gnostic Scriptures*, 254. (Layton renders "knowledge/gnosis" as "acquaintance," to stress its intimate [as opposed to cognitive] connotation.)

111. E.g., the Good Friday hymn *Pange Lingua* of Venantius Fortunatus, stanza 3.

112. *Gospel of Truth* 20.21-27, trans. Layton, *Gnostic Scriptures*, 255. (Note the use of Col. 2:14.)

113. E. Norden (*Die antike Kunstprosa*, 2 vols. [Stuttgart: Teubner, 1995 (repr. of 1915)], 2:545-47) expresses admiration for Valentinus' prose, based upon fragments preserved by Clement of Alexandria. Even such intemperately censorious writers as Jerome (*In Hos.* 2.10) and Tertullian (*Adv. Val.* 4) acknowledge Valentinus' literary and intellectual gifts.

114. J. Williams, *Biblical Interpretation in the Gnostic Gospel of Truth from Nag Hammadi*, SBLDS 79 (Atlanta: Scholars Press, 1988).

115. Williams, *Biblical Interpretation*, 191-99.

116. Williams, *Biblical Interpretation*, 199-204.

117. Allegory is a method of composition in which persons, events, and so forth, are symbols. Cf. Matt. 22:1-14 and works like John Bunyan's *Pilgrim's Progress*. Allegorism is a method of interpretation that views the details of a text as symbols. It is likely to emerge in any culture that possesses foundational texts (such as Homer) that are no longer relevant to the thought, values, and ethics of the current culture.

118. Williams, *Biblical Interpretation*, 186-87.

119. References, with the *Gospel of Truth* locations in parentheses: Rom. 1:21? (17.14-15); 3:23 (42.2); 5:5 (43.6); 8:3 (31.5); 8:29 (21.25); 1 Cor. 7:31b? (24.23); 15:28 (20.28); 15:45? (34.23-24); 2 Cor. 2:14 (34.1); 5:4? (25.18); Eph. 3:9? (24.15); 4:27 (33.19); Phil. 2:8? (20.28); Col. 1:16 (18.32; 19.8-9); 1:25 (18.11-12); 1:26? (27.8); 2:14 (20.20); Heb. 1:5 (38.11-12); 2:17 (20.10); 4:12? (26.2-3); 9:17? (20.14); 2 Tim. 2:20-21 (25.23-35).

120. See K. Koschorke, *Die Polemik der Gnostiker gegen das kirchliche Christentum*, NHS 12 (Leiden: Brill, 1978), 213–15. The best known of these works is Heracleon's *Commentary on John*, excerpts from which were preserved by Origen.

121. For text and details, see Layton, *Gnostic Scriptures*, 276–302.

122. Epiphanius, *Panarion* 33.3.1–7.10. For the text, see Gilles Quispel, *Ptolémée: Lettre à Flora*, SC 24; 2nd ed. (Paris: Cerf, 1966). (In references, the redundant reference to book 33 is omitted.)

123. Norden, *Die antike Kunstprosa*, 2:547 n. 2, 920–22.

124. If one thinks that divorce (33.4.4-10) is a major concern, it becomes somewhat more likely that an actual person is the addressee. See R. M. Grant, "A Woman of Rome: The Matron in Justin, *2 Apology* 2.1-9," *Church History* 54 (1985): 461–72. On the other hand, the material about divorce provides so fundamental an example that it could scarcely have been ignored.

125. On the distinction between "moral" and "ceremonial" law in the interpretation of Paul, see Wiles, *Divine Apostle*, 66–72.

126. Philosophers had earlier come up with a "tripartite theology," including that of the poets (mythology), that of the various civic cults (e.g., Artemis of Ephesus), and that of the philosophers.

127. Ptolemy's basic gospel texts appear to come from Matthew.

128. Justin, *Dial.* 44.2. A scheme very much like that of Ptolemy appears in the Pseudo-Clementines, *Hom.* 3.50-54. This is one mark of the Clementines' affinity with apologetic thought.

129. Quispel, *Ptolémée*, 23–26.

130. *Ptolemy to Flora* 5.9 (trans. Layton, *Gnostic Scriptures*, 312).

131. Cf. Heb. 8:5; 10:1.

132. 5.15, trans. Layton, *Gnostic Scriptures*, 312.

133. Trans. Layton, *Gnostic Scriptures*, 313.

134. Trans. Layton, *Gnostic Scriptures*, 314.

135. See p. 222.

136. Ptolemy held, as noted, that this tradition was transmitted secretly (Clement of Alexandria, *Strom.* 7.106). Many Alexandrian Christians accepted this, including Clement, who held that this tradition had been handed down orally (*Strom.* 7.61).

137. Grant, *Heresy*, 49–58 (51).

138. Trans. Layton, *Gnostic Scriptures*, 314.

139. Mark 12:26-27 defends resurrection by referring to immortality, a view enhanced by Luke 20:38. See Mikeal C. Parsons and Richard I. Pervo, *Rethinking the Unity of Luke and Acts* (Minneapolis: Fortress Press, 1993), 101.

140. Cf. *3 Corinthians* (p. 96).

141. Irenaeus (*A.H.* 5.13.2) says that 1 Cor. 15:50 is a favorite of the heretics. Cf. 5.9.1.

142. Wiles (*Divine Apostle*, 26) observes, "But Gnostic exegesis did not need to be wholly tendentious in order to claim the support of the great apostle for their belief in the evil character of man's bodily nature."

143. See the marginal notes in Layton, *Gnostic Scriptures*, 320–24. For Ptolemy's myth of origins, see pp. 214, 222.

144. See Layton, *Gnostic Scriptures*, 316–19, and Peel, ed., *Nag Hammadi Codex* I, 1:123–57; 2:137–215.

145. Trans. Layton, *Gnostic Scriptures*, 321.

146. On this, R. McL. Wilson, *Gnosis and the New Testament* (Philadelphia: Fortress Press, 1968), 119–21.

147. Trans. Layton, *Gnostic Scriptures*, 321.

148. Dassmann (*Stachel*, 203) is only formally and partially correct in stating that the Valentinians eliminated the tension between what believers have now and what remains "not yet." Final dissolution belongs to the future, necessitating a disciplined life.

149. Papias, Montanists, Irenaeus.

150. Irenaeus, *A.H.* 3.2.1.

151. Cf. Dassmann, *Stachel*, 217. The pattern of the orthodox creeds is also "mythical."

152. See Pagels, *Gnostic Paul*, 6.

153. For a translation, see Elaine H. Pagels and John D. Turner, in James M. Robinson, ed., *The Nag Hammadi Library in English*, rev. ed. (San Francisco: Harper & Row, 1988), 473–80. The full

edition is to be found by Pagels in Charles W. Hedrick, ed., *Nag Hammadi Codices XI, XII, XIII*, Nag Hammadi Studies 27 (Leiden: Brill, 1990), 21–88. Note also Koschorke, "Paulus," 185–87, and Lindemann, *Paulus*, 339–41. Codex XI is among the less well preserved books in the NHC. Only a few leaves are complete.

154. The earlier part of the treatise focuses upon Matthew.

155. Bracketed material in italics represents inserted transitional words rather than restorations, marked by Roman brackets.

156. The Coptic uses the Greek loan word χειρόγραφον (Col. 2:14—which does not speak of "condemnation").

157. Cf. *Excerpta ex Theodoto* 58.

158. Cf. Dassmann, *Stachel*, 220.

159. See the conclusions of Koschorke, "Paulus," 200–202.

160. Trans. Ron Cameron and Arthur J. Dewey, *The Cologne Mani Codex (P. Colon. Inv. Nr. 4780) "Concerning the Origin of His Body"*, SBLTT 15 (Missoula, Mont.: Scholars Press, 1979), 51. For another version, see Iain Gardner and Samuel N. C. Lieu, *Manichaean Texts from the Roman Empire* (Cambridge: Cambridge University Press, 2004), 166.

161. Consultation of the Greek texts of the two documents will reveal a number of precise verbal parallels. Note also the explicit citations of Gal. 1:1 in 60.16-24 (linked to a citation from 2 Cor. 12:1-5), and of Gal. 1:11-12 in 61.16-21, also linked to 2 Cor. 12.

162. For a general introduction to Irenaeus, with a good anthology of his writings, see Robert M. Grant, *Irenaeus of Lyons* (London: Routledge, 1997). See also John Lawson, *The Biblical Theology of Saint Irenaeus* (London: Epworth, 1948). For other bibliography, see Grant, *Irenaeus*, 199–201. On his utilization of Paul, see E. Peretto, *La Lettera ai Romani cc. 1-8 nell' Adversus Haereses d'Ireneo* (Bari: Istitutio di Letteratura Cristiano Antica, 1971); Dassmann, *Stachel*, 292–315; Rensberger, "As the Apostle Teaches," 208–13; David L. Balás, "The Use and Interpretation of Paul in Irenaeus' Five Books *Adversus Haereses*," *SecCent* 9 (1992): 27–39; and Richard A. Norris, "Irenaeus' Use of Paul in His Polemic against the Gnostics," in *Paul and the Legacies of Paul*, ed. William S. Babcock (Dallas: Southern Methodist University Press, 1990), 79–98. A major monograph representing the shift in the view of Irenaeus' understanding of Paul is Rolf Noormann, *Irenäus als Paulusinterpret: Zur Rezeption und Wirkung der paulinischen und deuteropaulinischen Briefe im Werk des Irenäus von Lyon*, WUNT 66 (Tübingen: Mohr Siebeck, 1994). See his history of research, pp. 4–21. Earlier studies include Johannes Werner, *Der Paulinismus des Irenaeus*, TU 6.2 (Leipzig: Teubner, 1889), whose negative judgments influenced generations of (especially) German scholarship, and Eva Aleith, *Paulusverständnis in der alten Kirche*, BZNW 18 (Berlin: Töpelmann, 1937). A contemporary statement of the view that Irenaeus failed to give Paul proper due is Dieter Georgi, "Irenaeus's and Origen's Treatment of Paul's Epistle to the Romans: An Assessment," in Kathy L. Gaca and Larry L. Welborn, *Early Patristic Readings of Romans*, Romans Through History and Cultures (New York: T&T Clark International, 2005), 206–12.

163. See p. 138.

164. Eusebius, *H.E.* 5.4.

165. See *A.H.* 4.6.2, which evidently refers to Justin's *Syntagma against All Heresies* (*1 Apol.* 1.26.8), often viewed as primarily an attack upon Marcion (Irenaeus, *A.H.* 4.6.2).

166. Eusebius *H.E.* 5.24.11.

167. Cf. *H.E.* 5.7, citing Irenaeus, *A.H.* 2.31.2; 32.4; 5.6.1.

168. Books 4 and 5 survive in an Armenian version, and there are some Greek and Syriac fragments.

169. The other is the *Epideixis, Demonstration of Apostolic Preaching*, available only in Armenian. The latter work is later than the *A.H.* and may represent the content of his instructions to candidates for baptism.

170. Irenaeus, *A.H.* 2.10.

171. Irenaeus uses the term "economy" (οἰκονομία), familiar from speculative Paulinism (e.g., Eph. 3:9), to explicate the divine plan.

172. Both "recapitulation" and "economy" (below) have a place in the realm of literary jargon. See Grant, *Irenaeus*, 29–31.

173. *Epideixis* 22.

174. In particular, Theophilus of Antioch.

175. The fascinating story of the reception of Paul by Clement and Origen is therefore left out of this survey.

176. Irenaeus, *A.H.* 3.14.1.

177. See *A.H.* 3.14.2, which speaks of Paul's address to "bishops and presbyters who came from Ephesus and the other cities adjoining..."

178. His arguments (*A.H.* 3.11.8) seem almost frivolous: the four corners of the compass, the four chief winds, and the four forms of the Cherubim (Ezek. 1:6, 10). The last has produced the conventional symbols (human, lion, ox, eagle) of the evangelists.

179. William W. Harvey, *Sancti Irenaei Episcopi Lugdunensis* (Cambridge: Typis Academicis, 1857). Counts vary, but the proportions are essentially the same.

180. In addition, the *Biblia Patristica*, vol. 1, *Des origins à Clément d'Alexandrie et Tertullien*, Centre d'analyse et de documentation patristiques (Paris: Editions du center national de la recherché scientifique, 1975), 519-24, cites 25 allusions to Hebrews, which Irenaeus evidently attributed to Paul, but few of these citations are explicit, and the document is not named in *A.H.* Western reservations about Hebrews may have dictated his caution. On Irenaeus' use of the Pastoral Epistles, see also James W. Aageson, *Paul, the Pastoral Epistles, and the Early Church* (Peabody, Mass.: Hendrickson, 2008), 167-70.

181. See p. 195.

182. In *A.H.* 3.21.2, Irenaeus summarizes the legend of the inspiration of the LXX, which he may have learned from Justin.

183. Theophilus of Antioch, for example, used a similar collection. See R. M. Grant, "The Bible of Theophilus of Antioch," *JBL* 66 (1947): 173-96.

184. See p. 284n13.

185. W. Bousset, *Kyrios Christos: A History of the Belief in Christ from the Beginnings of Christianity to Irenaeus*, trans. John Steely (Nashville: Abingdon, 1970), 446-53.

186. Bousset, *Kyrios Christos*, 451.

187. R. Martin, *Reconciliation: A Study of Paul's Theology*, rev. ed. (Grand Rapids: Zondervan, 1990).

188. Cf. the comment of Richard A. Norris ("Irenaeus' Use of Paul in His Polemic Against the Gnostics," in Babcock, ed., *Paul*, 79-98 [80]): "...[I]t is useless to inquire whether Irenaeus' Paul conforms to the image of the apostle that was later unveiled by the interests and perceptions of evangelical Protestantism."

189. For a discussion of Irenaeus' anthropology, see Noormann, *Irenäus*, 467-92. For Irenaeus, anthropology provided the foundation for understanding cosmology. To this extent he may be compared with Bultmann.

190. Luke, like Paul, used natural theology to level the playing field for both Jews and gentiles. See Pervo, "The Paul of Acts."

191. Irenaeus, *A.H.* 3.12.

192. Irenaeus, *A.H.* 3.16-18. See Norris, "Irenaeus' Use," 84-85.

193. See the discussion of Ptolemy, above.

194. See Norris, "Irenaeus' Use," 86-88.

195. Irenaeus, *A.H.* 4.33.5.

196. The final section of *A.H.* 3.16.6 (trans. *ANF* 1: 442).

197. See J. T. Nielsen, *Adam and Christ in the Theology of Irenaeus of Lyons* (Assen: Van Gorcum, 1968).

198. Irenaeus, *A.H.* 3.21.10, trans. A. Cleveland Coxe, *The Ante-Nicene Fathers*, vol. I (Grand Rapids: Eerdmans, 1973), 454.

199. Typology is less systematic than allegory in that it appropriates some biblical actualities, such as the ark as a model for the church, without developing all of the specifics.

200. See Susan L. Graham, "Irenaeus as Reader of Romans 9-11: Olive Branches," in Gaca and Welborn, eds., *Romans*, 87-113.

201. Cf. the citation of John 1:3 in *A.H.* 3.21.10.

202. On the Paulinism of Irenaeus' incarnational theology, see Noormann, *Irenäus*, 427-62, 487-89.

203. Norris, "Irenaeus' Use," 88–90.

204. On the last, see D. J. Bingham, "Irenaeus Reads Romans 8: Resurrection and Renovation," in Gaca and Welborn, eds., *Romans*, 114–32. Three of the essays in that volume (the contributions of Bingham, Georgi, and Graham) take up Irenaeus' use of Romans.

205. See Noorman, *Irenäus*, 39–67.

206. Noorman, *Irenäus*, 50–51.

207. See Noorman, *Irenäus*, 416–19.

208. Luke, for example, knew of Paul's doctrine of justification by faith, but saw it as limited to conflicts about Torah. See Pervo, "The Paul of Acts."

209. The author's intentions cannot be discovered with certainty. See Pervo, *Acts*, 18–20.

210. W. Schneemelcher, "Paulus in der griechischen Kirche des zweiten Jahrhunderts," *Zeitschrift für Kirchengeschichte* 75 (1964): 1–20.

Conclusion

1. Postmodern thought has tended to downplay historical differences, but it has played a major role in stressing the importance of minority views and in disrupting confidence in standard evaluations based upon a consensus that often amounts to little more than shared prejudices.

2. The contrast between the Pastoral Epistles and the *Acts of Paul* remains a useful example.

3. Paul did not invent the idea, as the prominence of Jerusalem and the desire for some uniformity was present during his lifetime (Gal. 1–2).

4. The vigorous—and often harmful—rivalry and competition among Greek cities contributed to the eventual rivalry for autonomy or dominance among Christian bodies in the various cities of the Roman Empire.

5. This tendency to limit the title "apostle" to the Twelve is characteristic of the Synoptic tradition (Mark, Matthew). It also appears in Revelation, but it is not found in John.

6. The exception—and it is not canonical—is the *Acts of Thomas*, probably composed in Syriac, although the Greek edition may have appeared almost simultaneously with the original.

7. In ancient terms Paul was more like Dio of Prusa (c. 100 CE) than the fourth-century BCE Diogenes of Sinope.

8. See the "Pauline Family Tree."

9. Amalgamation of genres: Mark (parables, miracles, pronouncement stories, passion narrative, etc.), Matthew (Mark, Q, a church order [?]); use of multiple texts: Matthew, Luke (?Justin), Tatian; editions of different sorts: ?Q, *Gospel of Thomas*, Marcion; "Apocrypha": the various non-canonical gospel texts.

10. Matthew 28:19-20 and Luke 24:49-53 exemplify this object.

11. The canonical Gospels already reflect an urban or urbanized environment, but the background of the tradition shines through. The least urban is John. Note also the *Gospel of Thomas*.

Index of Primary Sources

The Pastoral Epistles (1-2
Timothy, Titus), 5, 16, 29,
48, 55, 59, 80, 83-95, 102,
135, 223, 234, 305 n.25,
315 n.237

1 Timothy, 15, 197, 294
n.39
    1, 347 n.2791:1-2, 1
    1:3, 312 n.185
    1:4, 312 n.168
    1:8-11, 47
    1:10, 315 n.231
    1:11, 190, 289 n.53
    1:14-15, 168
    1:12-17, 14-15
    1:15, 290 n.73
    1:16, 50, 88, 290 n.67
    1:20, 313 n.193
    2:1, 289 n.53
    2:7, 190
    2:8-15, 306 n.38
    2:9-15, 91, 315 n.242
    2:11-13, 47
    2:15, 315 n.241
    3:1-6 316 n.262
    3:3, 300 n.145
    3:4, 90
    3:4-5, 314 n.227
    3:6, 312 n.168
    3:7, 90
    3:8-13, 316 n.262, 320
    n.376
    3:11, 315 n.236
    3:12, 314 n.227
    3:14, 288 n.38
    3:16, 92
    4:6, 138
    4:9-13, 296 n.69
    4:12, 312 n.180, 298
    n.119,
    4:14, 316 n.253
    4:19, 291 n.91
    4:19-21, 296 n.69
    5, 312 n.186
    5:5-6, 92
    5:9, 315 n.244
    5:16, 315 n.247
    5:17-22, 316 n.262
    5:18, 312 n.166
    5:23, 60, 312 n.181
    6:1-2, 90
    6:3, 315 n.231
    6:10, 351 n.17

6:20, 77, 310 n.146, 353
6:21, 316 n.268

2 Timothy 6, 16, 43, 84,
289 n.42, 291 n.97
    1:3, 303 n.202
    1:5, 316 n.261
    1:6, 316 n.253
    1:11, 289 n.53
    1:12, 14, 310 n.146
    1:13, 315 n.231
    1:14, 77
    1:15, 313 n.193
    1:15-18, 313 n.197
    2:8, 301 n.182, 353 n.45
    2:13, 50
    2:17, 313 n.193, 313
    n.193
    2:18, 317 n.278
    2:20-21, 356 n.119
    3:6, 91, 312 n.168
    3:10-14, 313 n.207
    3:16, 92
    4, 89
    4:3, 312 n.168, 315
    n.231, 339 n.93
    4:4, 320 n.360
    4:6, 138
    4:6-8, 314 n.217
    4:9-18, 313 n.199
    4:11, 327 n.56
    4:12, 305 n.15
    4:13, 313 n.198, 343
    n.184
    4:14, 313 n.193
    4:19, 291 n.91
    4:19-22, 313 n.205
    4:22, 316 n.268
    6:20, 312 n.168

Titus, 6
    1, 89, 316 n.262
    1-2, 312 n.171
    1:2, 350 n.96
    1:5, 312 n.185
    1:5-6, 316 n.262
    1:6, 314 n.227, 315
    n.235
    1:7-9, 316 n.262
    1:9, 315 n.231
    1:10-11, 311 n.156
    1:12, 300 n.145
    2:1, 8, 315 n.231
    2:1-10, 306 n.38

2:3, 92, 315 n.236
2:3-5, 92
2:4, 90
2:7, 15, 312 n.180
2:9-10, 90
2:9-15, 92
3:4-5, 312 n.182
3:12, 305 n.15
3:12-13, 300 n.145
3:15, 316 n.268

Philemon, 16, 30
    19, 80, 304 n.236
    22, 65
    23-24, 70, 305 n.12
    24, 126, 290 n.61, 307
    n.53

Hebrews, x, 27, 120-22,
213
    6:2-4, 326 n.25
    13:20-25, 121, 325 n.16

1 Peter, 125-26
    1:1, 34
    1:3-12, 41
    1:10-12, 319 n.318
    2:11, 328 n.60
    2:18-3:7, 126, 306 n.38
    3:1-2, 334 n.212
    3:19, 300 n.146
    5:1, 319 n.326
    5:12, 126, 343 n.187
    5:14, 126

2 Peter, 80, 143-45
    1:1-2, 143
    2:3-4, 14; 300 n.145
    2:9, 320 n.358
    3:1, 327 n.46
    3:7, 320 n.358
    3:15-16, 143

1 John, 28, 55, 119, 125,
192, 211, 244, 288 n.32,
333 nn.174, 180, 188.
    2:12-14, 306 n.38
    3:8, 141
    4:2-3, 141

2 John, x, 28, 55, 58, 59

3 John x, 28, 55, 58, 59, 295
n.52.

Apuleius, *Metamorphoses*
11, 302 n.207
11.8-17, 332 n.168

Arator, *On the Acts of the Apostles*, 2.1218, 347 n.285

Aristides,
Apology, 194, 296 n.73

Aristotle, 68
Politics, 1.2, 306 n.35

Athenaeus,
Deipnosophistae,
5.196A-203A, 332 n.168

Augustine, 235, 286 nn.12, 17, 294 n.37
Confessions 8.12.5; 5
Letter 153.14, 111
Barnabas, 119, 192-93
5:6, 318 n.302
5:9, 309 n.117
13:7, 192
20:2, 290 n.64

Chariton, *Callirhoe*
7.5-8.1, 346 n.249
8.6.8, 344 n.216

Chrysostom
Comm. In epistolam secundum ad Tim.,
10.3, 296 n.73
Homily on Acts 14, 315 n.246
In epistolam ad Hebraeos, arg. 1.1, 296 n.73

Cicero, 26
Ad Att.
6.72, 323 n.429
8.142, 323 n.429
De Natura Deorum
2.2.6, 324 n.448

Clement of Alexandria
Hyptoposeis
Stromata
1.94.4, 289 n.47
3.2.1, 355 n.94
3.80.3-81.3, 350, nn.91-

92
5.5.1, 289 n.47
6.7.61, 355 n.91
7.16,10607, 352 n.24
7.61, 356 n.136
7.106, 356 n.136

Commodian, *Carmen apologeticum*, 625-30, 341 n.139

Corpus Hermeticum
1, 209
13, 209

Correspondence between Paul and Seneca, 110-16

Cyprian,
De Exhort. Martyr. 11, 304 n.247
Testim. Adv. Jud. 1.20, 304 n.247

Cyril of Jerusalem,
Mystagogical Catecheses,
17.26, 296 n.74

Damascus Document 1.18, 285 n.4

Didache, 190 314 n.229, 348 n.18
4:9-11, 306 n.38
5:2, 290 n.64
11:1, 309 n.206
16, 299 n.133

Didascalia 6.7-9, 341 n.139

Dio of Prusa
Or. 8.11-13, 330 n.111

Diogenes Laertius, *Lives of the Philosophers*
7.183, 292 n.1

Diognetus, 119, 193-94
5:7, 194
5:12-16, 194
9, 194

Dionysus of Corinth,

145-48

Dionysius of Halicarnassus, *Ant. Rom.*
6.86, 328 n.75

Epictetus, *Discourses*
1.11.33, 330.n.111
2.1.10, 330 n.111
3.21.13-16, 289 n.53
3.22.69, 330 n.113

Epicurus
Epiphanius, *Panarion*
7.9, 296 n.74
28.1-8, 348 n.23
28.5.3, 189
33.3.1-7.10, 356 n.122
38.5, 347 n.4
42.1-2, 352 n.27
42.9, 109
49.9.4, 303 n.228

Epistula Apostolorum, 13, 164-66, 185

Eusebius; *Ecclesiastical History*
2.14, 341 n.138
2.16.1, 343 n.187
2.22.1-2, 296 n.72
2.22.1-3, 347 n.288
2.23.4-18, 191
2.23.18, 287 n.28
2.25.5-7, 347 n.283
2.25.8, 145
3.1, 296 n.73
3.3.1-2, 166
3.3.4, 142
3.3.4-6, 337 n.42
3.5.2-3, 191
3.11.1-12.1, 191
3.16, 328 n.61
3.16.1, 191
3.20.1-6, 191
3.21-22, 330 n.126
3.22, 134
3.25.2, 327 n.46
3.25.4-6, 337 n.42
3.27.4. 347 n.4
3.32.1-8, 191
3.33.3, 135
3.34-35, 135
3.36, 330 n.126, 331

INDEX OF MODERN AUTHORS

Holzberg, N., 292 n.8, 312 n.179, 324 n.458
Hornschuh, M., 340 n.120, 341 nn.130, 133
Horrell, D., 327 n.48, 328 n.66
Hovhanessian, V., 316 n.272, 317 nn.275, 277, 283, 284, 289, 290, 291, 294, 297, 318 n.309, 319 nn.321, 328, 333, 336, 339, 320 n.347
Hughes, F., 311 n.159
Hultgren, A., 312 n.170
Hultgren, S., 298 n.118, 304 n.243
Hunt, A., 350 nn.83, 85, 89, 96
Hurtado, L., 296 n.75, 301 n.179
Irmscher, J., 345 n.238, 346 nn.264, 266, 269
Jacobson, G., 291 n.95
James, M. R., 172, 322 nn.414, 415, 343 n.192, 344 n.193.
Jeffers, J., 327 n.59
Jefford, C., 286 n.11, 330 n.123
Jewett, R., 295 nn.62, 64, 296 nn.72, 75, 297 n.103, 301 n.169, 302 n.192, 310 n.136
Johnson, L. T., 312 n.187
Johnson, S., 337 n.47
Johnston, S. 317 n.296
Jones, F. S., 180, 345 nn.235, 238, 346 nn.252, 253, 254, 256, 257, 274, 347 n.277.
Junod, E., 343 n.192, 344 n.194
Kaestli, J.-D., 314 n.225
Kappler, R., 322 n.416, 323 n.437
Kelley, N., 345 n.236
Kennedy, G., 329 n.96, 351 nn.16, 18
Kiley, M., 290 n.61, 300 n.148, 305 n.12
King, K. L., 354 n.75
Kinzig, W., 353 n.58
Kitchen, M., 287 n.22
Klauck, H.-J., 191, 286 n.9, 287 n.22, 292 n.3, 293

nn.10, 11, 303 n.220, 304 n.4, 307 n.62, 310 n.128, 311 n.162, 325 nn.2, 4, 326 n.6, 334 nn.202, 205, 337 nn.40, 41, 343 n.176, 343 nn.188, 192, 345 n.238, 346 n.251, 348 n.28
Klijn, A., 316 n.272, 318 n.316, 347 n.3
Knox, John, 30, 36, 294 n.48, 297 n.90, 303 n.209, 351 n.21, 352 n.30
Knust, J. 311 n.156
Koester, H., xiv, 80, 125, 140, 288 n.33, 280 n.46, 294 n.45, 299 n.137, 304 n.237, 306 n.37, 310 nn.136, 142, 144, 312 n.168, 326 n.28, 327 n.43, 333 n.181, 334 n.208, 350 n.70.
Koschorke, K., 355 n.84, 356 n.120, 357 nn. 146, 159
Kovacs, D., 300 n.149
Krentz, E., 310 nn.133, 134, 311 n.158
Kuhn, K. G., 308 n.88
Kümmel, W. G., 287 n.19, 298 n.19, 326 n.34
Kurz, W., 299 n.133
Kürzinger, J., 331 n.130
Lambrecht, J., 298 n.109
Lampe, P., 33, 295 nn.64, 65, 325 n.16, 328 n.65, 329 nn.88, 97, 349 nn.64, 65, 66, 350 n.83, 352 nn.23, 40, 355 n.90
Lawson, J., 357 n.162
Layton, B., 208, 325 n.17, 354 nn.76, 77, 355 nn.101, 107, 356 nn.109, 110, 112, 121, 130, 132, 133, 134, 138, 357 nn.143, 144, 145, 147
Lee, M., 328 n.75
Leloir, L., 343 n.180
Lentz, J., 290 n.71, 336 nn.20, 21
Leppä, O., 310 n.127
Liénard, E., 322 nn.416, 424

Lieu, S. 286 n.15, 348 n.26, 357 n.160
Lightfoot, J., 149, 178, 294 n.46, 294 n.74, 320 n.353, 321 nn.387, 388, 390, 392, 395, 396, 322 n.422, 327 n.59, 330 n.112, 331 n.136, 335 n.4, 345 n.239
Lilla, S., 325 n.11
Lincoln, A., 286 n.11
Lindemann, A. 7, 126, 144, 192, 194, 285 n.5, 288 n.36, 289 n.46, 298 n.105, 299 n.122, 138, 303 n.208, 303 n.217, 305 n.19, 308n.75, 310 n.147, 311 n.162, 313 n.205, 325 n.20, 326 n.36, 327 nn.54, 58, 59, 328 n.62, 313 n.205, 325 n.36, 327 n.54, 327 nn.58, 59, 328 nn.62, 70, 329 n.77, 330 nn.112, 118, 122, 331 nn.135, 146, 332 n.154, 333 nn.185, 186, 189, 334 nn.195, 209, 210, 211, 214, 335 n.10, 340 n.120, 341 nn.126, 135, 345 nn.227, 229, 238, 347 n.9, 348 nn.18, 31, 34, 36, 37, 349 nn.42, 45, 47, 55, 58, 59, 61, 66, 350 nn.67, 72, 73, 82, 352 n.21, 354 n.84, 355 nn.86, 94, 357 n.153
Linton, O., 289 n.44
Lipsius, R., 170, 324 n.451, 333 n.55, 342 n.169, 343 n.175
Lohfink, G., 311 n.162, 316 n.265
Lohse, E., 64, 299 n.123, 304 nn.5, 14, 16
Löning, K., 335 n.7
Lona, H., 327 n.59
Lüdemann, G., 180, 345 n.238, 346 nn.254, 273, 347 nn. 277, 1, 348 nn.25, 31, 38
Lupieri, E., 354 n.73
Luttikhuizen, G., 317 n.273, 318 nn.299, 309, 320 n.347, 348 n.24

Luther, M., 4, 5, 122, 123, 235, 287 n.19, 308 n.81, 326 nn.34, 35.
MacDonald, D. R., 300 nn.153, 159, 301 n.160, 315 n.237, 339 n.84, 340 nn.107, 108, 117
MacDonald, M. Y.304 n.2, 306 n.50, 307 n.71, 309 n.108, 309 n.111, 315 n.239, 329 n.79
MacRae, G., 176 345 nn.227, 232, 233
Maier, H., 329 n.85, 332 n.152, 334 n.200
Malherbe, A. xv, 112, 292 n.3, 312 n.178, 314 n.222, 315 n.231, 322 n.416, 323 nn.427, 429, 324, nn.449, 456
Manns, F., 345 n.238
Marguerat, D., 157, 288 n.42, 335 n.7, 337 n.51
Markschies, C., 354 n.63
Martin, R., 358 n.187
Martyn, J., 346 n.254
Masson, C., 298 n.105
Matthews, S., 337 n.47
Mattill, A., 155, 336 nn.25, 32
May, K., 351 n.21, 352 n.23, 353 n.58
McGowan, A., 342 n.154, 352 n.37
Meade, D., 288 n.36, 320 n.352
Meeks, W., 306 n.35, 329 n.97, 346 n.254
Meier, J., 136, 331 nn.142, 145
Meinardus, O., 343 n.188
Melanchthon, P., 308 n.81
Merklein, H. 305 n.28, 307 n.62, 309 n.121
Merz, A., 311 n.162
Metzger, B., 294 n.42, 301 n.179, 302 n.200
Miller, J., 298 n.106
Mitchell, M., 125, 297 n.103, 326 n.33, 327 n.40, 329 n.85
Mitton, C., 299 n.127, 303 n.208
Mollenkott, V., 309 n.99

Momigliano, A., 322 n.416, 324 n.457
Moreschini, C., 294 nn.34, 37
Mount, C., 302 n.189
Mouton, E., 309 n.99
Muddiman, J., 192, 307 nn.60, 70, 348 n.39, 355 n.85
Müller, C., 334 n.204, 340 n.120, 341 nn. 126, 128, 134
Müller, D., 355 nn.101, 102
Müller, P.-G. 288 n.36, 335 n.3
Munck, J., 299 n.133
Munier, C., 330 n.118, 331 nn.135, 140, 146
Murdock, W., 176 345 nn.227, 232, 233
Musurillo, H., 286 n.1, 289 n.53
Nautin, P., 334 n.218, 335 nn.228, 233
Neyrey, J., 334 nn.202, 210
Nielsen, J. 359 n.197
Nienhuis, D., 293 n.22, 326 n.33
Nock, A. D., 344 n.203
Noormann, R., 357 n.162, 359 nn.189, 202, 359 nn.205, 206, 207
Norden, E., 213, 326 n.24, 330 n.121, 356 nn.113, 123
Norelli, E., 294 nn.34, 37, 354 n.69
Norris, R., 357 n.162, 358 n.188, 359 nn.192, 194, 203
Oakes, 334 n.196
Padovese, L., 347 n.1
Pagels, E., 211, 355 nn.87, 97, 357 nn.152, 153
Painter, J., 326 n.34, 346 n.255
Palagi, L., 322 n.416, 323 n.437
Parsons, M., 305 n.29, 336 nn.34-35, 357 n.139
Patzia, A., 303 n.208
Paulsen, H. 134, 330 n.124, 333 nn.172, 183
Payne, P., 300 n.158

Pearson, B., 288 n.36, 301 n.163
Penny, D., 103, 316 n.272, 318 n.314, 319 nn.331, 335, 320 nn.346, 348, 321 nn.387, 395
Pérès, J.-N., 340 nn.120, 121
Perkins, P., 341 n.124
Peretto, E., 357 n.162
Perry, B., 345 n.235
Pervo, R., 157, 285 n.11, 290 nn.8, 79, 291 n.80, 291 nn.86, 87, 90, 91, 98, 292 n.109, 293 n.9, 294 n.49, 296 n.70, 298 n.108, 299 n.136, 300 n.159, 303 nn.214, 222, 304 n.238, 305 n.29, 307 nn.51, 52, 68, 308 nn.86, 87, 93, 95, 311 n.102, 312 nn.169, 179, 313 n.201, 314 nn.215, 216, 220m 315 n.251, 316 nn.254, 263, 318 nn.304, 308, 319 n.341, 323 nn.435, 443, 324 nn.446, 466, 328 nn.61, 63, 69, 72, 329 nn.87, 95, 330 nn.100, 130, 332 n.150, 333 n.182, 334 n.206, 335 nn.2, 9, 336 nn.13, 14, 15, 21, 30, 31, 34, 337 nn.35, 36, 37, 41, 44, 51, 338 n.53, 339 n.93, 340 n.106, 341 n.127, 343 nn.188, 191, 344 n.94, 346 n.260, 348 nn.27, 28, 349 nn.49, 52, 350 n.68, 351 n.3, 352 nn.24, 25, 353 n.46, 355 n.99, 357 n.139, 359 nn.190, 208, 209
Pesthy, M., 337 n.47
Pfister, F., 296 n.73, 330 nn. 99, 112
Pfleiderer, O., 287 n.23
Pherigo, L., 330 n.112
Pietersen, L., 313 n.190
Pink, K., 321 n.389
Plank, K., 299 n.124
Plummer, A., 321 n.397
Poirier, P.-H., 317 n.296
Pomeroy, S., 315 n.243

Portefaix, L., 315 n.234
Porter, S. E., 287 n.22, 293 n.15, 303 n.208
Poupon, G., 341 nn.136, 137
Praeder, S., 291 n.95
Prieur, J.-M., 335 n.227
Pucci Ben Zeev, 352 n.24
Quinn, J., 291 n.80, 312 nn.165, 176, 313 n.205, 330 n.105
Quispel, G., 109, 321 n.404, 356 nn.122, 129
Radl, W., 291 n.95
Ramelli, I., 322 n.424
Ramsay, W., 297 n.96, 338 n.55
Reinink, G., 347 n.3
Reis, D., 331 n.146
Rensberger, D., 7, 335 n.237, 341 n.126, 348 nn.31, 34, 37, 38, 349 nn.43, 47, 55, 354 n.84, 355 nn.86, 94, 357 n.162
Reumann, J., 297 n.92, 307 n.69, 310 n.143, 311, n.162
Richard, E., 298 n.104, 310 n.131
Rigaux, B., 291 n.101
Robertson, A., 321 n.397
Robinson, J. M., 286 n.10m 299 n.121, 333 n.190
Römer, C., 322 nn.416, 418
Roose, H., 310 n. 129
Rordorf, W., 100, 157, 291 n.82, 316 n.272, 318 n.305, 337 nn.40, 50, 338 nn.52, 62, 64.
Rothschild, C., xv, 121, 287 n.22, 325 nn.4, 18, 20
Rudolph, K., 206 354 n.63
Sand, A., 288 n.36, 303 n.208
Sanders, E. P., 202, 352 n.33
Schenke, H.-M., 288 n.36
Schmeller, T. 288 n.36
Schmid, U., 351 n.21, 353 n.41
Schmidt, C., 318 n.315, 319 n.330, 338 n.60, 339 nn.75, 77
Schmidt, D., 301 n.165

Schmithals, W., 56, 296 n.76, 297 n.92, 302 n.192, 303 n.216
Schnackenburg, R., 299 n.131, 307 nn.66, 67, 69, 308 nn.72, 74, 77, 80, 82, 88, 310 n.125
Schneemelcher, W., 297 n.85, 316 n.222, 318 n.305, 321 n.394, 337 n.40, 338 n.54, 359 n.210, 297 n.85,
Schoedel, W., 134, 135, 313 n.195, 330 nn.118, 119, 124, 125, 331 nn.130, 137, 139, 140, 144, 332 nn.156, 160, 169, 170, 333 nn.173, 174, 179, 192, 334 nn.193, 199
Schrage, W., 316 n.255
Schröter, J., 314 nn.213, 216
Schubart, W., 318 n.315, 338 n.60, 339 n.75
Selwyn, E., 327 n.46
Sellin, G., 301 n.186
Sellew, P., xv, 107, 321 n.399
Semler, J. S., xi, 285 n.9
Simon, R., 285 n.9
Skarsaune, O., 349 n.66
Souter, A., 294 nn.34, 37
Sperling, D., 298 n.113
Speyer, W., 287 n.22, 345 n.223
Spicq, C., 289 n.53, 290 nn.65, 66,72, 314 n.217, 339 n.93
Staniforth, M., 142, 291 n.85, 334 n.198
Sterling, G., 308 n.79, 329 n.97
Stewart-Sykes, A., 353 n.42
Stone, M., 348 n.32
Stoops, R., 338 n.56, 341 n.140
Stowers, S., 292 n.3, 293 n.16, 300 n.149
Strecker, G., 345 n.238, 346 nn.264, 266, 269, 348 n.24
Strugnell, J., 301 n.187, 348 n.32
Stylianopoulos, T., 350 n.73

Sundberg, A., 297 n.91
Svenster, J. N., 322 n.416, 324 n.457
Swain, S., 308 n.95
Szepessy, T. 345 n.235
Tajra, H. 296 n.74, 316 n.271, 322 n.421, 340 n.98, 342 n.164, 343 n.173, 347 n.284
Talbert, C., 291 n.95
Testuz, M., 316 n.272, 317 n.297, 320 n.346
Theissen, G., 340 n.112
Thoma, A., 350 n.73
Thomas, C., 319 n.319, 341 n.136
Thomassen, E., 352 n.28
Thompson, T., 348 n.25
Thurston, B., 315 n.244
Tischendorf, C., 302 n.200
Tobin, T., 309 nn.101, 102
Trenkner, S., 345 n.235
Trilling, W., 310 n.135
Trobisch, D., 26, 56, 293 nn.12, 13, 16, 296 n.77
Troeltsch, E., 309 n.109
Trummer, P., 311 n.162, 312 n.173
Tucker, F., 349 n.53
Turner, J. 357 n.153
Turner, N., 312 n.165
Tyson, J., 302 n.198, 336 nn.29, 34, 351 n.21, 352 n.24, 353 n.48, 354 n.71
Van Voorst, R., 346 n.274
Verheyden, J., 293 n.30, 348 n.38
Versnell, H., 332 n.167
Vinzent, M. 353 n.41
Vouaux, L., 318 n.306, 319 n.329, 321 nn.387, 396, 400, 322 nn.409, 415, 422, 323 n.428, 430, 337 n.43, 340 n.115, 342 n.162,
Weinfeld, M., 314 n.229
Weiss, J., 303 n.213
Welborn, L., 328 n.61, 329 n.88
Wengst, K., 349, n.41
Werline, R., 196, 350 n.73
Werner, J. 223, 286 n.13, 357 n.162
Wesley, J., 5

CPSIA information can be obtained at www.ICGtesting.com
Printed in the USA
LVOW10s0621130716

495743LV00009B/53/P